Children *with* Exceptionalities

in Canadian Classrooms

Fifth Edition

Margret Winzer
University of Lethbridge

Prentice Hall Allyn and Bacon Canada
Scarborough, Ontario

This book is written for my mother

Canadian Cataloguing in Publication Data

Winzer, Margret, 1940–

   Children with exceptionalities in Canadian classrooms

5th ed.
Includes bibliographical references and indexes.
ISBN 0-13-792870-X

1. Special education—Canada. 2. Exceptional children—Canada. I. Title.

LC3984.W56 1999   371.9'0971   C98-930626-7

 © 1999, 1996, 1993 Prentice-Hall Canada Inc., Scarborough, Ontario
A Division of Simon & Schuster

Allyn and Bacon, Inc., Needham Heights, MA
Prentice-Hall, Inc., Upper Saddle River, New Jersey
Prentice-Hall International (UK) Limited, London
Prentice-Hall of Australia, Pty. Limited, Sydney
Prentice-Hall Hispanoamericana, S.A., Mexico City
Prentice-Hall of India Private Limited, New Delhi
Prentice-Hall of Japan, Inc., Tokyo
Simon & Schuster Southeast Asia Private Limited, Singapore
Editora Prentice-Hall do Brasil, Ltda., Rio de Janeiro

ISBN 0-13-792870-X

Vice President, Editorial Director: Laura Pearson
Acquisitions Editor: Dawn Lee
Marketing Manager: Christine Cozens
Developmental Editor: Carol Steven
Production Editor: Andrew Winton
Copy Editor: Kelli Howey
Production Coordinator: Wendy Moran
Permissions/Photo Research: Susan Wallace-Cox
Cover and Interior Design: Julia Hall
Cover Image: Helen D'Souza
Page Layout: Gail Ferreira Ng-A-Kien

1 2 3 4 5   03 02 01 00 99

Printed and bound in the United States of America.

Visit the Prentice Hall Canada web site! Send us your comments, browse our catalogues, and more at **www.phcanada.com**. Or reach us through e-mail at **phabinfo_pubcanada@prenhall.com**.

Table of Contents

Section 6: Children with Low-incidence Disabilities   401

Preface

Children with Exceptionalities is designed to serve as a comprehensive introduction to children with exceptionalities in Canada and to Canadian special education. It is intended to be a practical and readily understandable guide for those who are studying the problems of these children for the first time, as well as a resource for more advanced students. The text is useful for both education and psychology courses. It will interest students who are involved in special education, regular education, early childhood education, and early childhood special education. Students in rehabilitation, nursing, social work, and allied child-care disciplines such as audiology, speech therapy, and language pathology will also find *Children with Exceptionalities* of interest.

The text is essentially designed to present portraits of children with exceptionalities within Canadian special education. It is devoted to the portrayal of children with exceptionalities as learners with special needs rather than to generic or specific teaching and instructional practices. Most general educators do not have a thorough understanding of students with exceptionalities and their skills and needs. Research shows that knowledge changes attitudes toward people with disabilities. Teachers and others who hold a clear understanding of exceptional conditions tend to be more tolerant and accepting than those who know little about etiologies and developmental consequences.

Those hoping to intervene with children with exceptionalities must understand the psychological and cognitive differences that more and less able learners bring to the teaching/learning situation, the unique difficulties faced by children with disabilities, the developmental consequences of various disabilities, and the multiple types of interventions necessary to accommodate them effectively in local schools. With a strong base of understanding and knowledge, teachers and others can build specific educational and therapeutic interventions suited to the unique needs of each particular child.

Although Canadian special education shares much with that of other countries in both its historical development and contemporary practice, there is also much that is unique and special to the Canadian situation. This text sets out to capture the flavour of the Canadian services, to provide recognition of considerable Canadian achievements in the field, and to detail the exciting new advances that are occurring.

All of those involved in any way with children and education require knowledge of the philosophies, practices, and policies that determine the care and education of children with special needs in this country. This book aims to open a window on the Canadian experience through which students may discover the depth of the concern and care for children with exceptionalities being manifested in Canada. Throughout this text a categorical approach is adopted. Not only is this the most practical and logical manner in which to organize such a huge body of information, but it allows a focus on the specific needs of diverse groups of children who require additional educational, medical, and therapeutic services.

A multidisciplinary approach is maintained throughout the text; particular attention is paid to the medical, psychological, sociological, and educational aspects of the various categories of exceptionality. Within each chapter, the reader will find material dealing with etiology; developmental consequences; definitions and classification; prevalence; identification and measurement; and educational, medical, and technical interventions for each type of condition.

Of particular importance and relevance is an understanding of the ideology of special education. In this age of greater teacher accountability and increased teacher decision-making it is vital that those within the profession and those aspiring to join it fully understand the debates circulating in the field so that they can justify their own practice and explain it to others.

For example, the issue of inclusive schooling is one of the most controversial and even contentious debates in contemporary special education and one where the parameters are changing rapidly. When discussing inclusion—and other new movements and trends—we attempt to present all the arguments, based on the newest research and findings. Given the research base and their own readings and discussions, we hope that teachers and students will arrive at their own reasoned decisions on these issues.

New to This Edition

In this fifth edition, many of the features of earlier editions have been retained and expanded. The presentation includes highly current topics, events, and relationships from various fields as these affect what does—or does not—happen in the lives of children who are exceptional. For example, chapters feature research notes that present new findings or directions. Debates designed to present both sides of certain relevant issues have been expanded in this edition. Glossary terms are set in bold type for ease of reference.

A number of improvements and revisions distinguish the fifth edition. Even as the stress remains on the children, much more has been added about schooling, curriculum, and individualization. This aligns with emerging philosophies regarding inclusion and the need for every classroom teacher to be aware of methods, approaches, and techniques that enhance the learning of all students. Concrete examples and ideas are found in a new feature, the In the Classroom sections that close each chapter. These include developmental profiles, individual programs for specific children, and tips for teachers. Also found at the end of each chapter is a list of relevant Web sites where students can search for further information.

Supplemental Teaching and Learning Aids

A Student Workbook accompanies the text. This workbook is designed as a study guide for students and contains key terms, concepts and names, and summaries of each chapter. Review questions assist students in studying the material. Application questions and activities allow students to pursue areas of interest and research arising from the material presented. For the instructor there is an Instructor's Manual, a Test Item File, and a Computerized Test Item File written by Alan Edmunds of Saint Francis Xavier University.

Acknowledgments

Special thanks to the following reviewers, who provided many constructive recommendations: Riva Bartell, University of Manitoba; Clinton Davis, Brock University; Karen Bain, University of Alberta; Alan Bowd, Lakehead University; Alan Edmunds, Saint Francis Xavier University; Donald McKay, Ryerson Polytechnic University, Marilou Matthews, Fanshawe College; Carolyn Yewchuk, University of Alberta; Elizabeth Starr, University of Windsor; Elaine Jones, Fanshawe College; Sonia Masciuch, Mount Saint Vincent University; Susan Lollis, University of Guelph; and Jane R. Evans, Saint Francis Xavier University.

Margret Winzer

SECTION 1

Foundations of Special Education

In a philosophical and humanitarian sense, all children are special. All children have certain strengths and weaknesses, their own particular pattern of inter- and intra-individual differences. In most children, the strengths outweigh the weaknesses. In this text, however, we are concerned with children for whom the balance of strengths and weaknesses may tip a different way.

This book is about children with exceptionalities, those who have difficulty in realizing their full human potential. Their intellectual, emotional, physical, or social performance falls below that of other children. The differences may be related to physical, psychological, cognitive, emotional, or social factors, or a combination of these. Children who are gifted and talented are also included, although their patterns do not fall below but rise above those of average children.

In the past few decades, we have made such major gains in our ability to provide sophisticated services for individuals who are exceptional that the prospects for children and adults have altered dramatically. Medicine has made great strides in the prevention of disabling conditions, in intervention to ameliorate them, and in the care of children who must live with them. Genetic engineering and diagnosis are racing ahead. Closely linked to medicine, technological advances today provide a variety of adaptive devices and aids to help individuals with disabilities. In education, significant philosophical changes are ongoing in the areas of school responsibility, program delivery, and program implementation for special education.

For students with special needs, the most fundamental social change of recent decades has been the clear and unequivocal statement of the responsibility of educational authorities to provide all children equal access to an education in the manner most appropriate to their needs. As the concept of equal educational opportunities for children with special needs has become a dominant ideology, provincial governments and local school boards are increasingly obliged to develop appropriate programs for the entire school-aged population in the province. Outside the field of education, exceptional individuals are coming to be seen in a more positive light. Throughout Canada, public policies are changing as the authorities increasingly seek to develop the potential of individuals who are disabled and to make better use of their aptitudes.

This opening section of the text is designed to introduce children with exceptionalities, special education, and some general principles and practices that are germane to the care and education of individuals who are exceptional. The first chapter introduces the topic of exceptionality and children and adolescents who are seen to be exceptional within the school system. We consider the recognized exceptionalities; issues in classification, labelling, and prevalence; and the ways in which students with special needs are educated.

Educational services and the ideas that stimulate and direct their growth are never static. Changing needs lead to the formulation of new policies, legislation, and other administrative arrangements and practices. Nowhere is this more true than in the field of special education. In areas such as legislation, school placements, assessment, and teaching methodologies and approaches, today's special education is in a state of flux. Nearly all advocates for students with disabilities want "appropriate education in the least restrictive environment; public education that accommodates students with special problems; labels that carry the least possible social stigma; parental participation in decisions to provide special services; and collaboration among all service providers" (Kauffman, 1993). How these ends are to be achieved remains the subject of intense debate. Special education is grappling with new and intriguing philosophies, innovative practices and approaches, and new forms of collaboration.

Chapter 2 explores some of the major issues, trends, and movements that surround special education and exceptionality. We place particular emphasis on the trend toward inclusive schooling and what it means to classroom teachers.

Considerations of etiology (causes) are generally the domain of medical personnel. Nevertheless, teachers need a working knowledge of causes and their consequences for learning and behaviour if they are to instruct children adequately. In Chapter 3, we outline some of the major etiologies and look, albeit briefly, at a huge group of children subsumed within the generic category of *at risk*.

Introduction to Children Who Are Exceptional

Historical Notes

Society's attitude toward persons with disabilities has always been complex, fashioned at any given time by the prevailing culture, religion, government, and economic conditions. Because the care and training of exceptional individuals mirrored societal attitudes, the history of disability and the history of special education can be seen as following historical trends, rather than creating them.

The history of disability extends far back in time. Persons with disabilities were mentioned by the ancient Egyptians, Greeks, and Romans, and in the Bible. The greatest attention was directed toward those considered mad or insane, although this population included persons with mental retardation and those with epilepsy. Hippocrates and the Roman physicians Galen and Celsus also intervened in cases of people with deafness, blindness, and overt physical disabilities.

It is only very recently that an emphasis on the dignity and worth of each person has brought wider acceptance of all individuals who are exceptional in school and society. Although the historical record is murky, it seems that from humanity's earliest beginnings and through many ages persons with disabilities were grossly mistreated. Their conditions were considered hopeless, and in most cultures they were scorned as degraded and inferior beings. It was not until the mid-1700s that some humane concern was allowed individuals with disabilities.

Concern paralleled the beginnings of special education. Although the first documented reports of intervention with special students come from late-sixteenth-century Spain, it was not until the middle decades of the eighteenth century that Britain and Europe turned their attention to the education of their disabled populations.

In France, a new social philosophy, ushered in by Enlightenment thought, brought about major educational advances. The pioneer French educators such as Michel de l'Épée, Jacob Periere, Valentin Häuy, and Edouard Seguin adopted novel philosophical concepts about sensationalism, the psychology of language, and the use of alternate sensory stimuli, and joined them to the new concepts of social equality and individual rights. With their advances in establishing permanent schools and delineating specific methodologies, particularly for students who were deaf, blind, or mentally disabled, these French educators emerged as the founders of special education as we know it today.

North American special education began in 1817 with the founding of an institution for deaf students at Hartford, Connecticut. The first Canadian special school, again for persons who were deaf, opened near Montreal in 1831 but lack of funds forced it to close within five years, and it was not until 1848 that permanent residential schools were established in British North America. For reasons of economy and convenience, students who were exceptional were chiefly educated in institutional settings. However, very few children were actually served. Differentiation among exceptional conditions was murky, and energies were directed to those with obvious and overt disabilities. Schooling was open to children with sensory impairments (those deaf and blind); to those with intellectual problems (known then as the idiotic and the feeble-minded); and to those considered to be socially at risk (vagrant, neglected, and delinquent children). A concern for children with mild disabilities and the emergence of categories such as *emotionally disturbed, childhood psychoses, physical and health disabilities*, and *learning disabilities* came later; it was largely a phenomenon of the twentieth century.

Special segregated classes in the public schools began seriously in about 1910 and expanded rapidly in the first half of the twentieth century. However, the second half of the century brought vexatious questioning of the value of special education. The 1960s were a benchmark era. The decade saw the emergence of the philosophy of normalization as well as a series of efficacy studies that further probed just what special education was achieving. The 1970s saw intensive scrutiny of the knowledge and practices of special education, and discontent with special classes continued to mount. Agitation by parent and professional groups led to new legislation and many of the changes that are apparent in special education today.

With enabling legislation passed in the United States in 1975, the way was opened for large numbers of students with exceptional conditions to move into regular schools and regular classrooms. Then, throughout the eighties, there were dramatic increases in the number of students mainstreamed into regular classrooms so that by 1991 only 26 percent of students with disabilities in Canada attended a special school or a special class in a regular school (Oderkirk, 1993). Today we see continuing efforts by boards of education and other agencies to increase the universality of special education services.

A ll children differ from one another to varying degrees. The colour of their eyes, hair, and skin differs; the way they dress and speak differs; and their physical, cognitive, social, and emotional development and skills differ. Every child possesses a unique combination of abilities and problems, interests and fears, successes and failures. These individual differences fall along a continuum and are characteristic of all humans.

We all have certain strengths, we all have some limitations on our mental and physical ability, and we all have some disabilities, however minor, when it comes to learning. Most of these problems fall into common areas—a tendency to be easily bored, distractibility, poor study habits, poor memory, inadequate motor control, family interference, and so on. Some of us have problems learning a foreign language, others forget directions or people's faces. For most of us, a perfect backhand is an unreachable goal.

Classroom teachers see the same minor problems all the time. As they take these differences into account, teachers do not expect every student to learn the same things at the same pace, with the same materials, in the same time, and with the same amount of instruction. Good teachers always adapt to learning differences and minor learning difficulties.

In some students, the learning difficulties are more serious, and the children deviate more significantly in one way or another. These are youngsters who are exceptional, those whose learning and behaviour deviates significantly from the norm. They may show differences in the physical, intellectual, communicative, social, or emotional domains, or in some combination of these.

Because the child with an exceptionality is different from the average in some or many areas of functioning, the study of children with exceptionalities is the study of differences. However, it would be quite wrong to focus the study of these children solely on differences. It is equally important that the similarities among children be given significant emphasis. Children with exceptionalities do not differ in every way from their normally developing peers. They are children first and exceptional second. Individuals with exceptionalities share many attitudes, needs, and perceptions with everyone else. They desire acceptance, approval, and affection as much as do their normally developing peers. These similarities are important, and we must always be aware of the danger of seeing only the disability and losing sight of how much children with exceptional conditions resemble other children.

The study of exceptionality is a complex undertaking. Of the many factors that contribute to the complexity, the differences, similarities, and diversity of the population of persons who are exceptional are at the forefront. Many times, we are unable to make definitive statements about groups of children with the same exceptionality or even about a single child. Psychologists have not yet unravelled the mysteries of normal child development, so it is not surprising that understanding and explaining the course of development for children with disabilities poses a unique challenge to developmental researchers. Many of the aspects of atypical child development still remain unclear.

One commonality found in children and youth with exceptionalities is the need for skilled intervention and special care from trained professionals. Intervention may take many forms—medical, technical, therapeutic, and educational. In an educational context, children are considered exceptional only when their educational program must be altered to meet their unique needs. They must demonstrate a clear need for support to reach their full potential.

Special Education

Special education means instruction that is specially designed to meet the unique needs of children and youth who are exceptional. Special education is provided for many students displaying disparate characteristics. It encompasses students who are having problems adjusting to the regular school curriculum and those who encounter difficulties in conforming to the social needs of the classroom. Some pupils who are exceptional may require specific physical adaptations in the classroom and the school environment. Children who are gifted and talented are recognized as exceptional because they too need specialized help from professionals to fully develop their unique abilities.

Until quite recently, special education was chiefly identified with the school system and with school-age children and their teachers. This is no longer true. In the past two decades, special education has expanded dramatically. It now includes infants and preschoolers and reaches up to encompass adolescents and young adults. As well, recent demographic data suggest that public schools are faced with increasing linguistic and cultural diversity. One result of this change is that the special education system is increasingly serving students who are in the process of acquiring a second language or who come from home backgrounds where a language other than English is spoken. Today, special education could be a mother using sign language with her deaf infant in the home, a caregiver in a nursery school modifying an activity for a preschooler, a classroom teacher using remedial techniques in the school-room, a counsellor setting up a work experience program for a young disabled adult, or a teacher assisting a child from a linguistic minority.

Special education is founded on the proposition that all children can reach their full potential given the opportunity, effective teaching, and proper resources. Both traditionally and currently, special education has been undertaken by different personnel in different settings. While the current trend in North America is toward inclusive settings (see Chapter 2), a few children may be placed in special schools or special classrooms with specially trained teachers. Others may be in the regular classroom with adapted or modified instruction and with special assistance in the resource room. Today, in fact, the majority of students with exceptionalities are in regular classrooms, with instruction generally presented by classroom teachers who are increasingly required to tailor classroom instruction to the individual, not the group.

Although the onus for direct instruction is increasingly being placed on general education teachers, they are not alone in their efforts. Psychologists, speech therapists, physical and occupational therapists, counsellors, and other professionals consult and collaborate with teachers to help them to plan the best possible education for each student who is exceptional. These people form part of what is referred to as *related services, ancillary services, auxiliary services,* the *inter-disciplinary team,* or the *inclusion team.* We use the broad term **support services** to refer to those services that permit a child who is exceptional to benefit from special education. A sampling of the disciplines that may be involved is shown in Table 1-1.

Table 1-1 Sampling of disciplines involved with children who are exceptional

Medical	Paramedical	Educational	Psychological, social, behavioural
physician	audiologist	home-visiting teacher	intervenor
pediatrician	optometrist	infant stimulation therapist	social worker
neurologist	physical therapist	preschool teacher	school social worker
otolaryngologist	occupational therapist	regular classroom teacher	child care worker
ophthalmologist	public health nurse	special class teacher	guidance counsellor
dental surgeon	school nurse	remedial specialist	psychologist
psychiatrist		itinerant teacher	
nurse		learning assistant	
		school principal	
		speech therapist	
		language pathologist	
		paraprofessional	
		volunteer	

Definitions of Students Who Are Exceptional

Children who have differences that substantially change the way they learn, respond, or behave have been described in many ways. In fact, you will find these children referred to as children with exceptionalities, children with exceptional conditions, children who are handicapped, children with special needs, children with disabilities or disabling conditions, and children who are challenged. While the phrase *children with exceptionalities* tends to be the most encompassing, keep in mind that *exceptionality* can be defined and described in many ways, and that these ways constantly change in attempts to make descriptors more socially useful and relevant.

Precise definitions of individual disabling conditions are the vital first step in providing solid rationales for generating theories, formulating hypotheses, classifying disorders, selecting subjects, communicating with others (Hammill, 1990), and obtaining accurate prevalence figures. Nevertheless, the search for precise definitions is ongoing; in many ways, the area of disability and handicap is characterized by conceptual chaos. Children who are exceptional are constantly being reconceptualized, reconsidered, and renamed. But perhaps, given the broad range of disciplines providing information and input, the various classification systems, the ongoing changes in terminology, and the continuing discovery of new etiologies (causes), such chaos is inevitable.

Many disciplines contribute to research and intervention for children who are exceptional. Alongside the expected areas of education, social work, medicine, and psychology, information is generated from such varied fields as genetics, sociology, economics, law, ethics, and politics. Many professionals in disciplines allied with special education have different ways of looking at exceptionalities and use slightly different frameworks for classification. This means that the educational use of the term *exceptional* differs from that used in biology, medicine, psychology, social work, and other disciplines.

Some people assess differences according to how far development deviates from the norm. A psychologist, for example, may report that a child's score on an IQ test is two standard deviations below the mean. Others classify differences in terms of some underlying organic or functional cause; for example, medical personnel would determine whether a child has *spastic* or *athetoid* cerebral palsy. Educators, of course, describe exceptional conditions in terms of educational functioning and achievement. If a child with athetoid cerebral palsy or mild mental retardation is in a classroom, the teacher is more likely to be concerned with the activities and techniques that will help the child learn than with the exact number of the IQ score or the etiology of the condition.

Some Important Terminology

Today's terminology, both specific and general, is relatively non-stigmatizing. For example, we no longer use emotionally laden and essentially incorrect terms such as *deaf and dumb* or *feeble-minded*. We know that deaf people are not "dumb" in any way and that people who are intellectually challenged in our society can learn and contribute.

Contemporary society holds a more humanistic perception of the whole individual and sees the handicap, disorder, or disability as only one part of the total person. Always, we use terms that place the child first, the disability second. Hence, we speak of children with Down syndrome or children with intellectual disabilities rather than of "Down-syndrome children" and "mentally disabled children." Or by simply saying "a person who uses a wheelchair" one communicates information without using emotionally charged terms (McCrindle, 1995).

Further, *exceptional* is not the only generic term used to describe these children. Other terms are used synonymously, although the meanings are more restricted and slightly different. Some of the major descriptors are outlined below.

- *Impairments* are concerned with abnormalities of body structure and system function resulting from any cause.

- **Disabilities** reflect the consequences of impairments in terms of functional performance and activity by the individual; an individual who is disabled suffers from a disability or impairment of function in one or more areas, such as vision, hearing, or mobility (World Health, 1980). In other words, a disability refers to the behaviour relevant to the completion of a task and obviously implies a limited aptitude in that task.

- *Handicaps* are concerned with the disadvantages experienced by individuals as a result of impairments or disability and reflect an interaction of the individual with the environment (World Health, 1980). A **handicap**, then, refers to environmental or functional demands placed on a disabled person in a particular situation that are not met. A disability is always with a person, a handicap is not. A disability becomes a handicap when the person who is disabled is unable to meet environmental demands and achieve personal goals. For example, a bright child with spina bifida could function well in math class but would be handicapped on the ball field.

- *Atypical youngsters* are those who do not reach the norm in some functional area or areas.

- **Special needs** is an educational term used to designate pupils who require special education.

- The terms *high risk* or **at risk** are widely used in contemporary special education. Risk status is a mechanism for describing the likelihood that a particular individual will experience a specific outcome, given certain conditions (Planta, 1990). When the term *at risk* is used, children are seen to be vulnerable to some future condition. Some children are at risk for exceptional conditions that affect their functioning and achievement. Or a child may be at risk for learning and behavioural problems as a result of factors such as poverty or abuse, psychological disorders, or generally having an unproductive and unrewarding childhood. Older students may be at risk for dropping out of school or for delinquency. At-risk status is discussed in Chapter 3.

- The original construct of *developmental disability*, introduced in 1970 with the passage of the United States Public Law 91-517, included only individuals with mental retardation, epilepsy, and cerebral palsy. Amendments in 1978 broadened the concept and today a **developmental disability/delay** refers to a condition which represents a significant delay in the process of development. It does not refer to a condition in which a child is slightly or momentarily lagging in development or is at risk of a delay. The presence of a developmental delay is an indication that the process of development is significantly affected and that without special intervention, it is likely that educational performance at school age will be affected ("Developmental ...," 1991, p. 1).

- Students with *severe handicaps* are now generically defined as those who may possess severe language and/or perceptual/cognitive deprivations, and evidence abnormal behaviour such as failure to respond to pronounced social stimuli; self-mutilation; self-stimulation; manifestation of intense and prolonged temper tantrums; and the absence of rudimentary forms of verbal contact. Students also have extremely fragile physiological conditions (U.S. Federal definition 20 USC 1401(7)).

- Children with special health management needs (extremely fragile physiological conditions) are also referred to as **medically fragile** children. This category includes children who demonstrate a wide range of chronic and progressive illnesses and severe disabilities such as bronchiopulmonary dysplasia, cystic fibrosis, congenital malformations, neuromuscular diseases, and many others. Many of these children require technology, special services, or some form of ongoing medical support for survival (Nelken, 1987; Prendergast, 1995).

Major Categories of Exceptionality

The current classification systems used in special education evolved gradually, haphazardly, and inconsistently over the decades. Today, the search for universal or specific features of various conditions is ongoing, but remains futile and frustrating. Our classification systems remain imprecise. There is relatively little standardization in the study of children who are exceptional and a single consistent and universally accepted method of describing different groups of children with certain exceptional conditions does not exist.

Considerable overlap occurs in the classification of disabling conditions. Many children who are exceptional have more than one difficulty and, because they do not fall easily into one specific category, they are difficult to classify. Further, children who have been traditionally classified and grouped as mildly disabled—those described as learning disabled, mildly mentally retarded, and mildly emotionally disturbed—tend to share a variety of academic and behavioural characteristics that transcend traditional approaches to classification. These children often exhibit such similar behaviour that it is difficult to accurately differentiate the disability (see Chapter 5).

Keeping these caveats in mind, we can say that, in general, the special traits of children who are exceptional fall into the following categories:

- *Communication disorders*, which includes children with speech difficulties and language problems. In this text, we group children with learning disabilities into this category (although they could be placed in other areas) because so many of them manifest communication deficits.

- *Intellectual differences*, which includes children who are intellectually superior (gifted) and those who are intellectually disabled.

- *Behavioural disorders*, which includes a wide variety of problems—conduct disorders, anxiety and withdrawal, attention deficit/hyperactivity disorder, social maladjustment, and juvenile delinquency.

- *Sensory disabilities*, which includes children with auditory impairments and those with visual problems.

- *Physical disabilities and impaired health*, which includes children with neurological defects, orthopedic conditions, birth defects, and conditions that are a result of infection and disease.

- *Developmental disabilities,* an inclusive term. The category includes children with pervasive disorders such as severe mental retardation and infantile autism, and those with multiple disabilities such as such as cerebral palsy and mental retardation, or deafness and blindness.

Additional qualifiers may be used to provide more specificity to these general classifications. Degrees of severity are the most commonly used qualifiers. Conditions are described as mild, moderate, severe, or profound. When we speak of a child with mild mental retardation, we mean that the child has an IQ somewhere in the range of 55 to 70 and demonstrates deficits in **adaptive behaviour**—the ability to respond to and function in the environment according to age and social standards. On the other hand, a child with profound mental retardation would have an IQ below 25 and extreme difficulties in any form of adaptive behaviour.

Looking at Labels

A central theme of this book is that no two children are alike. Children who are exceptional should be viewed first as individuals, and then as people who differ from the norm in some way. A child's functional level and behaviour should be the critical components analyzed for intervention, and we should be wary of supplying labels that are arbitrary and that permanently assign a child to a specific category of exceptionality.

Despite this, and despite the distrust of labels and categorization that permeates today's special education, discrete categories of exceptionality and specific labels for particular conditions still abound.

Labelling refers to the categorizing of children on the basis of their primary disability. The practice evolved gradually; no one really planned it. Labels are products of the human mind—in special education they grew from a psychomedical model which encompassed diagnosis, classification, and placement. (The Historical Notes that open Chapter 3 explain the medical model and its genesis and development.)

The labels, and the influence they have, vary greatly, and often depend upon the labeller's perspective, which may be shaped by cultural and/or professional background. For example, professionals use the term *mental retardation* to describe children who are intellectually below the norm according to the standards of our society. However, in the United States Puerto Rican and African American parents reject the term, which is culturally offensive to them, as do parents in Pakistan (Harry, 1992; Mazurek and Winzer, 1994).

Much debate surrounds the use of labels in special education. People question whether labels are "necessary conceptual shorthand in a busy world" or whether they are "subversive disempowerment" (McCrindle, 1995, p. 16).

The research on labels has been inconclusive (Brantlinger and Guskin, 1987), and probably the best we can say is that while every situation has the potential for children to suffer adverse effects from labelling, in some cases labels may prove advantageous. Some of the many pros and cons of the labelling dilemma are shown in the Matter of Debate box.

Many of those opposed to the use of labels argue for generic or non-categorical approaches (such as *special needs* or *learning handicapped*), which focus on behaviours and

A Matter of Debate

Labels in Special Education

✓ Arguments for labels

A carefully considered classification can serve to simplify information for administrators, placement counsellors, educators, and parents.

Labels may be helpful to parents, especially when a condition is initially diagnosed. For parents, being able to use the name of a disability seems to give them some control over it (Akerley, 1975).

Categories are necessary to ensure quality services. For example, the rehabilitation system cannot disregard the fact that the unique needs of the visually impaired require the services of specialized professionals (Gallagher, 1988).

In England and Wales, where disability categories were completely abolished, there have been negative consequences (Feniak, 1988).

Labels permit us to identify children whose learning and behavioural characteristics cause them to require differentiated instruction.

Students with the same label may be assumed to share a common set of learning characteristics that may lead to efficient educational programming.

Labels may be a necessary administrative lever within the school system to obtain funding for special services.

Labels promote effective communication among agencies, services, and professionals that deal with individuals who are exceptional.

Labels result in increased visibility for groups of people with special needs.

Labels make others more tolerant of a disability. They may provide explanations for behaviour or appearance for which people may otherwise be blamed or stigmatized (Fiedler and Simpson, 1987).

Teachers react to children differently according to the child's classroom behaviour, not the label or handicap classification (Curci and Gottlieb, 1990).

The label gifted enhances a child's status in the family and affects the parents' perceptions of the child (Cornell 1983).

✗ Arguments against labels

Categorical definitions of exceptional children maintain the purity of each population by focusing on discrepant attributes, the unique and elusive characteristics that distinguish one defined population from other categories in special education.

The practice offers few benefits to the labelled individual. In general, classification systems are too often unreliable and inconsistent, and labels seldom adequately reflect a child's educational and therapeutic needs.

Too often, a label describes only the lacks, problems, and deficiencies of a person. It picks out a single quality, calls attention to it, and stresses how this quality differs from the norm. When development is different from the norm, it is assumed that there is something wrong either in the family, the child, or the culture.

An oversimplified label suggests that the child is an unhealthy, poorly functioning organism, deprived in some way. Strengths are obscured.

Although children may share a common exceptionality, they do not form homogeneous groups. Each disability ranges from mild to severe. A subgroup of children with intellectual disabilities, for example, is extremely heterogeneous: children exhibit different behaviours and are affected by the disability in various ways. Also, a child who is mildly disabled functions quite differently than a child with a severe disability.

Labelling engenders unfortunate and often unanticipated consequences. In the past, many children were misclassified and shunted into unsuitable educational environments.

The use of discrete categories for exceptional children tends to oversimplify the facts.

Sometimes the labels are incorrect, as in making dyslexia synonymous with learning disabilities. Or labels may exaggerate the severity of a disability, as in the labelling of a hard-of-hearing child as deaf or a visually impaired youngster as blind.

Labels do not automatically result in better services for a child.

A label suggests a permanent disorder requiring long-term professional treatment. Children must wear their labels everywhere and all the time, although they may not apply in all situations.

People tend to view a labelled person differently from a non-labelled one. People are more likely to expect deviant behaviour from labelled individuals.

Other students are sensitive to labels and to the differences between peers who attend different educational placements from their regular classroom. In one study (Bak, Cooper, Dobroth, and Siperstein, 1987) children responded to de facto labels of *resource room* and *special classroom* differently. They saw the students going to the resource room as significantly more capable than those in special classes.

Labels may affect a teacher's interactions with students and may tend to absolve teachers of their responsibilities. If teachers are predisposed to expect behaviour consonant with a child's classification, it may negatively affect interactions with the child. For example, a teacher may not even try to help little Jimmy with arithmetic because Jimmy has been labelled as mildly disabled and the teacher does not believe that disabled children can learn to add and subtract.

Labelling may filter down to affect perceptions of other children in a family. Richey and Ysseldyke (1983) conducted two investigations concerning teacher expectations of the younger siblings of students with learning disabilities. In the first study, teachers who had previously taught an older learning-disabled sibling were asked to predict their student's future academic performance in the first week of school. In the second study, teachers were asked to predict the academic performance of hypothetical siblings for the following year when they had older learning-disabled students in the class. In both studies, the investigators found that teachers held low expectations for the siblings of learning-disabled children. Similarly, Sydney and Minner (1984) found that teachers recommended placements in special programming for students with behaviour disorders more often for children with siblings identified as behaviourally disordered than for an identically described student with a non-disabled sibling.

High expectations communicated through the labelling process for a gifted child may contribute to feelings of failure; the child never quite measures up to expectations (e.g. Buescher, 1991).

Within the family, the presence of a child labelled as gifted has been found to have an ultimately negative impact on family dynamics and lead to adjustment difficulties among siblings. The gifted child may have a special position as family attention and resources are claimed for him or her, leading to increased competition in the family and sibling jealousy. (See Chapter 15.)

learning patterns rather than on diagnostic categories (such as *mild mental retardation*). The stress is on the functional behaviour of a child as the most important factor in that child's educational program. Such approaches, it is said, encourage educators to emphasize the common characteristics that exist among children with learning difficulties, and will do much to combat the stigmatization and stereotyping of individuals who are exceptional.

What do persons with disabilities themselves say about labelling? *The Disability Rag*, a U.S. disability activist publication, periodically editorializes against euphemisms created by non-disabled people. They point out that disabilities are real, and present policies are needed to enable real choice, not euphemistic terms that gloss over the need for action

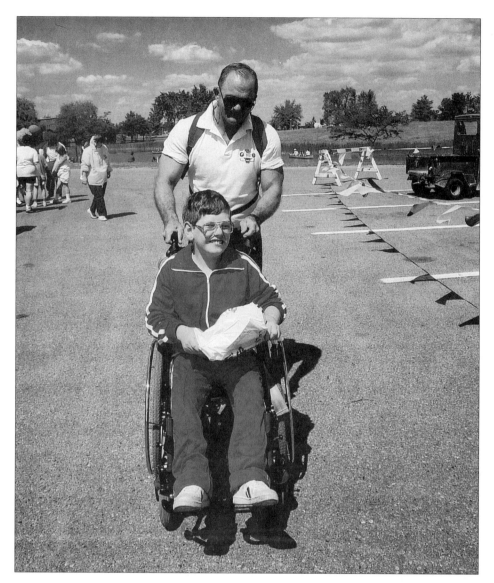

Approximately 15.5 percent of the Canadian school-age population is considered to be exceptional.

(Sleeter and Grant, 1994). As Kate McCrindle points out, many people with disabilities object to "'sugarcoated euphemisms' such as *handi-capable* and *physically challenged* because they are condescending and reinforce the idea that a disability can't be dealt with in a straightforward manner" (1995, p. 22). Expressions that emphasize abilities and mirror advances are more constructive. These include words such as *choice, empowerment, inclusion, self-determination*, and *independence*.

Prevalence

Recent United Nations surveys estimate that there are 290 million people with moderate to severe physical and mental disabilities in the world today and their numbers are expected to double in the next 35 years. In developing countries, the catastrophic rates may be even greater than present figures suggest. The numbers of people affected by largely preventable diseases, such as water-borne blindness, tuberculosis, and leprosy, and from chronic debilitating conditions that stem from malnutrition, impure water, and inadequate sanitation, is simply staggering (Mazurek and Winzer, 1994).

In the United States, approximately 35 million people are considered exceptional. The number of Canadians who have some form of disability jumped more than 27 percent between 1986 and 1991, from 3.3 million to 4.2 million or from 13.2 to 15.5 percent of the population ("Prevalence ...," 1995).

How many children among this number have disabilities? In 1986, there were an estimated 277 000 Canadian children with disabilities, representing 5 percent of all young people (Nessner, 1990). By 1991, numbers had risen. Of the 390 000 children who are disabled, 89 percent have a mild disability, and 8 percent a moderate disability. About 3 percent, or 11 500 children, have a severe disability ("Prevalence ...," 1995).

Estimates of the numbers of individuals who are exceptional are generally reported as either *incidence* or *prevalence*. **Incidence** refers to the number of new cases of a particular condition identified over a given period of time, usually a year. **Prevalence** applies to the total number of existing cases, old and new. Prevalence is also used to refer to the percentage or proportion of the population that falls into a given category.

During the school years, approximately 15.5 percent of the Canadian school-age population is considered to be exceptional. Among these children and adolescents, boys are more likely to be disabled than girls.

Table 1-2 shows prevalence rates drawn by the Canadian Council for Exceptional Children (1989) from some provinces. View these figures with caution. A precise determination of the incidence and prevalence rates for exceptional children and adolescents with specific conditions in Canada is very difficult. In general, estimates of the number of children with some identifiable special condition vary widely, particularly for those with high-incidence disabilities such as learning disabilities and behavioural disorders. It is easier to obtain accurate figures for low-incidence disabilities such as severe visual impairment. This is further illustrated in Figure 1-1, which shows severity rates.

Prevalence estimates are influenced by a complex set of interacting factors. Contributing to the difficulties in obtaining accurate figures are the varying definitions and descriptions of disabilities, the methods of data collection, and the interpretation of data. In addition, social factors related to stigmatization and public perception inhibit accurate prevalence estimates.

Definitional Problems

We noted earlier that children with exceptional conditions require services from a range of professional disciplines, chiefly medical, therapeutic, and educational. These necessary services sometimes confound prevalence rates simply because each discipline brings its own definitions and characterizations of what is exceptional.

In the educational system, students are only considered exceptional when their educational program must be altered to meet their unique needs. They must demonstrate a clear need for support services to reach their full human potential. Although heart disease is a serious condition, it may not impact on a student's learning, so a child with a heart disorder may not be counted among the special education population. On the other hand, a medical condition such as pediatric AIDS has major effects on learning, and a child would

Table 1-2 Proportions of children belonging to major categories of exceptionality

	Mental disability		Learning disability		Hearing impaired	
	▲	■	▲	■	▲	■
Newfoundland	0.59	7.87	6.38	85.6	0.14	1.9
Nova Scotia	1.21	10.89	7.14	64.32	0.1	0.9
Quebec	0.57	5.81	10.23	76.4	—	—
Ontario	1.73	22.85	3.10	40.9	0.8	1.15
Saskatchewan	0.35	12.10	2.95	60.92	0.12	4.18
British Columbia	1.05	8.83	1.29	10.95	0.15	1.31

	Gifted/ talented		Visually impaired		Behavioural disorders		Multiple disabilities	
	▲	■	▲	■	▲	■	▲	■
Newfoundland	—	—	0.15	1.97	—	—	0.15	1.97
Nova Scotia	—	—	0.08	0.78	0.44	3.96	0.08	0.79
Quebec	—	—	—	—	1.45	10.85	0.72	5.39
Ontario	1.3	—	0.03	0.37	0.45	5.94	0.16	2.08
Saskatchewan	—	—	0.039	1.33	0.26	9.10	0.22	7.55
British Columbia	1.9	—	0.08	0.66	0.5	0.42	—	—

▲ percentage of total school-aged population
■ percentage of population with disabilities

Source: Canadian Council for Exceptional Children, 1989

very likely require special education services.

Moreover, special education itself uses many vague and inconsistent definitions and, lacking clear definitions, it is almost impossible to estimate prevalence. Because school systems tend to interpret a child's condition according to services provided, a child may be called learning disabled in one school district and counted as a low achiever in another.

Changing Diagnoses

The diagnosis of a disabling condition is not, nor should it be, immutable. A diagnosis that is correct today could easily be inappropriate tomorrow. Frequently, children who are affected by speech defects, behavioural disorders, or learning disabilities improve to such an extent that they are no longer considered disabled (Hallahan and Kauffman, 1991).

Another factor that confounds efforts to estimate prevalence is ongoing research that brings new ways of looking at disabling conditions. For example, recent discoveries in neurology and genetics have altered traditional conceptions of the causes and nature of infantile autism; the condition is no longer classified as a severe emotional disturbance but as a neurological disability.

Figure 1-1
Prevalence of disability by severity levels

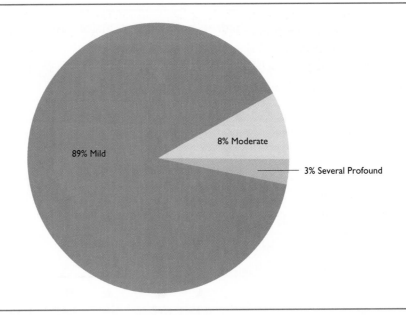

Sources: Oderkirk, 1993; "Prevalence of disability by severity levels," 1995

Multiple Disabilities

Confusion arises about the classification of particular children. With congenital anomalies or malformations, there can be a number of diagnoses. Further, many children have more than one pertinent set of characteristics: a child might be mentally retarded and hearing-impaired, or speech disordered and blind. Children with multiple disabilities are often classified according to their major condition (called the **primary disability**). For example, a child who is deaf with an emotional problem may be classified as hearing-impaired and receive services designed for deaf children; the emotional problem is presumed to be a secondary condition. Or, the child may be numbered in both categories, or simply as multiply disabled. Obviously, such varied counting and categorization makes rates unstable.

Early Identification

Low-incidence disabilities, such as severe retardation, serious physical impairment, or blindness, are usually identified early and involve more professional intervention than high-incidence conditions, such as mild intellectual disability. A mild intellectual disability, for example, may not be identified until the child has to confront the complexities of reading and writing in the classroom. As a result, low-incidence disabilities are more likely to be reported.

Changing Rates

Difficulties also spring from different prevalence figures at different points in the life cycle. As we just pointed out, children with mild intellectual disabilities are often not identified early. For these children, the most pronounced difficulties clearly relate to the structured environment of formal schooling. During the school years, therefore, the prevalence of mild intellectual disability tends to show a sharp increase. But since most of the adults who function in this range achieve personal and vocational independence, the estimated prevalence of mild disability decreases substantially as these adults enter the working world and assume their places as productive citizens.

The Stigma of Identification

Some parents are reluctant to have their child identified as exceptional. They may not report a condition, or they may opt for a different category. Parents seem to see labels that specify a particular problem as less stigmatizing than those that imply a global, developmental impairment. For example, many parents find the term *learning disabilities* far preferable to *mild mental retardation*.

Survey Problems and Sampling Errors

Epidemiology refers to the study of the distribution and determinants of diseases and disabling conditions in a population. Survey problems result when epidemiologists and other researchers use varied definitions of an exceptionality. Surveys can also be misleading when figures from a small area are extrapolated to the rest of the country. Newfoundland, for example, has a high rate of spina bifida, and to extrapolate Newfoundland figures to the rest of Canada would clearly be unwise.

Intervention with Children Who Have Exceptionalities

Intervention is a general term that refers to the application of professional skills to maintain or improve a child's potential and functioning. Early intervention, a major trend in current special education practice, refers to the establishment of educational and support services for young children who have disabilities or who are at risk for disabilities, and for their families. Although intervention is strongly associated with active educational programming, the term also includes medical intervention, mental health services, and welfare provisions for the family and the child.

A number of processes and terms are subsumed under the general rubric of intervention. First of all, there is habilitation, which comes from the Latin *habilitare*, to make skilled. In **habilitation**, people in medical, social, psychological, and educational fields support and assist children with disabilities in their development and daily lives. Closely aligned to habilitation is **rehabilitation**, a therapeutic term that refers to procedures that endeavour to restore an individual to normal or optimal functioning. **Remediation** is an educational term that refers to helping a child to overcome, or compensate for, specific deficits in learning and development.

For the child who is exceptional, the basic approaches to care and education include three of the major forms of intervention—medical, educational, and social. We discuss some basic intervention techniques here; these are expanded upon in later chapters.

Intervention with exceptional children can involve a variety of specialists.

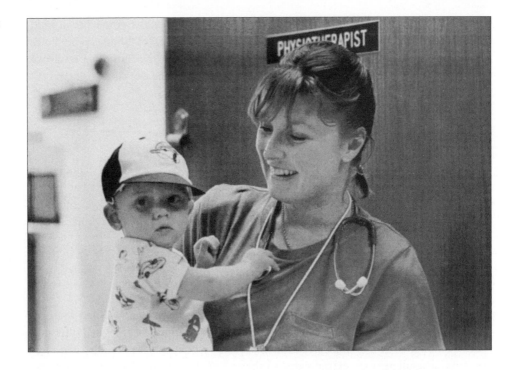

Medical Intervention

Medical intervention and treatment for children who are exceptional is a complex and highly sophisticated process that involves a variety of specialists with unique skills. Although medical treatment is extremely varied, the most common forms involve surgery; treatment that is life saving, such as insulin; the controlled use of medication; and supportive therapy.

Surgery

In recent decades, many forms of surgical treatment for children who are exceptional have emerged, leading to the development of subspecialties within the field of pediatric surgery. The most widely used surgical treatments currently include reconstructive surgery for repair of physical anomalies such as a cleft lip or palate; neurosurgery for disabling conditions of the brain and spinal cord; and orthopedic surgery for problems of the skeletal system that occur in youngsters with cerebral palsy or multiple physical anomalies. Other sophisticated techniques have also been developed to help children with Down syndrome, to insert cochlea implants in deaf individuals, and to transplant organs in children with cystic fibrosis.

Psychopharmacology

Of all the medical treatments for children with exceptional conditions, teachers are most likely to come into contact with *psychopharmacology*, or drug therapy. In 1937, Charles Bradley was the first to treat specific educational disabilities and hyperactive behaviour with a stimulant drug, Benzedrine. Bradley noticed an overall improvement in the children's mood, activity level, and educational achievement (Bradley, 1937). Since this seminal work psychopharmacological approaches to treatment have increased dramatically, and today drug therapy is used extensively with children who demonstrate physical and neurological complications. While the drugs administered to children vary widely in purpose and pharmacological action, in general, drugs are intended to manage problems of behaviour, activity level, emotion, or epilepsy. We discuss drug therapy fully in Chapter 8.

Therapy

Therapy, the treatment of an illness or disabling condition, consists of a broad range of interventions to help children adapt to their particular disabilities. Physical, occupational, and speech/language therapists provide many essential treatments.

Physical and occupational therapy can help children to develop hand skills, body coordination, and other physical skills, and can aid in gross motor development, muscle relaxation, and fine motor control. Speech and language therapists are trained in the evaluation and remedial treatment of speech and language problems in children and adults, and they may develop appropriate augmentative communication for children who cannot talk. Speech and language therapy may also be used with children who have difficulty in controlling the fine motor muscles needed for eating.

There are different types of therapy. Direct therapy occurs when therapeutic techniques are used in a treatment that only the therapist can safely carry out. Monitoring, in which teachers are involved, occurs when therapists monitor treatment carried out by parents, teachers, or classroom aides (Dunn, 1989).

Educational Intervention

Education for children who are exceptional may be provided through a variety of educational arrangements and instructional alternatives. We look at some broad ideas here; each chapter explores educational intervention for specific populations.

Educational Settings

When it comes to educational settings, the alternatives are determined by the unique needs of each child. Many different kinds and combinations of programs are required to accommodate the wide range of conditions that occur in varying degrees of severity and the need for different types and degrees of assistance at various age levels. Even with today's strong movement toward inclusion (see Chapter 2), many experts in the field (e.g. Marston, 1996) recommend that in order to provide appropriate education for students who are exceptional a cascade, or continuum, of services is necessary, as represented in Figure 1-2.

Settings on the cascade involve a series of options that move from contrived to more natural arrangements. Within a cascade of services, the wider the pyramid, the more children are encompassed; throughout are increasingly restrictive environments, with the point of the triangle generally considered to be the most restrictive because it denotes children on homebound instruction, who have little opportunity for social interaction with their peers.

Inclusion in the General Classroom

It is the general classroom that provides the child who is exceptional with the least restrictive environment and the opportunity for maximum integration with normally developing peers. When a child is included in the regular classroom, the classroom teacher holds

Figure 1-2
A diagrammatic model of a cascade of services

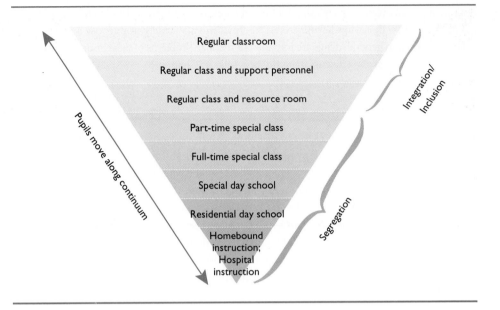

primary responsibility for that child and must ensure that appropriate programs and curriculum modifications are made. The classroom teacher also works with a number of professionals to tailor education to the needs of the individual child.

Students in general classrooms and their teachers are supported in a number of ways that vary according to the needs of the child, the type of program espoused by the school, and the resources of the school. In very general terms, supports by both personnel and institutional arrangements are:

- *Itinerant teachers.* These are specially trained educators who give individual assistance to a child for specific periods during the normal school schedule. The type and intensity of itinerant intervention depend on the needs of the child. Some children may simply need tutoring to keep up in regular school subjects; others may require a specific program in one area, such as speech and auditory training. Itinerant teachers may work with classroom teachers on program preparation and offer in-service training. They may also help prepare the child's classmates by explaining the child's disabling condition. In some instances, the itinerant teacher serves as an advocate to ensure that the special child receives the best education possible in the most appropriate environment.

- *Educational consultants.* In general, consultants do not have responsibilities but serve to assist classroom teachers throughout a school district to maintain children who are exceptional in their regular school programs. As an indirect service provider, the consultant may function as a diagnostician, a materials specialist, an administrator of various services, and as an advocate.

- *Paraprofessionals.* Variously referred to as teacher's aides, teaching assistants, classroom assistants, child care workers and so on, paraprofessionals are an integral part of the instructional team that shares responsibility in the area of learning facilitation. The aide must be able to develop and/or select daily elements of the curriculum as defined in an individualized educational plan, deliver instruction, provide for remedial experiences, and monitor a child's progress (Goodman, 1990). Aides are also used for

Research Notes

Paraprofessionals in Special Education

Assistance in the classroom is often offered by support personnel. These people have many titles, but more and more often are being called paraprofessionals "just as their counterparts in law and medicine are designated as paralegals and paramedics" (Pickett, 1989, p. 1).

Paraprofessionals first came into the schools in the 1950s. Since then, their roles have changed. What began as clerical and administrative supports for teachers has evolved from classroom helper to a greater emphasis on instructional support. Paraprofessionals now often fill roles that have traditionally been assigned to teachers (Jones and Bender, 1993).

In today's classrooms, para-educators may perform a variety of instructional and non-instructional tasks. They may provide direct instruction to individuals or groups of students following the teacher's guidelines concerning choice of material and the instructional plan, and/or observe and record data. They may also perform other duties such as maintaining inventory and ordering supplies.

As schools move toward inclusive programming, the roles of paraprofessionals will assume even greater importance. Nevertheless, while paraprofessionals are crucial to the success of inclusion, their use is not founded on a solid research base: the roles of paraprofessionals in the inclusive process have not been clearly delineated or even discussed in the literature on inclusion (French and Pickett, 1997), and there is little on what these people actually do all day. Jones and Bender (1993) found only 13 experimental or quasi-experimental studies on the effects of paraprofessionals on student outcomes in special education from 1957 to 1993.

There is much ambivalence about the proper role of paraprofessionals by teachers, administrators, and the paraprofessionals themselves. The small body of research does agree that non-teaching support personnel, whatever their title, are not meant to take away the authority of the teacher; they are to support the teacher.

In a BC study (Lamont and Hill, 1991), teachers, administrators, and the paraprofessionals themselves were asked which activities were appropriate for paraprofessionals to perform. There was general consensus that the tasks should be non-instructional and supportive in nature. Deemed inappropriate were tasks such as functioning as a substitute when the teacher was absent, and administering and scoring formal assessments.

Teachers saw the role of the paraprofessional as one of support, not instruction. Teacher assistants are not to replace the educational decision making or to make plans; they are to assist the teacher in enacting plans. They are not to teach, but to tutor and reinforce previously taught material. Activities such as modification of educational materials, one to one instruction, behavioural management support, administration of assessments, and involvement in IEP preparation, are activities that paraprofessionals are often asked to perform (Frith and Lindsey, 1980; Lamont and Hill, 1991).

The inclusive movement and the mounting involvement of paraprofessionals has brought its own set of problems. In fact, some current approaches to providing instructional assistant support might be counterproductive (Giangreco, Edelman, MacFarland, and Luiselli, 1997), and over-reliance on paraprofessionals might be a disservice to students (Udvari-Solnar, 1996).

First, the proximity and availability of aides can create a readily accessible opportunity for teachers to avoid assuming responsibility and ownership for the education of children with disabilities placed in their classes (see Giangreco et al., 1997). Successful teaching and learning may be compromised when para-educators, who have not received specialized training rather than as certified professionals, are providing services to students with disabilities ("Inclusion where...," 1996). This happens when aides have unfettered autonomy and are given ownership of children with special needs. Giangreco and colleagues (1997) found that aides were making and implementing virtually all of the day to day curricula and instructional decisions. Similarly, in a British Columbia study (Lamont and Hill, 1991), one respondent wrote that "Behaviour management is left entirely to the judgment of the paraprofessional." Another said that "My paraprofessional is totally responsible for the personal care and well being of the child"(p. 21).

Second, few teachers enter the profession with the expectation of having to direct adults. Certified teachers have little training in supervising paraprofessionals. When teachers have little or no preparation in the supervision of paraprofessionals, yet they hold responsibility for assignments and outcomes, this can cause dissonance in some teachers (Salzburg and Morgan, 1995). Many teachers are reluctant to supervise (French and Pickett, 1997).

Finally, aides regularly separate children with disabilities from the class group, and this is not in the spirit of inclusion. In this way, it may be that one-to-one aides are excessive and actually a barrier to inclusion by hindering interaction with classmates.

Many jurisdictions are working to overcome problems. For example, the Ontario CEC recently released a position paper on Professional Standards and Competencies for Educational Assistants. A major recommendation is that "all school boards should develop clear, written role descriptions for educational assistants that recognize their function as a professional member of the school team" (Ontario CEC, 1997, p. 7).

individual educational assessments and the recording of behaviour. The Research Notes provide more information about paraprofessionals in special education.

- *Therapists.* The speech/language, physical, and occupational therapists that we mentioned earlier are important in special education services. Often today, the therapeutic services will be brought to the child in the classroom rather than the child being removed to access services.

- *Resource rooms.* Before the advent of resource rooms in the mid-1970s, children with mild learning difficulties floundered in the regular classroom, were placed in special classes, or were sent to special schools. Today, resource rooms stand at the point between self-contained and regular classrooms. Pupils receive part of their education in the regular classroom and part of it in the resource room. This allows some learning to take place in a less distracting, less intense, and less competitive environment than the regular classroom. The regular classroom teacher still carries primary responsibility for program design but works in close co-ordination with resource room personnel.

  Resource rooms have been described as "an island of learning opportunities" (Vergason and Anderegg, 1993, p. 475). Resource room teachers design, alter, and present instruction across a number of curriculum areas, and address elements that facilitate students' success in the regular environment. They may provide support in academic learning of both the core and remedial curricula, and training in social and communication skills that will help the student to interact better in the regular classroom.

- *Collaboration and consultation.* Ideally, when children with disabilities are in regular classrooms, teachers receive support in the form of training, help, and consultation from special education teachers and other personnel, instructional aides, and so on.

Especially important is collaboration that forges a different relationship between special education and regular class teachers (Willis, 1995). By working with special education teachers, general educators learn about special education skills such as assessing learning styles and abilities, modifying curriculum, using various teaching strategies to meet student needs, and providing emotional support for students (Hanson, 1996).

- *Educational teams* are a concrete manifestation of the collaborative process. When teachers have students who are exceptional assigned to their classrooms, they accept assistance from a wide variety of support services; members of several disciplines pool their expertise in order to assist classroom teachers. The teacher may work on a school-based team with the principal, a psychologist, itinerant teachers, a speech therapist, a language therapist, and such allied child care personnel as audiologists and school nurses. Team collaboration provides a forum for regular and special educators to share ideas and concerns. The organization of a team is largely determined by the needs of a child and school policy (see Chapter 14).

One of the major duties of the team is to decide on both placement and program for a child who may be assigned to special education. First, the team considers a student's special difficulties in school and determines if the student is eligible for special education. Placement is carefully considered. Finally (and often following further assessment) the team discusses and documents the accommodations, adaptations, and modifications that a student requires in order to succeed (see Chapter 2). The process is formalized in the preparation of an Individual Education Plan (IEP). These plans are fully discussed in the In the Classroom feature at the close of this chapter.

Special Classes

Traditionally, the full-time special class was the most popular vehicle for serving students with exceptional conditions. During the late 1960s, the notion of special classes was critically examined, and the resulting debates and evidence added impetus to the movement toward inclusion. Nevertheless, special classes remain a setting for a small number of students who are exceptional.

In special classrooms, which are staffed by specially trained teachers and are located within the regular school, children with similar disabilities are brought together for instruction and social interplay. Partial integration, when feasible, is a major aim.

Special Schools

During the late 1940s, it was felt that a logical extension of the special class was the special school. Schools were designed and equipped to meet the needs of discrete populations of students who were exceptional. Day schools allowed a core of specially trained teachers and professionals to guide the child's education while the child continued to live at home.

A few special day schools still provide special education services, usually to specific groups of children with exceptionalities and often at the preschool level for young children who are deaf. Other examples for school-aged students are Alberta's Horizon School in Olds, which specializes in assisting children with severe physical disabilities, and the Christine Meikle School for children with mental disabilities.

Residential Schools

Special education in Canada began with residential institutions designed to serve the special needs of students who were blind, deaf, and mentally retarded. Provincially funded residential schools for children who are hearing impaired, visually impaired, and emotionally disturbed still function across Canada. In these settings, children live and are instructed with other youngsters who have the same exceptional conditions.

One of the problems with residential schools is that they separate the child from the home. However, the concept of full-time residential placement has changed substantially in recent years and many of these schools could more correctly be termed residential/day as more students have been encouraged to commute.

Home/Hospital Instruction

Homebound and hospital instruction are provided by local school boards for children who are confined because of illness, physical injury, or other problems (excluding suspension or expulsion). Intervention is initiated if the student's school absences begin to seriously affect progress.

Instructional Practices

There exists no universal conviction about how to teach children who are exceptional. There is no such thing as a panacea. Behaviour modification, individualized programming, and task analysis, along with children's own motivations and needs, cannot be administered through a generalized curriculum and set of techniques that are appropriate to all students and to all teachers at all times. Among educators, common ground is only reached concerning the necessity for a more detailed assessment of strengths and needs, greater individualization of instruction and curriculum, and more careful and systematic monitoring of performance (Winzer, 1989).

Many of the things that make special education special are done by good teachers every day. Good teachers recognize that all students have individual needs. They adapt materials, teaching techniques, and activities to the particular needs of their students. They build curriculum, use concrete techniques, generalize skills, apply learning at the appropriate level, and begin instruction at children's tolerance level. They provide individual and small group instruction, evaluate progress carefully by means of various evaluation techniques, and keep careful records (Winzer, 1989).

Still, there is no question that integrating students with exceptional conditions involves a wider range of organizational and instructional materials and alternatives than does regular teaching. Teachers are challenged to find innovative ways to enhance the learning environment in order to accommodate the learning differences and behavioural difficulties of pupils who are exceptional. Children may need special attention because of limited ability, poor motivation, sensory or physical impairments, or specific learning disabilities. Frequently their learning difficulties are related to a combination or interaction of a number of factors.

Changes made in the environment, in content, in instruction, or in evaluation differ according to the needs of a particular child. Not all students will require the same type or intensity of special education over the same period. Table 1-3 illustrates how it is possible for different children to receive special assistance in different areas.

Throughout this text, readers will find In the Classroom sections that provide examples for classroom implementation, give tips and strategies for teachers, and offer extracts from Individual Education Plans (IEPs).

Table 1-3 Areas of social assistance for different categories of children who are exceptional

Children with	IEP	Curriculum adaptations	Special devices	Special classroom arrangements	Counselling services	Speech/ language therapy	Occupational/ physiotherapy	Other therapies	Medical services	Social services
Mild mental retardation	X	X			X					
Moderate mental retardation	X	X			X	X				
Speech and language difficulties	X	X			X	X				
Learning disabilities	X	X			X					
Hearing impairments	X	X	X	X	X	X				
Visual impairments	X	X	X	X	X					
Health disorders	X				X			X		
Physical disabilities	X	X	X	X	X	X	X		X	
Behavioural difficulties	X	X			X			X		X
Psychoses	X	X			X	X		X		
Severe and multiple handicaps/ disabilities	X	X	X	X	X	X	X	X	X	
Giftedness	X	X			X					

Social Intervention

Social intervention covers a spectrum of services that can be grouped under the general category of child welfare. A primary concern is the care and treatment of the child within the family environment. A wide range of personnel are involved in service delivery —giving assistance to people who need it. They include social workers, family counsellors, foster parents, child advocates, child care workers, probation officers, and so on, who try to ensure that the child develops under the care of the family or surrogate family.

Child Advocacy

Child advocacy can be defined as any social, political, or legal action that is intended to achieve a better life for children from infancy to late adolescence (Lourie, 1975). A child advocate is anyone who pleads a child's cause or defends a particular child-related cause.

Child advocacy is a wide-ranging movement that functions at several levels. It involves a spectrum of activities that identify the needs of children and try to rectify unsatisfactory practices. A major goal of advocacy is to stimulate public and professional response to the child's needs and problems. Increasingly, advocates are playing an integral part in the education of children who are exceptional.

Advocacy is one function of parent organizations which have initiated services in education, residential living (most specifically group homes), and vocational alternatives. Some parent groups have started and operated services, while others have been catalysts and now work with community organizations. (See Chapter 15.) The efforts of parents have been supported and supplemented by professional and educational groups who also view advocacy as one of their primary functions. For example, parents are involved in the Canadian Association for Community Living (formerly the Association for the Mentally Retarded) and the Canadian Learning Disabilities Association (formerly the Association for Children with Learning Disabilities).

Parent Involvement

Teachers should stress parental involvement if they wish to enhance the educational experience for all of their students. When educators involve parents as partners in their children's education, parents appear to develop a sense of efficacy that communicates itself to children with positive academic consequences (Cummins, 1989). Particularly for students with disabilities, communication and collaboration are critical if a child is to make educational gains in a planned and co-ordinated manner (Perl, 1995). For example, as a result of being tutored in how to assist their children, parents of students with disabilities have been able to ensure appropriate programming in the least restrictive environment; facilitate successful vocational/special education programs through collaborative consultation with the schools (Elksnin and Elksnin, 1989); and improve mathematical ability (Minner, 1989).

SUMMARY

1. Children who are exceptional are those who deviate in some way from what society calls normal. However, the norm itself encompasses a wide range of behaviours from which everyone deviates to some degree.

2. Over the years, the way that professionals and society in general have described persons with exceptionalities has changed in a positive way. In the past, the terms used to describe people who were exceptional were value laden and tended to emphasize the person's handicap, disorder, or disability. Today's terms are non-stigmatizing and as clear and unambiguous as possible.

3. In spite of the proliferation of labels in the health and education fields, and despite the fact that child-based categorical systems retain their popularity, many professionals see the traditional system of labelling children by their primary disability as not always useful. However, labels probably both stigmatize and help students. Labels may broadly define categories of exceptionality, but no one classification can adequately describe the social, psychological, and physical qualities of an exceptional individual. Administrators and professionals will likely continue to use categories of exceptionality. In the classroom, alternative approaches may serve exceptional children better.

4. Children requiring special education may be taught in settings that range from the regular classroom to the residential school and hospital programs.

5. To fully accomplish the aim of individualizing instruction for children with exceptionalities, special education teachers and those involved in educationally integrating these students combine their resources with a wide range of personnel.

6. Many children with special needs require various types of therapy. A child with poor articulation may require help from a speech therapist; a child who has lost a limb will need physical therapy; an adolescent with cerebral palsy may benefit from occupational therapy.

7. Educational teams tend to be multidisciplinary in nature, with the major duties of planning, implementation, and evaluation of educational programs for special students. When a statement that details the individual program for a child with a disability is prepared, the document is called an Individual Education Plan (IEP). The IEP is a written planning document that outlines educational services and learning objectives to meet the specific needs of a child. It aims to co-ordinate plans and services, personalize and individualize a child's program, and integrate the individual plan with the overall plans for the classroom group.

8. By individualizing the program for students who are exceptional, we attempt to fit the curriculum and the program to the child, rather than vice versa. The individualization is in the planning, not necessarily in the instruction.

The essence of special education is individualization. When educators specifically adjust the nature of student programs in response to individualization, their students learn reliably and learn dramatically more (see Fuchs et al., 1995).

Some people think that individualizing programs for pupils who are exceptional means that the teacher must work with that child on a one-to-one basis at all times. This is patently untrue. Individualization is not a teaching method but a plan for instructional organization that may incorporate many methods. The defining characteristic of individual instruction is that each student works within learning plans designed to match his or her needs, interests, abilities, and pace of learning.

The process of adapting or modifying the regular curriculum and classroom environment often begins with an Individual Education Plan (IEP). The individual program is the manifestation of the philosophy of individualization as well as of pragmatic intentions concerning what to teach, who will teach it, and how it will be evaluated.

Each student's IEP is a broad statement that assists teachers by pre-specifying the goals and objectives of instruction and ensuring that the educational program is appropriate to the child's specific needs. The plan of action outlines the short-term objectives and long-term goals, describes the methods and techniques that will be used to achieve them, and details the responsibilities of various people, such as the classroom teacher, the resource room teacher, or the speech therapist, who will help the child along the way.

The IEP is a personalized program that is prepared annually, usually at an early point in the year. It is filled in before programming begins, and therefore writing the first Individual Education Plan for a child with a disability is largely guesswork. The goals and objectives are hypotheses about what a child can

and cannot do and about a child's critical needs. Moreover, the process of programming for needs is a dynamic one. An IEP is not a static document or a performance contract. Nor is it written in stone. The IEP is a communication document that is constantly modified and changed to match a child's progress and needs. A child who is visually impaired, for example, may in fact be visually impaired for life, but that child's needs will change, not merely each year but perhaps each week or even each day.

The major problem confronting teachers is determining and prioritizing the skills that are important to teach. Skill determination is easier for children with mild disabilities, who generally follow the curriculum designed for their normally developing peers.

An IEP is not necessarily lengthy or complex. Many students need minor changes that can be documented on one page (B.C., 1996). The most complex IEPs are for children with communication disorders, because language is composed of so many interdependent functions.

Individual Education Plans

The actual formats of IEPs differ markedly. Most, however, contain certain components. These are:

1. *IEP data.* Many plans contain information about the preparation of the IEP. It may state the names and positions of those attending the team meeting when the IEP was drawn up and whether the IEP is an initial document, a second IEP, or an evaluation document.

2. *Placement.* This is a statement of the educational setting considered most appropriate for the student with special needs.

3. *A summary of the student's present level of performance across a range of domains.* Each individual plan is founded on an assessment designed to discover the child's strengths and weaknesses

in the areas of cognitive development, physical and motor development, socio-emotional development, and adaptive behaviour. With a record of a child's performance based on information derived from an assessment or assessments, those preparing the IEP can pinpoint a child's present levels of performance and then determine the skills the child needs to acquire. That is, assessment data should tell us where a child is functioning and how that compares to normal developmental levels.

4. *The long-term or annual goals.* A *goal* may be defined as a stated outcome desired as the result of some action. On an IEP, goals are broad general statements that help to focus on the general areas for which individualized programming is to be provided. They indicate the priorities for intervention—the major learning experiences the child will have and the broad range of skills that he or she can be expected to attain. Long-range goals are usually written for one year, except in the case of children with significant disabilities, who may have long-range goals over a greater period, up to five years.

Taking assessment results, translating them into present levels of performance, and then using them in planning and individualized programming is not as straightforward as it may seem at first. In fact, the process is quite complicated and takes much careful thought. In using assessment information for IEPs, there are three basic steps. The present levels of functioning should provide a list of a child's strengths and weaknesses. These are divided into skills that need remediation, skills that are delayed, and skills within the normal ranges. Once this is done, skills are targeted for intervention (long-term goals). These are then written as short-term objectives. Typically, five to ten goals are identified in the domains of functioning where the child is showing the greatest lags. When they are written down, the goals should represent a specific expectation or skill (as opposed to a vague generic statement). For example, "Learn to read" is not specific enough, whereas "Will read books at grade one level" is.

5. *Short-term objectives for each annual goal.* An objective is a clear statement of exactly what a teacher wants a child to be able to do as a result of instruction. Objectives refer to increments in the progress of learning from the present level of functioning to the child's annual goals. Objectives are the steps toward achieving the goals, and they help to direct instruction and learning on a day-to-day basis. Short-term objectives are provided for each annual goal. There is no rule, but generally three or four objectives are provided for each long-range goal.

The way to turn long-range goals into short-term objectives is through task analysis, breaking skills down into their component parts. All of the small tasks that make up the larger skill are listed. The number of sub-skills depends on the task and the individual needs of the child. Good behavioural objectives are written as brief action statements that use verbs that lend themselves to observation and measurement. Appropriate verbs include *apply, describe, recognize, repeat, copy, reproduce, choose, draw, classify, match, identify,* and *select.*

6. *The specific educational and support services needed to attain each educational objective.* Once goals and objectives are identified, the next step is to select and sequence the most appropriate learning experiences to achieve those aims and objectives. However, in a sense an IEP represents a philosophy of what should be taught rather than illustrations of how it should happen. Examples of how to accomplish an objective may appear, but every approach, activity, or group interaction will not.

7. *The personnel who will hold primary responsibility for specific long-range goals and short-term objectives.* The program outlines the responsibilities of various people, such as teachers or therapists, who will assist the child. It shows the kinds of services required (such as speech therapy), the type

of instruction (individual or group), and the time to be spent in each activity (half an hour a day).

8. *The date for the beginning of special education services.*

9. *The anticipated duration of the services.*

10. *Specific evaluation procedures for each objective.* These are the criteria for determining whether the objectives have been attained.

11. *Procedures for re-evaluating the total IEP document.*

WEBLINKS

Disability Information for Students **http://www.abilityinfo.com/**

Special Needs Education Network **http://schoolnet2.carleton.ca/sne/**

The Integrated Network of Disability Information and Education **http://www.indie.ca/**

Disabled Peoples' International **http://www.escape.ca/~dpi/**

The Canadian Child Care Federation **http://www.cfc-efc.ca/cccf/**

CHAPTER 2

Issues and Trends in Canadian Special Education

Historical Notes

When special education began in North America, exceptional individuals were believed to differ from the rest of the population in almost every domain. Because of this, and for reasons of economy and convenience, children with exceptionalities were educated chiefly in institutional settings designed to protect the rest of society from the deviant child as much as to protect the children from an intolerant and prejudiced world.

Residential schools—variously referred to as asylums, institutions, colonies, or training schools—were first established in Canada in the 1860s to serve children described in the parlance of the day as deaf and dumb, blind, and idiotic or feeble-minded. In the United States and Canada these special schools were divorced from the general educational system and administered along with prisons, asylums, and public charities. Not until the early 1900s were special schools in most parts of Canada placed under provincial departments of education.

By the early 1900s, schooling had become the social norm for most children in Canada. As the public schools assumed responsibility for socializing and educating huge numbers of children, they were faced

with an unforeseen problem. How could schools best provide for children who could not be handled in the regular classes? These difficult students, labelled as truant, delinquent, incorrigible, and feeble-minded, were those with mild handicaps to behaviour and learning. More seriously disabled children were still relegated to institutional settings or excluded from education altogether.

To keep order in the schools and to protect the education of other students and the time of teachers, special segregated classes seemed the ideal solution. Special classes were first introduced in the 1880s, and by 1910 they were a feature of most urban education systems.

In Canada the first special day classes were started in 1906 for children with physical problems—those who were described as crippled, sickly, and malnourished. These were followed by provisions for pupils who were mentally retarded, sight-saving classes, home instruction, speech correction, and lip-reading classes. There were also orthopedic classes, vocational and advancement classes, and remedial reading programs.

The late 1940s saw a huge expansion of special

education due to simple demographics. The postwar baby boom increased the number of children with disabilities; advances in medical technology kept more children alive and limited degrees of impairment. Parents' associations formed and spearheaded a social movement to extend educational and treatment services to the most severely disabled children. For example, parents opened schools for children with moderate and severe disabilities. The polio epidemic of the 1950s and the rubella epidemic of the 1960s generated still more demand for special education.

Institutions, special classes, and special schools remained important in the education of students with disabilities into the 1960s. In that decade, parents, advocates, legislators, and educational systems began to reject the notion that exceptional students should be educated separately from their peers or that people with mental disabilities should be herded into large institutional settings.

The principles of normalization emerged (see the Research Notes later in this chapter). Within the education field, critics of special education claimed that special classes were too often used as dumping grounds. Gallagher (1972) pointed out that special education was often exclusionary rather than remedial and did not appear to be returning a significant number of children to the regular classroom. Critics also pointed to the inherent discrimination they saw in providing separate schooling for children based on presumed mental, physical, or behavioural incapacities. Still others castigated special education for the disproportionate number of ethnic and minority group children found in special segregated classrooms. Ethically, critics deplored labelling children and separating them from their normally developing peers.

Not only did special education classes cast a stigma on exceptional children, but they provided low quality education, and were often allotted inferior facilities and untrained teachers. Children from special classes were barely tolerated by regular classroom teachers and administrators.

Grave dissatisfaction with special classes was bolstered by numerous efficacy studies that compared the progress of children who were exceptional in segregated and regular classes. These studies found that children performed no better in special classes than in regular classrooms (e.g. Dunn, 1968; Gallagher, 1972; Myers, 1976; Reynolds and Birch, 1977).

The late seventies and early eighties was the period in which the practice of special education came of age and the true movement toward integration got underway. In the 1970s, enormous changes came about as a result of enabling legislation in both the United States and Canada. The dual philosophies of normalization and mainstreaming impelled many children with mild to severe disabilities into the orbit of the public schools.

While reform efforts in special education began in the 1960s, it is the 1980s and 1990s that can be seen as the decades of major school reforms in North America. In the 1980s, the Regular Education Initiative stressed the needs of children with mild disabilities in regular classrooms and called for a merger of regular education and special education. The 1990s are witnessing the inclusion movement, which seeks regular education advantages for all children with disabilities. Even the implementation of inclusion is changing. At first, it was intimately connected to a place; now it is more associated with a group of services and adaptations.

Social attitudes toward the education, care, and training of individuals who are exceptional usually reflect more general cultural attitudes toward the obligations of a society to its individual citizens. It is only recently that the creation of societies where persons who are exceptional can live productive and fulfilling lives has become an imperative, not just a dream. As a newly evolving social philosophy has emphasized the value of the individual and the rights of every citizen, the prospects for individuals who are exceptional have altered dramatically. Together with a significant increase in public awareness and understanding, current social philosophy aims to provide such individuals with an education and a lifestyle as close to normal as possible.

In Canada, the rights of persons with disabilities have emerged as key priorities: policies are formulated at the federal, provincial, and local levels of government. In general, how students are educated and policies related to special education are designed and implemented at the provincial and local level.

Special education describes an extremely complex social and conceptual system that is designed to assist all children in reaching their full potential. It is a field with a long and honourable history. Many of our current philosophies, legislation, techniques, and approaches arise from earlier precedents and activities. As well, special education is an integrative professional area that cuts across a spectrum of services, makes use of many different fields of knowledge, and depends upon the techniques, the concepts, and the practices of several allied disciplines.

A field as historically complex and as diverse as special education is bound to reveal controversial issues and to reflect major trends and movements. Today's most hotly debated issue concerns inclusion, or inclusive schooling. A broad spectrum of other trends and movements, all related in some way to inclusion, are germane to contemporary special education as educators continue their efforts to reform, revamp, and generally improve services for students with special needs. These include, but are not restricted to, teacher competencies, curriculum planning and delivery, individualization, consultation and collaboration, the use of paraprofessionals, assessment practices and procedures, early identification and intervention, transition services for adolescents, and legislation.

To do justice to these issues would take an entire book for each. We can only discuss some of the major issues quite briefly in this chapter in an attempt to alert readers to the movements and trends and to lay the groundwork for later chapters in this text. We direct the greatest attention to issues and trends that directly impact on the teacher in the classroom. Of these, inclusion tops the list, and it is important to understand the varied parameters of the movement. This includes the development, the terminology, the issues, and the ways in which inclusion can be best implemented.

Throughout the discussion, it should be kept in mind that reforms in education are continuous and reflect a society's views of what is important at a given time. In this sense, reform in education is an open-ended social issue and a definitive solution is illusory. As well, this text is a document written in a particular place at a particular time. It represents only a snapshot of special education and cannot faithfully reproduce the dynamic shifts that are occurring in the field. Finally, changes in special education are influenced by many external forces that include legislation, politics, medicine, ethics, and economics, to mention only a few.

Reforms in Special Education

In the past ten years, reform has become a major objective in North American education. Some believe that education is tottering on the brink of chaos and failure and that educational reform must be a top political priority. Parents, legislators, the general public, and educators themselves point to the gaps and deficiencies in the current educational system.

It was during the 1980s that the outcomes of education became a key concern of reform. Reformers called for greater accountability from schools and teachers; advanced academic achievement from our students, especially in mathematics and science; ways to improve literacy skills; ways to halt the dropout rates; ways to incorporate multi-ethnic and multicultural perspectives into classrooms and schools; ways to promote bilingualism and to teach students with limited English proficiency; and ways to ensure educational equality and opportunity for all students. Ideas to bring about educational reform ranged from administrative practices such as lengthening the school day to full-scale restructuring of education systems (for example, providing open enrollment options).

In the regular educational arena, a recent analysis of provincial and territorial reports provided by the Council of Ministers of Education shows specific educational trends. These include more co-operative efforts at the regional and national levels; more accountability to the public; information technology as an integral part of education; less funding to the administrative side of education to ensure that resources are allocated to classrooms; fewer school districts and boards; a focus on curriculum outcomes and standards to make education more relevant; improved levels of student achievement; more cost-effective ways to deliver programs; the implementation of comprehensive, multi-year assessment programs tied to curriculum standards and outcomes; transition programs; and the evaluation of current development and training programs ("Key trends...," 1996).

The reform movement did not pass special education by. On the contrary. In the late 1980s, special education became deeply embroiled in reform efforts and was subjected to enormous pressures for change. Rhetoric calls for special education to "break the mould," for "revolution," a "paradigm shift," a "fundamental reconceptualization," and "radical restructuring" (Kauffman, 1993, p. 10).

While many people say that contemporary special education is at a crossroads and in a state of flux, we must keep in mind that educational services and the ideas that stimulate and direct their growth are never static. The notion of reform embraces the idea of a need for change and is as old as the special educational system itself. Changing needs lead to the formulation of new policies and the adoption of new legislation and other administrative arrangements.

Prevailing social values define what is exceptional, different, or a problem, and how such issues should be dealt with. Therefore, reforms in education are continuous and reflect a society's views of what is important in education at a given time. A reading of the Historical Notes feature that opens this chapter and other chapters throughout this text and the summary of changes shown in Table 2-1 clearly indicates that special education has never been a quiescent enterprise.

Changing Views of Exceptionality

Traditionally, North American society has not shown a high tolerance for persons who are exceptional. In the past, individuals were stigmatized and stereotyped by prevailing attitudes toward their disabilities. Special education was a service delivery system that adhered to contemporary social attitudes toward deviance. When the old adage "out of sight, out of mind" held sway, persons with exceptionalities were placed in institutions for their care and training.

Recent decades have witnessed significant increases in public awareness and understanding of individuals who are exceptional. In general, our society has shifted from qualitative to quantitative conceptions of exceptionality. The qualitative model held that persons with disabilities were different and deviant—they learned, perceived, and thought in ways that were unlike the norm. Conversely, the quantitative model views differences as a matter of de-

Table 2-1 Changes in special education

1817	Establishment of an institution for persons who were deaf, soon followed by institutions for those blind and mentally retarded.
1860s	Reformatories established for children identified as delinquent.
1880s	Establishment of industrial schools for students identified as vagrant and neglected; very beginning of segregated classes in the public schools; movement to found day schools for pupils who were deaf.
1910	Segregated classes firmly established in the public schools. Segregated classes remained the most important vehicle to serve students with disabilities right into the 1960s.
1960s	Integration and the beginning of a movement away from special classes, based on civil rights, various exposés, and efficacy studies. New socially constructed categories such as *learning disabilities* emerged.
1975	Mainstreaming formalized with PL 94-142. The least restrictive environment and a continuum of services were put into place. Students with mild disabilities moved into regular classrooms and those with severe problems into local schools.
1980s	Regular Education Initiative (REI), which stressed that special education must redefine its relationship with general education. The REI was an intensive effort to mainstream students with mild disabilities, to merge regular and special education, and to restructure education.
1986	A new discipline, early childhood special education, was born, formalized in PL 99-457.
1987	Inclusion, as a merger of regular and special education, was mentioned in the mid-1980s (e.g. Stainback and Stainback, 1984, 1985; Will, 1986). In 1987 writers (Reynolds, Wang, and Walberg, 1987) called for "the joining of demonstrably effective practices from special, compensatory, and general education to establish a general educational system that is more *inclusive*, and better serves all students, particularly those who require greater-than-usual educational support" (p. 394, italics added).
1990s	Inclusion. The goal is to create a community in which all children work and learn together and develop mutually supportive repertoires of peer support while remaining aware of individual differences.

gree, not kind—people who are exceptional develop and function much as others do, but their progress may be slower and their achievements more restricted. Exceptionalities are no longer viewed as solely within the individual; a complex interplay of innate characteristics and environmental variables is instead considered.

The decade of the 1960s was a major crucible for change in public perceptions and portrayals of persons with disabilities. Today's efforts to provide surroundings, opportunities, and programs much like those provided for non-disabled persons stem from programs originally undertaken in the Scandinavian countries in the mid-60s, specifically the ideas of normalization and deinstitutionalization. (See Research Notes.) The new social philosophy

Supporters of normalization argue that all exceptional people deserve an educational and living environment as close to normal as possible.

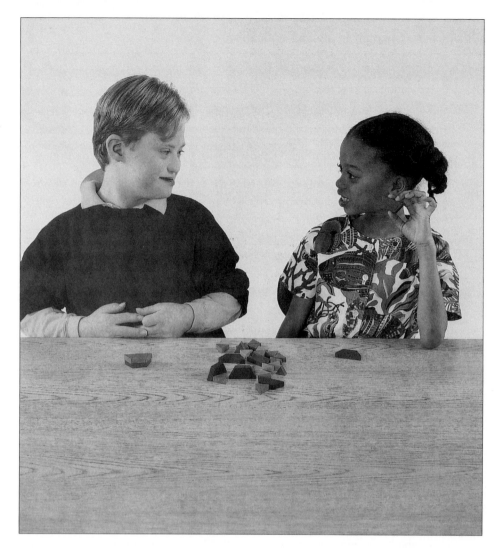

emphasized the value of the individual and the rights of every citizen. Since then, overcoming barriers to allow Canadians with disabilities to fully participate in social and economic life has become a major policy concern in Canada.

Educational Changes

For children with special needs, the most fundamental social change of the past two decades has been the clear and unequivocal statement of the responsibility of educational authorities to provide equal access to an education in a manner most appropriate to their needs. This statement of responsibility, embedded in legislation and supported by ethical and philosophical precepts, has meant that students who are exceptional are increasingly drawn within the orbit of the public schools.

Changes in the ways that schools conceptualize the needs of students with exceptional-

Research Notes

Normalization and Changes in Perceptions

During the 1960s, the civil rights movement brought about new conceptions of disability. Arguments held that persons with disabilities had a civil right to live, attend school, and work in the same environment as others. The principles of normalization and deinstitutionalization were articulated.

Normalization refers to the philosophical belief that all individuals who are exceptional, no matter what their level and type of disability, should be provided with an education and living environment as close to normal as possible. Bank-Mikkleson (1969) introduced the concept of normalization that was later defined by Benge Nirje as "making available to all mentally retarded people patterns of life and conditions of everyday living which are as close as possible to the regular circumstances of society" (Nirje, 1979, p. 173).

Normalization principles provide guidelines for the treatment of people with disabilities, as well as concrete suggestions for action. The major aim is for society to regard persons with disabilities as individuals and to treat them fairly and humanely. There will be a normal family and community life for all individuals as the traditional boundaries raised by disabling conditions are broached and people who are exceptional fill a variety of roles in general society and are offered the chance of a normal life routine, normal developmental experiences, independent choices, and the right to live, work, and play in normal surroundings. Ultimately, normalization will have occurred when individuals who are exceptional live

with members of the cultural group in a normal domicile within the community and have access to all the privileges and services that are available to others.

An obvious outgrowth of the philosophy of normalization is the process of deinstitutionalization. In the physical sense, deinstitutionalization is the movement of individuals from large institutions into community-based living arrangements such as group homes and half-way houses. In the broader social context, deinstitutionalization addresses a return to the community, maintenance in the community, the respect of other citizens, and acceptance by peers and others in the culture.

An institution is defined as a publicly supported, professionally managed facility housing fifteen or more people with similar disabilities. In Canada, most provinces and territories have policies supporting deinstitutionalization. Any building of new institutions is being strongly resisted by citizens' groups, who are demanding community supports and services instead. Today the residential institution is rarely considered an option for children who are disabled. In fact, most provinces now adhere to a "no new admittances" policy.

Numbers clearly illustrate the policies. In 1982 there were 1.4 million disabled Canadians of working age, of whom 45 000 were in institutions, 20 000 in sheltered workshops, and 1.37 million in the community ("Directions...," 1982). By 1991, the number of people living in institutions in Canada dropped to less than 16 000 (Fine, 1991; Richley, 1991).

ities and attend to those needs show a movement from institutionalization to full inclusion that spans almost two centuries. Students with special needs were first educated in large institutions. In 1910, segregated classes in public schools accompanied the rigorous enforcement of compulsory education laws. The normalization and civil rights movements of the 1960s affected education and brought about the trend toward mainstreaming. In the 1990s, we are witnessing a movement toward inclusive schooling.

Development of the Inclusionary Movement

Over the past four decades, there has been a gradual increase in the numbers and proportions of children with disabilities who receive their special education while enrolled in general education classes and schools. Table 2-1 shows the progression of settings for special education.

In the 1950s and 1960s, *integration* was the common term used to refer to the education of students with exceptionalities in regular classrooms. The term is still popular. *Mainstreaming*, often used as a synonym for integration, emerged in special education in the 1970s.

The basic goal of mainstreaming was the provision of free, appropriate education in the most suitable setting for all youngsters with exceptionalities. Philosophically, mainstreaming focused on the integration of children with exceptionalities with their non-disabled peers within the context of the regular neighbourhood school. As a process, mainstreaming provided services along a continuum so that a range of available services allowed pupils to be integrated in the manner best suited to their individual needs. It demanded individual programming, co-operative planning, as well as the range of educational options and support services.

Two major characteristics defined mainstreaming (as opposed to inclusion). First, it usually only applied to some children, most especially those with mild disabilities. Second, the target population generally consisted of students identified as needing special education services and often moving from special classes into regular classrooms.

During the 1980s, criticisms of the mainstreaming movement were legion. Only a small number of children were being mainstreamed, resource rooms were not functioning as effectively as they should, and the promises of the Individual Education Plan were not being met. As well, regular education and special education still functioned in the traditional way—as parallel rather than integrated enterprises. Many questioned the necessity for a dual system of education, particularly the high proportion of educational funding directed toward special education and the fragmentary nature of so much of special education's service delivery. Adding to this were arguments about the civil rights of children with disabilities. Many people saw segregated classes as inherently discriminatory and unequal, and expressed concerns about the stigmatization of children identified for special education.

The solution, the Regular Education Initiative (REI), was proposed by Madeline Will in 1986. Mainstreaming was reinterpreted under the REI: it did not seek inclusion but to restructure and improve and expand mainstreaming. Essentially, the REI had two major processes. First, it required a closer merging of general and special education resources that would bring about a system of education in which children with quite diverse, heterogeneous needs were educated in the same classroom (York, Vandercook, MacDonald, Herse-Neff, and Caughey, 1992). Second, the REI advocated the integration of students with low-incidence and severe disabilities into the general educational system and the retention of students with mild and moderate disabilities in general classrooms where general educators would assume unequivocal, primary responsibility for all students (Braaten, Kauffman, Braaten, Polsgrove, and Nelson, 1988).

Inclusive Schooling

The current movement to educate all children in general education is variously termed *inclusion, inclusive schooling*, and *inclusive education*. Inclusive schooling defies easy interpretation. There is no single model of inclusive education and it is not a fully developed structure with paradigms and a data base. Inclusion hosts a range of theoretical positions related to the underlying philosophy, the relationship of those targeted for inclusion, the nature of the general educational provision, and the manner in which supports are provided. The spectrum runs from radical or full inclusionists to those who would retain much of the status quo.

Inclusion or inclusive schooling implies subtle but real differences from mainstreaming, the least restrictive environment, and integration. Advocates of inclusive schooling argue that the social–cultural realities of mainstreaming and integration are that one group is viewed as the "mainstream" and one group is not; hence, one group must "push in" to the activities and settings occupied by the other (Salisbury, 1991). Under the principles of inclusion, children do not push into the mainstream because the underlying supposition in inclusive programs is that all children will be based in the classrooms they would attend if they did not have a disability.

Nevertheless, proponents of the various kinds of inclusion do not agree on definitions and there is no cohesive sharing of goals. Inclusion means different things to different people who want different things from it.

Full inclusion means the education of all students with identified disabilities in the schools and classrooms they would attend if not disabled, via collaboration by general and special educators to bring support and services to the student (Rogers, 1993). Those promoting full inclusion insist that the general classroom is appropriate for every child, regardless of degree and type of disability. A cascade or continuum of services is no longer necessary and regular classroom teachers, with support and collaboration, can teach all children.

Others are more cautious and promote partial integration. One version comes from the major special education organization, the Council for Exceptional Children (CEC). The CEC believes that

> individuals with disabilities should be served whenever possible in general education classrooms in inclusive neighbourhood schools and community settings. Such settings should be strengthened and supported by an infusion of specially trained personnel and other appropriate supportive practices according to the individual needs of the child (1993a).

This version points to education in normalized settings with the appropriate support and related services. It also stresses that all practices—placement, curricula, IEP, related services, and so on—should be geared to the individual needs of a specific child. However, the CEC also supports the retention of a continuum of services so that every child can be served appropriately.

In Canada, the Council of Administrators of Special Education (CASE) holds a position matching that of the CEC. To wit:

> CASE does *not* support any policy/practice in which *all* students with disabilities, *regardless* of the severity of their disabilities and needs for related services, receive their total education within the regular classroom setting in the school where they would attend if not disabled. A continuum of service delivery options must always be available (Council of Administrators, 1997, p. 3; original italics).

Note that CASE supports the philosophy of inclusion, as does the CEC, but adheres to the notion of individual decisions for each child.

Current Status

There is a general perception created by the literature, and perhaps the media, that inclusion is a universally accepted movement in special education. This is not true. At the moment, inclusion is something that is both evolving and changing. The ideal of full inclusion is not universally shared and it is not endorsed by all of those concerned with the education of children with exceptionalities. And, while most parents, teachers, and school administrators agree that the days of total segregation and institutionalization are long over, the manner in which the inclusion of students with exceptionalities can be most effectively attained has still not been worked out in practice.

Discussions on the merits of inclusion as a philosophy are not as prominent as apprehension about its implementation. Few dispute the contention that every child, regardless of type and severity of disability, has the right to a free and appropriate education in a setting as normal as possible. Nevertheless, our philosophical commitment far outstrips our practice. The barriers to successful and universal inclusion remain complex, diverse, and numerous. The question of how the integration of students with disabilities is to be accomplished remains a hotly debated issue among educators, parents, and child advocates. Most of the argument centres on how integration strategies can be implemented without deleteriously affecting the lives and educational programs of other students or impacting negatively on the professional lives of teachers.

The current debate is heated. We point out some aspects of the arguments and counter-arguments in the Matter of Debate box below.

What is clear is that the goal of inclusion for all students is inconsistent with views expressed by many in the special education community. Many parent and advocacy groups, as well as professional groups, primarily representing students with mild disabilities, speak against the elimination of a continuum of special education services.

Advocates for students with disabilities such as the Commission on the Education of the Deaf, the Learning Disabilities Association, and the National Education Association have issued statements supporting a strong separate special education system (Fuchs and Fuchs, 1994). Full inclusion is not endorsed by the Council for Learning Disabilities (1993), Learning Disabilities Association of America (1993), and the National Joint Committee on Learning Disabilities (1993). A policy statement of the New Jersey Commission on Learning Disabilities stated that "The regular education classroom is one of many educational program options but is not a substitute for a full continuum necessary to assure the provision of an appropriate education to all students with learning disabilities" (see Maloney, 1995, p. 330).

While the U.S. National Education Association supports appropriate inclusion (Gillet, 1994), other major organizations in general education strongly oppose the inclusive movement as a whole (Shanker, 1994). In 1994, Albert Shanker, president of the American Federation of Teachers, called for a moratorium on inclusive policies (Gorman and Rose, 1994). He advocated a halt to inclusion until issues concerning supports and the inclusion of students with behavioural disorders were addressed.

In the broadest terms, parents of children with significant disabilities are concerned with social integration, while parents of students with mild disabilities are more concerned with curricula and remediation (Borthwick-Duffy, Palmer, and Lane, 1996). Some parents voice doubts about whether their children will receive the necessary help. Parents of children with learning disabilities (Lieberman, 1991) and children with visual and auditory impairments have raised such concerns (Sandberg and Michaelson, 1993).

A Matter of Debate

Inclusive Schooling

✔ Arguments in favour of full inclusion

Students with disabilities are offered increased opportunities for interactions with non-disabled peers as well as meaningful curriculum content (Ford and Davern, 1989).

Much of the zeal for the practice of integration as a blanket policy stems from its anticipated effects in the socio-emotional domain. Children will be accepted because of contact and familiarity, will naturally model the appropriate behaviours of peers, will not suffer the stigma of special classes, and will be provided a more real-life environment for learning (Kaufman, Gottlieb, Agard, and Kukic, 1975).

Disabled students show increased rates of social responsiveness, increased numbers of social bids directed toward peers, and enhanced communication skills (see Staub and Hunt, 1993).

Contact between disabled and non-disabled children is associated with more positive attitudes and has the potential to promote relationships.

In inclusive education, students with and without disabilities have opportunities for interactions, which have many positive benefits for the social abilities of students with disabilities (Staub and Hunt, 1993).

All children can be taught successfully in regular classrooms.

Anecdotal reports of successful inclusion are emerging in the literature. Studies (e.g. Giangreco,

Denis, Cloninger, Edelman, and Schattman, 1993; Janney, Snell, Beers, and Raynes, 1995; Kozleski and Jackson, 1993; Salisbury, Palambaro, and Hollowood, 1993) have found increases in positive teacher attitudes following the experience of including children with severe disabilities.

All students need to learn in natural environments in which they are provided age-appropriate models for behaviour and communication.

The mere fact of school entry increases the probability of successful learning and allows a number of positive growth situations to occur for both special and regular students.

Special classes are discriminatory and unequal, and in violation of the democratic ethos that allows equal access to education for all students.

Equal opportunity implies equal educational rights for all youngsters.

Special children need equal opportunity and help to reach their maximum potential and every effort must be made to ensure that their ability to learn is stimulated.

Children in special classes or resource rooms suffer social stigma, which then affects their behaviour, self-concept, and learning.

Many teachers express support for the principles of integration.

✘ Arguments against full inclusion

Regular classroom placement alone does not produce beneficial effects for students who are exceptional. Evidence strongly suggests the possibility of some deleterious effects on a number of important peer-related dimensions (De Apodaca, Watson, Mueller, and Isaacson-Koiles, 1985).

Very young delayed children find it extremely difficult to form friendships. Although they are highly interested in their peers, discriminate among them, and develop preferences for specific playmates, these friendships are usually unilateral, rarely reciprocated. Few playmates whom they choose as friends choose them in return (Guralnick, 1990).

Evidence shows that disabled children are often perceived in negative and prejudiced ways by their non-disabled peers; integration may even increase prejudice and stereotyping and rejection.

Research does not support the contention that all students can be merged and taught successfully in general classes, and many disagree that regular educators can assume responsibility for special programming for all students with disabilities (e.g. Algozzine, Maheady, Sacca, O'Shea , and O'Shea 1990; Braaten et al., 1988; Lieberman, 1991; Walker and Bullis, 1991).

Reviews of the effects of placement do not suggest that location is the key to improvement in special education outcomes (Kauffman, 1993).

Comprehensive reviews (e.g. Carlberg and Kavale, 1980; Madden and Slavin, 1983) conclude that special classes and resource rooms contribute more to the academic achievement of some types of students with special needs, especially those who are learning disabled or emotionally disturbed, than do regular classrooms (see Fuchs and Fuchs, 1995).

There is very little empirical data on inclusion. For example, there is a paucity of research on the effectiveness of teaching children in mainstreamed classes (Brady, Swank, Taylor, and Frieberg, 1992).

If it is the function of schools to help individuals meet their needs and prepare them to lead productive and rewarding lives, then specialized instruction is necessary.

Skills should be taught in the environment where they are most likely to occur—the community, home, or work setting.

Students who are severely and profoundly disabled are best served in settings in which their cognitive development and social limitations can be addressed more intensively.

Equal educational treatment does not necessarily result in equal opportunity to learn.

In a recent study in Alberta (Alberta Teachers' Association, 1993), teachers identified critical problems in implementation. Many maintained that not all students could be integrated into regular classrooms.

By eliminating special education, general education will have to deal with children it has avoided in the past and will transform itself into a more responsive, resourceful, humane system (Fuchs and Fuchs, 1994).

Inclusion tells people with disabilities how to live, where they will be taught, and gives little credence to differences.

There is little evidence that general educators are receiving the kind of training they need to support students with disabilities comfortably (Heumann, 1994; Reiff, Evans, and Cass, 1991).

Very few, if any, general education teachers have received the ongoing professional development needed to include successfully (Schumm and Vaughn, 1995).

In the United States, less than 5 percent of all general education teachers have been formally prepared to work with students with special needs in inclusive settings (Smith and Luckasson, 1995). Currently few teacher training programs at Canadian colleges or universities focus on the educational practices required for inclusive education ("Action ...," 1993).

Nor do the traditional special education courses work very well. Goodlad and Field (1993) found in a national U.S. study that preservice teachers rated their own abilities to teach children with disabilities as the lowest of twelve domains of perceived instructional competence.

Even parents of children with significant disabilities hold widely divergent views about the efficacy of inclusion (Palmer, Borthwick-Duffy, Widaman, and Best, 1998). Parents believe that the two greatest benefits of inclusion are more opportunities for children with disabilities to be exposed to the real world and to be accepted by their communities (Green and Stoneman, 1989). But even as many parents seem confident about the social goals of inclusion, they are apprehensive about the impact on the quality of services their children receive (Palmer et al., 1998).

What do other parents say? While most parents accept the philosophy and practice of integration, others are reluctant. When asked about inclusion, the concern parents of both disabled and non-disabled children have is whether the special child will receive adequate attention and instruction (Stoneman, 1993). In a longitudinal study (Leyser and Gottlieb, 1996) of parents of normally developing children, parents in both 1981 and 1991 expressed strong negative feelings toward the idea of including children with severe disabilities in classes with non-disabled peers. Parents of normally developing children may believe that their children are being denied teacher time and intervention. The parents of children with disabilities may feel that their children's needs can be better met in a segregated setting with a structured curriculum and a low child–teacher ratio.

Many teachers support the philosophy of inclusion, but many identify critical problems in its implementation. A recent national study of 1 492 Canadian teachers found that more than two-thirds of teachers believe that inclusion is academically beneficial to children with special needs and their peers in regular classrooms, and 90 percent of teachers cite social benefits (Galt, 1997; "Resistance ...," 1997). Nevertheless, while a majority of teachers may support the philosophical underpinnings of inclusion, many express a deep concern that in too many cases the inclusive process is not working and is, in fact, creating educationally unsound situations (e.g. Alberta Teachers' Association, 1993; Buski, 1997; "Report ...," 1997)

Teachers are often resistant, but not because they dislike children with disabilities. Perhaps the most commonly cited source of resistance is a lack of skills necessary to teach students with disabilities (Minke, Bear, Deiner, and Griffin 1996). Teacher willingness to teach students with disabilities, consistent with their support for inclusion, appears to co-vary with the severity of the disability and the amount of additional teacher responsibility required (Scruggs and Mastropieri, 1996).

The social integration of exceptional children is essential to the success of inclusion.

Although many teachers support the concept of inclusion as an abstract principle, many prefer the current system (e.g. Coates, 1989; Semmel, Abernathy, Butera, and Lesar, 1991). For example, pull-out programs are sometimes perceived as non-preferred, stigmatizing, disruptive, and not leading to long-term academic gains for students. Studies indicate that both regular and special education teachers are not dissatisfied with the pull-out model. In fact, the majority of teachers in one study (Semmel et al., 1991) perceived special education classrooms as more effective and more preferred than regular classrooms for students with mild disabilities.

The three groups who present the greatest challenges to inclusion are those with significant disabilities, those with serious behavioural disorders, and adolescents at the end of their school careers. Some argue that it is deleterious to the child with behavioural disorders, the teacher, and other students to retain children in regular classes who cannot conform to the basic expectations of the classroom. There is even more disagreement within the field as to whether students with intensive educational needs belong in general education classrooms. In fact, the major placement issue of the day is whether students with severe intellectual disabilities should be based in regular or special education classrooms in home schools. Whether inclusion into regular secondary classrooms meets the needs of adolescents with disabilities is a third critical issue. Many argue that the regular curriculum does not match the needs or provide older students with the skills and competencies they require to negotiate a transition to the adult world and to be successful in occupation and living.

Together with the issue of who should be targeted for inclusion, concerns over practical implications on a wide scale have resulted in much divisiveness among parents and educators over the merits of the inclusionary ideal (Palmer et al., 1998). Implicitly, inclusion demands that supports be brought to the classroom to the child, not that the child be removed to the supports. The target of equal education cannot be met by placing students with disabilities in the regular system without these supports needed to accommodate their particular needs. However, maintaining such needed support is an enormous task that requires high degrees of commitment, communication, co-operation, collaboration, and funding.

Most regular classroom teachers do not feel that inclusion is possible without a strong support system in place (Lamond, 1995). Resources and supports include access to specialists, collaborative planning and decision making, appropriate environments and equipment, and the availability of paraprofessionals (see Miller, 1990).

Especially in the area of supports, the barriers to successful and universal inclusion remain complex, diverse, and numerous. The best intentions are dragged down by large class sizes, inadequate teacher training, lack of outside support for classroom teachers, and concern about the inclusion of certain groups of students (Galt, 1997).

Successfully implementing inclusionary practices is a major challenge to school systems in the 1990s. Diverse and complex threads must draw together if the most appropriate education is to be provided for every child who is exceptional. Some critical components are shown in Table 2-2.

Typical Services in the Late 1990s

In Canada, there is no legal mandate on, or consistent definition of, inclusion. Most Canadian legislation speaks to the idea of inclusion but not to the practice. All provincial and territorial education ministries and departments, based on a philosophy of integration,

Table 2-2 Making inclusion work

School	Restructuring to merge special education and regular education to create a more unified educational system School personnel are committed to accepting responsibility Accommodations made to the physical plant and environment Principal is supportive
Teachers	Positive attitudes; believe students can succeed Appropriate expectations Willingness to collaborate, adapt, and modify Tolerant of diverse student levels Real and perceived knowledge of students with disabilities Knowledgeable about and accepting of a child's problems and requirements Willing to plan learning experiences individualized to the child's needs
Team approach	Co-operation and collaboration Develop shared responsibility for students through regular and special education teachers working side by side with heterogeneous groups of students Team planning and teaching
Individualization	IEP Environmental adaptations Specialized devices and equipment
Curriculum	Curricular adaptations Curriculum matched to each student's needs Adapted regular curriculum Modified special curriculum Developmentally and age-appropriate curriculum Many strategies implemented such as co-operative learning and direct instruction Different grouping arrangements and lesson formats used
Evaluation	Appropriate policies for monitoring individual progress Accurate and ongoing assessment Adapted tests and grading practices
Supports	Individual supports for students with disabilities, including materials and personnel Appropriate teacher training Paraprofessional assistance Therapists and other related services
Social	Peer support Social skills training
Parents	Parents support program goals

offer a continuum of services and all promote the integration of students with special needs into the most appropriate and least restrictive learning environment. Only two ministry of education policies—those in Saskatchewan and the Northwest Territories—explicitly refer to inclusion.

Across Canada, the amount of integration into the regular classroom depends on provincial policy and the individual school district. Some Canadian school jurisdictions have adopted policies of full inclusion where all students, regardless of the severity of disabilities, are educated in regular classrooms with their age peers. A large number of school districts in Canada have chosen to maintain a continuum of services that includes segregated options and typically approach inclusion on a one-to-one basis.

It is held that case-by-case decisions are consistent with the essence of special education. Rather than a blanket policy, the special needs of each pupil must be carefully assessed and the most appropriate educational placement for that child judged.

Legislation

In Canada, except for the Declaration of Human Rights, there is no federal law to outline or guarantee the rights of children who are exceptional; the right of every child to education is not entrenched by any constitutional provision. The 1867 British North America Act (Sec. 93) was chiefly concerned with protecting the educational rights of linguistic and religious minorities. In the absence of constitutional provisions, the responsibility for education rests entirely with provincial legislation. Canadian jurisdictions have been slow to enact positive legislation guaranteeing educational rights. Only two provincial human rights codes (Saskatchewan and Quebec) list education as a right (MacKay, 1987a).

Each provincial government can develop its own legislation, regulations, policies, and procedures to ensure that all children receive a free and appropriate education. Educational goals and priorities occur in policy documents, the most relevant of which are issued by the ministries of education.

Each of the ten provinces and two territories has its own school system based upon provincial (or territorial) education legislation which springs from diverse sources—federal and provincial constitutional provisions, federal and provincial statutory law, administrative rules and regulations, and case law. Only a few schools and institutions are controlled by the provincial governments directly, such as provincial resource centres for the deaf. The rest are administered through local school boards, each of which is responsible for a geographical school district. Funding stems from a combination of property taxes and provincial government grants, according to formulae that vary from province to province (Clarke and Kendall, 1976).

Law may be defined as a system of rules and regulations relating to the behaviour of individuals and society as a whole (Warren, 1988). **School law** is the legislation, regulations, by-laws, and judicial decisions that apply primarily to all or part of the public school system (Nicholls and Martin, 1983). School-based laws are important, designed to support teachers, school administrators, and parents in providing appropriate interventions for students in need of assistance in regular and special education (Cole and Brown, 1996).

There are four main approaches to the development of legal rights in Canadian education. Some depend upon law decisions, others rely on statutory statements (Cruickshank, 1983). The four approaches are

1. Case law, which emerges from customs and legal precedents of earlier court decisions in which there were similar factual situations. Some legislation therefore arises from interpretations of existing statements in provincial education acts.

2. An express legislated statement on the right to education in provincial education acts.

3. An expressly legislated right to education in provincial human rights acts.

4. A right to education developed under the equality rights of the Canadian Charter of Rights and Freedoms.

Legislation for special education occurs because school boards fail to develop thorough and systematic policies on their own initiative. Varying practices mean that some boards go well beyond official mandates in assessment and placement but others do not establish policies and procedures and do not systematically identify, assess, and place children who are exceptional. Legislation makes school boards implement fair and equitable provisions for special education assessment, placement, and programming.

The relationship between legislation and litigation and the quality of services is not a direct correlation. Attitudes cannot be legislated, nor can responsibility. In the final analysis, the measure of responsible education will not be the number and length of laws, court cases, and interpretative regulations. The quality of education will be determined by the nature of the direction provided by educational leaders and the commitment to quality by teachers and others as they attempt to implement the intent of the directions provided. Legislation therefore may not reshape special education but it reflects the efforts that special educators have been working for years to achieve.

Legislation in the United States

In Canada, special education has tended to follow the American model. Canadian educational issues—legislative, administrative, and curricular—are directly influenced by events, philosophies, and pedagogy from the United States. As a result, Canadians have a touchstone against which to critically assess their progress and greater freedom to meld practices and philosophies to Canada's unique educational system.

The United States has a long history of relying on legislative and judicial remedies for social issues, including special education. In recent years, too, there has been an increasingly prominent role of the federal government in special education.

A number of important pieces of legislation related to children with disabilities at both school age and preschool age have been passed and then amended in various ways. Four particular laws work together to ensure that persons with exceptionalities are not discriminated against, receive a free and appropriate public education, and have access to facilities. One relates to people in general society; three are specifically educational.

A particularly important piece of legislation is the Americans with Disabilities Act (ADA) of 1990. This guarantees equal opportunity and access to all persons with disabilities, within and without the school system.

The first educational law is the oldest. Title V of the Rehabilitation Act, more commonly called Section 504, passed originally in 1974. Section 504 is a civil rights law that protects children and adults against discrimination. In the schools, it ensures that students can participate in educational programs. However, it only compels schools to make reasonable accommodations, not provide substantial or expensive services. Students not included under other laws, such as those with Attention Deficit Hyperactivity Disorder, are served under Section 504.

The major law came about in 1975 prompted by the civil rights movement, efficacy studies in special education, parent activism, professional pressure, and reports that four million of a total seven million youngsters with disabilities were being inappropriately or inadequately served (Meadow, 1980). When President Ford signed Public Law 94-142 (the Education for All Handicapped Children Act) into law in November, 1975, these children were ensured a free and appropriate education in the least restrictive environment. (Note that the numbers refer to the 142nd Bill in the 94th Congress of the United States.)

As a legislative remedy to some of the past failures of schools in providing appropriate education, Public Law 94-142 had a tremendous impact on the provision of services to children who were in some way exceptional. It represented official recognition by the Congress of the United States of the growing dissatisfaction with placing students with disabilities in special classes. The Act and its amendments legitimized the notion of placing such students in the public schools and in regular classroom settings. The legislation also led to the institutionalization of individualized instruction, increased the role of parents in the instruction of their children, and made education possible for previously unserved seriously disabled children (Will, 1986).

PL 94-142 was the broadest and most complex education law passed by the American government. Its terms are both specific and mandatory. Essentially, PL 94-142 has four major purposes:

1. To guarantee free and public special education programming to children who need it.

2. To assure fairness in decisions made about providing special education to children and youth with disabilities.

3. To establish management and auditing requirements and procedures regarding special education at all levels of government.

4. To help local and state governments implement the law by providing federal funds. PL 94-142 is a grant-in-aid law and responsibility for its implementation is shared by local, state, and federal governments. To be eligible for federal funds, state and local agencies must comply with the requirements of the law. All states have chosen to participate, so all are provided federal funds to support the education of students with disabilities.

Very specific groups of students are included under PL 94-142. The law did not apply specifically to gifted and talented students. Their needs for financial assistance and programs were originally addressed in PL 95-561, the Gifted and Talented Children's Education Act of 1978.

Public Law 94-142

PL 94-142 mandates that children with special needs must be educated in the least restrictive environment with an Individual Education Plan (IEP) developed, maintained, and evaluated for each child. States must assume non-discriminatory testing, confidentiality, and ensure due process procedures for all children with disabilities and their parents or guardians. As well, the states must actively attempt to identify children in need of special services and must provide a complete system of personnel development.

Although deeply significant, PL 94-142 is not model legislation and some of the promises have yet to be fulfilled. The prescriptive nature of the legislation has engendered its own special set of problems. One of the major areas of concern is the meaning of the least restrictive environment. The original 1975 law was never intended to force schools to educate all children with exceptionalities in the regular classroom. It was meant to ensure the most effective education in the most appropriate environment for each child based on that child's unique needs.

Particularly problematic is the requirement concerning Individual Education Plans, the accountability attached to these documents, and the amount of teacher time needed for preparation of the plans. Because of the legal basis for the IEP, every American teacher with an exceptional student in the classroom must have an IEP for that child.

However, the whole area of IEPs has become contentious and proven extremely difficult for the American system. Studies indicate that even with research and practice, the intent of the legislation of IEPs is not being met. Concerns about IEPs include increased work load, excessive paperwork, insufficient support, and lack of adequate training (Dudley-Marling, 1985).

Amendments

Like other comprehensive federal laws in the United States, PL 94-142 periodically undergoes re-authorization and amendments in response to changing circumstances. Under the original legislation, all states were mandated to serve children between the ages of six and eighteen. Ongoing amendments have extended the rights to preschool exceptional children and initiated transition programs for adolescents. PL 99-457 (1986) amended PL 94-142 to give full services for three-year-olds by 1992 and dramatically increased funding for preschool programs. PL 99-457 divided the preschool population into two groups—infants and toddlers (birth to three years) and preschoolers (three to six years). Part H of PL 99-457 refers to infants; Part B to preschoolers. The area of early intervention is further addressed in Chapter 15 of this book.

In 1990, the Individuals with Disabilities Education Act (IDEA) (PL 101-476) amended PL 94-142. IDEA retained all the basic provisions of the original legislation but expanded to include thirteen types of disability when it added autism and traumatic brain injury as categories. The title of the law was also changed to stress people-first terminology; that is, to say "a child with a disability," rather than "a handicapped child." IDEA was most recently amended on June 4, 1997, as PL 105-17.

Inclusion is a state-of-the art term; it is not mentioned in U.S. federal law. The IDEA of 1990 stipulates that children with disabilities must be provided with a free, appropriate public education in the least restrictive environment. They can be placed in special classes only when the use of supplementary aids and services in the general classroom cannot achieve a satisfactory education (Culross, 1997).

Legislation in Canada

Across Canada it cannot be said that the law clearly and unequivocally obliges the publicly supported school system to provide appropriate forms of education for all students, exceptionality notwithstanding. In fact, since the late 1960s, studies of special education have drawn attention to the shortcomings of Canadian legislation and the provision of special education services (Hall and Dennis, 1968; Poirier and Goguen, 1986; Poirier, Goguen, and

Leslie, 1988; Roberts and Lazure, 1970). Repeatedly authors contrast the progress made in American special education, particularly with reference to PL 94-142, with the lack of progress in Canada (Carter and Rogers, 1989). Rapid advances are apparent on the Canadian horizon, but the gap in the assumption of universal responsibility is not yet fully closed.

In recent years, all of the provinces and territories have elevated the concept of equal educational opportunity for all students to the status of the dominant educational ideology. Canadian provinces have recognized the right to an education for all children in different ways which can be broadly categorized as mandatory and permissive. The current legislation in each province and territory is summarized in Table 2-3.

Legislative activity has tended to focus on students with disabilities. Although gifted youngsters are considered to be exceptional in their need for special education, they have not fared as well in the legislative arena, perhaps because legal arguments for students who are gifted are different from those for children with disabilities; they are not fought on denial of access but denial of appropriate programs. In Canada, both territories and eight of the ten provinces include gifted students in some definition of exceptional pupil, either at the legislative, regulatory, or administrative policy level. The two provinces without a mention are Nova Scotia and Prince Edward Island (Ritchey, 1993).

Table 2-3 Canadian special education legislation and policies

Province/territory	Type	Policy
Newfoundland	Mandates boards to provide special education	"All students are entitled to programs designed to respond to their individual strengths and needs which are provided in the most enhancing environments. The policy promotes the idea of a continuum of supports."
Nova Scotia	Mandatory legislation; zero-reject policy. Education Act (consolidated, 1990)	"The issue is no longer whether students with exceptional needs should or should not be integrated, but what support is needed for integration to be successful."
Prince Edward Island	Mandatory, non-categorical, zero-reject	
New Brunswick	Mandatory legislation introduced 1986; inclusion	Legislation to improve "educational programs for exceptional students and emphasized placement of students with exceptionalities into regular classrooms."
Quebec	Mandatory; human rights approach with zero-reject and regulations	Amendments in 1979

Province/territory	Type	Policy
Ontario	Mandatory legislation	Education Amendment Act (1980)
Manitoba	Mandatory legislation; all-inclusive policy	Amendment to the Public School Act of 1975; under revision
Saskatchewan	Mandatory	"Education in Saskatchewan is based on the belief of the innate value and dignity of all people and the understanding that the inclusion of people with exceptional needs into every aspect of community life benefits all ... in society."
Alberta	Permissive. Mandatory legislation proposed under C26, the Amended School Act (1988). School Act amended September, 1990. Zero-reject. Policy formalized September, 1993	"There is a need for a variety of partners to work together as a team to meet each student's needs." Regular classroom is the first in a range of options. In Alberta, the School Act makes boards responsible for providing special education programs for students identified as having special needs, including those gifted and talented. When this is not possible, alternative (and presumably more expensive) arrangements are made by the boards.
British Columbia	Permissive; inclusive, non-categorical	"A board shall ensure that an administrative officer offers to consult with a parent of a student [with disabilities] regarding ... placement."
Yukon	Mandatory legislation; non-categorical School Act has sections based on least-restrictive environment and most-enabling environment.	"The Education Act 1990 requires that all students with exceptionalities be provided with an IEP implemented in the least restrictive and most enabling environment."
Northwest Territories	Mandatory legislation; zero-reject inclusion.	"Inclusive schooling shall be (a) characterized by equal access, (b) built on student strengths and needs, (c) community based, and (d) shall promote the involvement of parents ... in their child's education."

Source: Canadian CEC (1993)

Litigation

Legislation refers to laws or bills enacted by lawmakers. *Litigation*, a process that occurs through the court system, is one of the principal means by which society exerts pressure over, and provides direction to, public schools (Nicholls and Martin, 1983). Litigious influence has altered public policy and the functioning of the school system in areas as diverse as architectural barriers, assessment and classification, residential facilities, mainstreaming, custody of children, life management and sterilization, and appropriate educational practices.

Litigation involves an individual or a small group of people filing a suit against another group. The suit represents a complaint against the status quo. For example, a parent of a child who is intellectually disabled may sue a school board on behalf of the child or as a class action for all children who are intellectually disabled.

In Canada, the emphasis on using the power of the courts to settle disputes of an educational nature is less pronounced than in the United States, but nevertheless does occur with some regularity. Much litigation is initiated by parents. Sometimes, parents ask that a school district provide special educational services to a child or extend the amount of special education. In other cases, parents view the regular school as the most appropriate educational setting for the special child and disagree with the decisions regarding their child's placement in a particular program or exclusion from a program.

Other Canadian litigation has involved the rights of people with disabilities, sometimes brought by individuals or sometimes brought on their behalf. In 1982 the Adult Mental Incompetency Act came under close scrutiny in the case of Clark vs. Clark heard in County Court, Lanark, Ontario (Baker, 1983). In this case, Justin Clark, a youngster with cerebral palsy, won his rights. In British Columbia, the Stephen Dawson case involving sustaining life support was brought forward on Stephen's account (Savage, 1983).

At the moment, judicial activity seems to be stimulated by three things—the principles of the inclusion movement, the willingness of advocacy groups to support parents, and interpretations of the Charter of Rights and Freedoms.

The Charter is the federal and supreme law of Canada. Section 15 of the Charter, which came into effect in April, 1985, states that every individual is "equal before and under the law and has the right to equal protection of the law without discrimination and in particular, without discrimination based on … mental or physical disability" (s. 15 (1)).

With the Charter, the courts are entering into a period of complex and difficult decision making in which they will have a unique opportunity to significantly influence educational policy and practice. A number of challenges to the existing educational structure heard under the Charter have already occurred.

One of the earliest and most controversial cases was Elwood vs. Halifax County—Bedford School District. In October, 1986, the School Board insisted on a special placement for Luke Elwood, a lad with intellectual disabilities, and rejected the parents' requests for integration into the local school. The Elwoods went to court in 1987 in quest of the right of students with mental disabilities to be integrated into regular classrooms. When challenged on the grounds of discrimination on the basis of mental disability, the Board reversed its decision and negotiated under clauses of the Charter. A pretrial agreement signed between the Board and the family resulted in the child being integrated into the regular local public school classroom (MacKay, 1987b).

More recently, Ontario has seen Rowett vs. Board of Education of the Region of York

(Taylor, 1990) and the Eaton case against the Brant County Board of Education. Emily Eaton, at the time an eleven-year-old grade four student in Burford County, about 100 km southwest of Toronto, uses a wheelchair and a walker, cannot speak, and needs full assistance for personal care. After three years in a regular class, the teachers felt that Emily was increasingly isolated both intellectually and socially. The child's parents appealed the decision to place Emily in a special class and, after being frustrated at the board and district level, the case of Brant County Board of Education vs. Carol Eaton and Clayton Eaton was heard by the Ontario Court of Appeals. Here Madam Justice Louise Arbour ruled that under Section 15 of the Charter a placement cannot be made without parental consent as placement without consent is discriminatory (Smith, 1995). In a strongly worded statement, the judge found that Emily Eaton had a constitutional right to attend school with fully able children despite the insistence of the Brant County Board of Education that she be placed in a segregated setting (Makin, 1997; Smith, 1996).

In October 1996 and February 1997, the Supreme Court of Canada reached a different conclusion. The court decided that an individual child's needs are to be considered to determine the most appropriate placement from a range of options. As well, when an exceptional pupil has been placed in a general education class with appropriate supports and modifications and where objective evidence demonstrates that the child's needs are not being met, there is no violation of the Ontario Human Rights Code or the federal Charter of Rights and Freedoms in placing the child in a special class (Makin, 1997). Therefore, excluding some children from mainstream classes is an acceptable form of discrimination, provided that it is done in the best interests of the child. Unanimously, the Court rejected the idea of there being an automatic assumption that children with disabilities should gain entry into general classrooms if that is the wish of the parents. Instead, decisions should be made on a one-to-one basis, using the yardstick of the best interests of an individual child (Bogie, 1997; Makin, 1997).

In the United States, court actions have confirmed the rights of children who are exceptional to an appropriate education and have mandated public schools to provide that education. However, federal rulings about inclusion have also determined that the focus of an intervention should be on where a child can receive an appropriate education that meets his or her needs and that this may be a segregated classroom or a regular setting.

Trends and Movements

As we pointed out in the introduction to this chapter, there are a number of issues germane to current special education. Most of them either directly or peripherally revolve around the notion of inclusion for students who are exceptional. The following section outlines some of the most important and influential general trends.

Expansion of Services

As educational programming is provided for all youngsters, whatever the type and degree of their disability, there have been increasing pressures on special education to assume responsibility for the education of a greater proportion of the school population and a concomitant expansion of services. Programs are reaching down to encompass infants and preschoolers and up to provide transition programs and post-secondary education for students who are exceptional.

The early detection of a child's problems may prevent the development of more complex learning difficulties later in life.

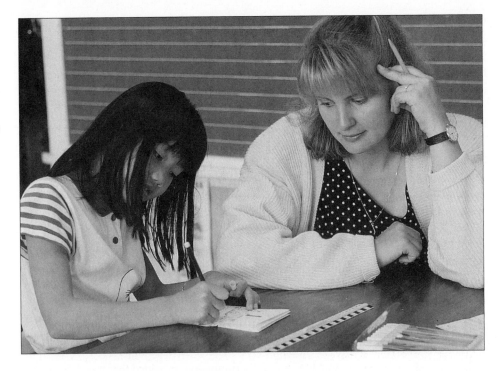

Early Intervention

Early identification and early intervention are two of the most promising areas of contemporary special education. Early identification is used to identify children with established disabilities, those who are at risk for problems, and those experiencing lags and delays. **Early intervention** refers to the establishment of educational and support services for preschool children and infants who are at risk for disabilities, and their families.

Early identification and intervention are part of the broader construct of early childhood special education. This new direction in special education truly emerged in 1986 with the passage of PL 99-457, an amendment to PL 94-142.

Of the many principles that underlie current early childhood special education, some of the most important are:

- both early intervention and its natural corollary, early identification, rest on the belief that children with disabilities can make positive gains if their problems are identified and diagnosed as early as possible and if they receive educational and therapeutic services attuned to their special needs.

- programs should be family-centred. They should establish the family as the focus of services; support and respect family decision making; and provide intervention services designed to strengthen family functioning (McBride, Brotherson, Joanning, Widdon, and Demmitt, 1993).

- parent involvement is critical. Research shows that early childhood special education is not as effective if parents are not involved and supported (Bricker, 1982).

- programs serve a broad range of children from birth to school age. Included are children with all types of disabilities, as well as children considered to be biologically or environmentally at risk for the development of conditions that can hinder learning or behaviour.

- early childhood special education should be thought of not as parallel care and education but as care and education that is embedded in and integral to early childhood education. The most appropriate settings for young children are comprehensive programs that promote regular contact. Children with special needs should be placed in a centre where they can achieve at their own level, where they are challenged to develop their potential but not swamped by a program beyond their grasp, where they can receive instruction in areas of need, and where they have opportunities to interact with normally developing children.

Transition

Many adults with disabilities do not fare well once they leave school. Increasingly, educators are becoming concerned with job placements, acquisition of a job, and maintenance of the job for young adults with disabilities. To ease the passage from school to work, transition programs are becoming more apparent in secondary special education.

Transition programs rest on the premise that the quality of life and the extent to which youth with disabilities achieve the desired goals of employment, community living, and social and leisure opportunities are dependent upon the effectiveness and appropriateness of secondary school experiences as well as on co-operative service planning and the availability of needed adult services (Johnson, Bruininks, and Thurlow, 1987). The area of secondary programming and transitions is discussed in Chapter 16.

Technological Advances

A broad range of technology is incorporated into the education and training of persons with disabilities. These are best seen on a continuum from high to low tech. High-tech solutions involve the use of sophisticated devices, such as computers and interactive multimedia systems. Medium-tech solutions use less complicated electronic or mechanical devices, such as videocassette players and wheelchairs. Low-tech solutions are less sophisticated aids, such as adapted spoon handles, Velcro fasteners, or raised desks that can accommodate a wheelchair (Blackhurst, 1997).

Computers are perhaps the technology that most obviously affects the lives of people who are disabled (Brody, 1989). Educationally, computer technology can provide reading for blind students, language for those who are deaf, and speech for students deprived by serious disabilities. As technology to improve lifestyles, computers provide sensory input, enhance mobility, develop cognitive and language skills, strengthen motor and perceptual functioning, and facilitate communication (Clements, 1985).

In the classroom, computers are an effective supplement to classroom instruction—a tool that helps students learn more and have fun doing so. In special education, Computer Assisted Instruction (CAI) has proven effective in influencing the educational outcomes of students of all ages. Computers seem to promote academic achievement and more positive attitudes about learning, particularly for disadvantaged students and other low achievers (Lepper and Gurtner, 1989). They are efficient and patient teachers that can repeatedly present material to those students requiring additional drill and practice. Children can work independently at their own pace and receive rewards and corrections as the program progresses.

In some ways, computers as instructional tools have been disappointing. In the early 1980s, the computer was seen as an educational godsend, the device to provide the greatest amount of assistance in the widest variety of areas to the maximum number of students. But much of the early optimism has evaporated. By the 1990s, critics were complaining that "the content and process of education remains unchanged and the computer revolution, which is radically transforming the office and factory, has not yet made its mark in the schools" (Kurzweil, 1990). In the particular field of the education of deaf students, for example, the early 1980s saw claims that "the microcomputer chip will be remembered as the technological product that changed the course of history for the hearing impaired population" (Stoker, 1983, p. 364). Not much later, a meta-analysis of the literature (Braden and Shaw, 1987) found a lack of evidence supporting the superiority of CAI over other instructional methods. The authors concluded that "there is no reason to believe that CAI is a panacea for deaf children, and in fact, there is no evidence to suggest that it is anything except an instructional placebo" (p. 191).

Assessment Practices

Diagnosis is a term derived from the Greek root *dia* (apart) and *gignoskien* (to know). By definition, **diagnosis** is the art of identifying disease from its symptoms. Differential diagnosis implies the precise specification that a given set of symptoms is indicative of one disorder rather than another.

The word **assessment** rather than *diagnosis* is used in education because it is more relevant to instruction by stressing the current level of developmental functioning. The term refers to the process of gathering "valid evidence to guide decisions about curriculum and instruction, and to evaluate the outcomes of instruction" (Calfee, 1987).

Assessment is undertaken with normally developing children and with those who appear to be making an inadequate adjustment in some aspect of their development whether it be behavioural, social, emotional, or communicative, or some combination of these. The process is not intended to label a child or to propel him or her toward special education. Rather, the basic purpose is to collect information, to clarify the "whys" of a child's performance and behaviour. It targets behaviours—social, communication, motor, or self-care skills—to determine how a child learns best, the behavioural characteristics that will affect learning, and whether there are any sensory or motor impairments relevant to achievement and performance. The process also helps in making decisions about the best educational placement for a child and is the first step in preparing an IEP.

The best way to view assessment is as a bridge between teaching and the psychological principle that every child is unique. If an educational program is truly to meet a child's needs, it must be based on assessment. Moreover, there is no clear line between assessment and intervention; we cannot devise a program for a child without a diagnosis, and we cannot arrive at a diagnosis without an assessment.

Over the years, the responsibility for assessing students with disabilities has come to be viewed as substantially different from assessment in general education. This is not correct: assessment in special education is best viewed as an extension of the measurement and evaluation techniques used by all teachers to assess student learning. However, the process in special education is more varied and complex. Assessment is not a one-time or single procedure. A single test, person, or occasion is not a sufficient source of information; instead, a valid description of a child's status is generated from data collected from several sources, instruments, and settings, and on multiple occasions.

In recent years, practices in assessment for learning problems have progressed considerably and a paradigm shift has occurred in assessment practices. No longer is assessment the sole responsibility of a psychologist in a clinic setting. Today, there are changes in the types of tools and measures preferred, the environment used for assessment, the flexibility of the procedures, and the greater involvement of regular and special education personnel in the procedures.

Increasingly, teachers are recognizing the importance of assessing student performance and learning outcomes in the context of the classroom and home environment. As they do, interest is being generated around methods that are relevant to the primary purposes of learning and that can be used to enhance teachers' instructional planning, such as curriculum-based assessment.

In this short section, we could not possibly detail all the new developments, which include authentic assessment, the use of portfolios, performance assessment, curriculum-based measurement, and so on. We can only point out some general procedures; assessment for special populations is further embedded in each chapter of the text.

Stages in Assessment

The actual assessment process can be conceptualized as three interrelated stages—*survey*, or screening; *specific*, or diagnostic; and *intensive*, or medical and paraprofessional. Each of these stages involves different strategies and is undertaken by different professionals. All, however, focus on developing efficient treatment and educational programs for an individual child. The primary goal is to gather and analyze enough pertinent information to teach the child effectively. Assessment addresses both diagnostic evaluations and the ongoing monitoring that is critical if the progress of a child's program is to be determined.

Screening

As a term, *screening* originated in the medical literature. As its use becomes more prevalent in the behavioural sciences, screening is now used in medicine and education to refer to developmental and health activities that are intended to identify those children who have a high probability of exhibiting delayed or abnormal development.

Screening in education refers to a classroom activity that generally occurs prior to direct testing. The procedures look at large groups of children and begin to identify those who may have difficulties in behaviour and learning. In this way, screening is a first step in determining whether children may need intervention or special services for a condition that could prove disabling, or whether children might profit from an adapted or individualized educational program due to disabilities or giftedness.

Interviews with parents form part of screening. In the classroom, procedures to screen in the intellectual and behavioural domains include first-hand observations, child interviews, past records, developmental checklists, behaviour rating scales, inventories, teacher-made tests, criterion-referenced tests, group achievement tests, and error analysis.

On average, most educational screening identifies about 85 percent of children with exceptionalities (Lerner, Mardell-Czudnowski, and Goldenberg, 1981). An exception is students who are gifted, where screening procedures are less successful (see Chapter 7).

Child interviews are one of many screening procedures used to identify students who might profit from a modified or individualized education program.

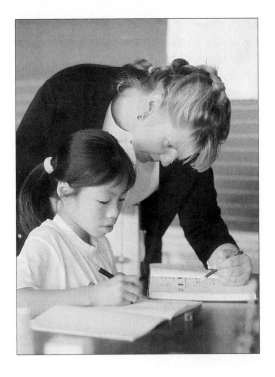

Note too that many students with severe or multiple disabilities do not pass through a screening evaluation, as they are obviously disabled, and the assessment process for them begins with psycho-educational testing (Gaylord-Ross and Holveot, 1985).

Parent Interviews

Interviews are part of the assessment process; in fact, an assessment is incomplete without the careful collection of data from parent interviews. Parents offer the singular advantage of providing information about specific types of behaviour in a variety of settings over a much longer time than is available to the examiner during a typical assessment session (Bagnato, Neisworth, and Musson, 1989). Parental insights about the child can complement information from other sources and paint a broader picture of the child's capabilities and educational needs.

Two caveats surround parent interviews. First, while valuable and oftentimes critical data are obtained through interviews, interviewers should be aware that the subjective and interpretative nature of interviews places limitations on their usefulness.

Second, parent conferences can be a source of apprehension for teachers, particularly when parents have requested the meeting or when the student is not adapting well at school (Perl, 1995). Conferences go more smoothly if teachers keep the following in mind:

- Schedule conferences well ahead of time, request that both parents attend, and indicate the amount of time available for the conference.

- Prepare some questions before the meeting. This helps keep emotionalism from obscuring your views and keeps the meeting on task. Throughout, keep the focus of the conference on school functioning.

- To facilitate communication, hold the conference around a table, rather than on opposite sides of a desk (Perl, 1995). If you have a classroom equipped for young children, do have adult-sized furniture for parents. It is not uncommon for parents to feel threatened at parent–teacher interviews sitting in a low chair around a paint-stained table with a timer ticking the seconds until their dismissal (Klapauszak, 1994).

- Begin the meeting with some pleasant informal talk to make participants feel comfortable. Offer coffee, a soft drink, or even water.

- Limit the number of professionals present. Parents can be overwhelmed by too many people.

- Interviews are most effective if the interviewer is a good listener. Parents have vital information professionals may not possess, so it is as important for professionals to listen and learn as to "explain" and "teach." Listening should be active rather than passive. Attending skills include body postures, squaring shoulders and looking directly at the listener, using a positive stance of open arms, leaning forward to the speaker, and maintaining eye contact (Studer, 1993/1994).

- Select and ask questions carefully and tactfully. Interviewers should ask questions that reveal information about the child from the parent's perspective. Questions serve three purposes: to obtain specific information, to clarify existing information, and to redirect the interview when it strays from pertinent topics.

- Avoid words that have a negative connotation such as *deficit* or *disability*.

- Ask the parents to tell you about their child, and to share their perceptions.

- Explain how you are trying to expand the child's abilities, rather than trying to make him or her "better."

Criterion-Referenced Measures

Criterion-referenced tests do not assess a child against some group norm but against the child's own individual progress toward preset criteria. Criterion-referenced tests may be commercially produced; many are designed by classroom teachers to assess the progress of an individual child.

Criterion-referenced testing is particularly easy to integrate with a child's individual educational program. The testing is performed simply to determine what needs to be taught. The teacher sets instructional objectives, or criteria, for the child to work toward. For example, if a short-term objective is for a child to learn the addition facts to nine, then the test would assess how that child achieved in that particular objective.

Curriculum-Referenced Measures

A special form of criterion-referenced test is referred to as curriculum-referenced testing or curriculum-based assessment (CBA). CBA is defined as a standardized measurement system used to monitor a student's academic growth and to improve instructional programs (Fuchs, Fuchs, Hamlett, and Ferguson, 1992).

Curriculum-referenced tools are similar to criterion-referenced, but they differ in that a predetermined criterion is not necessarily set and the test is always explicitly related to what was taught in the classroom. It does this by indexing student proficiency directly to the curriculum. CBA measures performance in a particular curriculum area and compares children's progress and performance with that of their peers in the same school or school division (Deno, 1985).

Although the fundamental question of CBA is "How is the student progressing in the curriculum of his or her school?" there are a variety of models of CBA in use. All are guided by the premise that curricula should serve as the basis for assessment, and all emphasize measurement that is brief, frequent, based on the student's classroom curriculum, and that can be used to monitor instructional programs and effectiveness (Potter and Wamre, 1990). To prepare CBA, teachers determine the annual curriculum goals for a student; devise and present short tests from the curriculum; and use this information to monitor student progress and to adjust programs.

The measurement of progress by using actual curriculum-based items and by direct daily measurement has been found to have a noticeable effect on academic achievement when the results are used to modify instructional planning (Overton, 1992). Apart from progress monitoring, CBA can be used for screening, referral, individual education planning, and program evaluation (Fuchs and Deno, 1992). It has been found an accurate screening measure for referral to special education, less influenced than other measures by teacher variables (Overton, 1992).

Ecological and Functional Assessment

Ecological assessment is closely related to the more general movement of authentic assessment, which insists that the content of testing should reflect the goals of learning in as far as they require students to think, decide, and act in the real world (Archbald and Newman, 1988). Classrooms are ecological systems where students and teachers are constantly interacting. From an ecological viewpoint, an individual's behaviour is the product of the interaction between the individual and all the variables in his or her environment. Hence, an ecological assessment focuses not only on a child but on environmental variables. For example, it may examine whether methods of presentation of content and classroom grouping match the learning style of an individual learner. A child from a Native culture will probably be far happier in co-operative learning groups than in competitive independent seat work (Winzer and Mazurek, 1998).

Functional assessment, a first cousin of the ecological model, is used for children with more severe disabilities. It stresses the assessment of specific observable behaviours that form the mode of the current and future existence of the child. It is based on the direct collection of performance data; the identification of factors that affect performance, such as those under teacher control; the presentation and examination of repeated teaching trials; and close assessment to assess the success of teaching (Sugai and Maheady, 1988). It looks at elements of the child's behavioural repertoire that interfere with instructional objectives; appropriate steps to reduce the skill-inhibiting elements of behaviour; conditions that motivate the child to attend or those that elicit a response; and the level of assistance that is required for a child to complete a task not accomplished spontaneously (Strain, Sainato, and Maheady, 1984).

There are two major areas to functional assessment. The first is to identify skills that will increase a child's ability to interact with people and objects in the daily environment. The second concerns whether the skill will have to be performed by someone else if the child has not been taught to do it.

Specific Assessment

Screening measures are not valid for diagnostics and should only be used to assist in referring a child for in-depth assessment. Direct testing (psycho-educational assessment) refers to testing children across a variety of domains relevant to social and educational

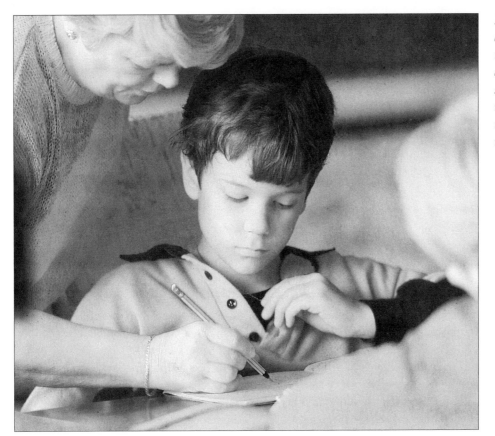

In dynamic assessment some teaching is allowed during the process so that effective instructional techniques can be identified.

performance. The aim is to gather further information on children who were identified as at-risk intellectually or behaviourally using primary screening measures. The process confirms or discounts the existence of a problem and helps determine what treatment and intervention are needed.

Psycho-educational assessment relies heavily on testing. In general, the term **testing** means that explicit criteria for performance are established in advance. **Tests** are defined as controlled and structured procedures that attempt to elicit particular responses that the child might not demonstrate spontaneously (Bailey and Brochin, 1989). Many tests are standardized—they use standard materials, administrative procedures, scoring procedures, and score interpretation. The purpose of standardization is to ensure that all children taking the test receive essentially the same experience, are expected to perform the same tasks with the same set of materials, receive the same amount of assistance from the evaluator, and are evaluated according to a standard set of criteria. The overwhelming majority of standardized tests are norm referenced—they indicate a child's developmental level in relation to that of other children of the same age, the normative group.

IQ tests (measures of mental ability) are probably the best-known and the most controversial of the norm-referenced measures. They provide an intelligence quotient (IQ), which is the relationship between a child's mental age (MA) and chronological age (CA). IQ reflects the difference between the child's performance on the tests and the normative performance for the child's age level.

Certain assumptions underlie the definition of IQ. The most crucial is the notion that intelligence, as measured on standardized tests of mental ability, is normally distributed. A normal distribution is a continuum of scores that vary from the average score by predictable amounts. Figure 2-1 shows the normal curve of intelligence, based on the scores of the Wechsler Intelligence Scale for Children-Revised (3rd. edition) (Wechsler, 1991). This widely used test of intelligence has an average score of 100 and a standard deviation of 15.

The subtests of the Wechsler scales are divided into two parts, a Performance scale and a Verbal scale. Subtests involve tasks such as mental arithmetic, word meanings, puzzles, tracing through mazes, showing what is missing in a picture, and reproducing a geometric design with blocks.

Teachers' involvement in assessing intelligence and cognitive functioning is usually limited to observation, screening measures, and determining instructional targets. Referrals are made to the appropriate services if deeper assessment is needed. Because IQ tests are delicate instruments and need careful interpretation, their use is restricted to psychologists and others who have received special training.

Many educators query the need for psychological services. They consider large-scale norm-referenced testing and grading systems to be of limited value in determining the needs and styles of inclusive classrooms (see Cullen and Pratt, 1992). Nevertheless, psychometric assessment is still widely used. Advocates stress that an assessment of a child's cognitive skills is essential to a complete understanding of his or her development because cognitive skills are closely intertwined with skills in other domains, especially language, social functioning, and behaviour. Further, when properly used and interpreted, tests perform important functions. The greatest advantage of standardized tests is their potential for comparing a child's performance to that of other children (the norm group), and they are still used with considerable success to predict academic achievement. As well, some school districts demand intellectual assessment as a major source of data in the designation and placement of students in special education (Wilson and Humphries, 1986).

Figure 2-1

The normal curve of intelligence based on the WISC–III

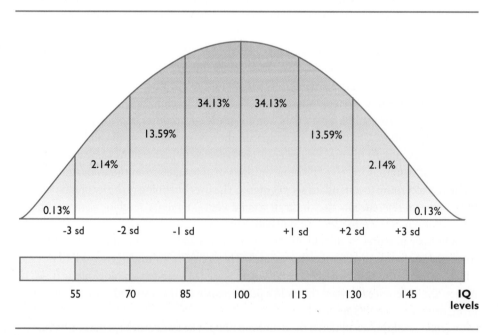

However, these measures are more important for defining delays than for program planning. Standardized measures tap isolated intellectual and language abilities but do not yield intervention-relevant information on functional skills that can be included in an individual child's program and easily integrated with daily activities.

Developmental Assessment

Development-referenced assessment is concerned with the location of a learner's skills within a specified hierarchy of skills (developmental milestones). The approach is founded on the assumption that children progress through specific patterns and that these patterns can be used in the detection of qualitative and quantitative differences between children.

The basis of the developmental approach is the use of developmental scales to establish lags or problems in one or more areas of growth. Sometimes teachers devise their own simple scales of developmental milestones that are compilations of developmental information taken from various developmental scales and charts. Just as often, they use norm-referenced tests to determine the extent of deviation from the norm.

The scales provide guidelines that give a baseline to tell whether a child is progressing through the normal sequences of development or whether there are delays in development. If a child fails an item in the normal developmental sequence, it is rewritten as an instructional objective and the skill targeted for intervention.

Dynamic Assessment

Dynamic assessment is an interventionalist approach to assessment that is in direct opposition to the one-tester, one-child norm-referenced approaches. A child is not asked to do something and marked right or wrong. Rather, a "test, teach, test" format is used. This process determines the amount and type of intervention that brings about change in a child, measures the amount of change that can be produced in a guided teaching and learning situation, and may identify obstacles that may be hindering a child's performance. Since some techniques are shown in the assessment to enhance the learning efficiency of the child, the observations and results lead directly to instructional suggestions because they specify the conditions under which learning and performance may be improved.

Medical Assessment

A huge variety of medical procedures are used with children with disabilities, often starting at birth or even before. Professionals involved at the medical level of assessment include school nurses, family doctors, pediatricians, neurologists, audiologists, and ophthalmologists, to mention only a few. The medical community uses a combination of testing devices, including clinical history, physical examinations, and laboratory tests to arrive at a diagnosis.

Medically, screening may begin as early as the prenatal period with the use of amniocentesis to determine the presence of certain genetic disorders. Immediately following birth, screening occurs as physicians check for obvious disabilities or genetic and metabolic disorders. Later, a public health nurse using a sweep test to check hearing or a Snellen chart for visual acuity is screening for physical problems.

For a school-age child, a complete look at the child's health history and current medical status must form part of the total assessment. Suppose, for example, that a grade one child, who appears bright and outgoing, cannot seem to comprehend such sound-symbol associations as "S is for snake." Before any specific psycho-educational diagnosis is undertaken, the child should be referred to an audiologist for a complete assessment of hearing acuity.

SUMMARY

1. Special education today is a vibrant and exciting area of education, alive with the pulse of new ideas. Issues, trends and movements apparent in the field are all designed to ultimately improve conditions of living and learning for all persons who are exceptional.

2. Many of the changes in attitudes and perceptions can be dated to the 1960s and the birth of the normalization movement. The ideological shift during the 1960s and the 1970s held that community settings were superior in their effects on social, vocational, and academic learning. By the mid-1970s, the treatment of persons with disabilities in non-restrictive, normalized settings gained priority.

3. Special education is deeply involved in reforming the system at various structural and theoretical levels. However, there is nothing new about reform in special education. In fact, since its inception in North America in 1817, special education has been constantly subjected to changes in educational settings, student eligibility, curriculum considerations, and so on.

4. Probably no question has occupied special education professionals more in past decades than the effects, real and potential, of integrating children with disabilities and children developing normally. While current reform efforts point in various directions and to various groups, the issues most germane to current special education still revolve around how thoroughly children with mental and physical disabilities should be integrated into the regular school system and how school districts can best include children with special needs into regular classrooms.

5. The most encompassing reform is within the paradigms and principles of what is referred to as inclusion, inclusive education, or inclusive schooling. While the concepts of inclusive schooling apply to all students, and include children with diverse backgrounds, abilities, and contributions, the most pressing issue concerns those students presenting intensive educational challenges to our schools who have historically been served outside the regular classroom and, in many cases, outside the community school.

6. The research literature supports inclusion for many groups of children. But, as with any new movement, many caveats are in order. While some professional organizations and many advocacy groups support full inclusion, others are more cautious.

7. Law and public policy have had a profound effect on the type and quality of education offered to children and youth who are exceptional. In some cases, they decide whether exceptional students are educated at all; in others, they determine how such children are educated.

8. Litigation and legislation underlie much of the process of educational integration witnessed today. Parent groups, court decisions, escalating educational costs, and the example set by PL 94-142 have all exerted pressure on governments. Movement has been toward giving school boards the duty, not the discretion, to provide appropriate programs for all students within their jurisdiction.

9. Recent trends in special education include the extension of programming to encompass children at the post-secondary and preschool and infant levels, new approaches to assessment, and transition programs for adolescents.

10. Before we can help children who are exceptional, we must accurately pinpoint their problems. For each child, we need a detailed picture of strengths and weaknesses in a variety of domains. Only then can we develop an effective educational program. Failure to incorporate diagnostic assessment results into program planning denies a child specially designed instruction and, without this, there can be no special education.

11. Assessment serves little purpose if the process is undertaken merely to collect data. Data from screening and psycho-educational diagnosis are only useful when used to initiate more effective services and programming for children.

12. With norm-referenced measures, the concern is how a child performs in comparison to a same-age reference group. Criterion-referenced and curriculum-referenced tests assess how a child performs related to a predetermined set of tasks or activities. Dynamic assessment provides information about the responsiveness of a learner to intervention. Developmental measures assess children in relation to normal milestones.

In the Classroom

Good teaching applies to an integrated class the same way that it applies to any class. For all students, it is the teacher's responsibility to provide warm and accepting learning environments. When students with disabilities are within these environments, they can experience success only when a range of supports is available.

Including students with special needs demands some changes in the standard learning environment. The teacher must be able to meet individual learning needs through appropriate changes in the environment, instruction, and content. Different adaptations and modifications are needed depending on the child's type and severity of disability. Teachers also need supports that include additional personnel assistance such as an aide or daily contact with special education teachers (Scruggs and Mastropieri, 1996), planning time, collaboration, and small class sizes.

While various changes can be incorporated to include students with disabilities in the regular classroom, changes in teaching methods are not that obvious or different. Specialized competencies and teaching methods are extensions and refinements of core competencies rather than new sets of teaching behaviour and skills (Ysseldyke and Algozzine, 1990).

Teachers will use procedures and techniques that, for purposes of clarity, we arbitrarily refer to as accommodations, adaptations, and modifications in the physical, instructional, and psychosocial environments. Distinctions between accommodations, adaptations, and modifications are subtle, and there is much overlap. We can say that:

- An *accommodation* is a minor change that assists a child's functioning in the environment. For example, an FM system for a child with a hearing impairment; seating close to the teacher for the child with a behavioural disorder; increased lighting, but no glare, for the child with a visual disability; or extra space between desks for the child with a physical disability.

- *Adaptations* are changes to the regular curriculum that retain the same outcomes as those for normally developing children. Adaptations refer to how teachers modify planned instruction beyond their routine adaptations in light of specific student difficulty (Fuchs, Fuchs, Hamlett, Phillips, and Karns, 1995). The array of adaptations from which a teacher may choose is enormous. Strategies such as precision teaching, cognitive strategy training, co-operative learning, monitoring of children's on-task behaviour, appropriate pacing of instruction, and peer tutoring have been shown to be effective in integrated classes. More specifically, teachers may employ a slower pace with many redundant questions and much drill and practice for children with learning difficulties; many diagrams, visual materials, and media for students who must grasp ideas without depending solely on language; maps, graphs, and so on in string, pasta, or raised glue for students with visual impairments; work sheets with only one type of activity or question for students with learning disabilities; self-tests and checklists so older students can monitor themselves; practice questions before an examination for older students; co-operative learning strategies for average and below average students; and independent studies for gifted learners. Elementary teachers report that the instructional adaptations used most frequently include shortened assignments, oral tests, study buddies, lower level worksheets, and preferential seating (Bacon and Schulz, 1991).

- *Modifications* step away from the general curriculum. Modifications have learning outcomes that are substantially different from the prescribed curriculum. They generally apply to children with significant disabilities for whom the regular curriculum may not be relevant.

- The process of change in environment and instruction is diagrammed below.

Providing appropriate adaptations for students with disabilities entails much more than finding a list of suggested adaptations for various subjects. It requires a great deal of advance planning, assessment of student ability and skill, consideration of resources, and curriculum planning. Particularly important is collaboration and input from the special education teacher.

Effective inclusion depends on the development of innovative and efficient ways of working with sup-

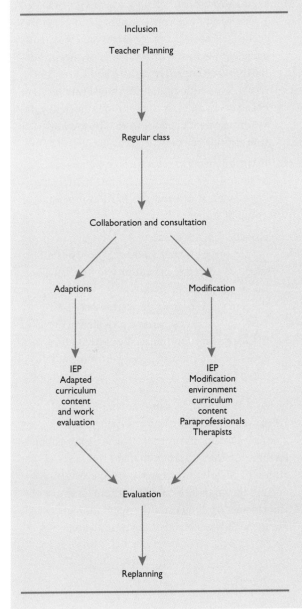

Inclusion

Teacher Planning

↓

Regular class

↓

Collaboration and consultation

↓   ↓

Adaptions   Modification

↓   ↓

IEP   IEP
Adapted   Modification
curriculum   environment
content   curriculum
and work   content
evaluation   Paraprofessionals
                     Therapists

↓   ↓

Evaluation

↓

Replanning

port disciplines involved with students with special needs. That is, procedures such as collaborative teaming and teaching and shared planning underlie the success of inclusion: "Teamwork among regular educators, special education teachers, support personnel, parents and peers is critical to the success of integrated education programs" (York and Vandercook, 1991, p. 22).

Teaming is the process in which two or more persons share information and expertise in order to meet a common goal (Morsink, Thomas, and Correa, 1991). Teaming will mean new forms of collaboration between parents, administrators, teachers, and others. *Collaboration* refers to any mutual effort to plan, implement, or evaluate educational programs for a student or students (Morsink, Thomas, and Correa, 1991). With collaboration, "multidisciplinary planning support is given to classroom teachers to improve the quality of instruction provided to learning disabled and other low achieving students presently receiving educational services in general education settings" (Bauwens, Hourcade, and Friend, 1989, p. 17).

One hallmark of an effective learning environment for students with mild disabilities is the degree to which the environment is constructively active. In an effective learning environment, the teacher engages in active teaching and the student is actively engaged in successfully completing academically relevant tasks. The teacher monitors student performance and provides informed feedback (Ysseldyke and Christenson, 1987). This approach is referred to as *conventional teaching* (Walberg, 1991) or *direct instruction*.

Direct instruction refers to activity-focused, teacher-directed classroom procedures that are systematic and usually conducted according to an individual plan. Direct instruction procedures include prompting, shaping, or reinforcing implemented in a precise and consistent fashion. Learning is achieved by identifying the specific objective to be attained, arranging appropriate stimuli to elicit the responses, programming learning sequences in small steps, and reinforcing desired behaviours.

Walberg (1991) argues that such a direct didactic approach has the best track record. He describes the teacher doing certain things:

- daily review, homework check, and if necessary, re-teaching;

- rapid presentation of new content and skills in small steps;

- guided student practice under close teacher monitoring;

- corrective feedback and reinforcement;

- independent practice in seat work and homework;

- weekly and monthly review (p. 44).

Making Adaptations

The problem is matching appropriate adaptations and modifications to student learning problems. This is facilitated when planning is individualized and documented in an IEP, as we discussed in Chapter 1.

It is simply not possible to adapt teacher-centred instruction to the diverse needs of every student, so teachers must select adaptations that suit a range of learners. As they make adaptations, teachers should ask the following questions:

- Can I do this in a reasonable amount of time with a reasonable amount of effort? Research shows that the less time and resources required to implement a change, the greater the acceptability to teachers.

- Can I fit this with my general teaching? In general, changes are not in core competencies, but in the techniques. In presenting instruction, teachers should alter the stress and pacing of lessons, the type and amount of seat work, and grading practices. Changes must often be made in the content of the lesson, which may be adapted to make it more concrete and relevant to children's recent experiences.

- If we teach this subject this way, will Jane be able to participate and learn the concept? Instructional arrangements and lesson formats include traditional lecture, demonstration, practice, whole class discussion, games and simulations, and ex-

periential learning, and range from large group instruction to co-operative learning groups and peer partners to individual and independent seat work. Since students with disabilities often have problems in large groups and in independent seat work, some type of small group or individual instruction can be an effective adaptation. For example, change a format from an independent research project into an arrangement such as group investigation in order to include Jane.

- If I use this format, will Joe participate? Compared to one-to-one and small-group teaching arrangements, whole class arrangements are consistently associated with the lowest levels of engaged behaviour (see Logan, Bakeman, and Keefe, 1997). As students with disabilities show lower levels of engagement in tasks than do their normally developing peers, a change to small-group instruction may also be beneficial for Joe.

- Is the adaptation relevant? To be effective, an adaptation or modification must match an evident problem or need of a particular student or group of students.

- How do I make the change? Inclusive practices do not presume that all teachers possess all the expertise needed to include all children; left alone, the solitary teacher cannot possibly know everything required to meet the learning needs of every student. Assistance must be provided in the areas of curriculum modification, participation, and social integration by special education teachers, paraprofessionals (aides), and non-disabled peers.

As mentioned, the range of adaptations is huge. Below we point out some generic changes that are suitable for many special learners. Each chapter contains further examples. Readers should keep in mind that although classroom accommodations, adaptations, and modifications are categorized according to a specific disability, this reflects the organization of the text, not the reality that changes suit many learners.

Examples of Generic Adaptations

CONTENT ADAPTATIONS

- Slow pace, wait time
- Teach to learning styles
- Use mastery learning

INSTRUCTIONAL ADAPTATIONS

- Use experiential learning that allows students with disabilities to be active rather than passive participants
- Use mnemonic devices
- Shorten directions
- Provide mediators
- Change format; for example, to a small group
- When large-group instruction is used, break the instruction up with an activity that allows all students to participate and move around
- Use advance organizers
- Preface all remarks with a title, or the main idea of the lesson
- Use cognitive learning strategies

GROUPING ADAPTATIONS

- Use co-operative learning, often recommended as a fundamental strategy in inclusive and multicultural classrooms
- Set up learning centres

ADAPTING MATERIALS

- Make materials self-correcting
- Highlight critical features
- Block out extraneous elements

CUEING, FEEDBACK ADAPTATIONS

- Provide response prompts
- Use corrective feedback
- Provide visual clues

INVOLVING STUDENTS

- Students appreciate it when teachers make changes in instructional techniques to allow for individual needs (Vaughn, Schumm, and Kouzekanani, 1993). Give older students some say in the adaptations that will be used.

INVOLVING OTHER CLASS MEMBERS

- There is clear evidence that children with learning and behaviour problems benefit from peer tutoring and co-operative learning. Use peer tutoring, defined as "a more able child helping a less able child in a co-operative working pair carefully organized by a teacher" (Topping, 1989, p. 489). Select peer tutors carefully. Not every student is suitable as a peer tutor. The optimal tutor is one who has mastered the skill to be taught and can follow the lesson independently of the teacher. A good tutor can reliably and accurately correct the tutee's errors and has the social skills necessary to form a long-term tutorial relationship (Grenwood, Carta, and Hall, 1988).

MANAGEMENT ADAPTATIONS

- Different delivery of reinforcers
- Use evaluative feedback. For example, "I like the way you formed your letters," rather than "Good work."
- Contingency contracts
- Change seating
- Counselling
- Social skills training

EVALUATION AND GRADING ADAPTATIONS

- Modify grades and report cards to reflect an individual student's level of improvement
- Use curriculum-based assessment

TEST TAKING

- Teach test-taking skills. Students are at a great disadvantage if they do not understand the format or the instructions of a test. From 5 to 14 hours of instruction time spread over 5 to 7 weeks appears to be the effective range of instruction time needed to improve test-taking skills and "test wiseness" (Grossman, 1995; Samson, 1985).
- Allow students to use different strategies in test taking.

STUDY SKILLS

- Teach study skills
- Note all assignments on a special bulletin board

 WEBLINKS

The Council for Exceptional Children **http://www.cec.sped.org/**

Internet Special Education Resources **http://www.iser.com/index.shtml**

Education Quality and Accountability Office **http://www.eqao.com/**

Office of Learning Technologies **http://olt-bta.hrdc-drhc.gc.ca/english.html**

The Canadian Charter of Rights and Freedoms **http://www.colba.net/~mgelinas/chrt/**

CHAPTER 3

Risk Factors and Children at Risk

People with disabilities have probably been in society since its beginnings. Responses to individuals who were different or deviant were influenced by many factors—culture, religion, government, and economics—and have included extermination, conversion, restraint, and cure. Educational and social intervention was little heeded until the middle of the eighteenth century.

Throughout history, the conditions were bounded by medical paradigms. Conditions requiring medical treatment were the first to be addressed; the recognition and care of intellectually and sensorially deprived persons had to wait for more enlightened attitudes regarding social care, which historically tended to lag behind purely medical concerns. The medical stress largely determined societal attitudes and legal mandates for persons with disabilities.

With the nineteenth century and the enormous interest in human genetics and heredity stimulated by Darwin's work, medical models became very prominent. For example, all of the early superintendents of institutions for persons with mental retardation were physicians. Today's American Association on Mental Retardation (AAMR) began as the Association

of Medical Superintendents of American Institutions for the Feeble Minded (Winzer, 1993).

In a time period that almost exactly matched the publication of Darwin's work (1859) and the birth of the Association (1856), major advances occurred in the etiology of disabilities, particularly mental retardation. One of the most important came when John Langdon Down in 1866 identified specific subcategories of retardation.

The medical model grew from concepts of disability that were purely biological in nature. They attributed disabilities almost solely to "bad stock" and assumed a qualitative difference between normal and abnormal. Persons with disabilities were thought to have traits and characteristics of a degree and type that made them fundamentally different from the general run of humanity and therefore could not be expected to want to have the same advantages as normally developing people.

In the late nineteenth century, biological theories of degeneracy and repressive theories of heredity ushered in a period of cruel and callous treatment. Eugenics, essentially founded on the idea that the future good of society depended on allowing only the average or superior to marry and procreate, developed as an important and influential theory. It determined to a large extent the treatment of persons with mental retardation until the 1930s. During this period, many persons who were disabled were locked away, forbidden to marry and procreate, and viewed as pariahs in society.

As special education developed, it adopted a medical model and, as new advances in medicine and genetics emerged, melded them into conceptions of disability. Disorders were seen to have primarily an organic or psychological basis; defects arose from things such as brain damage, chemical imbalance, or chromosomal abnormality. When the disabilities were attributed to various types of brain damage, terminology generally reflected a medical orientation. Common terms included minimal brain dysfunction, brain crippled, cerebral disordered, neurologically impaired, dyslexic, and dysphasic.

Past definitions of intellectual disability, for example, assumed a condition intrinsic to the individual; they emphasized the endogeneous, or internal, determination of defective intelligence. Mental retardation was seen as a condition that existed at birth; only a passing nod was given to negative environmental factors. Alfred Binet characterized idiots as being unable to talk or to understand language (Peterson, 1925). Tredgold (1908) defined mental retardation as "a state of incomplete mental development of such a kind and degree that the individual is incapable of adapting himself to the normal environment of his fellows in such a way

as to maintain existence independent of supervision, external control, or support." In the 1940s, Edgar Doll presented six criteria defining persons with intellectual disabilities: social and occupational incompetency; inability to manage affairs at an adult level; mental subnormality; intellectual retardation from an early age; intellectual retardation during maturity; and incurable (Doll, 1941).

Because disorders were seen to have distinct patterns of symptoms and signs that resulted from different disease entities and causes, they responded to different treatments. In the schools, medical models meant that a condition within a child could be diagnosed, the child could be labelled, and then placed in a class consonant with that label. Each condition was slotted into a separate pigeonhole, then a particular treatment was designed for each condition.

Well into the 1960s, there was a strict adherence to medical models in special education. The underlying assumption was that a diagnosis can be formed on the basis of observations and tests of the individual and that there is a corresponding treatment for a rehabilitating effect. We could find out what is wrong with a person and then "fix" it.

Medical models still remain important in special education. Today, however, educators focus on the learning styles and behaviours of a child rather than the presumed underlying etiology. Contemporary systems tend to describe or profile children's behaviour patterns and move the field closer to models in which descriptions of children's needs, not etiological labels, drive intervention efforts.

Dozens and dozens of factors surround children as they grow up. Some of them are related to the classroom; many, many more are familial or extra-familial factors. If teachers are to truly understand the pupils in their charge, they must be aware of a child's social world and a child's development, social skills, self-esteem, and interactions with parents.

This is even more key when a child has a disability. Not only must teachers be aware of the psychological, social, and educational factors related to a disability, but they must also have a working knowledge of biomedical causes.

At risk is a term used to describe a number of different categories of children. At risk refers to infants and young children who are physically, medically, or psychologically in danger of failing to thrive as well as children who are affected by diverse economic, environmental, and geographic factors. At-risk status includes, for example, young girls who become pregnant, adolescents involved in drugs and crime, those who have attempted suicide, school dropouts, and large groups of children for whom English is not the first language (Winzer and Mazurek, 1998).

Studies find that between 25 and 35 percent of all students are seriously at risk (Frymier and Gansneder, 1989). As it relates to school performance and success, at-risk status is associated with the factors we just mentioned as well as poverty in households, low-income families in which the parents' educational levels and occupational status are also low, single-parent families, and dysfunctional family backgrounds. Exceptional conditions such as intellectual disabilities or physical or learning difficulties that mask students' potential are also closely aligned with at-risk status. A further potent factor that places children at risk for a range of adverse educational outcomes is minority/ethnic group identity with or without limited English proficiency due to residence, immigration, or community norms (Winzer and Mazurek, 1998).

This chapter is concerned with risk factors, the biological or environmental causes of potential disabilities. When children are considered to be high risk or at risk, they are seen to be more prone to developing some form of disabling condition or for adverse effects on school learning and behaviour.

A huge variety of biological factors account for disabling or potentially disabling conditions in children. There are, for example, more than 200 known causes of mental retardation and perhaps nearly 2 000 inborn errors of metabolism (Berlin, 1983); in total, more than 3 500 genetic diseases have been identified. However, the etiology of a particular child's problem all too frequently remains obscure. Despite all that is known, nearly half of all childhood exceptionalities are attributable to unknown causes. Environmental causes that place students at risk are legion, although the most pervasive and important seem to be poverty, dysfunctional families, and cultural and linguistic differences.

We first consider a range of biological risk factors that cause disabilities in children. Etiological considerations relevant to specific disabilities are briefly re-addressed in following chapters. We also discuss emerging causes of disabilities, referred to as the new morbidity. Damage to, or deterioration of, the spinal cord and the brain are the most common causes of physical disabilities in children. Because serious brain insults produce such drastic reductions in children's development and functioning, we include a brief discussion of the human central nervous system.

Today's schools have become intervention sites for numerous learning and social problems affecting students which are growing more profound. Teachers deal with issues that were previously outside the realm of the school and must be knowledgeable about the social lives of students. Hence, we also examine, albeit briefly, some of the many environmental causes that increase the risk of a child developing a problem that affects learning and/or behaviour.

Risk Factors

Risk factors are the wide range of biological and environmental conditions associated with increased probability of cognitive, social, affective, and physical problems. Risk factors may be intrinsic or extrinsic, although to some extent this is an arbitrary distinction as variables under these two classifications often interact. Extrinsic refers to the environment that elevates risk—physical, cultural, and social. Intrinsic refers to aspects of an individual's make-up.

As increasing numbers of children with exceptional conditions move into regular educational milieus, teachers will encounter far more students with such medical problems as epilepsy, visual and auditory impairment, and orthopedic and urologic difficulty. If professionals are to successfully identify, diagnose, prescribe treatment for, teach, remediate, motivate, or generally improve the life of a child with an exceptional condition, they first require an accurate and clear idea of the nature of the disability—its causes, developmental consequences, and prognosis.

Teachers require a basic understanding of **etiology**, the process of finding causes to explain how a particular problem came into existence. Etiological considerations concern *symptoms*, the overt reactions or manifestations of the body to a certain condition and *symptomology*, the study of symptoms and characteristics. Etiology likewise involves *teratology*, generally thought of as the study of the agents involved in major congenital malformations (Kalter and Warkany, 1983). The concept has recently been broadened to include more minor malformations and behavioural difficulties, and now involves the causes of malformations and looking at outcomes of long-term importance in the medical and psychological functioning of a child.

Why is a knowledge of the pathophysiology, symptomology, and treatment of exceptional conditions important for educational professionals? There are many reasons that can be summarized as:

- The causes of disabilities cannot easily be separated from the developmental consequences—the psychological, social, and educational implications—which impact on learning and behaviour.

- Effective treatment requires an appropriate theoretical understanding of a problem and etiological knowledge leads to a better appreciation of a disability. Research attests that teachers and others who hold a clear understanding of exceptional conditions tend to be more tolerant and accepting than those who know little about etiologies and developmental consequences.

- Teachers' knowledge imparts confidence in their ability to program effectively for individual children. One teacher wrote, "The scariest thing about integration is the medical aspect of it. We're looking at giving out medication, injections, changing diapers and always having to be on guard for handicapped children's frailties in case they get a reaction to something or stop breathing for some reason" (Alberta Teachers' Association, 1993, p. 12). Understanding a condition leads to greater confidence in handling the medical aspects.

- Teachers' understanding of medical conditions aids them in becoming sensitized to the social, emotional, and educational problems resulting from a child's disabilities. It enhances an understanding relationship with the child, and creates an atmosphere of acceptance among classmates and others involved with the child. A child with spina bifida, for example, often requires an artificial bladder for urine drainage. The clinical manifestations of the child's urologic difficulties (incontinence) and the need for medical management (the bag worn on the stomach or flank) may create practical and psychological problems for the child. If the teacher is unable to assist and reassure the child, then the child's medical problems may create learning difficulties (Freund, Casey, and Bradley, 1982).

- Medical management for health problems can be a significant part of a child's daily life.

In order to adequately assist children with exceptionalities in the classroom, teachers must also be willing to provide necessary assistance beyond that of an educational nature.

• Some children with disabilities require medication on a regular basis such as anti-convulsants for seizures, muscle relaxants for spasticity, and a variety of medications for respiratory and cardiac problems. In 1986, 31 percent of Canadian children aged 5 to 14 with disabilities were taking medication at least once a week for their condi-tion or health problem (Nessner, 1990). Depending on school board policy, the teacher may be involved in the monitoring of drug dosages.

• Some children with disabilities have difficulty participating in certain physical activi-ties. In 1986, 30 percent of children aged 10 to 14 with disabilities were prevented by their condition or health problems from leisure-time participation in physical activities (Nessner, 1990). The teacher must be aware when certain activities are limited for a child who is exceptional, when to restrict the duration of an activity, and when to rec-ommend an alternative learning experience.

As well as etiological considerations, a general knowledge of the types of treatment that may be given children with disabilities is helpful. In general terms, treatment can be classi-fied into five categories:

1. Treatment that is necessary and lifesaving, such as insulin for diabetes. (See also Chapter 11.)

2. Treatment that is ameliorative and avoids secondary complications, such as surgery for contractures in children with cerebral palsy. (See also Chapter 12.)

3. Treatment that is adaptive and facilitates development, such as total communication for deaf individuals. (See also Chapter 9.)

4. Treatment that is unproven but potentially useful, such as drug therapy. (See also Chapter 8.)

5. Treatment that is controversial, such as special diets in the control of hyperactivity (Kessler, 1977). (See also Chapter 5.)

The New Morbidity

Before the advent of antibiotics in the 1940s, diseases such as whooping cough, measles, smallpox, enteric fever, meningitis, and scarlet fever seriously impaired, even destroyed, the vision and hearing of many children, and left a range of other disabling conditions. Scarlet fever and other such conditions are virtually eliminated, but a new group of disorders related to new etiologies has emerged. These new disorders have been characterized as "the new morbidity," referring to the fact that they result from new etiologies and include disorders such as Attention Deficit Hyperactivity Disorder (ADHD), Traumatic Brain Injury (TBI), Fetal Alcohol Syndrome (FAS), and fragile X syndrome.

Special education may be facing the emergence of what some are now calling a "bio-underclass," due in particular to pediatric AIDS and the use of drugs by pregnant women. AIDS is a "devastating epidemic disorder of extraordinary morbidity and mortality" (Church, Allen, and Stiehen, 1986, p. 423). Some researchers (e.g. Dokecki, Baumeister, and Kupstas, 1989) predict that pediatric AIDS—AIDS contracted by children under thirteen years of age—is destined to become a major cause of developmental and physical disabilities and death among infants and children in North America. In addition to children affected by pediatric AIDS, a frightening proportion of the next generation of school children will have impairments based on the physical and chemical damage done to fetal brains by drug-abusing mothers (Greer, 1990a).

Another group of children included in this category are those whom medical technology helps survive. Even twenty years ago, many of these children would not have lived. Extremely premature babies, rescued by aggressive medical treatments, are at high risk for a number of neurological and physical impairments. In addition, many children with severe and profound disabilities and those with severe chronic illnesses can today expect a normal life span (Batshaw and Perret, 1986). The lowered mortality rate means that more severely impaired children are surviving and attending school (Korabek and Cuvo, 1986).

The Central Nervous System

Structurally, the human nervous system consists of the brain, the spinal cord, and all associated nerves and sense organs. Structures are the fixed anatomical and physiological features of the central nervous system and are similar across the healthy brains of most individuals. How these structures respond to, organize, analyze, and synthesize incoming information varies with individuals and with the task involved. The way information is processed represents the problem-solving strategies of each person (Owens, 1996).

The spinal cord and the brain, the two major components of the central nervous system, are each composed of neurons and glial cells (the latter name is derived from the Greek *glia*, meaning glue). The number of glial cells is probably ten times the number of neurons (Groves and Rebec, 1988). Glial cells serve in a supportive role for the neurons—they transmit food (glucose and amino acids) from the blood supply to the neurons; some probably serve as scaffolding, and others manufacture a substance called myelin. The glial cells develop later than the neurons. They start to form at about thirteen weeks after conception, reach their peak of cell division from eighteen weeks after conception to four months after birth, and cease to form new cells by fifteen to twenty-four months after birth.

Neurons (nerve cells) are the basic units of neurological function; they undoubtedly hold the secrets of how the brain works. Researchers know their role in the transmission of nerve impulses and they know how the neural circuits work, but they are just beginning to unravel their more complex functioning in memory, emotion, and thought. See Figure 3-1 for an illustration of the human brain.

Neurons differ markedly in size and appearance, but they do possess some common characteristics. In common with nearly all cells, neurons have a cell body, a cell membrane, a nucleus, and a cytoplasm. Each neuron consists of three parts—the cell body, a simple long axon that transmits impulses away from the cell body, and several branching dendrites that receive impulses from other cells and transmit them toward the cell body. Neurons do not actually touch each other but are close enough to enable chemical electrical impulses to jump the minuscule space (synapse) between the axon of one neuron and the dendrites of the next. In short, the electrical charge of the neuron is changed by the release of neurotransmitters at its axon, which in turn effects the release of other neurotransmitters at the dendrite end of the second neuron.

Figure 3-1

The human brain

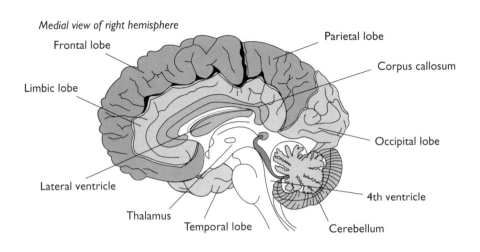

Medial view of right hemisphere

Frontal lobe

Limbic lobe

Lateral ventricle

Thalamus

Temporal lobe

Parietal lobe

Corpus callosum

Occipital lobe

4th ventricle

Cerebellum

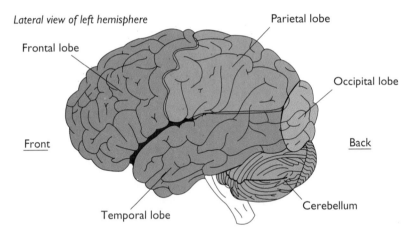

Lateral view of left hemisphere

Frontal lobe

Front

Temporal lobe

Parietal lobe

Occipital lobe

Back

Cerebellum

Half of the genes—50 000—are involved in the central nervous system in some way (Begley, 1996). There are approximately twelve billion neurons in the human nervous system. According to Cowan (1979), during the time the brain is growing *in utero* it must be generating neurons at a rate of more than 250 000 neurons per minute. Once the neurons are generated in germinal sites, they migrate to terminal locations where they are differentiated into appropriate neuron types. They are myelinated, form synapses with other neurons, and undergo some selective attrition (Rose, 1980). Unlike other cells, mature neurons do not reproduce. When they are destroyed, their loss is permanent.

What makes the nervous system work is a process in which the nerve fibres become sheathed with myelin in a process called *myelinization*. The myelin sheaths around individual nerves insulate them from one another and make it easier for messages to pass along the nerve pathways; they help speed up neural transmission and make the brain more efficient.

In one sense, the nervous system is complete at birth. That is, all the structures are present and the number of nerve cells does not increase, although the size of these cells does. At birth the parts of the brain most fully developed are those contained in what is usually called the *midbrain*. The cortex, the sophisticated part of the brain, is present at birth but considerably less developed than it will be later.

The central nervous system of newborn children contains the full complement of neurons, but comparatively few of the axons are covered with myelin. When a baby comes into the world, the brain is a jumble of neurons, all waiting to be woven into the tapestry of the mind (Begley, 1996). New connections continue to be built up by the process of myelinization, which occurs in different parts of the brain at different times and parallels brain development. For example, the part of the brain that controls gross motor skills is myelinated long before the parts that control fine motor skills. Four-year-olds can run, jump, and skip, but they must work endlessly to tie a bow or spread butter with a knife.

The Spinal Cord

The spinal cord is a pencil-thin, segmented collection of neurons that are related to specific parts of the body. Each segment contains both sensory and motor neurons. As damage to a particular portion of the brain will result in disability in the area of the body controlled by that part of the brain, so damage to the sensory cells in the spinal cord results in loss of sensation to the parts of the body affected by those cells.

The Brain

It is something of a paradox that the human brain is so complex that many scientists believe it is beyond its own ability to comprehend. The brain is a densely packed, incredibly complex organ that weighs about 1.4 kilograms and contains billions of neurons.

The cerebrum of the human brain—the grey matter that controls higher level intellectual functioning—is subdivided into two hemispheres. Joining the two cerebral hemispheres is the corpus callosum, a thick, boomerang-shaped band of fibres. The corpus callosum contains approximately 200 million neurons and is the massive midline conduit for processing and relaying information between the two hemispheres (Phillips, 1990).

Each hemisphere is divided into four *lobes—frontal, parietal, occipital,* and *temporal.* The occipital lobe is associated with vision, and the parietal lobe is involved in spatial orientation. The frontal lobe appears to be necessary in anticipatory activity; the temporal lobe has an auditory function. A fifth lobe, which is apparent only in a medial view of the brain, appears to be associated with sexual and emotional functions. The lobes may also perform other functions besides these primary ones. Indeed, researchers are finding that many parts of the brain contribute to functions hitherto associated with only one specific area.

The brain also contains four ventricles. At these sites, cerebrospinal fluid, the fluid that circulates around the brain and the spinal cord, is manufactured.

One of the wonders of human development is the manner in which the human brain, which consists of over 100 billion neurons, can develop so quickly from just a few initial neural cells. Cell differentiation within the brain of the fetus begins during the sixteenth week of gestation. Brain cells begin to multiply most rapidly after the first two months of fetal development, and progressively more slowly after birth. The last three months of fetal life and the first two months after birth are characterized by a spurt in brain growth. By adulthood, the brain is crisscrossed with more than 100 million neurons that, in reaching out to others, create more than 100 trillion connections (Begley, 1996).

Hemispheric Dominance

On casual examination, the two halves of the human brain look like mirror images of each other. However, there are both structural and functional differences. The left half is almost always larger. The right hemisphere contains many long neural fibres that connect widely separated areas of the brain, whereas the left hemisphere contains many shorter fibres that provide rich interconnections within a limited area (Geschwund and Galaburda, 1987).

Hemispheric specialization—cerebral lateralization—is evident from infancy (Kinsbourne and Hiscock, 1978). **Hemisphericity** refers to a person's tendency to rely more on one cerebral hemisphere to process certain types of information. Lateralization of the brain is not unique to humans, although the human brain may be the most asymmetrical. In humans, the right hemisphere is specialized for holistic processing through the simultaneous integration of information. It primarily houses, and is therefore dominant in, areas such as visio-spatial organization, orientation in space, perception, and recognition of faces, pictures, and photographs. The left hemisphere controls verbal function and the linear logical thinking associated with verbalization.

A hemisphere is said to be dominant if one process is primarily housed there. Yet overall, neither hemisphere is dominant over the other since each possesses specialized talents and brings different skills to a given task—neither hemisphere is competent to analyze data and program a response alone. Although they are responsible for specialized separate functions, the two hemispheres of the human brain are complementary and information passes readily between them through the corpus callosum and other subcortical bodies.

Risk Factors and Disability

Risk is basically a statistical concept. Risk status allows specialists to classify children in terms of the type and degree of potential disorders. Researchers who study risk identify the agent or situation, specify the effect, and then estimate the probability that they are associated.

There exist thousands upon thousands of risk factors. These can be slotted into three major categories—established risk, biological risk, and environmental risk (Tjossem, 1976). Much overlap exists between the categories. (See Table 3-1.)

Table 3-1 Sample of disabling conditions and sequelae

Condition	Classification	Timing	Major sequelae
CMV	Infection	Birth	Mental retardation; can be fatal
Cystic fibrosis	Hereditary anomaly	Conception	Involvement of digestive and respiratory systems
Down syndrome	Chromosomal aberration	Dysjunction at conception or soon after	Mental and physical anomalies

continued on next page

Condition	Classification	Timing	Major sequelae
Fetal Alcohol Syndrome	Intoxication	Throughout pregnancy	Mental and physical anomalies
Fragile X syndrome	Chromosomal aberration	Conception	Mental and physical anomalies
Galactosemia	Hereditary anomaly	Conception	Untreated will result in mental retardation
Herpes	Infection	Birth	Mental retardation; often fatal
Muscular dystrophy	X-linked genetic anomaly	Conception	Muscle degeneration
Phenylketonuria (PKU)	Autosomal metabolic disorder	Conception	Untreated will lead to mental retardation
Rh factor	Genetic problem	Conception	Jaundice, mental retardation, deafness
Rubella	Infection	First trimester	Deafness, blindness, mental retardation, multiple handicaps
Spina bifida	Perhaps multifactorial inheritance		Neurological impairments of varying degrees
Syphilis	Infection	Second and third trimester	Physical handicaps, mental retardation, sensory disabilities
Tay-Sachs disease	Autosomal hereditary anomaly	Conception	Fatal
Turner's syndrome	Chromosomal aberration	Conception	Mental and physical differences

Risk connotes a given probability but does not imply certainty, and not all children who fall within these categories of increased vulnerability become disabled. In fact, the majority of children deemed to be within the traditionally accepted categories of biological and environmental risk, such as those who were born prematurely and those who are raised by young unmarried mothers with low incomes, will develop normally (Shonkoff and Meisels, 1990). Nevertheless, when compared to the general population, a greater proportion of children who are exposed to risk factors will develop significant developmental difficulties. Present estimates indicate that between 30 and 70 percent of infants classified at birth as at risk eventually develop problems that require some form of intervention.

Established Risk

The established-risk category refers to medical conditions and anomalies that invariably result in a disability or developmental delay. Established risk is defined as a diagnosed medical disorder with a known etiology that bears "relatively well known" expectancies for developmental outcomes within varying ranges of developmental disabilities (Tjossem, 1976). This means that certain causes are known to relate to certain conditions and that there is a continuum of reproductive casualty; that is, the problems may range from relatively minor through to major difficulties. Established risk is most often related to genetic and chromosomal problems. Established risk includes conditions such as Down syndrome, fragile X syndrome, and infantile autism.

Genetic and Chromosomal Differences

All individuals are born with a unique combination of genes that is theirs alone from the moment of conception. Nothing will ever change. Individuals will die with the same number and set of genes and share these same genes with their offspring. Almost every human cell contains a complete package of hereditary instructions for the characteristics that comprise the individual. These instructions are located in 46 chromosomes, arranged in 23 pairs. Each pair carries one chromosome from each parent.

The first 22 chromosomal pairs are autosomal (identical) and determine the thousands of traits that make up a human being, whether male or female. The twenty-third pair determines the sex of the individual. Each chromosome consists of thousands of genes, and each gene is made up of deoxyribonucleic acid (DNA) which in turn consists of thousands of combinations of four chemical subunits. The order in which these subunits are joined together spells out the gene's message in the genetic code. Whether a particular cell will become facial skin or ankle bone depends on which genes are "switched on"—a process that is still a mystery (Montagu, 1977).

Many human traits such as skin and hair colour, height, and general body build, are controlled by the action of many genes operating together. Such interaction of numerous genes is known as polygenic inheritance. Genes are responsible for more than just physical traits: genetics is involved in intellectual factors, including IQ; specific cognitive abilities; academic achievement; reading disability and mental retardation; personality factors, including extroversion and neuroticism, temperament in childhood, and attitudes and beliefs; and psychopathology, including schizophrenia, affective disorders, delinquent and criminal behaviour, and alcoholism (Plomin, 1989).

About 3 to 5 percent of babies are born with a chromosomal abnormality, a clearly defined genetic disease, or a genetically influenced defect, such as malformation of the spine. Among these children, about 3 percent of newborns have some genetic birth defects and about one newborn in 200 has a chromosomal abnormality (Plomin, DeFries, and McClearn, 1990).

In recent decades, massive research has been undertaken in the field of cytogenetics, the study of the location and organization of genetic material from chromosomes. Research into genetic and chromosomal abnormalities has focused on the location, organization, and regulation of the genetic materials of the chromosomes, and on detecting a marker or unusual DNA sequence that is associated with a disease-causing gene (Nelkin and Tancredi, 1989).

Science tells us that just one misspelling in the DNA code throws off the entire process. But, even though a single gene has a dramatic effect on the development of an individual, it now seems that genetics involves far more complicated mathematics than the simple arithmetic of genetic transfer we associate with Gregor Mendel and his pea plants. Cystic fibrosis, for example, is no longer attributed to the action of one deviant gene; there may be as many as 60 different genetic differences that finally manifest as cystic fibrosis.

Genetic Disorders

As the embryo develops, DNA directs the chemical process within its cells. Scientists and researchers have looked for ways to locate and map defective genes to identify potential disabilities before birth. Much of the chromosomal territory is still unknown, but here and there are little pockets of well-covered ground. More than 800 of the estimated 50 000 to 100 000 individual genes have been mapped, and 200 of the 3 000 disorders known to be caused by a single gene have been diagnosed (Menolascino and Stark, 1988). The X chromosome is the most explored, with about 115, or 10 percent, of its genes now mapped.

One tiny flaw in the genetic structure can have tragic results. A change in DNA may repair itself or lead to spontaneous abortion (miscarriage). The flaw may also create abnormalities present at birth, called congenital abnormalities or hereditary anomalies. Because hereditary anomalies are in the genes, they may be passed on to subsequent generations, the rate depending on the type of inheritance. With dominant inheritance, a child usually has a parent with the same disorder. Dominant conditions tend to show marked variability, with different individuals having different degrees of symptoms, from none to severe.

The March of Dimes Birth Defects Foundation (1987) has catalogued about 2 000 confirmed or suspected dominant genetic disorders that can result in mental retardation and other disabilities. These include achondroplasia, a form of dwarfism; Huntington's disease, a progressive nervous system degeneration; and polydactyly, extra fingers or toes.

There are about 1 000 confirmed or suspected recessive disorders, which include cystic fibrosis, galactosemia, and Tay–Sachs disease. With recessive inheritance, the child must inherit a gene from both parents. Under simple Mendelian inheritance, each child runs a four-to-one risk of manifesting the disorder.

Some disorders are linked to the genes on the twenty-third pair of chromosomes. In X-linked inheritance, the sons have a fifty–fifty chance of inheriting the condition though the mother. Of the more than 250 types of X-linked inheritance disorders identified, colour blindness, hemophilia, and muscular dystrophy are probably the best known.

Multifactorial inheritance results from the interaction of many genes with other genes and/or environmental factors. Patterns of transmission are poorly defined; some conditions thought to be multifactorial are spina bifida, clubfoot, and cleft lip or palate.

In some cases, various types of transmission can account for a condition. For example, retinitis pigmentosa is a condition that affects the retina, the film-like layer in the back of the eye, and causes progressive visual loss. Retinitis pigmentosa is an inherited disease, transmitted through generations by a gene which may be recessive, dominant, or sex-linked. An estimated one person in eighty carries the gene for recessive retinitis pigmentosa. At present, however, it is rarely possible to detect the carriers ("Children should see ...," 1980).

Rh (Rhesus) Factor

A potential cause of childhood handicapping conditions is mother–child blood incompatibility called Rh factor. While the problem of Rh is rare among many groups—in Eastern Asia and the Pacific, for example—the factor for Rh is missing in about 15 percent of Caucasian and 5 percent of Black women in North America.

Since about 1968, when researchers discovered that administration of Rho-gam to Rhesus-negative women after a birth, miscarriage, or abortion would prevent Rhesus incompatibility in subsequent offspring, affected babies have been on the decline. Commonly associated sequelae include jaundice, retardation, and deafness.

Inborn Errors of Metabolism

While metabolic problems due to hereditary defects account for only a small percentage of disabilities, the study of these disorders has provided valuable knowledge for the prevention and treatment of disabilities due to other organic causes.

Most inborn errors of metabolism are the result of the action of a single pair of genes. Many result in missing or defective enzymes, which are the proteins that help the body convert one substance into another as, for example, in the transformation of nutrients to chemicals usable by the cells. The absence of, or defect in, one of the enzymes means that the normal chemistry of the cell is altered by the inability to provide or dispose of a critical chemical or protein, leading to unusual levels of particular chemicals in the body. Many of these conditions, such as phenylketonuria (PKU) and diabetes, can be treated or controlled; others, such as Tay–Sachs disease—a fatal deterioration of brain function—are untreatable.

Tay–Sachs disease is named after its discovers, Warren Tay, an English physician, and Bernard Sachs, an American physician who identified the condition in 1877. Tay–Sachs results from an enzyme deficiency caused by a single autosomal recessive gene. Infants appear normal at birth, but the nervous system is gradually destroyed because of the missing enzyme, hexosamidose A. The lack of this enzyme allows various fatty substances to build up in the body cells, including those of the brain. The excessive glycolipid in the cells of the nervous system causes the cells to swell, rupture, and finally die.

As the nerve cells die, the child becomes retarded, loses motor ability, and becomes deaf and blind. Effects of the condition can be seen at three to six months after birth. Death is inevitable, usually between four and six years of age.

About one in thirty Jews carries the defective gene. Tay–Sachs is also found in non-Jewish persons, but is a hundred times less frequent. The parents, who are heterozygous carriers, each have only about half of the regular amount of the enzyme, but this is sufficient for normal development.

Phenylketonuria (PKU), a relatively rare genetically transmitted metabolic disorder, was discovered in 1934 by a physician and biochemist, Dr. Ashborn Folling of Norway (Henderson, 1989). PKU is carried on a double recessive gene by about one in every 600 people, so the chance of two carriers marrying is statistically one in every 3 600. The condition affects about one child in every 14 000 and accounts for approximately one percent of all institutionalized mentally retarded individuals.

Phenylketonuria is primarily a condition that affects whites, with the highest incidence in the United States and Europe. It is rare in African, Jewish, or Japanese populations.

Some genes act on other genes. These modifier genes then determine how the other genes express themselves. This happens in PKU. The condition is marked by an inability to oxidize normally the amino acid phenylalanine, which is found in fish, dairy products, and most protein sources. Sustained hyperphenylalanin anemia in the early years is neurotoxic and almost invariably results in severe intellectual impairment (see Griffiths, Smith, and Harvie, 1997). The effects are irreversible.

The effects of PKU are eliminated or diminished by early screening and a special diet. The screening procedure includes urinalysis and blood tests shortly after birth. The most reliable test is the Guthrie blood test, developed by Dr. Robert Guthrie in 1961. It is performed between the third and sixth day after birth, with retesting after two weeks. Early detection of PKU is vital, because the infant must immediately be restricted to a diet low in phenylalanine. Although phenylalanine cannot be completely eliminated from the child's diet, it can be severely restricted with a phenylalanine-deficient formula, Lofenalac, a prepared milk substitute. Low phenylalanine foods include vegetables, fruits, juices, some cereals, breads, and starches. Milk and dairy foods are restricted and meat is eliminated from the child's daily intake.

Although the effects of phenylketonuria can be almost eliminated, some recent research has demonstrated mild problems even in children on strict diets. One group of researchers, for example, found that some treated children showed neurophysiological dysfunctions that interfered with academic functioning. Others discovered that in treated PKU children, the IQs are within normal limits but they tend to be lower than those of parents, siblings, and non-sibling control subjects (see Ozanne, Kaimmer, and Murdoch, 1990). Many females fail to maintain the diet; when they bear children, the elevated levels of PKU increase the probability of having an impaired infant (Henderson, 1989).

Another metabolic disorder that can result in mental retardation is *galactosemia*. In this case, the child lacks the ability to metabolize galactose. As with PKU, successful treatment depends upon early detection and a special diet.

Tuberous sclerosis is a complex disorder in which benign tumours grow in the brain, kidneys, eyes, and other organs causing seizures, mental retardation, and autism in about half of the affected group. The condition affects about one in every 6 000 people, usually starting in childhood. Researchers believe that a third of the cases are passed from parents to their children; in the other two thirds, a gene mutation arises spontaneously in a child with no affected parent (Painter, 1997).

Chromosomal Factors

Chromosomal problems result from chromosomal dysjunction, a malfunction in cell division. Problems occur when there is an extra chromosome, or when pieces or parts of chromosomes attach themselves to other chromosomes.

There are many different chromosomal disorders that affect children. Some reveal themselves in newborns through intra-uterine growth retardation, anomalies of the face and hands, or hypotonia, which is present at birth even when normal tone or spasticity develops later (Fenichel, 1980). The effects of the damage vary greatly. Wide variations occur in the onset of symptoms, the parts of the body involved, the nature of the symptoms, the degree of severity, and the possible multiplicity of impairments.

Down Syndrome

The most common chromosomal aberration is Down syndrome, which occurs in approximately one in every 1 000 live births (Plomin, De Fries, and McClearn, 1990). Down syndrome is an equal opportunity disability: it can occur in any family, regardless of race, socio-economic class, or the education of the parents. It usually happens only once in a family, and strikes most often when the mother is approaching the end of her child-bearing days.

The condition was first identified in 1866 by John Langton Down, a physician at the Earlswood Asylum in Surrey, England. The facial features of children with the condition prompted Down to refer to it as "Mongolian idiocy." He assumed that the condition represented a re-emergence of a more primitive evolutionary status, which he erroneously believed to also be that of the Mongolian race. The Mongolian resemblance, however, is due simply to the development of a fold in the upper eyelid, which is caused not by inheritance but by the failure of the root of the nose to develop normally (Montagu, 1977). Today we have discarded the term "mongoloid" as demeaning and developmentally inappropriate.

Down syndrome was one of the first conditions to be linked to a genetic abnormality. The major breakthrough came in 1959 when Swedish geneticists determined that the correct number of chromosomes in humans was 46. When they discovered the extra chromosome in Down, the link between Down syndrome and dysjunction was confirmed.

There are three major types of Down syndrome—Trisomy 21, translocation, and mosaicism. In each type, the mental and physical problems of the child are caused by extra chromosomal material which somehow disturbs the orderly development of both body and brain.

Chromosome 21 is the smallest human chromosome; it contains only about 1.5 percent of the total genetic material (Patterson, 1987). Yet cases of Down syndrome are somehow linked to this tiny chromosome. There are no individuals with the clinical symptoms of Down syndrome who do not have at least partial Trisomy 21.

Trisomy 21 accounts for the great majority of children afflicted with Down syndrome (about 93 percent). There are actually fourteen different types of Trisomy 21, but all are basically problems of dysjunction. In each case, the twenty-first pair of chromosomes contains three chromosomes instead of two. This may result from a mistake in chromosomal distribution in the egg or sperm, or because the chromosomes were distributed unequally when the fertilized egg began to divide.

Of the rest of the population with Down syndrome, 5 percent have *translocation*, in which only part of chromosome 21 is present in triplicate. In this condition, the extra chromosomal material most often attaches to chromosome 14, 15, 21, or 22 (Patterson, 1987). Although the actual chromosome count is 46, the affected child suffers from the same overdose of chromosome 21 as the child with standard trisomy. There may be hereditary components in translocation.

Mosaicism accounts for about 2 percent of Down syndrome cases. This condition results when there is a faulty distribution of chromosomes in later cell divisions. The child possesses some normal cells and some with a trisomy condition. Any resulting physical and mental anomalies depend on the number of affected cells.

More than 50 physical signs are listed as characteristic of Down syndrome. Some are apparent at birth, some appear much later, and some disappear with age. The number of physical features that a child displays bears no relationship to the degree of retardation. Few children have all the characteristics typical of the syndrome. Table 3-2 outlines the most common.

Table 3-2 Some observable physical characteristics associated with Down syndrome

Head	Hair	Face
distinctive shape; skull rounded and small	sparse, fine, and soft	flat profile
Nose	**Eyes**	**Ears**
small and "pug"; flat bridge; undeveloped or absent nasal cartilage; mucous discharge common	epicanthic fold; speckling of iris (Brushfield's spots); strabismus or nystagmus common	small and low-set; overlapping upper letices
Mouth	**Teeth**	**Tongue**
high arched; thick, fissured lips; narrow palate	small, irregularly aligned; late erupting	coarse, protruding
Hands	**Muscles**	**Feet**
broad, stumpy, with short fingers; palmar crease (simian line) on one or both hands; incurved little finger (clindactly)	general hypotonia; flexible joints	broad and short; excessive space between first and second toes
Skin	**Abdomen**	**Stature**
thick, dry, rough; mottled or flushed	prominent umbilical hernia common	short; average height: male – 152.4 cm female – 139.7 cm

The chances of having a child with Down syndrome increase dramatically with the age of the parents, particularly the mother. (Very young mothers are an exception to this rule: they are more likely to have a Down syndrome baby than women in their twenties or thirties.) For the woman over 40, the chances of bearing a Down infant are approximately one in 80. For women over 45, the chances increase to one in 60 (Hansen, 1978).

Many authorities believe that Down syndrome may result from a combination of two factors—chemical changes in the egg cells due to the mother's aging ovaries, and a reduction in the secretion of various hormones in older women (Montagu, 1977). The mother's age may not be the only factor, however. Researchers are discovering possible links between Down syndrome and the amount of the mother's exposure to radiation and certain viruses. They are also exploring the role of the aging father, who contributes the extra chromosome in 20 to 25 percent of the cases (Abroms and Bennett, 1983). For men aged 41 and up, there is an increased risk of fathering children with Trisomy 21, regardless of the age of the mother.

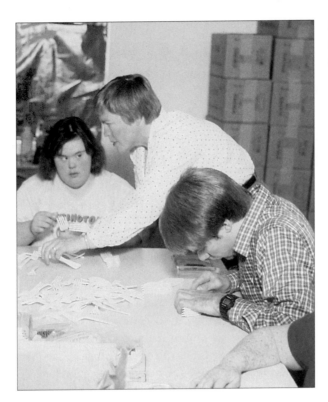

Down syndrome is the most common chromosomal aberration.

Fragile X Syndrome

Fragile X syndrome is a relatively recent addition to the catalogue of causes of retardation. The fragile X chromosome was first reported in 1969, but the syndrome was not consistently diagnosed until the 1980s (Hagerman, 1988). Identification uses a karyotype with a special culture medium low in folic acid.

Today fragile X syndrome is second only to Down syndrome among cytogenetic abnormalities associated with mental retardation (Simen and Rogers, 1989). The prevalence of individuals affected by the fragile X syndrome is approximately one in 1 000. The incidence among live male births is about one in 1 350; among female births, about one in 2 033 (Webb, Bundey, Thake, and Todd, 1986). The prevalence of carriers is higher. Reports of the prevalence of fragile X syndrome (those affected and carriers) in the general population ranges from 1.9 to 5.9 percent (Blomquist, Gustavson, Holmgren, Nordenson, and Paslsson-Strade, 1983; Jacobs, Mayer, and Abruzzo, 1986).

Fragile X is a marker on the X-chromosome at position 927. The syndrome is caused by an abnormal gene or genes at the lower end of the long arm of the X-chromosome (see Figure 3-2). The defective gene creates too long a stretch of DNA, which disrupts the structure of the X-chromosome and creates a fragile area. The chromosome is brittle in places and may even be separated into two or more pieces. Chromosomal analysis will demonstrate a fragile site (a narrowing of the chromosome in this region) in some cells of all affected males and in most females who are carriers.

The genetics involved in fragile X seem to be unlike those of most typical X-linked recessive conditions. Santos (1992) notes that fragile X runs through a family tree in a multi-step process, resulting two or three generations later in full activation of the mutation. During this

Figure 3-2
Diagram of fragile X

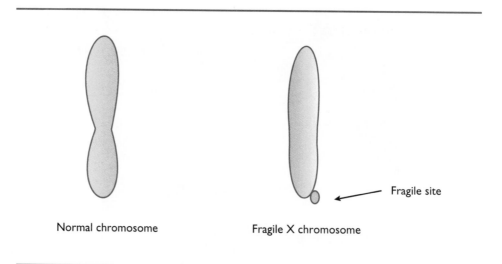

Normal chromosome   Fragile X chromosome

Fragile site

time many people can be affected to various degrees (physically, cognitively, and behaviourally) before a complete diagnosis is made. If this current theory proves true, says Santos, then physicians will have an increased ability to diagnose fragile X and this may have a significant impact on prevalence estimates. The number of people affected, either mildly or more severely, may be higher than originally thought (Santos, 1992).

Clinicians familiar with fragile X syndrome utilize physical findings to aid in diagnosis of affected males (see Table 3-3). Fragile X patients undergo changes in appearance from childhood through the adult years. During the growth period in males, testicular volume increases, the face grows in an elongated pattern, the forehead becomes more prominent, and the ears enlarge. The adult male patient typically has a long face, large ears, a prominent forehead, midface hypoplasia, and a prominent jaw. The most common feature seen in the postpubescent male is macro-orchidism (large testicles). However, among prepubertal males macro-orchidism is only reported in approximately 50 percent of the population (Simen and Rogers, 1989).

Some of the physical features typical of fragile X males can also be seen in female carriers, such as mildly prominent ears, a long face, and hyperextensible finger joints. Female carriers who are affected cognitively are more likely to show these physical features (Hagerman, 1988). Among fragile X positive females, however, facial features are exceedingly variable and do not serve as an aid in diagnosis.

Turner's Syndrome

Turner's syndrome (TUS) is a condition affecting offspring in one of approximately 2 000 live female births. Diagnosis is made by karyotype. Women with TUS either lack an X chromosome or have a structural abnormality in one of the X chromosomes.

The syndrome is characterized by short stature, growth failure, or gonadal dysgenesis (unformed reproductive systems) that inhibits spontaneous pubertal onset and fertility. Some women with TUS have abnormal appearances and/or medical problems such as problems of the aorta, hypertension, and renal abnormalities. Individuals with TUS also have a

Table 3-3 Features of fragile X syndrome

Physical	Non-physical
large head size	developmental delay
large flat ears	mental retardation
long narrow face	learning disabilities
prominent forehead	hyperactivity
broad nose	short attention span
high palate	autistic behaviours
large testicles	fearfulness, shyness
large hands; non-tapering fingers	rapid, repetitive speech
mitral valve prolapse (heart murmur)	talkativeness
increased birth-weight	difficulty adjusting to change
repeated ear infections	

characteristic pattern of cognitive abilities consisting of normal verbal IQ and relatively lower performance IQ due to difficulty with space forms and number concepts (Downey, Elkin, Ehrhardt, Meyer-Bahlberg, Bell, and Morishima, 1991).

Biological Risk

Biological risk relates to infants and toddlers with a history of prenatal, perinatal, neonatal, or early developmental events resulting in biological insults to the developing nervous system. Documented biological risk includes children whose pediatric history or current circumstances reveal significant biological conditions that do not lead inevitably to developmental delay or disorder but carry a greater probability of delay or disability than that found in the general population (Shonkoff and Meisels, 1990).

For purposes of discussion, it is useful to group biological causes of exceptionality into some major categories and then discuss them in specific developmental periods: the prenatal or gestation period; the perinatal, which extends from the seventh month of pregnancy and includes the delivery and birth period as well as the neonatal period, or first two weeks after birth; and the postnatal period.

Prenatal Period

Life begins not at birth, but at conception. At the beginning of life, a human being is smaller than the period at the end of this sentence. The individual is a single cell, barely visible to the naked eye, a tiny drop of fluid made up mainly of non-living material surrounding a miniscule nucleus of living matter. By the time of birth, some 38 weeks later, the individual weights about 3.5 kilograms and contains 200 billion specialized cells (Montagu, 1977).

The prenatal period encompasses three stages. The first two weeks are known as the period of the ovum, or zygote. Next, the period of the embryo lasts until the beginning of the third month. The remaining gestation time is known as the period of the fetus. The change of labels charts the organism's growth from a simple cell to a recognizable human creature. Specific changes occur to the developing human at specific times. Every cell, every tissue, and every organ has its own timetable for coming into existence, for developing, and for beginning to carry out its functions. So consistent are these functions that embryologists can determine them with great accuracy.

From the moment of conception until delivery nine months later, the human being is more susceptible to environment than at any other time. The opening third of pregnancy, the first trimester, is the most important to development. Here the die is cast, so to speak, in that the organism is immutably affected. During this time, major organs and basic tissues take shape and develop into their finished forms; after this stage, it is difficult to affect their growth in any fundamental way (Montagu, 1977).

Infections and Intoxicants

During pregnancy, the mother's health and adequate nutrition are vital to the development of the fetus. Any maternal condition that impairs the transport of oxygen and nutrients to the fetus or the exchange of metabolic waste products has the potential to act deleteriously on fetal development.

Etiologically, environmental agents that may harm the developing infant are known as *teratogens*, from the Greek *teros*, meaning monster. Teratogens that can cause damage include prescription drugs, hard drugs, nicotine, and alcohol.

Throughout the discussion, it should be kept in mind that a number of problems can occur at any time during the cycle. Moreover, a given teratological agent may have different effects depending on timing, severity, genotype, and unknown factors, while similar problems can be the result of various causes. Deafness, for example, can have pre-, peri-, or postnatal time of onset, and can be caused by agents such as rubella, syphilis, meningitis or, in the past, drugs such as streptomycin.

Rubella

Rubella (German measles) is a major cause of disabilities in children. The potential damage caused by rubella was first identified in 1941 by Australian physician McAllister Gregg.

Rubella provides an example of a critical period when exposure to a certain teratogen is most harmful to the fetus. A *critical period* is a part of the life cycle during which the developing organism is particularly sensitive or responsive to specific environmental forces. Outside this period, the same event or influences are thought to have little if any lasting effects.

The rubella virus crosses the placenta and affects the developing fetus. The fetal organs likely to be affected by rubella are those whose development is underway when the mother contracts the virus. The eye, ear, nervous system, and heart are especially vulnerable at early periods of fetal development. In cases where the mother contracts rubella during the first trimester of pregnancy, it is estimated that 50 percent of fetuses are damaged if the disease is contracted in the first month, while 20 percent of embryos affected in the second month are born with defects (Rosenblith and Sims-Knight, 1985). Severe sensorineural hearing loss is the major effect of maternal rubella (Hardy and Bordley, 1973); other major permanent features include cataracts, glaucoma, mental retardation, congenital heart disease, and cerebral palsy. As well, a number of reports (e.g., Menser, Forrest, and Bransky, 1978; Preece, Kearney, and Marshall, 1977) have documented a significant occurrence of late onset defects of rubella (conditions that are not apparent at birth but occur later), including vascular disease, growth hormone deficiency, thyroid dysfunction, and diabetes mellitus.

Rubella is often seen in epidemics that are estimated to occur in 25-year cycles. In 1964, the last major rubella epidemic created a phenomenal spike in the charts measuring the numbers of special children who were left deaf and blind or with other multiple disabilities as a result of the disease. Vaccines developed in 1969 make a rubella baby rare today, however.

Syphilis

Syphilis, one of the venereal diseases, is produced by the bacterium *Treponema pallidum* (also called *Spirocheta pallida*). It does not affect the developing organs as does rubella but produces destructive lesions (abnormal changes in structure) in already developed organs.

While rubella is most critical during the first trimester of pregnancy, syphilis affects the fetus after the sixteenth or eighteenth week of gestation. If the disease is controlled by penicillin before that time, only about two percent of fetuses will contract it. After the fifth month, uncontrolled syphilis will affect about 40 percent of fetuses. Twenty-five percent of affected babies die before birth; 33 percent of those who survive die in early childhood.

Infants who survive may exhibit many disabilities, including mental retardation, blindness, and deafness. Other affected infants show liver problems, peritonitis, central nervous system disorders, and pegged teeth (Montagu, 1977; Rosenblith and Sims-Knight, 1985).

Drugs

When we talk about drugs, we are referring to a wide assortment of potentially harmful agents that range from hard drugs such as heroin, through prescription and over-the-counter drugs, to drugs widely used in Canadian society—nicotine and alcohol. The problem is significant, and it is growing. Some studies report that as many as 15 percent of pregnant women admit to using illegal drugs or alcohol; experts fear that the real rate may be double that (Greer, 1990a). Because cocaine, for example, is illegal, only selected samples of children have been tested. The numbers of affected children could therefore be far higher than current estimates.

Chemicals can cause a wide range of congenital abnormalities, said to account for about 10 percent of birth defects (Schwartz and Yaffe, 1980). Dr. Harold Nickens of the American Society of Addiction Medicine has observed that the growing number of infants born to addicted mothers may require the medical community "to define an entirely new, organic brain syndrome" (Greer, 1990a). These children suffer from what Nickens calls "a well of yet to be determined birth defects" (Greer, 1990a). Experts anticipate that these children will form part of what has been characterized as a "bio-underclass" and will be prominent among the next generation of special education students. Many of the problems will arise because they are likely to experience the same dysphoria and thought and mood disorders as a recovering addict, which is essentially what the child is (Greer, 1990a).

Keep in mind throughout this discussion on drug use and abuse that it is extremely difficult to attribute specific characteristics to certain drugs, since abuse of multiple drugs is common. Mothers who are multi-drug users (cocaine plus other drugs) have children with the most adverse outcomes (Van Dyke and Fox, 1990). Infants of multi-drug users fare worse than infants exposed to single drugs in regard to birth-weight, gestational age, withdrawal responses, and length of hospital stay (Kaye, Elkind, Goldberg, and Tytum, 1989). In addition, prenatal exposure is often compounded by the presence of social factors such as poverty, neglect, or drug use by others in the home.

Prescription Drugs   Prescription drugs have been shown to have an adverse effect on fetal development. Research has linked some antibiotic, anticonvulsant, and anticancer medications to fetal malformations (Batshaw and Perret, 1986). There is also evidence that pain-relieving drugs administered during labour and delivery can result in behavioural differences in infants (Rosenblith and Sims-Knight, 1985).

Cocaine   The 1980s saw an increase in the use of cocaine for all socio-economic classes, races, ages, and sexes. Cocaine now surpasses heroin as America's leading street drug (Tarr and Macklin, 1987). In the United States, the president's National Drug Cohort Strategy Report estimated that 100 000 babies are born to cocaine-using women each year (Kusserow, 1990). With the increased use of cocaine, there is growing concern about the long-term effects of this drug on the fetus and the neonate (Van Dyke and Fox, 1990). However, researchers point out that "there is no typical profile of children prenatally exposed to drugs, though there seems to be a developmental continuum of vulnerabilities that persist into the preschool years" (Cole, Jones, and Sadofsky, 1990, p. 1).

Some neurochemical studies on cocaine *in utero* suggest that if it is present during gestation, it may affect developing fetal neuromotor systems, which could have a significant impact on the developing nervous system (Van Dyke and Fox, 1990). In the fetus, cocaine affects the vascular system causing the blood vessels to constrict in a state known as vasoconstriction (Chasnoff, 1987). This in turn puts increasing pressure on the heart and the blood vessels, increases blood pressure, and restricts the flow of oxygen (Schneider and Chasnoff, 1987). Babies are therefore more prone to intercranial hemorrhages.

Cocaine use during the last trimester may cause fetal hyperactivity, increased fetal blood pressure, or premature placental detachment from the uterus, which endangers both mother and child. Other research (Bingol, Schuster, Fuchs, and Iosub, 1987) has concluded that cocaine use in humans significantly reduces the weight of the fetus, increases the stillbirth rate related to *abruptio placentae*, and is associated with a higher malformation rate. Infants are likely to die before birth, to be born prematurely, and to be abnormally small for their ages (Brody, 1988; Rest, 1990).

Case histories of congenital abnormalities among cocaine-exposed children show missing fingers and forearm bones, cardiac anomalies, and microcephaly (Hoyme, Jones, Dixon, Jewett, Hanson, Robinson, Masall, and Allanson, 1990). Newborns may be born with deformed heads, lungs, digestive systems, or limbs. Researchers also describe children experiencing convulsions and stoppage of breathing (Chasnoff, Burns, Burns, and Schnoll, 1988; Chasnoff, Chisum, and Kaplan, 1988). Other reports of afflicted infants point to poor baby state, which includes tremours, chronic irritability, and poor visual orientation. Later, in learning situations, these children demonstrate poor abstract reasoning and memory, poor judgment, inability to concentrate, inability to deal with stress, frequent tantrums, a wide variety of behaviour disorders, and violent acting out.

In the late 1980s, crack, a relatively pure and inexpensive form of cocaine, emerged on the drug scene. As with cocaine, there is no single profile of an infant born to a crack-using mother. Some appear healthy; some are adversely affected.

Some crack-using mothers are giving birth to addicted babies who are having strokes and seizures, who are born with small heads, missing bowels, and malformed genitals. Crack babies are irritable, tremulous, and difficult to soothe for at least three months. They have a significantly higher rate of Sudden Infant Death Syndrome (SIDS) than babies who are not prenatally exposed. Many suffer neurological damage from prenatal drug exposure (Rest, 1990).

Too often, the infant's environment simply compounds the problems. Children born exposed to crack leave the hospital and enter homes often headed by poor, drug-addicted young mothers who are not able to cope with the demands of their own care, let alone the needs of a high-strung, difficult to soothe, unhealthy infant (Paciorek and Munro, 1995).

Heroin   Heroin passes the placenta so that infants of addicted women are born addicted. Withdrawal symptoms can prove fatal to the tiny infant. Survivors suffer a number of difficulties, but it is not known whether these extend beyond infancy. Methadone, the substitute that is used to withdraw heroin addicts, may cause even more physiological damage to the fetus. Children are small and subject to high mortality (Finnegan, Reeser, and Connaughton, 1977). They suffer more seizures and central nervous system damage, and seem to have altered breathing responses that persist 20 to 40 days after methadone is no longer detected in their systems (Rosenblith and Sims-Knight, 1985).

Fetal Alcohol Syndrome

Together with nicotine, alcohol is the drug most likely to be used and abused by Canadians. Alcohol in moderate amounts used to be thought safe during pregnancy. We now realize that even small amounts can damage the developing fetus. Alcohol ingestion by pregnant women has been found to be the culprit in a number of abnormalities in children.

A small proportion of children of drinking mothers are born with a **syndrome**—a constellation of findings similar from patient to patient—known as Fetal Alcohol Syndrome (FAS), first reported in France in the late 1960s and then described in 1973 by Kenneth Jones and his colleagues. FAS exists on a continuum ranging from the full-blown syndrome to minor developmental defects. Children may have the full-blown syndrome or Fetal Alcohol Effect (FAE). General estimates of the incidence of full-blown FAS are one to two per 1 000 live births. Children who exhibit only FAE effects are thought to number three to five per 1 000 (Sandor, 1981).

In children affected by FAS, mental retardation is a major characteristic and considered to be the second major cause of mental retardation (Williams, Howard, and McLaughlin, 1994). As the condition varies in intensity, there are also differences in outward expression and in the degree of mental retardation involved. Full-blown FAS affects the whole body system, causing malformations and anomalies in the nervous system, the musculoskeletal structure, and the internal organs, especially the heart and urinogenital tracts. Examples of anomalies are shown in Table 3-4. Other problems that may be associated with alcohol consumption on the part of the pregnant woman include spontaneous abortions and miscarriages. Children show a high rate of epilepsy, which may persist through the early school years (Williams, Howard, and McLaughlin, 1994).

Physical and mental anomalies occur because alcohol hinders fetal growth and produces

Table 3-4 Specific sequelae associated with FAS

Neurological	Craniofacial
mental retardation	low-set ears
microcephalus	short low-bridged nose
seizures	epicanthic folds
tremors	short lower jaw
irritability	long upper lip
poor fine co-ordination	droopy eyelids
hyperactivity	high-arched palate

Skeletal	Other
clubfoot	cardiac defects
spinal fusion	kidney defects
growth deficiency	genital problems
abnormal palmar creases	poor weight gain

small babies with small brains. Damage to the fetus is caused when the ethanol in the alcohol takes fluid from the developing brain, causing the death of brain cells. Children with FAS may have specific physical stigmata, such as small eyes, a flat bridge of the nose, retarded growth, and a small head circumference, known as *microcephaly*. The more physical disabilities that are evident, the more severe the retardation is likely to be (Montagu, 1977).

In the third trimester of pregnancy, the unborn child is gaining most of its eventual birth weight and the brain cells are rapidly multiplying and increasing in size. Some evidence indicates that the toxic effects of alcohol inhibit the development of major tissues, which may explain the presence of delays in growth and such conditions as congenital cardiac and kidney defects (McLeod, 1981). Iber (1980) postulated that craniofacial abnormalities occur because particular parts of the face are dependent upon a brain of normal size to fill out the face. The critical period for the development of the facial features associated with FAS seems to be the third or fourth week of prenatal development, when the head is starting to take shape.

Much is still unknown about FAS; the connection between alcohol consumption and reproductive risk is not clear. The medical profession has not yet determined a safe level of alcohol for the pregnant woman, and the influence of moderate drinking is unknown. Certainly, infants of mothers who drink heavily are at greater risk, but even in moderate drinkers there is evidence that the amount of alcohol consumed is related to infant's arousal levels and central nervous system functioning (Streissguth, Barr, and Martin, 1983).

It has been suggested that heavy drinking implies an intake of ninety millilitres of alcohol a day during pregnancy (Landesman-Dwyer, Martin, Smith and Streissguth, 1980). One study found that two ounces of alcohol in the first trimester (one six-pack of beer) led to 12 percent of the sample having infants with malformations, similar to children of chronic alcoholics ("Crisis…," [1986]). However, given the metabolic variations between individuals, there is no correlation between the quantity and frequency of the ingestion of alcohol and the number of defects in a child.

Maternal Smoking

When the mother smokes a cigarette, the fetus smokes it too. After the first few puffs its heart begins to beat faster, it feels a drop in oxygen (*hypoxia*), and an increase in carbon dioxide. It stops moving and increases its fetal breathing to try to make up for the hypoxia. All these responses have a severe enough cumulative effect in heavy smokers to contribute to spontaneous abortions, bleeding during pregnancy, premature rupture of the amniotic sac, fetal deaths, and deaths of newborns (Salkind, 1990). Smokers are twice as likely as nonsmokers to have low- birth-weight babies. The infants of smokers weigh an average of 200 grams less than infants of nonsmokers (Vorhees and Mollnow, 1987). Infants are shorter, have smaller head, chest, arm and thigh circumference, and have lower neurological scores than do infants of non-smokers (Metcoff, Cristiloe, Crosby, Sandstread, and Milne, 1989).

Coffee has also been implicated. One large-scale study (Linn, Schoenbaum, Manson, Rosner, Stubblefield, and Ryan, 1982) that analyzed the medical records of 12 205 women who gave birth over a three-year period found that birth problems were more common among heavy coffee drinkers (three or more cups a day). Problems, however, could not be attributed to coffee alone since it was often accompanied by cigarette smoking.

Maternal Nutrition

A mother's diet and nutrition play a significant role in the growth and development of her fetus. The importance of nutrition is suggested by the relationship between the mother's diet, the newborn's weight, and the child's eventual learning ability (see Salt, Galler, and Ramsey, 1988).

The period of intra-uterine development and the first 18 months after birth are crucial to the physiological development of every organ system. This is especially true for the brain. Inadequate prenatal nutrition can affect the relationship between the body's biochemistry and the functioning of the brain. Severe malnutrition can stunt brain growth and produce a significant lowering of intellectual ability. Nutrition in the mother seems to be particularly important in the third trimester, when the fetus should be making rapid gains in weight.

Postnatal nutrition, especially during the first six months of an infant's life, is also a critical factor in brain development. Various important neural structures and interconnections between the brain cells develop during this period. In the postnatal period, research indicates that severe chronic deprivation of either general nutrition or certain special diet substances can cause behavioural disorders as well as physical disorders and mental retardation (Lahey and Ciminero, 1980). When prenatal and postnatal malnutrition both exist, problems are likely to be much more severe.

Maternal nutritional deficiency covers a wide range of problems and developmental consequences. In general, malnourished women are much more likely to produce low-birth-weight babies although it may be that low birth-weight *per se* is not so much a problem as that maternal malnutrition increases the fetus's vulnerability to other risk factors. Severe malnutrition increases the risk of congenital defects, prolonged labour, stillbirth, and infant mortality during the first year. *Toxemia*, which refers to several common disorders of pregnancy, may well be related to maternal nutrition (Montagu, 1977).

Toxemias appear in the first trimester of pregnancy and are characterized by edema (water retention), hypertension, and protein in the urine. Toxemias are not passed on to the child but alter the intra-uterine environment in which the child is developing. Severe cases lead to extreme blood pressure and convulsions, known as *eclampsia*. Toxemias may impair normal fetal growth, and the drugs used to treat them may also harm the fetus (Berlin, 1983).

Unknown Prenatal Influence

There are a number of conditions present at or before birth for which there is no known cause. One such condition is *microcephaly*, a rare phenomenon in which brain development is impaired by an abnormally small cranium. Another is macrocephaly, which refers to an enlargement of the head, most frequently caused by hydrocephalus, a build-up of cerebrospinal fluid in the brain. Retardation may follow, but its severity can be reduced or eliminated by early diagnosis and treatment. To treat hydrocephalus, a shunt is surgically implanted to drain excess fluid away from the brain and into a vein behind the ear or in the neck. (See also Chapter 12.)

Prader-Willi was reported in 1956 by Prader, Labhart, and Willi in Switzerland. It is associated with obesity, small stature, oligophrenia (less than normal mental development) and small hands and feet. It affects one in every 10 000 to 25 000 children. There are more boys than girls affected. The etiology is unknown (Otto and Barber, 1992).

Birth and Neonatal Development

Birth is neither a beginning nor an ending, but a bridge between two stages of life. Birth takes place in three stages: labour, delivery, and afterbirth. It is a long process. An average first labour takes 14 hours; the average for later labours is eight hours. In many areas of life, too much or too little is not a good thing. This is true of labour—labours that are too long or too short produce a greater likelihood of problems.

Birth can be dangerous for the child and/or the mother. The fetus may be in an unusual position, such as breech or transverse presentations. The membranes may rupture too early, leading to infection. An incorrectly placed placenta may mean excessive bleeding. Drugs and forceps used during delivery may cause harm to the fetus.

Before the child is born, there is no contact with the atmosphere. The oxygen that is necessary for fetal survival and to the orderly development of the body reaches the fetus by way of the mother's bloodstream. However, when the time of birth draws near, the oxygen level in the placenta and in the child's circulatory system drops sharply. During the birth process, the human fetus is squeezed through the birth canal for several hours, during which time the head sustains considerable pressure and the infant is intermittently deprived of oxygen. Most infants tolerate this without difficulty; in spite of surface appearances, the stresses of normal delivery are usually not harmful (Lagercrantz and Slotkin, 1986).

Sometimes, however, inadequate uterine environments pose additional risks, and the infant cannot tolerate the normal changes of labour. If the child is overly deprived of oxygen, the condition is called *anoxia*. Most birth injuries result in deprivation of oxygen to the immature brain, which leads to abridgment of nervous system function. Pathologically and clinically, deprivation of oxygen in the infant brain is similar to cases of stroke in the adult brain (Fenichel, 1980). If supplies of oxygen to the nerve cells of the brain are too greatly reduced, brain damage or death can result.

When a portion of the brain is damaged, the part of the individual that is controlled by that portion of the brain is also damaged. Anoxia may be a villain in cerebral palsy, some types of epilepsy, and some mental retardation. Mild anoxia can also produce other subtle forms of childhood disability such as irritability, muscular tension, rigidity, learning disabilities, and motor defects.

Neurological Impairments

Neurological impairments can occur before, during, or after birth. Any factor that leads to hormonal, chemical, or blood-flow imbalances can cause central nervous system problems.

While pre- and perinatal causes are crucial, the incidence of infant and preschool brain injury is increasing. Causes include household and auto accidents, meningitis and encephalitis; anoxia caused through such events as near-drowning, inhalation of toxic fumes, and choking; and periventricular hemorrhage (Ewing-Cobbs, Fletcher, and Levin, 1985). Table 3-5 outlines some of the causes of damage to the central nervous system.

Damage to the brain may be so mild as to be undetectable or so profound as to reduce the child to a very low level of functioning. There may be focal brain damage that involves a very specific and delimited area of the brain, or diffuse brain damage involving a large or poorly defined area. Depending of the degree and location of the damage, the child's behaviour will be affected. For example, one of the traditional etiologies of learning disabilities is minimal brain dysfunction. On the other hand, generalized and diffuse brain damage results in mental retardation; damage to the motor areas causes cerebral palsy. Children with cerebral palsy caused by brain damage often have impaired vision as a result of loss of control of ocular muscles.

Preterm and Low-Birth-Weight Infants

Preterm or premature babies are generally defined as those born before the completion of 37 weeks, a week short of the full 38 week term. About seven percent of children are born preterm or of low birth weight. Prematurity occurs in ten or twelve births per hundred (Berlin, 1983) and is more likely to occur in multiple births. Premature babies generally weigh 2 500 grams or less, as compared to the usual birth weight of 3 000 to 3 500 grams. Because of possible difficulties with placental nutrition, babies may be of low birth weight but not premature.

The earliest stage possible for survival outside the womb is generally considered to be about 27 weeks. Fetuses born before this have little chance of survival, primarily because of lung immaturity. A preterm baby has very little surfactant, a substance that normally coats the lungs during the last three or four weeks of gestation to prevent them from collapsing. The most

Table 3-5 Some causes of damage to the central nervous system, with examples

Causes	Examples
neoplasms	brain tumour
oxygen deprivation	carbon monoxide poisoning, anoxia
maternal infection	rubella, syphilis
maternal intoxication	Fetal Alcohol Syndrome
child intoxication	lead poisoning
child infection	encephalitis
malnutrition	inadequate protein to fetus or young child
vascular accidents	brain hemorrhage
radiation	excessive x-rays
genetic defects	errors of metabolism
developmental errors	absence of brain substance
trauma	automobile accidents resulting in direct head injury
chromosomal abnormalities	Down syndrome
gestational problems	prematurity

critical problem for preterm babies is obtaining enough oxygen. Respiratory distress syndrome is responsible for about half of all newborn deaths in North America.

More than half the premature infants who weight less than 1 000 grams die at birth or shortly afterwards. Children born after 27 weeks of gestation have a survival rate of 60 percent, and those born at 28 weeks have an 85 to 90 percent chance of survival (Musgrove, 1984).

Research has clearly established that preterm infants have a higher incidence of developmental problems in childhood than full-term infants. Studies show that those infants classified as at risk more often develop problems than those classified neonatally as well babies. Yet current efforts to predict which individual infants will develop subsequent disabilities using perinatal medical factors are not very successful. Thus, in populations of four-month-olds, it is often impossible to distinguish those who will be functioning normally at age two from those who will display serious developmental delays (Bricker and Squires, 1989).

Full-term but low-birth-weight infants are also prone to a range of potentially dangerous conditions. In Ontario, Sagal (1982) studied the developmental progress of 294 low-birth-weight infants. Of the 179 children who survived, 30 showed neurological impairments, including microcephaly, blindness, deafness, mental retardation, and retrolental fibroplasia.

As they grow, small-for-term babies as a group tend to remain shorter and lighter than their agemates while preterm babies who survive are more likely to achieve normal heights and weights.

Additional risk factors can compound the original problems of preterm or small-for-term infants. For premature infants, the risk is a function of both gestational age and birth weight. Premature and low-birth-weight infants may experience central nervous system (cns) difficulties that inhibit their ability to develop normally. Such cns difficulties may be overcome in a stable family environment; in unstable low-income families lacking decent housing and enough money, the difficulties present at birth may result in developmental delays and learning problems (see Sameroff, Seifer, and Zax, M., 1987).

An overly long pregnancy can also be problematic. Infants born two weeks or more beyond the expected due date are said to be postmature. These children are in somewhat greater danger from anoxia and cerebral hemorrhage than children born at the normal 266 to 270 days. They also have a higher death rate and suffer more frequently from severe congenital abnormalities (Montagu, 1977).

CMV and Herpes

Some conditions are transmitted to the baby right at the time of delivery. Two potentially harmful or fatal conditions of this nature are cytomegalovirus (CMV) and herpes.

CMV, a form of herpes, is the most frequently occurring congenital virus among newborns. It affects about three percent of pregnant women (Kurant and Sever, 1977). The condition can cause a range of devastating problems in children, including deafness and mental retardation. When babies are born to mothers who have infections in the active stages, the mortality rate is about 50 percent. Of children that survive, about half suffer from conditions such as microcephaly, spasticity, paralysis, seizures, deafness, or blindness (McIntosh, 1984). It is difficult to know how many cases of each are caused by CMV because it is often difficult to diagnose (Schildroth, Rawlings, and Allen, 1989).

Herpes (HVH) is actually less prevalent than CMV, but it is potentially as damaging and can be fatal. Although it is a rare occurrence, babies are infected as they pass through the cervix or vagina. Affected infants are treated with an antiviral drug, but survivors are still at considerable risk for permanent damage (Hetherington and Parke, 1986).

Pediatric AIDS

Acquired Immunodeficiency Syndrome (AIDS) was first reported in 1981 as a mysterious ailment that seemed only to afflict particular groups in society. However, within a few years AIDS was recognized as a condition resulting from a viral infection that can afflict anyone of any class, any age, or either sex.

The T-cell lymphotropic virus, Type III, is commonly called the human immunodeficiency virus (HIV). HIV is the cause of the deadly AIDS. The virus attacks and seriously disrupts the body's immune system, its defence against disease. Without the protection of the immune system, AIDS sufferers are prone to fatal infections and cancers. HIV is taking many forms and, contrary to the usual evolution of infectious agents, it appears to develop within an infected individual toward more rather than less virulent strains (Cheng-Meyer, Seto, Tateno, and Levy, 1988). This finding suggests that HIV is an even more threatening virus than originally believed (Dokecki, Baumeister, and Kupstas, 1989).

AIDS in children may be the result of tainted blood transfusions or, rarely, it may be contracted through the mother's milk. The vast majority of children with pediatric AIDS have obtained their infection during birth from the mother, who used intravenous drugs or was sexually active with infected partners (Baumeister, Kupstas, and Klindworth, 1990). Placental passage *in utero* and newborn contact with the mother's blood or vaginal fluids during the process of labour and delivery are the two major routes of perinatal HIV infection (Dokecki, Baumeister, and Kupstas, 1989).

Children infected with HIV will likely develop symptoms of AIDS; between 30 and 60 percent of children born to HIV mothers will contract AIDS (Dokecki, Baumeister, and Kupstas, 1989). Pediatric AIDS is fully discussed in Chapter 11.

Postnatal Development

Postnatally, accidents are the most common cause of disabilities in children, followed by cancer in its various forms. As well, a variety of childhood diseases and infections can hinder children's progress.

Infections

Meningitis and encephalitis can be devastating. Both can result in mental retardation, visual impairment, deafness, cerebral palsy, and other disabling conditions. Meningitis attacks the meninges, or coverings of the brain and spinal cord; it is accompanied by a high fever. Spinal meningitis has a mortality rate of about 10 percent in young children and is often an offshoot of influenza B. Recently, a new vaccine became available to protect children from spinal meningitis.

Encephalitis can be caused by viral, bacterial, or parasitic infections. More encephalitic children suffer retardation than do meningitic children.

Prevention

The prevention of disabilities and potentially disabling conditions is usually classified as primary, secondary, and tertiary. Primary prevention is concerned with removing the causative factors that account for the initial occurrence of the disorder or strengthening the well-being of individuals in the population as a form of inoculation against the causes of subsequent problems. The focus is on the establishment of medical and social programs to reduce the occurrence of diseases and conditions that cause disabilities. The interventions are made available to the entire population and are targeted specifically toward groups and individuals who have not yet been identified as having the problem to be prevented (Planta, 1990). For example, providing medical care and fluoridated water to all children prevents childhood diseases and tooth decay (Planta, 1990). Other examples of primary prevention include measures to counteract poor nutrition, poverty, and prematurity (MacGregor, 1980).

Genetic counselling and educational programs on conditions such as Down syndrome are also part of primary prevention. Genetic counselling deals with the human and medical problems associated with the occurrence of risk or recurrence of a genetic disorder in the family. Counselling provides and interprets medical information based on our expanding knowledge of human genetics. The major goal is to convey an understanding of birth defects and genetic mechanisms to affected families and enable prospective parents to make informed decisions about child-bearing.

Secondary prevention refers to ascertaining, as early as possible, the evidence of disorders that may cause disabilities, as well as to allied attempts to reduce, remove, or reverse substantially complex aspects of disabilities. Successful secondary prevention programs provide services to high-risk groups to keep problems from becoming debilitating and to diminish the effects of dysfunctions that are identified early. There are two ways in which individuals are identified for secondary prevention. They manifest signs of potential dysfunction, or they are members of a high-risk group that has an elevated likelihood of having the problem but show no signs of problems as of yet (Planta, 1990).

In many cases, secondary prevention has proven very successful. For example, Tay–Sachs carriers are detected through a simple blood test. As a result of extensive testing and counselling, far fewer Tay–Sachs babies are conceived and born. In North America, the rate of Tay–Sachs among Jewish infants decreased by 95 percent in the 20 years from 1970 to 1990. As a result of prenatal testing, the incidence of Down syndrome has dropped from one in 600 twenty years ago to one in 1 000 today (Plomin, de Fries, and McClearn, 1990).

Many types of prenatal assessment of the developing fetus fall into this category. Currently, about 200 diseases can be detected prenatally. The major method used in the prenatal diagnosis of Down syndrome and other genetic disorders is amniocentesis, usually performed between the tenth and nineteenth week of gestation. Amniocentesis can be used to detect about 40 conditions, including abnormalities of the spinal cord such as spina bifida ("Prenatal" [1987]; Rosenblith and Sims-Knight, 1985). In this procedure, a needle is inserted through the mother's abdominal wall to extract ten to twenty millilitres of amniotic fluid. A chromosomal analysis then checks whether free-floating fetal cells have karyotypes (genetic patterns) typical of specific handicapping conditions. The procedure is relatively safe, with a total 2.5 to 3 percent risk of miscarriage, of which 0.5 percent is due to the amniocentesis itself ("Prenatal" [1987]).

Chorionic villi sampling (CVS) is a newer procedure with a risk factor of about 4 to 5 percent, but the portion of this risk due to the CVS itself is not known ("Prenatal" [1987]). CVS is performed between the ninth and twelfth week of pregnancy by removing a small amount of the tissue around the fetal sac that eventually becomes the placenta. The sample is removed using a catheter inserted through the vagina into the uterus under ultrasound guidance.

Other screening procedures include the new percutaneous umbilical blood sampling, ultrasonography, and fetoscopy. Ultrasound, which generates a picture (a sonogram), is used successfully in the prenatal diagnosis of hydrocephaly, anencephaly, and other multiple congenital deformities. Fetoscopy is a procedure used to evaluate fetuses that are at risk for certain genetic conditions. A fetoscope, equipped with a fibre-optic lens for viewing the fetus, is inserted into the amniotic sac. This process can be useful in determining whether a fetus has a congenital malformation that may be associated with mental retardation (Vitello and Soskin, 1985).

Secondary prevention also encompasses the management of conditions in order to ameliorate their impact. For example, certain organic conditions that cause mental retardation can be successfully managed when identified early. The effect of PKU can be prevented or diminished if a low phenylalanine diet is introduced in infancy. Hydrocephalus can be surgically treated, even in the fetus, by the insertion of a shunt to remove excess cerebrospinal fluid (Henig, 1982). Examples of secondary prevention in the schools include dropout prevention programs.

Tertiary prevention consists of intervention strategies after a negative outcome has occurred. The object of tertiary prevention is to minimize residual disabilities and maximize potential. Amelioration efforts seek to reduce the residual effects or adverse consequences of a disorder or failed outcome (Cowen, 1980). Methods of intervention may be medical, psychological, social, or educational.

Environmental Factors

It is almost impossible to determine the relative influences of heredity and environment on human behaviour, for every human life is a complex interplay of heredity and environment. The genes alone cannot produce a human being; an environment must also exist to provide nourishment, warmth, stimulation, and protection. Both heredity and environmental factors are crucial to child development. A child's growth will be seriously hampered by restricted sensory stimulation, deprivation, and impoverishment.

Types of environmental risk factors are legion, but we are increasingly able to identify the environmental conditions that increase the likelihood that a child will have a learning or a behaviour problem. Documented environmental risk includes children whose pediatric histories, caregiving circumstances, and current family situation contain risk factors that do not lead invariably to developmental delay but that carry a greater probability of delay or disability than that found in the general population (Shonkoff and Meisels, 1990). In this sense, environmental risk applies to infants and toddlers who are considered biologically sound but whose early life experiences (including maternal and family care, health care, nutrition, opportunities for expression of language, adaptive behaviour, and patterns of physical and social stimulation) are limited to an extent that creates a high probability of delayed development (Tjossem, 1976).

The two environmental problems that have been studied most are the lack of early psychological stimulation and the effects of severe malnutrition. These two factors are not always independent: in many cases, malnutrition and lack of early stimulation operate in the same child.

Environmental Risk Factors

Environmental risk refers to conditions that occur when a child is biologically normal but does not develop age-appropriate behavior at the normal rate. In this grouping, *at risk* refers to students who have characteristics, live in an environment, or have experiences that make them more prone to developing some form of disabling condition and/or more likely to fail in school. We cannot possibly describe here all the risk factors that exist; rather, we briefly examine three major environmental risk factors that are particularly relevant to classroom learning and behaviour. We touch on family structures, poverty, and cultural and linguistic differences. Examples of further important risk factors are shown in Table 3-6.

Table 3-6 Factors contributing to school achievement

Developmental	Family/social	School
Mental ability levels	Acculturation pressures	Equal opportunity to learn
Presence/absence of disabilities	Cultural beliefs	Teacher expectations
At-risk status	Culture conflict	Culturally relevant curriculum
Health status	Family interactions	Bilingual/ESL instruction
Ethnicity	Child rearing and management practices	Lack of realistic role models
Gender	Socio-economic status	Pre-referral and referral practices
Learning and communicative styles	Single-parent family	Assessment practices
Lack of communication skills	Religion	Concordance between learning styles and instruction
Lack of prior education	Social prejudice	Relevant textbooks and materials
Attendance rates	Parent involvement	
Motivation	Home/school relations	
Reading problems	Experiential background	
Dialect differences	Community interfaces	
	Grade retention	
	Peer pressures	

Source: Winzer and Mazurek, 1998.

While linguistic, cultural, socio-economic, and life style differences are not of themselves disabling conditions, the consequences may place children at higher risk. As well, phenomena such as family configuration, poverty, and cultural and linguistic differences interact and impact upon special education.

Most importantly, cultural and linguistic differences assume great impact given the rapid demographic changes seen in society and in our school systems. In cities such as Vancouver, Montreal, and Toronto, large numbers of students come from homes where English is not the first language. As the demographic composition of the school-age population shifts to encompass more students from diverse cultural backgrounds, bilingual homes, and economically deprived families, the need for special services in the schools increases.

Family Structures

Students receive about 900 hours of instruction in school each year. However, they spend a great deal more time out of school than in it; about 87 percent out of the classroom and only 13 percent in it (Monroe, 1991). What happens in the home, within the family, and in the neighborhood the other 87 percent of the time affects every aspect of a student's functioning and learning (Winzer and Mazurek, 1998).

Teachers must be aware that the child population of the late 1990s is different from earlier generations. Today's children are caught in the midst of rapid social changes. Many of the changes are positive; on the negative side are changing social and family structures that include everything from shortages in technical labour markets, to children living in poverty and homelessness, to destabilization of the institution of the family shown in mounting divorce rates and increases in the number of single-parent families.

High numbers of children (approximately 16 percent in 1985) are born to unmarried mothers. The Canadian divorce rate has increased 600 percent in the past 25 years. The number of single-parent families has likewise increased at a rate 2.5 times faster than two-parent families to 14 percent in 1995 (see Doxey, 1990). Many children now have blended families that include stepbrothers and stepsisters moving in and out of children's lives.

The family is universally recognized as a fundamental influence on child behaviour. The family structure establishes the norms of behaviour and teaches, explicitly and implicitly, social, moral and psychological lessons to the developing child.

As families change, new problems emerge. This is not in any way to suggest that non-traditional, non-nuclear families are dysfunctional. However, research does support the contention that increasing family instability leads to dysfunctional relationships. In children dysfunctional relationships during childhood and adolescence have been found to be related to verbal and physical aggression against others; school truancy and dropping out; behavioural disorders; learning disabilities; mental retardation; juvenile crime and delinquency; social isolation and withdrawal; and bad conduct discharges from the military (Bracken and Newman, 1994). The area of familial and non-familial influences on children's behaviour is discussed again in Chapter 8.

Poverty

In 1992, more than one half of Canadian single mothers and one in five children lived below the poverty line. Poverty is one of the greatest risk factors in the development of children. "Persistent and concentrated poverty virtually guarantees the presence of a vast collection of risk factors and their continuing destructive impact over time" (Schorr, 1988, p. 30).

Poor families may not utilize adequate prenatal and postnatal health care and poor children can be affected from the moment of conception. They are more likely to suffer the consequences of poor maternal nutrition, complications of pregnancy and delivery, prematurity, and low birth weight.

Lower SES negatively correlates with eight adverse socializing factors—harsh discipline, lack of maternal warmth, exposure to aggressive adult models, maternal aggressive values, family life stressors, mother's lack of social support, peer group instability, and lack of cognitive stimulation (Dodge, Pettit, and Bates, 1994). For example, children of lower SES families are much more at risk for abuse than children from higher SES homes (Dodge, Bates, and Pettit, 1990). There may be more stress in lower SES homes.

In school, children of poverty are at high risk for reading and writing difficulties because their parents are often unable to provide many of the emergent literacy experiences necessary such as printed materials and writing utensils in the home, adult–child interactions with literary materials, guided television watching, and interactive book reading (Marvin and Mirenda, 1993). Within the school system, children living in poverty make up a disproportionately large percentage of those who repeat a grade, are placed in special education, or drop out before completing school (see Winzer and Mazurek, 1998).

Cultural and Linguistic Differences

Today, more children from Asia and the Caribbean are entering our school systems. Chinese and other Asian students are especially highly represented in Vancouver and Toronto; one in nine residents in BC is of Asian ancestry (Renaud and Badets, 1993). It is estimated that by the year 2001 some 15 percent of the population will be members of a visible minority group; 20 percent by 2016 ("Projections ...," 1996; Ramcharan, 1988).

To live and develop in two culturally different systems is sufficiently challenging for students without exceptional conditions. The difficulties multiply for students who are culturally and linguistically diverse and also disabled. When special problems in cognitive functioning, sensory use, communication, mobility, or social and behavioural interactions combine with cultural and linguistic diversity, individual differences increase dramatically, as do the chances of school failure, even when special services are provided. So pervasive are the problems that this group has been referred to as triple threat students (Rueda and Chan, 1979); that is, they are subject to limited English proficiency, disability and, very often, poverty.

Culturally diverse students are more likely than those from majority backgrounds to be poor. In general, children from minority families who have limited English proficiency and are impoverished have historically done poorly in school (Dao, 1991). In both the United States and Canada, these students show an unacceptable pattern of social separation and isolation, a growing gap between their achievement and that of majority group children, disproportionate referrals to special education, tracking to lower streams, lower scores on tests, lower grades, high rates of school failure, high dropout rates, and lower rates of college attendance (Winzer and Mazurek, 1998).

Culturally Different Students with Special Needs

Many students of diverse cultural backgrounds may not fit exactly into any of the recognized categories of exceptionality and conventional definitions of exceptionalities do not always apply to these children, particularly those for whom English is not a first language. Special factors must be considered when defining a culturally different child who is also disabled. These include the role of language, the family's expectations, cultural attitudes toward disabilities, and the relationship between the child's cultural community and the larger society. The developmental consequences of a condition are related to the consequences of limited English; the consequences of the specific disability condition; and the additive nature of language deficiency and a disabling condition. Given these factors, disabled children from different cultures can best be described as children who have diagnosable disabilities that are recognized as such by their cultural community.

Culturally diverse students are represented in all categories of exceptionality and can experience any disability that is found in other children. In other words, disabilities of the same type affect children from diverse cultural backgrounds just as they do those of the dominant culture. Demographic information on the numbers of children with exceptionalities who have diverse cultural and linguistic backgrounds is difficult to extrapolate from sources because of a lack of consistency in identifying, defining, and reporting these populations. Hardman and colleagues (1993) estimate that among students with disabilities, 41 percent are from culturally diverse backgrounds.

The relationship between school failure, special education, and cultural and linguistic differences has not been a comfortable one. In the past, there existed little recognition or understanding of the cultural and linguistic variables that occur among culturally diverse populations. Special education has not given high priority to a positive recognition of individual differences relating to cultural backgrounds and attitudes, values and beliefs, learning styles, communication and language patterns, behavioural and response mechanisms, and family and community roles and involvement (Winzer and Mazurek, 1998).

In the past, immigrant and minority group children were over-represented in such classifications as slow learner, educably mentally retarded, and learning disabled (Cummins, 1984, 1986; Gelb and Misokawa, 1986; Sleeter 1986). Today, a high proportion of students served under *serious emotional disturbance* are from culturally and linguistically diverse groups. Far too many minority group children who have linguistic difficulties within the regular system are misconstrued as having special education problems, and the number of linguistic minority students placed in learning disabilities programs is growing disproportionately (Jacobs, 1991).

Minority group members resent the over-representation. For example, there seems to be a great deal of distrust in the area of special education in Native communities and schools. This has to do with inaccurate labelling, over-representation in special education, and the specialized nature of personnel (Hull, Phillips, and Polyzoi, 1995).

Today, most educators recognize that disability and cultural and linguistic concerns are not unrelated phenomena ; rather, they play interconnected and complementary roles in children's development and progress. Programs must address the interacting influences of all student variables.

SUMMARY

1. Medical research is bringing a more complete understanding of the ways in which a child's psychological, social and educational environments are related to learning. Teachers' understanding of the etiology, developmental consequences, treatments, and prognoses of exceptional conditions will serve to increase their interactions with and understanding of children with disabilities.

2. A huge range of disabilities affect children, the result of multiple etiologies. Disorders and diseases may arise from chromosomal or genetic aberrations, infections and intoxicants, malnutrition, deprivation of oxygen, and environmental hazards.

3. At-risk children are those not currently identified as disabled but more likely to develop some type of problem. Studies show that infants classified as at risk more often develop problems than those classified neonatally as well babies.

4. The child's physical condition is, of course, the proper concern of the medical profession. However, many physical problems have obvious implications for education.

5. The causes of childhood disabling conditions are changing; with the rapid advances in medical science, certain conditions have disappeared but others have filled their places. Premature babies are surviving, but a wide range of insults to the nervous and organic systems that can lead to mental retardation and other disabilities are possible with prematurity. As well, a frightening proportion of the next generation will be impaired by preventable causes, in particular pediatric AIDS and the use of drugs by pregnant women.

6. Biology is hardly destiny, and social influences combine with biological predispositions to shape behaviour and learning potential. Teachers must be aware of the myriad of factors that influence the lives of children with exceptionalities.

7. Changing demographics are accompanied by other major social changes such as pervasive violence, mounting divorce rates, increased foster care, and rising teenage pregnancies. Because of this, the schools will meet more students at risk for educational failure and dropping out, and special education is likely to serve a wider range of students.

In the Classroom

Profile: Monique

Monique has been in Canada for a little more than three years. Although the family came from French speaking Mauritius, they chose to settle in a large English speaking urban area. Monique's father has acquired fairly fluent English skills but her mother has only a few words. Her younger brother speaks and reads English fluently. Monique is in the middle. She has fairly fluent conversational skills, certainly good enough to play and communicate with peers and to negotiate through the community. To a large extent, though, she has rejected the French of the home and uses her English at all times, thereby closing off much communication with her mother.

Now eleven years old, Monique attends the regular grade five class of her local school. She no longer goes to ESL classes and spends all of her time in the regular classroom. Her poor grades in school are an increasing concern. In the past, they were attributed to lack of English and Monique was expected to "catch up" as her language improved.

This has not happened. Quite the opposite. Although Monique was well below grade level when she entered grade five, she is now falling further and further behind, especially in the language arts. In the context of the demands of the classroom, Monique's peer-appropriate communication skills are not adequate. Further, her reading skills are extremely poor and, now that she must apply reading skills in order to gain information in other subject areas, the content subjects are seriously affected. As well, her poor reading skills spill over to influence her spelling and, most specifically, her creative writing. In this last area, Monique seems to have many ideas but she can't get them onto paper and is functioning at least three years below grade level.

Moreover, as she tends to lag further and further behind the other children, Monique is losing friends as she becomes a friendly butt of jokes and mild ridicule. She reacts poorly to this teasing and is beginning to withdraw into herself. So serious is the situation that the teacher has made a referral for a full psycho-educational assessment and is beginning to feel that a special education placement may be more suitable for Monique at this point in her school career.

* * *

Once Monique was referred for psycho-educational assessment, her problems became more clear. Although she is a child of average ability, the psychologist identified her as having a learning disability. This is not as serious in the areas of receptive and expressive language as it is in written language, specifically reading and writing. When planning Monique's IEP, the team took into account the learning disability, the effects of cultural differences on learning styles, and her linguistic competencies in both languages. Specific strategies were used for reading (see Chapter 5). As well, the team looked at some overarching strategies that improve the functioning of students from diverse cultural and linguistic backgrounds, specifically pre-referred, grouping, and multicultural special education.

Special education is designed to accommodate students who are different from the average in some or many areas of functioning. The students served have traits and characteristics that demand unique and individual programming. When students are both culturally and linguistically diverse as well as exceptional in some way, they pose enormous challenges to the schools. Educators must accommodate the heterogeneous nature of the population, the diversity of cultures and languages, the unique combinations of disability and cultural/linguistic background, and the different socialization and values that students bring to the classroom (Winzer and Mazurek, 1998).

Pre-referral Interventions

Monique's referral to special education came late in her school career. However, the general trend is for too many students from diverse cultural and linguistic backgrounds to be referred for special education. And, once referred, studies show that anywhere from 54 to 92 percent of students are found eligible for special services (Algozzine, Christenson, and Ysseldyke, 1982; Fugate, Clarizio, and Phillips, 1993).

Before making such a referral, many authors suggest pre-referral interventions. Essentially, the teacher makes changes in the environment and instruction to see whether a child is not learning because of differences or because of disability. Pre-referral is based on the assumption that learning problems are contextual and exist within the context of the classroom, where the curriculum design and the instructional strategies employed by the teacher influence the degree to which student needs are effectively met. If needs are not being met, then the environment should be changed (Winzer and Mazurek, 1998).

Pre-referral interventions do not suggest that special education is imminent. They serve to gather data on a student's learning and behaviour. A major goal is "to minimize pulling the student out of activities by incorporating instruction that is meaningful to the student into general educational activities whenever possible" (Willams and Rox, 1996, p. 6).

To implement pre-referral procedures, a teacher should

1. Gather data on language and achievement. Here the teacher should teach and assess basic skills to attempt to clarify the problem and determine discrepancies between a student's abilities and the demands of the classroom.

2. Look for influencing factors by examining the student's language, instructional achievements, and cultural influences.

3. Collaborate with other professionals. A common way to begin the process is to bring the problem to the attention of a team which can actively brainstorm intervention options (Graham, 1989; Pugach and Johnson, 1989).

4. Select the best option and determine changes that can be made in the classroom. For example, pre-referral for Native students may include peer tutoring, co-operative learning, and additional wait time with questions. For another child, a teacher may use observations, work samples, and error analysis.

5. Plan ways to implement the best option.

Multicultural Special Education

It is not only that children from diverse backgrounds speak different languages or use different dialects, but that they have different cultural backgrounds which form their way of interacting in the environment. Monique, for example, is likely to have a learning style that responds well to techniques such as co-operative learning but not to a highly competitive classroom.

Children such as Monique need multicultural special education that celebrates the first language and culture while building a second language and accommodating to the new culture. Multicultural special education can be defined as

> A set of perspectives and skills that change the climate, curriculum, and interactions in
> schools and classrooms so that all students, whatever their cultural and linguistic back-

ground or type and degree of disability, have equal respect, the opportunity to learn, and are given the skills to develop cross-cultural sensitivity and the competencies necessary to function in a pluralistic society. Multicultural perspectives and skills meld with special education practices, are infused throughout the curriculum, and are tailored to the unique strengths and needs of each child who is exceptional (Winzer and Mazurek, 1998, pp. 104–105).

Classroom Grouping

One of the best ways to instruct students from diverse cultural backgrounds is through the use of reciprocal interactive teacher models such as co-operative learning and whole language. These promote empowerment and learning via verbal and written dialogue between students as well as between students and teachers (Figueroa, Fradd, and Correa, 1989; Ortiz and Yates, 1989).

Co-operative learning (also referred to as shared learning, collaborative learning, or small-group learning) is "a generic term for the instructional organization of children into small mixed ability study groups in which participants co-operate with one another to achieve academic goals" (Rich, 1986, p. 339). Within their groups, students know they can reach their goals if, and only if, peers in their group also reach their goals.

There are three basic formats of co-operative learning: peer teaching in which students explain material to each other, listen to others, and arrive at a joint understanding of the material; a group format where members pool information; and the jigsaw format in which each student is assigned a task. Within these three main formats, many different co-operative learning strategies have been developed in laboratory settings and in classrooms.

When teachers use co-operative learning, there are additional special concerns for students with language difficulties or special needs: special students' fear and anxiety; worries of normally developing children that their grades may be affected; and the passive attitude of some children. To overcome these fears, procedures should be carefully structured and explained, each team member assigned a role, students with special needs closely monitored to ensure that they don't become "hitchhikers," and specific learning outcomes targeted for each special student and identified as personalized instructional plans (Winzer and Mazurek, 1998).

EFFECTS OF CULTURAL AND LINGUISTIC DIFFERENCES	TIPS FOR TEACHERS
THE CHILD NEEDS CULTURAL AWARENESS	Be familiar with the home and community.
	Know the child as an individual.
	Be aware of differences in order to understand the behaviours and learning styles of students from diverse cultures.
THE CHILD NEEDS CULTURAL SENSITIVITY	Incorporate materials from a variety of cultures.
	While adding a second language and culture to the child's repertoire, do not try to replace the first language and culture; retain both.

THE CHILD HAS LINGUISTIC DIFFERENCES	Become familiar with features of students' dialects so as to understand better and distinguish miscues from errors. Know the stages of second language acquisition.
THE CHILD IS LEARNING ENGLISH AS A SECOND LANGUAGE	Assign students classroom roles that capitalize on their strengths and do not make unrealistic demands on English skills. For children with exceptionalities, try to get trained aides who speak the child's language. Use much oral language work. Garcia (1988) found that students learn math and literacy skills most effectively when student–student discussions take up to at least 50 percent of instructional time. Stress oral language and conversational skills before moving to reading and written language. Adapt English instruction to make it highly contextualized and multisensory, so that it is more easily understood by the students. Use general materials such as catalogues from Sears or Canadian Tire.

WEBLINKS

March of Dimes Birth Defects Foundation **http://www.modimes.org/**

Canadian Institute of Child Health (CICH) **http://www.cich.ca/**

Motherisk **http://www.motherisk.org/**

Campaign 2000: Child Poverty in Canada **http://www.web.net/~rpopham/ campaign2000/**

SECTION 2
Children with Communication Disorders

In all the enormous repertoire of human skills and abilities, communication is one of the most critical tools. Communication is the essence of human socialization, the link that provides reciprocal interaction between the individual and the environment. It is through communication that human beings make their impact upon the world and establish and maintain relationships.

Humans use communication to meet needs and desires, control environmental events, establish social relationships, and learn new skills and concepts. Communication includes written language and speech as well as a variety of non-speech forms such as sign language and many non-verbal forms such as gesture and body language.

Human language is incredibly complex, bound by structured rules and characteristic patterns of usage that change in different settings—intrapersonal, interpersonal, group, and societal (Levine, 1981). Yet for most children, the ready acquisition of their culture's language and speech is a natural part of early maturation. Small children learn language long before school age and do so with vivacity and playfulness.

All children show great variability in the age at which they will demonstrate a particular level of speech and language performance (Bernstein and Tiegerman, 1989). However, for children with communication exceptionalities, the variability falls outside what could be considered normal. These youngsters encounter serious difficulties in the acquisition and use of speech and language. Teachers may see children with phonological or articulation disorders or with voice problems, children who stutter, some who have delayed or deviant language, and some who have difficulties in expressive or receptive modes. Most often, there is a combination of these problems.

After learning disabilities, speech and language disorders are the most common seen in the schools. (In preschool children, speech and language disorders are the most common form of disability.) About eight to ten percent of school-aged children have some type of speech or language disorder. For some children, this is a short-term delay in acquiring articulation proficiency. Other children have chronic, recurrent speech and language difficulties, such as stuttering. For others, speech and language difficulties are part of a more complex constellation of disorders that may limit their lifetime options (Ilott, 1990).

This chapter on speech and language problems is the first of the categorical chapters because these types of problems affect almost all of the children we will meet in this text. That is, problems in speech and language are not only a field of exceptionality by themselves, but they cut across other areas. For many young children with disabilities, learning to communicate is not a simple or a naturally occurring task. Communication demands so much of the human organism that language learning is vulnerable to all the problems which can and do affect children.

As an example, many children diagnosed as learning disabled also suffer problems in the areas of speech and language. The term *language learning disabilities* refers to the language disorder syndrome associated with learning disabilities. Studies suggest that language is the primary deficit for 60 percent of students with learning disabilities (LD), while for all LD students language is one component of their disorder (Wesanko, 1990). This is why students with learning disabilities are included in this section.

In this section, we first introduce the subject of speech and language disorders and illustrate how they affect children who have these as their sole disabilities. We then discuss the very special problems of children identified as learning disabled, with particular emphasis on aspects of speech and language.

CHAPTER 4

Children with Speech and Language Differences

For centuries, parents, scholars, and teachers have been fascinated by the way children acquire and use language. Virtually all the major philosophers since Plato and Aristotle have considered the problems of the origin and role of human language. Debates centred on the role of language in the progressive differentiation of humans from other creatures and the way in which reason, if an original endowment of humans, manifested itself in language.

Eighteenth-century empiricists were particularly intrigued by language development in humans. (See the profile on Victor later in this chapter.) In the nineteenth century, the study of speech and language was known as *philology;* most of the research was in the form of diary studies. These soon gave way to an examination of children's vocabulary, which is perhaps the most traditional approach to the study of language acquisition. In the early twentieth century, the study of language development emphasized language form. In general, language forms were identified and classified into categories related to sentence types, parts of speech, and so on (Owens, 1996). By the 1930s and 1940s, data collection was more formalized. Then, when psycholinguistics emerged as a discrete discipline in the early 1950s, language became a favourite research area.

Today, the study of how children learn language is like many other academic pursuits in that different theories that attempt to explain the phenomenon compete for acceptance. Every theory advanced to explain language development has been criticized. The question is fiercely debated and there are champions of every conceivable position. Occasionally one theory predominates, but generally portions of each are used to explain different aspects.

Part of the problem in designing an overall theory is the complexity of both language and communication behaviours (Owens, 1996). Behaviourists consider language a subset of other learned behaviours and stress reinforcement in language acquisition. But even a rich learning environment cannot explain how children learn so much language so quickly and correctly. A social learning view of language extends the behavioural position to include the processes of imitation. Children are believed to learn to speak one language rather than another, and to speak it with particular vocabularies and idioms, because they imitate and are reinforced for imitating the language spoken in their homes and neighbourhoods.

Because children of all cultures learn language at about the same age and tend to learn it in similar ways, others question whether humans are born with a natural innate tendency to acquire language. Piaget believed that language acquisition is a direct result of cognitive development, that language is the handmaiden of thought. To Piaget, we cannot develop language skills until at least the last stage of sensorimotor development because it is not until then that a child's mental apparatus allows him or her to represent symbolically an object that is no longer present. Noam Chomsky (1965), also holding a cognitive–biological position, believes that a sense of grammar is innate, or native, to the human brain. Chomsky postulates an innate language acquisition device unique to and present in all humans that enables us to learn language simply by being exposed to it.

Enormously complex and comprehensive research into the nature and acquisition of language continues apace. The more that is discovered about language and language impairments, the greater the number of questions that emerge. Studies throughout the 1980s included all the traditional topics: phonology, morphology, syntax, pragmatics, and semantics. Stress was placed on the acquisition of pragmatics—an individual's ability to use language appropriately in social situations.

Recently, the functional definition of language has been expanded in important ways. First, communicative behaviour is seen as any behaviour that conveys a social message from one person to another. Spoken language, sign language, and the use of communication boards are considered diverse but legitimate modes of language. This accompanies the realization that formal language is only one of several forms of communicative behaviour. Gestures and actions (reaching, directed eye movements, use of objects) are other forms of communicative behaviour, which is defined by its function in a social interaction rather than by its form (Rogers-Warren and Warren, 1984).

O f all the achievements of early childhood, the acquisition and development of speech and language is one of the most remarkable. Tiny infants, initially able to produce only vegetative sounds and reflexive cries, rapidly acquire language and speech through exposure and experience. As children listen and respond to the language in their environments, they typically make enormous progress in speech and language development and quite unconsciously learn to produce an infinite variety of intelligible utterances.

The first three years are the crucial period for the development of speech and language: about twice as much language growth occurs between the first and third years as between the third and fifth years (Cratty, 1986). Without formal instruction, most children in their first two years develop a lexicon of spoken words and learn to form simple multilevel utterances.

The language explosion that occurs in the preschool years is most apparent in the growth of vocabulary—from about 50 words at 18 months to 200 words at age two, to between 8 000 and 14 000 words at age six (Carey, 1978). This means that from age two to age six the average child learns between six and ten words a day.

By the age of five, most children have acquired such mastery over language that they have a firm linguistic base on which teachers can formally build reading and writing. As children develop speech and language, they are also developing communicative competence—they know how to interact, how to communicate appropriately in various situations, and how to make sense of what others say and do in communicative interactions.

Language acquisition is a monumental task. Even though small children accomplish it with ease, linguists, psychologists, anthropologists, and many others either directly or peripherally involved in language research remain unsure of how the process actually occurs.

What happens in the early stages of acquisition of speech and language is critical and is reflected in the child's performance in the classroom later on. The use of language is closely tied to cognitive development and self-concept. Problems can impair a child's functioning in play and with peers and can result in the development of secondary behavioural problems. As well, unresolved difficulties will hinder a child's academic progress. For many school-aged children, inferior communication skills inhibit learning and contribute to feelings of failure (Wesanko, 1990). Too, competence with language has a direct influence on a child's ability to learn to read and write (Polloway and Smith, 1982), and young children with speech and language difficulties are more likely to meet problems in learning to read later on.

A basic understanding of the normal development of language and speech underlies an appreciation of the nature of communication disorders. We therefore begin this chapter with a brief overview of normal speech and language development.

Overview of Speech and Language

Communication may be seen as the process of exchanging information and ideas between participants. All living things communicate in some way and, in this sense, communication includes the entire spectrum of acts performed by living creatures in order to pass on and respond to messages.

Speech and language are the typically human activities in communication. Language is a system of symbols organized into conventional patterns to communicate meaning. Speech is essentially a mechanical production of language. Other methods than speech may be appropriately employed to express language—sign language and writing, for example. However, while it is possible to possess language and lack the ability to speak, it is not possible to have speech without language.

As children acquire speech and language they typically pass through certain stages. These should not be viewed as a set of discrete milestones through which children pass on the way to mastering adult communication; rather, language should be seen as a process that is generative, systematic, and rule-governed. Language learning begins in infancy and continues throughout life. Formal language use is one point on a continuum of communication behaviour that begins in non-verbal social exchanges during infancy and extends through the use of written language.

Another important aspect of language is the creativity involved. Children are not passive organisms into which language is poured; rather, they are catalytic agents. In other words, it is not so much that language develops but that language is acquired. The process is clearly marked by open-endedness and productivity. It is clear quite early that children do not put words together only if they have heard those words together in combination before; rather, they produce utterances they have never heard. As children develop vocabulary and internalize a knowledge of the rules of their native language they can potentially create an infinite number of unique utterances.

A further remarkable finding about language acquisition is that children acquiring language do so in essentially the same order. In English, children learn *in* and *on* before other prepositions such as *under,* and they learn the progressive form using *-ing* before other verb endings such as *-ed*. After they learn regular plurals and past tenses as in *horses* and *skated* they create some forms of their own, like *mouses* and *eated* (Gleason, 1985).

Elements of Language

Language consists of interrelated and intertwined components, all of which must be present or developing for appropriate usage. Children must simultaneously learn the sound structure of the language (the phonology), the rules that govern the ordering of words within sentences (the syntax or grammar), and the meaning of words and phrases (semantics). If their usage is to attain appropriate meaning, children must employ pragmatics—the use of language in its social context.

Syntax is the network of organizational principles underlying linguistic expression. Without syntax, language would become an incoherent jumble of vocabulary and sound (Crystal, Fletcher, and Garman, 1976). Syntactic rules govern what we call the grammar of language. The general term, **grammar**, refers to the sum total of conventions that govern the communication of meaning of a particular language; a person's total knowledge of the language's phonetics, morphology, syntax, and semantics.

Children do not learn syntax all at one time but progress through distinct stages. For example, in learning to express questions, children show a definite sequence of acquisition. In the first stage, the question is expressed by a slight rising of the voice. The second stage involves the use of an interrogative word, such as *who, what, where, which,* and *why.* These words are placed in front of a word, phrase, or complete sentence, resulting in such questions as "Who that?" "What this?" and "Why you cry?" (Byrne and Shervanian, 1977). The third stage involves the principle of inversion. The child places the verb before the subject of the sentence to ask "Is Daddy home?" and "Does it belong here?" Some children rely on the ubiquitous "Eh?" Tag questions, such as "You have one, don't you?" appear a little later (de Villiers and de Villiers, 1978).

Semantics is concerned specifically with meaning. The acquisition of words, their meanings, and the links between them does not usually happen at once. Words are clearly comprehended before they are spoken, and the number of words comprehended continues to be greater all through language development and in later life. Comprehension of the first word is about three months ahead of production of the first word, and the gap grows; comprehension of 50 words appears to occur five months before production of 50 words (Benedict, 1979). Moreover, children learn to produce 50 words before they string them together into sentences. Vocabulary growth begins slowly, but there is a great spurt in word learning between 24 and 30 months (Reich, 1986).

Morphology is the system of word building in the language. *Morphemes* may be words or significant elements, such as prefixes and suffixes. Sound units that are not words by themselves are called *bound morphemes* because they are units of meaning only when combined with words. For example, the suffix *-ness* can be added to many words in English.

Phonology is the sound system of language; the smallest sound units are called *phonemes.* Phonology encompasses the rules for using the sounds of language, for combining phonemes in particular ways to form identifiable language units such as the /s/ that we add to make words plural. People who speak American or Canadian English recognize about 44 phonemes. Other languages recognize different sounds.

Phonetics is the description of the speech sounds of a language. There are only 26 letters—vowels and consonants—in the English alphabet, but they are pronounced in different ways. Combinations of just 44 phonemes produce every English word.

Pragmatics is concerned with the ways in which we use language, the role of context in communicative interactions. Pragmatics develops from the early stages as children use their language to query, request, deny, and declare. How they use language—the content of their interactions—changes with the interaction and the situation. They can talk baby talk to infants, tell jokes and riddles, be rude to their friends and, usually, polite to their teachers and parents.

The Speech Mechanism

The act of speech is enormously complicated. English speakers talk at an average rate of 150 words a minute. A speaker produces 14 phonemes per second, using about 100 muscles that require 100 motor units apiece (Shames and Wiig, 1990).

The anatomical structures involved in the comprehension and production of language and speech include the nervous system, the respiratory system, the oral part of the digestive tract, and the auditory sense receptors. These physical structures function in a highly organized and integrated fashion. Each part is synchronized with other parts to produce a meaningful sequence of accurate speech sounds while maintaining proper levels of loudness, pitch, and a pleasing voice quality (Byrne and Shervanian, 1977).

In general terms, speech is produced in an airstream that is shaped and resonated by the lips, tongue, teeth, jaw, nasal cavity, larynx, and pharynx. Figure 4-1 shows the organs and musculature of speech.

More specifically, the physiological process of speech involves three stages—vocalization, articulation, and modulation (Byrne and Shervanian, 1977). *Vocalization* is the ability to produce sound. *Articulation* involves the generation of speech sounds by modifications of the vocal tract, which consists basically of the mouth and nasal and pharyngeal cavities.

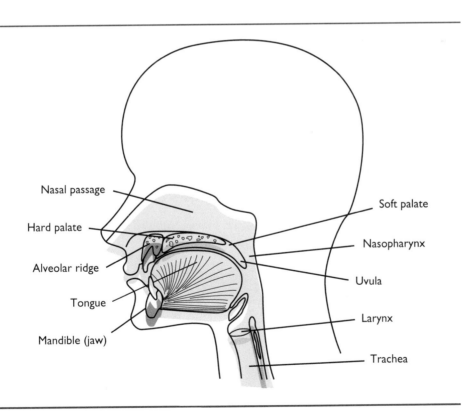

Figure 4-1
The sound-producing mechanism in humans

Changes in placement and manner of articulators (lips, teeth, tongue, palate, pharynx) cause changes in speech sounds. For example, /t/ and /d/ are formed by closing the lips and then opening them to allow air to escape. The only difference between /t/ and /d/ or /p/ and /b/ is that /d/ and /b/ are voiced, while /t/ and /p/ are voiceless. *Modulation* is the ability to control the loudness of the sounds produced.

Within these major processes, respiration, phonation, and resonance are the necessary components of the speech process. *Respiration* provides the airstream from which speech is developed; it depends on the lungs and various muscular and skeletal elements. *Phonation*, or vocal tone production, depends on the larynx, which produces a vibrating airstream (Moores, 1987). The larynx produces sound, and the pharynx modifies it, providing *resonance*. In addition to voice production, the larynx functions in crying, in keeping foreign objects out of the lungs, in coughing, and as a regulator of the exchange of oxygen and carbon dioxide in breathing (Leonard, 1982). The pharynx changes its shape, size, and tension, and combines with the nose or mouth to form the resonating chambers for speech. As the larynx and resonating cavities develop, the voice becomes louder, the pitch becomes lower, and the vocal tone increases in variety and range of inflectional patterns.

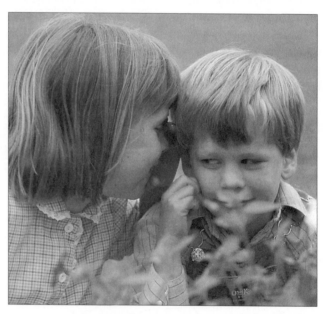

Early stimulation from parents and siblings aids in an infant's language acquisition.

Speech and Language Development

Language acquisition overlaps and relies upon social and cognitive growth. These aspects of development are closely intertwined, and really cannot be considered separately. Further, it is extremely difficult to separate speech and language development in the early years because language usage is expressed so cogently in speech forms in most children.

Language is first and foremost a social behaviour. At the outset, the quality of adult–child interactions is the single most important influence on the child's language development. Child–adult communicative interaction is sometimes called **motherese**, which is characterized by rather unique alterations in speech, meaning, form, and even language usage. When interacting with infants, both adults and children tend to use register changes—a higher pitch, exaggerated intonation, clear enunciation, a slower rate with more pauses between utterances, simplified speech sounds, repeated syllables, and simplified syntax.

How important is interaction in the early months? A recent report (Begley, 1996) notes that infants whose mothers spoke to them a lot knew 131 more words at 20 months than did babies of more taciturn, or less involved mothers. At 24 months, the gap widened to 295 words. When there is minimal or no social interaction, language acquisition will be severely hindered. Two children in quite different eras who were deprived of early stimulation are described in the profiles that follow.

Profile

Victor

Jean Marc Gaspard Itard (1755–1838), a French physician, is remembered for his intervention with Victor, the so-called wild boy of Aveyron. The boy was caught in the woods, and was reported to have been raised by wolves. When the lad finally reached Paris on Bastille Day, 1800, he was placed in the school for the deaf because of his muteness. Itard called him Victor, perhaps in anticipation of the victory that education would achieve (Seguin, 1864). Victor was stunted in growth, with a light complexion and scarred, pockmarked skin—probably the result of the smallpox he had caught in captivity. A huge scar ran across his larynx, suggesting that his throat had been cut before he was abandoned in the forest (Lane and Pillard, 1978).

Instead of resembling Rousseau's "noble savage," the boy was dirty, incapable of focusing attention, and insensitive to the basic sensations of heat and cold. He lapped his food, uttered inarticulate sounds, fixated on empty space, bit people who came too close, and spent most of his time sleeping or rocking back and forth. Observers concluded that Victor's constitution was defective; the boy was not an idiot because he had been left in the wilds, but had been left in the wilds because he was an idiot. Itard could not accept that Victor was irreversibly idiotic. Instead, he believed that the child was mentally arrested due to social and educational neglect; Victor had acquired idiocy through isolation, suffering a sort of mental atrophy from disuse of his senses. Despite Victor's appearance and lack of responsiveness, Itard believed that appropriate environmental conditions could humanize the boy and decided to try to educate him rather than sending him to a lunatic hospital.

Itard began his work with little concept of the complexities involved in working with a severely disabled child. Using crude diagnostic methods, he determined that Victor's sense organs were intact, though "dull" or insensitive. Victor would not, for example, respond to loud noises, not even to the sound of a pistol shot. On the other hand, he would react to such subtle signals as the cracking of a walnut.

Itard used a variety of means to make Victor aware of sensation—hot baths, massages, tickling, emotional excitement, even electric shock. Along with sensory stimulation and discipline, Itard presented Victor with a systematic series of specific sense training activities designed to improve his visual, auditory, and motor skills. He taught the activities in order and at a variable rate tailored to fit Victor's progress. Especially, Itard tried to teach the boy to communicate through speech and sign language.

In time, Victor became moderately socialized but not, as Itard had naïvely hoped, normal. Victor's ability to communicate continued to increase, and he learned the basic skills of eating and dressing. Nevertheless, after five years, Itard concluded that his work had been a failure and left Victor in the care of a friendly housekeeper.

Genie

The story of Genie illustrates the severe effects of emotional and social deprivation on language and speech development. Genie's father believed her to be hopelessly retarded, and from the time she was twenty months old, he confined her to a small room. The room was barren, completely unfurnished save for a small crib entirely covered with wire mesh and an infant potty. During the day, the child was strapped in the crib or tied to the potty chair. At night she was stuffed into a sleeping bag specially made to restrain her.

Genie's father never spoke to her and beat her if she made any noise. Sometimes, he pretended he was a dog, barking and growling and sometimes scratching the child with his fingernails. Genie's mother could only visit her for a few minutes each day to feed her. There was no radio or television in the house.

When Genie was thirteen and a half, the parents had an especially violent fight and the mother left. At about this time, in November 1970, Genie was discovered by the California authorities. Her father committed suicide on the day he was to be brought to trial.

When she was found, Genie weighed a mere 27 kg and was 137 cm tall. She could not chew solid food, was not toilet trained, was unable to stand erect, and could only shuffle, not walk. Genie was mute and could only understand a few simple commands. She appeared to have no comprehension of grammar. However, when tested at the hospital, Genie was found to have normal hearing, vision, and eye–hand co-ordination.

Genie was placed with a foster family who treated her much as they would a normal child. She began to develop speech, following a normal course of language development but with marked differences. After seven years of language acquisition, Genie continued to have articulation problems. She used two hundred words before she began making two-word combinations. She did not ask questions spontaneously and she demonstrated inconsistencies in word order. After many years of working with Genie, language therapists concluded that failure to acquire language during the normal period makes development laborious and incomplete, but that the similarities between delayed and normal acquisition outweigh the differences (de Villiers and de Villiers, 1978).

Speech development begins with the first sound following the birth cry and ends with full articulatory control. Infants begin to experiment with sound in the early months of life and increase their sound-making capacity in conjunction with other aspects of development, specifically neural, motor, and social. In the very early stages, speech and motor development are seen as occurring in a synchronous fashion so that acquisition follows an orderly progression, with advances in speech and motor skills intertwined to a considerable extent.

Newborns have a limited range of vocalizations. They cry, burp, cough, and make a few other sounds. For the later development of language, cooing is the most important. *Cooing* is the production of clear vowels, often in isolation. By their eighth week, infants can usually produce various of these vowel sounds. As the infant approaches the six-month mark, the nature of cooing changes and consonant–vowel patterns begin to appear. This incorporation of vowel and consonant sounds is known as babbling—random sound play of almost infinite variety.

Babbling is an almost universal response during infancy and does not seem to require exposure to language or other environmental auditory input. Even infants who are deaf babble, although they do not babble in the same way; their babbling is substantially delayed and these sounds usually stop around one year of age (Oller and Eilers, 1988; Pettito and Marenette, 1991; Stoel-Gammon and Otomo, 1986). The exceptions to the universal nature of babbling behaviour are children who are autistic or neurologically damaged, who may not babble at all.

There is considerable controversy over the relationship between babbling and later speech. Most researchers now believe that babbling and early speech are one continuous phenomenon (Gleason, 1985; Vihman, 1986) and that the babbling stage is a period of "tuning up" and establishing the necessary integrations between hearing/listening and sound production. Even if the sounds of babbling don't approximate speech, the intonation of babbling does. Babbling also helps to develop the musculature of the lips and the mouth necessary for the later articulation of speech sounds (Mysak, 1982). Further, children begin to babble the sounds unique to their own language. By six months of age, infants in English-speaking homes have different auditory maps than do those in Swedish-speaking homes (Begley, 1996).

At the same time that infants begin to babble, they also show the first indications of comprehension. Babies at about six months of age begin to associate certain sounds with people, events, and objects in the environment. Infant signals also take on a relatively consistent form and are produced in the expectation that they will promote a consistent response (see Roug, Lundberg, and Lundberg, 1989).

Because they require finer motor control of the tongue and lips, consonant sounds are more difficult to produce than vowel sounds. Once infants are using consonants in their babbling, they attempt to imitate adult sounds. At about eight months of age, infants begin to use **echolalic speech**—speech that is an immediate imitation of that of some other speaker. Soon infants move into the jargon stage; they begin to imitate adults consistently and are able to reproduce the intonation patterns or melodies of the language they hear.

At around one year of age, two new developments occur—expressive intonation in babbling and first words. By 10 or 11 months children are babbling in sentences, combining several incomprehensible "words" and uttering them with correct inflections (Reich, 1986).

At the same time, children are having a great many experiences with listening to language, and they rapidly become adept at discerning meaning from contextual as well as voice clues. Children show comprehension of words; they learn to follow simple directions and associate many environmental clues with speech that they have heard and with gestures (Acredolo and Goodwyn, 1988).

Then, after months of coaxing and prompting the meaningless babble of their babies, parents are rewarded by the emergence of the first word. First words emerge when the infant's motor system for speech production has become co-ordinated with breath control and the movements of lips and tongue. The age for first words ranges from nine to nineteen months for normal children. As children move into using single words, there is a corresponding decrease in babbling.

Children's first single-word utterances are remarkably efficient and maximally communicative. The speech is termed **holophrasic** because a single word is used to express a more complex idea. Although the first words may differ markedly from adult pronunciation, they are likely to be simplifications of adult usage involving the omission of final consonants, the reduction of consonant clusters, the omission of unstressed syllables, or the reduplication of syllables (Lindfors, 1987). Single words are used for naming favourite toys or foods, family members, or pets, and to make requests, comments, and enquiries. Children also incorporate single-word approximations of frequently used adult phrases such as "all gone" or "bad boy."

Several weeks after the first word, vocabulary begins to grow quite rapidly as new words are learned daily. Children learn to produce about fifty words before they string them together. Between 18 and 24 months of age, they begin to combine words. These early phrases (presentences) are the precursors of true sentences. For example, the child may express phrases such as: "Me Mike," "Bump table," "Daddy no," "Car now," or "No more milk." Children show a wide range of variation in the number of presentences they use. Some children use only a few; others as many as a thousand (Byrne and Shervanian, 1977).

The sentence is the key landmark in language acquisition. The first true sentences used by small children are described as **telegraphic speech** because they resemble a telegram in that only the essential aspects of the message, those possessing meaning, are included. In these utterances, children begin to use syntax and morphology. They also use inflections to signify plurality, possession, verb tense, subject–verb agreement, and comparative and superlative forms of adjectives. Children at this stage also use function words such as *in* and *on,* and the articles *a, an,* and *the.*

By the time they are using simple sentences, at about two years of age, children are about 70 to 80 percent intelligible in their speech. However, the full development of all of the sounds of English is a slow process. It is not until they are about eight years old that children are able to produce all the speech sounds: vowels, consonants, diphthongs, and blends.

By three years of age, most children demonstrate the construction of simple affirmative–declarative sentences. They put together a noun phrase for a subject and a verb phrase for a predicate (Elliot, 1981). As syntax develops, the child learns how to change word order and add and replace words to express more complex grammatical relationships. These changes are called *transformations*; as syntax becomes more complex, many transformations are used within the same utterances.

In first using language, young children tend to regularize the language because they have not yet learned the exceptions. A small child is likely to say, "He runned," or "He hurt his self." As well, small children often reach beyond the borders of word meaning and overextend their word usage, as in the little boy who calls every animal a doggie.

By the age of four, most children have achieved a great deal of language maturity. They have usually mastered the basic structures of their language and have developed an array of conversational skills that enable them to engage in extensive social and play interactions with their peers and others in the environment. Pronunciation improves as children gain greater control over the speech mechanisms. Speech is now more than 90 percent intelligible. Children still have difficulty with /r/, /s/, /j/, and /z/, and blends such as /ch/ and /sh/. The last English sound that most children acquire is the /zh/, as in *leisure* and *measure.*

By the time they arrive at school at about five years of age, children have a firm linguistic base, with a sophisticated grasp of semantic and syntactic rules, and an ever-expanding vocabulary. Six-year-olds are sophisticated language users. They can not only talk better, but they have become aware of how language is used. They can recognize its nuances, and begin to take delight in jokes and riddles that rely on ambiguity (de Villiers and de Villiers, 1978).

Compared to language during the preschool years, language during the school years is complex and sophisticated. In school-aged children, the developmental emphasis moves from semantics and syntax to metalinguistics and pragmatics. Once in school, children require a variety of language functions, a greater variety of discourse styles and organization, more abstract vocabulary, more complex syntax, and the ability to reflect on all the aspects of language (metalinguistics) (Westby, 1992). They learn to recognize instructional discourse—the language that gives them information about the curriculum and feedback on their efforts in mastering it.

During middle childhood, children improve in every subsystem of language. They begin to use a number of complex grammatical forms that did not appear in their earlier speech, and correct many of their syntactical errors. They use past participles such as *eaten* and perfect tense such as *has been,* personal pronouns, and passive voice. They develop wider **metalinguistic skills** and the ability to think about language; for example, nine-year-olds are more likely than five-year-olds to recognize grammatical errors in sentences and to be able to correct them. They also use the prepositions *as, if, so,* and *because* more accurately than earlier, although full development does not occur until later. Prepositions such as *although* and *therefore* don't come until the late elementary years or early adolescence.

Speech and Language Difficulties

Learning to communicate and understand the communication of others is one of the biggest challenges young children face. It is little surprise, then, that delays and disorders in speech and language are the most common and varied disabilities that teachers of young children will encounter.

Communication disorders encompass a wide range of problems in speech, language, and hearing. Within this generic classification, we find speech disorders and language delays and disorders. Speech problems include delayed onset of speech, speech usage below age-level expectations, oddities in articulation, peculiar usage of grammar, stuttering, unusual intonations or voice quality, paucity of speech, inability to recall familiar words, poor self-expression, or total absence of speech. Language disorders include delayed language, different language, deviant language, or even no language. Typically, language disorders are more complex in identification, diagnosis, and remediation than are speech problems. Table 4-1 lists some signs and effects of communication disorders.

The overlap between speech and language is considerable. For clarity, however, we describe speech and language disorders separately.

Definitions of Language Problems

Language problems refer to a range of difficulties with the linguistic code, or with the rules for linking the symbols and the symbol sequences. Children who demonstrate significant lags but whose language is still progressing according to the stages of normal language development are said to have **language delays**. Children with language delays characteristically

Table 4-1 Signs and effects of communication disorders

Disorder	Signs	Effects
Language delay	More than six months behind norm in reaching language milestones	Slower in all the elements of language acquisition and usage
Language disorders	May show impaired comprehension and poor verbal expression	Failure to understand instructions; withdrawal from group situations
Aphasia	Impaired reception or production of oral language	Failure to understand speech or to produce meaningful sentences
Apraxia	Inability to sequence the muscle movements needed for speech	Failure to produce meaningful speech
Articulation disorders	Abnormal production of speech sounds; speech not typical of chronological age	May be ridiculed by peers; may have decoding and comprehension problems with respect to specific words
Dysfluency	Impaired fluency and rhythm	Peer ridicule, oral difficulties
Voice disorders	Abnormal vocal quality, pitch, loudness, or duration	Self-confidence may suffer; withdrawal
Orofacial defects	Variety of clefts, such as cleft lip or cleft palate	May have problems in feeding, speech, or respiration
Dysarthria	Paralysis of the muscles associated with speech	Distorted speech

use language infrequently; by the time they reach preschool age, they talk approximately half as much as their peers and are much less responsive to inquiries from teachers and peers (see Roth, McCaul, and Barnes, 1993).

Language disorders are more complex than language delays. As defined by the American Speech and Hearing Association (1982), **language disorders** refer to impairment or deviant development of comprehension or of the use of a spoken, written, or other symbol system. These disorders may involve form, content, function, or any combination of these. Form refers to phonological, morphological, and syntactical elements. Content is semantics, and function refers to pragmatics.

Prevalence of Language Problems

Researchers and practitioners are no more adept at estimating the number of students with language delays and disorders than they are at pinpointing numbers for other forms of disability. The prevalence issue is particularly confused for language problems because:

- Researchers disagree on definitional and classification systems. Many types of language disorders remain ambiguous and controversial; a consensus has not been reached about the patterns of subtypes of language impairments or the criteria for classification.

- Many other terms are used to describe language disorders. These include *aphasia, dysphasia, communicatively impaired,* and *language learning disabled.* Some clinicians prefer the terms *aphasia* or *dysphasia* because they suggest fairly specific conditions. Others prefer the use of the general term *language disabled.*

- Some researchers (e.g. Shames and Wiig, 1990) define a language disorder as a form of speech disorder. Of children with speech disorders, they claim that three to five percent have language disabilities. Others (e.g. de Villiers and de Villiers, 1978) define language problems as separate from speech disorders. They estimate that 12 percent of children with communication problems have language delays or disorders.

- Surveys of language problems are often based on interviews of questionable validity, and there is likely a tendency to under-report the presence of communication disorders.

- Children in other categories of exceptionality often have language problems. For example, students who are learning disabled more often than not demonstrate deviations or delays in language; children who are intellectually disabled do not develop language commensurate with their intellectual ability; language problems are the chief difficulty of children who are hearing impaired.

As far as prevalence is concerned, the best we can say is that the overall number for communication disorders of all types may be as high as 12 to 15 percent, and speech and language disorders are estimated at between five and eight percent of school-aged children ("Children with communication…," 1995; Spitz, Tallal, Flax, Benasich, 1997).

Of all children with language disabilities, about two-thirds are boys (Silva, 1980). As well, there is an increase in communication disorders in people over the age of 40 as a result of stroke and other conditions.

Classification of Language Problems

Communication disorders in general are usually classified according to their symptoms, their causes, or their subtypes. This classification is shown in Table 4-2.

Specifically, language problems relate to disorders in the recognition and understanding of spoken language or in the ability to formulate well-organized grammatical sentences. As we noted, children may be characterized as having delayed or disordered language, a distinction that depends on the type, intensity, and duration of the difficulties.

Language disorders may also be classified as receptive or expressive. *Receptive disorders* are those that interfere with the comprehension of spoken language; *expressive disorders* are those that affect the formulation of grammatical utterances. Language disorders in children frequently combine both receptive and expressive problems. They range in severity from mild language learning difficulties to profoundly debilitating disorders.

Delayed Language Development

A child with delayed language development learns language in an orderly progression but more slowly and less proficiently than normal age peers. Minor delays in language development may

Table 4-2 Classification of communication disorders

Symptoms	Causes	Types
phonological disorders	organic-show a demonstrable pathology	language delay
articulation disorders		language disorder
voice disorders	functional—no identifiable pathology	aphasia
fluency disorders		expressive disorder
orofacial		receptive disorder
dysarthria		
dyspraxia		
language disorders		

be caused by generalized immaturity rather than a pervasive language problem. Clinicians sometimes use the "rule of six" in defining language delays; that is, if a child's language development lags six months behind what is considered to be normal, the child is said to have a delay.

Many young children who show minor delays catch up with their peers by the time they are five or six. Other children with language delays may not close the gap in functioning.

Language Deviations (Disorders)

Children who are language impaired or disordered show a developmental language disorder in the absence of other potentially contributing conditions (Casby, 1997). Some of these children show such difficulties in developing language in a normal progression that they may never attain adult levels. Others with language disorders may demonstrate bizarre language behaviour. The great majority meet such difficulties with acquisition that they require structured and systematic intervention. Another group show deviant language secondary to other disabling conditions.

Aphasia

Aphasia is a condition in which a child's primary impairment is the inability to communicate effectively with verbal language because of comprehension and/or production difficulties. Aphasia may be developmental (often referred to as dysphasia) or acquired. Children with developmental aphasia show severe delays in the development of receptive and expressive language but do not suffer from any apparent additional disabling conditions (Eisenson and Ingram, 1972).

Acquired aphasia refers to conditions (trauma) that occur after language has been developed. Acquired aphasia is a loss in linguistic ability that usually results from brain damage arising from serious illness, trauma to the head, or stroke. Verbal output and understanding are diminished but not always altogether absent (Leonard, 1982). Generally, children under eight years of age make excellent recoveries from aphasia (Zemlin, 1990; see also Chapter 12 on Traumatic Brain Injury).

Aphasia is also classified as receptive or expressive. Receptive aphasia is the inability to understand speech symbols. Children with receptive aphasia appear to talk in a free-flowing manner, but their words are incomprehensible. Expressive aphasia manifests itself as trouble remembering words (*dysnomia*), blocking on a word, and hesitating often when speaking. Severe global aphasia (both expressive and receptive present) refers to a condition where individuals experience a variety of other perceptual problems, even though they have normal physical sight and hearing (Byrne and Shervanian, 1977).

Etiology of Language Problems

Many factors account for language problems. The most prominent are brain dysfunction and psychological problems. Neurological dysfunction underlies the most severe types of speech and language disorders.

There are at least three well-established major language areas in the left hemisphere of the brain. The major sites for language and speech, Wernicke's area and Broca's area, are connected by a thick band of fibres. The standard model for language holds that language making and comprehension arise in Wernicke's area and then travel via the pathway to Broca's, where they call up the program that causes the phrases to be spoken (Phillips, 1990).

Damage to the speech/language centres of the brain can lead to aphasia or generalized communication disorders with varying characteristics depending on the site of the lesion. Head injuries, especially from motor vehicle accidents and diseases like encephalitis, are the most common causes of aphasia in children, with stroke the most common cause in adults (Holland, Swindell, and Ruinmuth, 1990).

Disruptions in early social interactions may contribute to the particular difficulties experienced by some children. Language disorders may be exacerbated by the child's interactions with the family. Children who are neglected, for example, show delays in language development (Allen and Wasserman, 1985).

Children with other disabilities are doubly disadvantaged because the original disability may lead to secondary language problems. Children with disabilities may have fewer opportunities to learn the social, play, and communication skills that are unique to and emerge from child–child social interchange (Guralnick, 1986) and from adult–child interaction. They may hear less language than other children; adults tend to speak less to non-verbal or low-verbal children but to talk more for them. Parents of children with language disorders also engage in fewer play and language activities. Mothers claim their children do not enjoy these games, but reluctance to interact seems reciprocal (Leonard, 1982).

Studies of children with Down syndrome, for example, suggest that their language acquisition and development is essentially similar to the language development of non-retarded children (Tager-Flusberg, Calkins, Nolin, Baumberger, Anderson, and Chadwick-Deas, 1990). They follow the same general path in acquiring language, but their language lags behind their non-verbal cognitive abilities and may proceed at a slower rate. In social interactions with their mothers, infants with Down syndrome show atypical interactive behaviours when compared with normal infants matched for mental age (Coggins and Morrison, 1981), and this may contribute to their language delays. Other studies have found that mothers of three-month-old infants with minor facial anomalies (cleft lip and palate) were less active during interactions with their infants than were mothers of normal infants (Barden, Ford, Jensen, Rogers-Salyer, and Salyer, 1989).

Speech Disorders

There is a huge variety of **speech disorders**, problems encountered in the oral production of language. All speech disorders, however, have one thing in common—an impairment of verbal communication such that the intelligibility of spoken language is reduced. That is, "Speech is abnormal when it deviates so far from the speech of other people that it calls attention to itself, interferes with communication, or causes the speaker or his listeners to be distressed" (Van Riper and Emerick, 1990, p. 34).

Speech disorders should not be confused with the speech errors that all young children make when learning to talk. In small children, mispronunciations and dysfluencies are common; children are about eight years of age before they are relatively stable in the sounds of the English language. Even then, about 10 percent of eight-year-old children still have some trouble with /s/, /z/, /v/, /th/, and /zh/ (Rathus, 1988).

Mispronunciations and dysfluencies only become disorders when they persist as characteristics in the speech of children who should have acquired certain sounds. We would worry more, for example, about the seven-year-old who talks about his "Wittle wellow wabbit" than the child of the same age who could not get her tongue around the /zh/ sound in *leisure* and *measure*.

Prevalence of Speech Disorders

In concert with language problems, reliable figures on the prevalence of speech disorders among children are difficult to obtain. This happens for several reasons:

- Criteria and definitions of communication disorders vary.

- Many speech problems, such as articulation problems, simply disappear as children mature. When minor delays are due to general immaturity, most children catch up with their peers without special intervention.

- Prevalence varies according to age. Milisen (1971) estimates that 12 to 15 percent of children in kindergarten to grade four suffer speech problems. In grades five to eight, the proportion drops to four to five percent and this remains constant after grade eight unless treatment intervenes.

- Speech problems are more common among boys than girls, especially in the early grades (Eisenson, 1971), and this is particularly true in the case of stuttering.

In 1986, 17 percent of Canadian children aged 5 to 14 with disabilities were reported to have a speech disorder (Nessner, 1990). Of speech disorders, articulation problems are the most usual type, accounting for approximately 75 percent of all speech disorders.

Clefts occur in approximately one in every 750 live births (Moran and Pentz, 1995). Incidence rates are higher among Native Americans and Asians, lower among Blacks (McWilliams, Morris, and Shelton, 1990). Among Black babies, the ratio is one in every 1 000 to 1 500. Usually more males than females are affected, except in the rare condition of a cleft palate only, in which case more females are affected.

Clear prevalence figures are also available for stutterers, who make up about one percent of the entire population.

Classification of Speech Disorders

There are many ways to classify speech disorders. For the sake of clarity and simplicity, we focus on specific major areas—phonological and articulation problems, voice disorders, problems with speech flow (dysfluency), orofacial defects, and problems associated with muscle control.

Articulation Disorders

The terms *articulation disorder* and *phonological disorder* are often used synonymously although they refer to slightly different problems. Phonological difficulties are present if a person does not understand how to use speech sounds according to linguistic rules and to communicate meaning accurately. When a child has a sound and pronounces it correctly in some contexts but not in others, the child has a phonological problem. Children with phonological impairments are aware of the effect of their errors on a listener's comprehension and will make adjustments to enhance verbal comprehension (Owens 1991).

Articulation problems are not related to use but to ability. With a phonological disorder, a child may have but not use a sound; with an articulation disorder, a child cannot actually make or produce a sound. Speech sounds are incorrect because of changes in the placement and manner of articulators. With a lisp, for example, the child's tongue is misplaced and says /th/ instead of /s/.

Some articulation errors result from problems such as cleft palate, but in the large majority of cases the disorders appear to result simply from deficiencies in learning (Winitz, 1975). When the child was first learning speech, for example, there may have been inadequate co-ordination of oral and facial muscles that eventually became habitual.

Articulation disorders are characterized by omissions, substitutions, distortions, and additions of speech sounds which may occur in the initial, medial, or final position in a word. The most commonly misarticulated sounds are /s/, /z/, voiceless /th/ as in *bath*, /r/, /l/, /sh/, and /j/ as in *judge* (Gearheart, Mullen, and Gearheart, 1993).

Omission errors are those in which one or more sounds are left out of words. Omissions occur most frequently with blended sounds, such as /bl/,/pl/, /pr/, /st/, /dr/, and /tr/. When words begin with a blend, children may drop one sound so that *smell* becomes *mell*, *break* is *reak*, *play* is *pay*, and *school* is *kool*.

Substitutions of speech sounds occur when one consonant is replaced by another: /b/ for /v/, /w/ for /r/, or /w/ for /l/, or *thunshine* for *sunshine*. A lisp is a substitution where /th/ is used for /s/ or /z/. Some children may substitute sounds in some words but not in others. A child may be able to say the word *yes* correctly, but substitute /l/ for /y/ in the word *yellow*.

Distortions involve deviations from normal speech sounds, often caused by placing the tongue or lips in the wrong position for the production of a particular sound, as *shoup* for *soup* or *ideer* for *idea*. Addition of sounds refers to the adding of a sound to a word. The extra sounds are usually added between blended sounds such as *terain* for *train*.

Voice Disorders

Voice disorders are probably the least understood of all the various communication disorders. A voice that lacks power, is unpleasant, or abuses the vocal mechanism is likely to be considered defective (Perkins, 1978).

Voice disorders include hoarseness (too nasal or rough), breathiness, loudness (too loud or too soft), pitch (too high or too low), and sudden breaks in pitch. They are frequently combined with other speech problems to form a complex communication disorder. Deviations may impair both speaking and singing.

The most common deviations in pitch seen by speech and language clinicians are levels that are too high or low and levels that are monotonous with little variation of pitch (Moore, 1986). Children who do not speak loudly enough for their needs may suffer from hearing loss, an organic disorder, or reticence about speaking. Some children do not know how to use a "big" voice without abusing the vocal mechanism (Moore, 1986).

For some people, pitch problems are caused by too small a larynx (too high) or too large a larynx (too low). Some may result from overall slow maturation. In children, however, most voice disorders are functional, related to poor learning of voice control. Children who scream or talk loudly are in danger of abusing their vocal cords (Perkins, 1978). Vocal abuse can lead to vocal nodules or polyps that may have to be removed surgically.

The child who "talks through the nose" has hypernasal speech. This may result from a cleft palate, or from partial paralysis of the soft palate rendering the necessary closure of the nasal passages impossible.

Dysfluency

Fluency is the smoothness with which sounds, syllables, words, and phrases flow together; the opposite, dysfluency, describes conditions in which the flow of speech is interrupted with blocking, repetitions, or prolongations of sounds, words, phrases, or syllables. *Stuttering*, the major subcategory of dysfluency (speech flow) disorder, affects approximately one percent of the entire population. Two to ten times more males than females stutter. The condition is not related to social class or cognitive functioning; stuttering is found among all ethnic and socio-economic groups. Many famous people were stutterers, including Aesop, Aristotle, Demosthenes, Charles I, Winston Churchill, Charles Darwin, and George VI (Taylor, 1976).

As a serious communication problem, stuttering is both complicated and multidimensional. In terms of severity, it should be seen on a continuum, rather than as a limited set of behaviours. At one end is normal dysfluency, which is not stuttering but a part of speech development in young children at about three years of age. The progression is then to primary stuttering, which is characterized by breaks in speech caused by repetitions of syllables and sounds, and sometimes prolongations, but which is not usually accompanied by physical signs. The final stage is secondary stuttering, which is terse, non-fluent speech in which the rate and rhythm are severely affected. Secondary stutterers show symptoms such as eye blinking, head jerking, facial grimaces and tension, other types of body distortions, muscular tension, and forcing when they try to speak. Secondary stuttering is much harder to overcome than primary stuttering.

In terms of age of onset, the earliest time of onset of stuttering is generally around eighteen months, just when children begin to speak in short phrases. However, a child may begin to stutter at any time; the mean age of onset is 3.6 years and the incidence of onset declines each year from 18 months on (Bloodstein, 1975). In some cases, stuttering progresses from a sporadic to a chronic problem. In others, it spontaneously disappears by adolescence; a greater number of females than males recover spontaneously. In another group, stuttering disappears, only to resurface later.

Cluttering

Cluttered speech should not be confused with stuttering. *Cluttering* involves rapid, jerky, stumbling speech with marked omissions. Speakers may clip off speech sounds, omit sounds, and have rapid-fire bursts of speech. Cluttered speech shows excessive speed combined with disorganized sentence structure and articulation problems. It lacks appropriate phrasing or grouping of words within an utterance and is difficult to understand. In severe cases, the speech is confused, disorganized, and even chaotic (Van Riper and Emerick, 1990).

Muscle Control

Dysarthria refers to a group of speech disorders resulting from disturbed muscular control over the speech mechanisms (La Pointe, 1982). The articulation of speech sounds is disturbed when there is a partial or complete paralysis of the muscles associated with speech. When a child with dysarthria tries to talk, consonant sounds are distorted and efforts at speech may not be successful. Indeed, the harder the child tries to speak, the more difficult speech becomes.

Apraxia is the inability to program, position, and sequence the muscle movements involved in speech. The child with apraxia can produce the movements involved in articulation, but often fails to combine these movements into meaningful speech (Byrne and Shervanian, 1977).

Orofacial Defects

Clefts are known as midline defects. They are only one of the wide variety of craniofacial anomalies, but they are also one of the most common and generally least severe. There are several patterns of clefting—for example, cleft mandible, double mouth, cleft tongue, cleft uvula, undeveloped tongue, cleft lip, cleft palate, and cleft lip and palate (Shah, 1985). Clefts also vary in severity. A cleft lip can range from a slight notch in the vermillion (coloured portion of the lip) to a complete separation of the lip extending up and into the nose. When there is a cleft lip, the alveolar ridge (upper gum ridge) may also be separated. Lip clefts can occur on one or both sides. Clefts may also be part of a disorder such as Crouzon's disease or Treacher Collins syndrome, both which are accompanied by facial anomalies.

The palate separates the respiratory and the digestive systems. Many children with clefts are born with a gap in the roof of the mouth (palate) which opens into the nasal cavity. Children with unrepaired cleft lip/palate have difficulties in the feeding process because of interruptions in the rhythm of feeding, or in mastication, swallowing, choking, and regurgitation.

There may be *malocclusion* (abnormality in the coming together of the teeth). As well, between 25 and 60 percent of children with cleft palates also have a degree of hearing loss due to intermittent occurrence of middle ear disease (Harrison and Philips, 1971).

Mutism

The condition where there is no voice is known as *aphonia*. This is different from **mutism**, the total absence of speech. Mutism is a rare condition, related to severe emotional, neurological, or sensory deficit. The term **elective mutism** describes emotionally disturbed children who do not speak or who speak only in certain circumstances. Elective mutism may be associated with a traumatic event and is always symptomatic of a deep disturbance of psychological functioning.

Etiology of Speech Disorders

Most often, children with articulation and voice disorders do not differ from others in anatomical variables, auditory variables, intelligence, or personality. Nor is there any clear evidence that stutterers are biologically different from non-stutterers (see Research Notes).

Research Notes

Stuttering

One of the most difficult things about stuttering is the inability to confidently point to a precise cause. The search for causes is long-standing and the assumptions underlying the research, theories, and therapies related to stuttering range from obvious to obscure. Reich (1986) points out that twentieth-century explanations include lack of cerebral dominance, neurotic symptoms arising out of psychodynamic conflicts developed in early childhood, biochemical causes, perseveration, lateral auditory dominance, laryngeal dysfunction, and auditory feedback dysfunction.

Genetic predisposition is a popular, but disputed, explanation. Some studies lean to learning rather than genetics. For example, Farber (1981) studied ninety-five sets of identical twins raised apart. A genetic predisposition would find pairs of stutterers, but only five individuals in the group stuttered, and in each case only one member of the pair stuttered. On the other hand, clear evidence of genetic transmissions of susceptibility have been reported since the 1960s. Stuttering is found in families as shown by analysis of pedigrees (family trees). For men who stutter, the chances of their children having the condition is 9 percent for daughters and 22 percent for sons. For stuttering women, the figures are 17 percent for daughters and 36 percent for sons (Andrews, Craig, Feyer, Hoddinott, Howie, and Neilson, 1983).

Therefore, no one can be confident about the precise causes of stuttering (or about current treatment of the disorder). Probably the most useful approach is to view stuttering as the result of multiple causative factors including potential constitutional vulnerability, biochemical and physiological factors, the cumulative results of faulty learning, and resultant apprehension and anxiety related to speech.

In correction, current practices tend to focus on three broad groupings of etiology. Some speech pathologists regard stuttering as a symptom of physical impairment or instability; others look at it as a symptom of personal maladjustment or emotional instability; still others are of the opinion that it is symptomatic of neither but simply a form of learned behaviour found in normal individuals.

When stuttering is regarded as a symptom of an underlying emotional problem, psychotherapeutic intervention is in order. The objective of treatment is to eliminate stuttering or decrease its effect. Treatments that focus on organic causes include air flow techniques—breathing manoeuvres that release the laryngeal spasm (a locking of the vocal cords as speaking begins)—together with stress reduction and procedures that build confidence and develop self-motivation (Schwartz, 1988). Biofeedback, counselling, and speech therapy are also widely used. Free-token response–cost programs have been used successfully to modify stuttering during speech therapy (Salend and Andress, 1984).

Whatever the intervention, the trend is to attempt to remediate the condition early. Clinicians stress the elimination of stuttered speech at the time it first appears (Onslow, Costa, and Rue, 1990). Researchers hold that optimal intervention involves early detection and prevention, and that there is less risk involved in overdiagnosis than underdiagnosis of stuttering (Moore and Perkins, 1990).

Structural inadequacies are a major cause of speech disorders in children. These may be structural inadequacies in the vocal folds (larynx), tongue, teeth, lips, palate, and resonating cavities. Most defects of this type are of a developmental nature, although they can result from physical injury or disease.

Damage to or maldevelopment of the central and/or peripheral nervous system is another major cause. Dysarthria, for example, results from a fundamental disturbance in the movement or motoric function brought about by damage to the nervous system. Children with cerebral palsy often suffer from dysarthria. The motor impairment that affects the lips, tongue, jaw, and soft palate hinders the intelligibility of their speech (La Pointe, 1982). Inadequacy of the hearing mechanism, causing hearing impairment, is a third major cause of speech disorders.

The causes of clefts are not known, but it is generally agreed that most result from an interaction of genetic and environmental influences (Moran and Pentz, 1995). Numerous villains have been suggested, including alcohol, acetylsalicylic acid, certain foods, and an excess or lack of vitamin A (Shah, 1985).

Stuttering is known to have both biochemical and physiological indicators. There is also clear evidence of genetic transmissions of susceptibility that have been reported since the 1960s. Analysis of pedigrees—family trees—have found that much stuttering is familial (Ambrose and Yairi, 1997).

Identification and Assessment of Speech and Language Problems

We must identify delays and disorders in speech and language as early as possible because such disorders affect other areas of development, impact negatively on social integration, and hinder educational and personal achievement. Because language and speech are so intimately connected, assessment usually includes both areas. However, language is far more complex both in assessment and remediation. Robert Owens, Jr. (1991) describes the evaluation of language as "part science and part art" (p. 290). This statement reflects the multiple contexts in which communication assessment should be implemented, the variability in children's functioning, the vast range of areas to be assessed, and a relative shortage of appropriate tools. Moreover, the types of measures used, the domains sampled, and the targeted skills are quite different for children with mild delays and for those with severe disabilities of which language is only one component. Students with severe or multiple disabilities may be functioning at prelinguistic or minimally linguistic levels (see Chapter 14).

Assessing Language Problems

Language problems are generally assessed by a team comprising a psychologist, a speech clinician, a physician, an educator, and possibly a neurologist. All physical and psychological disturbances to normal language development, such as hearing loss or low IQ, must first be ruled out. After that, assessment involves both linguistic and cognitive skills, since both are necessary for language competence.

A comprehensive assessment consists of:

- An interview with the family to gather all pertinent developmental and behavioural data.
- Measures of cognitive ability (IQ tests) and achievement data when the child is school aged.
- Formal tests to evaluate a child's language abilities and disabilities and to determine the presence or absence of communication disorders. Standardized language tests are available for both screening and diagnosis.
- Informal assessments, including a sample of the child's language. A spontaneous or elicited language sample should consist of at least 50 and preferably 100 utterances.

Assessing Speech Disorders

Assessment of articulatory, voice, and fluency disorders is undertaken by a speech/language therapist in the school or in a clinic setting.

Articulation assessment is a rapid and effective way of obtaining a sample of a child's speech. In its crudest form, the articulation test is a test of a child's ability to pronounce correctly, in the view of the investigator, a certain number of words. Children under age four are usually tested on their ability to echo or imitate the clinician's model. Children over four are usually asked to name either objects or pictures. Older children may be asked to read words or sentences or to describe objects (Byrne and Shervanian, 1977). During the assessment, the clinician may test the child's production of phonemes in isolation and in the initial, medial, and final position in words. The clinician also tries to determine whether there is a consistency in the child's error patterns.

Developmental Consequences

Language is inextricably intertwined with our mental life—our perceiving, remembering, attending, comprehending, and thinking—in short, all of our attempts to make sense of our experiences with the world. All types of speech and language disorders affect the ease with which children can communicate with people in their environment. Children who communicate poorly, whether because of speech problems or language disorders, may be hindered in their academic performance and in almost every aspect of functioning.

Cognitive Development

Children with language disorders often perform within normal limits on non-verbal intelligence tests (Leonard, 1981). Even children with aphasia, dysphasia, and apraxia, caused by a disturbance of brain function, are often near or within normal range in most other respects (Mysak, 1980).

However, many cognitive abilities are clearly language-dependent and children with language problems tend to be more rigid and literal in their thinking. They lack the flexibility required for pretending, for playing word games, for laughing at riddles and jokes, and for effective social interaction. Children with language disabilities may continue to overextend words into inappropriate contexts. For instance, a child may call all liquids that can be poured into a glass "juice" as opposed to milk, water, or soda. Or the child may learn to call all articles of clothing that have sleeves "sleeves" rather than shirts, sweaters, or coats because something about the sleeve is meaningful to him or her. Symbolic play in children with language impairments is different from that of normally developing children, although the differences seem quite small (Casby, 1997).

Children with clefts may exhibit delayed language development and are more likely to have language-based learning disabilities (Moran and Pentz, 1995). As well, delayed articulation is not uncommon in children with clefts who may have difficulty building and sustaining enough air pressure in the mouth to make pressure consonants such as /p/, /b/, /s/, /z/, and /ch/. Many of the children who exhibit delayed language development are more likely to have language-based learning disabilities (Moran and Pentz, 1995).

Neurological disorders such as aphasia have more severe effects. Aphasia in children negatively impacts on comprehension, the formation of grammatical utterances, word usage, and the expression of meaning (Byrne and Shervanian, 1977).

Academic Achievement

As one would expect, children with language problems perform poorly in those aspects of learning that rely on language. Literacy skills suffer because children with problems in language acquisition and use invariably have difficulties learning to read. Further, the abstract and symbolic material that becomes important by about grade four makes it increasingly difficult for children with language disorders to cope with academic subjects.

Many students with speech disorders also face difficulties. For example, students with articulation disorders, particularly those with multiple sound errors, also have difficulties with comprehension, syntax, and vocabulary (Bernthal and Bankson, 1981).

Social and Emotional Development

Any degree of disturbance in our communication with others in the environment has an impact on social adjustment. It is not surprising, then, that there is a fairly strong relationship between communication disorders, emotional disorders, and behavioural disorders in children and adolescents (Giddan, Melling, and Campbell, 1996). In some students, more serious psychiatric problems also emerge. As disorders of the development of language are likely to be central to the development of human personality, researchers observe that "There appears to be a strong association between developmental language deficits and severe psychiatric disorders" (Gualtieri, Koriath, Van Bourgondien, and Saleeby, 1983, p. 168).

Children with articulation problems and those with language problems tend to show a high prevalence of behavioural problems (Baker and Cantwell, 1982). Teachers may observe behaviours such as short attention span, excitability, tantrums and solitary behaviour. Some children find it so difficult to communicate that they become frustrated, withdrawn, and depressed. They may withdraw from social contact and talk only when absolutely necessary because of the negative feedback they have received in the past. They use physical means to gain others' attention, by relying on gesture and body language—a shake of the head or a shrug.

The longer people stutter, the more likely they are to have associated emotional problems (Shames and Florance, 1982). In general, stutterers tend to be more anxious, less self-confident, and more socially withdrawn than non-stutterers (Block and Goodstein, 1971). Students may respond to their difficulties with aggression or by denying that they have a problem (Shames and Florance, 1982). Others may avoid situations where talking is expected.

The reactions of others in the environment add to the frustration. For example, young stutterers become rapidly aware of listeners' reactions and often feel embarrassed, guilty, frustrated, and angry. Both elementary and secondary students tend to see classmates who have articulation disorders in a more negative light (Hall, 1991; Silverman and Paulus, 1989). Some children with clefts may meet social discrimination from peers and teachers (Moran and Pentz, 1995).

Intervention with Children Who Have Speech and Language Disorders

Language specialists and educators have developed many new forms of treatment for children with speech and language disorders, both for the classroom and for the clinic. Nevertheless, a guaranteed method to correct speech and language difficulties simply does not exist, and diversity in remediation programs characterizes the status quo.

A range of methods are used depending on the needs of the child, the severity of the disability, the setting for intervention, the targeted skills, and the expertise of the teacher. Here we provide only an overview of approaches used with children with mild and moderate disabilities. We return to the topic of intervention for children with severe disorders in Chapter 14.

Medical Intervention

When speech disorders result from structural defects or inadequacies, medical intervention is often the first step in habilitation. Surgery is used for speech disabilities that result directly from defects of the respiratory, oral, and facial musculature involved in speech production. Corrective and plastic surgery can largely prevent the wide-ranging speech problems associated with cleft palate and other orofacial defects.

Clefts of the primary and secondary palates and velopharyngae (lip and palate) inefficiency require special examinations and treatments by a number of different professionals over many years (Paynter, Jordan, and French, 1990). The lip is typically repaired early in the first year of life. The time for surgical repair of the cleft palate is more variable, but is most commonly performed before the child is two years of age (Moran and Pentz, 1995). When other facial–skeletal anomalies accompany the cleft palate, prostheses designed to facilitate speech are prescribed. Dental surgery may also be necessary.

Therapy

Speech/language pathologists or therapists are concerned with communication, its normal development, and its disorders. They are trained in the evaluation and remedial treatment of speech and language problems in children and adults. In most provinces, a qualified clinician requires a master's degree in speech pathology and a year of closely supervised clinical work. Speech pathologists work as consultants to schools and special education programs; they are also employed in hospitals and rehabilitation centres. The speech/language pathologist works with teachers to identify potential communication disorders, assesses and diagnoses problems, and plans and recommends intervention activities. The pathologist works with children to teach them how to speak and listen effectively and how to overcome the effects of communication disorders. To treat articulation disorders, therapists teach children to listen, recognize, and discriminate consonant sounds; to produce articulated speech sounds; and to retain the memory of speech sounds (Winitz, 1975).

Major areas of emphasis in voice therapy include listening and articulatory adjustments and breath-control training. Breath control includes training to relax and reduce laryngeal tension as well as other specialized techniques (Van Osdol and Shane, 1982).

Although the many studies of the symptoms and treatment of stuttering have not revealed all of the possible underlying causes, many effective therapeutic methods have been developed to treat the problem. Psychotherapy, behaviour modification, and biofeedback are used to reduce the intensity of stuttering or eliminate it (Perkins, 1990). Some therapists combine a variety of techniques, including new therapies such as desensitization, parent–child verbal interaction, and fluency shaping (Shames and Florance, 1982). The Research Notes on stuttering in this chapter outline other major treatments.

Technical Intervention

One successful use of computers in the classroom is to promote social interaction in children with language difficulties. Studies have found higher levels of social interaction and social play from delayed children (McCormick, 1987). Others found that three preschoolers demonstrated significantly more turn taking, pro-social behaviour, and cognitively complex and imaginative verbalizations during a computer activity than during lunch or free play periods (Villarruel, Martin, and Dickson, 1985).

Technology is a boon for individuals unable to use speech. Elaborate computer-driven devices enable children and adults who have language disorders to communicate more complex and subtle messages. These devices offer multiple outputs, such as print-out, screen, or speech synthesized voice. They are easily activated by a variety of volitional movements, including eye control, finger contact, or sipping and puffing on a blow stick. Further technical devices are described in the section on augmentative communication in Chapter 14.

Educational Intervention

Language is the primary medium through which much classroom learning takes place, and the acquisition of socially and academically appropriate forms of both oral and written language in general is seen as one of the principal goals of education (Reagan, 1997). As efficient speech and language underlie academic success, the goal of any language intervention effort is to enhance a child's ability to use language as an effective means of communication in everyday life and to develop academic skills.

A second goal is bolstering peer acceptance in school-aged children. Training is important because various communication skills have been found to predict social acceptance in middle childhood (Dodge, Pettit, McCloskey, and Boron, 1986). Finally, "Understanding and correcting deficiencies of language can improve behaviour and help a child resolve at least some of his emotional dilemmas" (Gualtieri et al., 1983, p. 169).

Inclusion

The key word in recent language intervention trends is *natural*. Natural procedures take place in naturally occurring situations and pay attention to functional communication and conversational skills. As much as possible, settings should be natural environments and all those close to the child—parents, peers, and teacher—should be involved (Bernstein and Tiegerman, 1989; Lahey, 1988). This means that the regular classroom is the most appropriate setting for almost all children who have speech and language difficulties as their sole impairment.

Several reasons underlie the use of natural environments as the best settings for language assessment and training:

- Much language is learned in a social context. Language production is necessarily the result of an interaction between the skills of the speaker and events in the environment, and language is best taught through social interaction and naturally occurring events.

- The problems of generalizing skills are circumvented. A major problem in language training concerns the transfer of learned language from the training setting to the natural environment. The generalization of language skills appears to be more restricted in children with language disorders, and it is uncertain whether language learned in clinical settings will generalize to other environments (Spradlin and Siegel, 1982).

Children with minor speech and language disorders can often receive adequate assistance within the school from a learning-assistance teacher or speech-and-language clinician.

- Persons in the child's natural environment can be the chief intervenors. Teachers and peers facilitate strategies.

- Because training occurs in natural settings, it is bound to be functional, and this enhances the likelihood that new language will be maintained and generalized.

Educational Approaches

All educational approaches attempt to improve a child's linguistic competence. Although some approaches are designed for special classes or clinics, contemporary intervention, as we have just seen, focuses on natural interaction in natural settings—that is, intervention from the teacher in the regular classroom. The procedures used in naturalistic language intervention vary extensively (Hepting and Goldstein, 1996). Research has not indicated which strategy for teaching communication is the most effective. Skilled teachers use descriptive feedback, directing, telling and explaining, question asking, modelling, and prompt and coaching statements. When necessary, they use teacher-mediated and peer-mediated strategies and direct teaching.

Remediation of speech problems specifically is the venue of speech therapists/pathologists, although the classroom teacher should work proactively with the therapist to reinforce elements the child attains in therapy sessions. For language remediation, there are several defined approaches which teachers may follow or from which they may draw components. The major approaches can be grouped as diagnostic–prescriptive, syntax-based, performance-oriented, or interpersonal–interactive (see also Chapter 9).

Diagnostic–prescriptive approaches are designed for specialized settings. There are two forms of the diagnostic–prescriptive approach—the process or ability model and the task analysis model. In the process or ability model, intervention focuses on all the abilities involved in perceiving and discriminating speech, interpreting spoken language, and formulating language and speech. Intervention may also encompass short- and long-term memory, verbal reasoning, word retrieval, and the visual and motor processes involved in speaking, reading, and writing (Wiig, 1982). In the task analysis model, every task involved in speech, language, and communication becomes the focus of intervention. The task analysis approach is often derived from the child's performance on criterion-referenced tests, such as the Clinical Evaluation of Language Functions (CELF) (Semel and Wiig, 1980).

Syntax-based programs may be taught in regular classrooms or special settings. Syntactic disorders seem to respond best to direct teaching, and direct language instruction might be initially used to introduce a new structure that can then be generalized through the use of more interactive techniques.

Programs based on syntax teach the child specific language structures, such as subject, verb, and object, and word order relationships, such as question forms. Studies have shown that these structured language programs are effective with children who are linguistically delayed (Illebrun and Leong, 1981).

A number of commercial tests and programs support syntax-based programs. For example, the Language Assessment, Remediation and Screening Procedures (LARSP) (Crystal, Fletcher, and Garman, 1976) provide a systematic methodology for the description and treatment of syntactical problems. The Fokes Sentence Builder (1976) is another example of a syntax-based remedial language program. SOS—Sound, Order, Sense (Semel, 1970) is designed to help children develop listening skills in order to better comprehend spoken language. Stress is on perception, order, and the sense of what is being said.

Performance-oriented approaches attempt to modify, decrease, or increase language behaviours. They are designed for regular classrooms. Intervention is aimed at overt, measurable disordered communication behaviours. Since much language is learned by imitation, imitation, modelling, and expansion of correct communication behaviours are stressed.

Interpersonal–interactive approaches, also used in regular classrooms, are similar to performance approaches. They aim to strengthen a child's ability to use language and to develop communicative competence. Children learn what language is by learning what language can do. Specific objectives include helping the child to interpret contextual clues, strengthening role-taking and role-playing abilities, and increasing the range of verbal and non-verbal communication styles (Wiig, 1982).

Much of the teaching is incidental—it comes up in normal classroom interactions, rather than in direct instruction. With younger children, teachers use a group of closely interrelated strategies for oral language, which we explain below. Examples are found in Table 4-3.

Table 4-3 Examples of strategies to use in a natural approach to language intervention

Imitation	The teacher may say "Show me," or "You say this now."
Expansion	The child may say "Car go," and the teacher expands it to "Yes, the car goes." Or if the child says, "Camera takes pictures," the teacher can expand to, "Yes, he has a camera to take pictures, like your grandma does." The child may say "In woods," which the adult expands to "Yes, he is in the woods."
Extension	Similar to expansions. The child says "Cat in the Hat" and the adult responds "Yes, that Cat in the Hat is making a big mess." Or if a child says "I miss the bus," the teacher may respond with, "You missed the bus. Were you late for the dentist?"
Paraphrasing	Responding, for example, to "Want ball," with "You want the ball."
Recast sentences	If a child says "That boy hitted me," the teacher responds with "That boy hit you."
Open-ended questions	Examples include, "Why could the man be angry?" "Where is my book?" "Why did the man go to the store?" "Where is he going next?" "Who did the cat scratch? Why?" "What is he going to bring when he plays baseball?" "How many clowns rode on the bicycle?" "How will he get down from the tree?"
Indirect commands	For example, "Tell Tommy what you want."
Praise	"I like how you did that." "That's right!"

Sources: McNeill and Fowler, 1996; Winzer, 1997.

To promote language development, strategies include imitation and modelling. Teachers also use expansions; an expansion is a restatement of what the child has just said, with the addition of information. When teachers or parents use expansions, the complexity of children's language increases more rapidly over time (Hoff-Ginsberg, 1986) because children learn to speak in better sentences by listening; the teacher understands a child's meaning more easily; and children may talk in longer sentences and talk more often. And, when teachers add more words and information, they are expanding a child's comment, which lets the child know that they like to talk to him or her.

In paraphrasing, the adult repeats a statement or question to elicit a reply. Extension follows the child's statement with different words. Using recast sentences involves repeating or restating a child's words in the correct form. Open-ended questions are genuine requests for information requiring more than a "yes" or "no" response. Praise is a statement describing the child's prior verbal or non-verbal communication as correct, acceptable, or good (McNeil and Fowler, 1996; Winzer, 1997).

Curriculum

No special curriculum apart from the above models exists for children with speech and language disorders. Generally, language teaching for delayed children should be based on normal language acquisition processes. Teachers provide the motivation to communicate, many opportunities for teacher–child and child–child interactions, and much peer and adult modelling. They create realistic conversational atmospheres, focus on children's interests, and help them to use language to promote or regulate social interaction and to develop skills that refine listening, attention, and memory. They also stress the language arts curriculum of listening, expressive language, and reading.

SUMMARY

1. Human communication is incredibly complex. As a component of communication, language is a typically human activity. Even though language is one of the most distinctive features of humans, it remains poorly understood.

2. Language is a complex system of symbols and rules for using these symbols. It is the product of all aspects of development—physical, sensory, social, and neurological. Speech is essentially a mechanical production of language.

3. Speech and language disabilities interfere with the ease with which a child interacts with the world. Speech disorders are problems in the articulation of language sounds, voice production, and fluency. Language disorders are problems in the acquisition, comprehension, and formulation of language. Youngsters with language disorders may have the rudiments of a language code but show large gaps in linguistic development and display little consistency in their various deficits.

4. Speech and language problems are a separate category of exceptionality. They also cut across other categories. Many, if not most, children with other disabling conditions also manifest speech and language problems that further hinder their optimal development. Children with hearing impairments, learning disabilities, intellectual disabilities, and severe emotional disturbance often have speech and language problems.

5. With language, all the major developmental milestones are reached in infancy or early childhood.

6. A linguistic environment, an intact cognitive/perceptual system, and normal social interaction all underlie the development of language. If the child does not hear language, has some impairment of the cognitive/perceptual mechanism, or has a troubled family background, then the child's development of language will reflect these problems.

7. Speech development depends on having something to say (language) and the opportunity to say it (social interaction). It also depends on the development of the speech mechanisms and articulators—the pharynx and larynx, the tongue, the palate, the lips and the teeth, and the production and modulation of breath flow.

8. Many types of speech and language disorders remain ambiguous and controversial. They are manifested in a staggering array of distinct forms. Language disorders may manifest themselves in speech and writing, either at the phonological or grammatical level, or both; in the comprehension of specific concepts, or of language structures; or in some combination of these areas. Speech is defective when it is conspicuous, unintelligible, or unpleasant.

9. Dysarthria and aphasia are related to brain dysfunction. Children with clefts may show delayed language and speech development. While the search for definitive causes of stuttering has been extensive, the results have been largely negative.

10. Communication disorders can have painful consequences for all aspects of a child's development. Disorders of speech and language socially isolate those who have them, impoverish their lives, and impact on school success. When children with communication disorders are considered as a group, it becomes evident that they have an increased prevalence of learning problems and psychiatric disorders.

11. Language develops in the framework of family associations, social interactions, and interpersonal relationships. This belief underlies the use of natural environments (regular classrooms) for almost all children with speech and language differences.

In the Classroom

Profile: Bennie

Bennie is seven-and-a-half years old with normal hearing and no deviations in his speech mechanisms. When Bennie is nervous or in a hurry, his speech becomes difficult to understand. He is easier to understand when his sentences or replies are short.

Before referring Bennie for an assessment, the classroom teacher undertook some observations and measures. Bennie's English composition on teacher-selected topics showed a marked academic delay of two years and many writing difficulties at the sentence and discourse levels. Oral language performance likewise showed deficits. However, when a psychologist assessed Bennie, his performance on standardized tests showed a child of average-level abilities.

During a later speech/language assessment, the clinician asked Bennie to name the objects in a series of pictures. Bennie correctly produced all the phonemes in the initial, medial, and final word positions up to approximately the developmental level of a five-year-old. He produced substitutions and distortions of certain sounds, such as /ts/, /s/, and /z/ in all positions. He consistently mispronounced the sounds /s/, /th/, /l/ and blended sounds such as /tr/, /pr/, and /cl/. He could not correctly pronounce /th/ and usually substituted an /f/ sound. He also had problems with /r/ sounds and sometimes substituted /w/ for /l/. Nor was the clinician able to detect a clear /s/ in Bennie's conversational speech. To assess receptive language, the therapist used the Peabody Picture Vocabulary Test. On this test, Bennie scored at the 84th percentile.

The speech clinician, Bennie's teacher, the psychologist, and his parent met to discuss a program for Bennie. Bennie's mother explained that he was the baby of the family, the youngest of four children. His parents both work outside the home and are away all day. The speech therapist explained that speech problems are developmental rather than physiological and respond well to remedial instruction. She felt that Bennie's problems were caused by a combination of immaturity, lack of opportunity to practise speaking, and self-consciousness. Bennie does not have enough chances to talk at home, and his self-consciousness at school further deprives him of necessary practice. She also noted that Bennie knows he does not speak clearly. He told her that he tries hard, but was bashful about speaking because the children at school made fun of him.

The team agreed that Bennie does not need an Individual Education Plan at this time, although he does need strategies to "catch up" in the language arts, such as placing stress on a sight word vocabulary that will circumvent the articulation problems. Far more important right now is individual speech training. The team arranged an hour of speech therapy for Bennie every second day at school. The therapist will teach Bennie how to correctly produce the mis-articulated sounds and give him a great deal of speaking practice.

As he attains new sounds, the teacher will promote correct use and reinforce it in the classroom. She will also ensure that Bennie has many opportunities to use oral language and she will use incidental teaching strategies to improve both his speech and his language. It is hoped that as Bennie gains confidence and improves in oral skills, there will be a positive spill-over to areas such as written language.

* * *

There are three main prongs to Bennie's program: individual speech therapy to learn new speech sounds and improve language, much practice in the broader context of academic and social communication, and remediation in academic areas.

The goal of language intervention efforts for Bennie, as for any child with similar problems, is to enhance his ability to use language as an effective means of communication in everyday life. The goal of training is not absolutely correct grammar or pronunciation. Rather, training should accelerate general communicative development and help Bennie communicate in a way that is understood by others and that seems comfortable for him.

EFFECTS OF SPEECH/LANGUAGE DISABILITIES	TIPS FOR TEACHERS
THE CHILD NEEDS MULTIPLE OPPORTUNITIES FOR ORAL LANGUAGE USE	Use experiential units in which the teacher modifies instruction to focus on tasks such as building things, setting up household tasks, or preparing food. This gives a child constant repetition of specific language.
	Ask questions meaningful to the child in a way that activates the child's thinking and promotes problem-solving. This is one of the most potent methods teachers can use to foster language.
	Arrange classrooms so that there are materials and activities of interest to children. The function of language depends on its effects on the environment. Teachers must set the scene, provide materials, and prompt dialogues that children can use with each other.
	Focus on making language a part of a child's routine.
	Provide access to interesting materials and activities.
	Create realistic conversational atmospheres where speech is valued; language is learned in social interactions.
	Focus on the children's interests.
THE CHILD HAS A RESTRICTED VOCABULARY	Present new words with incidental teaching. Cazden (1988) suggests that word meanings are most easily learned through interactions and conversations with an adult who introduces new words.
	Present new words in many contexts. The likelihood that a child will learn the meaning of a new word from a single exposure in a meaningful context ranges from 5 to 20 percent.
THERE IS A NEED FOR PROACTIVE WORK BETWEEN CLASSROOM TEACHER AND THERAPIST	Work with the therapist to find out what sounds the child is stimulable for (ready to learn). Target these sounds in individual sessions and give the child real-life opportunities to produce them.
THE CHILD NEEDS RECOGNITION AND REINFORCEMENT FOR USING CORRECT FORMS	Use formal reinforcement such as praise or stickers.
	Follow the child's lead and reply to the child's initiations or comments. Communication is maintained by conversational responses, not "good talking." For example, "I saw monkeys" is related to "Monkeys are funny," not "Good talking" (Owens, 1991).
	Use much modelling, imitation, and expansion of the child's utterances as well as paraphrasing, extending, and recasting sentences.

THE CHILD HAS POOR COMPREHENSION OF SPOKEN LANGUAGE	Give directives that are as explict as possible. Avoid using unnecessary words. After giving a direction, have the child repeat it to show comprehension.
	Speak clearly and at a moderate speed to be more easily understood. However, research confirms that rapid sound changes cause dysphasic children problems that impair their ability to identify and discriminate consonants. For these children, speak at a slower rate to improve their comprehension.
	Repeat and reword if the child seems confused.
	Speak at a normal pace and loudness and avoid over-enunciation.
	Stress important points in a lesson with "Watch now," or "Listen carefully."
THE CHILD GIVES SLOWER RESPONSES	Avoid placing pressures on the child to use oral language.
	Avoid speaking for the child.
THE CHILD FEELS EMBARRASSMENT ABOUT POOR PERFORMANCE	Use puppets; young children tend to be braver in their use of language when they are protected by the puppet.
	When asking questions, wait patiently for an answer. For children with language problems, teachers should respond to the content rather than the correctness of the language. That is, stress the content of the answer, not the grammar.

WEBLINKS

Canadian Association of Speech-Language Pathologists and Audiologists **http://www.caslpa.ca/**

The Canadian Hyperlexia Association **http://home.ican.net/~cha/**

Aphasia Hope Foundation **http://www.aphasiahope.org/**

Speak Easy Inc. **http://www.vibrate.net/speakeasy/**

CHAPTER 5

Children with Learning Disabilities

Historical Notes

It is probably true to say that there have always been people with learning disabilities—if we are referring to persons of average intelligence who suffer some dysfunction that hinders their learning by traditional methods. By definition, however, learning disabilities are tied to academic achievement. Therefore, when pushing a plough was more important than pushing a pen, and when schooling was not a social norm for all children, the unique problems of individuals with learning disabilities would simply not have existed.

It was at the opening of the twentieth century, when compulsory school laws propelled all children into some form of education, that the particular difficulties of students with learning disabilities came to the fore. Many different disciplines contributed to the new field. Physicians, neurologists, ophthalmologists, speech therapists, psychologists, and educators all brought their own professional orientation and focus. Early research, conducted by physicians and psychologists who emphasized clinical investigation rather than practical application in the schools, focused primarily on three disorders—spoken language, written language, and motor and perceptual

problems. In 1877, for example, Kaussmaul first described congenital "word blindness." In 1896 James Kerr, a British physician, and W. P. Morgan, an ophthalmologist, also reported cases of word blindness. Eye surgeon James Hinshelwood investigated cases of word blindness, word deafness, and mind blindness. He published *Congenital Word-blindness* (1917), the first true monograph on the unique problems of children we now refer to as *learning disabled*.

In the early 1920s, Samuel Orton, an American psychiatrist, noted that children with learning problems often displayed mixed laterality and suggested that the failure of one hemisphere of the brain to become dominant caused the disorder. Orton coined the term "strephosymbolia" for individuals who saw "mixed symbols" when they tried to read (Orton, 1927).

Although these early researchers made some provocative and relevant findings, it was the work of Alfred Strauss, a neurologist, and Heinz Werner, a developmental psychologist, that established the conceptual base and the research and theories in the field. Strauss and Werner investigated the impact of brain damage on children's behaviour and psychological development. When they began to study children of normal ability who were experiencing learning difficulties, Strauss and Werner were able to delineate a group of common behaviours—a behavioural syndrome—that they believed characterized children suffering from minimal brain damage. The Strauss Syndrome, as this was called later, has five principal components: hyperactivity, hyper-emotionalism, impulsiveness, distractibility, and perseveration. While these components have been expanded, subdivided, and made more specific over the years, they still describe the core behavioural characteristics of children with learning disabilities.

The actual term *learning disabilities* came into use in 1963 to describe students who experienced continual school failure yet did not fit into the traditional categories of exceptionality. It was first used as a standard description for children of normal intelligence with learning problems by Samuel Kirk, one of the pioneers in the field, at a Chicago parents' meeting in 1963. Kirk defined his term carefully:

> Recently, I have used the term "learning disabilities" to describe a group of children who have disorders in development in language, speech, reading, and associated communication skills needed for social interaction. In this group, I do not include children who have sensory handicaps, such as blindness and deafness, because we have methods of managing and training the deaf and the blind. I also exclude from this group children who have generalized mental retardation (Kirk, 1963, p.3).

Kirk's speech had three major effects. First, it isolated the general characteristics of the population to be subsumed under the label of learning disabilities. Second, it precipitated a vote to reorganize diverse groups into the Association for Children with Learning Disabilities (ACLD), renamed the Learning Disabilities Association (LDA) in 1989. Primarily a forum for parents of learning disabled children, the ACLD expanded rapidly and became a powerful lobby group in both Canada and the United States.

Third, the creation of a new term served as a catalyst to stimulate interest in the field. Kirk's conception created an entirely new area of special education and set it on the road to an astonishing expansion. Such growth has never been experienced by any other area in special education in such a short time. The massive interest in the area, the number of students identified and served as learning disabled, the development of parent and professional organizations, and the contributions of allied disciplines has been little short of phenomenal. Today, learning disabilities is the largest single focus of special education in many Canadian school districts.

Perhaps more than any other field of exceptionality, learning disabilities have generated controversy, confusion, misconceptions, and polarization among concerned professionals. While some categories in special education can be easily identified by a common trait, such as hearing loss, visual impairment, or speech dysfunction, learning disabilities do not concern a single, easily identifiable disability and children with learning disabilities do not form a unified homogeneous group. On the contrary. *Learning disabilities* is a syndrome, a group of related and overlapping conditions that includes vastly different populations who reveal a wide variety of behavioural, learning, social, and interpersonal problems.

Although individuals who are learning disabled differ in many critical ways, they do share some common problems. First of all, they show a marked discrepancy between their potential and their performance. These students have average or above average intelligence but they seem unable to learn through regular channels and cannot reach their full potential when taught through traditional instructional methods. Second, students with learning disabilities show academic lags, often compounded by hyperactivity, inconsistent performances, memory and attention problems, and perceptual deficits.

Even while many of these students appear bright and receptive in all sorts of ways, they still fail in school. They earn report cards larded with comments such as "Could try harder," or "Should apply herself," or "He is not working up to his potential." But many of these young people *are* applying themselves, and the more they try and fail, the more unhappy and frustrated they become. Eventually they are caught up in a cycle of frustration and failure that threatens their entire educational career and engenders lack of motivation, social problems, increasingly less acceptable classroom behaviours, and dropping out, or even being subtly pushed out, of a school system that cannot accommodate their unique needs. The Profile on this page offers a particularly poignant example of a child whose learning disability was not identified. The letter was written many years after the person had left school.

In the past, children with learning disabilities have been described as hyperactive, distractible, inattentive, brain damaged, slow learning, dyslexic, perceptually disabled, aggres-

Profile

Dear Teacher,

You will not, I am sure, remember me. I am the child you failed in the second grade many years ago. That failure had profound effects on my life. It was my first, but not my last, bitter taste of defeat. I never found out from my mother why I failed that year. I was told only that "it was thought best."

The full implication of repeating a grade did not dawn on me until the day school started that next autumn. I had once felt like my younger sister's smart older brother, but now I felt like her slow, retarded brother. From that day onward, she and I were both in the same grade until we parted company in high school.

I hated school after that first day of my second go-round in grade two. Teacher, I hated you. I hated being the same mental age as my younger sister. I hated authority. I had done my best to please you the year before and my best was not good enough. I quit trying to please anyone in school.

You never asked me why I was hyperactive and could not sit still. You never wondered how it felt to be in the "Blue Birds" slow reading group. You never asked how I felt about math, which I just could not do. I wanted to be good at numbers, but I could just not cope with the anger that math provoked in me. To some people, numbers are friendly little creatures that love you. To me, numbers were mean ugly biters that bullied me every chance they got. Hell, I thought, must be having to do numbers forever by working them out in your head. Spelling was also a painful subject. I used to avoid your eyes, and prayed that you would not call on me.

As a young teenager, I thought I had found the answer to all my problems in the power of alcohol. I relied on alcohol to change my fear into temporary courage, and to turn my feelings of low self-worth into Superman-like confidence. At first my answer worked. But in time it became a one-way ticket to training school, jail, and personal defeat. Only by luck did I meet a counsellor who understood my learning problems and helped to set me on the right path.

In closing, I'd just like to say that today you have other children like me in your classroom. They may be the shy wallflower types or the loud performers that get on your nerves and disturb the rest of the class. They may be the ones with hidden secrets who daydream all day long. One thing is certain—they are already awake and the nightmare will not go away.

Thank you for listening, Teacher,
Brian

sive, and emotionally labile. More unsavoury terms have included *dull, lazy, inept,* and *disturbed*. Because of difficulties in identification, youngsters with learning disabilities were often shunted into classes for children either mentally retarded or emotionally disturbed. Others were placed in non-stimulating settings where their problems and progress were improperly evaluated.

Students with learning disabilities are neither emotionally disturbed nor intellectually disabled. They stand in good company with similarly affected historical figures. Thomas Edison's teacher, for example, described him as "addled." Auguste Rodin's father complained that he had "an idiot for a son." Woodrow Wilson had severe problems with reading and writing (Thompson, 1971). Albert Einstein did not speak until age three; he found school so difficult that one teacher predicted that "nothing good" would come of him (Patten, 1973). Nelson Rockefeller, who became vice president of the United States, encountered great difficulties with reading. Rockefeller later wrote that he "just struggled to understand words that seemed to garble before my eyes, numbers that came out backward, sentences that were hard to grasp" (Rockefeller, 1976).

Definitions of Learning Disabilities

Learning disabilities remains a puzzling condition—one of the least understood and the most difficult to deal with. This is partly the result of the field's evolution, its accelerated growth, and its interdisciplinary nature. More importantly, the extremely heterogeneous nature of the identified population defies easy categorization or description.

Since its beginnings, the most challenging issue in the field of learning disabilities has been the search for an appropriate definition. One study (Ysseldyke, Thurlow, Wesson, Algozzine, and Deno, 1983) found more than 42 definitional criteria in the literature. Yet a universally acceptable definition remains elusive. Lack of a clear definition in turn creates confusion in estimates of prevalence, considerations of etiology, and presents major difficulties in the design and use of tools and tests for assessment.

Many reasons contribute to the difficulties facing parents and professionals attempting to identify and define a child's learning disabilities. Chief among these are the following:

- while the term *learning disabilities* implies a distinct syndrome of behaviours, the components of the syndrome itself are varied and confused. So many behaviours are included as a learning disability that the term is often applied to students who could more accurately be described as slow learners, as children who misbehave in class, or as those who are absent often or who move from school to school.

- closely related to the above are the disparate characteristics of the population, which muddies clarity between categories of exceptionality. Often, these children are confused with those with mild mental retardation, behavioural disorders, or with Attention Deficit Hyperactivity Disorder. The overlap among categories of mild disabilities is shown in the Research Notes.

- learning disabilities is often referred to as a socially constructed category. At the outset, it applied to children from middle class backgrounds with no discernible mental or physical anomalies who were nevertheless failing in school (see this chapter's Historical Notes). Recently, there has been much movement among the categories of mild disability, and "Learning disabilities classes appear to be shifting from protective areas for

Research Notes

Overlap of Categories

In the past, students with mild disabilities—those traditionally labelled as learning disabled, mildly mentally retarded, and mildly behaviourally disordered—were not thought to share common etiological factors and behavioural characteristics. Among the three groups, differences were said to exist in the level of cognitive ability, in academic achievement, in patterns of cognitive performance, in degree of underachievement, and in adaptiveness of social and emotional development.

Ongoing research finds that, in many respects, these students cannot be reliably distinguished from one another. As Ysseldyke (1987) observed: "There are no characteristics of behaviour specific to learning disabilities, there are no characteristics that students labelled as learning disabled evidence that are not demonstrated with equal frequency by low-achieving students who are not learning disabled." Multiple studies confirm this point. Research shows no differences between students who are learning disabled or low achieving students on psycho-educational measures, on reading and phonological processing measures, and more similarities than differences in measures of reading (Gresham, 1997).

Not only is there almost no differentiation between learning disabilities and low achievers, but researchers (Fensler, Rosenberg, and Rosenberg, 1991) continue to find a considerable degree of overlap between the diagnostic areas of learning disabilities and behavioural disorders. Similarly, those with intellectual disabilities often exhibit behavioural disorders (e.g. Gresham, MacMillan, and Bocian, 1996).

In differential diagnosis, children with mild problems are difficult to categorize through diagnostic methods such as diagnostic tests, WISC-III profile analyses, or behavioural checklists. Treatments and instructional methods often overlap. One study (Algozzine, Morsink, and Algozzine, 1988) found that instruction in 40 classrooms serving groups of students designated as behaviourally disordered (emotionally disturbed), educable mentally retarded, or learning disabled did not differ to any degree.

Specific domains of development and the overlap of behaviours and learning are shown in table form below.

	LEARNING DISABLED	MILDLY MENTALLY RETARDED	BEHAVIOURALLY DISORDERED
Cognitive	Average or above average IQ	IQ below 75	Average IQ, mean around 90
Learning	Deficits in attention, memory, achievement	Deficits in memory, attention, and achievement	Deficits in memory, attention, and achievement
	Significantly more off-task behaviour	Significantly more off-task behaviour	Significantly more off-task behaviour
Social	Ignored or rejected by peers	Ignored or rejected by peers	Often actively disliked by peers
Physical	No physical anomalies	No physical anomalies	No physical anomalies
Communication	Speech and language difficulties	Speech and language difficulties	No language difficulties
Self-concept	Poor self-concept, outward locus of control	Poor self-concept, outward locus of control	Often outward locus of control, poor self-concept
Gender	4:1 boys to girls	5:1 boys to girls	6-12:1 boys to girls

white, middle-class, failing children to remedial classes for students previously classified as retarded or slow" (Sleeter, 1986, p. 46; see also Chapter 6).

the movement among categories is partly prompted by the greater social desirability of the term *learning disability* as compared to *slow learner* or *intellectually disabled*. As learning disabilities generally reflects the notion of an impairment that is specific rather than global in nature, it is therefore less stigmatizing to the image of the child as a whole person (Harry, 1992).

With all of the above, it is not surprising that learning disabilities are ill-defined in the minds of many educators, psychologists, and parents, and the implications of the condition are neither fully understood nor adequately conceptualized. Learning disabilities cannot be simply measured by a numerical designation, such as an IQ score or a decibel loss.

With such confusion about definitions, perhaps no other area of special education has expended so much effort to define itself and its population. Even today, some people think that there is no such thing as a learning disability. Others use the term to label every learning problem.

Despite these problems, many definitions of learning disabilities have emerged and all have their advocates and their opponents. Most modern definitions echo Kirk's original model, quoted in the Historical Notes. Among the current crop, the one proposed by the National Joint Committee on Learning Disabilities (NJCLD) seems to have the best chance of becoming the consensus definition (Hammill, 1990). According to the NJCLD,

> *Learning disabilities* is a general term that refers to a homogeneous group of disorders manifested by significant difficulties in the acquisition and use of listening, speaking, reading, writing, reasoning, or mathematical abilities. These disorders are intrinsic to the individual, presumed to be due to central nervous system dysfunction, and may occur across the life span. Problems in self-regulatory behaviour, social perception, and social interaction may exist with learning disabilities but do not by themselves constitute a learning disability. Although learning disabilities may occur concomitantly with other handicapping conditions (for example, sensory impairment, mental retardation, severe emotional disturbance) or with extrinsic influences (such as cultural differences, insufficient or inappropriate instruction), they are not the result of these conditions or influences (National Joint Committee on Learning Disabilities, 1988).

This definition stresses that learning disabilities is a syndrome of behaviours that manifests differently in different individuals. The disabilities are intrinsic to the individual, affect learning and behaviour, and are directly related to problems in school learning. Social, emotional, and motor difficulties may accompany the learning disability but do not constitute disabilities by themselves.

Even though the NJCLD definition has much credibility, it is not universally accepted and there is continuing debate on the matter. It therefore makes sense to examine common elements that are found in most definitions of learning disabilities.

Neurological Dysfunction

Much of the theoretical understanding of learning disabilities grew out of work with children described as *brain damaged*. In the 1930s and 1940s, Alfred Strauss argued that children with brain injuries are subject to major disorders in perception, thinking, and behaviour that reduce their ability to read, write, spell, and calculate.

Many theorists still attribute learning disabilities to some type of brain impairment or central nervous system (cns) dysfunction. This pathological emphasis is particularly evident among medical professionals; in educational circles, the tendency over the years has been to de-emphasize pathological aspects of the problems and stress behavioural ones. Many educators today would like to see the concept of presumed neurological impairment dropped entirely. They prefer to focus on each child's particular perceptual, cognitive, learning, and motor problems and skills so that appropriate educational programming can be developed.

Uneven Growth Pattern

Students with learning disabilities are presumed to have irregular or uneven development of the various domains of development. While some of the components mature quickly, others lag behind. Uneven development manifests as peaks and valleys in a student's performance. Some children, for example, are precocious verbally but far behind in motor and hand skills. While ahead of their age group in the use of oral language, these children may find it hard to hold a pencil or crayon, make shapes, or learn to print.

Difficulty in Academic Tasks

Academic problems are perhaps the clearest indication of a learning disability. A child may encounter difficulties with a wide range of learning tasks. Specific problems may occur in the acquisition of speech and oral language, in reading, in written language, in handwriting, in spelling, or in arithmetic. Depending on the definition, thinking, motor skills, perceptual skills, and psychosocial skills could be added.

Discrepancy Between Potential and Performance

Children with learning disabilities are most often described as those who manifest educationally significant discrepancies. In the United States, about 98 percent of states use a discrepancy notion in their definitions (Gresham, 1997).

There are three ways of looking at a discrepancy. It can be seen as a discrepancy between age or grade level expectations, such as reading two levels below grade placement. Or it can be seen in terms of differences between and among achievement areas such as reading comprehension versus listening comprehension (Gresham, 1997). The most common discrepancy measure is between a child's tested potential for academic tasks and the child's performance in academic and social domains (between what a child is capable of learning and what the child actually achieves). In theory, such a conception allows educators to distinguish children who are learning disabled from those who fail because of low intelligence, behavioural disorders, or other disabling conditions. This does not always follow; see the Research Notes on the overlap between categories.

A child's potential is judged by the mental age obtained on standardized tests of mental ability, which is then compared to performance on achievement tests. A difference of two years between the estimated potential and the performance is frequently used as an indicator of academic retardation.

Exclusion of Other Causes

Most definitions of learning disabilities exclude children whose exceptionality is primarily the result of other causes. Children who are learning disabled are not intellectually disabled, behaviourally disordered, visually or hearing impaired, or socially or economically disadvantaged. This is not to say that children with other disabilities cannot also be learning disabled. However, by excluding other disabilities, the field of learning disabilities gains clarity regarding its special population of learners.

Often, the exclusionary clauses simply add more confusion. This happens when we simply define learning disabilities by another type of exclusion—if you don't have any other problems, then you must be learning disabled. As we pointed out when discussing definitional problems, today learning disabilities is somewhat a residual category that includes many students who would have been classified differently in the past. For example, the learning disabilities category has come to include language minority children who are not necessarily disabled at all (see Jacobs, 1991).

Average or Above Average Intelligence

Inherent in the whole concept of learning disabilities, and closely associated with the exclusionary clause, is the notion that the child who is learning disabled is of average or above average intelligence.

Social Deficits

Some definitions define learning disabilities strictly in terms of intellect and achievement; others include emotional and social complications that may adversely affect school learning and achievement. Whether to include social deficits in definitions remains controversial. Arguments for the inclusion rest on data that show that social interactions are often difficult for children with learning disabilities, and that social skill deficits are common (Haager and Vaughn, 1995; Tur-Kasper and Bryan, 1995).

Terminology

The roots of the field of learning disabilities are embedded in the areas of neurology, ophthalmology, and other medical specialties. Although the terminology drawn from neurology is less popular today, some terms are still in general use and warrant explanation. In the following, the prefix *a-* means an absence of and *dys-* means a disturbance of.

- *Agnosia* is a lack of knowledge, an inability to recognize the significance of sensory stimuli.
- *Dysgraphia* means a disturbance in the ability to express thoughts in writing.
- *Dyscalculia* is a disturbance in the ability to use and remember numbers and do arithmetic.
- *Dyslexia* is a disturbance in the ability to read.

Of all these terms, *dyslexia* is the one that has become part of the common language. Precise definitions vary but generally "dyslexia refers to a severe difficulty in learning to read" (Mercer, 1987, p. 374) or to "an inability to read normally as a result of damage to the brain" (Myers and Hammill, 1990, p. 63).

Prevalence rates for dyslexia as a reading disorder range from 5 to 10 percent of the entire population, although rates as high as 20 to 30 percent are also reported (Pennington, 1991). DSM-IV (APA, 1994) estimates the rate among school-aged children at 4 percent, with 60 to 80 percent of these male.

Dyslexia and *learning disabilities* are not synonymous terms. Many children with reading problems are not categorically identified as learning disabled and most reading difficulties stem from factors such as poor instruction, lack of reading readiness, and/or cultural differences ("Reading difficulties...," 1997). And, while up to 80 percent of children who are learning disabled have reading difficulties, learning disabilities is best viewed as a syndrome of a number of behaviours.

Although the general public still clings to the term, educators have long wished to dispense with the term *dyslexia* in favour of *reading disability*. As early as 1969, the National Advisory Committee on Dyslexia and Related Reading Disorders in the United States set out to examine its terminology. The next year, the Committee stated: "In view of ... divergencies of opinion, the Committee believes that the use of the term *dyslexia* serves no useful purpose" (p. 38).

Prevalence of Learning Disabilities

Estimates of the prevalence of students who are learning disabled are so high (but vary to such a great degree) that it seems that the school system has fallen in love with the notion. Since 1963 the numbers of students identified and categorized as learning disabled has been astronomical. Between 1976–77 and 1992–93, the number of students in the United States served as learning disabled has increased by 198 percent (Gresham, 1997). In Canada, too, students with learning disabilities make up the largest single group of children with disabilities.

Figures depend upon the definition and the procedures used, so definitional problems and inconsistent identification procedures render exact proportions impossible. By definition, though, learning disabled students are atypical, so numbers could not be in very high ranges. Generally, the best Canadian estimates place the number of students with disabilities serious enough to hamper their educational progress at from two to four percent of the school-age population.

Boys outnumber girls with learning disabilities about four to one (MacGregor, Rosenbaum, and Skoutajan, 1982). The reasons for this are somewhat unclear. It may be that boys tend to indulge in more overt acting out behaviour, and are therefore more likely to be referred for in-depth diagnosis.

Classification of Learning Disabilities

Efforts to classify specific subtypes of learning disabilities can be traced back almost as far as the concept itself. But even after years of intense research, a consensus has not been reached about how to define or classify learning disabilities. These children and youth do not fit into any of the traditional categories of disabling conditions. Moreover, learning disabilities is not a unitary concept; it represents a group of students displaying disparate characteristics who fail to learn appropriately for diverse reasons. Because learning disabilities encompass a complex constellation of behaviours and conditions, they can be classified and categorized in many ways, with some support for each classification scheme (Samuels and Miller, 1985).

In Canada, the severity classifications of mild, moderate, and serious learning disabilities are widely employed. Severity classifications are founded on the belief that learning disabilities are less a question of kind than degree and consequences and can occur on a continuum from severely learning disabled to subtle differences in attention and performance (Little, 1980).

Learning disabilities are also classified as general or specific. With general learning disabilities, a student's academic progress is lagging behind that of normal peers in most areas. Specific learning disabilities may imply that the student has difficulties in particular areas but performs adequately in others. The term is also used to refer to students who have very serious and deep-seated disabilities.

Etiology of Learning Disabilities

Experts do not agree on the causes of learning disabilities any more than they agree on definitions. Complex and varied etiologies have been proposed. Some say that learning disabilities result primarily from physiological factors. Others stress that the school tasks we expect students to accomplish contribute to learning disabilities by making demands on their maturity levels or learning styles that they are unable to meet. Still others blame environmental factors such as inadequate nutrition, inappropriate diet, or allergies. Moreover, various suspected causes interact in subtle ways, rendering etiology even more difficult to determine. In most cases, the cause of a child's learning disability remains unknown.

Minimal Brain Dysfunction

Following the lead of Alfred Strauss and other pioneer neurologists, a presumption of some type of brain injury is still found in many of today's definitions of learning disabilities. It is described as neurological dysfunction, and is sometimes called *minimal brain dysfunction.*

Some researchers believe that minimal brain dysfunction is the root cause of all learning disabilities. They suggest that slight damage to the brain hinders its most efficient functioning and point to disruption of neural cell development during early fetal development (Hynd and Semrud-Clikeman, 1989).

Although the findings from neurological studies are not yet conclusive, a small but increasing amount of data does point to some neurological abnormalities as a cause of learning disabilities (Hynd and Semrud-Clikeman, 1989). An easily identified pattern of neurological disturbance has not, however, been found.

Biochemical Disturbances

Other researchers hold that children with learning disabilities suffer from physiological problems or biochemical disturbances. Commonly mentioned sources are diet or environment-related allergies that adversely affect learning.

Food allergies were theoretically linked to hyperactivity by Benjamin Feingold (1975,

1976) who noted that artificial flavours, artificial preservatives, and artificial dyes were consumed in increasing quantities by North American children. Feingold argued that approximately 50 percent of hyperactive children can be helped by eliminating from their diet artificial food colourings and dyes and foods such as apples, oranges, tomatoes, and strawberries that contain certain natural salicylates, Aspirin-like compounds found in some fruits and vegetables.

Genetic Factors

Genetic factors are extremely prominent in research directed specifically to dyslexia. Researchers know that reading disabilities tend to run in families, especially among male members. Their questions: "What is the rate of familial dyslexia?" and "Are familial reading problems due to hereditary factors or to similar learning environments?"

Ongoing research into rates clearly identifies the familial nature of some reading problems. One investigator (Scarborough, 1989, 1990) found that a family history of dyslexia accounted for 30 to 36 percent of the variance in reading. Another large-scale study (Decker and Defries, 1980, 1981) that compared the families of 125 children with reading disorders to a control group of average readers found common reading problems in the families of the poor readers, especially among the male members, which led the investigators to argue that learning problems were familial in nature. Studies of twins generally show that when one twin has a reading disability, the other twin is also likely to have a reading disability if the twins are monozygotic rather than dizygotic.

Genetic researchers theorize that dyslexia is linked to a glitch in the brain's wiring that interferes with the ability to translate a written word into units of sound (phonemes) (Wingert and Kantrowitz, 1997). The problem seems to be inherited and the influence of the genes operates at several levels. But a child is not born reading disabled in the same way that a child is born redheaded or female. Writing, spelling and reading problems per se are not biological features that can be inherited. Yet, if present, they may stem from some underlying cognitive or neurological defect based on genetic transmission.

Reading ability or the language skills underlying reading ability will be linked to many genes. So far, research shows linkages between chromosome 6 and phonemic awareness and phonological decoding skills ("Reading difficulties ...," 1997). It also appears that a genetic abnormality is found on chromosome 15, although the mechanism of transmission is still in question, as is the strength of the genetic influence (Smith and Pennington, 1987; Wenar, 1994). As well, the B2 microglobulin gene, which is thought to influence the immune system and male sexual development, is also found on chromosome 15, which may help explain the high prevalence of males among the reading disabled population (Smith and Pennington, 1987).

Maturational Lags

A **maturational lag** means that a child is slow to reach some developmental milestones. Such a developmental lag does not necessarily imply a structural deficiency or limited potential. Some children may simply be progressing at a slower rate in language, motor, cognitive, or socio-emotional development. Most of these children overcome their behaviour and learning problems as they grow older, although some may continue to lag behind their agemates. For example, developmentally young children who appeared to be reading disabled at grade three but responded by grade five developed into low–average readers by grade eight (Badian, 1988).

It may be that the effects of schooling on children with developmental lags itself creates the appearance of mild disabilities (Shank, 1990). Schools assign children to a grade level based on their age, assuming that children of the same age possess the same levels of ability. This is simply not true; children reach their developmental milestones at different times, and to expect all children to be ready to learn the same things on the same schedule is clearly not reasonable. When children are behind the expected schedule, they will manifest characteristics of a child with learning disabilities, such as behaviour, reading, and attention-span problems (Senior, 1986). These developmentally young children are penalized if they are drawn in by procedures intended to find potential problems and then labelled as learning disabled.

Environmental Factors

Children do not "catch" a disability when they enter school. In most cases they bring with them unspecified cognitive, behavioural, linguistic, and affective characteristics that have developed over time, which interact with the academic and social ecology of the classroom (Cooper and Speece, 1990). Nevertheless, when there is a mismatch between children's learning styles and readiness and classroom expectations, some children may indeed catch learning disabilities when they enter school.

Lloyd (1975), who describes this phenomenon as **dyspedagogia** (maleducation), suggests that children in this category do not have learning problems, but their schools do. Coles (1978) went so far as to assert that learning disabilities are a way to blame a group of students for the failure of the schools. In the same vein, Englemann (1977) argued that "Perhaps 90 percent or more of the children who are labelled 'learning disabled' exhibit a disability not because of anything wrong with their perception, synapses or memory, but because they have been seriously mistaught. Learning disabilities are made, not born" (pp. 46–47).

Proponents of the maleducation point of view believe that if teachers were better prepared to handle the special learning problems of children in the early school years, many learning disabilities could be avoided. They point to inappropriate teaching settings, narrow bands of acceptable behaviour, inflexible grouping practices, and narrow curricula. Studies (e.g. Cole, Dale, Mills, and Jenkins, 1993; Mills, Dale, Cole, and Jenkins, 1995; Yoder, Kaiser, and Alpert, 1991) suggest that one curriculum may not be best for all children and that programs should match the individual needs of the child.

Dyspedagogia implies more than poor teaching and a mismatch between instruction and a child's needs. It also includes poor curricula, poor health in the child, and poor attendance at school. Poor parental and professional attitudes may also function to weaken a child's motivation and hinder learning.

Identification and Assessment of Learning Disabilities

While there is little agreement on definition, prevalence, or remedial procedures in the field of learning disabilities, there is almost universal agreement on the need for the efficient diagnosis of this population's members. Before setting up remedial programs and deciding on the most appropriate educational placement, it is incumbent on educators to conduct a thorough evaluation of the student in order to pinpoint the kind and degree of specific disabilities present as well as the strengths and weaknesses in each developmental domain.

The identification and assessment of children with possible learning disabilities is anything but easy. Assessment practices are fraught with problems. An acceptable assessment framework is lacking, appropriate instruments are not available, and many of the assumptions that have traditionally underlain assessment practices are under attack. Often, too, the process suffers from lack of co-ordination. Many professionals within and outside the school system become involved and each of these people may hold very different views regarding the nature of learning disabilities. The pediatrician may stress minimal brain dysfunction, the psychiatrist behavioural disorders, and the psychologist intellectual inadequacy. Even within the school system, identification and assessment is often a rather hit and miss process. There is currently no single procedure to identify learning disabilities. Clinicians use a variety of tests and rely heavily on personal diagnostic judgment. As well, there is little consensus regarding when children should be tested, by whom, and to what purpose.

Children with learning disabilities may show deficits and lags in specific developmental tasks in several or all of the following functions: sensorimotor abilities, language, perception, thought processes, emotions, and social behaviour. A comprehensive and detailed examination of a child's physical and psychological make-up depends upon a battery of psychological and educational tests. Measures are supplemented by observations of the child, a physical examination, an evaluation of hearing and vision, interviews with the child and the parents, and information gathered from other sources. School records and the comments of earlier teachers are potent sources of data.

Generally, identification involves two processes—screening and psycho-educational diagnosis, as shown in Table 5-1. **Screening** procedures examine large groups of children in order to identify those who fall below or rise above specified levels of behaviour and attainment. Diagnosis follows screening and investigates selected children to determine the precise nature of their difficulties.

By definition, a learning disability involves a discrepancy between a student's potential

Table 5-1 An overview of the assessment process

Medical	Informal screening	Formal/psycho-educational
observations	observations	IQ measures, e.g. WISC-III
physical examination	interviews	
hearing assessment	school records	achievement tests
vision assessment	case histories	visual, auditory, motor, motor, sensorimotor functioning
	inventories	
	rating scales	
	teacher-made measures	diagnostic tests
	portfolios	language measures

and his or her performance. Therefore, one of the first steps in the formal diagnosis is an assessment of intellectual potential to rule out the possibility of mental retardation and simultaneously to establish the fact of normal mental ability.

Broad-coverage tests such as the Wechsler Intelligence Scale for Children-III (WISC-III) are usually given first. The Wechsler scales have proven both valid and reliable in the assessment of children with learning disabilities. Once intelligence is judged to be normal, clinicians use more specific measures in a range of areas—auditory, visual, and motor processing; achievement, most particularly in language arts and mathematics; diagnostic tests to pinpoint specific areas of weakness; and perhaps tests of vocational skills and adaptive behaviour.

Achievement tests are used to measure a spectrum of tasks such as oral reading, reading comprehension, language, spelling, math, and general knowledge. In addition, tests are often administered to identify the specific psychological processes in which a child is deficient. For example, a child's reading problems may be the result of a processing problem in auditory discrimination or visual figure–ground processing.

Psychological processing refers to how an individual processes sensory information and puts it to meaningful intellectual use. Theories about learning disabilities have long taken into account the possibility of processing deficiencies; indeed, this has been the major position in the field for the past 30 years.

The use of tests to diagnose underlying processing deficits was introduced at the same time that learning disabilities developed as a category of exceptionality. These measures have generated much concern and controversy. Opponents argue that because psychological processes are not directly observable and must be inferred from a child's performance, it is almost impossible to accurately assess underlying psychological processes. Nevertheless, a wide variety of measures that purport to assess such areas as auditory and visual processing, motor subskills, and kinesthetic functions are available. Table 5-2 shows the auditory and visual subskills upon which many of these tools focus.

As language problems assume greater importance in learning disabilities, there is a concomitant emphasis on assessing language competencies. Teachers use observations, language samples, and standardized tools. (See Chapter 4.)

Developmental Consequences of Learning Disabilities

Individuals who are learning disabled simply do not seem to learn in the same way as everyone else does—they sometimes do complicated things very well and then amaze and puzzle us with their lack of competence in areas that seem elementary. Sometimes these youngsters seem to remember incongruous items—they know all the words of TV jingles but forget simple spelling words from one day to the next. Their performance is inconsistent; they show great variability in areas of functioning—large differences between skill areas. Often, the energy levels of these students frustrates teachers; they may spend more time out of their seats than in them and have a higher rate of motor activity than other class members.

Learning disabilities represent a constellation of widely varied behaviours and conditions. The problems take a different course in each individual. In some students, the effects are global; in others, they impinge on specific areas of functioning. Certain displayed be-

Table 5-2 Examples of visual and auditory processes

Process	Ability	Implications and problems
Visual perception	The ability to make visual stimuli meaningful	The child may have problems attending to and interpreting visual stimuli.
Visual discrimination	The ability to perceive dominant features in different objects or symbols	The child may confuse letters and words that look alike.
		The child may not see the internal detail, as in rid/red, or may fail to see the general configuration as in ship/snip.
Visual closure	The ability to identify a common object from an incomplete visual presentation	The child may have difficulty assembling puzzles and objects, identifying missing parts, or completing words by closing spaces between letters, as in rab-bit.
Visual figure–ground	The ability to focus on the foreground and ignore the background visual stimuli	The child may not be able to distinguish words; for example, the child may be unable to point to the first word of the second paragraph.
Visual memory	The ability to recall the dominant features of the stimulus item	The child may not be able to copy patterns or arrange blocks in a series.
Visual sequential memory	The ability to recollect the sequence of a number of items presented visually	The child fails to recognize visually familiar words and forgets the arrangement of letters in a word.
Auditory perception	The ability to recognize and interpret stimuli that are heard	The child may have problems attending to and interpreting auditory stimuli.
Auditory discrimination	The ability to recognize differences between sounds and to identify similarities and differences between words	The child may not hear the similarities in initial or final sounds in words or be able to discriminate short vowels such as pin, pan, pen.
Auditory closure	The ability to identify sounds and words from an incomplete auditory presentation	The child may have problems in sound–symbol association and especially in blending sounds.
Auditory figure–ground	The ability to focus on the foreground sound and ignore other sounds	The child may not focus on the dominant sound; the fan on the overhead projector may be more important than the teacher's voice.
Auditory memory	The ability to recognize and recall previously presented auditory stimuli	The child may have problems retaining and recalling auditory experiences.
Auditory sequential memory	The ability to reproduce from memory sequences presented auditorily	The child may forget or confuse oral directions, the sequence of events, the sequence of letters in a word, and the sequence of words in a sentence.

haviours may be more apparent in individuals with mild and moderate disabilities, while others are manifested in students with severe problems (Shaughnessy and Mahan, 1991).

Some common characteristics are shown in Table 5-3. This list certainly does not cover all the behaviours that have been attributed to students with learning disabilities and it should be regarded with extreme caution. No child with learning disabilities will display all the behaviours, while the disparate characteristics of the population means that additional behaviours may exist in some children. Most importantly, one attribute or behaviour does not a learning disability make; we probably all have at least one or two of the listed behaviours.

Table 5-3 Some common characteristics seen in children who are learning disabled

Attitudes and behaviour

- Intelligent but fails at school.
- May be reluctant to try anything new, be frightened by change.
- Lacks flexibility and is upset when routine is different or the schedule changed.
- Has difficulty in changing from one task to another.
- Says "I don't care" or "I won't" and really means "I can't"; would rather be called bad than dumb.
- Impulsive—says what first comes to mind; calls out in class.
- Forgets assignments and homework as well as books, coats, and pencils.

Language

- Hears the dog barking, a truck honking, the scratching of pencils, the sound of the air conditioner, and footsteps outside, but barely hears mother calling and does not hear what the teacher says.
- Forgets names of people, places, things, own address and telephone number, but does remember the ads on television.
- May be an expert strategist in checkers or chess but cannot understand a riddle or joke.
- Many hesitations and repetitions in oral language; blurred pronunciations in speech.
- Poor verbal expression; language is jumbled and shows poor usage of syntax and semantics. Stops and starts in the middle of a sentence or idea, talks about hospitals, animals, and enemies all at once. Has trouble in relating a story or incident.
- Difficulty in concept formation. Calls breakfast lunch and is confused by yesterday, today, and tomorrow.
- Asks the same thing over and over; asks constant questions but does not seem interested in the answers.

Academic performance

- Rushes headlong into work; is the first one finished, and did all the problems wrong.
- May read *on* for *no*, write 41 for 14, *p* for *d*, or *q* for *b*, and cannot remember the sequence of letters that make up a word.
- May be able to add and multiply but not subtract or divide; or can do math mentally but cannot write it down.
- Skips words, omits them, or adds them when reading aloud.
- Frequently confuses directions, both oral and written.
- Needs instructions explained for each assignment.
- Can't plan studies and assignments.
- Sloppy and disorganized book work.
- Has difficulty beginning or completing tasks.
- Doesn't complete lengthy assignments.

continued on next page

Co-ordination

- May hug the cat too tightly but can't hold a pencil; may get frostbite in the snow and not feel the hot water until it burns.
- May be a good swimmer but stumbles up the stairs.
- Does not look before walking, bumps into the door, swings lunch boxes into the nearest legs, and trips easily.
- Has trouble lining up, cannot help bothering the child ahead in the line.

Social

- Relates poorly to peers; may be socially inept and always on the fringe of a group.
- Poor self-esteem and self-concept.
- Lacks judgment.
- Does not seem to understand the affective status of others derived from facial expressions, body movements, and tone of voice.
- Cannot keep a friend and prefers to play with younger children.

Cognitive Development

Cognitive delays are associated with intellectual disabilities. A learning disability is not a cognitive delay. By definition, students with learning disabilities possess average or above average intelligence. Also by definition, students with learning disabilities do not acquire academic skills at grade expectancy and at a normal rate, and will lag in some or all academic areas. They show a marked discrepancy between potential and performance.

Thinking requires the ability to conceptualize and solve problems. Because children who are learning disabled are of normal intelligence, they are clearly able to think. Yet significant numbers of these students exhibit memory and thinking disorders; they have problems remembering information over long or short periods of time and demonstrate memory deficits for both auditory and visual stimuli (Swanson, 1987; Torgensen, 1988). They have trouble recalling what things sounded like or looked like and forget math facts, spelling words learned only the day before, and directions. These children forget basic personal information, such as their telephone numbers and their addresses.

Many researchers consider the development of memory to be synonymous with the development of memory strategies (Howe and O'Sullivan, 1990), which include strategies for learning and for problem solving. Self-regulated learners are flexible problem solvers who plan, select, correct, and monitor effective strategies for learning, anticipate problems, and reflect on tasks when they are finished (Corno and Mandinach, 1983; Paris and Cross, 1983). When students monitor and orchestrate their own learning strategies, the processes form part of a cognitive procedure referred to as **metacognition**, the awareness of basic learning strategies and one's own awareness of how one learns.

In most cases, students with learning disabilities do not have deficits in the actual ability to learn. They seem to have performance deficits rather than ability deficits; that is, they are weak in the development of learning and problem solving strategies and have deficiencies in metacognitive skills. Their learning strategies—or lack of them—prevent them from using their basic abilities to the best advantage.

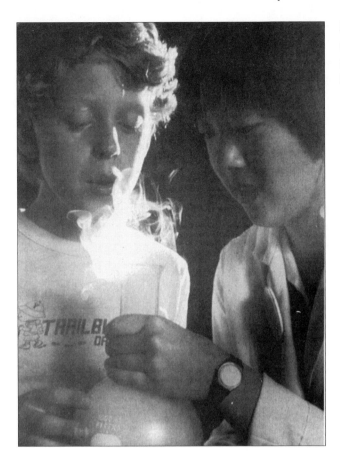

Peer tutoring is usually helpful to students with learning disabilities

Students who organize information poorly tend to be impulsive when solving problems, miss a logical train of thought, and fail to consider appropriate alternatives before embarking on a course of action. Their responses to problem situations indicate an inability to generalize and apply what they have learned in other situations. Lacking the skills to direct and monitor their learning and behaviour, students who are learning disabled flounder in traditional classrooms.

Communication

Language disabilities are closely connected with learning disabilities of all types. So apparent is the connection that some researchers use the term *language learning disabilities* to refer to students with language disorders that adversely affect academic performance. In the classroom, these may be the students who sit at the back and hope that the teacher won't call on them. They rarely volunteer answers and when they are asked to speak they may be hesitant, stumble over words, and use a sparse vocabulary.

Students with learning disabilities tend to reach a plateau of language abilities in the areas of semantics, syntax, memory, and pragmatics at levels expected of children between eight and ten years old (Wesanko, 1990). All the elements of language overlap and must develop in tandem if students are to be communicatively competent, so deficits in one area affect the others. In language, students with learning disabilities show deficits in:

- *Listening.* The teaching learning process proceeds on the assumption that participants listen to each other. When instructing, teachers use an initiation-reply-evaluate mode. They ask questions, listen, and then evaluate whether or not children have mastered the task through the reply.

  Listening (and therefore responding accurately) is a problematic area for children with learning disabilities. When listening, they tend to misperceive phonemes requiring very fine discrimination such as /m/ and /n/. They also confuse voiced and unvoiced consonants, such as /f/ and /v/ (Wiig and Semel, 1976).

- *Expressive language.* Although they have problems with both expressive and receptive language, students with learning disabilities seem to have greater difficulty using expressive language (Hessler and Kitchen, 1980; Noel, 1980), particularly with semantics and pragmatics.

  As well, children with learning disabilities often have difficulties with articulation (Montgomary, 1981) and may show immature speech patterns, mild speech irregularities, general unintelligibility, and cluttered speech. They may substitute inappropriate words, repeat the same phrase over and over, or use a monotonous voice.

- *Semantics.* The vocabulary used by these students tends to be small, superficial, and reflective of reductions in the development of underlying concepts. Normally developing children of eight or nine years of age recognize the multiple meanings of frequently used words; adolescents who are learning disabled may not perceive multiple meanings and misinterpret when they read or listen. They often take things very literally, missing the subtle nuances of the language. For example, one adolescent went to a Laundromat for the first time with a small load of washing. On a towel, he read the instruction, "Wash colours separately." He proceeded to do exactly that, using a separate washing machine for each shade of colour. He spent nine dollars and infuriated the other patrons. Another student was handed a tape by a frazzled teacher and asked to "Put it on the video." The boy set it neatly on top of the machine.

  Some children cannot remember the meanings of new words whether the words are identified by the teacher as necessary for general vocabulary acquisition or discovered by the students when attempting to read English literature, social studies, science, and so on. Research indicates that 43 percent of students with learning disabilities have word finding problems (Wesanko, 1990). Because of limited vocabulary or the inability to absorb the full significance of words, students with learning disabilities tend to be seriously affected in the areas of generalization, conceptualization, and abstraction.

- *Syntax.* Students with learning disabilities may have problems organizing phrases and words into sentences and are more likely to make syntactical and grammatical errors (Bryan and Pflaum, 1978). They may talk about things out of order, produce rambling and repetitive utterances, and make unrelated statements.

- *Pragmatics.* Pragmatic problems in the social use of language are seen in students who fail to communicate intent, show an inability in turntaking in conversation, and fail to cue their listeners to the topic of discussion (Hasenstab, 1985).

Academic Development

Academic underachievement is the hallmark of the learning disabled population. Some children show deficits in all areas; for others, only a few specific academic skills may be affected. Reading, writing, and mathematics are the three major areas affected.

Students with learning disabilities appear to reach a plateau at about a fourth or fifth grade achievement level (matching their achievement in language). This level is at the point at which basic skill instruction generally ceases and students move on to apply their skills to reading comprehension, math applications, expository writing, and greater use of textbooks in science and social studies. Moreover, the gap between achievement scores and grade expectancy level seems to widen as students with learning disabilities progress through high school. Even when placed in secondary school resource programs, students do not seem to recoup basic skills. Despite intensive instruction, many adolescents with learning disabilities do not master the higher-level skills involved in reading and written expression (see Chapter 16).

In 1989, 2.7 million Canadian adults—15 percent of the population aged 16 to 69 with reported abilities in either English or French—had limited reading skills so that they could not deal with the majority of written material that they encountered (Montigny, 1990). Among all children, reading problems are the major cause of poor school performance; about four percent of children have serious reading disorders (APA, 1994).

Reading disorders rank high on the list of academic problems of students who are learning disabled; the figure could be as high as 80 percent. One sample of 200 elementary students with learning disabilities found that 54.5 percent had deficits in reading (Rivers, 1986). Using the Wide Range Achievement Test (WRAT), another study (Weiner, Harris, and Shirer, 1990) found elementary students with learning disabilities to have a mean percentile of 7.74.

Students with hard-core reading difficulties manifest a variety of problems. Comprehension is the main purpose of reading, but comprehension is not possible unless a reader can translate the printed words into the language they represent (decode). At the secondary level, the primary reading disability of students who are learning disabled is in the area of reading comprehension.

Word-attack skills are often deficient; students may be unable to deal with symbols, unable to synthesize parts of a word into a whole, or unable to organize words into meaningful clusters. Most children show difficulty with **phonological awareness**—the ability to blend, segment, rhyme, or in other ways manipulate the sounds of spoken words. They also have difficulty in understanding the sounds of the letters (Hatcher, Hanline, and Ellis, 1994).

When reading, students often miss or confuse important details, such as *and* or *but*, resulting in confused interpretation of meanings. When these students read aloud, their reading may be stilted and full of substitutions, omissions, and additions. Individuals with learning disabilities also seem to lack sensitivity to various patterns of textual organization and to the relative importance of major and minor ideas (Vallecorsa and Garriss, 1990).

Many students also show marked impairments in all forms of written expression. Poor spelling correlates with reading difficulties; good readers can be deplorable spellers but poor readers are always certain to be bad spellers. Spelling for students who are learning disabled has been described as a "seemingly impossible task" (Leuenberger and Morris, 1990), and their spelling achievement usually lags far behind their grade placement. On the spelling subtest of the WRAT one study found a mean percentile of 7.52 (Weiner, Harris, and Shirer, 1990).

Some children who are learning disabled can speak well yet cannot write a simple sentence. Students with a writing disability tend to write little or laboriously, using incorrect grammar, syntax, and punctuation. They show confused or truncated sentences, with an incorrect sequence of tenses, pronoun reference, and word order. Figure 5-1 shows the written work of an eleven-year-old student with many constraints in his written expression and handwriting.

Figure 5-1

*Work of an
11-year-old with
difficulties in
written expression*

Jan. 21. 1987

dear mrs windsor,

I met Brenda nine o'clock wednesday
morning we talked about DINOSAWRS and School
and ingsects. then me played Connect Four,

we played Five games and I beat Brenda three,
times   She lost,

I must go it is allmost recess time,

G̲

Good-bye
Chris

During the writing process, students with learning disabilities do not have a plan that they consistently refine; instead, they have a less sophisticated approach to composing, one that minimizes the role of planning and operates largely without metacognitive control (De La Paz and Graham, 1997). Writing is characterized by shorter and lower-quality stories than those written by normal students. While students with learning disabilities may have a basic understanding of story structure, their stories often lack organization and coherence and contain relatively few story elements over all (see Montague and Graves, 1993). Students convert writing tasks into telling what they know about a topic and do not rework or evaluate the information. They generally include basic story elements such as setting, plot, and resolution, but they frequently omit the critical elements of good stories such as the internal responses or plans of the characters (Leavitt and Ioannides, 1993; Montague, Maddux and Dereshiwsky, 1988).

Many problems in written expression result from a lack of understanding of linguistic rules. Some students with learning disabilities may be unable to classify and categorize information into coherent sentences; others are unable to produce sentences displaying correct syntactic and grammatical order. One study (Linn, Algozzine, Mann, and Schwartz, 1987) that used standardized competency tests found that adolescents with learning disabilities in general performed poorly, specifically on communication items requiring identification of an irrelevant statement in a selection, use of apostrophes, and use of *s* to show possessives.

Students with a handwriting disability tend to write laboriously and as little as possible. They may produce clearly deviant writing, with scrawling letter formations, reversals, transformations, uneven slant, and inability to keep to the lines on the paper. Unco-ordinated motor movements and difficulty in judging the writing space are the most common causes of penmanship problems (Gerard and Junkula, 1980).

It follows that areas such as note taking, so important in secondary level programs, suffer. Students are often unable to identify important information, write fast enough to keep up, or make sense of the notes later. Rather than a record of pertinent information, the notes are often scribbles, single words, and drawings that have little relation to the content covered (Weishaar and Boyle, 1997).

Math for students with learning disabilities is typically characterized by high failure: these students experience much greater difficulty in most aspects of math performance than their non-disabled peers (Carpenter, 1985; O'Melia and Rosenberg, 1994). Basic skills such as counting, writing numerals, and basic addition and subtraction are deficient.

Homework accounts for about 20 percent of student time spent on academic tasks. However, it is estimated that 56 percent of students with learning disabilities have difficulty completing homework (Bryan and Sullivan-Burstein, 1997). Similarly, children with learning disabilities and behaviour disorders exhibit higher levels of test anxiety than do their non-disabled peers (Rizzo and Zabel, 1988). Test anxiety has been associated with depressed academic performance and self-defeating interpersonal and intrapersonal behaviour. It contributes to the development of detrimental motivational, coping, and task strategies such as dependence, self-deprecation, and conformity (Swanson and Howell, 1996), negative self-evaluation, difficulties in concentrating, and off-task thoughts.

Academic deficits are exacerbated by the significant problems students with learning disabilities experience in social perceptions, self-concept, and motivation (Schrader and Valus, 1990). Compared to their peers, students tend to hold lower self-concepts about academic performance, even in areas in which they have had little experience or instruction. They tend not to attribute their learning to their own ability, and develop an **external locus of control**. When this happens, students view themselves as controlled by outer rather than inner forces. They hold lower expectations for success, credit any successes to luck or the ease of the task rather than their own abilities or efforts, and view failure as further verification of their own persistent lack of ability (Licht and Kistner, 1986). Such pessimistic appraisals lead to less optimism about improving their performance in the future, even when they receive special education services, and to reduced levels of effort and negative affect.

Students who retain an outward locus of control may revert to *learned helplessness*, an important individual difference that appears to affect children's performance in a variety of settings (Fencham, Hokada, and Sanders, 1989). Children who display learned helplessness have no faith that their efforts will result in desired outcomes. Because they expect to fail, they lose their motivation.

With all of this, it seems little wonder that students often develop secondary emotional problems. Children with learning disabilities may develop an **emotional overlay**, an adverse reaction to learning problems and academic failure. In many cases it is extremely difficult to determine whether the learning or the adjustment problem came first, and the exact interaction of these in a child's functioning.

Perceptual Development

Perceptual and processing difficulties in the auditory and visual modes, together with problems in co-ordination and motor skills, are part of the traditional conception of learning disabilities. Also included are haptic disorders which concern the information transmitted through touch, body movement, and position.

Perception involves the use of the senses to recognize, discriminate, and interpret stimuli. Students unable to process perceptions accurately are said to have perceptual disorders, sometimes referred to as *psychological processing deficits*.

Visual perception problems are most commonly associated with learning disabilities. Many early studies (e.g. Calfee, 1977; Satz, Taylor, Friel, and Fletcher, 1978) indicated that visual perception problems are common and that, as a group, children with learning disabilities perform poorly on tasks designed to assess visual perceptual abilities. Visual perceptual problems lead to difficulties with oculamotor co-ordination, with spatial relations, with figure–ground perception, with the discrimination of differences, and with the recognition of likenesses. Children find it difficult to discriminate symbols, and may reverse letters and shapes in their printing and drawing. They have problems in identifying the letters of the alphabet, reading the printed page from left to right, drawing basic shapes, and staying on the line when printing or writing.

Other studies (e.g. Flynn and Byrne, 1970; Harber, 1980; Henry, 1975) showed that auditory disorders occur with greater than normal frequency among children who are learning disabled. This problem is often recognized when children attempt to spell words. Their poor spelling results from their inability to discriminate sounds, to blend sounds, and to encode (spell) or decode (read) words. The child with an auditory dysfunction may have difficulty synthesizing sounds into words, analyzing words into word parts, and associating sounds with symbols.

Behaviour

Between 24 and 52 percent of children with learning disabilities are reported to have significant social, emotional, and behavioural problems (Rock, Fessler, and Church, 1997). Children show many externalizing behavioural disorders such as aggression, antisocial behaviour, and conduct problems (Richards, Symons, Greene, and Szuskiewicz, 1995).

Compared to normally developing students, those with learning disabilities behave in a less appropriate fashion in both regular and special classes. They are less task oriented, show more problem behaviours, and often display maladaptive styles of responses during instructional activities, possibly as a result of their poor cognitive performance (Bender and Smith, 1990; Cosden, Gerber, Semmel, Goldman, and Semmel, 1987). One study found a learning disabled sample to be on task only 57 percent of the time, as compared to 70 percent for the non-disabled sample (McKinney, McLure, and Feagans, 1982). Others (Roberts, Pratt, and Leach, 1991) reported that a group of students with mild disabilities were off task twice as often as were non-disabled students.

Off-task behaviour, lowered motivation, and externalizing behaviour raise further barriers to successful learning. They limit a child's ability to profit from instruction (Richards et al., 1995).

Motor Development and Co-ordination

Haptic problems, which encompass touch, body movement, and position in space, are thought to be relatively uncommon (Mercer, 1979). Haptic problems may be important in handwriting, because tactile information dictates the grasp of the pen or pencil. As well, researchers suggest a relationship between visual motor and haptic abilities, and body image and laterality (Hallahan, Kauffman, and Lloyd, 1985).

Laterality refers to an internal knowledge of the differences between left and right; **directionality** is an awareness of left and right in the environment outside the body. Out of an infinite number of motor experiments, children learn the differences between an activity on the right side of the body and the same activity on the left. The pattern thus becomes a skill, and the skill becomes a habit. At approximately five or six years of age, most children establish complete cerebral dominance and consistently prefer to use one side of their bodies in dealing with the world.

Laterality is the motor basis for spatial concepts. When children have developed laterality, they can project this to directionality concepts in external space such as up and down, and in front and behind. **Body image** refers to a person's awareness of the body, its capabilities, the interrelationship of body parts, and the relationship of bodies to the environment.

The laterality theory maintains that learning is adversely affected if the child does not establish a tendency to perform most functions with one side of the body. In the past, many left-handed children were considered to be at high risk for learning disabilities. While it is true that among the learning disabled population (and indeed among nearly all populations of problem learners) there is a far higher proportion of left-handers than in the general population, the hand dominance in itself does not seem to be the problem. The difficulties arise

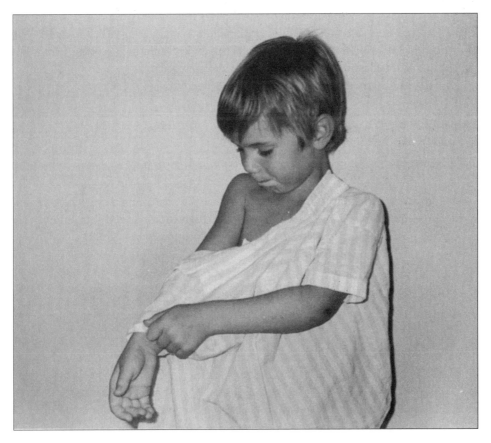

Children with body image problems often have difficulty with tasks such as dressing.

with incomplete or mixed dominance, which translates into confusion in directionality or right and left discrimination.

The failure to establish laterality, directionality, and dominance may account for many reversals and similar confusions in children's reading and writing. When mixed dominance is encountered with other signs, such as *enuresis* (bed wetting), preference for play with younger children, or infantile speech patterns, it may suggest a maturational lag or developmental immaturity which can interfere with a child's abilities to function in academic work (Murray, 1981).

Children with body image problems may not be able to organize themselves within their environment. They may be clumsy; slow in dressing and undressing and have difficulty in putting on a sweater; be unable to walk across the classroom without knocking into chairs and desks; and unable to draw figures.

General unco-ordination refers to a lack of muscular control. Motorically disordered children may walk with an awkward gait, are unco-ordinated in physical activities, and have difficulties in running, skipping, or throwing and catching a ball. Overflow movements, which occur when the child wants to perform a movement with one hand and the other hand involuntarily follows in a shadow movement, may be present.

Attention Problems

Attention problems are endemic among youngsters with exceptional conditions, and those with learning disabilities are no exception. There is evidence of considerable overlap between the diagnostic categories of learning disabilities and attention deficit disorders (see the Research Notes earlier in this chapter and Chapter 8). Attention problems and hyperactivity in children identified as learning disabled are estimated to range from 9 to 80 percent (McKinney, Montague, and Hocutt 1993; Shaywitz and Shaywitz, 1987).

Social and Emotional Development

Research since the early 1970s has documented the social difficulties encountered by many students with learning disabilities. It suggests that the social interaction and social acceptance of children with learning disabilities remains deficient in comparison with other children. This seems to be true regardless of whether the judgment of a child's social competence is based on teacher perceptions, parent perceptions, peer perceptions, or the actual behaviour of the child observed in social interaction (Coleman and Minnett, 1992).

Students who are learning disabled in inclusive settings interact with teachers and students at much lower rates than do their non-disabled peers (McIntosh, Vaughn, Schumm, Haager, and Lee, 1994). One study (see Weiner, Harris, and Shirer, 1990) found that approximately 50 percent of a sample of 90 children with learning disabilities in suburban schools had peer relationship problems, with about 35 percent being neglected and 15 percent rejected. Especially problematic for these children are name calling and being laughed at by other students when performing poorly at a game (Conte, Andrews, Loomer, and Hutton, 1995).

The reasons why individuals with learning disabilities inspire negative responses are not clear. Studies suggest that inadequate skills in social perception, specifically in skills em-

Profile

John

John is seven years old and in a grade two class. His teacher describes him as fidgety, as boundlessly energetic, as an excessive talker to the point of perseveration. According to his teacher, John only attends to tasks for a very short period and often fails to complete work at all. He draws attention to himself in the classroom by being awkward and clumsy and acts out his anger rather than verbalizing it. John also has trouble making and keeping friends. He seldom engages in constructive play, alone or with classmates.

John's mother found similar behaviour in the home. John could never seem to sit still. He talked from morning to night, wandering aimlessly from one topic to another. In the social domain, he showed extreme frustration when corrected and often embarrassed his family in public. He was also very hard on his personal possessions.

Because John was an only child, his parents had no other children with whom to compare his behaviour. However, they were deeply concerned about his behaviour and were reaching the point of exhaus-

tion. They readily agreed when school personnel suggested an in-depth diagnostic work-up.

A psycho-educational assessment confirmed the observations of John's teacher and parents. Although the psychologist found John inattentive, distractible, and unable to control his continuous activity, he did manage to complete a WISC-R and a number of other tests. The psychologist concluded that John displayed normal intelligence. His severe learning deficits, such as his inability to learn to read, were due to his disturbing classroom behaviours. The psychologist found that John had not yet developed laterality and experienced left–right confusion. John performed poorly on auditory tasks involving discrimination, sequence, and memory. This may have accounted for his anomalies in articulation and syntax, as well as his failure to learn basic reading skills through a phonics approach. The psychologist suggested that further medical evaluation of John's hyperactive behaviour be undertaken. (Adapted from Darnforth, 1984)

ploying empathy, role taking, and making social inferences, contribute to the difficulties (Holder and Kirkpatrick, 1991). These children perform less well on role taking in interpersonal tasks that require taking an alternative viewpoint (Horowitz, 1981). They tend to ignore interpersonal signals from their peers, have trouble perceiving the moods of others, and are less accurate than non-disabled children in interpreting the non-verbal behaviour of others. An inability to interpret facial expressions is probably central to the problem (Holder and Kirkpatrick, 1991). It has also been suggested that students with learning disabilities possess the necessary social skills but lack the motivation and cognition to apply them when necessary (Perlmutter, 1986). Or it may be that students with learning disabilities differ along temperamental dimensions and these influence social interactions with teachers. Differences may then influence teachers' management and instructional strategies.

With rejection and dislike to the forefront, it is little wonder that children with learning disabilities develop emotional problems. Adolescents with learning disabilities are at risk for emotional difficulties and are more likely to experience depression (Kaplan, 1996). Often, as already mentioned, students develop an outward locus of control, learned helplessness, and/or an emotional overlay.

Intervention with Children Who Have Learning Disabilities

Since a learning disability can be highly deleterious to a child's academic and social functioning, as well as future success in life, treatment becomes a critical issue. A wide variety of intervention approaches have been employed with children with learning disabilities. Some approaches are controversial; others contradictory. For example, some early studies supported training for visual perceptual functions (Brod and Hamilton, 1973; Meikle and Kilpatrick, 1971) but other research suggested that such training is not in the least helpful (Camp, 1973; Chapman and Wedell, 1972). It is the disparate characteristics of students who are learning disabled that confounds intervention. Given the extremely heterogeneous nature of the population, no single approach, method, or technique can be expected to offer a solution to every problem.

Medical Intervention

Historically, medicine and learning disabilities have been closely linked, particularly in the area of diagnosis. Until quite recently, learning disabilities were conceptualized in relation to biophysical disorders—specifically some form of minimal brain dysfunction. Today, the field has moved away from a medical model to a diagnostic and educational model for remediation. However, the medical profession continues its active interest in learning disabilities. The current foci of medical interest are drug therapy and diet management.

Psychopharmacological Management

Drugs were first used in the treatment of hyperactive children in 1937. In the last few decades, synthetic compounds have rendered the effects of drugs more predictable, and today psychopharmacological treatment for children diagnosed as hyperactive and/or with attention deficits is the most frequently used method of management. A comprehensive discussion of drug therapy for children identified variously as learning disabled, behaviourally disordered, and Attention Deficit Hyperactivity Disordered is found in Chapter 8.

Diets

One theoretical source of biochemical disturbance is allergy to foods, food dyes, artificial flavours, and preservatives. For example, Kittler (1970) reported studies in which the behaviour of some children improved when foods such as chocolate and milk were excluded from their diet.

Benjamin Feingold (1975) popularized the notion that some substances in foods are linked to hyperactivity in some children. Feingold hypothesized that artificial colourings and flavourings were pharmacologically active substances that produced or aggravated hyperactive symptoms in children. He proposed a diet (the K-P Diet) to restrict the intake of artificial food colours, flavours, preservatives, and foods with natural salicylates. After a stabilization period, foods would be gradually reintroduced to identify the particular items that affected a child.

Informal clinical evaluations and parent testimony suggested that Feingold's diet relieved hyperactivity in 30 to 40 percent of the children who tried it (Swanson and Kinsbourne, 1980). Results of controlled studies have shown equivocal results. Some studies indicate that Feingold's diet may only help a small percentage of hyperactive children (Spring and Sandoval, 1976); others suggest that claims for the importance of food allergies in causing learning disabilities are exaggerated (Henker and Whalen, 1980).

But while skepticism concerning Feingold's hypothesis persists, concerns about the diet's adverse effects seem unwarranted. Rimland (1983) warned that we must be careful of abandoning something with few, if any, ill effects and the potential for some good results.

Technical

Computer technology has much to offer students with learning disabilities. The computer has infinite patience for daily review. There are program learning packages, voice printers, programs to teach logic, and programs to develop self-concept. Some programs have been designed to provide supplementary drill and practice in academic skills. Others attempt to overcome passivity and help the child take a more active part in the learning process by developing active learning styles and problem solving strategies.

Educational Intervention

The challenge for those involved with students who are learning disabled revolves around how to prevent learning failure, how to individualize education for a particular child, and how to provide special education programs for students who are not responding to traditional instructional approaches. Educators must be deeply concerned about how and what to teach pupils who have demonstrated that they learn differently and not very readily the things with which education is charged with teaching them.

The regular classroom–resource room combination is a common method of program delivery. However, intervention in educational settings varies, largely determined by how learning disabilities are defined and understood in a particular school. Disparities in approach, program delivery, procedures, and teaching tactics also occur from situation to situation and from teacher to teacher according to personal preference and training.

Inclusion

Within the public school system, almost all students with learning disabilities are educated in regular classrooms. In the United States during the school year 1989–1990, for example, 98.5 percent of children with learning disabilities were in regular settings (McLeskey and Pacchiano, 1994).

For most students, this is appropriate. Do be aware, however, that serious concerns exist among parents, professionals, and advocacy groups regarding inclusion for students with serious learning disabilities (see Chapter 2). All call for responsible and selective inclusion and a full continuum of services. For example, a policy statement of the New Jersey Commission on Learning Disabilities stated that "The regular education classroom is one of many educational program options but is not a substitute for a full continuum necessary to assure the provision of an appropriate education to all students with learning disabilities" (see Maloney, 1995, p. 25).

Research also supports a continuum of services. For example, a recent study of settings where students with learning disabilities were included (Zigmond, Jenkins, Fuchs, Deno, Fuchs, Baker, Jenkins, and Couthino, 1995) failed to find academic benefits for students. Rather, they found that the achievement outcomes were "neither desirable nor acceptable" (p. 539).

Not all parents are convinced about the inclusion option, especially if it means moving the child from a special class. Some parents are reluctant to return the child to the regular classroom (Green and Shinn, 1994).

Another line of research finds that few teachers in general education classes presently possess the breadth of knowledge or the competencies to meet the individual needs of students with learning disabilities (Wagner, Newman, D'Amico, Jay, Butler-Nalin, Marder, and Cox, 1991). Teachers recognize the low achievement of students with learning disabilities but do very little that is different instructionally when these students are assigned to regular-content classes. The one adjustment that is commonly made is moving to lower grading standards so that the students have a good chance of passing the course (Zigmond, Levin, and Laurie, 1985).

Educational Approaches

In a field as important as learning disabilities, one would think that the way to teach these children most effectively has been the subject of intense investigation and practice. Such is not the case. Issues of definition, etiology, referral, and identification seem to have taken precedence over issues of actual classroom practice, and educational intervention has been somewhat ignored. In a survey of eight major special education journals between 1978 and 1987, for example, the researchers (Lessen, Dudzinski, Karsh, and Van Acker, 1989) found that only 119 of 3 106 articles (4 percent) addressed academic intervention for students with learning disabilities.

A diverse range of general and specific approaches exists in educational intervention for students with learning disabilities. General approaches refer to techniques such as adapting curriculum and grading requirements in the regular classroom or providing resource room assistance in areas of academic lag. Specific approaches refer to a great deal more program adaptation and direction, such as teaching to subskill deficits or metacognitive training.

In instructional terms, learning disabilities may be seen in three ways. Programs focus on underlying problems (processing), observable problems (skills), and strategy problems. Twenty years ago, educators stressed process training approaches that sought to remediate processing deficits. Such an emphasis is quite rare today, and the focus is now on behavioural (skills) or cognitive (strategy training) approaches. Modern techniques that stress careful instruction in the academic areas as well as strategy training tend to be more successful than the earlier indirect approaches that attempted to train students in the dysfunctional processes interfering with learning (Lloyd, 1988).

Behavioural (Skills) Approaches

Behavioural approaches, also referred to as a skill model or task-based perspective, assume that a child's problems are external and result from some gap in instruction. The major focus, therefore, is on the mismatch between school tasks and the unique ability patterns and learning styles of students with learning disabilities and their ability to perform academic tasks. Teachers provide direct instruction in weak academic areas and focus on the skills needed for academic success such as word decoding and basic number facts.

Within each skill subject, a hierarchy of skills is defined. Briefly, teachers would:

1. Determine the student's current repertoire of skills and information through informal and formal testing, school records, and medical data.

2. Determine the skills and informational deficits of the student.

3. Specify the long- and short-term goals of the instructional program for each student.

4. Break these down into small, measurable, and more immediate objectives.

5. Select instructional procedures and techniques.

Task analysis—analyzing the behavioural components and prerequisite skills of a task—plays an integral role. When a teacher task-analyzes an objective, the elements of the task that a child must master are clearly identified. For example, reading skills are broken down into the smallest possible steps and taught one step at a time. Instruction begins at the level of the simplest skill not mastered by the child.

Especially for young children, skills approaches can be very successful. Recent American studies, for example, show that when students with severe reading problems are given early, intensive instruction, almost 95 percent can reach the national average in reading ability ("Reading difficulties ...," 1997).

Not every curriculum area suits such a structured approach based on specific, building steps. While content subjects such as math and handwriting lend themselves quite nicely to such a developmental model, subjects like social studies are more problematic.

Cognitive Approaches

Advances in cognitive psychology have resulted in the development of programs that focus on learning and thinking skills. They focus on *metacognition*, simply defined as an individual's awareness of his or her own cognitive performance and the use of this awareness in altering one's own behaviour.

Cognitive approaches are founded on the belief that learning is a mentally active and constructive process that involves the learner's use of strategies to acquire, store, retrieve, and apply knowledge (Andrews and Violato, 1996). Self-regulated learners have developed metacognitive competence, which begins to develop around ages five to seven and improves throughout school. They own a combination of academic learning skills and self-control. They have both the skill and the will to learn (McCombs and Manzano, 1990).

In contrast to efficient and self-directed learners, poor learners fail to develop efficient metacognition; they simply do not understand the relationship between strategic learning and successful performance. Many students with learning disabilities fit into this group. They have metacognitive deficits; that is, they do not lack the processes entirely, but they seem to use them inefficiently and ineffectively.

What Are Metacognitive Processes?   Before we discuss strategy training, it makes sense to be clear about what metacognition is and the processes involved. Within the general concept of metacognition, there are two types of behaviour. The two behaviours comprising metacognition are knowledge and skill, alternatively referred to as cognitive strategies (control executive strategies) and learning strategies. Metacognitive processes are illustrated in Figure 5-2.

Knowledge is the overarching organizing process—the general strategies used in accomplishing a learning goal. It includes how a person thinks and acts when planning, executing, and evaluating performance on a task. The outcomes of executive strategies are an indicator of how well a person uses methods and strategies to control and promote his or her own learning. The ability is shown when competent readers reduce their reading speed when they reach a difficult passage, for example (Befring, 1997).

Learning strategies refer to an individual's approach to tasks that are either generic or domain specific. Generic strategies are problem-solving skills that apply across many areas of the curriculum such as planning, setting goals for studying, skimming information, locating information, generating questions, note taking, and test writing. Included are mechanisms such as tracking attention to task, asking questions such as, "Am I understanding this?" monitoring speed, and assessing the amount of time it takes to learn and understand certain material. Specific strategies are those used in one situation such as remembering a /sh/ combination in reading or a principle in geometry.

Strategy Training

Research findings indicate that children with learning disabilities in general lack comprehension monitoring skills and efficient task strategies. They fail to maintain and generalize learned strategies, do not understand the relationship between learning strategies and successful performance, and do not apply efficient strategies such as verbal rehearsal and chunking spontaneously (Brown and Palinscar, 1982; Chan, 1988; de Bettencourt, 1987).

Individuals with learning disabilities show significant improvement following strategy training (also known as learning–thinking instructional programs, cognitive training, and

Figure 5-2

Metacognitive processes

Metacognition
awareness of your mind's activity

Cognitive strategies
regulation and control processes; e.g., deciding to switch to problem-solving strategies; knowing how to order a series of strategies to solve a complex problem.

Learning strategies
awareness of strategies and resources needed to perform a task; e.g., mnemonic strategies.

Strategy training
Includes organizational skills, study skills, application of information, problem-solving; selecting correct strategies; knowing when and why to use a strategy.

cognitive behaviour modification) which typically provides the learner with a set of self-instructional steps to increase effectiveness in the acquisition, organization, and expression of information. Training teaches the strategies needed for acquiring information from written material, techniques for remembering information, and methods for improving written expression. The ultimate aim is to provide students with tools that will enable them to become autonomous learners and devise their own strategies.

There are several important sequenced areas in strategy training:

- *Teaching students to consider the many variables involved in problem solving.* Students must analyze the task at hand; identify the steps necessary to complete the task; identify the effective strategies; delineate the necessary steps; and decide how to go about implementing the strategies.

- Teaching students to regulate the processes involved in problem solving, such as planning, checking, testing, revising, and evaluating. Here students reflect on what they already know; they devise a plan for attacking the new problem; they monitor their progress; and they evaluate the outcome of the plan (Lowenthal, 1986).

- *Increasing student effectiveness in the use of specific cognitive skills employed in problem solving.* Simply telling students about effective strategies is not enough; practice is essential. In teaching a strategy for math, for example, one way to teach the procedures is for an adult to first perform the specified task while verbalizing aloud, covering questions about the task, self-guiding instruction on how to do the task, and self-evaluating performance on the task. The student then performs the task while the adult instructs aloud. Following this, the pupil performs the task while verbalizing aloud. The student can now perform the task while using self-verbalization in a whisper and, finally, perform the task using merely subvocalizations. Throughout, the student should be provided with feedback about the utility of the self-instructions for performance.

- *Keeping tasks within the learner's repertoire.* Metacognitive ability is dependent on the interaction between person, task, and strategy variables (Driscoll, 1994). Students must be able to accomplish the tasks they are self-instructing themselves to do; self-instructional support for reading will be of little use if the passage is too difficult for the child.

- *Learning appropriate strategy use and generalization.* Teachers can explicitly point out other tasks and settings in which self-instruction can be used and use a variety of trainers, settings, and tasks to increase the chances that the student will learn to use self-instruction successfully outside of training sessions.

Teachers need also to define when certain strategies are used. For example, mnemonic devices can be extremely valuable in aiding student recall of important information because they strengthen the relationship between what is known and what is to be learned (Levin and Levin, 1990). When Scruggs and Mastropieri (1989) taught adolescents with mild disabilities information about the First World War using either a variety of mnemonic strategies or the more traditional drill and practice, students who learned through mnemonics recalled substantially more content than the traditionally taught group and retained the information for a longer period. While mnemonic strategies have emerged as one of the most powerful instructional techniques in special education for promoting the acquisition of academic content (Scruggs and Mastropieri, 1990), students must know when mnemonics are suitable. They may help with science content but may not be as applicable to learning a passage of Shakespeare.

Strategy instruction is not a quick fix but it does work. For training in the use of learning strategies to have a significant impact on student success, the instruction must be intensive and extensive (Pressly, Levin, and McDaniel, 1987). Students should be trained in the techniques until a reasonable criteria for performance has been reached, then followed up with booster sessions in order to give a better chance that the trained skills will be maintained. Extensive instruction may be necessary to foster the use and transfer of appropriate strategies.

A number of other techniques have grown from cognitive strategy training. For example, attribution training is relevant to students with learning disabilities who often develop an outward locus of control. *Attributions* are the reasons that people give for what happens to them. In strategy attribution training, students are guided to think of their success or failure in terms of the use or non-use of a strategy. For example, "I wrote a good paper because I used a writing strategy" (Stevens and Englert, 1993).

Instrumental Enrichment

Mention should be made of the innovative approach devised by Feuerstein, whose work began with children in post-war Israeli refugee camps. Over the past 40 years, Feurstein has been concerned with assessing the untapped cognitive potential of deprived children so as to remedy their deficiencies through an active intervention program which attempts to build a more effective cognitive structure. The acquisition of such a structure will enable a person of low mental ability to become more adaptable and flexible and therefore more capable of comprehending, planning, and solving problems (Lewis and Samuda, 1989).

Feuerstein calls his program Instrumental Enrichment and describes it as "active modification," because he sees children's performances as modifiable under appropriate social, cultural, and educational policies (Harth, 1988). The aim of instrumental enrichment is to "change the overall cognitive structures of the retarded performer by transforming his passive and dependent cognitive style into the characteristic of an autonomous and independent thinker" (Feuerstein, 1980, p. 1).

Instrumental Enrichment is a paper and pencil curriculum administered three to five times a week over a two to three year period. Each lesson takes about one hour and is typically used as part of a school program. The program is taught to a whole class in a specific sequence (Harth, 1988). The more than 500 pages of exercises are divided into 15 instruments. Each instrument primarily focuses on one deficient cognitive function, although it addresses other cognitive functions as well. Each of the instruments is content free; it does not address any specific curricula skill or content area but rather focuses on the processes of learning directly (Harth, 1988).

Curriculum

A major characteristic of pupils with learning disabilities is an inability to learn adequately in the regular classroom through traditional teaching techniques. Because of the heterogeneous nature of the learning disabled population, schools must provide different administrative arrangements and varied approaches. In addition, they must be willing to permit adaptations to the regular curriculum and assessment procedures.

Adaptations include differentiated assignments, focused questions, intermittent tutoring, grouping, and supplementary instruction. If possible, curriculum adaptations should stress changing the format rather than watering down the curriculum.

Specific ideas for teaching are found in the In the Classroom feature at the end of this chapter. Remembering the blurring between categories, readers will also find relevant techniques for students with learning disabilities in the In the Classroom sections of Chapters 4, 6, and 8. Secondary programming is discussed in Chapter 16.

SUMMARY

1. The term *learning disabilities* first appeared in 1963. As it implied an educational rather than a medical orientation and was also relatively non-stigmatizing, it appealed greatly to parents and educators.

2. Learning disabilities are found in children who do not have any marked cognitive deficits or emotional problems, and do not come from home environments that could be used to explain a reason for their behaviour. Students with learning disabilities exhibit an entire syndrome, or collection, of symptoms. Their problems lie well outside the normal range for their age level and persist despite repeated efforts to correct them. They are handicapped by their disabilities and prevented from realizing their full potential.

3. Controversies continue to plague the field of learning disabilities. These chiefly revolve around the formulation of a universally acceptable definition. Although the term *learning disabilities* has gained wide recognition among educators and the general public, a precise definition has not yet surfaced. Current definitions fail to reflect any consistency, and this spills over to influence critical areas such as classification, identification, prevalence, and instructional approaches.

4. Many more children are moving under the learning disabilities umbrella, although the term may not accurately apply to them because their problems are of a different nature.

5. Learning disabilities adversely affect a child's functioning across domains. The common thread is the inability of these students to learn adequately in regular classrooms under traditional teaching approaches and methods. Youngsters who are learning disabled cannot conform to normal educational demands—there is a marked gap between capability and performance on academic tasks. Children are sound in mind and body but still cannot seem to get the hang of reading, writing, and arithmetic, and therefore lag noticeably in school. Students who have difficulty learning often have problems adjusting to the school, classroom routines, the pressures of daily life, peer groups, and a range of different teachers.

6. The reasons why students with learning disabilities fail are not easily discerned. The condition is generally regarded as a multifaceted concept in terms of etiology and clinical manifestations.

7. The difficulties that students with learning disabilities face in dealing with various types of information may cause them to be less task oriented, less verbally facile, and less responsive than their peers. Children are likely to show attention problems, be more distractible, and exhibit poor self-esteem, an external locus of control, poor motivation, and learned helplessness. They are often disorganized, unco-operative, slow to adapt to change, and overly active. Many children with learning disabilities experience negative social relations with significant people in their lives—parents, teachers, peers—as well as with strangers.

8. Reading deficits are endemic. Arithmetic problems occur with less frequency than reading disabilities and have traditionally received less attention. Problems in visual per-

ception and visual processing include difficulties with oculamotor co-ordination, spatial relations, figure–ground perception, the discrimination of differences, and the recognition of likenesses.

9. Metacognition refers to higher-order thinking processes. Metacognitive strategies serve to support, guide, and extend the thinking processes of their users.

10. Recently, educators have begun to reconceptualize students who are learning disabled as those who have not developed effective learning strategies. They see a need for strategy training to teach students how to use metacognitive skills which involve self-monitoring, practising, reality testing, and co-ordinating the processes of studying and learning.

11. Cognitive instructional programs stress information processing, organizational skills, study skills, application of information, and problem solving. Essentially, the procedures are designed to improve learning effectiveness and social performance in school settings and to teach students to become independent learners.

In the Classroom

Profile: Danny

School is really hard for eight-year-old Danny. He tries and tries but just can't seem to learn as easily and quickly as his classmates. When he was younger, Danny loved going to school and was always eager and excited. Now he approaches each day with apprehension.

In the classroom, Danny is very passive, rarely responding to questions or participating at all. He attempts seat work but is often distractible and off-task. When he is, he more and more often bothers other children and engages in minor misdemeanours. Danny's social skill deficits are becoming more prominent; for example, he exhibits discomfort when given a compliment and has poor eye contact.

Early in his school career the teachers suspected that Danny had learning problems, but it was not until the end of his grade two year that he was formally referred and then administered a battery of psycho-educational measures. At a team meeting just at the close of the school year, the psychologist spoke with some certainty about Danny's problems and described him as a rather typical child with a learning disability.

On the WISC-III, Danny scored a little above the normal range (Full Scale score 122). But on academic work, specifically reading, spelling, and arithmetic, Danny showed serious lags. He is far behind in math and has not yet really mastered rational counting skills, basic place value, or any number facts. He is further ahead in reading, and has quite a broad range of sight word knowledge. However, he needs much work in phonics and phonological awareness. His weaknesses here hinder his reading and make his spelling very much a hit or miss procedure. His printing is poor, as are attempts at creative writing. Here he has problems in generating ideas, in understanding cause and effect relationships, and in using sequential thought processes that are compounded by the poor printing and spelling.

The psychologist suggested a skills approach with much small-group direct teaching for Danny. As in any teaching approach, the skills model should be tailored to Danny's individual needs. The teacher may need to adjust the materials, change the timing, alter the lesson format, or adjust evaluation techniques to help Danny. An extract from Danny's IEP appears below.

* * *

Danny is fairly typical of children with learning disabilities who often enter into a cycle of frustration and failure. Their production deficiencies, the self-helplessness syndrome, and the inactive characteristics of these children all interact to produce learners who are passive, who are incapacitated with feelings of self defeat, and who have a fear of learning. Ineffective coping skills include not asking questions, resisting making choices, being poor risk takers, failing to use effective study skills, and failing to use self-monitoring strategies (Kay, 1986).

Improvements in reading may be accomplished by a word family approach. This will build on Danny's strong sight word vocabulary while strengthening his weak phonic skills. Rather than focusing only on sound symbol association, Danny may benefit from much work in structural analysis of such items as prefixes, suffixes, and compound words. In the early grades, children like Danny also need more intense instruction in phonological awareness.

Proficiency in writing relies on an expanded experiential and knowledge base and the development of adequate listening, speaking, and reading skills (C. R. Smith, 1990). To improve writing, the teacher must first build Danny's motivation to write and his confidence that his thoughts are worthy of communication. A writing program should include daily writing and sustained writing. As well, peer collaboration will allow Danny to use talk to elaborate writing and to become more familiar with words, ideas, and composing procedures (Daiute, 1989).

Remediation of arithmetic problems requires an

individual math program with step by step instruction, beginning at Danny's level of performance and advancing at his rate. Danny must learn the basic skills in which he is deficient. He must master the number facts to 19 and develop a concept of place value before he can learn the four arithmetic processes. To master the number facts he needs daily oral and written drill as well as many opportunities to generalize these facts to other solutions.

In learning math, he needs practical associations. Whenever possible, concrete materials should be used, but Danny will need much practice to translate concrete sums into numerical notation. Place value should be taught with many concrete materials, such as Popsicle sticks, Cuisenaire rods, and a calculator.

Later, decimals should be taught as related to money, and integers can be taught with the temperatures on a thermometer.

Danny's passivity is a mounting problem. Students who respond actively and often to ongoing instruction learn more than students who passively attend. For Danny, the teacher can use many methods of student participation.

Danny's social problems appear to rise directly from his academic frustration. Learning tasks should be structured to allow him much success. He must demonstrate mastery of each step before progressing onward. To build his self-esteem, praise should be realistic and consistent. Danny's progress should be charted with some type of graphic display.

Extract from Danny's IEP

Name: Danny
CA 8-1
Grade: 3
Teacher: Mrs. Als
School: Warren Place

PRESENT LEVELS OF FUNCTIONING

In arithmetic, Danny exhibits a marked discrepancy between his potential and his performance. He functions more than two years below his grade level in this area. He is also delayed in his reading, though not as severely. By using his extensive sight word vocabulary, he is able to partly camouflage his deficits in word attack skills. Danny's academic problems seriously frustrate him, and he is increasingly resorting to overt, acting-out behaviour.

PLACEMENT

Regular classroom. Individualized math program. Although Danny should try to remain in the same reading program as the rest of his class, his success and attitudes to reading might improve with a special set of high interest, low vocabulary readers presented in small-group instruction.

LONG-RANGE GOALS

- Danny will improve decoding skills in reading.
- Writing skills will be stimulated through daily and sustained writing with a peer.
- Danny will improve math skills by learning basic facts.
- Danny will learn about days and months, time, and simple money exchange.

SHORT-TERM OBJECTIVES

- Using a listening station, Danny will decode 15 to 20 selected words.
- Danny will use the words in his own stories.
- Danny will read the decoded words in short paragraphs.
- In a paragraph, he will capitalize and use periods.
- Daily, Danny and a peer will write together for ten minutes on a teacher-selected topic.

- Using a software program on calendar skills, Danny will recognize the days of the week and say them in order.
- Using concrete objects, he will say and write numbers to 100.
- With a peer tutor, Danny will practice number facts to 19 to 100 percent accuracy.
- When given short addition and subtraction problems, Danny will align them on the page correctly and solve to 100 percent accuracy using concrete objects.

EFFECTS OF LEARNING DISABILITIES	TIPS FOR TEACHERS
THE CHILD HAS READING LAGS OR DIFFICULTIES	In order to provide pacing and ensure better understanding, read orally to the class. State a purpose for reading, such as looking for specifics. Use various models for reading, such as in-class text reading, semantic maps, pre-teaching new vocabulary, silent reading (Schirmer, 1997).
THE CHILD HAS POOR COMPREHENSION OF WRITTEN MATERIAL	Use reciprocal teaching, which involves students and teacher in a dialogue for discovering the meaning of a written passage. The steps are 1. Summarize: identify and paraphrase the main ideas of the text. 2. Question generating: self-questioning about comprehension. 3. Clarifying: discerning where and if there has been a lack of comprehension. 4. Predicting: what will happen next (Palinscar and Brown, 1986).
THE CHILD HAS DIFFICULTY READING/ COMPREHENDING CONTENT AREA TEXTS	Highlight textbooks. Provide supplementary content written to a lower level than the textbook. Provide outlines of textbook chapters and outlines of lecture presentations for older students. Teach textbook structure, such as headings, subheadings, differing print, introductory and summary paragraphs.
THE CHILD HAS LANGUAGE DIFFICULTIES	Allow short answers to questions.
THE CHILD HAS PROBLEMS IN PERCEPTUAL PROCESSING	Use visual and auditory cues and prompts to enhance students' ability to discriminate between various stimuli (Polloway, Patton, Payne, and Payne, 1989).
THE CHILD HAS A NEED FOR MUCH REPETITION	Use Computer Assisted Instruction.
THE CHILD EXHIBITS INEFFICIENT STRATEGY USE AND POOR MONITORING OF PROGRESS	Children with learning disabilities have a difficult time choosing the correct strategy (Butler, 1995). Provide cognitive support to help them learn and remember information.

EFFECTS OF LEARNING DISABILITIES	TIPS FOR TEACHERS
	Teach strategies to improve memory.
	Have students explain concepts and skills in their own words.
	Use cognitive frameworks (also called story maps, critical thinking maps, cognitive maps, semantic feature analyses, induction towers, flow charts, study guides, and structured outlines (Boyle and Yeager, 1997). These highlight the salient points of an academic activity and are anchors for knowledge around which students build new information (Boyle and Yeager, 1997).
	Pre-teach and preview major concepts.
	Use advance organizers.
THE CHILD EXHIBITS LOW OR FRAGMENTARY ACHIEVEMENT	Emphasize co-operation rather than competition; effort over achievement.
	Use peer tutoring, an effective instructional alternative for students with learning disabilities, especially when the tutoring program emphasizes repetition and incorporates review, and when the tutee reaches mastery level before advancing to the next tasks (see Bierne-Smith, 1991).
THE CHILD IS A PASSIVE LEARNER	Let students use response cards (a card they hold up on a Popsicle stick) rather than calling on individual students.
	Think "pair share." After posing a question to the class, ask the students to find a partner, make eye contact, share their responses to the question, and remember their partner's response.
	Use free-write, free-tell, or write-alongs. Stop an activity for five minutes and have the students write or tell you about any item that confuses them, what they've learned, and their questions.
THE CHILD DEMONSTRATES OFF-TASK BEHAVIOUR	Seat students near the front of the room so that distractions are behind them, or use carrels to cut down on distractions.
	Divide teaching into small modules; teach in small building steps.
	Students are led to persist longer if they are given attribution feedback on effort ("You've been working hard") or ability ("You're good at this"), or some blend of the two, particularly ability feedback combined with teaching particular strategies in math and reading comprehension (Dohrn and Bryan, 1994).
	Define all requirements of a completed activity. For example, "Your math is complete when all five problems are complete and corrected."
	Provide multiple written prompts such as "To answer this question, look on page 12" (Boyle and Yeager, 1997).

EFFECTS OF LEARNING DISABILITIES	TIPS FOR TEACHERS
	On worksheets, use lots of spacing; provide ample space for writing or drawing; avoid crowding and extraneous print; limit the type of questions; provide clear and concise directions; provide examples; use typing or printing in place of handwriting.
THE CHILD HAS BEHAVIOURAL PROBLEMS	Be specific, consistent, and systematic in expectations and actions.
THE CHILD HAS AN OUTWARD LOCUS OF CONTROL	Maintain a warm and supportive emotional climate. Be honest but liberal with praise. Use consistent reinforcement and provide continuous and immediate feedback.
THE CHILD IS DISORGANIZED AND FORGETFUL	Have students keep an assignment notebook. Use many organizational devices to assist student learning such as dates for assignments written on the board, reminders about homework.
THE CHILD EXHIBITS TEST ANXIETY	Teach students to focus on the types of questions that are likely to arise, to answer the easy questions first, to allot time properly during a test, to answer all the questions, and to check their work. They need to know how to carefully read all the questions and how to develop an outline before writing an essay. Allow children to take tests using different formats. For example, a youngster may respond more easily if allowed to tape record test answers. Allow slow writers extra time to finish tests. Administer practice tests before the real thing. Give alternative forms of the test—oral, essay, short answer, multiple choice, fill-in-the-blank. Use clear, readable, and uncluttered test forms.
HOMEWORK	If homework is important to your program, keep in mind that too much can overwhelm the student who is learning disabled. Use a homework planner (Bryan and Sullivan-Burstein, 1997). Never give homework as a punishment. Listen to what students say about their homework experiences. Put smiling, frowning, and neutral faces on the cover of homework assignments. Have students circle the one that describes their feelings about the assignment. Discuss.

WEBLINKS

Learning Disabilities Association of Canada **http://edu-ss10.educ.queensu.ca/~lda/ldachome.html**

Instrumental Enrichment **http://www.maidenet.co.uk/hope/enrich.html**

Wechsler Intelligence Scale for Children—III **http://edcen.ehhs.cmich.edu/~mnesset/wisc2.html**

Dyslexia, Learning Disabilities, and Literacy Resource Site **http://www.greenwood.org/**

SECTION 3

Children Who Have Intellectual Differences

Intellectual differences is a category that includes two very different groups of children. Children who are intellectually disabled are markedly slower than their agemates in using memory effectively, associating and classifying information, reasoning, and making judgments. Gifted children are exactly the opposite. They learn more, faster, and more thoroughly than their peers. Yet both these groups are considered exceptional and require special education and related services to develop their full potential.

In the past 30 years, education for gifted children and youth and for students with intellectual disabilities has advanced considerably. Positive changes have occurred in public perceptions, terminology, identification and assessment, educational administrative arrangements, and service delivery. However, a broad range of issues and problems remain to be solved. Some of these problems are due to the lack of any universally accepted definition of either giftedness or intellectual disability. Others are more complex and lie at the heart of our societal and personal values.

In the field of intellectual disabilities, issues revolve around normalization and deinstitutionalization and the manner in which individuals can be most effectively integrated into schools, communities, and work places. The major issue in the education of students who are gifted is whether an egalitarian school system should provide special services for children who are already well-endowed. This single issue will determine the fate of education for students with special gifts and talents.

CHAPTER 6

Children with Intellectual Disabilities

Historical Notes

As a human condition, mental retardation has been acknowledged in literature for 2 500 years. Only sparse and scattered information about the actual living and social conditions of persons with mental retardation exists before the seventeenth century. It does appear that little was done for those in society who appeared different or deviant. Generally, superstition and myths surrounded persons with mental retardation. Often they were treated cruelly, sometimes as buffoons, and sometimes as special conversants with higher powers.

Actual teaching of students with mental retardation began in France in the early 1800s. It rapidly translated to the New World, where special facilities were established in Boston in 1848 and Ontario in 1873. In the early 1900s, special classes developed in the public schools to extend schooling to larger numbers and a more varied clientele of students for longer periods.

Right into the 1960s, segregated classes, euphemistically titled "opportunity classes," or "auxiliary classes," or "classes for slow learners," remained the most important vehicle to serve the needs of children who were mentally retarded. Students were trained in manual arts, practical skills, handiwork, and personal and social adjustment skills. In the 1950s, the curriculum for students with mild retar-

dation changed and began to represent an extension of the general school curriculum. At the same time, there was more interest in people with deeper disabilities and curricula for those with moderate and severe retardation emerged.

The 1960s were the turning point in the education of persons with retardation. In that decade a matrix of factors persuaded the educational system to embark on a search for more appropriate ways to educate children with mental retardation. Parent pressure, legislation, litigation, a panel on mental retardation called by U.S. president John Kennedy, and exposés of the deplorable conditions in institutions for mentally retarded persons and for juvenile delinquents created a climate for change. As well, a series of efficacy studies indicated that children in special classes were doing no better in school than they would have been in the regular classroom.

With the 1975 passage of Public Law 94-142 in the United States, the notion of educating all students in the least restrictive environment emerged. The advent of mainstreaming philosophies and practices proved particularly advantageous for children classified as intellectually disabled. Legislation was joined to litigation, civil rights, parent pressure, and normalization and deinstitutionalization. Soon, mainstreaming in the regular classroom became the most common option for the education of these children.

In the 1980s, the Regular Education Initiative in the U.S. stressed the needs of children with mild disabilities in regular classrooms and called for a merger of regular education and special education. The 1990s are witnessing the inclusion movement, which seeks regular education advantages for all children with disabilities.

Intellectual disability is not an illness, nor is it a disease. Essentially, the term refers to delayed intellectual growth which is manifested in immature reactions to environmental stimuli and below average social and academic performance.

As with many areas of special education, the field of intellectual disabilities is characterized by constant change, evolution, and growth in attitudes; in research; in expectations; and in education and training. Compared to even 30 years ago, present attitudes toward individuals who are intellectually disabled are strikingly positive. As a result of new research, professionals now entertain rising, but realistic, expectations for their clients who are intellectually disabled.

Definitions of Intellectual Disabilities

Intellectual disabilities have long been recognized as an exceptional condition, and numerous attempts have been made to define retardation within various disciplines including medicine, psychology, social work, and education. Still, definitions have never been standardized and a universally accepted definition does not exist.

Although recent definitions are very flexible, they are still rooted largely in medical models of disability. (See the Historical Notes in Chapter 3.) The concept of mental retardation is still captured within intelligence and adaptive behaviour scores used with labels.

Today's primary definition of mental retardation is that first adopted in 1959 by the interdisciplinary American Association on Mental Deficiency (AAMD) (today known as the American Association on Mental Retardation (AAMR). The criterion for adaptive behaviour, not in the 1959 version, was added later. Under this widely accepted definition, mental retardation refers to

> substantial limitations in personal functioning, characterized by significant subaverage intellectual functioning, existing concurrently with related limitations in two or more of the following adaptive skills: communication, self-care, home living, social skills, community use, self-direction, health and safety, functional academics, leisure, and work. Mental retardation is manifested before age 18 (AAMR, 1993).

The three important points in the definition are those that refer to subaverage intellectual functioning, deficits in adaptive behaviour, and manifestation during the developmental period.

Subaverage General Intellectual Functioning

Individuals are not considered intellectually disabled unless they score below 70 IQ on a standardized test of mental ability; that is, two or more standard deviations below the mean. This is a relatively recent cut-off point—before the 1970s children who fell between one and two standard deviations below the norm (IQ 85 and below) were included in the mentally retarded category. The definition adopted by the American Association on Mental Deficiency in 1973 limited the category of mental retardation to those with an IQ of 70 or less (Moores, 1987). With this change, 80 percent of the mentally retarded population was eliminated (Zetlin and Murtaugh, 1990). Today, students whose IQ scores fall between 85 and 70 are considered borderline or perhaps slow learners, but not mentally retarded.

Adaptive Behaviour

Since the 1950s, changing definitions of mental retardation have given increasing prominence to the concept of adaptive behaviour. The construct was first delineated as a component of mental retardation by Edgar Doll in the early 1940s and formally added as a criterion in 1961 (Heber, 1961). The phenomenon of adaptive behaviour was expanded by Mercer (1973) who described the "six-hour retarded child"; that is, the one who cannot cope with the methods, pace, and materials of the regular educational classroom but functions quite adequately in other environments.

With the addition of the adaptive behaviour construct, the concept of mental retardation broadened. Adaptive behaviour is crucial to today's definitions. Individuals must demonstrate poor adaptive behaviour as well as subaverage intellectual functioning before they can be classified as retarded. Students who manifest deficits in adaptive behaviour but score within the normal range on IQ tests are usually labelled emotionally disturbed or learning disabled (Reis, Levitan, and McNally, 1982).

Nearly all conceptions of adaptive behaviour use the basic definition formulated by the AAMD, in which adaptive behaviour is seen as "the degree and efficiency with which an individual meets the standards of personal independence and social responsibility of his age or cultural group" (Grossman, 1977, p. 11). In other words, **adaptive behaviour** refers to how well a person is able to adapt to environmental demands, and differs according to the individual's age group and particular situation.

Adaptive behaviour is a dynamic construct influenced by cultural norms and age-related expectations. The preschooler, for example, needs sensorimotor skills, communication, self-help skills, and socialization to adapt to the environment. We do not expect the preschooler to be interested in vocational prospects and an expanded peer group; these are the adaptive concerns of the adolescent.

The dynamic nature of adaptive behaviour implies that, over time and with experience, adaptive behaviour can change. Specific adaptive limitations often co-exist with strengths and other personal capabilities; with appropriate supports over a sustained period, therefore, the life functioning of the person with intellectual disabilities will generally improve.

Adaptive behaviour is a controversial concept. Some interpretations include academic and more cognitively oriented skills; others intentionally omit these types of behaviour. Generally, adaptive behaviour includes social functioning and interpersonal relationships, functional academic competencies, and vocational/occupational competencies. Competencies related to functional independence are perhaps the most widely accepted component of adaptive behaviour. Skills involved relate to toileting, dressing, feeding, avoiding danger, and maintenance of a minimal level of health and safety (Reschley, 1989).

Although adaptive behaviour has been critical in the identification of mental retardation for more than 40 years, lively debate about and criticism of the construct remains common. Some researchers want to disregard adaptive behaviour and focus solely on subaverage intellectual functioning (e.g. Zigler, Balla, and Hodapp, 1984); others (e.g. Barnett, 1986) stress adaptive behaviour and see the interaction between individual characteristics and societal demands as absolutely vital. Other recent issues concerning adaptive behaviour revolve around a definition, the integration of the construct with broader models of personal competence, empirical investigations of the nature of the construct, and assessment of adaptive behaviour (see McGrew, Bruininks, and Thurlow, 1992).

Developmental Period

Under the AAMR definition, the developmental period refers to the time between the child's conception and his or her eighteenth birthday.

Terminology

If you have been reading this chapter carefully, you will have noticed that we use the term *intellectual disabilities* and only refer to *mental retardation* when explicitly discussing information that comes from the AAMR. This usage reflects new trends in labelling.

Over the centuries, persons with intellectual disabilities have been described by a plethora of labels, many of them offensive. In 1910, Henry Goddard, an American psychologist, divided retardation into the categories of *feeble-minded, moron, idiot,* and *imbecile.* These terms lingered until the 1950s, when the term *mental retardation* became generally accepted. Today, however, that term suffers its own problems. Because it is used for individuals with the most severe disabilities, it evokes in many people the impression of a condition that is always a permanent and comprehensive incapacity. However, especially in the case of mild conditions, mental retardation does not include the expectation of biologically based, permanent, and comprehensive incompetence (Harry, 1992). The current AAMR definition sees mild mental retardation as a condition that can improve as a result of changes in either the individual or the environment.

As well, the term *retardation* suggests a deficit within the individual (Harry, 1992). Some people today prefer *intellectually challenged*, which reflects the social aspects of the disability; that is, people find difficulties in meeting the challenges of our highly industrialized, technologically oriented, and fast-paced society. Others in the field prefer to use the more inclusive term *developmental disability.*

Classification of Intellectual Disabilities

Most professionals agree that the most useful system to classify retardation is that proposed by the AAMR, which considers the condition along a continuum, or scale, of severity. The AAMR's categories—*mild, moderate, severe,* and *profound* retardation—describe the individual's functioning clearly. The AAMR system carries no negative stereotyping and little stigma. As adjectives, the words mild, moderate, severe, and profound apply to many other things besides retardation (Hallahan and Kauffman, 1991).

When severity classifications are employed, it is important to remember that there will probably be as much variability within any one group as there is between the groups and between or within groups of normally developing individuals. As well, the cut-off scores leave room for clinical judgment. An IQ of 54 may be judged as moderate or mild mental retardation. Table 6-1 indicates, in broad terms, the educational expectations at each severity level.

While many educators prefer the AAMR classification system, we still occasionally hear the more traditional terms *educable* and *trainable,* which educators have used over the years to try to describe the educational needs of children who are intellectually disabled. This terminology reflects the ability of children labelled as educable mentally retarded (EMR) to benefit from academic instruction, whereas those called trainable mentally retarded (TMR) are presented with a more non-academic program that focuses on training in life skills and skills for independent living.

Classification by Needs

Recently, a new set of qualifiers arrived in the field of mental retardation. The Diagnostic and Statistical Manual (DSM) (APA, 1994) still uses severity levels and, as we just saw, they are still used by the AAMR. However, in 1992 the AAMR attempted a change.

Table 6-1 Degrees of intellectual disability and expected developmental and academic characteristics

IQ level	Expectations
70–90	Not classified as intellectually disabled. Capable of competing in school in many areas.
55–70 (mild)	Capable of basic academic subjects up to advanced elementary levels; will achieve about half to two thirds of what normally developing peers do. General achievement ranges from second to fifth grade. Gap widens in secondary school.
40–55 (moderate)	Capable of attaining self-help skills, communication skills, and social adjustment. Limited academic achievement but can attain many functional skills and basic functional academics. Can achieve economic usefulness later in routine jobs under supervision or perhaps in sheltered workshops.
25–40 (severe)	Can attain basic communication and self-help skills. May or may not be ambulatory. Additional disabilities hinder attainments.
below 25 (profound)	With intensive training, may learn basic self-help and communication skills. Often not ambulatory; may be medically fragile and/or technology dependent.

Rather than severity, the proposed system changes dependency to support needs, keys terms to the level of services required, and describes them in ways that are prescriptive for programming needs. Specifically, it replaces the levels of mild to profound with *intermittent, limited, extensive,* and *pervasive,* terms which refer to the supports needed. In this classification on supports, an individual's needs are classified in several domains; for example, communication (McLean, Brady, and McLean, 1996).

A child needing intermittent supports would require only a little extra assistance in the classroom. In contrast, a child needing pervasive supports would require supports characterized by constancy and high intensity, that are provided across environments, and that are of a potentially life sustaining nature (Kaplan, 1996).

In Chapter 1 we discussed the use of labels and the controversy that often surrounds labelling. But in this case, the change in classification by the AAMR seems to have passed most people by. These new AAMR terms have been largely ignored by the field (Vergason and Anderegg, 1997).

Prevalence of Intellectual Disabilities

Any attempt to estimate the incidence rate of a relatively common disorder almost invariably fails to take into account some affected individuals. This occurs in the case of mental retardation, where mild conditions prove elusive and difficult to accurately pinpoint and many cases go unreported.

It is extremely difficult to obtain true and accurate prevalence figures for intellectual disabilities. Specific reasons are outlined in the list below.

- Different IQ cut-off points are used. Whereas the AAMR uses an IQ of 70 as the beginning of the designation of mild mental retardation, a school system may use an IQ of 75.

- Methods of gathering data for prevalence studies differ.

- Different definitions of adaptive behaviour are used.

- Different regions and social classes show different prevalence. The majority of children labelled as intellectually disabled come from a lower socio-economic bracket—children from lower socio-economic strata have a greater risk of incurring brain damage because of factors such as malnutrition, poor prenatal and postnatal care, and environmental hazards during infancy (Baumeister, Kupstas, and Klindworth, 1991; Dunlap, 1989). Hence, large urban areas with a high lower-class population show a higher proportion of mental retardation.

- There are gender differences within prevalence estimates. A higher percentage of boys than girls are found among the population considered to be mildly intellectually disabled, somewhere between five to ten times as many boys as girls. This may result from a higher probability of adverse biological factors affecting male children. It may also result from the fact that expectations tend to be higher for males, or it may be that the more aggressive behaviour usually found among males can lead to the label of mental retardation.

- Different age groups show different prevalence figures, especially among the group classified as mildly mentally retarded. Prevalence is low in the preschool years (less than one percent in children below the age of five), increases dramatically during the school years, and declines later (Drew, Logan and Hardman, 1992). The high rates among school-age children are no doubt a reflection of the environmental demands of school. As a social system, the school has a certain set of expectations, which some of these children fail to meet. In fact, some researchers contend that high-functioning mentally retarded children do not officially become retarded until they enter school and encounter reading, writing, and math. They pass through the school system labelled as intellectually disabled but then go on to occupy normal roles in society.

- There has been a redistribution among categories that is a direct result of the birth of the field of learning disabilities in 1963 and the redefinition of retardation ten years later. This led to a kind of hydraulic relationship among the mild categories of exceptionality, with the most significant movement occurring between learning disabilities and mild mental retardation. Today, many youngsters who previously wore the label of mild mental retardation are being propelled into the classification of learning disabilities.

- The concept of mild mental retardation is particularly controversial since children in this category are drawn almost exclusively from poor families, often of minority origin. Although gender and racial imbalance (more males and ethnic children) continue (Polloway, Epstein, Patton, Cullinan, and Lueble, 1986), there is also a greater hesitancy to label children as EMR.

- Jurisdictions are developing stricter criteria for diagnosing mental retardation and, as this happens, the number of children identified as learning disabled increases.

- In the United States, there is quite a deal of reluctance to label children as mentally retarded because of court cases such as Larry P vs. Riles (see Winzer and Mazurek, 1998).

- With stricter criteria and a reluctance to label, mental retardation is a shrinking category. This relates to both within the number of children identified and labelled and within the amount of research directed toward it (see Edgar, 1987).

Reduction in the rate of mental retardation has not resulted from any significant change in rates for severe and profound—and perhaps moderate—retardation, but from dramatic changes in the way we now define and label the condition of mild retardation.

Given a normal curve, a theoretical 2.27 percent of the population might be expected to fall two or more standard deviations below the mean. In reality, this does not happen. Only about 1 to 1.5 percent of the population meets the AAMR definition of retarded in both intellectual functioning and adaptive behaviour.

More than 75 percent of the mentally disabled population are mildly retarded. For the moderate, severe, and profound levels (IQ of 50 or below), a review of 20 studies found three or four persons per thousand (McLaren and Bryson, 1987). Severe and profound intellectual disabilities are extremely low-incidence conditions. Note, however, that there is evidence of a recent increase in the number of children with severe and profound conditions as children who may not have survived in the past are now saved by medical advances (Alper, Schloss, and Schloss, 1994). Figure 6-1 shows the prevalence and severity of mental retardation.

What this means for the schools is that the current population of children considered to be mildly mentally retarded, or educable mentally retarded (EMR), has changed quite dramatically. Today, we find that pupils identified as mildly mentally retarded tend to have greater disabilities than those of previous years (Epstein, Polloway, Patton, and Foley, 1989; MacMillan, 1988; Polloway, 1985). If children are in special EMR classes, their average ability level is lower than before. Today, EMR classes serve children with Down syndrome and those previously classified as trainable mentally retarded (TMR) (Robinson, Patton, Polloway, and Sargent, 1989).

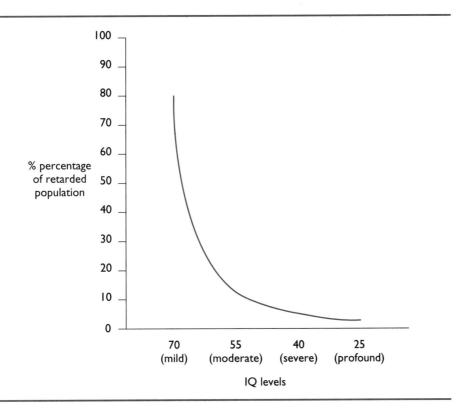

Figure 6-1
Prevalence and severity of mental retardation

Etiology of Intellectual Disabilities

In both historical and contemporary contexts, etiological considerations have been prominent in the field of mental retardation. Nevertheless, the causes of intellectual disability remain highly controversial. Even though our knowledge has increased a hundredfold, we are still unable to answer some of the most fundamental questions and are frequently powerless to explain the condition of a specific child.

The agents that cause intellectual disabilities are legion and include genetic and chromosomal differences, infections such as maternal rubella, intoxicants such as drugs, postnatal diseases such as meningitis, and childhood accidents. In all, more than two hundred causes of mental retardation are known. Some of the etiologies are also the villains in other disabilities. Rubella, for example, can leave a child with a range of disabilities that affects almost every organ.

The cause of retardation can actually be specified in about 20 to 25 percent of cases, which are almost exclusively of the moderate to profound severity levels. When causes can be pinpointed, they are referred to as organic causes, classed into two very broad categories—genetic factors and brain damage. Children retarded by organic causes are usually diagnosed well before school entrance because their conditions are readily apparent.

Far more problematic in diagnosis are those children who show no clear-cut evidence of an organic cause. The condition, referred to as non-specific mental retardation, is found most often among individuals with mild intellectual disabilities.

The following brief discussion on the etiologies of intellectual disabilities supplements the information presented in Chapter 3. Table 6-2 presents a sample of etiologies, some common and some rare, that can lead to mental retardation. Note that some conditions occur within more than one classification.

Genetic Defects

Problems due to heredity account for only a small percentage of mental retardation. The study of these disorders, however, provides valuable knowledge that can lead to the prevention and treatment of retardation due to other causes.

Phenylketonuria (PKU) and galactosemia, two genetic disorders that are potential causes of mental retardation, result from the body's inability to metabolize essential proteins. Children with untreated PKU have intellectual levels below 50 IQ and may also be subject to noisy and destructive psychotic episodes (Robinson and Robinson, 1976).

Chromosomal Problems

Chromosomal abnormalities include too many chromosomes, too few chromosomes, and chromosomes that are attached to one another. Abnormalities in the structure and number of chromosomes can be caused by natural mutation of genes, by radiation, and by a host of other factors that are only partly understood. Apart from Down syndrome, the number of children with intellectual disabilities due to chromosomal abnormality is quite small.

Down syndrome is by far the most common and widely known form of chromosomal aberration. Worldwide, Down is the most common clinical cause of mental retardation (Manfredini, 1988). Intellectually, the Down syndrome child can fall anywhere in the retardation spectrum, but most tend to be classed as moderately retarded. Down syndrome accounts for approximately 10 percent of all cases of moderate and severe mental retardation (Hallahan and Kauffman, 1991). Individuals with Down syndrome who have normal intellectual development are exclusively those with the mosaic form of the condition.

The fragile X (Fra (X)) syndrome has attracted the interest of health, education, and human service professionals because it is common, its inheritance pattern is unique, and it presents a wide variety of disabilities. Frequency estimates indicate that Fra (X) may be second only to Down syndrome as an etiology of mental retardation in males. Among males with fragile X, approximately 30 percent may be severely or profoundly retarded; the majority are moderately or mildly retarded, and 10 percent have borderline or low–normal IQs (Dykens, Leckman, Paul, and Watson, 1988; Hagerman and Sobesky, 1989). Lesser degrees of impairment are found in fragile X females. Research indicates that they are usually less cognitively affected than males, although one-third have mental retardation, usually in the mild range (Reiss and Freund, 1990).

Whether they are intellectually disabled or fall into the normal range, a significant number of fragile X children display specific and behavioural learning difficulties (Forness and Kavale, 1994). In addition, fragile X is associated with greater risk for a range of disorders involving social relations (Dykens, 1996).

A controversial finding relates to the possibility of a decline in cognitive skills with age. Various studies have reported significant drops in IQ over time. The reason may involve progressive neurological degeneration (Simen and Rogers, 1989).

Table 6-2 Some causes of mental retardation

Infections and intoxicants	Infections: rubella, syphilis, toxoplasmosis, herpes simplex, bacterial infections, viral infections, parasitic infections
	Intoxicants: drugs, poisons, smoking, caffeine, alcohol, lead
Trauma or physical agents	Anoxia, irradiation, trauma
Metabolism or nutrition	Lipid storage diseases: Tay–Sachs disease, Hurler's, Hunter's
	Carbohydrate disorders: galactosemia, hypoglycemia
	Endocrine disorders: hypothyroidism
	Amino acid disorders: phenylketonuria
	Other: Prader-Willi syndrome, malnutrition
Gross brain disease	Neurofibromatosis (von Recklinghavsen's disease), Sturge-Weber syndrome, tuberous sclerosis (epiloia), Huntington's chorea
Unknown prenatal influence	Anencephaly, microcephaly, Apert's syndrome, meningomyocele, hydrocephalus
Chromosomal abnormality	Chromosomal aberrations: Down syndrome, Klinefelter's syndrome, *cri-du-chat*
	Autosomal dominant gene disorders: neurofibromatisis, tuberous sclerosis, Sturge-Weber syndrome
	Autosomal recessive gene disorders: phenylketonuria, congenital hypothyroidism, maple syrup urine disease, Tay–Sachs disease, Smith-Lemli-Optiz syndrome
	X-linked disorders: Lasch-Nyhan syndrome, fragile X syndrome
Gestational disorders	Prematurity, postmaturity, low birth weight
Psychiatric disorders	Psychoses
Environmental influences	Psychosocial disadvantage, sensory deprivation

Sources: Aase, 1979; Grossman, 1977; Vitello and Soskin, 1985

Infections and Intoxications

Infections and intoxications that lead to mental retardation can occur in the pregnant mother, the infant, or the young child. Rubella is particularly dangerous. The virus can cross the placenta and damage the developing fetus during the first trimester of pregnancy. Syphilis in the mother is another infection that can cross the placental barrier and damage the fetus. Unlike rubella, syphilis is most dangerous after the fifth month of pregnancy.

Pediatric AIDS is the fastest growing infectious cause of mental retardation and brain damage in children (Gray, 1989). Of infants born with HIV infection, 78 to 93 percent become developmentally disabled through central nervous system involvement (Gray, 1989).

Intoxicants and poisons in the pregnant mother or the child can also cause mental retardation. One of the most important outcomes in this category is Fetal Alcohol Syndrome (FAS), which joins Down syndrome, fragile X syndrome, and spina bifida as one of the most common currently known causes of mental retardation. Of these conditions, FAS is the most directly preventable, at least in principle.

Mental retardation appears to be associated with the more severe cases of FAS. One study of 20 patients found that 60 percent had IQs more than two standard deviations below the mean (Streissguth, Herman, and Smith, 1978). Other researchers have reported an average IQ of 65, with a range from 16 to 106 (Landesman-Dwyer, Martin, Smith, and Streissguth, 1980). Still others note that although the structural deformities caused by a mother's drinking during pregnancy are permanent, the behavioural problems of alcohol-exposed children seem to increase with age (Vorhees and Mollnow, 1987).

In the developing child, meningitis and encephalitis can lead to mental retardation and other anomalies. More encephalitic children than meningitic children suffer retardation. Childhood accidents involving cerebral assault or prolonged loss of consciousness can also cause brain damage that leads to retardation. Child abuse is increasingly being cited as another cause of brain damage (see Chapter 11).

Environmental Influences

The great majority of children with identified intellectual disabilities are categorized as mildly retarded with the etiology "causes unknown." These children often come from deprived backgrounds and many of their problems spring from psychosocial disadvantage, poverty, inadequate nutrition, family instability, lack of educational opportunity, or an unstimulating infant environment.

Subtle genetic factors may interweave with socio-economic deprivation to further affect a child's development. The relative influence of genetic factors to environmental ones is, however, unknown.

Identification and Measurement of Intellectual Disabilities

The identification and assessment of intellectual disabilities fulfills several major needs. Medical diagnosis leads directly to necessary treatment regimes. A full pediatric medical evaluation of the child is vital to pinpoint secondary conditions and allow the physician to recognize and identify the child's strengths. The physician searches for whatever potential-ities will help the child achieve more efficient functioning. This includes all the sensory and motor strengths that can be used for later training and development.

Within the educational milieu, identification must determine if the child's mental abil-ity and adaptive behaviour fulfill the definitional criteria. However, the most important use of data is the provision of an appropriate program and/or treatment plan and the estab-lishment of objectives and remedial strategies.

But even with the thousands of tests, measures, inventories, and scales available, identi-fication and assessment remain problematic. Diagnosticians still encounter grave difficulties in arriving at an accurate assessment of the learning potential and adaptive behaviour of many children who are intellectually disabled.

Formal diagnosis is not one short affair. Assessment incorporates a range of medical, formal, and informal processes using a variety of assessment instruments, different types of procedures, and different personnel. In an extreme case, as an example, a child with a severe intellectual impairment and co-occurring disabilities may be seen by a physician for phys-iological assessment, an audiologist for hearing acuity, an ophthalmologist for visual efficiency, a physical therapist for gross motor functioning, an occupational therapist for fine motor skills, a psychologist for intellectual ability, and a teacher for educational achievement.

Procedures may include direct testing, ecological or functional assessment, or some other assessment procedure. The tools administered depend on the strengths and needs of the child. A test that suits a child who is mildly disabled, for example, will likely be inap-propriate for one with severe retardation.

Educational Screening

In the school system, educational screening often precedes psycho-educational diagnosis. For children with moderate to profound intellectual disabilities, screening may not take place simply because many of these children will have overt and obvious problems that were diagnosed well before school entrance. The clear-cut organic or psychological signs that ac-company severe disabilities make it possible to identify them in infancy.

On the other hand, many cases of mild intellectual disability are not suspected until children enter school. Teachers are often the first to recognize that these children have prob-lems and are at the forefront in identifying their needs and referring them for further as-sessment. Not only can teachers observe students over a period of time and note academic performance in the classroom and social behaviour in and out of the classroom, but they also have access to pertinent school records and to the observations and comments of other teachers who may have encountered the child in earlier grades.

Assessment of Intelligence

In the formal assessment of intellectual disabilities the initial two major areas of concern are IQ and adaptive behaviour. IQ is the pivotal concept. Moreover, IQ has been around longer and a range of measures are in use.

With children suspected of intellectual disability, an assessment of intelligence is im-portant in order to meet the definitional criteria of an IQ level two or more standard devi-ations below the norm. Children in the more severe ranges of intellectual disability are often untestable through the usual standardized IQ tests such as the WISC-III. In cases where organic brain pathology and physical disabilities are present, IQ levels are estimated through the use of developmental scales, measures of adaptive behaviour, observations, and other tools. (See Chapters 13 and 14.)

Assessment of Adaptive Behaviour

The inclusion of adaptive behaviour in the definitions and assessment of intellectual disabilities has led to the development of numerous scales. Still, no single, quantifiable, and reliable assessment procedure exists and almost all of the scales designed to measure adaptive behaviour have been criticized.

One problem is the rather murky definition of adaptive behaviour; another relates to the relative newness of the concept. As well, there exists no simple relationship between adaptive behaviour and chronological age in children who are intellectually disabled (Volkmar, Sparrow, Gourdeau, Cichetti, Paul, and Cohen, 1987).

Many adaptive skills are very visible, such as using the toilet, feeding oneself, dressing, and peer relations. Adaptive behaviour scales, used with children in all severity ranges, generally consist of lists or inventories of these and other common behaviours, as well as maladaptive behaviours. The scales are completed by someone close to the child—a parent, teacher, or primary caregiver.

Many scales are in common use. These include the Balthazar Scales of Adaptive Behavior (Balthazar, 1973, 1976), the Adaptive Behavior Checklist (Allen, Cortazzo, and Adams, 1970), the Cain-Levine Social Competence Scale (Cain, Levine, and Elzey, 1963), the AAMD Adaptive Behavior Scales (Lambert and Windmiller, 1981; Nihira, Foster, Shellhaas, and Leland, 1974), the Vineland Adaptive Behaviour Scale, Revised (Sparrow, Balla, and Cicchetti, 1984) and the Battelle Developmental Inventory (Newborg, Stock, and Wnek, 1984).

Prevention of Intellectual Disabilities

Research suggests that for the moderate, severe, and profound levels of retardation, postnatal causes account for about five percent, perinatal causes for about 15 percent, and prenatal causes for about 80 percent (Milunsky, 1975). While prevention is not possible in many cases, various estimates claim that about 20 to 30 percent of cases could be prevented with the intensive application of current knowledge (National Prevention Committee, 1982).

Great strides have been made in identifying contributing causes and developing preventative measures. One of these is genetic counselling, and more than 40 genetic conditions are now detectable through amniocentesis. Conditions such as FAS are preventable and those such as PKU are controllable by diet.

Developmental Consequences of Intellectual Disabilities

Intellectual disabilities cover a variety of physical, intellectual, academic, and behavioural characteristics. Individuals who are described as intellectually disabled vary widely in almost every aspect of human behaviour, human personality, and human temperament. Despite their intellectual limitations, youngsters who are intellectually disabled show more similarities to other children than they do differences. They feel, think, hope, play, have fun, and find mischief, just like everyone else. While they will have difficulties with complex academic material, many children who are intellectually disabled develop into productive and self-sufficient adults. They marry, have children, assume mortgages, hold down jobs, and participate in social activities. Of course, the amount and degree of the retardation is of prime importance; within the various levels of disability is found a wide range of behaviours and abilities.

Viewing intellectual disability on a continuum, we can place children who are mildly disabled and having trouble with academic subjects at one end and profoundly retarded youngsters who may be non-ambulatory and non-responsive to their surroundings at the other. However, when discussing the population of persons with intellectual disabilities, we must keep in mind that categories of severity often overlap and are subject to change. Very early intervention allows teachers and parents to reduce the impact on child development.

When IQ can be changed, this is called *trait plasticity*. Experts say that IQ is malleable by about 20 points. Early intervention with children with Down syndrome, for example, has shown that the condition need not always cause moderate to severe mental retardation. The psy-

Profile

Jane

Jane L. is seven years and ten months old. She was diagnosed as having Down syndrome at birth. When she was six months old, she and her mother began to attend an infant stimulation program for developmentally disabled children and their families. At age three, Jane was enrolled in a nursery school for developmentally disabled children. During these preschool years, her mother spent a great deal of time with her, carrying out the suggestions of the infant therapist and then the preschool teachers.

A recent psychological testing of Jane indicated that, both cognitively and socially, she is functioning in the high end of the moderately retarded scale. While Jane's verbal and non-verbal intelligence scores were similar, her social age was somewhat higher, as measured by the Vineland Social Maturity Scale. Her use of receptive language, measured by the Peabody Picture Vocabulary Test, was more advanced than her expressive language. Jane's language problems are compounded by speech problems associated with

the physical anomalies of Down syndrome.

Jane loves school. She attends the local public school in a self-contained classroom. Her teacher is using a language experience method to expand her receptive language vocabulary. Jane enjoys this approach, and also finds integrated activities great fun—preparing simple non-cooked recipes, dusting, sweeping, and "playing house." Jane is less enthusiastic about her sessions on articulation with the speech therapist. However, she is always eager to attempt any of the motor tasks suggested by the physical therapist to improve the quality of her movements.

Jane's social aptitude serves her well. She is well liked by the other children in the class and could be considered the class leader. At first, on the playground, she was very shy of other children in the school. Recently, however, she has begun to join the games of some of the kindergarten children, who accept her quite readily.

chological profile of babies with Down show that they seem to develop normally in early infancy. The rate of development slows after six months of age and by ten months these infants receive lower scores than normally developing infants on measures of intellectual development (Kopp, 1983). For children with Down syndrome, early and sustained intervention halts the decline in cognitive development. It also appears to prevent further decreases throughout the remaining early childhood years (see Guralnick and Bricker, 1987; also Chapter 15). The profile on Jane illustrates the success of early intervention for one student with Down syndrome.

Physical Development

Individuals who are mildly intellectually disabled present few if any divergent physical symptoms that differentiate them from their peers. Minor differences may be seen in measures of health and of physical and motor performance.

The range in age at which motor and language milestones are attained is far greater than for normally developing children. In early childhood, children with intellectual disabilities reach developmental milestones later; they may take up to nine months longer to learn to walk, talk, eat, and toilet themselves. These children are also likely to be somewhat below the comparative standards for height, weight, and skeletal maturity. In motor areas, they perform below the standards of non-disabled children (Bruininks, 1977).

Physical impairments become more complex in children with moderate retardation. These children tend to be markedly less able physically and more unco-ordinated.

Traditionally, researchers and practitioners have tended to group people who are severely and profoundly intellectually disabled together, although these groups differ in several ways. Of course, the categories do overlap, as do severe and moderate disabilities. Common to both groups are the presence of additional conditions. Blindness, deafness, cerebral palsy, epilepsy, and other physical anomalies are the rule rather than the exception.

There exists a strong negative correlation between IQ level and the presence of organic brain pathology, central nervous system impairment, and other disabilities. In other words, as one proceeds down the scale, the incidence of co-occurring disabilities increases, which then serves to compound the original retardation. A British Columbia study of non-specific retardation (Herbst and Baird, 1983) found that 27 percent of people with mild intellectual disabilities had additional conditions. In contrast, 73.1 percent of profoundly retarded individuals suffered additional conditions.

Individuals who are severely retarded may show poor speech, inadequate social skills, poor motor development or non-ambulation, incontinence, sensory impairments, seizures, and cerebral palsy. The population of persons who are profoundly retarded can be divided functionally into two groups (Miller, 1976). "Relative" profoundly retarded persons have less organic damage and are capable of some degree of ambulation, communication, and self-help skills. "Absolute" profoundly retarded individuals are some of the most seriously impaired of all people with disabilities. The nature and degree of their disability is so great that, without various forms of intensive training and therapy, they exhibit virtually no adaptive behaviour. As well, many of these people exist in a medically fragile state.

Survival rates vary with the level of retardation. Herbst and Baird (1983) found the death rate among mildly intellectually disabled persons was twice as high as that of the general population. It was seven times higher among those severely retarded, and 31 times higher among those profoundly disabled. Moreover, the mortality rate among people who are profoundly retarded is almost 50 percent higher than among those with severe retardation. Mortality rates for non-ambulant persons are significantly higher than for those who are ambulant (Balakrishnaw and Wolf, 1976).

Down Syndrome

Apart from their physical stigmata, children with Down syndrome are prone to a range of sensory impairments and very serious health problems. Only within recent years has the life span of children with Down syndrome begun to approach that of the general population. In 1929, these individuals had a life expectancy of nine years; by 1980, it had advanced to more than 30 years; now 25 percent of individuals with Down syndrome live to the age of 50 (Patterson, 1987). The mortality rate is still high, however, especially perinatally and in the first years of life, largely due to congenital heart conditions and increased susceptibility to infections (Burgio, Fraccaro, and Tiepolo, 1981). After age one, mortality is considerably reduced. Between ages five and ten, life expectancy is only six percent below normal.

About 40 percent of children with Down syndrome have congenital heart defects. Gastrointestinal malformations and reduced resistance to respiratory infections are com-

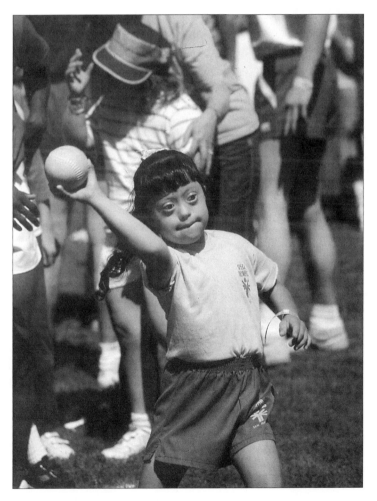

Down syndrome is a cause of mental retardation, ranging from mild to profound.

mon. Children are especially susceptible to otitis media and the resultant conductive hearing loss; as many as 75 percent of children with Down syndrome may have significant hearing losses, and the detrimental effects of hearing loss are believed to be greater for these children compared to non-retarded youngsters (Northern and Lemme, 1982; Whitman, Simpson, and Compton, 1986; Yarter, 1980).

Children with Down syndrome have biochemical differences as well. Recent research on chromosome 21 has shown that its genes are linked not only to Down, but also to susceptibility among normal individuals to cancer, Alzheimer's, congenital heart defects, and vision problems (Kolata, 1989).

If individuals with Down syndrome survive to middle age, they are more likely to develop cataracts, leukemia, and Alzheimer's (Patterson, 1987). There is a twenty- to fiftyfold increase in the risk of developing leukemia, probably because of a gene on chromosome 21 that is known to cause leukemia if improperly activated (Patterson, 1987; Siwolop and Mohs, 1985). There is a link between Down syndrome and Alzheimer's disease; adults with Down are predisposed to Alzheimer's, with a prevalence rate of 54.5 percent in the sixth decade (see Prasher, Chowdhury, Rowe, and Bain, 1997).

Cognitive Development

Cognition is the process of recognizing, identifying, associating, and inferring meaning beyond the figural information provided by the environment that allows an understanding of a concept and application to new conditions (DeRuiter and Wansart, 1982). **Cognitive development** implies orderly changes that occur in the way children understand and cope with their world.

By definition, intellectual disability equates with deficiencies in cognitive development. Nevertheless, an intellectual disability only means slowing down, not stopping. Individuals with intellectual disabilities have impaired or incomplete mental development; their problems are specifically a retardation in the development of intellectual and adaptive behaviour. Their ability to learn and their capacity for putting learning to use is limited but certainly not non-existent.

More and more research evidence indicates that retardation is quantitative rather than qualitative. That is, children who are intellectually disabled pass through the same cognitive developmental stages in the same order and manner as non-disabled children. In studies of Down syndrome children compared with non-disabled children of the same developmental level and socio-economic status, for example, investigators have found no differences in the sequence of sensorimotor development (Rogers, 1988).

Children with intellectual disabilities pass through the stages more slowly and attain lower levels of achievement. On Piaget's periods, those who are mildly intellectually disabled function no higher than concrete operations; those who are moderately disabled do not surpass pre-operational stages, and those who are severely and profoundly disabled are at the sensorimotor stage (Robinson and Robinson, 1976).

Learning and Memory

The most specific consequences of intellectual disability involve its effects on an individual's potential to learn and to progress academically. Although individuals basically learn in the same fashion as do other people, students have difficulties in all aspects of intellectual functioning including concept learning, attention, and language. Children with intellectual disabilities have particular trouble with memory, a key aspect of learning. Memory efficiency decreases as the level of retardation increases.

Memory is often explained through the constructs of **information processing,** which holds that we process information in different ways and at various levels of analysis. Essentially, information processing looks at the sensory register where information is perceived and attended to; at short-term memory where information that has been passed through the sensory register is held for about five seconds; and long-term memory where retained information is stored, probably permanently. We could use the example of a young child hearing a catchy jingle on TV. The child attends to the jingle (sensory register), takes it into short-term memory, and then sings along and repeats the jingle over and over (rehearsal and elaboration) and in this way passes it to long-term memory where it is stored for retrieval later when the child, perhaps, wants to sing it for Daddy.

For information to move from short-term to long-term memory, we must do something to help us retain the information. Memory strategies include such things as rehearsal, subvocalization, and mnemonics. For individuals with disabilities, the greatest difficulty seems to be with short-term memory, which may result from an inefficient use of memory strategies. In addition, students often do not understand why they are memorizing certain information, in what context the information is meaningful, or how to internalize the structure provided by teachers (Gerber, 1988).

Students can be taught to use strategies successfully and thereby improve their memory functioning. (See Chapter 5.) And, once individuals with intellectual disabilities have thoroughly learned information, their long-term memory is comparable to that of non-disabled learners.

Difficulties with memory are compounded by problems with observational learning, organization, selective attention, generalization, and motivation. Students with intellectual disabilities find it very hard to select learning tasks and attend to all of their relevant dimensions. They also have difficulty paying attention and keeping on task. In the classroom, they tend to be less attentive, spend less time on academic tasks, and spend more time out of their seats than non-disabled children (Finkelstein, Gallagher, and Farran, 1980; McGee and Richgels, 1990). As well, they are less able to apply the knowledge or the skills they have learned to new tasks, problems, or stimulus situations; they have problems in generalizing and transferring skills.

Concepts are the building blocks of human knowledge, but children with intellectual disabilities show difficulties in concept development, especially at abstract levels. For example, children with mild disabilities have significant deficits in the understanding of basic concepts such as *above, always, other*, and *different*.

As the degree of retardation increases, problems with learning and memory become more severe. However, learning is both possible and common for children with moderate to profound mental retardation. Using classical and operant conditioning procedures, educators have taught many skills in the domains of adaptive behaviour, simple academics, and vocational skill formation to severely retarded, and some profoundly retarded, individuals.

Academic Achievement

Pupils categorized as mildly intellectually disabled form the largest group of retarded learners and possess the widest range of skills and needs. In general, these students are slower in developing motor and social skills. In the classroom, these children tend to underachieve

Figure 6-2

Differences in functioning of mildly retarded and non-retarded children in school

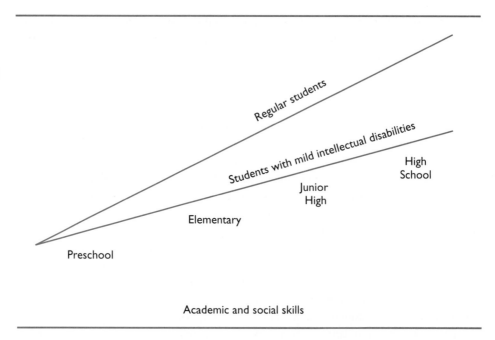

in all academic areas. In fact, they do not achieve in school at a level commensurate with their intellectual potentials. In school, students who are mildly retarded achieve about two-thirds of what other children will accomplish in an academic year. This lag presents challenges to secondary level educators, as we discuss in Chapter 16.

Apart from limited cognitive ability, the reasons why students underachieve are legion. We have already mentioned poor motivation, problems with short-term memory, lowered ability to generalize and transfer skills, and failure to use the strategies needed for successful learning. These students also have short attention spans and become quickly frustrated by academic tasks. They cannot gain insight easily or reason as well as non-disabled children and find it more difficult to remember abstract ideas than concrete information. They often require more time than their normally achieving peers to attain accuracy and speed of performance.

Reading and all the language arts suffer. Math and arithmetic are not easy for students with mild disabilities. They often have difficulty with such basic skills as counting, writing numerals, and learning basic associations, and may not be competent even in the basic addition and subtraction facts. Students will meet particular difficulties in comprehending arithmetic concepts that involve abstract notions and symbols, and are unlikely to follow systematic strategies for solving word problems.

Individuals who are moderately retarded have limited intellectual ability, difficulties in working with abstract ideas, and problems in generalizing learning to new situations. They are not ready for much academic work until their early teens.

Children and young adults who are severely or profoundly retarded experience major challenges to successful adaptation. Their intensive instructional and technological needs must be met if they are to overcome the intellectual and adaptive demands of their homes, schools, and communities. Many individuals suffer such serious problems that they will likely require life care and supervision. Individuals who are severely retarded can acquire basic skills;

they may learn to regulate toilet habits, to eat with a spoon or fork, to throw a ball at a target, to understand simple verbal directions, and to participate in simple play and games (Anderson and Greer, 1976).

Communication Development

Youngsters with intellectual disabilities acquire language more slowly. Typically, their language levels remain below those of non-disabled children and are often below their general mental age.

Children demonstrate delays in sentence length, sentence complexity, and speech sound discrimination. Their expressive language tends to be less complex than that of peers, and some children meet difficulties in generalizing the rules of grammar. They do not gain as much information from verbal or non-verbal receptive language; both children and adults who are mentally retarded do not decipher affective facial expressions as well as their peers (Adams and Markham, 1991; Maurer and Newbrough, 1987).

Language problems are not related to the etiology of the retardation, but to its severity. Youngsters who are mildly intellectually disabled may be delayed in talking, but mutism is rare. Individuals who are moderately mentally retarded use stereotypical language, rarely free of defects. Among persons who are profoundly retarded, expressive speech and language skills are extremely limited. Mutism is common among individuals who are severely and profoundly retarded, as are primitive levels of speech such as babbling and jabbering (Jordan, 1976).

In children with Down syndrome, speech and language acquisition is often significantly delayed (Pruess, Vadasy, and Fewell, 1989). Babies with Down vocalize less frequently. Many of these children do not acquire two word phrases until three or four years of age; some do not acquire functional speech until eight years (Drash, Raver, Murrin, and Tudor, 1989).

It is estimated that speech disorders affect about 55 percent of the total population of persons with intellectual disabilities. Some speech problems are the result of structural differences or malformations. For example, children with Down syndrome often have oral problems that affect articulation—an overly large tongue over which they have less muscle control than other children, or an inability to close the passage from the nose to the mouth, resulting in hypernasal speech.

Social and Emotional Development

In some children with mental retardation, social skill deficits are marked. These children often have special personal and social problems and exhibit atypical development patterns in socialization. The more severe the disability, the lower the percentage of social interactions with non-disabled peers (Guralnick, 1981).

Children initiate far fewer social exchanges and tend to engage in shorter sequences of reciprocal interaction than do their normally developing counterparts (Beckman and Lieber, 1994). They may fail to respond readily to initial overtures from others; this lack of response further isolates the child as it serves to discourage interaction.

The social outcomes of placing students with mental retardation in regular classrooms have been disappointing, and their mere physical presence in the class does not seem to enhance their social competence (Leffert and Siperstein, 1996). Often children with mental retardation occupy a marginal position in the social network of the regular class (see Siperstein and Leffert, 1997), although certainly not always.

In general, students with intellectual disabilities are not well accepted by their non-disabled peers and often have trouble making friends (Luftig, 1988; Zetlin and Murtaugh, 1988). These children are frequently the subject of teasing, which serves to diminish their self-concepts and further compounds the problems in self-esteem that accompany low achievement. Children may be rejected because they look different or show unusual behaviour, and then don't try again because of low motivation.

On the other side of the coin, studies of how children with disabilities feel about peers (Wenz-Gross and Siperstein, 1997) find that children with disabilities were less likely to view their peers as a source of support than normally developing children. This is particularly strong in the area of emotional support. In friendships, children reported less intimacy, loyalty, self-esteem, and contact in their friendships than did normally developing peers.

Students who are moderately retarded have rather clear-cut deficits in adaptive behaviour; they have problems with interpersonal relationships, social concepts, emotional instability, and communication. As these children grow older, the progressive widening of their developmental lag tends to make their retardation more obvious. This is in contrast to persons who are mildly retarded whose condition becomes less obvious in adulthood.

Behavioural Development

Children with mental retardation have a higher rate of behavioural disorders than do other children (Einfield and Tonge, 1995). In a study of the relationship between intellectual deficits and aggression (Huessman, Eron, and Yarmel, 1987) results indicated that childhood aggression was correlated with low intellectual and scholastic aptitude. Children with low intelligence abilities had difficulties learning needed skills for non-aggressive problem solving and probably experienced increased frustration and stress.

As well as behavioural disorders, there exists a significant correlation between the level of retardation and psychiatric processes. The prevalence of mental illness has been estimated to occur in from 14 to 64 percent of the retarded population (see Galligan, 1990). One of the most serious disorders is schizophrenia. Note that adults with Down syndrome seem to have more depression and dementia than other adults with mental retardation (Dykens, 1996).

Especially in children, it is extremely difficult, if not impossible, to determine whether the emotional disturbance caused the mental retardation, or vice versa. Children who are emotionally disturbed in early childhood may be deprived of the normal sources of intellectual and social development. A low IQ (especially if below 50) increases the probability that an infant will have problems in perceiving, understanding, and responding to the environment and is therefore associated with the pathology of psychoses (Bhatara, 1980). Conversely, the child who is retarded may withdraw and display the behaviours characteristic of children who are emotionally disturbed.

Maladaptive behaviour, which includes both inappropriate behaviours and self-injurious behaviours, is found across the spectrum of the population of intellectual disabilities but is more common in persons who are severely and profoundly retarded. As with skill development, the frequency of maladaptive behaviours is extremely variable. (See also Chapter 13.)

Inappropriate behaviours include aggression toward other people and objects, tantrums, and such stereotypical behaviour as meaningless repetitive movements, rocking, and hand waving. Hand–mouthing (finger and hand sucking) is common. Less prevalent behaviours include vomiting and rumination, disrobing, pica and coprophagy (eating inedible objects, including feces), stealing, and material hoarding (Whitman and Scibak, 1979).

Self-injurious behaviour, defined as any self-inflicted, repetitive action that leads to laceration, bruising, or abrasions of the client's own body, is common. Persons who are severely and profoundly retarded may engage in head banging, eye gouging, biting, scratching, self-pinching and hitting, and rectal digging. The prevalence of self-injurious behaviour ranges from 8 to 19 percent (Gedye, 1989). Higher frequencies are found among those who are severely retarded (49 percent) and profoundly retarded (40 percent) as compared to individuals who are mildly retarded (12 percent) (Murphy and Corbett, 1987).

Intervention with Children Who Are Intellectually Disabled

Many different types of intervention are used with individuals who have intellectual disabilities. Medical and pharmacological interventions are especially important for individuals with organic etiologies. Social and early intervention is critical for infants and preschoolers and their families (see Chapter 15). Various therapists may intervene to improve secondary motor, language, or speech disabilities. It is in the schools, however, that the major focus occurs. Most students with mild disabilities are placed in regular classrooms, and the crux of education for students with moderate to profound mental retardation has altered in recent years to greater placement in the public schools.

Medical Intervention

No surgical procedures or miracle drugs are known to actually improve intellectual ability or adaptive behaviour. In general, medical intervention attempts to prevent or correct the organic causes of retardation rather than alleviate the condition itself. We have already discussed the values of screening in cases such as phenylketonuria.

Surgical intervention has been used with children who have Down syndrome in an effort to alleviate speech and eating problems and to render their appearance more normal. Increasing numbers of families are seeking this option, especially for tongue reduction to improve speech and looks.

Technical Aids

Technological advances have resulted in the development of devices designed specifically for persons with intellectual disabilities. A range of instructional technology is employed in classrooms; independent functioning is supplemented with aids for self-help skills and environmental control. These include a device that produces a signal for a non-toilet-trained child to go to the bathroom, a self-feeding tray for persons who are multiply disabled, and special bathing devices. Adaptive equipment is discussed in Chapter 12. Instructional technology primarily involves microcomputers and innovative software. (See Chapter 2.)

Educational Intervention

Intellectual disabilities are related to delayed intellectual development in areas considered important for school success. Students classified as intellectually disabled achieve below grade level and usually experience difficulties throughout their school careers.

Inclusion

Within the school system, the current trend is to include students with intellectual disabilities in the regular classroom, especially those with mild disabilities. A student's success in the classroom depends on a number of additional factors that include support services, curriculum adaptations and modifications, acceptance by the other students, the classroom teacher's experience with and exposure to children who are exceptional, the availability of community resources, and the age of the student.

In the past, children with moderate and severe intellectual disabilities attended special schools. Although these schools provided an appropriate curriculum, a controlled learning environment, and a suitable daily schedule, they had the drawback of segregation. Today, students who need special education arrangements may be in the regular classroom with assistance or perhaps placed in small, self-contained special classes in the regular school.

There is often much more intervention at elementary than secondary levels. Although services for a majority of students with disabilities have significantly improved and expanded in the years since the passage of Public Law 94-142 in the United States (see this chapter's Historical Notes), the provision of appropriate educational services remains problematic for many secondary-school-aged students with disabilities (Edgar, 1987; Zetlin and Hossenini, 1989). Secondary education programs tend to be more explicitly vocationally oriented than those at elementary levels and are directed toward securing employment upon graduation. In some cases, such programs are operated in conjunction with sheltered workshops. (See Chapter 16.)

Educational Approaches

There are three major goals in the education of students with intellectual disabilities: productivity, independence, and participation. To accomplish these goals, students are presented with instruction in the areas of academic, social, self-help, community living, and vocational skills. Depending on the extent and severity of the disability, the major goals are not always fully achievable; success may be only fractional for children functioning at the low end of the continuum.

Students with Mild Intellectual Disabilities

The actual curricula objectives are the same for students with mild intellectual disabilities as for their peers. Students require instruction in basic academic skills, particularly basic literacy and numeracy. Teachers must also stress the cognitive, language, and social domains. Each program will be individualized, based on a student's unique set of strengths and weaknesses.

In the early grades, children who are mildly disabled are taught readiness skills in such areas as math and reading. At the intermediate school levels, educational emphasis may be placed on activities for everyday life such as functional reading, writing, and math, and areas such as learning about the local environment, transportation, budgeting, peer relationships, personal hygiene, and personal and recreational interests. At the secondary level, students with mild disabilities are taught personal–social adjustment, health and self-care skills, citizenship skills, and occupational skills, along with basic academics.

Children with Moderate Intellectual Disabilities

For students with moderate disabilities, the curriculum is less academically oriented than for children who are mildly disabled. In general, children who are moderately disabled do not learn to read beyond the first grade level. Children are taught to read names, directions, labels, and to write relevant names and words. They are also introduced to numbers, time, and simple money exchange.

The ultimate goal of education is functional independence. Recent trends in public school curricula for students and young adults who are moderately and severely disabled have seen a movement away from the specification of curricular goals on the basis of developmental age; teachers now direct instruction toward chronological-age-appropriate skills that students need to meet the demands of their community environments (Wiggins and Behrmann, 1988). When functionality is the core of the curriculum, it is referred to as a *functional approach* or *life-skills instruction*. Adaptive behaviour, self-help skills, life skills, and social skills are the important components of this approach.

Functional Approaches

Functional skills are those that help children to get along in their current and future environments. The skills are displayed throughout a lifetime and tend to be performed in progressively more complex and varied forms as children grow (Wolery, 1991). Functional skills include dressing, eating, and toileting, as well as the skills needed for participation in routine home and community activities such as playing with siblings, helping with simple chores, and eating at a fast-food restaurant.

Self-help skills are functional. They include the ability to care for oneself, which is fundamental in achieving independence and self-sufficiency. The collected nouns for self-help skills are divided into those related to eating, dressing, bathing, grooming, and toileting. Training is undertaken in such skills as independent eating, dressing, toileting, washing, combing hair, brushing teeth, and using a handkerchief. Students also learn simple home-making skills, such as dusting, sweeping, setting and clearing a table, washing and drying dishes, washing and ironing clothes, sewing, using simple tools, and using the telephone. They are taught safety rules and how to use public transportation.

For all children, the functional approach becomes more important as they grow older. Life skills essentially include all the components a student requires to successfully negotiate life as an adult. Programming identifies the myriad demands of adulthood, relates the demands to specific skills, and bases the curriculum on teaching these skills (Robinson et al., 1989). A variety of job-related skills are presented. Deficits in student performance during the school years and beyond suggest that skill instruction is best conducted in real-world settings in the presence of non-disabled people and using naturally occurring situations and materials (Hamre-Nietupski, Nietupski, Bates, and Maurer, 1982). Natural environments include stores, restaurants, public transportation, banks, and drug stores.

Communication training is designed to help the child develop the skills necessary for everyday communication. Personal and social skills include consideration for others, common courtesy, obedience, and self-judgment. Students also learn perceptual-motor and

Training in life skills is essential for students with mental handicaps.

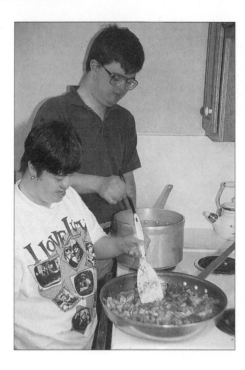

physical skills which include sense training in the visual, auditory and tactile modalities, eye–hand co-ordination, balance, and gross and fine motor movement.

Within a functional approach, targets for instruction are selected by analyzing the child's environment. Teachers identify specific skills to immediately improve the child's ability to interact with the environment and to increase the probability that the child will perform functionally critical behaviours for success and survival in future environments. Important skills are then broken down into small, building steps in a task analysis. Skills are taught for generalization as well as for functional usefulness. Teaching a child to grasp a toy may, for example, generalize to grasping a hair brush or a tooth brush, both necessary self-help skills. Or, if the objective is to teach students to operate a musical device during their leisure time, it is more functional for a fifteen-year-old to use a CD player than a gaily coloured Fisher-Price music box.

Students Who Are Severely and Profoundly Disabled

While almost all students with mild intellectual disabilities will be educated in regular classrooms, and most trainable students will be in regular classes or schools, the placement of students who are severely and profoundly disabled is more controversial. For these youngsters, there exist conflicting and extreme ideologies that revolve around the issue of inclusive schooling. (See Chapters 13 and 14.)

There is no question that for children who are severely and profoundly disabled we must redefine the term *education* beyond its traditional academic limits. The goals of education are different than those for non-disabled students and for those with milder disabilities. Many more personnel are involved: these children often require a range of other services from professionals such as doctors, speech therapists, social workers, and psychologists.

The major educational goals are to decrease dependence on others, increase awareness of environmental stimulation, teach basic communication and self-help skills, and push achievement levels higher. The training of individuals who are severely and profoundly retarded begins with basic survival and self-help skills, along with the elimination of undesirable behaviour.

Repetition and simple conditioning are primary teaching strategies. At first, teachers focus on obtaining responses to environmental stimulation; these responses include head and trunk balance, sucking, swallowing, chewing, grasping, movement of body parts, and vocalization. Later training includes imitation, language acquisition, self-feeding, ambulation, dressing skills, toilet training, social and recreational behaviour, and functional academic skills (Stainback, Stainback, and Mauer, 1976).

Although behaviour modification is used with virtually every type of disability, it is particularly useful in the education and training of children with severe and profound disabilities. Behavioural methods seem to succeed where others fail, and the behavioural emphasis on specific task analysis is particularly well suited to the problems of individuals who are severely disabled. Behaviour modification has been successfully used to teach a diverse array of skills, including self-help skills, eating, toileting, dressing, socialization, and language acquisition. As well, a range of behaviour modification techniques have been employed in the elimination of maladaptive behaviours.

Social Intervention

Advocacy groups of parents and professionals exist for the sole purpose of improving life conditions for the population of persons who are intellectually disabled. The Canadian Council of Community Living (CCCL) (formerly the CAMR) is typical. Essentially, the CCCL performs the following functions:

- Encourages the acceptance of all intellectually disabled people into the life of the community.

- Promotes the enactment and implementation of legislation to improve the welfare of intellectually disabled people.

- Promotes improved educational and vocational training for intellectually disabled people.

- Furthers the education and training of personnel for work in the field of intellectual disabilities.

- Provides centres for the gathering and distribution of information about intellectual disabilities.

- Fosters research concerning all aspects of intellectual disability.

- Develops better public understanding of people who are intellectually disabled and their needs (CAMR, 1980).

SUMMARY

1. Under the AAMR definition, three factors must be present before an individual can be considered within the category of mental retardation—subaverage general intellectual functioning, deficits in adaptive behaviour, and manifestation during the developmental period.

2. Adaptive behaviour is a difficult construct to operationalize, define, and measure. In

the broadest sense, adaptive behaviour refers to an individual's ability to cope or deal effectively with personal and social demands. The existence of limitations in adaptive skills occurs within the context of community environments typical of the individual's age peers and is indexed to the person's individualized needs for support.

3. In current definitions of mental retardation, there is considerable controversy about terminology, adaptive behaviour, and the use of IQ tests. Today's definitions, especially of mild disability, do not see it as a permanent condition but one that improves with sustained intervention and also one linked to the demands of formal schooling. There is a higher incidence of retardation during the school years, with lower incidence figures during the preschool years and adulthood.

4. The redefining of children labelled as mentally retarded in 1973 to omit those functioning between one and two standard deviations below the mean accompanied increasing numbers of students being categorized as learning disabled. Learning disabilities is today the largest focus of special education in many school districts and mental retardation, per se, seems to be a category of declining importance.

5. New terms introduced by the AAMR use different levels of support—*intermittent, limited, extensive*, and *pervasive*—rather than severity levels.

6. The agents that cause mental retardation are legion and include genetic and chromosomal differences, infections such as maternal rubella, intoxicants such as drugs, post-natal diseases such as meningitis, and childhood accidents.

7. In trying to pinpoint the existence and severity of intellectual disabilities, clinicians are challenged to find a range of observations and measures that are appropriate for individual children. Data on a child's levels of cognitive functioning (IQ tests) are employed as one measure used to determine an individual educational program.

8. Although youngsters with mild intellectual disabilities may consistently lag in academic areas such as reading, math, science, and social studies, they learn in the same way as other pupils. Studies on the learning characteristics of these children show that even if their rate of learning is slower and the level reached not as high, their learning curves approximate those of non-disabled pupils. Individuals who are severely and profoundly retarded must often struggle to achieve ambulation and simple physical activities. For individuals in these two levels of severity, physical development is often impaired and co-occurring conditions are common.

9. Children labelled as mildly intellectually disabled form the greatest proportion of the retarded population. Today, the majority of these students are educated in regular classrooms. Following graduation, many such individuals blend into the social fabric of their neighbourhoods, holding jobs, marrying, and having families. Once that adjustment is made, they are no longer retarded according to the AAMD definition.

10. Children with moderate levels of intellectual disability are being educated in regular schools, either in regular classrooms or in special self-contained classrooms. Teachers present limited academic curricula with a stress on functional skills in all domains. The inclusion of students who are severely or profoundly retarded is beset by controversy. These children have grave barriers to learning, often demonstrate maladaptive behaviour, and are often multiply disabled. Although structured behavioural programs can impart useful skills, argument rages about the most appropriate placement in which to present these skills.

In the Classroom

Profile: Nicholas

In his grade two classroom, Nicholas is far behind his peers in reading and math. He has a short attention span, poor on-task behaviour, low motivation, and generally seems to find school very trying and difficult. His teacher attempted a number of adaptations such as peer tutoring in reading and a token economy to improve on-task behaviour, but to little avail. He eventually referred Nicholas to the school principal, asking for an assessment and some assistance in developing an appropriate program.

A school psychologist administered a number of measures to Nicholas including the WISC-III, a measure of receptive language (Peabody Picture Vocabulary Test, PPVT), a test of language usage (Test of Language Development, Primary TOLD-P), a reading test (Test of Early Reading Ability, TERA), and a measure of math readiness (Test of Early Mathematical Ability, TEMA). She also carefully noted Nicholas' presenting behaviour—the way he approached the situation and the measures, and the way he interacted with her.

In some ways, the test results confirmed the teacher's suspicions. Nicholas showed a Full Scale IQ score of 76, with very little difference between the Verbal and the Performance scales and very little scatter between the subtests. The raw scores on the other measures were all reported as percentiles and the psychologist found that Nicholas scored in the 21st percentile on the PPVT, the 14th on the TOLD-P, the 4th on the TERA, and the 8th on the TEMA.

What surprised the psychologist was Nicholas' interactions during the testing sessions. Although he seems to dislike classroom work, he really enjoyed the one to one situation with the psychologist and readily attempted everything presented him. And he talked throughout. He particularly wanted to tell the psychologist about his hockey and how the night before his team "had just killed those guys from Medicine Hat," and gone on to win the trophy. Nicholas demonstrated (quite surprisingly, given the teacher's referral) adequate vocabulary and good logic and sequencing in his stories, although he showed many problems with syntax.

When the psychologist, the classroom teacher, and the parents met to discuss Nicholas' program, the psychologist stressed this area. She asked the parents many questions about Nicholas' activities outside the classroom and how he performed in the home and the neighbourhood. His competence outside school did not match his obvious lacks in classroom learning which, even with somewhat restricted ability, should be higher. The psychologist later noted that he showed the profile of what has been described as a "six-hour retarded child."

The program developed for Nicholas focuses very heavily on functional skills and uses materials from his own experiences and interests. An extract from Nicholas' IEP is given below.

* * *

Nicholas has an abundance of "street smarts" but demonstrates little knowledge of reading and writing in his grade two classroom. To stimulate his interest, a program should be built on his personal likes. For example sports, especially hockey, are of major interest to Nicholas, and an individual reading program can be based on this.

There is much documentation of the success of accomplishing specific academic objectives through direct instruction. For a child who has poor memory, low task commitment, and poor language, this is a necessary component. Nicholas needs structured direct teaching daily with much repetition.

In all areas, concrete materials should be used. Persons who have mental disabilities will often learn better if the stimuli they encounter are real and not symbolic. For example, money skills should be taught using real money, and social skills with real people.

Many of the ideas and techniques suitable for Nicholas appear in Chapter 5, and readers are urged to review the In the Classroom feature in that chapter.

Extract from Nicholas' IEP

Name: Nicholas
Teacher: Mr. McPhee
C.A.: 8-2
Grade: 2
School: St. Basil's

PRESENT LEVELS OF FUNCTIONING

Nicholas was referred by his classroom teacher for psycho-educational assessment as he is falling further and further behind his classmates especially in the core areas of reading and math.

COGNITIVE

On the WISC-III, Nicholas showed a Full Scale score of 76 (+ - 5). While still within the average range, this is well below the norm.

LANGUAGE

Nicholas appears to have below average language ability based on results of the PPVT-R and the TOLD-P. However, the psychologist noted his strong use of appropriate language when talking about things that really interested him, although syntactical lags were obvious.

READING

Nicholas has barely made a start in formal reading. He is at a beginning grade one level.

MATH

All math concepts seem to be difficult for Nicholas. He does not seem to understand place value. However, he knows the names of coins and seemed further advanced and far more interested when using real money.

PLACEMENT

Regular classroom

ADAPTATIONS

IEP
direct instruction in reading and math
peer tutoring
promotion of social interactions
modified report cards

LONG-RANGE GOALS

• Stimulate interest in school activities by building on relatively strong language based on his own experiences.
• Correct syntax and expand language incidentally.
• Develop a sight word vocabulary.
• Read very short paragraphs and books (e.g. Sports Illustrated for Kids) about sports.
• Use coins as the major manipulative to teach rational counting, place value, addition and subtraction facts, and basic computation.

SHORT-TERM OBJECTIVES

- Learn ten sight words related to sports with the teacher, in a small group, or with a peer tutor.
- Read and discuss short paragraphs about sports in small group.
- Use written exercises (fill-the-blank, draw, underline the word) to stress sight words and to teach reading directions.
- Use pennies for rational counting to 99, forward and backward.
- Use coins for simple equations.

EFFECTS OF INTELLECTUAL DISABILITY	TIPS FOR TEACHERS
THE CHILD HAS DIFFICULTIES IN ACADEMIC SUBJECTS	Use peer tutoring in the classroom. Arrange cross-age tutoring, where students with special needs tutor younger children.
THE CHILD HAS DEFICITS IN SPEECH AND LANGUAGE	Use co-operative learning strategies. Use incidental teaching (see Chapter 4).
THE CHILD HAS MEMORY PROBLEMS	Students with memory problems tend to be passive learners; they learn more easily if good demonstrations and visual aids provide them with a concrete model to watch and imitate. Use a variety of alternate approaches to instruction; that is, many methods to present material and reinforce learning.
THE CHILD EXHIBITS POOR PROBLEM-SOLVING AND LEARNING STRATEGIES	Specifically teach learning strategies.
THE CHILD NEEDS MUCH REPETITION	Ensure mastery of new material through repetition and overlearning. Provide many opportunities for *drill* (repeating a task) and *practice* (applying the task to similar situations). In math, for example, students may be drilled on number facts through rote repetition, work sheets, and games. They may then practice the skills through the actual performance of a task, such as applying the number facts to addition problems. Computer Assisted Instruction (CAI) has proven to be particularly effective for children with intellectual disabiities.
THE CHILD HAS DIFFICULTIES IN ABSTRACTION AND GENERALIZATION	As a general rule, the more abstract the learning experience, the less these students will be able to experience success. Emphasize concrete, meaningful content, especially in initial instructional presentations. Present tasks in an uncomplicated, brief, and sequential fashion. Sequence from the simple to the more complex.

EFFECTS OF INTELLECTUAL DISABILITY	TIPS FOR TEACHERS
	Promote transfer of learning by applying learning to other situations, objects, and problems in the learner's environment.
THE CHILD HAS AN OUTWARD LOCUS OF CONTROL	Promote an atmosphere of success.
	Motivation increases as competitiveness decreases. Rewarding effort rather than ability is likely to serve as a motivator for all students.
	Motivation also involves allowing students opportunities to control and monitor their own learning and behaviour. Allow some degree of freedom in selecting tasks or assignments.
	Feelings of personal competence and self-esteem are closely tied to experiences of success. Through individualization, provide for success in academic domains.
	As these students are more limited in their learning, they require more reinforcement.
THE CHILD SHOWS DEFICITS IN ADAPTIVE BEHAVIOUR	Teach social skills, if necessary (see Chapter 8).

WEBLINKS

Canadian Down Syndrome Society **http://home.ican.net/~cdss/index.html**

Fragile X Syndrome **http://www.metronet.com/~thearc/faqs/fragqa.html**

CHAPTER 7

Children Who Are Gifted, Creative, and Talented

Historical Notes

Cultural values have always determined the attitudes of society towards its outstanding members. Different eras have valued achievement in different fields of endeavour. Ancient Greece admired the philosopher, Rome the soldier and orator, and Renaissance Italy the artist.

In the modern age, remarkable early development, or precocity, was seen in many major historical figures. Beethoven performed in public at age seven, Thomas Jefferson began serious study at five, and Pablo Picasso drew before he could walk. Others who contributed significantly to our cultures bloomed later and only after surviving hardships or overcoming disabilities. Winston Churchill was a sickly child with a speech impediment; Edison's teachers described him as "addled"; and Auguste Rodin had a learning disability. Vincent van Gogh suffered crippling bouts of depression that eventually led to his suicide.

Before the mid-nineteenth century, giftedness was a visible, yet poorly defined and understood, phenomenon. Even as much honour was paid to individuals who made significant contributions to their own or succeeding cultures, genius was often mis-

understood and popularly viewed as directly related to insanity.

Francis Galton, an English scientist and eugenics advocate, was one of the first to research and write about giftedness. Galton proposed that motivation to achieve was innate and inborn and claimed that genius would actualize itself despite external circumstances (Galton, 1869), a position that led to the enduring and dangerous myth that "the cream will rise to the top" regardless of difficulties or lack of environmental support.

As a descriptive term for a specific group of individuals who are highly intelligent and strong academic achievers, *gifted* was first used in the literature by Guy M. Henry in 1920. In the following years, behavioural scientists used *gifted* as the sole designation to describe people with high intelligence. As a wider conception of the array of human potential developed, the constructs *talented* and *creative* came into use in the 1960s.

Special day classes for gifted pupils emerged in the United States during the 1890s, but the movement was small and the classes scattered. By the mid-1930s, there were still only 75 such classrooms in the country. Canada also established classes, but again the movement, compared to that for children with disabilities, was small. Community-based gifted education was founded in London, Ontario, in the late 1920s, when concerned teachers and parents worked together to design an enrichment program for the elementary grades (Bain, 1980). On the Prairies, the Enterprise Method developed and trained students in learning and community-oriented group activities. The Major Work Program, first adopted in Alberta, flourished briefly across the country. It offered selected children greater intellectual stimulation, along with training in advanced creativity and problem solving (Bain, 1980).

Over the decades, other programs have developed in Canada, many of them based on the philosophy of Samuel Laycock of Saskatchewan. From the 1930s to the late 1960s, Laycock championed the cause of those exceptional children who were capable of creativity and leadership but were too often ignored by society. Saskatchewan, in fact, has had a continuous program since the 1930s for very gifted learners (Lipp, 1988).

In the 1970s, concern for the special needs of children who were gifted was reawakened, in large measure by the evidence that many of these youngsters were bored with the lockstep of mass education and were turning into chronic underachievers and dropouts. Another major spur was the mounting pessimism of North American educators as they saw their educational standards drop far below those of the Japanese and the Europeans. Another was an offshoot of the women's movement that began to open avenues for females to enter less traditional roles.

But even today, attempts to provide appropriate programs are undermined by popularly held stereotypes and myths. Galton's myth that "the cream will rise to the top" has been perpetuated as educators have persistently argued about whether special programming for individuals already well endowed violates the ethics of a democratic school system. Funding, willingly ceded to children functioning below the norm, has been only grudgingly allowed to those with superior abilities. Compared to that for disabled children, education provided for those gifted and talented has been a very small-scale enterprise.

ifted is a somewhat abstract term applied to people who, by virtue of outstanding abilities, are capable of high performance (Clark, 1988). A variety of variables figure in the scenario of giftedness, including aptitude, creativity, personality, and motivation (Friesen, 1997). Some individuals soar to great heights in the talent domain, others in intellectual ability, and still others in creative endeavours. A few individuals achieve remarkably high levels across several domains.

Gifted individuals have greater ability in some areas than most of us. Generally, we admire such people, but occasionally we are a little envious of their talents and achievements. We seem to have to work much harder than they do to achieve only mediocre results.

Special education attempts to provide for any child markedly different from the average, even if this difference is a positive one. Gifted, creative, and talented students have special educational needs—they may learn in ways different from other students; they are more curious; and they think more abstractly. At the same time, students who are gifted are vulnerable to the same forces that affect other children and youth and can become frustrated and bored in unstimulating learning environments.

To reach their full potential, children who are gifted, creative, and talented must be confronted with suitable challenges and stimulating educational experiences. However, the provision of special services to this population has always been a difficult undertaking that poses many complex issues and problems for educators. A great deal of professional skill and sensitivity is required to identify the special needs of gifted students, while the development of appropriate programs taxes the skill, resourcefulness, and empathy of teachers as they walk a tightrope between equity and excellence.

The restrictions placed on programs for students who are gifted are both academic and attitudinal. All are associated, to a greater or lesser extent, with the notion that "the cream will rise to the top." Many people still believe that children who are gifted are smart enough to make it on their own. They see students who are gifted typically doing well in school, easily meeting age and grade levels for achievement, and tending to be well-behaved. They therefore rationalize that pupils who are gifted will develop their abilities even if not provided with special education: If students don't do well, then they're not gifted, anyway.

Myths about students who are gifted being able to do well regardless of environment and the amount of stimulation and opportunity are compounded by the fact that most of these children demonstrate no immediate problems that can serve as a basis for an emotional appeal for special services. Traditionally, special education has been viewed as a way to help children who perform poorly in school, and children with outstanding abilities rarely arouse the same level of concern as do youngsters who are disabled. Children with gifts and talents are not perceived as suffering from social stigma or unhappiness; rather, giftedness is considered highly desirable and a boon to social status.

Many educators feel that although we are morally obliged to help children with disabilities, there is no moral necessity to assist those children who are already advantaged. They question the ethics of a society that labels a select few, that provides special opportunities for the elite, and that attends "to the exclusive needs of only a small segment of learners" (Sapon-Shivin, 1984, p. 79).

The underlying concern is that special education for the gifted might subvert our commitment to egalitarianism and jeopardize the principle of democratic education by creating an overadvantaged elite or meritocracy within the school population. Because of this attitude, we direct our special education programs, and the taxes that support them, largely into programs for students who are disabled. Our regular education programs serve the needs of average children. The gifted we leave to fend for themselves, even when this involves a waste of their potential.

Yet an increasing number of educators, administrators, legislators, parents, and researchers support the idea that giftedness needs to be fostered and nurtured. They argue that children who are gifted have the same right as other children to develop to their full potential and therefore require special education and appropriate related services. Without educational opportunities and challenges, children who are gifted may hide their abilities or bury them in underachievement. In fact, probably half of the gifted population do not match their tested ability with comparable achievement in school.

Most thinking individuals would agree that Canada's youth who have gifts and talents form one of the country's greatest undeveloped resources. Many of the leaders, scientists, and artists of the next generation are likely to emerge from the current crop of children who are gifted and talented. Nevertheless, debates surround the issue of egalitarianism versus special programs and are germane to today's education of these students. Educators are challenged by the philosophical and practical problems of how to educate children who are gifted adequately in a public education system that is philosophically and administratively egalitarian in nature. But if education for the gifted is to survive, this issue will have to be resolved.

Definitions

To be *gifted* is to be superior in some way to the average. But beyond this almost meaning-less statement, no definition of giftedness has been agreed upon. In fact, the importance of adequately defining giftedness as a precursor to identification and as an indicator of preva-lence has led to a multiplicity of definitions. In one publication, 17 different conceptions of giftedness were identified (Sternberg and Davidson, 1986).

Many factors underlie the definitional problems found in the field. These can be sum-marized as follows:

- Perceptions of giftedness and beliefs about what abilities should be recognized and de-veloped in Canadian schools have changed dramatically over the years (Gardner, 1983; Renzulli, 1979; Sternberg, 1981; Treffinger, 1991).

- There is no such thing as a typical child who is gifted; particular talents and social envi-ronments give rise to varying personality patterns. Some students who are gifted, for example, may have only average aptitude in math, and some students who are mathe-matically gifted may not do well on tests of verbal abilities.

- Although many different gifts and talents have been identified and creativity can be, at least partly, explained and measured, gifted, talented, and creative individuals are typi-cally lumped together as a single category.

- Definitions of giftedness have changed. When the roots of the field of gifted education were laid down by pioneers such as Francis Galton and Lewis Terman, high IQ was viewed as the critical dimension of giftedness. Because children with high IQs were the most deeply investigated, early definitions tended to be narrow and restricted. They relied on psy-chometric measures and limited giftedness to specific performance on an intelligence test. Over time, definitions have become much more liberal in terms of both the types of behaviours attributed to individuals who are gifted and the degree of behaviour that must be elicited before the label *gifted* is applied.

- Identification of signs of giftedness, of potential for high-quality creative achievement, remains a relatively inexact science (Feldhusen, 1989). There is no consensus on how to measure superiority or how to recognize potential giftedness.

- There are two quite different views about the definitions of giftedness. One looks at gift-edness as potential; the other looks at it as the actual production of outstanding work. The giftedness-as-potential view often uses an IQ cut-off between 120 and 140 or restricts giftedness to a percentage of the population, ranging from the top 1 to the top 20 percent. When giftedness-as-product is used, definitions dismiss the idea that IQ alone deter-mines giftedness; they focus on the attributes of identified individuals who are gifted and their potential value to society. This is because "school-house giftedness," connoted by high test scores and good grades, is only weakly associated with adult eminence or creative contribution (Siegler and Kotovsky, 1985; Sternberg, 1987). Product definitions therefore base giftedness on an individual's consistently remarkable performance in some socially useful area and only assign the term *gifted* to people who have attained outstanding achievements.

A widely employed definition, originally adopted by the United States Office of Education in 1977 and revised in 1981, states that children who are gifted are those who give evidence of high performance capability in areas such as intellectual, creative, artistic, leadership capacity, or specific academic fields, and who require services or activities not ordinarily provided by the school in order to develop such capabilities (PL 97-35, sec. 572).

This definition manages to be inclusive, specific, and practical. It encompasses a wide range of gifts, talents, and creative aptitudes; stresses the necessity for special education provisions for students identified as gifted; and ties identification to the necessity for programming. Newfoundland has adopted this definition; Alberta's 1983 Minister's Task Force on Gifted and Talented Pupils recommended a similar definition. Ontario has quite a specific definition that includes characteristics and programming (Ontario, Ministry of Education, 1981). British Columbia has adopted an official definition, and the Yukon has adopted the model proposed by Renzulli (1978).

Joseph Renzulli, who believes in defining giftedness largely as product, holds that in the end, giftedness is determined by the contributions an individual makes to humanity. Renzulli studied adults known to be gifted and concluded that three characteristics were required for remarkable achievement: high intellectual ability, high creativity, and the ability to carry tasks through to completion. The interaction is shown in Figure 7-1.

It is not enough to possess only one of these traits; as the figure shows, it is only where the circles intersect that the three traits come together and that, according to Renzulli, true giftedness is found (Renzulli and Reis, 1991). Renzulli (1978) feels that children who are gifted and talented "are those possessing or capable of developing this composite of traits and applying them to any potentially valuable area of human performance" (p. 261).

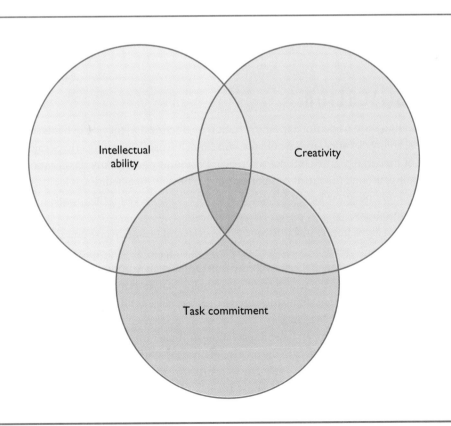

Figure 7-1
Interaction of Renzulli's characteristics

Terminology

To compound definitional problems, a host of other terms are used to describe individuals who are gifted. Words such as *precocious, talented, creative,* and *genius* are all popular, and the terms *gifted* and *talented* are frequently used interchangeably.

As the Historical Notes that open this chapter point out, *genius* was the original term used to indicate a particular aptitude or capacity. Today, we reserve the word for those persons who demonstrate extremely rare intellectual powers. In the early 1920s, the term *gifted* evolved to describe high-achieving students. It may be defined as a combination of above average general ability, a high level of creativity, and a high level of task commitment (Renzulli and Reis, 1991).

During the 1960s, definitions began to add components of creativity. Barbara Clark (1988) observes that "creativity is a very special condition, attitude, or state of being that nearly defies description" (p. 46). Creativity may be seen as the "activities and products invented in the interest of solving a problem" (Cole and Sarnoff, 1980, p. 6).

Sometimes, young gifted children are said to be **precocious**. This word comes from the Latin *preacox,* meaning to precook or to boil beforehand. Precocity refers to remarkable early development. Many children who are highly gifted show precocity in particular areas of development such as language, music, or mathematical ability. The fields that have produced the most prodigies are music and chess (Feldman, 1993).

If giftedness is above average competence, then talent is above average performance. **Talent** refers to a specific dimension of a skill in areas such as music, visual arts, drama, athletics, and particular academic domains. Canadian psychologist François Gagné calls talent "the developmental product of an interaction between aptitudes and intrapersonal and environmental catalysts" (1991, p. 66).

Classification

Classification systems do not appear in relation to giftedness as they do in fields such as intellectual ability. Severity levels would not make much sense. We could perhaps call a person mildly or moderately gifted but not severely or profoundly gifted. Any classification, therefore, revolves around the varied components that contribute to giftedness. It is closely aligned with the terminology we have just explained and takes into account that people may possess many components.

The term *gifted* implies the possession of special abilities in diverse areas; however, it is most often used to refer to students with above average academic endowment. This happens because, educationally speaking, the most important components of giftedness are those defined relative to the school in which an individual finds himself or herself. *Academic ability* refers to intellectual ability measured by performance on IQ and standardized tests of academic achievement (Marland, 1972). Academically talented students are generally considered to be those scoring at the 95th percentile or higher on these measures.

Essentially, **creativity** refers to the process of bringing unusual and unexpected responses to bear on given situations; it is a capacity to restructure the world in unusual or useful conceptual terms. Creative thinking includes fluency of ideas, or producing a number of responses to a given stimulus; flexibility, or shifts in thinking from one category to another;

originality, or unusual and clever responses; and elaboration, or the addition of details to basic ideas or thoughts (Torrance, 1969).

Divergent thinking, a type of thinking in which considerable searching about is done and a number of answers are produced, is part of creativity. It seems to be only a component, however, as divergent thinking in childhood is not highly correlated with creative abilities in adulthood (Feldhusen and Clinkenbeard, 1987). Divergent thinking is the basis of creative problem solving and is in some ways the opposite of *convergent thinking*, which focuses on one right answer, or toward a relatively determined answer. This relationship is diagrammed in Figure 7-2.

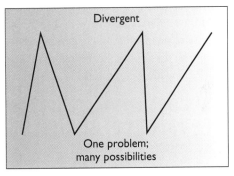

Figure 7-2
Convergent and divergent thinking

The link between intelligence and creativity is difficult to pinpoint. Above a threshold score of about 120 IQ, the correlation between giftedness and creativity disappears. A Canadian study (Kershner and Ledger, 1985) found that highly intelligent boys and girls aged nine to eleven were, as a group, more creative than less intelligent children. Not all of the children who were gifted were more creative than their peers, however, and girls were significantly more creative than boys, especially on verbal tasks.

Creativity may very well be an innate trait that can be stimulated or quashed. Creativity seems generally to decrease as children get older, a tendency that may be accounted for by both age and culture. As well, creativity tends to occur in spurts. During the first three years of school, most children increase their creativity, perhaps because teachers in these grades allow much freedom of expression. After grade three, a sharp drop in creativity occurs, followed by a gradual decrease during the remaining elementary and middle school years (Bernard, 1973).

Research has not yet shown the relationship of talent to giftedness. Gagné (1985) presented one of the first major attempts to delineate talent as distinct from giftedness. He suggested that talent is an ability focus that emerges out of general ability. Therefore, giftedness is a prerequisite for talent, but an individual who is gifted is not necessarily talented. Some children have unusual talents in one field and limited abilities in other areas.

Talented children begin to nurture their special traits early and children are often encouraged by their parents and extensively tutored or coached by experts. But there seems to be more to talent than that. Some of us may practise our pitches and putts forever but will never play with Tiger Woods. Why? It seems that certain aptitudes make it easier to learn certain skills and genetic factors may influence one's abilities in a particular area (Gagné, 1991). As well, the direction of an individual's talent depends on many factors such as experience, motivation, interest, emotional stability, hero worship, parental urging, and even chance.

There seem to be three phases in talent development. First there is playful exploration that entices the learner into further involvement. Then there is acquisition of skills and attention to detail, with rigorous practice. Finally, a commitment to excellence is made (Bloom, 1985).

Leadership is defined as the ability to effect positive and productive changes that are self-enhancing or group-enhancing. Plowman (1981) described leaders in these terms: charismatic, intuitive, generative, analytical, evaluative, and synergistic. Those with high leadership abilities demonstrate empathy and sensitivity, personality and proficiency, and possess *charisma*, the ability to actualize values to the extent that dynamic group change is effected (Lindsay, 1978). Children who display early leadership qualities will interact easily with a variety of people; be sought out by others; possess confidence; establish the mood of the group; be sensitive to the feelings of others; show others how to improve on a task; and generate many ideas and solutions (Karnes and Strong, 1978).

Prevalence of Giftedness

The lack of a universally accepted definition of giftedness makes it very difficult to estimate its prevalence in the population at large and in school-aged children. However, we can reasonably assume that only a small percentage of a school population will require special programming for the gifted. In this general sense, giftedness is said to occur in two to five percent of school-aged children.

Only Ontario specifically includes students who are gifted in its special education legislation. Of school-aged children, about 1.3 percent are educated in the gifted category. British Columbia identifies 1.9 percent of school-aged students as gifted (Canadian Council for Exceptional Children, 1989).

The relative contribution of genetic and environmental factors with respect to giftedness is not clearly understood.

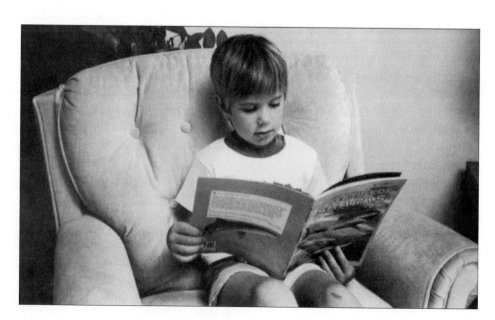

Factors Contributing to Giftedness

Children with gifts and talents are found at every economic level and in every stratum of society, throughout all ethnic, cultural, and racial groups. However, we do not yet understand what contributes most to giftedness, or why some gifted people achieve eminence and others fade into obscurity. The multiplicity of factors that bring a Tiger Woods or a Margaret Atwood to prominence have not yet been untangled and identified.

The effects of heredity and environment are both important in the development of children who are gifted and talented, but the relative contribution of genetic and environmental factors is not clearly understood. Genes carry potential for various characteristics from parent to child down through the generations, but the genes alone cannot produce a human being. Each of us is born in a unique environment in which conditions act and react with one another. The individual human being is the total expression of all these complex and constantly interacting forces.

Genetic Factors

The proposition that intelligence and abilities are inherited is not popular in our egalitarian society. Francis Galton and other early researchers maintained that most human traits were passed down through the generations on "germ plasm." When the dangers of a purely genetic view of development became obvious, the pendulum swung toward a strong emphasis on environmental conditions, especially after the 1930s.

Nevertheless, it is now abundantly clear from the field of behavioural genetics that there is a significant role played by genetic transmission in the development of intelligence (Gallagher, 1991). Most authorities in the area of behavioural genetics hold that genetic factors are at least as important as environmental factors in determining intelligence (e.g. Bouchard and McGue, 1981; Scarr-Salapatek, 1975). Among Caucasian children in North America and Europe, it is estimated that half to three-quarters of intelligence variation is due to genetic factors (Eysenck, 1979; Scarr-Salapatek, 1975). There is also no doubt that some of us have more inborn capabilities in music or visual perception or linguistic ability than others (Plomin, 1989).

Environmental Factors

The complex study of genetics has not yet revealed how genes influence giftedness. Moreover, even the strongest hereditarians acknowledge the great influence of environment on the development of intelligence.

Giftedness is not just a condition bestowed on some and denied to others. Rather, it is a set of traits that must be nurtured in order to reach their full development (see Gagné, 1985). The unique development of gifted traits can only occur through specific interactions within family units and later with appropriate training and education.

The importance of nurturing is clearly evidenced by the many deprivation studies that have demonstrated the negative effects of malnutrition and lack of stimulation on infant functioning. The high proportion of first-borns among the gifted population further suggests the importance of environment to the full development of intellectual potential (Laycock,

1979). Unlike younger siblings, first-borns receive full attention and much stimulation from their parents, even if only for a short time.

No race, ethnic group, or culture holds a monopoly on giftedness. However, the statistical probability of giftedness increases when a child's parents have higher than average intelligence and provide a better than average home environment. Bright children are more likely to be born to bright parents, although some children who are gifted are born to slow learners. Other factors in the environment that seem most clearly to affect the development of giftedness are the values and expectations of the culture; the socio-economic level of the family, with accompanying nutritional and other health variables, attitudes, and values; the number of children in the family; and the presence of environmental stimulation (Eysenck, 1979; Laycock, 1979).

Using the family as a starting point, many investigators have attempted to unravel the specific family variables associated with gifted-level abilities in children (e.g. Colangelo and Dettman, 1983; Cornell, 1983, 1984). What they find are many favourable qualities in these families, particularly parental interest in child-rearing and a strong commitment to the development of the child's talents and abilities. When Benjamin Bloom and his colleagues (Bloom, 1985; Bloom and Sosniak, 1981) examined the home environments and the early training of exceptional people in the arts, in athletics, and in cognitive skill areas, they found that the home environment and the person's parents were almost entirely responsible for nurturing the child's early interests and the development of his or her skills.

Highly educated parents are more likely to produce children who are gifted and to provide them with enriching environments. On the Stanford-Binet Individual Intelligence Test, the average score for children of college graduates is more than 10 points above the mean, whereas for children of parents with less than high school education it is about 6 points below the mean (Kaplan and Saccuzzo, 1993). In a Canadian study of gifted kindergarten children, Perks (1984) found that 59.5 percent of their fathers and 50 percent of their mothers had post-secondary education. This compared to 30.9 percent of fathers and 27 percent of mothers for non-gifted children. Perks compared the reading material available in the children's homes and found that 61.9 percent of the families of children who were gifted had more than 300 books, as compared to 18.4 percent of families of non-gifted children.

Certainly, bright children come from lower socio-economic homes, but not as often as we would expect. Intervening factors may include lack of motivation, family expectations, neighbourhood aspirations, and financial pressures.

Identification and Assessment of Giftedness

Much of the success of programs for students who are gifted is contingent upon sound identification procedures. At first glance, the identification of gifted and talented children and youth may seem to be a relatively simple task. Nothing could be further from the truth. From the outset, one of the major concerns in gifted education has been the problem of identification and its measurement correlates. Even today there is much confusion, and the issue of identification and assessment remains highly problematic.

The heterogeneity of the population, the plethora of available definitions, and the administrative problems make identification particularly difficult and uncertain. Problems can and do occur at various points in the process. This led Borland (1989) to suggest that the process of selecting students and placing them in appropriate programs is the most difficult, controversial, and thankless of all the tasks involved in developing and implementing programs for the gifted.

Part of the difficulty lies in the wide range of areas to be assessed. Outstanding ability comes in a number of different forms and requires a variety of ongoing identification procedures as well as a variety of special educational programs. There exists no single adequate identification procedure or combination of procedures that addresses all important areas and therefore effectively taps a high proportion of students who are gifted.

Another problem with all forms of identification systems is that they are less than perfect. The younger the child, the less confidence can be placed in the reliability and validity of the measures. So when the term *gifted* is used to describe young children, it essentially applies to potential rather than accomplishment and is making guesses about the future with limited information (Colangelo and Fleuridas, 1986).

In addition, the selection of students for gifted programs should be a recurring activity, not a one-shot affair. Both IQ and interests can change and specific abilities can emerge. The correlation of the IQ of a child at age six or seven with the same person's IQ at age seventeen is approximately +0.7 (Bloom, 1964).

The process of identifying learners with gifts and talents is becoming more diversified, especially in terms of the instruments used. In the past, giftedness was viewed as a univariate construct, basically consisting of those traits that were measured by IQ tests. Children with high IQ scores formed the bulk of the population identified as gifted. Conceptions of giftedness as IQ were established by Lewis Terman, who conducted an important longitudinal study into giftedness. See the Research Notes on these pages for more on Terman's study.

Terman's study represented the first full-scale longitudinal study of the nature of gift-

Research Notes

The Terman Studies

Lewis Terman, an American educator and psychologist, expanded the concepts and procedures related to IQ developed by Alfred Binet in France at the beginning of this century. Terman believed the Binet scale assessed a wide range of performance and could be adapted for use with high-functioning children. In 1916, he published the Stanford-Binet Individual Intelligence Test in conjunction with Stanford University.

Terman held that intelligence was manifested essentially in the ability to acquire and manipulate concepts. He defined the gifted as those who scored in the top one percent of general intellectual ability as measured by the Stanford-Binet Scale or a comparable instrument (Terman, 1926). Terman carefully dis-

tinguished giftedness from talent and creativity. He viewed talent as the potential for unusual achievement, but only when combined with high IQ scores. Creativity, he believed, was a personality factor, and thus differed from both giftedness and talent (Wolf and Stephens, 1982).

In 1922, armed with the Stanford-Binet tests and a single-measure concept of intelligence, Terman embarked on a massive study of giftedness among California school children. This study, which included 1 528 children, "was designed to discover what physical, mental, and personality traits are characteristic of gifted children as a class, and what sort of adult the typical gifted child becomes" (Terman and Oden, 1951, p. 21).

To determine his population, Terman relied on teacher nominations and group intelligence tests. He then identified his gifted children from those scoring at or above 140 points on the Stanford-Binet Individual Intelligence Test.

Although Terman died in 1956, the study continues today. The remaining "Terman kids" are now in their eighties. The longitudinal research found the following:

- Most students in the sample came from a middle or higher socio-economic group, with a low incidence of broken homes.

- Nearly half of the children could read before entering kindergarten.

- One in five children skipped part or all of the first grade.

- On average, the children finished school 14 percent faster than normal students.

- The children averaged 40 percent higher than their agemates on achievement tests.

- They preferred abstract subjects, such as literary debate and ancient history, and were less interested in such practical concerns as penmanship and manual training.

- They read more and better books, made numerous collections, and had many hobbies.

- When retested as adults, they were found to have retained their intellectual superiority.

- As adults, they were ahead in terms of occupational status, incomes, publications, and patents. They earned more money, had more managerial jobs, and made more literary and scientific contributions than the average adult (Terman and Oden, 1959). When checked in 1959, Terman's group had published over 2 000 scientific papers and 33 novels and taken out 230 patents (Sprinthall and Sprinthall, 1990).

- Middle-aged people in Terman's sample maintained their superior physical characteristics (Terman and Oden, 1959). They were far above their agemates in general health, physique, mental health, and emotional adjustment. Fewer than five percent of Terman's population were rated as seriously maladjusted, and the incidence of problems such as ill health, psychiatric disturbance, alcoholism, and delinquent behaviour was but a fraction of that normally observed in the general population.

- Although reaching college age just before the Great Depression, when college attendance was not common for women, over 67 percent of the Terman women earned at least a bachelor's degree.

- The female sample contained more childless women than normative samples of similar ages and as a group had relatively higher incomes and levels of employment than women of comparable ages (Holahan, 1991).

edness; it legitimized the field, and the serious inception of a gifted movement began with Terman. Many of Terman's findings remain remarkably relevant; so far, his study is unsurpassed in the field of giftedness. The one area that has been disputed and altered is Terman's establishment of IQ tests as the sole measure of giftedness.

Psychologists are no longer satisfied with intelligence defined simply as what IQ tests measure. Today's researchers are finding evidence of multiple intelligences rather than a single general intelligence. J. P. Guilford (1988) and Howard Gardner (1983) are the most modern proponents of the concept of multiple cognitive abilities.

Multiple Intelligences

Psychologist J. P. Guilford of the University of Southern California was one of the first to propose a multidimensional theory of intelligence. Guilford's Structure of Intellect analyzes intelligence in terms of its specific skills and divides intellectual performance into three dimensions: operations, contents, and products. Each of these dimensions encompasses several abilities. The first, *operations*, stresses the methods people use to process information. Guilford's second dimension, *contents*, has to do with how a learner classifies processed information. The third, *products*, refers to the forms and structures that people use to organize information.

Guilford's novel and distinctive approach was widely influential within the psychological field. It prompted researchers to reconsider intelligence as a diverse range of intellectual and creative abilities. Within gifted education, Guilford inspired interest in the characteristics of creative thought processes, in tests of creativity, and in other psychometric measures based on the 120 factors of the Structure of Intellect. For example, a test called the Structure of Intellect–Learning Abilities (SOI–LA), is classified as an intelligence test. There is also a Gifted Screening Form (GSF), which consists of ten areas that Guilford determined to be most related to the characteristics of individuals who are gifted (Meeker, 1979).

When Howard Gardner (1983) proposed an alternate theory of multiple intelligence, he departed from the more traditional psychometric approach of Guilford. In essence, Gardner holds that many forms of thinking are prominent both inside and outside of school. He sees intelligence as involving the use of problem solving skills that enable people to resolve genuine problems, create effective products, and find or create new problems. Both the problems and the products must be relevant to the particular cultural context (Maker, Neilson, and Rogers, 1994). That is, individuals develop competence in different domains which are independent of each other, and society plays a role in shaping and defining the competencies through its value system.

The capabilities which people develop fall into seven areas—linguistic, logical–mathematical, spatial, bodily, kinesthetic, musical, and interpersonal–intrapersonal. Most people are not gifted or even highly competent in all seven areas. Gardner believes that development of high level competence requires innate capacity, motivation, and opportunity. Environment, cultural context, and language may also influence all of these important factors (Maker, Neilson, and Rogers, 1994).

Although research on multiple intelligences is in its infancy, Gardner's work, like Guilford's before him, has had an impact on the education of students who are gifted. Today, those involved in the identification and assessment of children who are gifted are strongly persuaded to look not only for children with high IQs but also for those who are gifted in other dimensions as well.

Assessment Measures

In the field of gifted education, "the ideal identification system has not been developed" (Feldhusen, Hoover, and Sayler, 1990). Identification of signs of giftedness and of potential for high-quality creative achievement "remains a relatively inexact science" (Feldhusen, 1989, p. 8).

When educators define giftedness in terms of potential, they use identification procedures that emphasize IQ tests and other predictive measures such as academic achievement, creative products, and critical thinking. When giftedness is seen as current achievements, identification procedures stress observations and nominations, performance in academic subjects, performance assessment, or a review of a portfolio. Diagnosticians may incorporate information from many sources: nominations (teacher, parent, peer, self); previously demonstrated achievement; school grades; family histories and interviews; case studies; tests of creativity; and observations of physical, personality, and social traits.

Whichever focus is taken, the most common identification approaches involve one of four general procedures: cut-off scores; two-stage screening which uses a cut-off score and a teacher recommendation or a test; pools in which several areas are targeted for assessment using a variety of measures such as standardized tests and achievement in the classroom; and a matrix, which is broader than the above. It uses several scores from various instruments but weighs the scores (see Tuttle, Becker, and Sousa, 1988). Various procedures and a sampling of measures are shown in Table 7-1.

There is little to indicate that any one identification procedure is better than another. For example, researchers (Shore and Tsiamis, 1986) compared two groups of children either on the basis of traditional measures of achievement or on that of parent and teacher identification. They found that the groups were not distinguishable and concluded that formal selection by testing was not necessary for a substantial number of students who are gifted.

Observation

Screening involves a broad range of procedures that may use different instruments and procedures. Especially for young children, observation is one of the most potent ways to identify those who are potentially gifted. A three-year-old may be observed to tackle mathematical problems that are taught in grade three. A four-year-old may be able to read and draw maps as well as most adults (Robinson, Roedell, and Jackson, 1979). High verbal ability is a good indicator of IQ; children may show early and extensive vocabulary development. An 18-month-old child may use language like most children at 30 months. Older children ask many questions and have good memories. Many children with advanced vocabularies have an intense interest in books. They learn to read relatively early and easily and carry out the task fluently. One-half to three-quarters of verbally talented children are reading by the age

Table 7-1 Identification of children who are gifted, creative, and talented

Intelligence	Screening nominations	Creativity	Other	Formal intelligence	Achievement
Group IQ tests	teacher parent peer self Gifted Screening Form rating scales	tests of creativity and divergent thinking (e.g. Torrance Tests, Creativity Assessment Package)	school grades case history interviews observations performance tests portfolios exhibitions	IQ tests (e.g. Structure of Intellect Learning Abilities, WISC-III, Stanford-Binet)	Achievement tests (e.g. Canadian Test of Basic Skills)

of five (Piirto, 1994). (Parenthetically, very advanced reading in the early grades does not guarantee that students will still be outstanding years later [Mills and Jackson, 1990].)

Parents and teachers should not expect very young children to be gifted in everything. Especially in preschool children who are potentially gifted, we see **dyssynchrony;** that is, uneven development. This applies particularly to motor skills. Some children learn their letters from some combination of teaching by parents, older siblings, and preschool teachers and try to write early. But even if children know the letters, they probably do not possess the fine motor skills to form them well.

Group Tests

Because giftedness has traditionally been defined on the basis of intelligence, identification procedures have typically involved some measures of intellectual ability. Some schools begin by screening students with standardized group intelligence tests. However, all currently available group intelligence tests have a high prevalence of underidentification and overidentification of exceptional children, particularly with reference to creative divergent thinkers and very young children. It is not unusual for scores on group intelligence tests and individual IQ tests to vary as much as 30 points (Martinson, 1975). In addition, group intelligence tests may identify proficient tests takers at the expense of those who may score somewhat lower but who are highly creative and original thinkers (Renzulli, 1979). Group intelligence tests also appear to penalize children from lower socio-economic and minority groups.

Teacher Nomination

Teacher nomination has traditionally been, and remains today, a major method for identifying youngsters who may be gifted, talented, and creative. It is an inexpensive screening method founded on the premise that teachers know their students well enough to spot those with strong abilities. But even as teacher nominations are appreciated for their apparent relevance to children's educational experiences and functioning, they are criticized for their ineffectiveness in accurately identifying children with gifts.

Teacher nominations are suspect because they may result in the correct identification of as few as one in five children who are gifted (Martinson, 1975). Teachers, who are fairly efficient in rating students' academic levels and identifying students requiring special help, are relatively poor in identifying youngsters who may be gifted, talented, and creative (Perks, 1984). Teacher nomination proves no better than conventional group screening. One early study (Renzulli, 1979) found that teachers were only 50 percent successful when requested to identify those students whom they considered to be gifted and talented. Others (Haywood Gear, 1976; Perks, 1984) discovered effectiveness rates of between 10 and 57 percent with effectiveness measured as the number of pupils correctly identified as gifted.

Why are teachers, who know their students well, so poor at identification procedures? Teachers may look for the wrong things. Some tend to choose one sex over the other; others tend to choose conformist high achievers and overlook creative or divergent thinkers (Martinson, 1975). Or teachers may not understand giftedness. A recent study (see Reis and Westberg, 1994) found that 61 percent of public school teachers and 54 percent of private school elementary teachers reported that they had never had any training in teaching students who are gifted.

When teachers are given specialized training in teaching gifted students and asked to identify children on the basis of clearly defined characteristics, accuracy in identification can be improved up to 40 percent (Haywood Gear, 1976; Perks, 1984). Too, attitudes and teaching strategies improve greatly (Hansen and Feldhusen, 1994; Reis and Westberg, 1994).

Together with training programs, questionnaires and rating scales increase effectiveness. Rating scales are particularly helpful in objectifying teacher judgment. Measures such as the Scale for Rating Behavioral Characteristics of Superior Students (Renzulli, Hartman, and Callahan, 1975) are designed to obtain teachers' estimates of student traits in specific areas. The teacher is asked to rate each pupil in the areas of learning, motivation, creativity, leadership, communication, and the arts.

Parent Nomination

Parent nomination questionnaires are another economical means of identifying children who are gifted and talented. Parents see their children make up games and stories, invent and build things, solve problems, and create all sorts of products. From these observations, parents may identify high performance. One study found that parents' implicit beliefs about their children's ability levels closely related to the children's actual tested IQ. Parents were especially accurate in their assessment of creative thinking, abstract thinking, and memory abilities (Louis and Lewis, 1992). In another survey in the United States of 1 039 parents of gifted children, 70 percent of the children were identified accurately by age three. Of all the characteristics that caused parents to suspect giftedness, "early verbal expression" was mentioned most frequently (Gogel, McCumsey, and Hewitt, 1985).

Studies have shown that parent accuracy varies from 11 to 76 percent (Khoury and Appel, 1979), which still tends to be better than teacher nomination. Nonetheless, problems do exist. Parents from lower socio-economic neighbourhoods are more likely to report their child as gifted than parents from higher socio-economic locales, partly because well-educated parents tend to set higher intellectual standards for their children. Other parents may be unaware of their child's outstanding abilities, especially if they have little chance to compare his or her accomplishments with those of other children of a similar age.

Peer Nomination

Peer nominations have been judged very favourably by experts in the field and are growing in popularity as a screening technique for giftedness (Gagné, 1989). One survey (Cox, Daniel, and Boston, 1985) found that 25 percent of school boards surveyed in the United States used peer nominations. Davis and Rimm (1985) wrote that "peers are extraordinarily good at nominating gifted and talented students" (p. 78), while others (Richert, Alvino, and McDonnell, 1972) have judged peer nominations to be the most adequate technique for screening leaders and creative individuals. Peer nomination may be especially helpful in identifying rural gifted and minority children, as well as those who are disadvantaged or disabled (Banbury and Wellington, 1989).

Self-Nomination

Self-nomination forms have been used with students who have strong artistic, creative, scientific, or other interests and talents. They are especially recommended at the junior and senior high school levels, where peer pressure may cause youths to mask special talents (Davis and Rimm, 1994).

Tests of Mental Ability

Following screening, promising students are often administered individual intelligence tests. The Stanford-Binet Individual Intelligence Test and the Wechsler Intelligence Scale for Children (WISC-III) are the most commonly used measures.

In many ways, individual IQ tests appear to be the best single method for identification of children with superior cognitive abilities. They possess high validity as predictors of success in academic settings and their scores are relatively stable over time. Assuming that motivation remains constant, these tests can reveal not only a child's present abilities, but those that will develop in the future. IQ tests can also identify those children who are gifted but still underachieving.

Even with these finer points, the tests are not a panacea and a number of problems exist. IQ measures may reflect a racial or a socio-economic bias and reinforce existing inequalities in selection of children for special programs. As well, giftedness seems to be characterized by qualitative differences in thinking and insightfulness, which may not be clearly reflected by performance or intelligence tests (Reis, 1989). The tests may fail to measure some traits, behaviours, and potentials that are significant indicators of giftedness and thereby fail to identify some of our most promising and potentially capable students.

Achievement Tests

Achievement tests can be employed systematically to identify children with gifts and talents who are already achieving at a high level academically. These tests have been used very successfully to identify school children who are performing extremely well in specific fields, such as mathematics (Stanley, 1979).

Measuring Creativity

Children who are gifted, especially academically gifted, may be identified by their high levels of achievement and motivation. Omitted from the equation here is creativity, which is difficult, if not impossible, to measure accurately.

An instrument that yields a single score or index of children's creativity or creative giftedness simply does not exist. This is hardly surprising. First, creativity is so varied and shown in so many ways that it is not reasonable to try to use a standard measure to assess what is in reality such a nonstandard trait. Second, there is still no unifying theory of creativity embraced by all researchers and practitioners, and it seems unlikely that a general theory will ever emerge.

Despite these difficulties, more than 60 instruments for measuring or assessing creativity exist (Treffinger, 1986). Many are based on Guilford's work. For example, Torrance used Guilford's assumption that the most important factors in creativity are fluency, flexibility, and originality in his Torrance Tests of Creative Thinking (Torrance, 1966). Designed to measure divergent thinking, not creativity per se, the Torrance has two subtests—"Thinking creatively with words" and "Thinking creatively with pictures." Guilford's SOI Gifted Screening

Form is used in many districts as an instrument for screening students for special programs and as an approach to individualizing curriculum (O'Tuel, 1983).

The Group Inventory for Finding Creative Talent (GIFT) and its update (Rimm and Davis, 1976) contain a five-level inventory with items to measure perseverance, interests, biography, independence, and curiosity. For example, on the perseverance measure, a child responds to the statement, "Easy puzzles are the most fun." Those who agree are considered to be less creative than those who disagree.

The Creativity Assessment Package (CAP) (Williams, 1980) consists of two group tests for children: a Test of Divergent Thinking and a Test of Divergent Feeling. A third instrument, the Williams Scale, is a rating measure for parents and teachers. All three instruments can be used to screen, identify, and evaluate the most important factors of creativity among all children.

Portfolios

Portfolios, a type of performance test made up of continual collections of a student's work, are emerging as a promising measure in the assessment of learners who are gifted. A portfolio (sometimes called a *process folio*) is a folder of representative work that meets certain criteria or purposes. Portfolios are joint projects between the teacher and a student. They include information selected by the student under the guidance of the teacher as well as a series of statements that reflect a student's thoughts about the contents (Wolf, Bixby, and Gardiner, 1991). The portfolio will include work samples and projects, and may include the results of tests.

As the portfolio is a continual collection of a student's work, developmental growth is evidenced through the work presented (reports, artwork, poetry, and video, for example). In using portfolios, students are expected to participate fully in assessment and are provided with access to the results of such evaluation (Nixon, 1990).

Leadership

Leadership does not describe inborn characteristics but cumulative capabilities that result from an intermixing of the child's innate abilities and experience. To assess leadership, observation of performance together with some rating checklist is most appropriate.

Visual and Performing Arts

In this field, talent is still most often assessed by expert judges in an audition setting. Experts in the arts are not enthusiastic about the use of tests to determine artistic ability and prefer exhibitions, performances, auditions, and interviews. Nevertheless, a range of measures are available to assess potential and aptitude, especially in the areas of music and visual art (Khatena, 1982).

Problems in Identification

You can judge from the above section that identification problems abound in the field of gifted education. Not only are there questions about how and what to identify, but in any procedure some special populations tend to be overlooked, and then these children who are gifted pass through school unidentified, their gifts and talents uncultivated. Especially open to non-identification are gifted underachievers; gifted females; atypical children who are gifted, a population that includes children who are disabled; those from minority backgrounds and children who are culturally different from the majority population; and children with learning disabilities.

Gifted Underachievers

To some people, the phrase *gifted underachiever* is an oxymoron. Yet we cannot contradict the body of research data that shows that many children with gifts and talents do not develop to their full potential. Intellectually gifted students especially, in contrast to those gifted in athletics, arts, or leadership, may be at risk for learning difficulties in school (Whitmore, 1988).

Academic underachievers are those about whom we can make a reasonable prediction of academic potential that is not fulfilled. These are children who are gifted on IQ tests but whose academic achievement is grade level or less (Yewchuk, 1984). Such performance does not necessarily equate with failure or underproduction; children may indeed work at an average level but not at one commensurate with their ability. Others, of course, do not even attain average levels.

A complex of factors contributes to the high proportion of underachievers among the population of persons who are gifted. These include:

- *impossible expectations.* Pervasive misunderstandings of the nature of giftedness may result in inappropriate expectations and consequent adult responses that place students at risk (Whitmore, 1988). For example, when parents and teachers believe that learning and school achievement are easy for all students who are gifted, they tend to demand more effort and tolerate little error or imperfection. Or, when adults believe that such children are so much more mature than their peers developmentally, they tend to expect more mature behaviour than is reasonable and forget the childishness that is necessarily present in all children.

- *conflict between giftedness and creativity and the typically rigid classroom.* Children who are gifted are turned off by conformity to precise directions, excessive repetition, memorization and drill, uniformity of assignments, and the lack of opportunity to pursue interests and work independently. In a classroom that requires a high degree of conformity and achievement on schedule with a restricted and often dull curriculum, these children may feel stifled and frustrated. They can't or don't conform to classroom mores, feel that there is nothing to learn that is interesting and challenging, and gradually sink into underachievement.

- *learning not to learn.* In the early years, a child may need to make little, if any, effort to make good grades. Consequently, when academic demands become greater, the student does not know how to apply effort. Such children may then lack confidence, have poor study habits, and do inconsistent work.

- *social and emotional factors.* Some students may underachieve because it is socially safe. If they feel that peer relationships are jeopardized by expectations of superior performance, they may not want to be singled out as different. Other students may have unfavourable self-concepts that distort their perceptions of the world and undermine their motivation and goal orientation.

One father described his underachieving son as "an emperor and a Renaissance man at age four, dethroned by age six, and a behaviour problem and underachiever thereafter" (in Rimm and Lowe, 1988, p. 358). We can see the same pattern in the Profile of William, a student with high potential who became an underachiever by early adolescence.

Females Who Are Gifted

Both in school and in the working world, more males than females are considered gifted and talented. By an overwhelming margin, men achieve high status and recognition more frequently than women of the same age. There is no conclusive evidence that this disparity is the result of biological differences; rather, available research points far more clearly to social and cultural expectations as an explanation for the disproportionate number of males recognized as gifted. Society encourages narrow role definitions and behaviour options for women and broader ones for men. It is considered neither proper nor advantageous for girls to be too superior. Girls who insist on their giftedness are encouraged to become musicians or artists, rather than physicists or engineers.

Females have not been encouraged to enter academic disciplines and careers historically dominated by males. Certainly, more women are entering such non-traditional professions as chemistry, engineering, dentistry, and physics, but the numbers are still very small. Fewer than one-quarter of senior male and female high school students take math and science (International Association, 1988), and talented girls are even less likely than tal-

Profile

William

William was identified during fourth grade as a gifted child. On the WISC-R he scored 162 on the Verbal Scale and 108 on the Performance Scale for a Full Scale of 134. Achievement testing showed his reading to be at grade level, although his math was only at grade four. During the testing sessions, William was resentful and manipulative, and stated that he "did not appreciate having his brain examined." He eventually complied with the examiner's requests and finally confided that "When I was five I was an optimist; at seven a pessimist. Now I'm a cynicist."

Although William revealed outstanding abilities in verbal tasks and abstract thinking, he showed a severe deficit in visual-motor dexterity functioning. He had an aversion to written classroom assignments, which had begun to significantly lower his achieve-

ment. William also had a tendency toward acting-out behaviour and poor peer relations, chiefly attributable to his bossy and directive attitude. This was compounded by his inability or unwillingness to comply with expected school behaviour in matters of dress and personal hygiene.

William was accelerated and skipped grade six. At the same time, he was given special help to compensate for his visual-motor deficits. However, William increasingly failed to achieve at levels commensurate with his potential. By grade nine, he was functioning in a slow-moving junior high school stream. When William was sixteen, he dropped out of school. Currently, he is unemployed with few prospects for work in the future.

ented boys to pursue a career in the sciences. In fact, young women's interest in the sciences has actually declined in the past two decades, despite the women's movement and a range of efforts to encourage young women to pursue careers in these fields (Astin, Green, and Korn, 1989). Women tend not to pursue math to the same extent as mathematically gifted males. Kerr (1988) contends that girls who are gifted are rewarded for intellectual achievement at early ages but by adolescence they are rewarded for social conformity, which may include seeing math as masculine.

Even in careers traditionally assigned to women, men tend to achieve high status and recognition more frequently than women of the same age by an overwhelming margin. For example, men are disproportionately represented in positions of power and influence in education. The 1970 Royal Commission on the Status of Women in Alberta found that "a man was 7.5 times more likely to become a principal, although he was only 2.5 times as likely to have higher qualifications than a woman" (Nixon, 1989). Nearly thirty years later, educational leaders are still male.

The reasons forwarded to account for the smaller proportion of girls identified as gifted are legion. Barriers may come from the protection of a feminine self-image (Meece, Parsons, Kaczada, Goff, and Futterman, 1982), non-assertiveness (Hollinger and Fleming, 1984), fear of success (Lavach and Lanier, 1975), conflicts arising from achievement versus self-concept (Fox, 1977), or fear of loss of social acceptance (Casserly, 1979). Girls who are gifted find it difficult to reconcile their academic interests with the areas of excellence traditionally seen by society as sex-role-appropriate for women (Schwartz, 1980). As high achievers, girls who are gifted are expected to be active, assertive, and exploratory; as females, they are encouraged to be nurturing, passive, and dependent (Handel, 1983).

It is during early adolescence, the age when sex roles are heavily reinforced by parents and peers, that girls generally begin to encounter problems that obscure their giftedness (Dishart, 1981). Often, parents of girls who are gifted are more concerned about their daughters' social adjustment than their academic boredom. Teachers tend to reinforce quiet, non-aggressive and non-competitive behaviour among girls.

Gifted Students Who Are Disabled

A child who is both gifted and disabled may be described as one who demonstrates at least one attribute of educational, emotional, or physical/sensory impairment.

The spread of intelligence in the population of persons with disabilities matches that of the general population, so the prevalence of giftedness is about the same. It is estimated that two percent of all children with disabilities are gifted (Whitmore and Maker, 1985), although some authorities argue that a five percent cut-off is probably more realistic (Davis and Rimm, 1994).

Why, then, are so many children with disabilities overlooked in identification procedures? The answer is entwined with common perceptions, the traits of disability, and the identification procedures themselves.

A gifted child who is also disabled fails to meet stereotyped expectations of giftedness. Many teachers, administrators, students, and parents have trouble accepting that a child with a disability may also have outstanding abilities: they focus entirely on the child's disability to the exclusion of his or her individual potential and capabilities.

The individual student probably exhibits many contradictions by deviating substantially

Gifted females should be encouraged to participate in traditionally male-dominated activities.

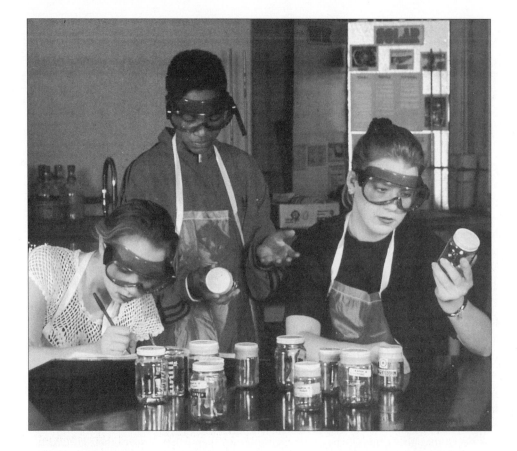

both above and below the norm, showing both strengths and weaknesses that are very pronounced. With the current identification procedures, gifted children who also have disabilities may lack the opportunity to reveal superior mental or creative ability. No one instrument or checklist is capable of identifying the range of characteristics and conditions that may be present in a gifted child with a disability.

Teacher observations of a child's behaviour are critical in identifying those who are both gifted and disabled. Observations must be made over time rather than in isolation (Pledgie, 1982).

Gifted Students Who Have Learning Disabilities

Little research exists on gifted students with learning disabilities. We do know that these students have talents and strengths in some areas and disabling weaknesses in others. They have unique characteristics related to persistence and individual interests and possess lower academic and self-efficacy than their peers who are not identified as being gifted and learning disabled (Baum, 1995; Baum and Owen, 1988).

Children who are both gifted and learning disabled are often not identified (Gyndereson, Maesch, and Rees, 1987). The reasons parallel those we mentioned for children with disabilities, with an added glitch. Sometimes, when giftedness and learning disabilities co-exist, they tend to mask one another so that neither the giftedness nor the disability is immediately

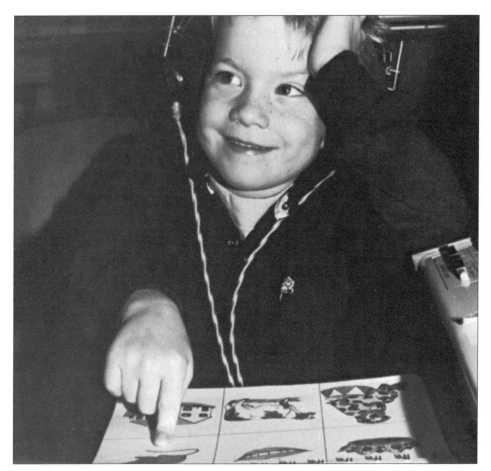

Children who are disabled in one way may be exceptionally gifted in another area.

evident (Silverman, 1989). The disability may depress the IQ and achievement scores so that these students are not eligible for gifted programs, yet their giftedness allows them to compensate well enough for their weaknesses to maintain grade level expectations, which prevents detection of their learning difficulty (Silverman, 1989). The result is that they frequently do not qualify for special education services.

At other times, the child may be receiving special education services, and the giftedness is completely overlooked. This is clearly illustrated in the case of Richard, profiled on the next page.

The Culturally Different Gifted Child

Two of the most troubling issues in special education are the persistent over-representation of minority and economically disadvantaged populations in special education and their under-representation in programming for gifted students. Many students who are non-white, non-middle-class or from language minority groups are not identified and taught as gifted learners.

A major reason accounting for under-representation is an implicit demand that children always manifest giftedness in the same way—*the same* equating with the majority cul-

Profile

Richard

The school that Richard attends has a small pull-out program for children identified as gifted beginning at the grade three level. The teacher of this program is very popular with all the students, and because she insists on always presenting the products of the gifted class, the whole school is aware of her program and many children are eager to enter it.

Eight-year-old Richard, however, seemed an unlikely candidate. He was identified in grade two as having a learning disability that affected his ability in reading and written language. He attends the resource room daily for additional assistance in these areas. When the teacher of the gifted students asked classroom teachers to nominate children for her program, Richard was not mentioned. However, the teacher used a group of rating scales—parent, teacher, peer, and self-nomination.

While the teacher's nomination scale gave no indications of gifted potential in Richard, the teacher was puzzled by the peaks and valleys in performance that emerged as she filled out the scale. Richard has excellent reasoning ability but difficulties in memorizing, paying attention, and following several directions at once. Solving oral math story problems is often easier for him than remembering multiplication facts. He frequently talks about complex ideas but writes slowly and illegibly. He seems to have difficulty in managing time and is slow in processing information.

Similar ups and downs were indicated by his parents. They agreed, for example, that Richard suffered serious lags in reading but judged him highly in his oral language abilities, his commitment to projects once started, and his interest in a range of hobbies and collections. Richard did not rate himself highly, but his peers did. In the peer nominations, they agreed overwhelmingly that Richard was the child who could think up unusual and interesting stories and games.

With such contradictory evidence, the teacher of the gifted class decided to have the school psychologist present Richard with a WISC-R. On this, he was above average on both the Verbal and the Performance scales for a Full Scale score of 141. To Richard's delight, he was admitted to the gifted program while still attending the resource room daily.

Today, all three teachers speak well of his progress. The resource room teacher reports that Richard is really applying himself to improving his reading and written language skills, and the classroom teacher is pleased that incipient behavioural problems have muted. Richard now wears his glasses without prompting, for example. In the gifted program, Richard achieved on a level with the other students.

ture's definitions of giftedness. The demand is not reasonable, as children from other cultures are shaped by different value systems, and certain traits that define giftedness in the dominant culture may not even be allowed to appear because culturally different children show different interests and attitudes.

For example, definitions of giftedness in a First Nation context are quite different from those usually utilized by psychologists and educators who primarily function in the institutions of dominant society (Friesen, 1997). What is clever and creative for the child on a reserve, where different value systems are in operation, will not be the same as for the child growing up in a suburb. White, middle-class gifted children tend to display a high level of verbal ability; in contrast, Native children raised on reserves are normally very quiet and verbal precocity would not be an indicator for Native gifted children. But knowing about spirituality—the sacred traditional ways—is a manifestation of giftedness (Friesen, 1997).

Standardized tests are inappropriate in the identification of most culturally diverse students, including those with giftedness. Instead, teachers should use a collection of instruments and procedures that include observations, nomination forms, dynamic assessment, and rating scales. Assessment and identification procedures should measure how a child meaningfully manipulates a symbol system held valuable in the culture; thinks logically when given appropriate data; uses stored knowledge to solve problems; reasons by analogy; and extends or extrapolates knowledge to new situations or unique applications (Clark, 1988).

Developmental Consequences of Giftedness

Like every population, individuals who are gifted form a heterogeneous group. Differences run the gamut of possibilities; among persons who are gifted will be found the active, the lethargic, the healthy, the infirm, high achievers, low achievers, the painstakingly patient, and the lightning quick. The one thing, however, that students who are gifted have in common is "the ability to absorb abstract concepts, to organize them more effectively, and to apply them more appropriately than the average youngster" (Gallagher, 1975, p. 19).

Table 7-2 outlines some of the common characteristics of students who are gifted, talented, and creative. View this list with caution; probably no child displays all of these traits. Rather, each child possesses a unique subset of descriptors, which come from, but do not include, all the behaviours of the larger set. As well, attach no credence to the notion that these are wunderkind, adept in all areas of functioning. Like everyone else, children who are gifted have their warts, and teachers must accommodate problems as well as potentials. Also be aware of the great variance in the gifted population that renders many other characteristics possible. The true extent of that variance is not even known, because of our inability to identify all children who are gifted.

Physical Development

Throughout history, there has been a persistent stereotype of the individual who was gifted as an "egghead." The person with gifts was viewed as physically weak, homely, socially inept, narrow in interests, and prone to emotional instability. Such stereotypes were shattered by Lewis Terman, who found that as a group, individuals who are gifted exhibit superior physical traits. The children in Terman's study were larger at birth, walked sooner, went through puberty earlier, had fewer diseases and operations, and reported less nervousness than average persons (Terman and Oden, 1959). Although children who are gifted tend to physically outstrip their agemates later on, their superiority is seldom detectable at birth or even during the first year. Nor do children who are gifted show advanced motor skills as a general trait. Teachers are very likely to find young children who can read far above level yet are unable to write their own names legibly.

Academic Development

Three general characteristics seem typical of the learning behaviour of students who are gifted—an internal locus of control, independence, and self-motivation. In fact, one of the

Table 7-2 Some common characteristics of children who are gifted, creative, and talented

Traits common in children who are gifted

- Wide range of ability
- High academic achievement
- Insatiable curiosity
- Good observational skills, with a willingness to observe both the usual and the unusual
- Verbal fluency and a large vocabulary; may talk a lot and have many ideas; often use metaphors and abstract ideas and enjoy debating issues
- Ask a lot of questions; inquisitive about the world and want to know the why and how as well as the what
- Committed to finding out what happens if something is done, as in a science experiment
- High motivation with persistent goal-directed behaviour and high task commitment; stick to a topic to completion
- Long attention span; become absorbed in self-selected tasks
- High energy level, with an intense concentration of activity
- Organizational and planning skills
- Innovative, creative, divergent responses
- Ability to synthesize large amounts of diverse information; ability to think and perform in an interdisciplinary manner
- Superior reading ability
- Ability to grasp and retain knowledge
- Ability to convey ideas effectively
- Ability to work independently, with little or no need for adult monitoring
- Ability to assume and discharge responsibility; possess decision-making capabilities and leadership qualities
- Avid collectors and hobbyists; join many clubs
- Easy adjustment to new situations
- Mature sense of humour
- Appreciation of social values; show advanced ethical thinking; often prize integrity, independent judgment and social values and ideals; are interested in political and social issues
- Tend to be task- and contribution-oriented more than recognition-oriented
- Superior in height, weight, health, energy, and vitality
- Establishment of favourable relationships

Traits common in children who are creative

- Tendency to ask many questions that may be embarrassing, advanced, or controversial, often challenging the teacher and the textbook
- Production of work that is off the beaten track, with much humour and playfulness
- Boredom with recitation and memorization of facts; preference for talking about ideas and problems
- Good problem-solving ability with new and unusual ways of solving problems; show a variety of approaches to problem solving; are resourceful and can solve problems through ingenious methods
- Keen sense of humour and a fine sense of the absurd; reputation among teachers and students for wild and silly ideas
- Skill in abstract thinking
- Use a wide variety of resources
- Considerable energy

- Unexpected answers on examinations
- Pleasure in working alone
- Apparent lack of hard work, coupled with good performance in examinations
- Unusual capacity for originality, concentration, and hard work on special projects
- Imagination and inventiveness; show playfulness in experimentation
- Versatility and diversity of interests
- See associations and innovations

Traits common in children who are talented

- Persistent goal-directed behaviour and high task commitment
- Imaginative and inventive; acute observational skills
- Perceptive and imaginative in the interpretation of stimuli
- Pronounced intuitive sense combined with a high degree of artistic integrity
- Ability to interpret and interconnect to a refined degree
- Attack drawing, painting, or sculpting in non-prescribed ways, often not taught by the teacher
- Use of technical ability as a foundation for reinterpretation, refocusing, and retranslating, chiefly for personal satisfaction
- Ability to detach oneself from the surroundings and focus intently on the task at hand. This is especially true of auditory attention in musicians.

most ubiquitous traits of both productive students who are gifted and eminent adults is high motivation and persistence.

Students who are gifted like learning, enjoy difficult subjects, and are willing to spend extra time on projects that stimulate their interest. They learn more, faster, and more easily than do their agemates. They also learn to read sooner and continue to read at a consistently more advanced level. Children at this level of functioning are also more adept at critically evaluating facts and arguments. Because they more readily recognize relationships and comprehend meanings, they can reason out problems more effectively.

All these factors place children who are gifted far ahead in academic achievement. They can master the curriculum content of a grade two or three times faster than the average child. In elementary mathematics, for example, a good rule of thumb for students who are gifted is that two years of standard content can be covered in one year (Van Tassel-Baska, Landau, and Olszewski, 1985).

Behaviour

Like other children, students who are gifted are not always well behaved. They may interrupt others, fail to listen, be argumentative, refuse to comply with requests they view as trivial, be excessively critical, teasing, or bossy, or display a high energy level that results in perpetual motion and disorganized work habits (Whitmore, 1979).

Research has not found significant differences in the attitudes of gifted and non-gifted students toward school (Schneider, Clegg, Byrne, Ledingham, and Crombie, 1992). However, students who are gifted are often impatient with the routines in a regular classroom: chalk and talk, endless drill and practice, and repetition, along with a concomitant lack of stimulation and challenge, can bore and frustrate advanced learners. In fact, children who are gifted and talented complain a great deal about the boredom of their classroom experiences. They say they are forced to spend a lot of time being taught things they already know, doing repetitive drill sheets and activities, and receiving instruction on new material at too slow a pace (Feldhusen, 1989).

Especially for girls, perceived academic competence is an important factor in global self-worth of children who are gifted from grade four to grade eight (Hoge and McSheffrey, 1991). By the age of 13 or 14, some of these youngsters have a motivation to avoid failure at any cost rather than a motivation to succeed.

Perfectionism is a common trait in children with gifts and talents (Parker, 1997). These children are often too critical of others and of themselves and need help in accepting failure.

Creativity leads to a set of personality traits characterized by a strong self-concept that gives little credence to outside academic and social sanctions. Creative children tend to have high independence and be less conforming than their peers. This is especially true of boys. In junior high school classrooms of students with gifts, creative boys are eight times as likely to quarrel with the opinions of peers and teachers as are creative girls.

Social and Emotional Development

One common and persistent myth regarding individuals with gifts, especially those in the arts, is that they are prone to mental disease. The question of whether individuals who are gifted are more emotionally stable, self-sufficient, and less prone to neurotic and psychotic disorders than average people has been the subject of intense research which offers modest support for the superior adjustment of persons who are gifted (Grossberg and Cornell, 1988). In a study of gifted students in grades five, eight, and ten, Ottawa researchers (Schneider et al., 1992) found that the children who were gifted were relatively well-adjusted individuals. This relates to students who are moderately gifted. Those who are extremely precocious may be at greater risk for social problems than their modestly gifted peers (Dauber and Benbow, 1990). Students with very high IQs are less popular and have more difficulty with peer relations than their agemates. Possibly their unusually high intelligence makes it difficult for their agemates to relate to them intellectually or socially. One study (Dauber and Benbow, 1990) discovered that extremely gifted students viewed themselves as more introverted, less socially adept, and more inhibited. The extremely gifted adolescents also reported that their peers saw them as much less popular, less socially active, less athletic, and less active in the crowd.

Modestly gifted children tend to be well liked by their peers, although popularity may taper off in secondary school settings. Sometimes they alienate peers simply by the discrepancy between them or by their eagerness to demonstrate their unusual talents. Tannenbaum (1962) reported that bright students most favoured by peers were intelligent, athletic, and non-studious. The least-favoured gifted students were intelligent, studious, and non-athletic. In the Tannenbaum studies, boys rated more highly than girls. A later study (Cramond and Martin, 1987) of teachers and preservice teachers found much the same. Respondents did not value academic brilliance but athleticism as a critical determinant in a person's likability. Males were rated more highly than females.

Ethical Development

Students who are gifted develop steadfast values quite early, with strong concerns for right and wrong (Piechowski, 1991). They wrestle with problems that we often associate with adults. When Derevensky and Coleman (1989) asked 70 children aged 7 to 13 in a Toronto school for the gifted, "What are the things to be afraid of?" the students gave fears generally expressed by chronologically older students, such as death and nuclear war. Nicholas Colangelo (1989) asked 125 gifted children to define problems that were important to them. More than 50 percent chose typical teenage dilemmas of friendships and love relationships. However, they also identified 36 issues dealing with more adult themes such as public welfare and life and death scenarios.

Intervention with Students Who Are Gifted, Creative, and Talented

The basic educational goals for children with gifts and talents are the same as for all other students: to develop their abilities in ways that are consistent with their personal needs and the best interests of society. At the same time, schools must develop mechanisms to identify children who are gifted and provide them with appropriate educational programs.

Children with gifts and talents cannot just fend for themselves; they possess no magical ability to help them overcome the obstacles to their growth. Like other exceptional children, these youngsters need special assistance to fulfill their potential for achievement.

Technical

For most children who are gifted, technical aids, in the sense of hearing aids and wheelchairs, are not relevant. Children who are gifted should, however, be able to take advantage of the new advances in information and communication technology, specifically as related to computers. For students who are gifted, computers can become idea engines, their tool to discovery, exploration, and collaboration. They can do research and apply thinking skills by working with real problems and computer simulations.

Educational Intervention

Inevitably, educational models and approaches are a function of definition, be they implicit or explicit. Reflecting the difficulties in pinpointing the most effective definition of giftedness and gifted individuals is the wide variety of practices and programs that have been devised over the years to cater to children with gifts. In 1985 a nationwide survey of gifted programming in the United States found 16 different types, from simple enrichment programs within the regular classroom to full-time special schools (Greer, 1990b).

Nobody is sure of the best way to educate students with gifts, and it is true to say that there is a lack of systematically developed models and systematic experimental evaluation of programs and program models with explicit goals, objectives, and specified outcomes (Busse and

Mansfield, 1986; Renzulli, 1980). Numerous programs have been attempted, all intended to come to grips with three major problems: the balance between the quest for excellence and a zeal for equality; the wide range of abilities among the gifted population; and teachers' lack of special instructional methods.

Inclusion

With the exception of classroom enrichment, all of the practices recommended for academic achievement of students with gifts and talents focus on separate programs or different curricula. This, of course, is the opposite of inclusionary practices.

Some research has found "disturbing evidence of neglect" in regular classrooms (Culross, 1997, p. 24). Advocates of special programming contend that "gifted education and gifted students are in deep trouble without grouping practices" (Davis and Rimm, 1994, p. 10). Opponents simply argue that special programs for the gifted run counter to the spirit of the inclusive classroom.

Teachers' voices are important in this debate, as are their attitudes about and perceptions of students who are gifted. In fact, so critical are teachers' attitudes that some researchers argue that children who are gifted should only be placed in regular classrooms if the teacher is prepared to assist them (see McCarthy, 1994).

In a review of the literature (Cramond and Martin, 1987), researchers found that teachers had conflicting attitudes toward students with gifts. Some studies found that teachers view students who are gifted positively and give them preferential treatment; others found teacher discomfort and resentment that could lead to apathy toward gifted education. In a sample of 98 parents of gifted children, Kaufman and Sexton (1983) found that 45 percent had encountered a teacher who they felt was unsympathetic to the special needs of the child who was gifted.

Some teachers disagree with special programming on both philosophical and pragmatic grounds. Bransky (1987) found negative attitudes among classroom teachers, which she attributed to a poor foundation of knowledge about the pull-out programs for students who are gifted. Others realize that teachers of students who are gifted need special traits, but are unaware of the traits or have little confidence in their ability to develop them (see the Research Notes on teachers below). Archambault and Hallmark (1992) found that 42 to 62 percent of the 7 000 teachers in their studies had absolutely no exposure to methods for teaching the gifted.

Some teachers argue that the classroom that loses children who are gifted is robbed of leadership. Others express concern about the fragmentation of their programs or the need to reschedule lessons (Meyers, 1984). Occasionally, teachers are averse to designing programs for learners who are gifted.

Educational Approaches

The education of students who are gifted is replete with different models offered in varied settings. Typically, more program options are available in urban and suburban areas and in the elementary schools. The four most common types of educational provisions used in Canada are enrichment, ability grouping, mentoring programs, and acceleration.

Research Notes

Teachers of Students Who Are Gifted, Creative, and Talented

Should gifted children be taught by gifted teachers? This is one of the controversial questions that exist in the field of education of gifted students. If it is decided that gifted children should be taught by gifted teachers, then what exactly is a gifted teacher? Is it the teacher who possesses gifted traits? Or is it the teacher who is gifted at the profession of teaching?

Research on gifted teachers has generally looked at three areas: the personal characteristics of outstanding teachers of the gifted; their competencies; and those behaviours that set outstanding teachers apart (Whitlock and Du Cette, 1989).

An early study (Bishop, 1968) found that gifted students opt for teachers who are older and experienced and well above average in intellectual pursuits, who enjoy their profession and are respectful to students and other teachers. Later research has bolstered these findings, showing that gifted students preferred teachers with creative and positive personalities and high intelligence (e.g. Webb, Meckstroth, and Tolan, 1982).

The characteristic most often described as desirable is that of being a facilitator of learning. Additionally, traits such as flexibility, creativity, good self-concept, depth and breadth of knowledge, sense of humour, counselling ability, maturity, teaching experience, and resourcefulness were deemed important (Story, 1985). These characteristics, of course,

are the mark of any good teacher. Certainly, the teacher of gifted children should possess all the traits common to good teachers. But they should also possess knowledge, understanding, and sympathy for the gifted population. The teacher should have a high level of creativity and energy to meet the special demands of gifted children. As well, teachers of gifted students need to be lifelong learners; to possess superior mental abilities; to be divergent thinkers; to be well educated in the liberal arts; to demonstrate competence in effectively individualizing instruction; to demonstrate skills in teaching science and arts; to have excellent skills in communication; and to have a healthy self-concept (Bell, 1986; Whitmore, 1985). Teachers also need knowledge of subject areas, an eagerness to be with bright children and dedication to students, and they must believe in the importance of enhancing pupils' self-image and maturity (Whitlock and Du Cette, 1989).

It is only recently that teacher-training programs have presented more than a cursory overview of the education of gifted students. Across the country, special education faculties are increasingly offering special courses and diploma programs related to the education of gifted and talented students. Richert (1991) recommends that all education students should have a three-hour course in gifted education as a bare minimum.

Acceleration

Acceleration means moving faster through academic content. Students speed up their progress through the existing curriculum to complete a prescribed program in a shorter time period. Included within acceleration models are early school beginning, grade skipping, ungraded classes, high school courses for credit, extra load, seminars for college credit, early admittance to post-secondary programs, and honours programs.

Two general characteristics define acceleration models. First, acceleration is one of the most time-honoured options in gifted education and has been practised throughout the history of providing educational provisions for this population. Second, there is probably no other area in the education of students who are gifted that is more controversial.

Supporting acceleration practices is a body of data that "are unanimous in their support of the benefit of accelerative alternatives, both academically and socio-emotionally" (Keating, 1980, p. 56). From the point of view of its proponents, even the word *acceleration* is a misnomer; the process is really one of bringing youth who are gifted and talented up to a suitable level of instruction commensurate with their achievement levels and readiness so that they are properly challenged to learn new material (Felhusen, 1989).

Opponents of acceleration marshal an impressive array of arguments that focus on psychosocial rather than academic reasons. They view the practice of allowing students who are gifted to progress through the educational system at their own rate as potentially hazardous to social and emotional adjustment.

Hence, we have a situation where the literature on the academic acceleration of students who are gifted consistently demonstrates a lack of harmful effects, but many educators and administrators resist the implementation of the model in their schools (Feldhusen, 1989; Southern, Jones, and Fiscus, 1989). The major arguments from both sides of the debate are presented in the Matter of Debate feature on the next pages.

Ability Grouping

Students who are gifted need interaction with peers who share their interests and concerns. The general tenor of research indicates that they require social and emotional support from a group of true peers in order to maintain a positive self-concept and intellectual interaction

A Matter of Debate

Acceleration for Students Who Are Gifted

There is no argument more contentious in gifted education than that revolving around acceleration. Opponents of acceleration have marshalled an impressive array of arguments. The psychosocial reasons for hesitation in implementing acceleration programs are more numerous than the academic reasons (Swiatek and Benbow, 1991). On the other hand, advocates cite 80 years of positive research findings.

✔ Arguments in favour of acceleration

Acceleration programs reduce the time that students need to complete the curriculum; by accelerating, students can maximize their intellectual potential and maintain their interest and motivation. Students can enter high school, college, and graduate studies earlier, and get a faster start on their careers.

A meta-analysis of the results of 314 studies of the academic, social, and psychological effects of acceleration at the elementary and secondary levels (Rogers, 1990, cited in Davis and Rimm, 1994) found that "no form of acceleration led to a decrease in any area of performance—academic, social, or emotional," and that "There appears to be generally positive effects from most forms of acceleration."

Literature reviews (Swiatek and Benbow, 1991) show that no studies yield evidence that accelerated students exhibit deficits in knowledge or achievement. Most gifted children are psychosocially mature. Little research evidence links forms of acceleration to socioemotional adjustment problems (Cornell, Callahan, and Loyd, 1991).

Empirical research indicates that acceleration provides academic settings that are well suited to the needs of high-ability students (Benbow, 1991).

Gifted youth may have self-concepts which clearly relate to and recognize giftedness, and their self-concepts may be influenced positively by participation in a gifted program (Feldhusen and Hoover, 1986).

A body of literature spanning five decades has consistently associated the acceleration of precocious children with positive change in their academic achievement and a lack of negative effects on social and emotional growth.

Studies do not indicate that acceleration is harmful, and many indicate that it is beneficial (Southern, Jones, and Fiscus, 1989).

Academically, acceleration promotes intellectual achievement. It allows gifted students to learn more efficiently (Feldhusen, Proctor, and Black, 1986) and increases effectiveness (Davis and Rimm, 1994).

Accelerated students perform as well as older students with whom they are placed and exceed the achievement of non-accelerated students of the same age and ability by almost a year (Kulik and Kulik, 1984). "Failure to advance a precocious child may result in poor study habits, apathy, lack of motivation, and maladjustment" (Feldhusen, Proctor, and Black, 1986, p. 27).

With acceleration, "boredom, restlessness, frustration, underachievement, and disruptiveness can be replaced by enhanced motivation, improved self-concepts, and improved study habits and productivity" (Davis and Rimm, 1994).

Both early admission and later acceleration have been extensively studied and no reliable research exists that documents harm (Daurio, 1979; Kulik and Kulik, 1984; Pollins, 1983; Proctor, Black, and Feldhusen, 1984).

Acceleration is supported by an analysis of costs (Weiss and Gallagher, 1982). It costs little to implement and may actually save school systems money if students spend fewer years in the system (e.g. Stanley and Benbow, 1982).

Not one study exists showing that acceleration is harmful to social or emotional development (Benbow, 1991)

(X) Arguments against acceleration

Students may burn out if they are placed in classes that are advanced for their chronological ages.

Acceleration may lead to gaps in knowledge of the participants or poor retention of material learned at an accelerated pace (Van Tassel-Baska, 1989).

Children cannot escape the physical and emotional limits imposed by chronology. Gifted children may show deficient or retarded psychosocial development. Children will not fit in with more mature classmates.

Special education opportunities lead gifted students to become conceited and self-centred; children will become contemptuous of their age peers and may suffer negative emotional and social consequences (Southern, Jones, and Fiscus, 1989).

Acceleration programs emphasize the differences between gifted and average students, thereby jeopardizing the social acceptance of gifted students; those enrolled in special classes will lose the ability to function in the larger world of average people (Swiatek and Benbow, 1991).

The self-concepts of gifted students will suffer if they are set apart from their average counterparts. Accelerated pupils will not socialize with older children, will have fewer friends, will not be happy, and will miss important social interactions (Southern, Jones, and Fiscus, 1989).

Research knowledge only sporadically finds its way into educational practice, even when the research has produced substantial knowledge related to problems of real-world importance (see Malouf and Schiller, 1995, p. 414).

Acceleration conflicts with the school's perceived role to socialize students and make them good workers.

and to transform abilities into productive reality. True peers are simultaneously the student's intellectual and chronological equals.

As the name suggests, ability groupings (pull-out programs) refer to changing the environment to bring students who are gifted into contact with each other. They are removed from heterogeneous settings and placed in special groups. In some cases, children go to special classrooms. In others, independent groups of students progress at different rates within the same classroom. Special groups may meet full-time or only part-time. They may be made up of students from a single school or from several schools within a district. Groups may meet during regular school hours or on an extra-curricular basis.

Certain criteria ensure the success of pull-out programs. These include integration with the regular curriculum; daily program experience; placement with intellectual peers; pace of program matched with the student's learning rate; a complex and higher level curriculum; and excellent teachers (Belcostas, 1987).

As with acceleration, pull-out programs are far from universally accepted. Opponents claim that the practice is undemocratic because it fosters intellectual elitism and limits contacts between gifted and normal children. Pragmatically, they contend that pull-out programs are often frivolous. Programs often diverge from the regular school curriculum, do not give grades, do not have instruction in traditional subject matter, focus on the affective rather than the academic, and do not have written curricula (Van Tassel-Baska, 1987).

In contrast, advocates argue that only when children who are gifted are grouped together can they be provided with truly effective instruction. As far as curriculum is concerned, they believe that since separate gifted programs provide for students who differ from the norm, the programs also should differ in their adherence to the conventional structures associated with education.

Mentor Programs

Mentor programs are designed to allow students to work, at a specified time, with adults in the community with whom they share a special interest. Usually the teacher, the mentor, and the student set up a project with the final results to be presented to the class in some form.

Mentor programs are particularly cost-effective and serve as a liaison between the school and the community. They allow students to pursue special interests. Other benefits include career and interest advancement; an increase in knowledge and skills; the development of talent; enhancement of self-esteem and self-confidence; development of a personal ethic or set of standards; establishment of long-term friendships; and enhancement of creativity (Edlind and Heansly, 1985).

The Best Approach?

The research does not provide clear evidence for or against ability grouping in terms of academic achievement. When Goldring (1990) analyzed 23 studies on delivery methods, he found that students who were gifted in special classes achieved more than students of high ability in regular classrooms, but the benefits of the special classes depended on the subject. The largest effects were in science and social studies, with smaller effects in math, reading, and writing. The higher the grade level, the stronger the advantage of special classes. Others (Kulik, 1992; Kulik and Kulik, 1991, 1992) have shown that children of medium and low ability are either not affected or are negatively affected by ability grouping, but that the achievement of high-ability students is positively affected by ability grouping that includes curriculum modifications directed to their learning characteristics. Vaughn and colleagues (1991) analyzed the research and found small to medium positive effects on academic achievement and critical and creative thinking.

Gifted programs may be most justifiable when the content of the special program is truly an accelerated curriculum, not just add-ons. The most popular subject for acceleration is math, while language arts or social studies are usually the focus of enrichment programs.

Whether special programs affect children's self-esteem is unknown. In a Calgary study (Bourque and Li, 1987), the researchers assessed 60 students with gifts between the ages of nine and eleven who were placed in regular and segregated settings to see if they differed in perceived competence, social adjustment, and peer relations. As rated by teachers, educational setting did not appear to have any differential impact on social adjustment, on peer relations, or on socio-metric nominations, and was not an important factor for self-esteem, social adjustment, or peer relations. Note that what students like most about being in a special program is freedom of choice and self-directedness.

Finally, research on enrichment programs does not yield clear evidence that they adequately stimulate children who are gifted. It generally does not find achievement benefits.

Enrichment

In many situations it is impossible and perhaps unnecessary to take children who are gifted from their assigned classrooms. Enrichment programs provided by regular classroom teachers are the solution.

Enrichment involves providing special activities in the regular classroom setting. These activities, which involve a broader range of skills and deeper understanding than the regular curriculum, are designed to challenge and interest children while focusing on their unique patterns of strengths and weaknesses. Of course, enrichment activities are good for all students, and it must be kept in mind that for students who are gifted there must be higher order objectives outlined within enrichment.

We can see this in the sample enrichment unit presented here. This example examines seeds and plants and is loosely based on Benjamin Bloom's taxonomy of educational objectives (1956). This type of unit can be used effectively with students who are gifted as a group assignment or as independent study.

Advocates of enrichment programs maintain that the programs allow a child to remain in the regular classroom with age-level peers. Detractors point out the difficulty of meeting individual needs with a few extra activities in a generally inadequate learning environment. They contend that enrichment often promotes the false impression that something substantial is being done for the gifted. In fact, enrichment has been referred to as "busywork and irrelevant" (Stanley and Benbow, 1986).

Curricula

The difference between the regular program and the program for students who are gifted is one of degree. Some classroom practices currently being studied include independent projects, creative writing on self-selected topics, teaching thinking skills, encouraging discovery, and using classroom questioning that encourages reasoning and logical thinking (Gubbins, 1991).

Enrichment activities include a number of recognized instructional models, including the Enrichment Triad, the Revolving Door, and the Autonomous Learner Model.

The Enrichment Triad delineates three types of enrichment activities for students. Type

Sample Unit

Plants and Seeds

KNOWLEDGE

- List all the parts of a seed plant you can find.
- Define the following terms (related to seed plants): bulb germination, dormancy, dicotyledon, dissemule, root hair.
- List the many methods of seed dispersal.
- Name the conditions necessary for germination and development in a plant.
- List the enemies of plants (as many as you can find).
- Look at several beauty magazines to see how plants are used in make-up and other beauty aids.

COMPREHENSION

- Why do leaves change colour in the fall?
- Explain how a plant takes water from the earth and uses it in its living processes.
- Explain the difference between coniferous and deciduous.
- Describe how a plant grows, from fertilization through to maturity. If you like, you can use an example to help you.
- Describe the role of chlorophyll in photosynthesis, explaining why green plants turn yellow and die if they do not get enough sunlight.
- Describe the role of a seed plant in the ability for life to exist on earth.

APPLICATION

- Using a microscope, diagram the cell structure of a leaf.
- Diagram the different parts of a seed plant.
- Show how you can tell how old, and how tall, a tree is.
- Make your own perfume, using the leaves of flowers.
- Show how a seed plant takes root and begins to grow.

ANALYSIS

- Conduct an experiment to see how far seeds can travel.
- Compare and contrast coniferous and deciduous trees, and the way they grow.
- Conduct an experiment to see what happens when seeds are crowded too close together.
- Compare past and present uses of plants in the field of medicine. Are there any similarities?
- Conduct an experiment to see what will happen to a leaf when it is coated with Vaseline. Why does this happen?
- Conduct an experiment to determine the lengths to which plants will go so that they can get sunlight?

SYNTHESIS

- Design an environment possessing ideal conditions for the growth of seed plants.
- Choose two plants and, using your knowledge about genetics and plant breeding, predict the outcome of a cross between them. Describe the new creation. What are its strength and weaknesses, if any?
- Grow several bean seeds, controlling different environmental conditions in each instance. Predict the outcome in each case, and compare it with the actual results.

EVALUATION

- Decide whether or not the commercial use of greenhouses can be beneficial to people in the long run.
- Acid rain has a great effect on plants. What exactly is that effect, and what can we do about it? Are we doing all we can right now?
- Assess the value of gardens in space. Are they worth the trouble?

Source: Hicks, 1987

I, General Exploratory Activities, is appropriate for all students. Type I activities expose pupils to exciting topics, ideas, and fields of knowledge not ordinarily covered by the regular curriculum, and include visiting speakers, field trips, demonstrations, interest development centres, and the use of many different kinds of audio-visual materials. Type II, Group Training Activities, is also appropriate for all children. It consists of methods, materials, and instructional techniques designed to develop thinking processes, research and reference skills, and personal and social skills. Type III activities, Small Group Investigations, are very rigorous and challenging. Students self-select areas of study and take responsibility for initiating, conceptualizing, and planning the activity or project. They investigate real problems and topics using appropriate methods of enquiry (Reis and O'Shea, 1984).

The Revolving Door model (Renzulli and Smith, 1984) is designed to identify giftedness, to provide enrichment activities, and to overcome many of the problems related to student selection, motivation, and interests. The model is essentially a resource room adjunct program. Students participate as their interest and motivation dictates; they are not permanently in or out of the program, but can apply for special consideration to work on projects of their own choosing. Renzulli claims that this approach teaches students they must earn the right to participate.

The Autonomous Learner Model (ALM) (Betts, 1985) is designed for secondary-level special classrooms but can also be used at elementary levels. It is usually presented during one period at specified times throughout the week. While not a total program, ALM meets the socio-emotional needs of learners who are gifted and encourages independence in the learning setting. In a three-year sequence, students move through five major dimensions:

- orientation: understanding giftedness and group building activities;
- individual development: learning skills and career involvement;
- enrichment activities: exploration and investigation;
- seminars: general interest and advanced knowledge;
- in-depth study: independent projects and mentorships.

SUMMARY

1. There is not another category in special education as fraught with political, emotional, and educational issues as that of giftedness. Difficulties revolve around just who is gifted, how to identify gifts and talents, how to offer special programming, and how to balance the needs of students who are gifted within the parameters of an egalitarian school system.

2. Giftedness is considered as a component of special education because students who are gifted require appropriate educational opportunities and challenges if they are to develop to their full potential.

3. Not the least of the problems that plague the field of gifted education is the lack of a universally accepted definition. It is very difficult to find a definition that encompasses all children and youth who are gifted, talented, and creative because these students demonstrate such a broad array of characteristics and behaviours. As well, a consensus has not been reached on whether to define giftedness as performance or potential.

4. Although we no longer claim that giftedness springs entirely from the genes, it is only reasonable to assume that genetics have some effect. Environment is important, but beyond the obvious general advantages, it is not known what specific factors in upper- and middle-class homes encourage giftedness.

5. For a long time, the study of giftedness was dominated by the single variable of a child's tested IQ. Today, the most prevalent identification models used call for multiple means of identification. When nominations are used, the process is guided by effectiveness and efficiency.

6. Within identification procedures, many children with gifts go undiscovered, particularly those who are culturally, ethnically, linguistically, socially, or economically different from the norm; gifted females; and gifted children with disabilities.

7. Children who are disabled in one way may be exceptionally gifted in another. When the child has a learning disability, his or her superior intellectual ability is working overtime to compensate for the weaknesses caused by the disability. Culturally different children should not be expected to demonstrate the same strengths as white, middle-class children.

8. Students who are modestly gifted seem to have more favourable profiles in terms of personality and peer acceptance and interaction than do students who are exceptionally gifted.

9. The provision of programs for students who are gifted is one of the most controversial issues in special education. Research on the efficacy of any particular administrative model is somewhat inconclusive, but acceleration appears to have a strong edge. However, practitioners seem to regard acceleration in general, and early entrance in particular, as risky approaches in serving the needs of children who are gifted. As well, there is strong support in the literature favouring segregated settings on academic and intellectual grounds. The special classroom provides opportunities for acceleration and for horizontal expansion of the curriculum.

10. Enrichment in the classroom implies more than tacking on a few activities to the existing curriculum. A number of models assist teachers in planning and presenting classroom enrichment.

In the Classroom

Profile: Troy

In his early years in school, most of the teachers saw Troy as an almost perfect student. He always finished his work, performed at a high level, and was well behaved, compliant, polite, and helpful. Early assessment showed Troy to be functioning well above his peers in all academic areas (Full Scale IQ 144) and each teacher attempted to put in place different types of enrichment activities for Troy. That he was sometimes bored and a little frustrated was masked by his good behaviour and happy nature.

This changed once Troy was in grade seven. Mr. Jane, Troy's teacher, did "not believe in giftedness" and insisted that Troy do exactly the same work as everyone else. At first, the teacher decried some mounting behavioural problems simply as "puberty kicking in." However, as time went on, Troy frustrated and angered the teacher, especially when he contested the information being presented. This happened so often that Mr. Jane finally referred Troy for special assistance as a student with a behavioural disorder.

When the team met to discuss Troy, the teacher was a little surprised and somewhat disconcerted to hear the results of another psycho-educational assessment and from the school counsellor. These results indicated that Troy was functioning at a very high level both academically and socially but was growing increasingly miserable within the constraints of the traditional classroom.

The psychologist explained that students who are gifted require structured and systematic programming that allows them not only to delve deeper into the regular curriculum but also to pursue topics of their own interest. A deeper examination of the regular curriculum cannot be achieved by adding a few tasks. Rather, it needs a consistent and structured curriculum expansion founded on broad goals directed at their specific needs. Curricula should be designed to allow children of high ability such as Troy to master important conceptual systems that are at the level of their abilities in various content fields.

It was recommended that enrichment activities be available for Troy in the regular classroom and that he spend some time with the resource room teacher, who would put a special program in place for him. An extract from Troy's IEP is found below.

* * *

To educate students who are gifted, a school can make changes in the learning environment, in the content of lessons, and in the skills taught (B.C., 1995; Gallagher, 1985). Environmental changes include acceleration and ability grouping. Content includes both what students study and the rate at which they study it. Skills relate both to process—how the students work with information, and to products—how they represent what they know.

Various processes are used to provide enrichment in the regular classroom:

- Curriculum compacting (telescoping) is used to bring the content up to the level of the child (Reis, 1995) and to move students through the curriculum far more rapidly. It is designed to adapt the regular curriculum to meet the needs of above-average students by either eliminating work that has been mastered previously or streamlining work that may be mastered at a pace commensurate with the student's ability. A major goal of curriculum compacting is that students' time be used more efficiently on appropriate topics or activities rather than completing tasks they already know.

- Horizontal enrichment involves examining a certain curriculum area in greater depth. Students who are gifted don't need more work, but different work that is challenging and interesting. They should do the regular curriculum, but may delve into it in deeper ways. For example, a child in grade three may do all the addition problems set for the other students but then go on to do another set in Roman numerals.

- Vertical enrichment refers to students doing additional independent work of their own choosing in the classroom.

- Research skills. For students who are gifted, we need to add a fourth R—research skills—to the curriculum. Students must be assisted in developing skills and strategies that enable them to become more independent, creative, and self-sufficient seekers after knowledge. Lacking research skills, students cannot undertake self-directed learning (also called autonomous learning, self-teaching, individualized education, independent learning, and personalized teaching).

- Self-directed learning. There are almost as many conceptualizations of self-directed learning as there are researchers and theorists. Essentially, self-directed learning means that students are given autonomous control of their own instruction. Included are library research projects, scientific research projects, and independent study in art, music, and drama, learning centres, and field trips.

Extract from Troy's IEP

Name: Troy
Teacher: Mr. Jane
Date: November 12, 1999
Grade: 7
School: Ourtown Junior High

RESULTS FROM FORMAL ASSESSMENT ADMINISTERED 21 OCTOBER, 1999

Test	Results
WISC-III	Full Scale 93rd percentile
	Performance 91st percentile
	Verbal 95th percentile
	Key Math 91st percentile
Diagnostic Arithmetic Test: Test of Adolescent Language Development	98th percentile

STRENGTHS

Works well alone
High achiever
Strong oral language
Is very popular
Is inquisitive
Searches for significance
Seeks to organize
Enjoys problem solving
Exhibits intense concentration
Has high energy, alertness, eagerness
Diverse interests and abilities
Independent

WEAKNESSES

Perfectionist
Bored with classroom work
Constantly argues with teacher on things and people

MAJOR NEEDS

- Opportunities to make use of high level thinking skills
- Activities that build on logical and thinking skills

- Research skills
- Self-selected projects

SETTING

- Regular classroom/resource room

LONG-RANGE GOALS IN PULL-OUT PROGRAM

- Learn basic research skills
- Explore a topic of own choosing in depth
- Communicate findings to grade seven class

IN-CLASS GOALS

- Complete general classroom work before moving to own projects
- Adhere to a contract for an independent project prepared with the teacher

SPECIAL PROGRAM

- Take part in debating club

EFFECTS OF GIFTEDNESS	TIPS FOR TEACHERS
THE CHILD IS INDEPENDENT WITH HIGH INTERNAL LOCUS OF CONTROL	Individualize as much as possible.
	In the classroom, the degree of conformity should be reasonable and flexible. The young child, for example, may not listen intently when you read to the class, but neither should that child be permitted to divert the attention of others.
	Make assignments that allow some choice.
THE CHILD IS SELF-MOTIVATED	Use individual reading assignments with self-selection of materials.
	Use written expression for a variety of purposes—informative and persuasive as well as narrative.
	Provide opportunities for choices in assignments
	Design a curriculum that facilitates the movement from teacher-directed to self-directed learning styles.
	Provide time for students to do their own work at school.
THE CHILD HAS HIGH-LEVEL SKILLS	Introduce important ideas as early as possible.
	Teach to the highest cognitive level possible.
	Teach students to utilize all of their thinking processes.
CHILD NEEDS MORE RAPID PACING	Since pace is one of the most important variables in teaching, and these students may learn fifteen times faster than others, present material more rapidly and with less practice than for average learners.

EFFECTS OF GIFTEDNESS	TIPS FOR TEACHERS
	Do not work in a qualitatively different way than for other children; just present more advanced material.
	First teach the basic structure of a discipline, but then try to have the students approach it as the specialist approaches it.
	Provide an appropriate time span for learning activities that is consistent with the child's style.
THE CHILD NEEDS COMPETITION	In special programs, competition may be important, especially for older students. Some educators disagree with competition in the classroom and many have moved toward a greater emphasis on co-operative learning strategies. However, the value of co-operative learning is questionable when heterogeneous groups are used for highly able students (see Feldhusen and Moon, 1992). A study of the preferred learning styles of 169 gifted high school students showed that both males and females preferred individualistic learning styles over co-operative learning for all subjects (Li and Adamson, 1992).
THE CHILD NEEDS RESEARCH SKILLS	Stress technical writing. For example, teach children how to phrase research questions.
	Teach methods by which the children can discover knowledge for themselves.
	Teach students how to write proposals and how to present primary research data in graph, table, diagram, and statistical form.
	Stress the processes of problem solving as well as the products of work.
THE CHILD NEEDS INTERACTION WITH INTELLECTUAL PEERS	Let students teach each other through small-group work and ability-group learning activities.
THE CHILD HAS VARIED INTERESTS	Try to find mentors.
THE CHILD NEEDS SOCIAL INTERACTION	Have students regularly share with the class what they are doing.
THE CHILD IS HIGHLY CREATIVE	To stimulate creative students, allow learning by exploring, testing the limits, searching, manipulating, and playing.
	Tell students you appreciate their creativity.
UNDERACHIEVERS	Provide support and respect for the child's efforts.
	Establish standards and provide instruction, guidance, and support, with encouragement and co-operation rather than competition (Whitmore, 1980).

EFFECTS OF GIFTEDNESS	TIPS FOR TEACHERS
	Begin in the early grades, before the patterns of resistance in underachievers become too ingrained.
FEMALE STUDENTS	Provide early entry into stimulating and challenging programs.
	Provide models that contradict sex-role stereotypes.
	Provide information about scholastic requirements for career alternatives to stereotypical disciplines.
STUDENTS WITH DISABILITIES	Provide a nurturing environment that values individual differences and encourage strategies such as advance organizers, the development of test-taking skills, and special notes that help to compensate for the disability.
CULTURALLY DIVERSE STUDENTS	Gain parental involvement and support and develop program models, goals, and objectives that are meaningful for the local culture.

WEBLINKS

Gifted Education: A Resource Guide for Teachers **http://www.educ.gov.bc.ca/.specialed/www/gifted/title.html**

Newfoundland and Labrador Association for Gifted Children **http://calvin.stemnet.nf.ca/Community/NLAGC/nlagc.html**

Structure of Intellect (J. P. Guilford) **http://www.gwu.edu/~tip/guilford.html**

Student Leadership Diving Board **http://www.sentex.net/~casaa/**

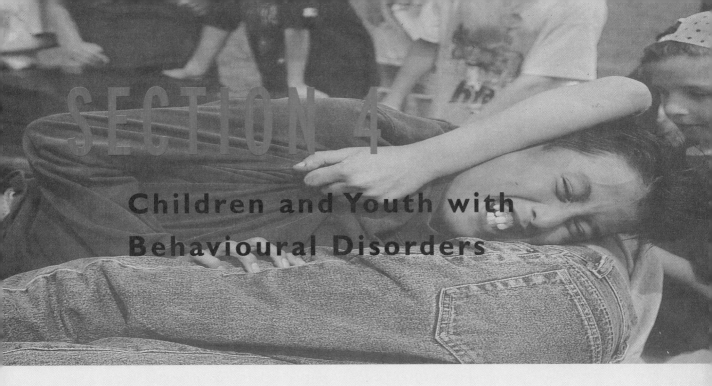

SECTION 4

Children and Youth with Behavioural Disorders

Just about every parent has, at some time or another, been frustrated and annoyed with the behaviour of his or her child. In the classroom, on an almost daily basis, every teacher confronts minor misdemeanours and unacceptable behaviours from students who seem intent on satisfying impulses that are incompatible with the kinds of classroom control and academic activities that the teacher has in mind. Behavioural excesses include physical and verbal aggression, defiance, temper tantrums, lying, swearing, stealing, throwing chairs, spitting, wearing attention-getting T-shirts, and generally disrupting the classroom.

When the behaviours become chronic, excessive, and far beyond the norm expected at a certain age, they are known as *behavioural disorders*, and the children demonstrating them are grouped in the broad category of *behaviourally disordered*. These children are not rare and most of us have had some experience with children and youth that we would characterize as behaviourally disordered. These troubled children create problems for almost everyone with whom they interact. They exhibit, to a marked and prolonged extent, behaviour that is clearly undesirable, inappropriate, and maladaptive in its social context. Some children withdraw; the great majority strike out with hostility and aggression. Their behaviour affects their own learning and social interactions as well as the equilibrium of those in their environments.

The category of behaviourally disordered is of increasing concern in our schools. The concern is reflected in a number of fundamental questions that seem to be asked more frequently today by parents, educators, the public, and the media. Questions such as:

* How are behavioural disorders precisely defined?
* How many young people show behavioural disturbances?
* How do we best understand and treat behavioural problems?
* Is the prevalence of behavioural disorders on the rise?
* How likely is it that the disorders will persist in later life?
* Should violent and aggressive children and youth be educated in regular classrooms?
* If so, what are the ramifications for teachers and children?

Teachers are particularly concerned with children and youth displaying behavioural disorders, those who are aggressive and bullying, and those who add to violence in the schools. One of the major tasks of teaching is to establish and maintain order in the classroom, and discipline is usually the number one issue facing individuals who are responsible for any classroom, particularly if they are new teachers. In fact, research has repeatedly found that new teachers list maintaining classroom discipline, motivating students, and interacting with parents as among their greatest concerns. In one survey (Feitler and Tokar, 1982), chronic student misbehaviour was noted as the main source of job stress by 50 percent of the respondents.

When faced with aggressive or non-compliant children, teachers turn to special education. As students with behavioural disorders seem to be among those least preferred by regular classroom teachers, and as many teachers feel that such students should be segregated in special classes (Johnson, 1987), classroom behavioural problems are the most common reason children are referred to special education. One study (Phipps, 1982) reported that 82 percent of the boys referred for special education were referred primarily because of their behaviour.

Nevertheless, many students with mild behavioural disorders can function in regular classroom settings. Once educators understand the behavioural difficulties likely to be seen in children and youth, they may better appreciate that these children are not in direct control of their deviant behaviours. Among the diversity of symptoms seen in these children runs an undercurrent of anxiety, inhibition, apprehension, depression, and overcontrol (Edelbrock, 1979). Understanding of the problems can also help teachers to formulate expectations, plan assessment strategies, and develop programs for behaviour and learning.

In this section, we address behavioural disorders that include conduct disorders, anxiety and withdrawal, delinquency, and Attention Deficit Hyperactivity Disorder. The more profound disorders of behaviour, such as childhood schizophrenia, are discussed in Chapter 13, on pervasive developmental disorders.

CHAPTER 8

Children and Youth with Behavioural Disorders

Historical Notes

Children and youth with mild behavioural disorders gained the attention of reformers and educators in the middle decades of the nineteenth century, becoming a part of what was referred to as the child rescue movement. Child rescue advanced in tandem with the stress on free and compulsory education for all students that began in Canada in the late 1840s and became law in the 1870s. At the same time, legislation was gradually passed in the areas of child labour, family courts, juvenile courts, and children's aid societies.

When compulsory school laws sent all children to school, the schools were forced to find ways to accommodate students who were unruly, recalcitrant, or truant. The solution was the establishment of segregated classrooms where such children could obtain special instruction and where they would not disrupt other pupils or take a teacher's time. The first segregated classes in the public schools, called unruly classes, opened in the 1880s. By 1910, segregated special classes were a permanent feature of most urban school systems. These classes remained the most important vehicle for providing services to children and youth with behavioural disorders into the 1960s.

Along with segregated classes, there were also placements in reformatories and industrial (training) schools. When the preferred treatment was psychiatric in nature, education required changes in the child's total living environment, which often meant placement in an institution. Very often, too, school exclusion, expulsion, or suspension was the solution to a behaviourally disordered pupil.

In the early 1970s, a number of provincial and national reports on education stressed the need for expanded and more effective educational services for children with behavioural disorders. They urged the federal and provincial governments to assume educational responsibility, and asked local education authorities to provide educational services for all children within their jurisdictions (Csapo, 1981a).

After that, service for students with behavioural disorders developed rapidly. Nevertheless, educational programs have not shown particularly positive outcomes. Students show excessive dropout rates, high rates of academic failure, poor achievement, low graduation rates, high numbers of institutional placements, and poor post-school adjustment (Eber, Nelson, and Miles, 1997).

Children and adolescents with behavioural disorders are not rare, and most of us have come into contact with or observed such young people. These disturbing, different, and disapproving individuals test the limits of our society in ways that challenge the wisdom of convention. They are often harmful and destructive in their actions, and they never permit us to rest comfortably in our routines (Wood, 1982). These students are some of the most difficult to handle, and they lack the appeal that others have. They frequently withdraw from proffered help or reject it outright.

Special education for students with behavioural disorders is a fairly modern development. It was not until the 1950s that special education services for mildly and moderately disturbed children and youth really emerged. Even today, however, this field is in many ways both confused and confusing. Terminology is inconsistent and much dissatisfaction exists with current definitions (Hallahan and Kauffman, 1991). Treatment regimes and interventions vary. The majority of current intervention practices, administrative arrangements, and teacher training programs have been developed with younger children in mind, and most special programs for behaviourally disordered children are found in elementary schools. Fewer provisions have been made for students at secondary levels who are disturbed.

Of all the deviant behaviours exhibited, the two most common are aggressive acting-out behaviour and social withdrawal (Heward and Orlansky, 1992). In the classroom, aggressive, acting-out, and disruptive children are unlikely to escape attention. Such youngsters challenge and frustrate teachers, disrupt classrooms, and hinder the achievement of everyone in the environment. Children who are anxious and withdrawn are more likely to be overlooked at the outset, but most teachers will quickly respond to their unusual patterns of behaviour.

No single approach suits each child with a behavioural disorder, and the approach that works today may not work tomorrow. Teachers employ various methods of discipline and management. They combine these with teaching children specific prosocial behaviours through methods such as modelling, shaping, coaching, and cognitive problem-solving skill development (Gresham, 1986; Hollinger, 1987), and prompt children to engage in interactions and role playing. Teachers also attempt to change the attitudes of normally developing children toward their peers with disabilities through role playing, peer tutoring, and reinforcement.

Definitions of Behavioural Disorders

The original term for behavioural disorders, *emotionally disturbed*, first appeared in the literature about 80 years ago without being defined (Reinert, 1980). Numerous definitions of this complex condition have emerged in the intervening years, but a universally accepted definition of behavioural disorders is extremely problematic.

Abnormal behaviour has an obvious referent in normal behaviour, but there is a continuum that runs from mental health to mental illness. Therefore, behavioural disorders are an open-ended area of deviance rather than an entity, and problems in identification occur when we try to pinpoint just where on the continuum behaviour becomes aberrant. Lack of a precise and universally accepted definition of just what a behavioural disorder is then creates problems in estimating prevalence, in identifying characteristics, in assessment, in etiology, in devising treatments, and in educational approaches.

Traditionally, the study and treatment of behavioural disorders has been the domain of clinical psychologists, researchers specializing in abnormal psychology, psychiatrists, and, more recently, educators. It follows that deviant behaviour is defined and conceptualized in many ways, and definitions proposed come from a variety of perspectives and disciplines.

The many attempts to define disturbed child populations and to define disturbed behaviour have had varying degrees of success. Much definitional confusion remains, all related in some way to the following:

- There is not a single symptom that is common to all pupils who are behaviourally disordered, or even to a subgroup of these children, because there is no such thing as a typical student who is behaviourally disordered.

- Behavioural deviance necessarily has a referent in normal behaviour. But human emotions and behaviour are so varied that a precise notion of normalcy is difficult to derive. Lack of an adequate definition of mental health makes behavioural disorders an open-ended category of deviance.

- If we cannot define normalcy, then it is difficult to define behavioural disorders. All behavioural disorders are abnormal in the sense that abnormal means *away from the norm* and behavioural disorders are deviations from average or standard behaviour. Any deviation in behaviour should, however, be viewed along a continuum from normal to markedly abnormal. But it is very hard to draw a line between serious behavioural disorders and problematic behaviour that is fairly common in childhood.

- Varying behaviours are exhibited by all children. Deviant and unusual behaviours may exist in the repertoires of normal children, usually as transient outlets for tension. At the same time, children who are disturbed may sometimes behave quite normally. Distinctions between normal and disturbed behaviour are generally in the amount or degree rather than in kind. Children with behavioural disorders perform certain behaviours too often or too intensely, or not often or intensely enough, but specifying this amount and degree is difficult.

- The patterns of behaviour exhibited by children with disorders are often unpredictable and subtle, rendering their conditions even harder to define. Children with behavioural disorders are likely to display a wide variety of inappropriate behaviours, which may or may not be associated with particular situations. In some children, for example, a certain subject in school or a specific object will trigger an anxiety attack.

- The behavioural problems change as children grow older. Four-year-olds may disobey their parents; as teenagers, they may engage in vandalism and delinquency.

- Behavioural disorders cannot be measured quantitatively. We have no instruments to determine a mental health quotient analogous to the IQ test.

- Varying professional perspectives exist. Many disciplines work with children who are behaviourally disordered, each with its own theories concerning the causes, definitions, and treatment of the disabilities.

- Legal and educational terms differ, and while the educational and the legal system are not at odds, their perspectives and their solutions may be different. *Delinquency* is a legal term applied by the criminal justice system to indicate that a youth has been adjudicated by the courts and found guilty of criminal behaviour. The educational term, *antisocial behaviour*, is less restrictive than delinquency because it includes behaviours that are norm-violating but not necessarily delinquent (Nelson, Rutherford, Center, and Walker, 1991).

- Social and cultural expectations differ. Behavioural disorders occur among the rich, the poor, the gifted, the intellectually disabled, and members of all racial and ethnic groups. There are, however, varying reactions to certain behaviours. Deviance is defined by social groups that recognize some behaviours as infractions of the rules and label as deviant persons who do not conform to these socially defined rules. Minority group children, for example, may bring to school different skills, different expectations, and different competencies than those valued by the dominant culture. Behaviour considered normal and adaptive in a subculture may be looked upon as deviant or inadequate by members of the dominant group (Hallahan and Kauffman, 1991). When classroom management procedures do not match cultural mores, students are less likely to change their behaviours, teachers become more frustrated, and a cycle is set in motion.

- Children rarely decide for themselves that they are behaviourally disordered; that determination is made by teachers and parents. But to some degree at least, behavioural disorders correlate with teacher tolerance levels, and varying teacher tolerance levels of deviant behaviours result in a high degree of variability in the teacher decision-making process (Shinn, Tindel, and Spera, 1987).

- Disruptive behaviour is often in the eye of the beholder, and any individual's interpretation of a situation is precariously subjective. Teachers place different demands on students depending on their own behaviour standards and the degree to which they are accepting of specific maladaptive behaviours. Students regarded as disruptive by one teacher may be ignored by another; rules might be enforced by one teacher but not by another.

- There is often a relationship between behavioural disorders and other disabling conditions. For example, some children with intellectual disabilities also manifest behavioural disorders. In an early study of hearing-impaired children (Schlesinger and Meadow, 1972), researchers found five times as many children with severe emotional disturbance and three times as many with moderate disturbance as they found among hearing students. As discussed in Chapter 5, many students who are learning disabled develop an overlay of emotional problems that compound their learning difficulties and conceal their primary disorder.

Of the many definitions of behavioural disorders currently available, the one proposed by James Kauffman (1991a) is particularly relevant from an educational point of view. Kauffman notes that

> children with behaviour disorders are those who chronically and markedly respond to their environments in socially unacceptable and/or personally unsatisfying ways but who can be taught more socially acceptable and personally gratifying behaviour. Children with mild and moderate behavioural disorders can be taught effectively with their normal peers (if their teachers receive appropriate consultative help) or in special resource or self-contained classes with reasonable hope of quick reintegration with their normal peers.

This definition focuses on behaviours that are inconsistent with current societal standards and ones that are personally unsatisfactory. Kauffman recommends specific educational settings and maintains a positive outlook for children's success through appropriate educational intervention. Kauffman's definition also has much in common with other current definitions that usually include the following statements about behavioural disorders:

- They deviate in an extreme way from the norm.
- They recur chronically. The chronic nature of the behaviour is a differentiating and important item. In children with behavioural disorders, the behaviours are not transient and episodic; rather, they last six months or longer, and interfere with expected age-appropriate functioning (Paul, 1987). In normally developing children, behaviour problems fluctuate and decline as children get older and are not necessarily signs of clinical deviance. Lying, for example, is reported to be a problem for the majority (53 percent) of 6-year-old boys; by the age of 10, lying decreases to 10 percent of boys. In girls, the pattern is more dramatic with a high rate (about 48 percent) at age 6 and no lying reported as a problem at age 11 (see Kazdin, 1989).
- They violate social or cultural expectations. Too often, a student's linguistic and cultural background is perceived as a disability and he or she is then diagnosed and treated as learning disabled or behaviourally disordered.
- They affect a child's self-esteem, interpersonal relationships, and probably school achievement, and therefore require special education intervention.

Terminology

As in many areas of special education, the field of behavioural disorders has seen evolving terminology over the years. At the outset, a variety of names, largely arising from a psychiatric base, were used: these included *neurotic, psychotic, obsessive,* and *emotionally disturbed.* Current educators prefer to dispense with psychiatric terms, but still debate whether to call these children emotionally disturbed, behaviourally disordered, socially maladjusted, deviant, psychologically impaired, educationally handicapped, character disordered, or delinquent.

In the past, the general category of behavioural disorders was referred to as *emotional disturbance,* with two severity levels differentiated. Children with milder conditions were referred to as *mildly emotionally disturbed*; those with serious problems, such as infantile autism and childhood schizophrenia, as *seriously* or *profoundly emotionally disturbed.*

Today, the terms *emotionally disturbed and behaviourally disordered* are often used interchangeably for those with milder disorders. (The American IDEA uses the former term.) However, most professionals opt for *behavioural disorders* because this term focuses on the most obvious problems (Huntze, 1985). Some suggest that the term *children in conflict* is more appropriate (Reinert and Huang, 1987).

Classification of Behavioural Disorders

With the difficulties we have already pointed out in regard to definitions and terminology, it is not surprising that consensus does not exist about the classification of these disorders into types and degrees of deviance. Research is giving some direction, but there are more problems than clarity. Classification difficulties concern not only how and what to classify, but the value of any classification system at all.

Researchers have tried to find meaningful classifications in various ways. The most important are described below.

Clinical Classification

The principal modern clinical classification scheme is that provided by the American Psychiatric Association (APA) in its *Diagnostic and Statistical Manual of Mental Disorders*. DSM is a clinical manual that describes behavioural symptoms of all disorders currently recognized by the APA and defines the symptoms and signs required for the diagnosis of each disorder.

The problem with the DSM classification is that disorders are judged as either present or absent. They are not defined as deviations from the norm and evaluated on a continuum. Too, the DSM diagnostic criteria were originally developed for adults (Clarizio and Klein, 1995) and there may be more valid systems for use with children and youth.

Classification by Severity

When severity levels are used, classification is not an either-or proposition; rather, it is based on how much behaviour differs from what is considered normal. As deviations from the norm, behavioural disorders are classified in terms of the severity of the condition—as mild, moderate, severe, or profound.

Dimensional Classification

Dimensional classification systems see behaviours overlapping to form a syndrome or cluster that contributes to a specific condition. Groupings or clusters of specific behaviours are usually derived from observer descriptions of deviant behaviour, quantified into groupings using the statistical procedure or factor analysis.

Perhaps the most widely used dimensional system is that of Quay and his colleagues (1972, 1986), who used behaviour ratings by teachers and parents, children's life history characteristics, and children's questionnaire responses to statistically derive six behavioural dimensions. These begin with conduct disorders, anxiety and withdrawal, socialized aggression, and immaturity/attention problems. Quay's fifth category of motor excess refers to states where a child is restless, unable to sit still, tense, unable to relax, and overly talkative. The sixth dimension includes those children who display psychotic behaviour—those who express far-fetched ideas, have repetitive speech, and show bizarre behaviour.

The dimensional classification provides a relatively reliable basis for description. We discuss the first five dimensions later in this chapter when we look at the characteristics of children with behavioural disorders. The sixth dimension, psychotic behaviour, is reserved for Chapter 13.

Classification by Behavioural Type

Definitions of behavioural disorders are based on excesses or deficits of social behaviour. Following this, behaviours are often described as externalizing or internalizing. This is not a formal classification but it does provide a useful description. For example, children with conduct disorders externalize their behaviour through such acts as disobedience, lying, stealing, fighting, sexual delinquency, and destructiveness. In contrast, anxious and withdrawn children internalize their behaviour. They may suffer from nausea, pains, headaches, phobias, fears, obsessions, shyness, nightmares, crying, depression, self-consciousness, and withdrawal.

Prevalence of Behavioural Disorders

In ever-increasing numbers, children are being identified as behaviourally disordered. It seems that the incidence of hyper-aggressive, undercontrolled behaviour has increased dramatically during the past few decades. Violence in our schools is a mounting concern, and there appear to be accelerated rates of juvenile crime, with the age of children committing delinquent acts decreasing. (See Research Notes.)

Research Notes

Violence in Our Schools

Whoever thought a teacher would be afraid of a student? Unfortunately, in too many of our schools today, this is a reality. Teachers are seeing more children who exhibit violent and aggressive behaviour at an earlier age, more children who show defiance, and more aggression toward property and persons ("The discipline ...," 1996). As more students are exhibiting violence, aggression, and defiance in the classroom than ever before, "Youth aggression and violent behaviours are among the most challenging issues facing educators and mental health professionals" (Cole, 1995, p. 108), and schools and teachers are struggling to find answers to a problem that shows no signs of going away ("The discipline ...," 1996).

The youth violence observed in North American communities is increasingly present in Canadian schools (MacDonald, 1997). A survey of police services and school boards across Canada found that 80 percent of respondents felt that there is more violence in schools now than ten years ago. Since 1986, the number of young people charged with violent crimes has increased 131 percent, although 1986 was also the year that 16- and 17-year-olds began to be charged under the Young Offender's Act, which meant that previously adult crimes became juvenile charges (Campbell, Grange, Cernetig, Ha, and Galt, 1997). Nevertheless, educators, police, and lawyers agree that youth crime is more sophisticated and more terrorizing than ever before (Campbell et al., 1997).

The violence phenomenon must be understood in the context of changes in society at large. These include demographic changes (refugees and immigrants), family changes, economic restructuring, access to firearms, involvement in antisocial groups, and drug abuse (see Cole, 1995).

School violence includes those behaviours that seriously disrupt the safe learning environments of classrooms and schools. To address violence, a program must be part of a wider school change, if only because a teacher usually has a class for only one year. Needed are school-wide programs; an acknowledgment of cultural and ethnic differences; ecological perspectives; and collaborative consultation.

There are common features of school-wide behavioural management systems, which include:

- a total staff commitment to managing behaviour, whatever approach is taken;

- clearly defined and communicated expectations and rules:

- consequences and clearly stated procedures for correcting rule-breaking behaviours;

- an instructional component for teaching students self-control and/or social skill strategies;

- a support plan to address the needs of students with chronic, challenging behaviours ("School-wide ...," 1997, p. 2).

Dire as these generalizations may be, researchers cannot provide accurate prevalence figures for behavioural disorders, chiefly because of the lack of a clear and precise definitional construct. Prevalence estimates vary tremendously. Cotler (1986) notes that in middle childhood (elementary school) about 7 percent of children have severe to moderate behavioural disorders and 15 percent have mild disorders. Coleman (1992) says that 2 percent of all children have severe behavioural disorders and another 7 to 10 percent have disorders that are mild but require intervention. Others note that 6 to 10 percent of the school-aged population exhibit serious and persistent behavioural problems (Kauffman, 1991; Kazdin, 1989).

The vast majority of children identified as behaviourally disordered fall into the mild and moderate categories. Boys exhibit more behavioural deviance than girls, including learning difficulties, hyperactivity, bed wetting, and antisocial behaviour (Wicks-Nelson and Israel, 1991). First-born males are more likely than later-borns to exhibit behavioural disorders and to be rated by teachers as anxious and aggressive toward their peers (Lahey, Hammer, Crumrine, and Forehand, 1980).

Many children with behavioural disorders come to the attention of professionals in the middle childhood and early teen years. The prevalence of behavioural disorders is low in the beginning grades, reaches a peak in the middle grades, and begins to fall off in high school. Delinquency, however, peaks during adolescence.

Children from lower socio-economic levels are more likely to be regarded as problems. There is a reported higher prevalence of aggressive behaviours among lower-class children as opposed to those from the middle and upper classes (Hallahan and Kauffman, 1991), and a higher proportion of those identified as behaviourally disordered are from minority groups (Rich, 1982).

Etiology of Behavioural Disorders

Psychiatrists, psychologists, and educators have traditionally placed great emphasis on identifying the causes of behavioural disorders in children, hoping that an understanding of the origins of the disorders would lead directly to their treatment and cure. Despite a vast amount of research, investigators still do not fully understand the causes of any type of psychopathology, and there exists no empirical evidence linking behavioural disorders to any specific causes. Deviant behaviour usually involves the interaction of several factors rather than a single cause. Each additional variable increases the risk of behavioural disorders, and the risk is greater when several factors combine (Rutter, 1990).

Most major developmental theories have been used to explain behavioural dysfunctions. They are founded on certain conceptual models that represent the different theoretical orientations of allied disciplines. As etiology is closely linked to conceptual models, there are considerable differences seen in both the presumed causes and in the importance that researchers attach to finding the causes of disturbance. The psychodynamic model, for example, focuses almost exclusively on causation while the behavioural model is concerned with the outward manifestations of deviancy. Table 8-1 presents an overview of the models.

These conceptual models are not just theoretical; they guide and direct interventions with students with behavioural disorders. However, as you examine the models, you will notice that the components of some models are compatible, others are not. But teachers know that no one intervention exists for every troubling behaviour that is manifested in the

Table 8-1 Conceptual models in the area of behavioural disorders

Approach	Assumption
Biophysical	Behavioural difficulties arise directly from constitutional, genetic, neurological, or biochemical problems. Disease, malnutrition, and substance abuse are included here.
Psychodynamic	Deviant behaviour is determined by past experiences; students with behaviour disorders are suffering inner turmoil; they can be helped by being made aware of their feelings and how to deal with them.
Psycho-educational	An eclectic approach that sees behaviour as having various causes. Focuses on academic achievement with therapy and counselling to seek the roots of the problems.
Behavioural	Emotional or behavioural deviance is the definable consequence of either mislearning or restricted learning. Normal, healthy, and desirable behaviours may be acquired to supplement or replace undesirable behaviours by consistently applying established behavioural principles of learning.
Ecological	Behaviour disorders are a function of the reciprocity between the child and the environment; that is, problems are the result of agitated transactions between the child and those in the environment.
Psychosocial	Can be seen as part of an ecological model although the focus is on the child's relationship to family, peers, and others in the environment.
Holistic	Behavioural disorders have diverse etiologies that interact with each other.

classroom. Because a single cure-all strategy is not out there waiting to be discovered, educators tend to draw ideas from a number of approaches.

Biophysical Model

As the name indicates, a biophysical approach holds that behavioural disorders relate to biological causes. Some evidence suggests that certain biological factors—genetic conditions, constitutional conditions, prenatal and birth factors, and environmental hazards—do increase the risk of behavioural disorders. But despite accumulating data, researchers remain wary. Information about the relationship between biophysical factors and behavioural disorders is scattered, and it is rarely possible to demonstrate a relationship between a behavioural disorder and a specific biological factor.

Geneticists maintain that no genes directly determine behaviour. Nevertheless, some genes do determine enzymatic and biochemical functions that, in turn, can have both major and subtle behavioural effects. Some very specific genetic defects may cause dramatically disturbed behavioural functioning. Children with untreated PKU, for example, often show deviant behaviour along with mental retardation.

From another line of genetic research, we know that temperaments are inherited, and temperamentally difficult children are more likely to become antisocial adolescents and adults (Baum, 1989). Boys and girls who are moody and ill-tempered at age ten tend to be ill-tempered adults whose relations with their spouses and children are generally unpleasant and full of conflict (Caspi, Elder, and Bern, 1987).

Also available are genetic studies on family relationships. Twin studies, for example, suggest that heredity is involved in behavioural disorders, but little is known about the mechanisms. As well, there is a greater risk among biological siblings of children with Attention Deficit Hyperactivity Disorder (ADHD)—approximately 20 to 30 percent have the disorder (Murphy and Barkley, 1996). Recent work with the biological parents of children with ADHD show that the parents are themselves more likely to have psychiatric disorders and to report greater distress than parents of children in normal and non-clinical groups. Parents of ADHD children seem to have more stressful events and are more likely than other parents to have marital disturbances (Murphy and Barcley, 1996).

Mounting evidence further suggests the possibility of a relationship between behavioural disorders and neurological disturbances. But researchers are baffled by the exact relationship; they point out that "the evidence linking behavioural characteristics to brain dysfunction is circumstantial, speculative, and in most cases clearly not documentable" (Smith and Robinson, 1986, p. 223).

Along with genetic problems and neurological disturbances, disease, malnutrition, and brain trauma may predispose children to develop emotional problems (Baumeister, Kupstas, and Klindworth, 1990; Lozoff, 1989). Substance abuse can also lead to serious emotional and behavioural problems (Newcomb and Bentler, 1989).

Psychodynamic Model

The psychodynamic model and approaches originated with the extremely complex theory first defined by Sigmund Freud in the early 1900s. Today psychodynamic models continue to exert a strong and persuasive influence on the terminology, definitions, and taxonomies of behavioural disorders.

Essentially, a psychodynamic approach is concerned with the development of and interaction among the intrapsychic (mental) processes believed to underlie human behaviour. Behavioural disorders are observable symptoms reflecting inner turmoil created by abnormal intrapsychic processes, so psychodynamic approaches attempt to locate the origins of behaviour within the context of psychological development.

Psycho-educational Model

Advocates of the psycho-educational model agree that children with behavioural disorders may have dealt unsuccessfully with developmental problems. Efforts are made to discover why children demonstrate deviant behaviour; there is a simultaneous stress on the acquisition of academic and daily living skills.

Behavioural Model

Early twentieth-century investigations of reflexive and voluntary behaviour, arising particularly from the work of Ivan Pavlov and John B. Watson, laid the groundwork for modern behavioural psychology. Bolstered by B. F. Skinner's principles of operant conditioning, the behavioural model has exerted a profound influence on psychotherapy, counselling, education, and special education (Cullinan and Epstein, 1982).

While the behavioural model includes a number of theories and points of view about human behaviour, two points most clearly define it. First is the assumption that behaviour—including deviant behaviour—is acquired and is regulated by certain identifiable principles of learning. Second, the behavioural model has a commitment to scientific methods of studying behaviour and behaviour change (Powers and Franks, 1988).

Behaviourists believe that all behaviour is learned and that behavioural disorders represent inappropriate learning. In general, behaviourists do not define and classify behavioural disorders. Instead, they try to understand their origins by observing, describing, and measuring deviant behaviour, by noting the conditions under which it occurs, and by detailing the relationship among the complex environmental factors that elicit and support deviant behaviour. By changing these conditions, behaviourists attempt to extinguish the undesirable behaviours and shape appropriate responses.

Ecological Model

Ecology refers to the overall pattern of relationships involving an organism and its environment (ecosystem) (Cullinan, Epstein, and Lloyd, 1991). From an ecological point of view, problem behaviour does not simply reflect inappropriate action by the student; rather, it is influenced by undesirable interactions and transactions between the student and others. That is, the behavioural disorders of children and youth arise when there are disturbances in the "goodness-of-fit" between a child and the ecosystem (Cullinan, Epstein, and Lloyd, 1991). Some characteristics of a child (usually the behaviour) agitate the ecosystem and the ecosystem responds in ways that lead the child to provoke further agitation. For example, a student's temper tantrums in school might be the problem, but from an ecological perspective, the behaviour of the student's teachers, peers, and parents—their expectations, demands, and reactions to the tantrums—must also be taken into consideration (Kauffman, 1991a).

The ecological approach reduces the danger of assuming that behavioural problems reside wholly within the child. It may be that the environment is not providing the necessary supports to enable the child to progress in adaptive development. In order to overcome the disturbance in the interaction between child and environment, changes may need to be made in both.

Psychosocial Model

The psychosocial model focuses both on the family and on **extra-familial influences**, those agencies outside the family that influence a child's cognitive, social, and emotional development. Three important extra-familial agents of socialization are schools, peer groups, and television.

Research and theory that focus on family patterns as possible sources of behavioural disorders find that family conditions may predispose a child to develop behavioural disorders or precipitate maladaptive behaviours. Predisposing conditions include maladaptive families characterized by harsh discipline, little parental involvement with the child, and poor monitoring and supervision of a child's activities. Precipitating factors are an immediate stress or incident such as divorce, separation, or the chronic illness of one or both parents.

Parental attitudes and child-rearing techniques are often critical in the development of aggressive behaviour. As a predictor of an antisocial adult personality, having an antisocial parent places the child at significant risk for antisocial behaviour; having two antisocial parents puts the child at even greater risk (Robins and Earls, 1985). There also seems to be a high degree of intergenerational similarity for antisocial behaviour: children in aggressive families are more likely to be aggressive and, in turn, their children are more likely to be aggressive (Farrington, 1987; Huessman, Eron, Lefkowitz, and Walder, 1984).

Research has also concluded that there is a significant cause-and-effect relationship between television violence and aggressive behaviour. The effects of TV are discussed in the Research Notes.

Research Notes

The Influence of Television

In this electronic age, children face external influences as great as school has ever been—probably greater. Of all extra-familial influences on young children, television is one of the most critical.

Television was introduced in 1939 when President F. D. Roosevelt broadcast the first transmission at the New York World's Fair. In the 1950s, TV permeated the market. Since then, researchers, parents, teachers, and legislators have debated the effects of television on children. Concerns centre on the impact of television on children's reading skills and attention levels and, most importantly, on the influence of media violence on the development of aggression.

Eighty percent of all prime time television programs contain at least one incident of physical violence. On average, prime time programs portray 7.5 violent acts an hour (Gerbner, Gross, Morgan, and Signorelli, 1980). With the high rate of violence that characterizes so much contemporary programming, child viewers are consistently exposed to examples of antisocial behaviour.

Until quite recently, researchers would not state a definite connection between television violence and aggressive behaviour in children. However, a growing body of empirical data supports a relationship between aggression and violence viewing. For example, the American Psychological Association Commission on Violence and Youth (1993) concluded that higher levels of viewing violence on film or TV are correlated with increased acceptance of aggressive attitudes and increased aggressive behaviour. Children who initially tend to be high in aggression seek out violent programming and respond to it with greater aggression.

The age of children at the time of viewing is crucial in developing aggressive attitudes. The strongest relations between television violence and both simultaneous and later aggression have been reported for children in the eight- to twelve-year-old range (Eron, 1982). Leonard Eron (1982) speculates that because aggressive children tend to be unpopular they spend more time watching television. The violence they see then serves to reassure them of the appropriateness of their behaviour while teaching them new coercive techniques.

A steady diet of violent programming may convince a child that the outside world is a violent place inhabited by people who rely on aggressive strategies to solve conflicts. One research team (Eron, Heusmann, Brice, Fisher, and Mermelstein, 1983) looked at seven- to nine-year-old boys and girls who were judged to be highly aggressive by their peers. These children not only preferred violent programming but believed that violent shows were an accurate portrayal of everyday life.

Television programs also tend to maximize violent incidents and stress the impersonal nature of crime. Viewing violence may not only arouse emotions associated with aggressive thoughts, but at the same time may reduce emotional reactions to the negative consequences of aggression for the victim (Rule and Ferguson, 1986).

Not only is television a likely cause of aggressive behaviours in children, but the effects are long-lasting (Eron, 1982). A longitudinal study (Eron and Huesmann, 1987) followed subjects for 22 years and found that television viewing habits measured in children related to aggressive behaviour in adulthood. Probably, continued viewing of aggressive programs contributes to the development of certain attitudes and norms of behaviour and teaches youngsters ways of solving interpersonal problems that stay with them over the years. The study also found that the more violent the programs the children watched at age eight, the more aggressive they were at age 19, the more serious were the crimes for which they were convicted at age 30, the more aggressive was their behaviour while under the influence of alcohol, and the harsher they were in the punishment of their own children (Eron and Huesmann, 1987).

Holistic Model

The holistic approach attempts to encompass the other models by viewing behavioural disorders as essentially indivisible phenomena that are more than just the sum of separate parts (Cullinan, Epstein, and Lloyd, 1991). The holistic model therefore acknowledges that the etiology of inappropriate behaviours may be illness, childhood traumas, poor relations with others, inappropriate learning, problems in socialization, any combination of these, and many other factors.

Characteristics of Children with Behavioural Disorders

Children with behavioural disorders exhibit a spectrum of behaviours ranging from disruptive and cantankerous outbursts to severe withdrawal from social interaction. Over a hundred different characteristics have been attributed to children and youth who are behaviourally disordered. Table 8-2 lists the most common characteristics and behaviours, grouped within the dimensional classification system. Keep in mind that all children demonstrate some of these traits at one time or another; they only become problems when they occur chronically, acutely, and in tandem. Also note that even though these children are categorized on different dimensions, there is considerable overlap between groupings, especially between conduct disorders and socialized aggression and between immaturity and anxiety and withdrawal. In addition, the problems of attention deficits may be seen in a number of populations of learners who are disabled.

In very general terms, students with behavioural disorders

- show an inability to learn that cannot be explained by intellectual, sensory, or health problems;

Table 8-2 Some behaviours seen in children and youth with behavioural disorders

Conduct disordered

- Fighting, hitting, assaults
- Destructive behaviour
- Impertinence and impudence
- Attention seeking
- Unco-operative and negative behaviour
- Hyperactivity
- Poor relationships with others
- Distractible, short attention span, and less task oriented than other children
- Lags in all academic areas, especially reading

Socialized aggressive

- Assaultive
- Delinquent activity
- Gang vandalism
- Destructive, disobedient, hostile, truant
- Lying
- Substance abuse
- Verbally abusive
- Sexually precocious

Anxious and withdrawn

- Anxious, fearful, shy, timid, tense, and withdrawn
- Depressed and sad
- Self-conscious and hypersensitive
- Cries frequently
- Short attention span
- Poor self-esteem that affects interpersonsal relationships and academic achievement

Immature

- Clumsy
- Easily frustrated
- Lacks initiative
- Passive
- Messy
- Short attention span
- Socially inadequate

Motor excess

- Overtalkative
- Unable to relax
- Accelerated rates of motor movement
- Short attention span
- Impulsivity
- Distractibility

While temper tantrums in preschoolers are expected, the same type of behaviour in an older child may indicate a conduct disorder.

- demonstrate behaviours that do not compare favourably with those manifested by normally developing children;
- exhibit inappropriate types of behaviours or feelings under normal conditions;
- exhibit behaviours that are generally unacceptable to the child, to normal peers, and to adults;
- exhibit a comparatively high number of problem behaviours;
- show behaviours that interfere with their expected performance relative to chronological age
- continue and even increase the behaviours unless structured and systematic intervention occurs;
- show an inability to build or maintain satisfactory interpersonal relationships with peers and teachers;
- show a tendency to develop physical symptoms, pains, or fears associated with personal or school problems.

Conduct Disorders

Conduct disorder is the term used to describe hyper-aggressive and highly disruptive children who form the major portion of those identified in the schools as behaviourally disordered. These students exhibit **antisocial behaviour**, which refers to overt, aggressive, disruptive behaviour, or to covert antisocial acts that are repeated infractions of socially prescribed behavioural patterns and that violate social norms and the rights of others (Kauffman, 1991a; Loeber, 1985).

Students with conduct disorders refuse to comply with requests, school rules, and the conventional limits of behaviour. They display problem behaviours that are acute, chronic, and characterized by various forms of aggression such as hitting, biting, and kicking. These students frequently suffer low self-esteem and poor self-concept, which may manifest in numerous other deviant behaviours, including dependency, crying, and whining (Walker, 1983).

Children with conduct disorders have failed to develop reliable internal controls; their behaviour is impulsive, distractible, hyperactive, and disruptive. They have short attention spans and sometimes seem not to know right from wrong. Their behaviour is not age-appropriate. For example, temper tantrums are common among two- and three-year-olds, as these young children strive toward independence. Among normally developing children, unfocused temper tantrums diminish during the preschool period and are uncommon after age four (Hartup, 1974). In children who are behaviourally disordered, tantrums are more likely to continue; a twelve-year-old throwing a temper tantrum is demonstrating clearly inappropriate behaviour.

Aggression, which may be defined as any form of behaviour designed to harm or injure another living being who is motivated to avoid such treatment (Baron and Byrne, 1981), is of more concern to teachers than any other aspect of behavioural disorders. In DSM-IV, two specific disorders involving aggression are mentioned. *Oppositional defiant disorder* is a condition in which children argue repeatedly with authority figures, show resentment, and often throw temper tantrums, although aggression is limited. The other condition is called *conduct disorder*, of which aggression is one of the most overt manifestations. The precursors, development, and outcomes of childhood aggression are discussed in the Research Notes below.

Research Notes

Childhood Aggression

Among all human emotions, aggression is probably the most studied; it has been a favourite topic for psychologists for all of this century. Explanations for aggression have come from evolution (no group in the animal kingdom is free of aggression), social learning (aggressive behaviour is learned and often rewarded), and modelling (children do what they see). All theories agree that although aggression in moderation is a useful survival tool, it becomes a problem when it is prolonged, frequent, and severe.

Aggression, behaviour aimed at harming another person (Perry, Perry, and Boldezar, 1990), seems to be one of the true differences between the sexes. It is found more strongly in males (Cummings, Ionatti, and Zahn-Waxler, 1989) and is also more tolerated in boys.

Aggression is developmental in nature. The early part of life is a particularly critical time when techniques for controlling others by aggressive means are rapidly acquired (Maccoby, 1980). Patterns of aggressive behaviour in children frequently seem to be well established before age nine (Patterson, 1982).

To be aggressive, children must know that they can get others to do what they want by causing them distress. The knowledge that other people can serve as obstacles that block one's intended course of action probably comes very early, and between the ages of one and two this knowledge seems to be extended (Maccoby, 1980). Anger in two-year-olds is distinctive and intense, usually expressed through undirected temper tantrums, hitting, and angry cries. Between the ages of three and five, children become more retaliatory and begin to express their anger verbally by scolding, insulting, or threatening others (Harris, 1986).

After age three, when many children have their first social encounters, disputes with playmates, rather than their parents, are the primary cause of angry outbursts (Harris, 1986). However, children's conflicts are brief, usually lasting between 12 and 31 seconds (Eisenberg and Garvey, 1981).

There is more overt aggressive behaviour in younger children, and younger children have more disputes over objects than do older children (see Peterson, 1992). Older children have more conflicts over behaviour and territory; they are in conflict over another child's actions or lack of action and factual disputes as to who's right or wrong (Shantz, 1987).

Aggression becomes more acceptable with age. Seven- to ten-year-olds who can easily discriminate accidental from deliberate harm-doing may react aggressively to almost any provocation, even one that they know is unintentional (Sancilio, Plumment, and Hartup, 1989). Older children (eighth graders) judge aggression to be less reprehensible than do younger children.

Antisocial behaviours such as aggression, truancy, and vandalism show relatively high continuity, and there is substantial stability of aggression over time. Highly aggressive three-year-olds are likely to become aggressive five-year-olds (Cummings, Ionatti, and Zahn-Waxler, 1989). Children's level of physical and verbal aggression at ages six through twelve are fairly good predictors of their tendency to threaten, insult, tease, and compete with peers at ages ten to fourteen (Olweus, 1979). Antisocial or non-compliant behaviour is particularly likely to be stable over time when the first antisocial behaviour appears at a young age, is frequent, appears in more than one setting, and consists of several distinct forms of antisocial behaviour (Loeber, 1990).

The major influences on aggression are temperament, the family, peers, and television, which we discussed in the Research Notes earlier in this chapter. In relation to temperament, the temperamental traits that make infants difficult may be related to behaviour problems of aggression and anxiety (Bates, 1987), but infancy is at best a modest predictor of later problems.

Parents' attitudes and child-rearing strategies play an important role. Cold and rejecting parents and those who are hostile and punitive often apply physical punishment erratically and permit their children to express frequent aggressive impulses. In early life, stress and constant threats seem to rewire emotional circuits, as in the mother who screams at a child who falls down, "It's your own fault," as opposed to the soothing parent (Begley, 1996). Aversive behaviour and physical punishment provide models and a partial sanctioning of aggressive responses. It may reinforce a child's aggressive behaviour toward others and teach patterns of attack and counter-attack so well that children become blind to alternative ways of solving conflicts.

Eventually, children who live in highly coercive family settings may become resistant to punishment. The use of arbitrary, high-intensity tactics elicits defiance from young children, rather than the compliance that parents want (Crockenberg and Litman, 1990). Children learn to fight coercion with coercion, often defying their parents by repeating the same acts for which they are punished (Shaffer, 1985). If they are spanked, for example, the spanking serves as a model of the very aggressive behaviour that the parents are trying to suppress. One of the few longitudinal studies (Herronkohl, Egolf, Ellen, and Herrenkohl, 1997) found that the severity of physical discipline in the preschool years to be related to assaultive behaviour in late adolescence. Males were more assaultive than females; people with higher intelligence and women are more likely to break the violence cycle (Kaplan, 1996).

Most children learn to use aggressive behaviour to overcome resistance and do become more aggressive as they develop, but not approaching the degree seen in children with conduct disorders. For these youngsters, aggression becomes a dominant theme in their social interactions. In today's schools, childhood aggression, as manifested in classroom and schoolyard bullying, is a mounting problem. See more on bullying in the Research Notes below.

Research Notes

Schoolyard Bullying

Think back to your own school days. Were you ever intimidated and frightened by the school bully? Perhaps you were. But even though bullying has been around for a long time, it has only recently been recognized as an enduring and underrated problem in today's schools (see Bentley and Li, 1995). Too, the bully you may remember bears little resemblance to the bully of today. As Campbell and colleagues (1997) report, "The schoolyard bully has gone big time, and he's more likely than ever to be carrying a weapon" (p. A6). They go on to say that the child stealing lunch money is passé, mainly because it is rare today for a student to work alone, and the money involved often exceeds the price of a burger and fries.

Bullying is a form of aggression, a particular kind of violence to which children are exposed. There are different kinds of bullying, but most have three things in common. Bullying is a repeated action that occurs over a prolonged period of time; there is an imbalance of power; and the verbal, psychological, and/or physical negative actions of bullying are unprovoked (see Bentey and Li, 1995).

Campbell and colleagues (1997) report on a study that found that bullying is pervasive; children in elementary school playgrounds indicate that bullying

occurs frequently, once every seven minutes. The same study found that 15 percent of students acknowledged bullying others once or twice during the term, and 20 percent reported that they had been bullied more than once or twice.

In Toronto, Ziegler and Rosenstein-Manner (1991) found that 20 percent of students in grades four to eight reported being bullied, whereas 15 percent reported bullying others now and then or more frequently. In Western Canada, a study found that 42.4 percent of students have suffered from bullying at least once over the previous eight months (cited in Bentley and Li, 1995). In a Calgary study of 379 grade four to six students (Bentley and Li, 1995), the results indicated that bullying/victim problems among upper elementary students are quite prevalent. One in three children run into bullying with some regularity. Youngsters in the sample, both boys and girls, were at risk for being bullied by both classmates and older students. When researchers (Perry, Perry, and Weiss, 1989; Perry, Williard, and Perry, 1990) studied patterns of aggression in American elementary third grade children, they found that one child in ten was severely and repeatedly abused by highly aggressive classmates.

Socialized Aggression

Youth characterized as *socialized aggressive* are chronic violators of broad cultural mores and social values. They are hostile, destructive, disobedient, and often verbally and physically abusive. They tend to lie, steal, and vandalize, sometimes assaulting people as well as property. They view social problems in hostile terms, do not seek explanations, generate few solutions, anticipate few consequences for aggression, and see violence as a legitimate way to solve problems (Guerra and Slaby, 1990).

These traits match those of children characterized as conduct disordered, except in one area. The difference is that students who are socialized aggressive are active in delinquent groups and loyal to delinquent friends. Delinquent behaviours are rewarded by peer attention at the same time as they attract some form of punishment from adult society. Thus a vicious circle is set in motion: more delinquent behaviour and more reward from the peer group, catalyzed by more punishment from the adult community and more anger on the part of the adolescent.

Children and youth within the classification of socialized aggressive are sometimes classed as *socially maladjusted* rather than *emotionally disturbed* or *behaviourally disordered*. This is because the United States Public Law 94-142 and its recent amendments specifically exclude "children who are socially maladjusted, unless it is determined that they are seriously emotionally disturbed" (US Dept. of Health, Education and Welfare, 1977, p. 42478). The distinction is subtle and depends upon the effect of the condition on the student. It is felt that behavioural disorders are persistently distressing to the child, while social maladjustment may not be. Within their gangs, socialized aggressive youths may enjoy considerable prestige as a result of their aggressive and norm-violating behaviours. Nevertheless, scholarly opinion holds this exclusionary clause in the U.S. federal definition of emotional disturbance (behavioural disorders) to be ill-founded (Kauffman, 1991a; Nelson et al., 1991). The ways of acting exhibited by these youths are clearly indicative of problems in socialization and ethics development that fall within the scope of the broader concept of behavioural disorders.

Socially maladjusted students take part in behaviours that include gang vandalism, stealing, fighting, truancy, sexual precocity, and substance abuse. These actions often fall under the rubric of delinquent behaviour, which implies any illegal act by a juvenile, regardless of whether the perpetrators are apprehended (Nelson et al., 1991). Once children and youth come to the attention of the courts they gain a new label—*juvenile delinquents* or *young offenders.*

The problems surrounding delinquency are of grave concern to parents, the juvenile justice system, and law enforcement agencies, as we explain in the Research Notes below.

Research Notes

Juvenile Delinquency

Delinquency refers to a set of antisocial behaviours acquired over time. Delinquency is viewed as a social and a legal concern, and the term *juvenile delinquency* has a legal connotation, not an educational one.

In Canada, corrections are the responsibility of the federal government, which enacts legislation outlining juvenile offences, age limits, court procedures and penalties. Provincial governments administer the legislation, supply containment facilities, provide probation officers, and carry out court judgments.

Correctional programs extend along a continuum of levels of intervention, with diversion at one end and containment at the other. Programs may be open, residential, or community based, and are located wherever there is a substantial population of young people (see Reist, 1991).

Few human behaviours have been subject to as many varied and contradictory explanations as juvenile delinquency. All the possible etiologies we have presented for behavioural disorders, plus quite a few more, have been proposed. For example, Patterson and Banks (1989) investigated the paths that children at risk follow in their acquisition of delinquency and concluded that a sequence of aggressive behaviour begins with incompetent and harsh parenting. This leads to an antisocial behaviour pattern that, in turn, is associated with school failure, peer rejection, membership in a deviant peer group, and ultimate socialization into a delinquency subculture. Similarly, Loeber (1985) reported that the two best predictors of delinquency were composite measures of parental family management techniques and child problem behaviour. Expanding on this, a number of researchers (Patterson, 1982; Quay, 1986; Wahler and Dumas, 1986) observe that students at risk for juvenile delinquency are exposed to negative, harsh and incompetent parenting practices and, in some cases, have been aware of the commission of criminal acts by family members. They have well-developed patterns of antisocial and aggressive behaviour and are rejected by normal peers. In school, they have low academic performance, poor grades, and substandard achievement.

Others see low self-confidence and fear of failure as characteristic of young offenders. Still others attribute at least some responsibility for delinquency to poor self-concept and school failure; organizational structures that bring tracking, large school size, depersonalization, large classes, and poor communication between the school and the home may add to the problems (Gage and Berliner, 1986). Some researchers believe that delinquent youth have a character trait known as *social anomie*, a lack of entrenched societal norms and values; students do not appear to internalize a coherent set of values and standards for regulating their own behaviour. Others adhere to the appealing theory of an innate criminal personality type.

One controversial theory links learning disabilities with juvenile delinquency. Research finds a significantly greater prevalence of learning disabilities reported in delinquent youth populations than in non-delinquent populations, and that students with learning disabilities are more at risk for adjudication regardless of race or socio-economic level (Keilitz and Dunivant, 1986).

In Canada, a review of the prevalence of learning disabilities among adolescents in trouble with the law indicates a range of 4 to 36 percent, with the lower incidence figure reflecting strict identification criteria and the higher one reflecting relatively lenient levels of discrepancy between ability and achievement (Murphy, 1986). Other Canadian studies have found that 20 to 30 percent or more of young offenders have academic problems (Crealock, 1984, 1986), and that learning problems may be a predisposing factor in delinquency in some cases (Pihl and McLarnon, 1984).

The nature of the relationship between the constructs of learning disabilities and juvenile delinquency is not clear. Most support comes from the continual school failure that characterizes both conditions.

Early forms of antisocial behaviour are linked to the early onset of official juvenile offences: childhood aggression is recognized as a strong predictor of behavioural difficulty in adolescence and early adulthood (Griffin, 1987). About half of antisocial children become adolescent delinquents and roughly half to three-quarters of these individuals become adult offenders (Blumstein, Cohen and Farrington, 1988; Farrington, 1987).

Olweus (1987) found that children described as aggressive at 13 and 15 years of age were more likely at 24 to be engaged in criminal and antisocial activities. A Swedish study of more than 900 youths (Magnusson, 1988) found evidence that hyperactive/hyperaggressive behaviour in childhood predicts adult psychopathy. Teachers rated boys at the age of 13 on aggressiveness, motor restlessness, and lack of concentration. Of the 85 boys they rated as extremely aggressive, almost half were registered for criminal offences between ages 18 and 26. Of the 123 boys rated least aggressive, only 14 percent were registered, and then only a very small portion for serious crimes.

The course of chronic delinquency follows an anticipated path, a progression from less serious to more serious incidents. Boys starting their criminal careers in late childhood or early adolescence are at the greatest risk for becoming chronic offenders (Farrington, 1983; Loeber, 1982). Boys first arrested between ten

and twelve years of age average twice as many con-
victions as later starters (Farrington, Gallagher,
Morley, St. Ledger, and West, 1986); this comparison holds into early adulthood. In contrast, the late
starter is someone committing his or her first offence
in middle to late adolescence. Lacking the early training for antisocial behaviours, this individual has not
experienced the dual failure of rejection by normal
peers and academic failure (Patterson, De Baryshe,
and Ramsey, 1989).

Anxiety and Withdrawal

The problems of anxiety and withdrawal are estimated to affect about five percent of the
child population (Kauffman, 1993). There is not nearly as much literature on children who
are anxious and withdrawn as there is on those with conduct disorders, and much is inconclusive, especially in regard to later outcomes.

Anxiety can be described as a fear with a future reference. It is vague, undifferentiated, and
uncertain, relating to futuristic events that have not yet occurred. In some instances, anxiety may be an adaptive response to threats from the environment. Many people, for example, are anxious about entering a new situation and meeting new people. But while many of
us are apprehensive of new situations, we are able to deal with them after some initial anxiety. Anxiety is considered abnormal when it happens in situations that most people can
handle with little difficulty.

A **phobia** is a persistent and irrational fear of a specific object, activity, or situation
(Comer, 1992), an intense fear with no rational basis. Some of the most common phobias are
fear of the dark, of animals, of vehicles, and of school. Among children, school phobia is
one of the most common. Although phobias in general are found more often in girls than in
boys, (Erickson, 1992), school phobia affects about 2 percent of the school-aged population and has the same incidence in boys and girls (Wolman, 1978).

School phobia seems to be more than simply an irrational fear of school. Children not only
fear school but they suffer nausea, abdominal pain, and other physical difficulties associated with tension and extreme agitation. Children with severe school phobia may simply
refuse to attend school. If forced, they may spend most of the time either mute or crying.
Sadness and deep depression are not uncommon (Freedman and Doyle, 1974). Symptoms
subside if the child is allowed to stay home and on weekends.

Children who are anxious and withdrawn do not necessarily suffer phobias. But because
they have low self-concept and little self-esteem, and are self-conscious, hypersensitive, and
sad much of the time, they may be so shy that they find it painful even to go to school.

Even if children do not develop phobias, per se, they do tend to develop a pattern of adjustment to cope with anxiety. In doing so, they forgo assertive, independent behaviour; become excessively withdrawn, fearful, secretive, and apathetic; and often spend large amounts
of time fantasizing and daydreaming instead of interacting with those around them. Some children who are withdrawn regress to earlier stages of development and demand constant help
and attention; others become depressed for no apparent reason (Klien and Last, 1989; Kovacs,
1989). Their depression is similar to that seen in adults (Hallahan and Kauffman, 1991).

Both negative aggression and poor peer co-operation are outer-directed (externalizing)
behaviours which can disrupt others. In contrast, anxiety is inner-directed (internalizing) and
typically not disruptive to other students, so that anxious and withdrawn children may be

Some anxious children become extremely withdrawn.

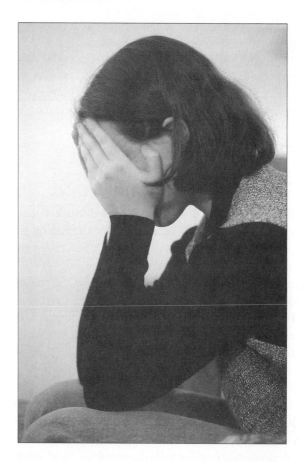

overlooked in the classroom. For these youngsters, the greatest threats are to themselves, not to those around them. The depression that often accompanies the condition is more than just a feeling; it is accompanied by cognitive, motivational, and physical symptoms. The most extreme manifestation is suicide. Severe behavioural disorders, in fact, are by far the most prevalent conditions associated with suicidal behaviour, and many studies have confirmed the link between suicidal behaviour and emotional instability (e.g. Pfeffer, 1986).

Adolescents are a generally healthy group. They have survived childhood diseases and not yet encountered the complaints of adulthood, although there are the developmental hazards of substance abuse and teenage pregnancy (Pagliaro, 1995). Suicide has become the second leading cause of death for young people (Cole, 1992) (accidents are the first). Worse, for every successful suicide it is estimated that there are 50 to 100 attempts (Pagliaro, 1995).

Suicide rates are higher in Canada than in the United States. The highest rates are in the Yukon and Northwest Territories (Cole, 1992).

Immaturity

Not much is known about the special nature of children who are characterized as *immature*. While similar in many ways to those who are withdrawn, immature children seem even less able to function in the regular classroom. They demonstrate many of the characteristics that we discussed in the chapter on learning disabilities in relation to maturational lags and attention deficits. They appear to be very clumsy, socially inadequate, passive, easily frustrated, messy, and lacking in initiative. They have short attention spans and frequently fail to finish assignments. Often they show a preference for younger playmates.

Attention Problems and Motor Excess

Two very similar (and very controversial) conditions fall into this category—Attention Deficit Disorder (ADD) and Attention Deficit Hyperactivity Disorder (ADHD). Together they have become the most popular conditions of the past decade. Writers observe that "not since the establishment of learning disabilities as a special education category has a condition so captivated both the professional community and general public as has attention deficit hyperactivity disorder" (Reid, Maag, and Vasa, 1993, p. 198).

The condition is not new to the fields of education, psychology, and pediatrics, but the interest is. There have always been children who couldn't sit still, who wriggled and fidgeted, and seemed not to concentrate on anything for longer than a few seconds. In the past, teachers and parents might have called them Fidgety Phils; psychologists and other health professionals used terms such as *neurological dysfunction, anatomical dysfunction of the right cerebral hemisphere, cognitive memory deficit, soft neurological signs,* and *minimum brain dysfunction syndrome* (Campbell, 1997; Meents, 1989).

Hyperactivity was first described in 1845 by a German physician, Henrich Hoffman. In the intervening years, hyperactivity became one of the most deeply investigated and controversial disorders within the fields of pediatric medicine, clinical psychology, and education (Gadow, 1979). Hyperactivity has also been identified as the most common childhood behavioural disorder presented to doctors, psychiatrists, teachers, and other related professionals, not to mention parents (Weiss and Hechtman, 1979).

In 1968, DSM-II provided the first official diagnostic classification of hyperactivity, which was characterized as hyperkinetic reactions of childhood. The disorder was given a specific name in 1980 and, since then, every new version of DSM has presented a revision of the ADD/ADHD criteria. The term Attention Deficit Disorder was first used in DSM-III in 1982. In 1987, DSM-III-R used the term Attention Deficit Hyperactivity Disorder.

Initial research defined two conditions—Attention Deficit Disorder and Attention Deficit Hyperactivity Disorder. Recent studies indicate that ADD without hyperactivity is uncommon, and today there is more use of the composite syndrome, ADHD. There are suggestions, however, that ADD occurs more often with students who are learning disabled, while ADHD may be more frequent among children with disruptive behavioural disorders (Barkley, Du Paul, and McMurray, 1990; Lahey and Carlson, 1991).

Following its introduction as a diagnostic category, research and interest in ADHD increased dramatically. Nevertheless, the procedures for identification, assessment, and treatment have been embroiled in controversy (see Reid, Maag, and Vasa, 1993). There are numerous definitional and diagnostic problems, not the least being a lack of consensus about an exact name for the condition, the characteristics that accompany it, and its prevalence rates. There are also criticisms of the distinction between ADD and ADHD (see Stewart, 1994), and controversy over which version of the DSM criteria is preferable (see McBurnett, Lahey, and Pfiffner, 1993).

Increasing numbers of children are reported as ADHD. Up to 3.5 million children in the United States are said to have Attention Deficit Disorder or its cousin, Attention Deficit Hyperactivity Disorder ("New developments ...," 1995). In Canada, the growth in diagnosis of ADHD has been staggering. An estimated half million Canadians, most of them school children, have been diagnosed (Campbell, 1997).

Many people look askance at the high number of children being diagnosed as ADHD. Child misbehaviour is changed into child pathology and, as one psychologist chides, "The diagnosis has become a wastebasket into which any misbehaving child can be tossed" (in Campbell, 1997, p. 30). There is little doubt that the diagnosis is popular, more so in North America than anywhere else. Five percent of children in the U.S. have been diagnosed; in Britain, the diagnosis is only about 0.03 percent for the same age group (Campbell, 1997). Australia is currently experiencing local epidemic outbreaks of ADHD. But in Victoria, an Australian state, an average school of a thousand children would not have one receiving treatment for ADHD. In two other states, Western Australia and New South Wales, approximately 10 students in every thousand would be treated for ADHD (Slee, 1997).

Within the special education community, critics of the role of clinical diagnosis of ADHD have pointed out that it does not lead to special placement and does not predict response to instruction. They believe that adding ADHD as a disability category is unnecessary because students diagnosed as ADHD who manifest symptoms severe enough to impair educational performance currently are eligible for educational services under existing categories such as learning disabilities or behavioural disorders (e.g. Ysseldyke, Algozzine, and Thurlow, 1992). Other educators object to ADHD because it may divert resources away from children with serious disabilities and it is difficult to define and identify (Aleman, 1991).

ADHD is characterized by three primary features—inattention, impulsivity, and hyperactivity. These three major criteria for ADHD are not situation-specific; rather, they are displayed by affected children at all times. It is important to understand the behaviours that make up each component. In brief:

*   Attention disorders are characterized by difficulty in concentrating. The child has problems with **attention**—the process of tuning in to sensory information, and with engagement or active participation.

    Attention and engagement are developmental: the younger the child, the lower the rates of engagement. Very young children flit from activity to activity, show high rates of movement, and are easily distracted by visual and auditory stimuli. The parts of the brain that allow the child to sustain attention and screen out distractions become increasingly myelinated between the ages of about four and seven (Higgins and Turnure, 1984). Children's ability to control their attention and to discriminate between what is and what is not important are developmental: the younger the child, the lower the rates of engagement. Very young children flit from activity to activity, show high rates of movement, and are easily distracted by visual and auditory stimuli. The parts of the brain that allow the child to sustain attention and screen out distractions become increasingly myelinated between the ages of about four and seven (Higgins and Turnure, 1984). Children's ability to control their attention, to discriminate between what is and what is not important, and to adapt their attention to details of the situation improves as they mature. They are able to maintain attention for longer periods because they are less easily distracted.

    This seems to be the difficulty for children with attention disorders. They find it hard to focus their attention for appropriate lengths of time and are unable to concentrate on a task because they have not learned to screen out irrelevant stimuli. They cannot sit still long enough to initiate and sustain the thought processes needed for school work and are repeatedly unable to concentrate on specific tasks long enough to complete them.

- *Impulsivity* represents a child's difficulty in withholding active responses such as blurting out statements or grabbing materials (Zentall, 1993). Impulsive students do things without thinking and do not learn from experience. They have difficulty organizing themselves, need much supervision, speak out of turn, and don't wait their turns in games or groups. They may show angry outbursts, be social isolates, blame others for their problems, fight with others quickly, and be very sensitive to criticism (Alderson, 1993). They are poorer at tasks requiring sustained attention and meet difficulties in problem solving and planning (see Reardon and Naglieri, 1992).

  Impulsive students do not double-check their work. They ignore details, write before thinking and planning, leave off word endings, do not organize compositions, copy sloppily from the board, and do not self-correct. These students (and others with ADHD) may *perseverate*—they purposelessly and sometimes disadvantageously repeat an activity. For example, a child may finish addition problems on page one and continue to add on page two, even though the instructions clearly indicate a switch to subtraction.

- *Hyperactivity* is defined as "a child's frequent failure to comply in an age-appropriate fashion with situational demands for restrained activity, sustained attention, resistance to distracting influences, and inhibition of impulsive responses" (Routh, 1980, p. 57). Hyperactive children display rates of motor behaviour that are too high for their age groups. Boys are more prone than girls. It is estimated that hyperactivity occurs in 3 to 20 percent of all elementary school children, with a sex ratio of three or more boys with the disorder to every girl (Wicks-Nelson and Israel, 1991).

  The accelerated rates of activity and the excessive, non-purposeful movement disturb others, worry teachers, and cause their families discomfort and even despair. Young hyperactive children are constantly on the move, pushing, poking, asking questions, but never waiting for answers. In the classroom, they are unable to sit still. When confined to a seat, they translate their need to be active into finger and foot tapping, as well as other disruptive activities. Hyperactive teenagers may drum their fingers, shuffle their feet, open and close their desks, and continually visit the pencil sharpener, other desks, and other areas of distraction. Even when asleep, the child shows excessive activity and other sleep problems (Alderson, 1993).

  Children with generalized hyperactivity have a very early onset of problems. Typically, signs are evident in early childhood, often by the age of three and even in infancy. There is a mean onset age of four years (Alderson, 1993; Barkley, Fisher, Newby, and Breen, 1988).

  ADHD is a medical diagnosis. The prevalent opinion about causes is that ADHD is an invisible function with a basis in the central nervous system that involves a faulty regulation of a particular neurotransmitter, norepinephrine (Alderson, 1993). Some researchers have documented a genetic factor in ADHD; they report findings of similar characteristics for anywhere between 60 and 75 percent of the relatives of children with ADHD and for 30 to 50 percent of their siblings (Goodman and Sevenson, 1989). Nevertheless, the efforts expended to find a biological etiology of ADHD have been generally inconclusive and often contradictory.

  Approximately 50 percent of children with ADD/ADHD qualify for some other diagnosis.

They have a higher incidence of anxiety, depression, mood disorder, learning disabilities, and Tourette syndrome than do children not so diagnosed ("New developments ...," 1996).

Typically, ADHD has been the domain of active prepubescent males. Females are often unidentified, for they express the disorder through talking or being busier, which is more socially acceptable than the gross motor activity often seen in boys. This means that girls are less likely to be hyperactive and also less likely to receive special education services for the condition. Only very recently have researchers begun to study girls with ADHD.

Identification and Assessment of Behavioural Disorders

Behavioural disorders are easier to identify than to define or classify. Children with conduct disorders attract attention with their overtly disruptive behaviours. Immature and withdrawn children are a little harder to identify but are still fairly recognizable.

Within the educational system, children with behavioural disorders are so readily identified by school personnel that few schools bother to use systematic screening procedures (Hallahan and Kauffman, 1991). Teachers are fairly accurate in identifying behavioural disorders; both experienced and inexperienced teachers can accurately perceive difficulties among children on the basis of behavioural deviations (Schwartz, Wolfe, and Cassar, 1997). A teacher's informal judgment has therefore served as a fairly reliable means of screening these children (Hallahan and Kauffman, 1991).

When it comes to referral for diagnosis and additional assistance, teachers tend to over-refer children showing conduct disorders. Childhood aggression accounts for a disproportionate number of referrals to special education programs and to mental health and child guidance centres (Epanchin and Paul, 1987). On the other hand, teachers tend to under-refer children with internalizing problems such as anxiety and withdrawn behaviour (Hallahan and Kauffman, 1991).

Once teachers have identified and referred a child, it is not a simple task to find out what is wrong, what is not connecting. Nor is it easy to determine whether a behavioural problem is serious enough to warrant further diagnosis. Many temporary behavioural disorders occur in normally developing children, and we do not want to identify a child incorrectly any more than we want to overlook a child who needs help.

The characteristics of children with behavioural disorders are so varied that no single measure or tool can pinpoint all of the symptoms or all of the causes of the behavioural and learning deficits. Further, the approaches used by educators to identify and diagnose behaviourally disordered students are determined by both philosophical and pragmatic considerations—the conceptual model favoured and the availability of personnel for psycho-educational diagnosis.

A complete assessment includes clinical interviews (with the child and parents); observations; rating scales (teacher ratings, peer ratings, and self-ratings by the target child); personality tests; and formal and informal tools to assess a child's mental ability, academic achievement, oral language development, perceptual–motor development, and auditory and visual acuity.

Before a child is referred for psycho-educational diagnosis, teachers may use a variety of procedures devised to help identify youngsters who deviate significantly in intra- and interpersonal learning and social behaviours. One of the most potent processes, teacher observation, tries to answer the question: When is a behavioural disorder a behavioural disorder? Teachers look for form—the form or shape of a behaviour that involves a description of the behaviour itself, such as a temper tantrum. They also look for chronicity and frequency. It is important also that observations take into account a variety of settings and circumstances, such as different times and subject areas in the classroom, the playground, and other school activities.

Direct observation is a more structured behavioural analysis technique in which observers record instances of specific behaviours in order to establish the frequency, durability, and age-appropriateness of a behaviour. Data recording may be as simple as a narrative system, or it may be more sophisticated with codes to score behavioural deviations, language skills, motor behaviour, and so on. There are limitations on the amount of behaviour that can be documented. We cannot observe all behaviour and must sometimes be content with a sample to make observations more manageable. With the different sampling techniques, systematic observations of a child are undertaken over a period of not less than a week, and preferably longer.

Event sampling is used to determine the frequency or length of a specific behaviour. The procedure includes two types—frequency counts and duration recording. A frequency count is used for behaviour that is of relatively short duration, such as the number of times a child hits another child. A duration measure (duration sampling) is an indication of how long something occurs and is used for behaviours that vary considerably in length, such as negative or positive peer interaction or self-stimulating behaviour.

Suppose, for example, that a teacher is particularly worried about the physically aggressive behaviours shown by James. In the course of a school day James slaps, punches, and generally annoys the other children in the room. In using direct observation techniques, the teacher would begin by measuring James's behaviour and comparing it to that of three other somewhat problematic children in the class. Over a period of at least five days, the teacher would enter a checkmark on a tally sheet each time James and the other three children exhibited physical aggression. The average number of aggressive behaviours in the five days provides a baseline. The teacher can profile James's baseline, compare it to those of the other children, and decide whether to refer him for intensive assessment. In addition, when a behaviour reduction program is begun for James, the teacher can quickly measure his progress by comparing his current status to the baseline. Figure 8-1 shows the baseline for James and the three other children.

When more formal procedures are used, teacher judgment measures (teacher ratings of behaviour) are the most widely used tools for diagnosing conduct disorders in a classroom setting (Hoge and Andrews, 1992). These tools have been found to be quite accurate. (See Table 8-3.)

Psycho-educational Assessment

Following screening, a child may be referred for psycho-educational diagnosis. An estimation of potential based on an IQ test, assessment of communication skills, and pupil performance in academic, social, psychomotor, and self-help skills provides a basis for sound instructional decisions. Do keep in mind that although a formal psycho-educational diagnosis will contain components that assess a child's potential and performance, the overall assess-

Figure 8-1

Baseline graph for charting physical aggression in children

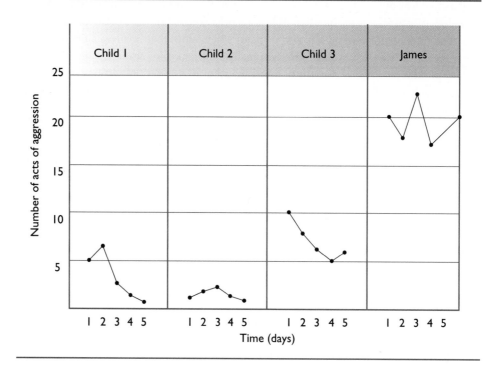

ment remains subjective. No measure of behavioural disorders can parallel the IQ; emotions are simply not defined by objective parameters.

Ecological Assessment

Ecological assessment views an individual's behaviour as a function of the values of the social system within which he or she is being evaluated, and includes the child's total ecological system (the various environments in which the child functions). Assessment includes an examination of the materials, methods, and curriculum, as well as teacher expectations, discipline, cultural and social factors, and so on.

Assessing ADHD

ADHD is classified as a neurological disorder. Measurement is particularly difficult, with few well-defined markers to separate normal behaviour from that requiring professional help (Campbell, 1997).

   To be diagnosed as ADHD, a child must exhibit eight of fourteen symptoms appearing in DSM-IV that reflect attention difficulties, impulsivity, or motor hyperactivity, with onset before the age of seven. Assessment needs parent and teacher interviews, parent and teacher rating scales, and direct observation. Diagnosis is conducted by matching parents' and teachers' descriptions of a child's behaviour with the inventory of behavioural descriptions provided in DSM-IV.

   A proper diagnosis requires more than six hours of interviews with the child, the family,

Table 8-3 Identification of behavioural disorders

Classroom screening testing	Educational measures	Psychological measures
Direct observation	Achievement in reading, math, and so on	IQ tests
Interviews	Perceptual/motor functioning	Personality measures
Teacher ratings	Auditory/visual processing	Projective tests
Peer ratings	Language development	
Self-ratings	Social Skills Rating System-Elementary and Secondary (Gresham and Elliott, 1990)	
Q sorts	School Social Behavior Scales (Merrell, 1993a)	
Social skills assessment	Behavioral Assessment System for Children (Reynolds and Kamphus, 1992).	
Sociometric measures	Conners Teacher Rating Scale (Conners, 1969, 1973)	
Rating scales on attitudes toward school, academics, and so on		
Behavior Problem Checklist, Revised (Quay and Peterson, 1987)		
Behavior Rating Profile, 2 (Brown and Hammill, 1990)		
Child Behavior Checklist (Achenbach, 1991)		

and teachers. But with many family doctors making the diagnosis, a child may be labelled as ADHD after a 20-minute examination (see Campbell, 1997).

Social Skills Assessment

Socially competent individuals have certain groups of skills—interpersonal and self-related behaviour, academically related skills, skills related to peer acceptance, communication skills, and assertiveness skills (Gresham and Elliot, 1987). The purpose of social skills assessment is to ascertain whether or not children possess these skills. It attempts to answer certain questions, to wit:

- What is the child's social status?
- What are the child's social/behavioural deficits?
- What, if any, behaviours interfere with the acquisition or performance of social skills?
- What are the antecedents preceding and consequences following performance of a skill? (Elksnin and Elksnin, 1997).

Once teachers have answered these questions by assessing the extent to which particular skills are being used, or not used, by a child, they can identify target skills to teach.

Prevention of Behavioural Disorders

If the specific causes of behavioural disorders were known, prevention would be greatly simplified. Only general preventative measures can be delineated; these revolve around broad areas such as nutrition; the family climate and family interaction; and the prevention of child abuse and neglect.

Developmental Consequences of Behavioural Disorders

Children and adolescents with behavioural disorders deviate significantly from their peers in the quantity, quality, and modes of their emotional expression. Apart from this overarching trait, there is no symptom common to all pupils who are behaviourally disordered, or even to a subgroup of these children. That is, there is no such thing as a typical behaviourally disordered or disturbed student. Behavioural disorders may take one or many specific forms and can be manifested in various ways. The severity of disturbance ranges from mild to serious and debilitating.

Cognitive Development

Studies show that intelligence and scholastic achievement are negatively correlated with aggression and delinquency for both boys and girls (Jarvelin, Laara, Rantakillio, Moilanen, and Isohanni, 1994). Compared to the normal distribution of intelligence, many children with behavioural disorders fall into the slow learner or mildly intellectually disabled category. Most have IQs in the dull normal range—around 90—and very few score above the bright normal range (Hallahan and Kauffman, 1991).

Academic Performance

Only rarely is a child who is disturbed academically advanced; the few children who do seem competent academically are seldom able to apply their skills to everyday problems (Hallahan and Kauffman, 1991). Many of these youngsters are underachievers at school, as measured by standardized tests (Kauffman, 1991a). They often experience difficulty with basic school skills and do not achieve academically at the expected level for their mental or chronological ages. They are usually behind in reading, arithmetic, and spelling (Lewis and Doorlag, 1991).

Research supports a relationship between underachievement and externalizing behaviour (Richards, Symons, Greene, and Szuskiewicz, 1995) as well as reading disabilities and aggression (Cornwall and Bawden, 1992). This is not surprising, as students with conduct disorders tend to be non-compliant and uncontrolled, alienating teachers and other students.

Because they create such problems in classroom management, teachers tend to instruct children who have conduct disorders with fewer academic questions, less extended feedback, and fewer dyadic work interactions. With non-compliant behaviour and less instruction, students may rapidly enter a pattern of severe academic failure that quickly becomes cyclical. When children do not learn the skills needed for coping with academic pressures, they react by withdrawing or lashing out in angry frustration. They soon learn to dislike the learning process and resent the school experience, and often resort to truancy.

Co-occurring problems that compound academic underachievement are common. For example, about 38 to 75 percent of children and adolescents with serious behavioural disorders are also identified as having learning disabilities or severe learning problems (Rock, Fessler, and Church, 1997).

At first glance, anxiety may not seem as academically and socially debilitating as aggression from the point of view of both the child and the teacher. But for children, timid, passive behaviour, dependency, isolation, and withdrawal interfere with the development of potential (Conger and Keane, 1981). Children tend to develop a defeatist attitude along with feelings of worthlessness and excessive self-criticism.

Different problem behaviours evoke different attitudes among teachers, and some writers contend that acting-out behaviours are viewed more negatively than withdrawn ones (Li, 1985). Others find that teachers consider socially withdrawn behaviours and non-communication (negative aggression and poor peer co-operation) to be the most difficult type of behaviour to manage (Safran and Safran, 1987).

Whether considered the most difficult or not, it does seem that children who are anxious and withdrawn may be ignored in the classroom. A recent study (Finn, Pannozzo, and Voelkl 1994) that measured the academic achievement of compliant, disruptive, and withdrawn fourth graders found that the withdrawn children scored considerably lower than the other two groups. The investigators surmise that the attention that teachers give to disruptive children actually helps these youngsters but withdrawn children do not disturb the classroom and therefore tend to be more ignored (Saad, 1997).

The general characteristics of ADHD—inattention, distractibility, impulsivity, and hyperactivity—can cause or compound academic problems. Obviously, children who are easily distracted from learning tasks learn less than those who pay attention and, by definition, children diagnosed as ADHD are easily distracted, don't stay on task, and have short attention spans.

When compared to normally developing students, students with ADHD are more likely to receive lower grades in academic subjects and lower scores on standard measures of reading and math (Zentall, 1993).

More than 80 percent of eleven-year-old students with ADHD are reported to be at least two years behind in reading, spelling, math, or written language. Over one-third of students with ADHD fail to finish high school (Weiss and Hechtman, 1986).

Communication

Speech and language disorders cut across all areas of exceptionality and are likely to be found among children with behavioural disorders. In fact, a higher prevalence of behavioural disorders are found among seriously language-delayed children. Children who are not successful in communication often demonstrate negative, resistant, or attention-getting behaviour and are at risk for both psychiatric and learning disorders (Baker and Cantwell 1987; Owens, 1991). And vice versa. Of psychiatric outpatients, 24 to 65 percent may suffer speech and language problems (Giddan, Melling, and Campbell, 1996). When investigators (Gualtieri, Koriath, Van Bourgondien, and Saleeby, 1983) surveyed 40 consecutive admissions to a child psychiatric inpatient facility, they found—after in-depth speech, language, and intelligence testing—that 20 of the 40 had moderate to severe language disorders.

On the other hand, teachers sometimes feel that children who are behaviourally disordered communicate *too* well. They interrupt in class, swear, use aggressive language, speak defiantly to adults, and indiscriminately vent their emotions. They often use language to disrupt and control social situations. This excessive use of language may not be a communication disorder, but it is certainly a social problem.

Social Development

Socialization is the means by which individuals become reasonably acceptable and competent members of their society. Through socialization, children acquire the discipline and the skills, the knowledge, the ambitions, and the empathy for those around them that allow them to participate in the life of the family and later the school and the community.

A number of related terms and concepts arise from the general idea of socialization. **Social cognition** is the knowledge and cognitive activities employed by people in dealing with the social world (Pearl, 1987). **Social competence**, "the ability of children to successfully and appropriately select and carry out their interpersonal goals" (Guralnick, 1990, p. 4), includes the development of meaningful and productive relationships with peers, social and communication development, degrees of independence, and other factors that may contribute to becoming socially acceptable. Socially competent individuals perform behaviours that they believe will effect rewarding outcomes and avoid acting in ways that might cause negative outcomes (Schunk, 1987). **Social skills** are "those responses which within a given situation prove effective; or ... maximize the probability of producing, maintaining, or enhancing the positive effects for the interactor" (Foster and Ritchey, 1979, p. 626). **Sociability** is a term that describes a child's willingness to engage others in social interaction and to seek their attention or approval.

All of these concepts are relevant to students with behavioural disorders in the sense that such students exhibit deficits in socialization, social cognition, social competence, and social skills. Instead of being sociable, these children show excessive aggression and defiance and develop intense and far-ranging interpersonal problems with teachers, peers, parents, and others in their environments. Compared to samples of normally developing children, those with conduct disorders are usually less responsive to social reinforcement, less empathetic, and less sophisticated in their understanding of and responses to their peers' behaviour (Baum, 1989). Those who are anxious and withdrawn fail to respond appropriately to those in their environments.

At both elementary and secondary levels students with behavioural disorders are seldom socially accepted; they are often actively rejected, not just neglected. This is especially true for highly aggressive children, who are less likely to make friends, are disliked by most of their peers, and more likely than others to be attacked by peers.

Accepted children display high frequencies of sociable behaviour, whereas rejected children show aggressive and disruptive behaviour (Siperstein and Leffert, 1997). Aggressive children provoke a large number of fights, and are also more likely to become the targets of aggression. Non-aggressive children who are harmed under ambiguous circumstances are much more likely to retaliate if the harm doer has a reputation as an aggressive child (Dodge and Frame, 1982; Sancilio, Plumment, and Hartup, 1989).

When aggressive children do make friends, they tend to gravitate toward other peers with more equal levels of aggressive, disruptive, antisocial behaviour. As early as middle childhood, antisocial children tend to associate with other antisocial and/or rejected peers either by choice or default (Dishion, Andrews, and Crosby, 1995; Farmer and Hollowell, 1994).

Social problems also affect children with ADHD. In fact, the time periods required for peers to notice and disapprove of children with ADHD are distressingly brief, measurable in minutes or hours (Bickett and Milich, 1990).

Prognosis

The problems created by and for children with behavioural disorders should not be underestimated. Rejection and low levels of peer acceptance place a student at substantial risk for a wide variety of negative outcomes (Parker and Asher, 1987).

Socially unacceptable behaviour in adulthood is most likely to be seen in individuals classified as *conduct disordered*. Antisocial behaviour in childhood generally leads to poor adjustment and mental health in later years, especially for boys. The continuation of antisocial behaviour in school is likely to lead to increased risk of school failure, membership in deviant peer groups, dropping out of school, and eventual delinquency (Walker, Shinn, O'Neill, and Ramsey, 1987).

In school, withdrawn children have acceptance problems (Siperstein and Leffert, 1997), but outcomes for students with anxiety and withdrawal are not as clear as they are for the conduct disordered population. Some (e.g. Coie, 1995) conclude that withdrawn children are not at any greater risk for the development of maladjustment than are any other children. Many others (e.g. Parker and Asher, 1987; Vargo, 1995) find that children with low peer acceptance are at risk for concurrent and later difficulties.

Intervention with Children Who Have Behavioural Disorders

Methods of intervention for students with behavioural disorders have been largely developed according to various theoretical perspectives. No one method has proven effective for all behavioural disorders. Successful behaviour change is related to the additive effects of multiple interventions based on diversified treatment modalities.

Medical Intervention

Medical intervention for students with behavioural disorders rests almost entirely on psychopharmacology (drug therapy). In recent years, drugs have become the standard treatment regimen, and an increasing number of children are being prescribed drugs for use at school.

Drugs administered to children vary widely in purpose and pharmacological action. Generally, the drugs fall into three major categories—stimulants, major tranquillizers, and anti-depressants. For children with ADHD, stimulants are the drugs of choice among physicians. Stimulant medication seems to be the least complicated of the possible medications and seems to produce the fewest side effects. Tranquillizers and anti-depressants are reserved for a smaller group of patients. The major tranquillizers such as thioridazine (Mellaril), chloropromazine (Thorazine), and haloperidol (Haldol, Serenace) may be prescribed for children with very serious behavioural disorders. Antidepressants, such as imipramine (Tofranil) and amitriptyline (Taroxyle, Tryptant, Elevil) may be administered for problems such as enuresis (bed wetting) and childhood depression.

Of the stimulant drugs prescribed to control hyperactivity and inattentive behaviour, the most commonly recommended are the psychostimulants—methylphenidate hydrochloride (trade name, Ritalin) and dextroamphetamine (Dexedrine, Deanol, and Cylert). Ritalin is the first choice of doctors, probably because it seems to produce fewer side effects. Ritalin is prescribed about ten times more than the other two combined (Gadow, 1986).

Perhaps 60 to 90 percent of children diagnosed with attention deficits and/or hyperactivity receive stimulant therapy for prolonged periods during their school careers (Copeland, Wolraich, Lindgren, Milich, and Woolson, 1987; Lambert, Hartsough, Sassone, and Sandoval, 1987; Safer and Krager, 1988). And the numbers are increasing. Health Canada estimates that the amount of Ritalin consumed in Canada in 1996 was 4.6 times more than in 1990 (Campbell, 1997). In Alberta, the use of Ritalin has increased tenfold since 1986. From 1992 to 1993, there was a 40 percent jump (Bell, Fisher, and Rodriguez, 1994).

Psychotropic drugs affect the neuron cells of the central nervous system either by increasing or decreasing their excitability (Ross and Ross, 1982). They are prescribed to control hyperactive and inattentive behaviour in the hope that their effect will produce better peer relationships, improved self-image, and pleasure in acquiring competencies.

There seem to be two conditions that respond well to psychopharmacology—poor selective attention and concentration and impulsivity (Levine, 1982). When used in carefully controlled dosages along with educational programs, stimulants do facilitate academic functioning (Douglas, Bari, Amin, O'Neill, and Button, 1988). The majority of youngsters show medication-related improvements, and there is little question that drugs are often successful in reducing hyperactive behaviour and increasing attention skills.

While chemical treatment is celebrated in the professional literature as successful, we should also consider possible adverse affects, specifically the ethics and advisability of wide drug use with children. Ethical problems revolve around the drugs and their illegal use in our society. Do note that some students prescribed Ritalin refuse the medication, but others sell it; in fact, the move from therapeutic to recreational use of the medication is common.

Other concerns focus on the short- and long-term effects of drug therapy. Long-term effects may include growth inhibition and sleep and diet disturbances. In the short term, drug therapy seems effective for many children. But because any beneficial effects dissipate rapidly upon discontinuation of the medication, researchers are concerned about what they refer to as "short-term efficacy."

Given the short-lived effects, it can be argued that prescribing medication as the sole method of behaviour management seems inefficient. Medication is best viewed as one component of a comprehensive treatment program; an adjunct to other interventions such as special education and behaviour management. The Canadian Pediatric Society (1988) advocates a thorough interdisciplinary approach with teachers playing a major role in the entire process (Fishburne, 1989). The teacher has an essential role in monitoring the effects of the therapy (Alderson, 1993).

Therapy and Counselling

The developmental histories of many students with serious emotional and behavioural disorders have often been characterized by turmoil, uncertainty, abuse, neglect, unclear family communication, abandonment, and ineffective modelling (Jones, 1996). Because many students suffer a serious lack of self-esteem, depression, or anxiety impairment, the importance of interventions in the affective domain, which help students understand themselves and their environment, cannot be overestimated. Providing students with an understanding of their own dysfunctional perceptions and clarifying their own reality lays the basis for healthy self-esteem and productive self-talk (Jones, 1996).

Affective domains are addressed through various therapies and counselling techniques. Many occur in clinical settings; some are applicable to the classroom.

Individual psychotherapy implies a transaction between a child and a therapist. Techniques rely heavily on discussion and the probing of feelings and attitudes. Simply because young children may not realize that what they are experiencing is different from what other people feel, traditional therapeutic approaches have not been entirely successful with children. Children do not have adequate labels for internal experiences, and so they are unable to properly describe their feelings of anxiety, depression, or resentment.

As children have a difficult time with traditional "talk" therapy, indirect methods such as music, art, and storytelling are used instead to help children to communicate about therapeutic issues. Young children communicate more easily through play than through words, so various forms of play therapy have also evolved.

In play therapy, the therapist creates an atmosphere where a child can freely express feelings, concerns, and conflicts. The therapist, who assumes the role of co-player, model, or observer, then interprets the child's play to find the source of fears and problems, or tries to reflect back the feelings expressed by the child.

In addition to different therapies, counselling has proven effective for children with behavioural disorders and their families. The major goal is to help the child eliminate unacceptable behaviours and learn more appropriate ways of responding to people and the environment.

Individual, group, family, guidance, and career and vocational counselling are used. Although individual counselling is popular, many counsellors suggest that group therapy—the simultaneous treatment of several children, usually in the same age range—is a more natural way to work with children. By treating children in a group, the therapist can use group processes and face-to-face peer interactions as primary vehicles for change (Suran and Rizzo, 1983).

Group techniques make use of modelling, play, verbal interactions, peer influence, socialization, experience, and mutual support. Within the context of the group, children can unlearn inappropriate behaviours and learn new ways of relating more easily through the interaction and feedback in a safe practice situation with peers. At the same time, children learn to help other people, to accept help from others, and to talk openly about themselves and abandon facades. They take more risks and accept responsibility for their growth and the growth of others (Ohlsen, 1977).

Educational Intervention

Two critical elements characterize current services for children and youth with behavioural disorders. The first is the development of the various conceptual models, which we discussed earlier in this chapter. The second relates to placement issues. When full inclusion is discussed, the two groups of students who force educators to consider carefully the most enabling environments are those with severe and multiple disabilities and those with serious behavioural disorders. Especially for the latter group, inclusionary practices are contentious and unresolved. At issue is not only the learning of the individual child, but also the progress of other class members and the safety of the teacher and others in the environment.

Inclusion

For many school-aged children with mild behavioural disorders, the regular classroom is the common milieu. With support, appropriate programming, and individualization, regular teachers can teach and manage these students. But what about students with serious and violent behaviour? For these children, there is "a murky picture as to the future of inclusive education" (Bassett, Jackson, Ferrel, Luckner, Hagerty, Bussen, and MacIsan, 1996, p. 365). Whether they belong in the regular classroom is an ongoing argument, as shown in the Matter of Debate box below.

A Matter of Debate

The Educational Placement of Students with Serious Behavioural Disorders

 Arguments for Inclusion

Studies (e.g. Farmer and Farmer, 1996; Glassberg, 1994; Meadows, Neel, Scott, and Parker, 1994) on the effectiveness of traditional pull-out and self-contained classes for children with behavioural disorders tend to support the use of general education settings. Researchers contend that in the regular classroom students are provided with appropriate models of behaviour and the interaction improves children's self-image and casts doubt on the utility of self-contained settings as catalysts for critical socialization processes.

 Arguments against Inclusion

Efficacy studies on the inclusion of students with serious behavioural disorders suggest that such placements are not as successful as special education classes or that the energy and resources needed for success in the regular classroom may be commensurate with the questionable gains achieved (see MacMillan, Gresham, and Forness, 1996).

said that exceptional students were often highly disruptive in their classes and failed to learn in any meaningful way. A 1994 follow-up study found that teachers still broadly supported integration but that the fears expressed by regular educators had grown even more acute (ATA, 1993, 1994). A report from Manitoba suggests that teachers hold that little is gained academically by including these students (Report of Task Force, 1990).

Other facets to address are teacher effectiveness and the precise relationship between teacher effectiveness and tolerance for behavioural and academic deviance. In the volumes that have been written about the profiles of effective teachers, it is axiomatic that more effective teachers are distinguished by different ways of instructing and managing students. As well, a substantial body of research exists about the type of behaviours teachers consider critical for success in their classrooms (standards), and the types of behaviours they find the least acceptable (tolerance). Teachers' belief systems determine the standards they maintain for students, what behaviour they will tolerate, how they expect individual students to behave, and the way they approach the tasks of instruction and management (Kauffman and Wong, 1991).

This body of research indicates two things—effective teachers are distinguished by the way they handle and manage students, and teachers vary greatly in their attitudes, standards, tolerances, and expectations. On the other hand, even effective teachers may find themselves unable to accommodate the varied needs of some of these children (Kauffman, Gerber, and Semmel, 1988).

For one thing, teachers who use very effective teaching techniques tend to be characterized by higher standards for students and lower tolerance for behavioural excesses. These teachers are often those who are least accepting of the behavioural and cognitive difficulties that characterize students with disabilities (Gersten, Walker, and Darch, 1988; Walker and Rankin, 1983) and resist accepting such students into their classes (Lundrum, 1992). Second, while competency in classroom management is a major, if not the major, competency necessary to be successful (Bullock, Ellis, and Wilson, 1994), the needs of students with behavioural disorders may fall outside the limits of most effective general education teachers. Effective teaching of students with behavioural disorders may require skills, attitudes, and beliefs that are different from those of teachers who work effectively with more ordinary students (Kauffman and Wong, 1991).

• *Supports.* If children are placed in regular classrooms, there must be adequate supports in the form of personnel and instructional adaptations. Records show that most students who are violent are not special education students. Nevertheless, for these students we need a full continuum of services. For those placed in inclusive or general education classes, teachers should individualize their curriculum so that it meets their academic needs and presents the material in the students' preferred instructional mode. Classes that contain even one violent student should have at least two adults in attendance, whether it be another teacher, an aide, or an adult volunteer. However, what is the feasibility of providing the number of trained personnel needed to ensure benefits to the child with severe behavioural disorders being included?

All teachers have to devote some time to classroom control; typically about 10 percent of their time (Crealock, 1983). When a child raises classroom management from a chore to an obsession, disrupts the learning of other students, and demands too much teacher time, we must confront alternative programming for that child.

More restrictive placements include a regular classroom with a full-time or part-time aide; a regular classroom on a part-time basis with some special class placement; placement in a special classroom with some regular classroom integration; or full-time placement in a self-contained classroom. These should be considered temporary placements. The ultimate goal of segregation is rapid return to a regular classroom once the child has learned to behave less aggressively and less disruptively.

Educational Models

As we pointed out, the conceptual models from various disciplines are used to explain and treat behavioural disorders. Many programs relate to one specific model; studies support the belief that programs with a solid philosophical base and with staff who believe in that philosophy are the most likely to be effective (Beare, 1991). On the other hand, no single method has proven adequate in the management of all children who are behaviourally disordered and teachers select strategies from various models. An outline of common interventions related to the various conceptual models is shown in Table 8-4.

Psychotherapeutic Intervention (Psychodynamic Approach)

The psychotherapeutic approach holds that the guiding principles of psychoanalysis should be employed in educational intervention with children who have behavioural disorders. The essential element among the numerous theoretical orientations and practical approaches to psychotherapy is an attempt to relieve a child's distress and encourage development. Underlying this approach is the belief that traditional psychoanalytic concepts can be used to find the underlying causes of behavioural disorders and emotional disturbance. There is little value in changing a person's overt behaviour; instead, intervention should alter the underlying psychopathology by helping the person remember unfortunate experiences from infancy and early childhood. These memories provide insight, allowing the patient to come to grips with the causes of disturbed behaviour.

When translated into educational settings and intervention, therapists focus on uncovering the underlying psychology to improve a child's psychological functioning through revealing and relieving the child's unconscious psychic emotions and inner conflicts. The teacher's major concern is to help the child overcome inner turmoil rather than alter behaviours or focus specifically on academic skills.

Psycho-educational Approaches

When approaches are termed psycho-educational, the supportive atmosphere, concern for underlying problems, and therapies match psychotherapeutic models. But a far greater emphasis is placed on educational success; teachers focus on academic skills and work closely with therapists to come to the root of a child's problems.

Teachers are trained to focus on their students' positive learning goals rather than on their defects and problems. This philosophical framework leads to a more positive, learning-directed approach than many other forms of mental health treatment.

Behavioural Approaches

During the 1960s behavioural psychology was systematically incorporated into work with students with behavioural disorders. Today, behavioural approaches are the preferred intervention of many educators.

Behaviourists do not concern themselves with the deep-rooted probing of psychody-

Table 8-4 Approaches to intervention with students with behavioural disorders

Approach	Treatment	Sample of methods
Biological	Alter the child's physiology	Drug therapy; change in diet. The only intervention from the model of causation that has a research base is drug therapy.
Psychodynamic	Discover the underlying conflicts that cause problem behaviour	Various therapies and counselling techniques. Verbalization and clarification of previously repressed thoughts; corrective emotional experiences resulting from the child's relationship with understanding adults; presentation of alternate modes of behaviour.
Psycho-educational	Create trust while helping the child to meet academic goals	Therapies, crisis intervention, success in academic pursuits. Preventive classroom planning; permitting or sanctioning certain types of behaviour; tolerating behaviour beyond the child's control.
Behavioural	Rearrange environmental events. Focus on the behaviour, not the underlying causes	Reinforcers, punishments, time-out, contracts, and so on. Selecting instructional programs on the basis of objectives to be achieved through practice with reinforcement and measurement until criterion performance is reached.
Ecological	Change the nature of the interaction between the child and the environment	Counselling and a team approach. Crisis intervention; environmental modelling; curriculum planning. Identifying whatever norms happen to be used in the class setting; finding means for children to meet classroom goals.

namic approaches. Nor do behaviourists categorize children's behaviour as abnormal, evil, mysterious, or deviant. Rather, they assume that the same principles that guide the development of normal behaviour are involved in the development of inappropriate behaviour. That is, all behaviour is caused and controlled by environmental events outside the child. All behaviour is therefore observable, measurable, and subject to change through a change in the environment. With this in mind, behaviourists attempt to use the principles of behaviour therapy (behaviour modification) to alter the inappropriate behaviour. Examples of behaviours that can be modified include hyperactivity, aggressiveness, distractibility, bed wetting, excessive fearfulness, and harmful anxiety.

Three basic interrelated forms of treatment characterize the behavioural approach. The first uses teaching and training techniques to create behaviours that do not already exist. The second uses a number of techniques to maintain and generalize behaviours that are already established. The third uses other techniques to confine, reduce, or eliminate problem behaviour. Typically, all three modes of treatment are undertaken simultaneously.

Behavioural techniques can be simply conceptualized on the ABC rule. The procedures attempt to change the events (antecedents) that precede problems (behaviours) as well as the events that follow (consequences). Compliance is not the sole goal of a child's socialization. Changing antecedents and consequences means bringing about more appropriate behaviour, not just eliminating poor behaviour. This is referred to as the fair-pair rule, which states that when a behaviour is decreased teachers should select a desirable behaviour to increase at the same time.

Under the fair-pair rule two questions need to be addressed in developing procedure for behavioural changes: "What do I want the student to do instead?" and "What is the most effective and efficient means to help the student reach his or her goals?" Regardless of whether the student is withdrawn or aggressive, the first objective is to exhibit a positive response instead of the current behaviour; that is, give students a repertoire of appropriate responses rather than merely eliminating behaviours. For example, we may want a student to play with peers on the playground instead of playing alone and to play appropriately with groups instead of hitting peers during games. For both behaviour patterns, we have identified what we want the child to do instead of the current problem behaviour. Providing reinforcement for playing in a group may result in an increase in this behaviour along with a simultaneous and connected decrease in the inappropriate behaviour of hitting others.

Reinforcers (rewards) are used to increase desirable behaviour, and aversion techniques are used to decrease or extinguish undesirable behaviour. Reinforcement can be provided by anything that a child finds pleasurable. Reinforcers are usually divided into three types: primary reinforcers are candy and food; secondary reinforcers include objects that have no intrinsic value of their own, such as tokens and stars. Whether a child receives a primary or a secondary reinforcer, it is always accompanied by a social reinforcer such as a smile, a hug, or a pat on the back. Intervention is represented in Figure 8-2.

Selecting and using reinforcers is not as simple as it seems. As Mossish (1997) points out, the Achille's heel of the reward and consequences system is that it only works if children care about the rewards and the consequences. If children develop an immunity, they can defeat the system, as in, "Send me to the office. I don't care."

Still, positive reinforcement is far more effective than punishment, which is a poor deterrent to unwanted behaviour and should be used sparingly. Punishment generates students' anger, bringing greater conflict. Punishment does not answer the "why" of poor behaviour, does not teach appropriate behaviour, and does not suppress behaviour. In fact, it may lead to other unacceptable behaviours emerging, and may be used by children as a negative means of gaining attention from adults.

Some forms of behaviour modification are more suitable for general classrooms; others work better in self-contained settings. Token economies are widely used. The following profile, Class 7B, presents a token economy system employed with an entire class. Such systems are equally applicable to individual class members.

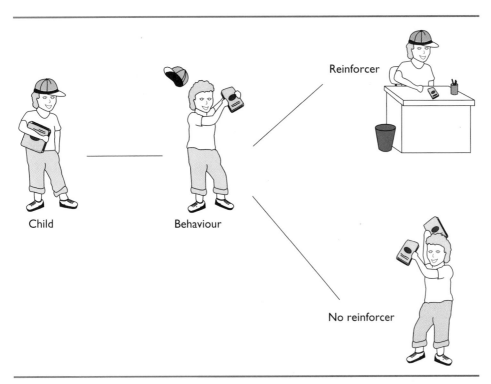

Figure 8-2
How reinforcement works

Reinforcer

No reinforcer

Profile

Class 7B

The grade seven class at the end of the hall was well known to all the students and teachers in the school. Any trouble, vandalism, or disruptive behaviour could generally be traced to that group of nine children. Although each child in the class was unique, they all behaved in ways that were unacceptable to the school and the community.

The children in this class had been punished so often that such disciplinary measures as detentions, time-out, and suspensions had little meaning for them. Indeed, such punishments usually resulted in increased resentment toward school personnel and an even more active dislike of learning. Rather than using further aversive measures, the grade seven teacher decided to institute a token-economy behavioural program.

Because of her students' age, the teacher invited and incorporated their suggestions for every step of the program. From some students, she won immediate co-operation. She decided to focus only on on-task behaviour because the students' problems were so diverse.

During the first weeks of the program, the children were told exactly how much seatwork would earn a token. For example, three math problems earned a poker chip. On Friday afternoon, students with ten chips could trade them in for a reinforcer, such as the viewing of a special film.

As the program continued, the teacher shaped her students' behaviour by making them work longer to earn tokens and by raising the token price of reinforcers. Wisely, she changed tokens and reinforcers often. She soon saw positive changes in behaviour, more on-task behaviour, increased learning, and a new sense of pride and achievement in the class.

Ecological Approaches

The usual positive aspects of life in school and community are not present for students with behavioural disorders. Ecological approaches focus on how a student functions in the classroom environment and on altering the match between the child and the environment. They use group processes such as discussion groups, class meetings, and role playing, and may also include the teaching of the social skills and adaptive interpersonal behaviours.

Role playing involves both emotional and cognitive components. Participants assume a specific role in a demonstration or simulation. Some students may perform better with a script that shows the roles played by the members, the sequence of activities, and the reward structure.

Teachers may use *bibliotherapy*, a procedure based on the concept that books serve a therapeutic purpose, especially for children with disabilities (Pardeck, 1990), and that reading stories with positive role models can affect an individual's attitudes and behavioural responses. Not only are books relaxing, but they help children work through a crisis, and they can help children see how others have confronted problems and gain insight into alternative solutions.

TVDRP (TV or other media, discussion, rehearsal, and guided practice) is another procedure used to assist students with behavioural disorders. TVDRP stresses self-control, group participation, social awareness, social decision making, and problem solving (Elias and Taylor, 1995).

Promoting Social Skills

Social skills are specific behaviours that people perform when interacting with others. Training in social skills is a particularly important academic feature for children with behavioural disorders because instruction helps children make and keep friends and get along with adults, and helps aggressive children to modify their behaviour (Weissberg and Allen, 1986).

In the classroom, a teacher can promote communication skills, prosocial skills, collaborative skills, and group maintenance skills. These include:

- Greeting behaviours;
- Ways to extend and receive invitations;
- Positive listening skills such as listening attentively, sharing and encouraging, and engaging in verbal and non-verbal interaction with others;
- Conversational skills, such as asking about other people's interests, responding to others' questions, and maintaining an extended conversation by taking turns to comment on a topic;
- Giving verbal and non-verbal compliments and positive feedback;
- Using positive methods of gaining teacher attention (for example, when asking about a work assignment);
- Acceptable habits of cleanliness, grooming, and health;
- The ability to inhibit reactions to stimuli to stem inappropriate outbursts;
- Self-management skills which enable children to select appropriate choices based on probable consequences.

When teachers are asked to rate social skills, they assign most importance to skills such as following rules and directions, volunteering answers, and interacting with teachers and peers about school work. Less important to teachers are skills involving conversation, initiating social contact with peers, and assertiveness.

The type of social skills that teachers perceive as critical for classroom success has implications for their selection of skills for intervention. But, as the range of social skills need to be addressed, the best way for teachers to determine which social skills to teach is to conduct informal natural observations (Cartledge and Kleefeld, 1989).

One way to promote social skills is to introduce a social interaction program within the context of the entire classroom. Alternatively, training can be directed solely at children who show deficits, with the training taking place in settings where the social behaviour would most naturally occur. Lessons are best implemented in groups of three to five students, which optimally include socially competent peers to serve as models. The first group lesson should focus on three things: an explanation of why the group is meeting, a definition of what social skills are, and an explanation of what is expected of each student during the lesson. It may also be helpful to implement behaviour management procedures for the group, such as contingencies for compliance and non-compliance. As lessons continue, it is important to prompt the students to use newly learned skills throughout the day and across settings to promote maintenance and generalization, and to reinforce the students when they use new skills (Lewis, Heflin, and DiGangi, 1991).

Quite a number of commercial programs have been developed for children and adolescents that incorporate effective methods of behaviour modification, modelling, role playing, feedback, and transfer of training. Skills range from how to have a conversation to learning to resist peer pressure. The Early Childhood Social Skills Program (Odom, Kohler, and Strain, 1987) is a well-validated procedure for normally developing children and those with developmental delays for classroom implementation. Skills include making offers and requests to share, offering play suggestions, making offers and requests to give assistance, showing affection, and giving compliments. There are two phases in the program—formal teacher instruction and practice. For instruction, the teacher places children in groups during play and teaches a skill. Sharing is the first skill taught. To teach, the teacher demonstrates the strategy and then monitors as all children perform. For adolescents, the ASSET program (Hazel, Schumaker, Sherman, and Sheldon-Wildgren, 1981), developed at the Kansas Institute for Research in Learning Disabilities, provides a set of training procedures to help students gain social interaction skills.

The teaching of social skills and fostering of children's social competence has become a major curriculum emphasis in both general and special education (Rutherford, 1997). The strategies employed in teaching social skills are varied, as are the targeted populations, and the rate of success (Fox, 1989). Intervention to increase social acceptance has been attempted with low-status children in regular classrooms (Bierman, Miller, and Stabb, 1987); with children labelled as mentally retarded, learning disabled, and behaviourally disordered (Zaragoza, Vaughn, and McIntosh, 1991), and with mildly disabled children integrated into regular classrooms (Sasso and Rude, 1987). Specifically for students with behavioural disorders, the effectiveness of social skills training effects have been modest at best and the long-term generalized effectiveness remains uncertain (Rutherford, 1997).

Curriculum

Coherent, comprehensive descriptions of educational programs for students with behavioural disorders are relatively rare in the professional literature. Nevertheless, the curriculum for students with mild disorders will generally parallel that for normal youngsters, although alternate methods for basic academic skills development may be required. To the extent that the curriculum is not a powerful enough tool, the teacher needs to compensate with other methods. For students with behavioural disorders, academic curricula must come to terms with their affective needs. Besides academic success, disturbed children need a warm supportive atmosphere that promotes an increase in self-esteem and self-concept.

In the area of ADHD, only a handful of projects have contributed to more effective educational practices. Research into behaviour management for students with ADHD has focused on increasing on-task behaviour, task completion, compliance, impulse control, and social skills, while reducing hyperactivity, off-task behaviour, and disruptive behaviour and aggression (Fiore, Becker, and Nero, 1993).

Social Intervention

Social intervention encompasses a variety of methods and services to help children with behavioural disorders and their families. Children's Mental Health Centres provide a range of treatment programs. Foster care may also be used to remove a child from home for a period of time. This can be done if the family is unable to cope with the child's behaviour or if the home atmosphere is considered to be damaging for the child.

SUMMARY

1. We use the term *behaviourally disordered* to describe children and youth who are meeting difficulties in adjusting to normal behavioural expectations.

2. While deviant behaviour has been conceptualized in many ways and definitions have been proposed from a variety of perspectives and disciplines, a universally accepted definition does not exist. The expectations of teachers and other observers play a key role in defining behavioural disorders.

3. While classification systems may use the severity system proposed in DSM-IV, it is most common today to establish clusters or dimensions of behaviour. Behaviour can also be seen as internalizing or externalizing.

4. Of the many variables contributing to human experience, none has been conclusively shown to underlie emotional problems, and many factors can lead young people to act out in ways that are unacceptable and reprehensible. Causes may be genetic, biophysical, disturbed family climate, deleterious environment, academic difficulties, faulty learning, and other school factors, to mention only a few. A combination of risks has far more negative effects on children than any single source of risk.

5. It would seem that the overt behavioural disorders would be easy to identify and define. This is not true. The most fundamental and pressing question in the field is how to find a precise definition for behavioural disorders. In identification, a major problem when evaluating behaviour centres on what is normal behaviour as opposed to what is abnormal in the classroom.

6. Children with conduct disorders attract attention with their overtly disruptive behaviours. Those who are anxious and withdrawn internalize their behaviour: they may exhibit nausea, pains, headaches, phobias, fears, obsessions, shyness, nightmares, crying, depression, self-consciousness, and withdrawal. Children with ADHD tend to be dis-

tractible and to spend more time in off-task behaviour than do their peers. Delinquent youth are shaped through contact with a variety of social and emotional factors that increase the likelihood that they will become or continue to be adjudicated offenders.

7. ADHD is a new focus for special education. With mounting research interest more children are being diagnosed, the term has entered educational parlance, and researchers are directing considerable attention to the condition.

8. Parents who rely on physical punishment to counter child aggression are likely to have children who are highly aggressive. Although aggression is a stable trait, the character of childhood aggression changes dramatically with age as do children's perceptions of what is hostile.

9. Teachers must be deeply concerned about children and youth who fail to comply with the demands of the school and the classroom and who indulge in various forms of criminal and antisocial behaviour outside the school environment. They must be aware that in our rapidly changing society the elements of delinquency and delinquent behaviour have changed.

10. One consistent finding is that antisocial children show poor academic achievement. Aggressive children are more likely to be disliked; they lack social skills and possess unfortunate personality traits that elicit dislike and rejection from others.

11. Faced with rambunctious, contrary, or unfocused children, some people leap to the conclusion that drugs can solve the problem. The use of psychotropic drugs to control behaviour and increase academic functioning is a matter of deep concern and considerable controversy.

12. Specialized therapies employ music, art, pet therapy, or other approaches.

13. Placement decisions must take into account the needs of the child as well as the boundary conditions—the classroom teacher and the other children in the class. Educators must determine the extent to which a student's learning or behaviour deviates from what is considered typical for age and grade; they must then address the teacher's tolerance and ability to deal with the child's difficulties. Many of these youngsters can be well served in regular classrooms provided teachers are given assistance regarding how to manage misbehaviour. No student should be removed from the regular class until it is clear that effective programming cannot be provided there.

14. All psychotherapeutic approaches search for the child's inner conflicts and motivations while trying to explain current or past events. Behavioural approaches are more concerned with producing desirable behaviour. The ecological approach to behavioural disorders emphasizes the need to look at the total interaction of the child with the social environment in order to know how the youngster's ecological system functions and how his or her behaviours fit or do not fit these ecosystems.

15. Those intervening with behaviourally disordered youngsters require a spectrum of different approaches and techniques. Teachers require a range of strategies and techniques and should be familiar with the components of all models.

16. Social acceptance involves more than tolerance. The use of skill-streaming instruction can increase prosocial and positive behaviour. Training includes skill identification, modelling, role playing, reinforcement, and generalization. The development of social skills has important implications for children's academic and vocational success as well as for long-term mental health adjustment.

In the Classroom

Profile: Gary

As a preschooler in nursery school, Gary aggressively bit, fought, and scratched his way through the program. He threw terrible temper tantrums, and did not stop throwing tantrums until he was about ten years old. He spent much of his time in elementary school ejected from the classroom or in the principal's office.

Gary seemed totally unresponsive to external pressure, whether in the form of a reward or punishment. In fact, it seemed the more he was rewarded, the worse he behaved and the less he learned. Likewise, the more he was punished, the worse he behaved and the less he learned.

During Gary's first year in junior high school, his disruptive behaviour, fighting, and irrational conduct led to a number of suspensions. His achievement was at a very low level, hardly surprising given his behavioural problems, his apparent lack of academic interests, and his resentment of school and authority. Gary had large gaps in reading skills, both for word attack and comprehension. His spelling was poor and creative writing exercises were beyond him. Only in math did he show any interest or potential.

By the middle of Gary's first year in junior high school, his behaviour had resulted in severe penalties. After he lit a fire on the school bus, he was transferred to a special class for children with problems. Even among this smaller group, Gary's behaviour continued to be outlandish. His achievement and academic interests were minimal, and he developed a more pronounced pattern of physical assault, swearing, truancy, and smoking.

Gary worked at math and achieved at level. During math periods, his behaviour was also relatively serene.

* * *

Managing children of any age, any grade, and any functional level can be a challenging and often frustrating task. No matter how well teachers manage their classrooms or centres, or how conscientious,

consistent, and fair they are, there will inevitably be some children who fail to respond as positively as others and who consistently test the teacher's authority.

Gary requires structured and consistent behavioural intervention in a supportive environment that offers much opportunity for success. However, developing successful behavioural interventions for a student such as Gary is a complex process that must take into account the child's motivation for misbehaving, his or her likes and interests, and positive as well as negative reinforcements. When devising an intervention program, it is critical that educators develop realistic goals for student behaviour. Initially, teachers may need to accept behaviours that would ordinarily be deemed inappropriate. For example, when a student exhibits explosive anger, a realistic first step might be to accept screaming or cursing as long as the child is not physically aggressive.

For students with behavioural disorders, placement is the critical issue. Before placement decisions are made, a teacher's tolerance must be considered. The match between teacher characteristics, including standards and tolerances, and a student's behavioural and learning needs must become a priority if difficult-to-teach students are to enjoy a reasonable opportunity to achieve success in regular class settings (Lundrum, 1992). Mismatches between teacher expectations and standards and child behaviour may result in teacher resistance. Decisions on inclusion must first ask whether we can place students without regard to the type and degree of condition, to the ability to behave appropriately in a regular classroom, to the educational benefits, and to the effect on other students.

These students are disliked by most of their peers. If a child's behaviour is so aggressive and disruptive that it entails active rejection and dislike for the child, then the regular classroom may be a more restrictive environment until the behaviour improves. Active rejection in a regular placement may only serve to further heighten the distress and lower the self-esteem of some students with behavioural disorders.

In the special placement, observations by Gary's teacher showed that his behaviour during math was calm, while his behaviour during reading or language was at its most violent. In light of this, the teacher mounted a two-pronged program to alter Gary's behaviour and improve his academic functioning.

Gary's classroom environment was changed so that students worked in cubicles on individual programs for the first half of the morning. At the same time, a token economy was established with the co-operation of all students in the class.

The teacher also decided to stress Gary's strengths in order to help his weaknesses. Reading, as a specific subject area, was eliminated from his timetable. Math became the fulcrum of Gary's education. For example, as Gary tackled math word problems, his reading comprehension improved; he later enjoyed writing math problems for the class. Math concepts, such as distance and scale, were extended to other areas, such as social studies.

Classroom Management

Controlling behaviour and teaching discipline and self-control are aspects of the broader construct referred to as *classroom management*. In general terms, classroom management refers to "the way in which teachers manipulate the classroom environment to minimize disruptions and give all children the optimum opportunity to engage in appropriate behaviour and reach learning and social goals" (Winzer, 1995, p. 627).

Classroom management includes curriculum planning, organizational procedures, resources, arranging the environment, maintaining child progress, and anticipating potential problems. Within the construct of classroom management, behaviour management refers to all the ways in which teachers control inappropriate and disruptive behaviour, as well as ways in which children are taught discipline and to control their own behaviour.

The word *discipline* derives from *disciple*, a follower of the master's teaching. **Discipline** means helping children to learn to guide their own behaviour in a way that shows respect and caring for themselves, other people, and the physical environment. Self-discipline involves being able to consider an outcome and select the behaviour that will achieve it (Glenn and Nelson, 1987). Discipline must be taught, learned, and internalized because discipline is necessary if the classroom and the children it contains are to function properly.

In classroom situations, there are three approaches to behaviour management—prevention, defusion, and follow up.

- *Prevention*. The best way to handle inappropriate behaviours is to prevent them from happening in the first place. **Preventative discipline** refers to strategies and procedures that militate against any discipline problems arising. Good preventative discipline includes providing a warm and interesting environment, logical routines, clear rules, much positive reinforcement, children's knowledge of consequences for misdemeanours, and a curriculum matched to the needs of the child. When the curriculum is meaningful and well presented, students are less inclined to engage in disruptive behaviour.

- *Defusion*. Defusion is an approach that is helpful with students who are continually confrontational (Colvin, Ainge, and Nelson, 1997). When students are confrontational, teachers need strategies that defuse the behaviour, rather than increasing it. They must not allow the student to pull them in the direction of confrontation or a cycle will be set in motion (Colvin, Ainge, and Nelson, 1997). Defusing strategies lessen the likelihood that the situation will escalate.

  For minor problems, ignore, redirect the student, or give a choice between behaviour and the loss of a privilege (Colvin, Ainge, and Nelson, 1997). State the rule or expectation, or request explicitly that the student "Take care of the problem."

In the presence of serious threatening behaviour, disengage and break the cycle of successive interactions by delaying responding. Delay—briefly look at the student, look at the floor, look detached, pause. Disengage—for example, say "Excuse me," and move to your desk and pick something up. Return to the student, redirect, and withdraw.

- *Follow up.* Defusion is not all that is needed; there must be later follow-up. This provides consequences for the behaviour and helps the student to find alternate ways of behaving. When following up, forgive and forget the past; do not allow past misdeeds to form the basis for present interactions. Convey the idea that you like the child even if you do not find the behaviour acceptable.

Extract from Gary's IEP

Name: Gary S.
Age: 12
Grade 7
School: Green Middle
Teacher: Mrs. Potts

PLACEMENT

At this time, Gary will be placed in a special class. He can return to the regular classroom when his aggressive and violent behaviour decreases.

NEEDS/ADAPTATIONS

No physical adaptations. Needs warm, supportive environment with structured program and much reinforcement. Intervention by counsellor.

LONG-RANGE GOALS

- To decrease/eliminate violent behaviour.
- To decrease aggressive behaviour and learn alternate responses to frustration.
- To follow reasonable adult requests.
- To decrease time required to begin assigned academic tasks.
- To implement a social skills program.

SHORT-TERM OBJECTIVES

- To learn alternate responses to aggression, such as ignoring, through role playing.
- To role play on following adult requests; to use token economy with daily child and teacher evaluation.
- To use a commercial social training package for social skills.
- To use a timer for beginning work on time.
- To learn to set goals for himself for each set of tasks.

EFFECTS OF BEHAVIOURAL DISORDERS	TIPS FOR TEACHERS
THE CHILD NEEDS SUPPORTIVE ENVIRONMENTS	Establish supportive interpersonal relationships with students.
	Try to create a warm atmosphere characterized by acceptance without permissiveness.

EFFECTS OF BEHAVIOURAL DISORDERS	TIPS FOR TEACHERS
	Bear in mind that each child is unique. Children must be treated as individuals regardless of their behaviour patterns.
	Allow older students to be involved in setting up reinforcement systems
THE CHILD NEEDS CONSISTENT EXPECTATIONS	The need for consistency is very high; whatever system of classroom management is used, it can be successful only if it is implemented in a systematic and consistent fashion. Provide clear expectations: students need to know what to expect of the teacher, what is expected of them, and what the consequences are for success and failure.
	Establish routines; set clear limits to behaviour.
	Make class rules sparingly. Remind students of the rules often.
	Be consistent. When teachers are consistent in enforcing rules, children learn self-control.
THE CHILD NEEDS MONITORING OF BEHAVIOUR AND LEARNING	Determine why the student is acting in a certain way. If you can discover what a child is trying to get with a behaviour, then you can find an alternative behaviour that meets the needs.
	Keep rigorous documentation of behavioural interventions.
THE CHILD COMMITS CHRONIC CLASSROOM MISDEMEANOURS	Keep a sense of humour.
	Share your problem students with a buddy. When you reach the breaking point, send the student to the buddy with something to do. Return the favour.
	Seat disruptive children among others who are well behaved.
	Remove objects or toys that cause problems.
	Keep a careful eye on scissors, pencils, and other potentially dangerous objects.
	Immediately remove the results of poor behaviour.
	Consider the timetable: if a certain time or subject seems to cause disruption, alter the scheduling.
	To eliminate aggression, eliminate the payoff for aggression; model and coach, create non-aggressive environments, and teach social skills.
THE CHILD IS CONFRONTATIONAL OR MAKES THREATS OF VIOLENCE	Develop the ability to show a flat face (no emotion).
	Give the student a change to save face and cool down. For example, "It's your call. Take a minute to think about it."

EFFECTS OF BEHAVIOURAL DISORDERS	TIPS FOR TEACHERS
	Send for help; get the names of participants and witnesses.
	Make the office aware of the incident.
	If in doubt, do nothing. Take a minute to think over the options.
	Provide models of non-aggressive responses to aggression-provoking behaviour.
	Provide reinforcement for non-aggressive behaviour; do not allow positive reinforcement for aggressive behaviour. For example, reward students when they are doing something well, even in the middle of misbehaving. For example, you might say "You're very angry and I appreciate that none of those books are going in the direction of people."
	If you step into an aggressive act, devote as much attention as possible to the victim and ignore the perpetrator as much as possible.
THE CHILD EXHIBITS A LACK OF ATTENTION, IS DISTRACTIBLE	Children with ADHD are driven by their interests. Increase interest in what they are working on.
	Provide high levels of feedback, praise, and reinforcement.
THE CHILD IS HYPERACTIVE	Be organized and consistent. Disorganized and chaotic classrooms can elevate hyperactivity in children, as can unpredictable classroom schedules.
THE CHILD EXHIBITS OFF-TASK BEHAVIOUR	Set a beeper to go off at various intervals. Every time the beeper sounds, students earn points if they are on task.
	Break up long lessons by changing the pace and allowing some physical movement.
	For ADHD students, teachers can hold attention for longer periods by facing the student and establishing eye contact.
	Use concrete aids such as flow charts, flip charts, and overhead projectors. Students may also attend more closely if they are provided with a lesson outline or a glossary of key terms prior to the lesson (Winzer, 1989).
	Children with intrinsic attention problems are difficult to handle in groups, and teachers may consider reducing the amount of time these students spend in group settings. Proximity control—seating the student near the teacher—may also help to sustain attention (Winzer, 1989).

EFFECTS OF BEHAVIOURAL DISORDERS	TIPS FOR TEACHERS
	Children need and respond to outside stimulation. Allow the child to move, doodle, or squeeze a small ball while in class. This can actually increase concentration. Seat the child in the front of the room.
THE CHILD EXHIBITS ANXIETY AND WITHDRAWAL	Help anxious, withdrawn, and immature children to view themselves more positively. Do not call on withdrawn students to answer questions unless they volunteer. When an anxious student does answer and makes a mistake, be supportive with "That's a good try," or "You almost made it," and move onto another student immediately.
THE CHILD EXHIBITS POOR ACADEMIC FUNCTIONING	Focus on academic skills. Provide children with experiences in which they can succeed. Use organizational folders Use thematic projects that allow children to pursue their interests and be active participants.
THE CHILD NEEDS TRAINING IN SOCIAL SKILLS	Teach social interaction skills. Ensure that students participate, as far as possible, in all aspects of school programs at the elementary and secondary levels. Involve the child's parents: make daily communication with the home or issue daily report cards.

WEBLINKS

The Challenge of Difficult Children **http://www.smu.edu/~egibson/**

Attention Deficit Disorder Library **http://qlink.queensu.ca/~3dw18/add.htm**

Canadian Professionals' ADD Centre **http://www.usask.ca/psychiatry/CPADDC.html**

Diagnostic and Statistics Manual Criteria for ADHD **http://www.chadd.org/dsm_iv.htm**

Canadian Journal of Behavioural Science **http://www.cpa.ca/ac-main.html**

SECTION 5

Children with Sensory Impairments

Hearing and vision connect us profoundly with our environment. Because of this, they are known as the distant senses. Even when we are not aware of it, and even when we are asleep, these two senses, especially hearing, keep us connected and in touch with the world. With this in mind, it is easy to realize how the loss of hearing or vision isolates an individual from family, friends, the community, and the physical environment. Nor is it surprising that such isolation has the potential to damage a person psychologically, socially, emotionally, and educationally. The greater the loss, the greater the potential isolation for the affected individual.

Few children of school age are completely blind or deaf. Far more common are children who see poorly or who are hard of hearing. As these hearing and vision problems are mild, many go undetected until children reach school age. Some children's problems are never identified, which places children at risk for being mislabelled as learning disabled or dismissed as dull, stupid, or lazy.

In areas that suffer from a lack of efficient identification procedures and appropriate services, such as rural or remote areas, children with vision or hearing problems are especially likely to go undetected. Among the Native population, for example, hearing and visual impairments are widespread; they are endemic throughout the Northwest Territories, and most prevalent in the eastern and central Arctic (Watters, 1980).

As we have found in much of contemporary special education, the education of students who are visually impaired or hearing disabled is beset with issues. For example, whether or not to stress braille in the education of students who are blind, the issue of bilingual education for those who are deaf, and the problems of curriculum and setting for those who are deaf-blind (see Chapter 14).

Of all the contentious issues, placements stand front and foremost. Many students with sensory impairments have moved from special institutions and schools to integrated programs within public schools where they may be supported by resource-room and itinerant-teacher programs. Nevertheless, the debate on inclusive schooling remains prominent.

Integrating students with sensory disabilities is challenging to teachers, especially when the student has a hearing impairment. Techniques and approaches to include hearing impaired or visually impaired students are, of course, quite different. The main difference is in language and communication: children with visual impairments use language to keep in contact with their environments; those with hearing impairments use visual means that may include speech reading and sign language.

CHAPTER 9

Children with Hearing Impairments

Historical Notes

It is to the Abbé Michel Charles de l'Épée (1712–1789), a French cleric, that people who are deaf owe their sign language. In 1760, de l'Épée opened a school for deaf students in his own home in Paris. At the outset, the abbé knew little about deaf people, their education, their language, or the impact of deafness. But as he studied his pupils closely, de l'Épée noticed that without any teaching or guidance, they evolved a language of simple signs by which to communicate. Building on these basic signs, he developed a system of what he called "natural signs." Then, to teach his students metaphysical and abstract concepts, as well as the grammar of French, the abbé also created a system of "methodological signs." In systematizing the signs into a structure, l'Épée provided persons who were deaf their own language of signs.

The first American teacher of students who were deaf, Thomas Hopkins Gallaudet (1787–1851), trained at l'Épée's school, the National Deaf Mute Institute, in Paris in 1816. When he returned to the United States, Gallaudet and a French teacher, Laurent Clerc, established the American Asylum for the Education and Instruction of Deaf and Dumb Persons in Hartford, Connecticut. In 1857, Gallaudet's youngest son, Edward, became president of the National Deaf Mute College in Washington, D.C. In 1864, the college, with Abraham Lincoln as patron, became a degree-granting institution. In 1893 its name was changed to Gallaudet College in memory of Thomas Hopkins Gallaudet. Now called Gallaudet University, the facility remains the world's foremost degree-granting institution for students who are hearing impaired.

The education of students who were deaf was the first form of special education to be undertaken in Canada. In 1829, Ronald McDonald, a reporter with the Montreal Gazette, was sent by the government of Lower Canada to train with Gallaudet in Hartford. In 1831, McDonald opened a school for deaf children in Champlain, Quebec, but lack of funds closed the establishment after only five years. Later, the Catholic Church in Quebec opened schools for deaf boys in 1848 and deaf girls in 1851.

The most prominent pioneer in the early history of Canadian special education was John Barrett McGann (1810-1880), who arrived in Toronto from Ireland in 1855. With assistance from Egerton Ryerson, McGann's work culminated with the

Ontario Institution for the Education and Instruction of the Deaf and Dumb, established at Belleville in 1870, and the Ontario Institution for the Education and Instruction of the Blind, at Brantford in 1872.

Residential schools to serve the needs of students with serious hearing impairments were eventually established in all provinces, and most remain today. Because deaf parents often prefer to send their children to residential schools, these facilities have helped foster the concept of a deaf community and a deaf culture (Meadow, 1980; Winzer, 1993).

Hearing loss is silent, painless, and invisible, one of the least recognized and most misunderstood disabilities. Severe and profound hearing loss (deafness) is a low-incidence condition; however, milder forms of hearing impairment (hard of hearing) are widely prevalent.

Most people think of deafness as simply a lack of sound, but this is one of the least of the problems. The greatest single result of serious hearing impairment is the concomitant impairment in communication skills. Hearing loss, a physical ailment, spills over to affect the development of speech and language, the most important components of interpersonal communication. As Helen Keller (1933) pointed out, deafness also means "the loss of the most vital stimulus—the sound of the voice that brings language, sets thoughts astir, and keeps us in the intellectual company of men" (p. 68). When Beethoven became hearing impaired, he wrote that he was "soon obliged to seclude myself and live in solitude" (Freeland, 1989, p. 1).

For children, hearing impairment poses a serious threat because hearing is so critical for learning. In normal child development, speech and language are acquired spontaneously and almost effortlessly. From their earliest days, normally hearing infants process language, preparing to become competent communicators. They have intact auditory processes on which to build an early mastery of the sound, shape, and sense of language. Babies do not merely listen passively to the language around them; they take in, process, and organize the language they hear and, like miniature linguists, they recreate for themselves the language of their culture. For babies who are deaf, life is devoid of sound effects and spoken script. Children who are hearing impaired do not hear the sounds made by themselves and others. They are isolated from the human voice, and this inevitably hinders or halts their acquisition of speech and language.

In the past, few children with serious hearing impairments were admitted to regular classrooms. However, the vigorous advocacy of the past 20 years on behalf of all children who are exceptional has wrought profound and fundamental changes in the particular area of the education of students with hearing impairments. Although provincially funded schools remain an important instructional vehicle, the current emphasis on appropriate integration with support services has meant shifts in program locations, student placements, and greater possibilities for regular class participation for youngsters who are hearing impaired.

Nevertheless, educational integration is an issue (only one of many) that remains beset with controversy. Many deaf people, advocacy groups, and some professionals working with students who are deaf reject the practice (see Rodda, Grove, and Finch, 1986) and see little benefit for students who are deaf within the present inclusive practices. The issue is intertwined with the continuing viability of deaf culture and the deaf community as well as with the mode of communication and bilingual education for young children who are deaf.

The Human Ear

The human ear, a truly marvellous instrument, is designed to collect sound, process it, and transmit it to be decoded in the brain. The ear is one of the most complex organs in the body, a triumph of miniaturization, fitting into a space not much larger than a hazelnut. It can detect sounds much softer than the dropping of a pin but still filter sounds a million times louder.

Hearing impairments are caused by interference with any part of the ear's transmission system. Impairment may take the form of restriction in the range of frequencies received, distortions along the frequency spectrum, or a failure to perceive sounds.

The ear's anatomy is usually discussed in terms of the external, the middle, and the inner ear. Figure 9-1 illustrates the major parts of the human hearing mechanism.

The External Ear

The outer ear is the visible cartilage structure on the side of the head, referred to as the **pinna**. This is the least complex part of the hearing mechanism and the least important for hearing. An external canal, or *meatus*, runs obliquely from the pinna to the ear drum. The ear drum, or **tympanic membrane**, is a tough, tightly stretched tissue that separates the outer from the middle ear. It is at the ear drum that hearing really begins.

The pinna serves to collect sound waves and filter them into the meatus. The external canal is lined with coarse hairs and four thousand wax glands that secrete cerumen. The wax traps insects, dust, and other irritants, guards against infection, and lubricates the canal and the ear drum. The ear drum is a concave mechanism that vibrates freely when struck by sound

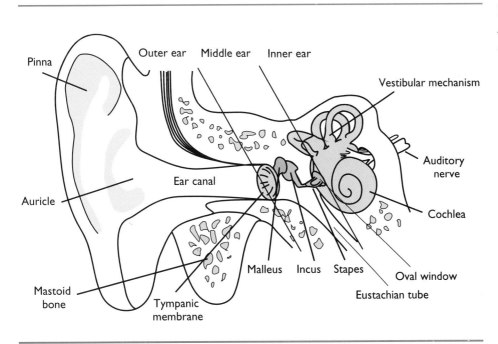

Figure 9-1
Anatomy of the human ear

waves. Even the faint vibrations of a whisper cause it to vibrate, but perhaps only a millionth of a centimetre.

The Middle Ear

The inner surface of the ear drum is located in the air-filled cavity of the middle ear. The middle ear drum surface holds three small bones, the *malleus*, the *incus*, and the *stapes*, also called the hammer, the anvil, and the stirrup. These tiny bones, the smallest in the human body, form a bridge, the *ossicular* chain, between the ear drum and the inner ear entrance at another drum called the oval window. There are two muscles in the middle ear, one joined to the stapes and the other to the ear drum. The **Eustachian tube** connects the middle ear to the nasopharynx.

In the middle ear, the transmission of sound becomes more sophisticated. When sound waves strike the ear drum, it vibrates and moves the three small bones. These bones transmit the vibrations across the middle ear cavity to the inner ear through the oval window. The middle ear amplifies the sound about 22 times, and also protects the inner ear from very loud noise.

The Eustachian tube serves to equalize the pressure on both sides of the ear drum. You may have experienced the discomfort of unequal pressure in an airplane descent. To clear the Eustachian tube, and to make the ears "pop," passengers yawn deeply, suck on hard candy, blow their noses, or swallow.

The Inner Ear

The inner ear, the real organ of hearing, is located in a cavern of the skull. It is about the size of a pea, an intricate mechanism with thousands of moving parts. Because it looks like a complex maze of passages, the inner ear is called the *labyrinth*. It contains the cochlea and the vestibular mechanism, which are independent in their functioning.

The **cochlea** is a tiny, snail-shaped structure filled with a fluid similar to cerebrospinal fluid. Its twisting interior is studded with thousands of microscopic hair cells, each one tuned to a particular vibration which responds to a particular fragment of sound. Within the cochlea are highly specialized structures, such as the organ of Corti and Reissner's membrane. The auditory nerve, which is about the diameter of a pencil lead and consists of more than 31 000 nerve fibres, relays messages to the brain (Clark and Tong, 1985).

Behind the cochlea lies the **vestibular mechanism**, composed of three fluid-filled semicircular canals. These loops of tubing are the organs of balance. Information regarding movement and balance is fed to the brain through the vestibular mechanism. Other nerve endings in the body also contribute to the sense of balance—those in the eyes, feet, muscles, and joints.

The intricacy of the inner ear structure is matched by the complexity of its function. When air-carried (conducted) sound pushes on the ear drum, it causes the stapes to vibrate on the oval window leading to the inner ear, which makes the fluid in the cochlea begin to move. A low-pitched sound pushes at the top of the cochlea and a high-pitched sound at the base. For example, if middle C is sounded, then the cochlea's middle C hair cells vibrate, waving in the fluid. The waving produces a wisp of electricity that feeds into the auditory nerve and is transmitted to the brain. There the signal is unscrambled and converted into meaningful sound. An overview of the sequence is provided in Table 9-1.

Table 9-1 The sequence of hearing

---

1. Sound waves enter the ear, travel through the external canal, and vibrate the ear drum.

2. The vibrations of the ear drum move the bones of the middle ear.

3. The footplate of the stapes moves the oval window and sets the cochlear fluid in motion.

4. The movement causes the hairs immersed in the cochlear fluid to move. This stimulates the attached cells to send a tiny electrical impulse along the fibres of the auditory nerve to the brain.

5. In the brain, impulses are translated into meaningful sound.

Most sound travels on air (air conduction). With bone conduction of sound, sound travels directly through the jawbone and the mastoid bone to the inner ear fluid. Because we hear our own voices by bone conduction, we hear ourselves quite differently from how our listeners hear us and often have trouble recognizing our own voices on a tape recorder.

Definitions of Hearing Impairment

The broad category of *hearing impairment* stretches from marginal hearing losses that may only be a real concern in noisy situations to profound deafness where individuals cannot hear voiced sounds, even with amplification (hearing aids), and must resort to speech reading and, often, sign language. A number of definition and classification systems are used in the field of hearing impairment.

A general definition states that:

- *Hearing impairment* is a generic term indicating a hearing disability that may range in severity from mild to profound. It includes the subsets of deaf and hard of hearing.

- A *deaf* person is one whose hearing disability precludes successful processing of linguistic information through audition, with or without a hearing aid.

- A *hard-of-hearing* person is one who, generally with the use of a hearing aid, has residual hearing sufficient to enable successful processing of linguistic information through audition.

Classification of Hearing Impairments

The distinction between deaf and hard of hearing is not as clear-cut as the above definitions imply. Both groups are heterogeneous, and subcategories of each are often used.

The classifier's orientation often determines the system of classification. Those with a strictly physiological perspective are interested primarily in the measurable degree of hearing loss. On the other hand, educators want to know how hearing impairment will affect a child's functioning. Because hearing loss is closely linked to language delay, educators tend to categorize chiefly on the basis of language ability.

Four major, though closely interrelated, classification systems for hearing impairment are in use. These are founded on the degree of hearing impairment, the cause, the site of the deficit, and the age at which the impairment developed. Table 9-2 shows the classification of hearing impairments.

Classification by Severity Levels

Hearing loss is classified according to the amount of hearing (acuity) in a person's better ear. Acuity is measured by the subject's response to loudness across a range of frequencies. Decibels and hertz are used to measure loudness and frequency, respectively. Individuals are classed as deaf or hard of hearing depending on whether they hear sounds at certain intensities of loudness across a range of frequencies. This classification is further structured by designation as mild, moderate, severe, or profound hearing loss. Table 9-3 illustrates the levels of hearing impairment.

A *bel*, named after Alexander Graham Bell, is the unit of loudness intensity. Each bel is broken down into ten parts, known as decibels (dB). A **decibel** represents the smallest difference in loudness intensity that can be perceived.

Hearing loss is measured on a decibel scale, beginning with 0 dB, a figure that designates the point at which people with normal hearing can detect the faintest sound. Inability to hear sounds of 25 to 30 dB or more is considered to be a hearing loss. However, a loss of 60 dB is not merely six times greater than a loss of 10 dB. The figures are logarithmic, not arithmetic, so that 60dB is 10^6 times louder than 10dB. Figure 9-2 shows the decibel (dB) level of some common sounds on an audiogram, a chart on which hearing is recorded.

Sound waves are produced by the to-and-fro waving movement of molecules. One complete to-and-fro movement makes a cycle; the number of cycles per second determines the frequency of a sound. Cycles per second are measured in hertz (Hz)—a frequency of 1 000 Hz indicates 1 000 cycles per second. As the frequency increases, the pitch of the sound becomes higher.

Although the human ear is sensitive to frequencies between 50 Hz and 20 000 Hz, most human speech falls between 500 and 2000 Hz. This range of pitch is known as the **speech range**. Middle C on a piano is about 500 Hz.

Classification by Site of Loss

Hearing impairment is also classified according to the part of the hearing mechanism that is affected. Problems in the mechanical transmission of sound waves through the outer and middle ear are called **conductive hearing losses** because something stops the air conduction of sound. Conductive losses generally affect the intensity of sound reception but do not distort the sound. Most conductive losses, affecting the outer and middle ear only, usually respond favourably to medical or surgical intervention.

Impairment in the inner ear is caused by abnormal sense organs (sensory) or defective auditory nerves (neural). These **sensorineural hearing impairments** interfere with the conversion of sound waves into neural impulses for the brain. Not only is sound intensity hampered, but any sound received may also be distorted. Sensorineural hearing loss is most common among children with serious losses.

Table 9-2 Classification of hearing impairment

Severity	Time of onset	Etiology	Site
mild	prelingual	congenital	conductive
moderate	post-lingual	adventitious (deafened)	sensorineural
severe			
profound			

Table 9-3 Levels of hearing impairment

Range	Severity	Implications
0–25 dB	insignificant	
25–40 dB	mild hearing loss; hard of hearing	May have difficulty with faint or distant sounds. May have problems in conversations, groups, or settings with much ambient noise.
40–60 dB	moderate hearing loss; hard of hearing	Frequent difficulty with normal speech, especially in conversations, groups, and class discussions.
60–90 dB	severe hearing loss; hard of hearing	Great difficulty with even loud or amplified speech, which seems faint and distorted. Requires amplification and intense speech and language training.
90 dB+	profound hearing loss; deaf	May be aware of loud sounds and vibrations, but generally cannot understand even amplified speech.

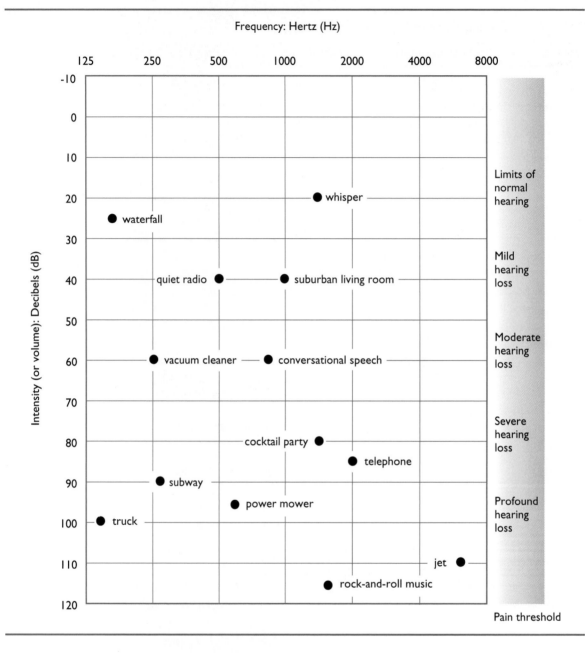

Figure 9-2
Chart showing the hearing level of some common sounds

Classification by Etiology

A **congenital hearing impairment** is one that is present at birth; an **adventitious hearing impairment** is acquired some time after birth, through accident or disease. People with adventitious hearing losses are sometimes described as *deafened*.

Classification by Age of Onset

Closely connected to the classification of adventitious and congenital hearing impairment is that concerned with age of onset. Children with **prelingual deafness** are those who were deaf prior to the development of speech and language. Children with **post-lingual deafness** became deaf after the development of speech and language. The cut-off point is often set at two years of age (Meadow, 1980). Note that fewer than one child in ten loses hearing after the age of two.

Children with prelingual (congenital) hearing losses do not have the opportunity to practise the listening skills essential to developing speech and language. Inevitably, prelingual impairment affects every aspect of communication development from birth onwards. Children who acquire hearing impairments after they develop speech and language usually find it easier to develop communication skills. The later in life an impairment occurs, the greater the child's linguistic capabilities are likely to be.

Prevalence of Hearing Impairments

Approximately one in ten Canadians, or about two million people, have some form of hearing impairment. Perhaps one in 40 has an impairment serious enough to affect daily life and communication, and one in four hundred, or about fifty thousand, suffers from profound deafness. Hearing loss among the aged is especially common. Serious hearing problems affect one in ten people over 65 years of age, and four out of every ten over 75 (Ontario, Ministry of Health, 1978).

Hearing loss is most tragic when it strikes the very young. Its incidence at birth is quite low, however. About one infant in every 1 000 is born profoundly deaf, or is deaf before the age of three. But when infants with mild losses are included, the numbers go as high as one in 750 (Ruppert and Buhrer, 1992).

It is extremely difficult to arrive at a true determination of the prevalence of hearing impairment, and estimates vary considerably. One widely accepted estimate holds that five percent of school-aged children have hearing outside the normal limits. Of this number, 10 to 20 percent require some type of special education ("Children with communication ...," 1995).

Of the many factors that hinder researchers from arriving at accurate prevalence and incidence figures for hearing loss, the most important are

- Inconsistent definitional data.

- Confusion regarding identification and reporting.

- Methodological problems in surveys. For example, after comparing surveys in Canada and the United States, Jerome Schein (1994) found that hearing impairment in the United States has a prevalence rate of 86 per 1 000 as compared to 41 per 1 000 in Canada, which reflects the younger overall age of the Canadian population. Schein also found that rates vary considerably across the Canadian provinces from a low of 34 per 1 000 in the Northwest Territories to 61 per 1 000 in Prince Edward Island and Manitoba.

- Difficulties in accurate early identification of hearing loss.

- Increasing prevalence of hearing impairment with age.

- Difficulties in estimating hearing impairments among individuals with multiple disabilities, who are often reported according to their primary disability.

- A shortage of research in some areas. An extensive body of research deals with deafness; much less exists in relation to hard-of-hearing individuals. While hard-of-hearing children are much more common, their true numbers are unknown, as many cases are misdiagnosed or simply overlooked.

Etiology of Hearing Impairments

Etiological and diagnostic considerations in hearing impairment are the venue of medical and paramedical personnel. Audiologists are chiefly involved in the assessment of hearing and in recommending and fitting amplification equipment. Otolaryngologists are medical personnel concerned with the problems of the ear, nose, and throat that affect hearing and speech. They also handle voice disorders through medication and surgery.

Impairments of the Outer Ear

External otitis, or swimmer's ear, is an infection of the skin of the external auditory canal. Also in the canal, an excessive build-up of wax can result in decreased hearing acuity. Infrequently, a child is born with missing or undeveloped auditory canals. This condition, known as *auditory atresia*, interferes with the air conduction of sound and requires medical or surgical intervention before it impedes a child's education. *Microtia* refers to a misshapen or extremely small pinna. Perforation of the ear drum, resulting from any number of causes, can also produce hearing impairment.

Impairments of the Middle Ear

Middle ear hearing impairments are more serious than those affecting the outer ear, but most are surgically correctable. The great majority of middle ear conditions are conductive hearing losses, meaning that the conduction of sound by air is hindered. The result is a loss of intensity of sound, though not usually a distorted pattern. Conductive losses do not exceed 65 dB.

The most common form of ear infection in children is **otitis media**, a condition in which the mucosal lining of the middle ear becomes inflamed and the cavity filled with fluid. Infections use the Eustachian tube to reach the middle ear from the nose or throat.

Otitis media is most extreme in infancy, when the Eustachian tube is shorter, wider, and in a more horizontal position. It is estimated that 50 to 75 percent of children have one episode of otitis media in the first year of life (Roberts, 1997). The peak prevalence for otitis media is between 6 and 36 months (Bluestone, 1982). After six years of age, the incidence steadily decreases. However, in the normal school environment, 20 to 30 percent of children between the ages of 5 and 12 will have at least one bout of middle ear effusion. Of these, 10 to 20 percent will probably develop chronic middle ear problems (Brooks, 1977).

Otitis media is more common in some groups than others. It is found more often in males than in females. The prevalence is higher among lower socio-economic groups, in children with cleft palates, and in those with other cranio-facial anomalies. Children with Down syndrome are especially susceptible to otitis media and its resulting conductive hearing loss (Whitman, Simpson, and Compton, 1986).

Researchers have also found a higher prevalence among Native children, but a lower prevalence among Blacks (Robinson, Allen, and Root, 1988). When Scaldwell and Frame (1985) examined children in six Ontario Native communities, they found a higher incidence of otitis media among school-aged children. The reasons for the higher prevalence among Natives is unclear but it may be a combination of genetic, socio-cultural, environmental, and economic factors (McShane, 1982).

Otosclerosis is a hereditary condition characterized by the destruction of the capsular bone in the middle ear and the growth of a weblike bone that attaches to and restricts the stapes. Otosclerosis, which is twice as common in females as in males, affects two percent of the population and is clinically active in more than 0.5 percent ("Hearing loss," 1982). The condition is rare in children and is not usually noticed until adolescence or the early twenties. Resultant hearing losses can be at the 50 or 60 dB level, necessitating the use of a hearing aid or corrective surgery.

Other middle ear problems can be caused by blows to the head or a fall. They can also result from congenital defects.

Impairments of the Inner Ear

The most devastating hearing impairments are caused by sensorineural problems of the inner ear. While a great many childhood sensorineural impairments are attributed to "causes unknown," in recent years the five major causes of sensorineural deafness have been heredity, maternal rubella, meningitis, mother–child blood incompatibility (Rh factor), and prematurity. The most profound losses stem from meningitis, maternal rubella, and hereditary factors.

Estimates of the number of children with hearing loss due to hereditary factors range from 30 to 60 percent (Moores, 1982). There are about 65 types of hereditary deafness. Hearing problems may be inherited on a dominant trait (14 percent), a recessive trait (44 percent), or as a sex-linked disorder (2 percent) (Lowenbraun and Thompson, 1982). Hearing loss can be inherited alone or in combination with other abnormalities in a syndrome. Hearing loss accompanies skeletal deformities in Treacher-Collins syndrome and abnormal skin pigmentation in Waardenburg's syndrome, and it is sometimes part of the multiple disabilities of Down syndrome. Approximately four to five percent of congenitally hearing-impaired individuals suffer from Usher's syndrome, which results in hearing impairment and a progressive deterioration in the visual field through retinitis pigmentosa (see Chapter 14). Pendred's syndrome and Jervell and Lang-Neilson syndrome are also associated with hearing impairment.

Maternal rubella is the most common identifiable cause of deafness from an external source. Rubella (German measles) is acquired by pregnant women via an airborne virus. The infection may cause the child to be born with hearing loss, defective vision, heart irregularities, and disorders of the nervous system. Children whose hearing impairment is due to rubella may show progressively more severe hearing loss as they grow (Anvar, Mencher, and Keet, 1984). There may also be a late onset of other disabilities, such as strabismus.

Meningitis is a major cause of acquired sensorineural hearing loss because the high fever that accompanies the disease is very dangerous to the inner ear. Incompatibility of blood type between mother and infant may also cause hearing impairment, along with several other disorders.

Prematurity itself does not cause deafness. However, premature and low-birth-weight babies are at higher risk for hearing disorders. Deafness can also result from birth complications such as prolonged labour, abrupt birth, or the use of obstetrical instruments. Failure to breathe immediately after birth—apnea—is another commonly reported cause of hearing problems.

Among adults, progressive nerve deterioration, known as *presbycusis* (deafness of age), is the most common cause of auditory defect. The older one gets, the more one is prone to presbycusis. As well, inner ear fistula (a build-up of inner ear fluid), acoustic neuroma (tumour on the auditory nerve), and viral infections and vascular spasms in the inner ear can cause permanent or temporary Sudden Hearing Loss Syndrome. Intracranial tumours, cerebral hemorrhages, and prolonged exposure to tones of high intensity are also increasingly recognized as causes of sensorineural hearing loss. Ménière's disease, a condition characterized by nausea, vertigo, and tinnitus, is a particularly devastating problem for adults.

Both deaf and hearing individuals can suffer from tinnitus. The word derives from Latin, meaning to "tinkle or ring like a bell." For some sufferers it may be hearing a ringing or a hiss, but for others it is living constantly with the noise of a squeaking door hinge, the squealing of an unoiled metal bearing, or the sound of fingernails being dragged across a blackboard (Agnew, 1986). The chronic nature of the condition causes great distress and becomes the central issue in the lives of some affected people.

Tinnitus is not an audiological phenomenon but a medical condition. The actual mechanism is not known. Tinnitus does not have a specific site of origin; it can be produced anywhere along the auditory mechanism, or it may not be generated by the auditory system at all. Anything that can go wrong with the ear may have tinnitus associated with it as a symptom—wax against the drum, tumours on the nerve, otosclerosis, Ménière's disease, and exposure to excessively loud sounds (Agnew, 1986).

Prevention of Hearing Impairments

If you were to take a casual survey of a hundred people and ask who had had a medical checkup, dental checkup, eye examination, or hearing assessment in the past 12 months, only a very few would mention a hearing test. Why? Because in North America we pay less attention to hearing loss than to almost any other medical condition. But we ignore our hearing at our own risk. Certainly, not all hearing loss can be prevented, but increased awareness can serve to prevent or ameliorate many problems.

People should be aware that noise levels sufficient to cause hearing damage are a growing problem in society. For example, a power lawnmower emits 100 dB, a subway train 90, a riveting gun 130, and a jet take-off 105 or more. Modern music also causes hearing impairments: rock bands often reach 115 dB. Muscles in the middle ear protect the inner ear from excessively loud low-pitched sounds, but no such action protects the ear from the new high-pitched sounds.

The problem of foreign objects in the ear has always existed and probably always will. Nature designed the ear to clean itself. An old saying claims that if a finger were intended to go in the ear, it would have been made small enough to fit. Unfortunately, many other things do fit—the ends of pencils, beads, carrots, peanuts, and bobby pins. Even cotton swabs can do enormous damage, either by puncturing the paper-thin ear drum or pushing accumulations of wax further into the ear.

For acquired deafness, problems associated with mother–child blood incompatibility have decreased since the 1968 advent of anti-Rh gamma globulin (RhoGam). If injected into the mother within 72 hours of birth, she will not produce the antibodies that can harm later infants. A rubella vaccine, developed in 1968, is given to preschool children. A vaccine to prevent some forms of meningitis in children has also been developed.

Identification and Measurement

Measuring a hearing impairment is quite complicated because measurement must incorporate the physical, psychological, and educational aspects as well as the impact on speech and language acquisition and development (see Table 9-4). To assess the various domains, a number of professionals and paraprofessionals need to be involved—physicians, audiologists, psychologists, educators, and speech and language therapists.

Table 9-4 Assessment of children with hearing impairments

Audiological	Psycho-educational	Communication/educational
Sweep test	WISC–III (Performance scale)	Language sampling—spontaneous and elicited
Pure-tone audiometry	Leiter International Performance scale	Tests of oral and written language
Auditory brainstem evoked response	Goodenough–Harris Draw-a-Person Test	General standordized tests in reading and math
Reflex audiometry	Raven's Progressive Matrices	
Impedence audiometry		
Play audiometry		
Speech audiometry		

Measurement of Hearing Loss

Audiology is the science of detecting and correcting hearing impairment. The major purposes of audiology are to assist in medical diagnosis; to provide an overall assessment of hearing in order to ascertain the need for supportive services; and to detect changes in hearing that may have resulted from exposure to hazards.

Audiologists use many sophisticated methods to assess hearing. In general, three major categories of hearing tests are used—pure tone audiometry, speech audiometry, and specialized tests for very young and difficult-to-assess children.

Screening

The most common screening procedure is the sweep test, which uses a portable audiometer to present tones at 20 to 25 dB across a range of frequencies. Children who show problems at the screening level are then referred for in-depth audiological testing.

Screening may not identify all children requiring in-depth assessment. School screening has been known to fail to identify at least half of children with otitis media (Gdowski, Sanger, and Decker, 1986), and especially children who suffer a recurrent "on-again, off-again" otitis media and therefore present inconsistent responses. Screening may also fail to detect students with high-frequency losses.

It is estimated that 80 percent of children with hearing impairments are identified through informal means, usually observations by parents or teachers (Barringer, Strong, Blair, Clark, and Watkins, 1993). Table 9-5 outlines some of the behaviours that suggest mild hearing loss. Teachers and parents should be alert to these behaviours and send children with suspected problems for audiological evaluation.

Pure Tone Audiometry

An individual's degree of hearing loss, measured in decibel and hertz units, can be ascertained through pure tone audiometry, a procedure designed to establish an individual's **threshold of hearing** at different frequencies. A threshold of hearing is the level at which a person first detects a sound.

The procedure for pure tone testing is relatively simple. The audiologist presents a variety of tones at levels from 0 to 110 dB across a range of frequencies, usually 125 Hz to 8 000 Hz, testing each ear individually. The person being tested responds by raising a hand when a sound is detected, and the data for each ear are plotted on a chart of hearing called an **audiogram**. Figure 9-3 shows an audiogram on which is plotted the average loss (both ears) of three individuals.

Person A has a flat loss of about 70 dB. In other words, Person A only begins to detect sounds at the level of 70 dB and would be regarded as moderately hearing impaired. Because of the amount of residual hearing, especially across the speech range (500 to 2 000 Hz), a hearing aid would help this individual.

Person B suffers a hearing loss described as a "ski slope loss" because of its shape. This person, with little usable hearing above 90 dB and none across the speech range, would be categorized as profoundly deaf. Person C displays a saucer-shaped audiological pattern, which

---

Table 9-5 Possible signs of mild hearing loss in children

- There appears to be a physical problem associated with the ears, such as buzzing, earaches, discharge, or frequent colds and sore throats.
- The child has poor articulation, particularly missing some of the consonant sounds.
- The child cocks the head or turns the body toward the speaker in an obvious effort to hear more accurately.
- The child has more than usual trouble in following directions.
- The child frequently asks for information to be repeated.
- The child appears to be inattentive when spoken to in a normal voice.
- The child speaks or sings too loudly or too softly.
- The child talks too much and appears not to want to relinquish control of the conversation.
- The child is withdrawn and unwilling to mingle with classmates or neighbours.
- The child gives incorrect answers to simple questions.
- The child is functioning below potential ability in school.
- The child is becoming a behaviour problem at school or at home.

Figure 9-3
Audiogram

a number of researchers (e.g. Anderson, Barr, and Wedenberg, 1970) have found common in children with hearing loss due to rubella.

Speech Audiometry

Speech audiometry is designed to assess an individual's ability to detect and understand speech. The *speech detection threshold* refers to the intensity level at which a person can hear, but not necessarily understand, speech. Much more important is the **speech reception threshold** (SRT), the level at which an individual actually understands speech.

To ascertain the speech reception threshold, the tester presents the person with a list of two-syllable words (called *spondees*) that have equal stress on each syllable—*baseball* or *ice cream* are examples. Each ear is tested separately, and the level at which half of the words are understood is the speech reception threshold.

Tests for Young Children

Pure tone audiometry can only be used with people who understand what is expected of them. The diagnostic process requires a person to discriminate among sounds of different intensity and tone and then communicate their discriminations. For a child under the age of about four, the process is too complicated. So that hearing impairment can be identified as early as possible, a number of special tests have been devised for very young children. Special tests have also been developed for those whose disabilities do not suit standard pure tone audiometric testing. The two most common forms of specialized hearing tests are electrophysiological and behavioural assessments. (See also Chapter 14.)

Electrophysiological Assessment

Electrophysiological procedures include electroencephalography-evoked (EEG) response audiometry (also known as auditory brainstem evoked response) and impedance audiometry. EEG assessment measures responses to auditory stimuli but requires no active participation on the part of the child. In this relatively new approach, electrodes are attached to the scalp, sounds of varying intensities are delivered through an earphone placed over the infant's ear, and brainwave activity is recorded. By evaluating the brainwave patterns, an estimate of hearing, or hearing loss, can be made (Murray, 1988).

Acoustic impedance audiometry assesses conductive hearing losses by measuring the movement of the ear drum and middle ear muscles and bones in response to auditory stimulation (Northern, 1980). The audiologist can detect fluid in the middle ear, a sign of otitis media, for example.

Behavioural Assessment

Behavioural testing includes observation of behaviour and reflexes and play audiometry. Infants show an orienting response by turning their heads toward the source of a sound. Diagnosticians can therefore gain a crude measure of hearing status by observing infants' reactions to loud sounds. Under the age of five or six months, infants also display reflexive behaviours that are useful for testing hearing. A startle movement, a reflex that affects face, arms, trunk, legs, and eyes, is present at birth and elicited by loud sound.

Play audiometry is used with children over two years of age. It involves an audiometer and a game in which the child performs an activity in response to the sound. The child may respond by building a stacking toy, dropping blocks into a box, or putting pieces into a puzzle.

Psycho-educational Assessment

A range of measures is needed to assess the psychological and educational functioning of students with hearing impairments. The one commonality among tools and procedures is that they circumvent the effects of the hearing loss and match the linguistic deficits of the child.

Non-verbal tests are the most appropriate for children who are deaf. The most widely used IQ test is the Performance Scale of the Wechsler Intelligence Scale for Children (WISC-III), which is believed to yield fairly valid IQ scores for children who are deaf aged nine to sixteen. The Verbal Scale is usually omitted from the battery, and an IQ score is calculated on the basis of the Performance Scale alone.

Other popular measures include the Goodenough Harris Drawing Test (Harris, 1963) and Raven's Progressive Matrices (Raven, 1948) for children nine years of age and older. The Leiter International Performance Scale (Leiter, 1948) has remained popular for young children because it can be administered by pantomime and needs no verbal cues or responses.

Critical among educational measures are those assessing speech and language. General types are shown in Table 9-4.

Developmental Consequences of Hearing Impairments

The major handicap of hearing impairment is its impact on the development of speech and language. This can, and often does, spill over to adversely affect other developmental domains.

Cognitive Development

The cognitive development of individuals who are hearing impaired is a provocative and challenging area of research. Studies dating back to the nineteenth century have considered IQ levels, the relationship between language and thought, concept acquisition and development, perceptual processes, and memory function. As 150 years of research findings accumulated, ideas about the cognitive development of individuals with hearing impairments changed, sometimes quite dramatically.

For example, studies before 1950 showed school children who were deaf to be three or four years behind hearing children and about ten IQ points below the norm (Meadow 1980). However, the reason for past perceptions of poorer intellectual development lay not within the child but in the testing procedures used. When testing procedures are matched to their linguistic capabilities, students with deafness score within the normal range of the performance scales on tests of mental ability. In general, the hearing-impaired population fits on the same curve for intelligence as does the rest of the population (Quinsland and Vanginkel, 1990).

The relationship between language and thought has fascinated psychologists for decades, and different views have emerged. Benjamin Whorf (1956) took an extreme view, holding that

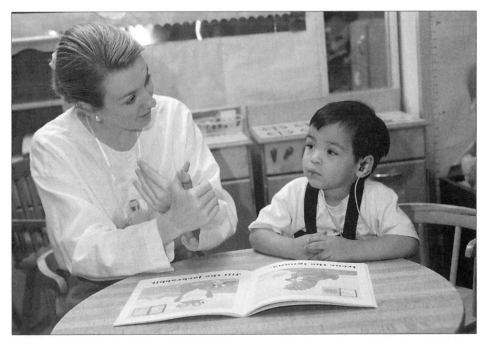

Students with hearing impairments have special needs in the classroom.

thought could not really exist without language. Jean Piaget characterized language as "the handmaiden of thought," but Jerome Bruner gives it a central place in cognitive development.

If cognitive development is not dependent on language, then one would expect children who are hearing-impaired, despite their linguistic deficits, to develop the same abilities in much the same manner as hearing children. Some researchers have found that children who are deaf consistently demonstrate the same thinking processes as hearing children when the tasks involved are not dependent on language (Furth, 1966, 1971). In a study using Piagetian tasks with preschoolers, Bond (1987) found children with hearing impairments to lag slightly but not significantly behind hearing children. Others have found that children who are deaf and who have acquired some language consistently outperform those with less language ability (Schlesinger and Meadow, 1972; Silverman, 1967).

Studies of the performance of children who are deaf on memory tasks show conflicting results. For example, children are more likely to retain words that have a sign equivalent than words that do not, and they are more likely than hearing children to remember geometric forms better than digits.

Early researchers (e.g. Mykelbust, 1960) argued that the perceptual and conceptual processes of children with congenital deafness failed to develop normally. Persons who were deaf were said to lack abstract thinking capacity and to function normally only if restricted to concrete activities. While recent comparisons of concept formation and abstract thinking skills between hearing-impaired and normally hearing children yield somewhat inconsistent results, many educators and researchers now accept that children who are deaf can think logically without a linguistic system. Braden (1987), however, asserts that all children who are deaf suffer metacognitive deficits. These may result in part from the memorization, drill and rote learning so characteristic of programs for the education of students who are deaf.

Communication Development

Speech and language are the areas of development most severely affected by a hearing impairment. Deficits vary considerably as a result of many factors. These include the degree of hearing loss, the training and use of residual hearing, the child's age at the impairment's onset, the etiology of the impairment, the family climate, the early mode of communication, and the educational setting.

For children with mild or moderate hearing losses, the effect on speech and language may be minimal. Communication for the child who is hard of hearing has more in common with that of the normally hearing child than with that of the child who is deaf, because both hearing and hard-of-hearing individuals use audition rather than vision as the primary mode for speech and language development (Berg, 1986). Children who are hard of hearing use their residual hearing to develop speech and language, and so they use spoken language adequately to transmit and receive information although they may speech read as a supplement to auditory skills.

Even so, children who are hard of hearing may still be at risk for educational failure. Some research suggests that a mild to moderate hearing loss (10 to 40 dB) impairs the listening performance of a young child to the extent of becoming an auditory handicap (Gdowski, Sanger, and Decker, 1986). Moreover, many environmental variables such as extraneous noise, the distance from the speaker, and even the child's language capacity can adversely affect a child's auditory comprehension.

There is conflicting evidence about the effects of early otitis media on speech and language development. It does seem that otitis media causes temporary to chronic mild conductive hearing losses. Because of the nature of the condition, the degree of hearing loss may fluctuate. Under certain conditions, such as when the child has a heavy cold, the loss may be much greater. As well, certain environments, such as a noisy classroom, can compound the effects of a mild conductive hearing loss.

Therefore, children who have suffered mild losses due to otitis media often demonstrate language and learning difficulties in the preschool years and otitis media may be implicated in later speech disorders (Roberts, Burchind, Koch, Fodto, Henderson, 1988; Wallace, Gravel, McCartan, and Ruben, 1988). Children with recurrent middle ear disease are at considerable risk for losing high frequency auditory sensitivity; psycho-acoustic studies have found that intensity discrimination is adversely affected by the presence of high frequency hearing losses (Fausti, [1987]). Children with early onset otitis media may be left with permanent effects, such as inefficient listening skills, that persist in later life. These children may demonstrate sporadic misunderstandings in speech; they may, for example, confuse the markers -*ed* and -*ing* and misunderstand small words in connected speech such as *are, to,* and *in.*

It is during infancy that children who are born deaf most closely resemble their hearing peers. Deaf infants follow the normal patterns of visual exploration and motor development. They also cry and coo and vocalize like other children during the first few months of life. Not until they reach the babbling stage at about six months do their sound patterns become differentiated from those of hearing infants. By the age of ten months, infants who are deaf show a significant decrease in babbling behaviour. This happens because they cannot hear their own babbling and do not receive reinforcement from the speech of adults.

For children who are deaf, most loud speech is inaudible, even with the most sophisticated hearing aids. Children therefore have significant problems in learning language, as well as significant articulation, voice quality, and tone discrimination problems. Because children who are deaf cannot hear the words of people around them, they have no language models. Even with optimal intervention, their language levels are seriously retarded.

Every element of language is affected—semantics, syntax, morphology, pragmatics, and phonology. As well, constructions such as phrasal verbs (*turn off, run in*) pose great difficulties. Similarly, figurative language (idioms, similes, metaphors, proverbs, and so on) involves every area of comprehension and semantics and is beyond most students who are deaf (see Arnold and Hornett, 1990). An idiom such as "hit the road" transgresses the laws of logic and is almost impossible to justify for a literal-thinking deaf person. One teacher tells how a young child who was deaf looked bewildered when she signed to him, "Your nose is running." To the child, running was something done on the playground and not something that noses did.

Speech is another area of great difficulty. In an early study (Jensema, Karchmer, and Trybus, 1978) teachers rated the intelligibility of the speech of their students who were hearing impaired; more than 42 percent of the children were rated as unintelligible or barely intelligible. According to the survey, approximately 13 percent of the children would not even try to use their voices for speech.

Lip reading or **speech reading** is the skill of understanding speech through watching the lips and face. The latter term is more accurate because facial expressions impart to spoken words a whole spectrum of feelings, attitudes, and visual clues.

It is a commonly held myth that individuals who are deaf are endowed with a compensatory speech reading ability that atones for their loss of hearing. Yet school leavers who are deaf can speech read no better than hearing peers (Conrad, 1979). In fact, hearing persons may be better at speech reading simply because they possess a strong linguistic base to fill in missing information.

Speech reading is a difficult skill to acquire because only about 30 percent of English sounds are visible on the lips (Stewart, 1984). For example, the colour words *red*, *white*, and *green* all look pretty much the same on the lips, as do *bat* and *mat*, *manic* and *panic*, and *measure* and *pleasure*. The difficulties with such look-alike words are almost insurmountable. Imagine a child trying to distinguish between "a red bat" and "a green mat." When words look the same, speech readers must anticipate them and fill them in, but this takes sophisticated language knowledge—an area of deficit for most people who are deaf. To add to the problems, the average speaker makes about 13 articulatory movements a second during normal conversation. The average observer, however, can only visually record eight or nine movements a second (Sanders, 1971).

Academic Achievement

The academic achievement of students with hearing disabilities is closely aligned to their acquisition of language. With the difficulties that most of these students meet in acquiring language, it is perhaps not surprising that their academic performance compares poorly with documented potential. Pupils who are hard of hearing who rely primarily on residual hearing and speech for communication have well-documented language deficiencies that limit their reading comprehension as well as their oral communication skills (Gearheart, Weishahn, and Gearheart, 1992). Students who are deaf uniformly appear to lag educationally by three to five years.

Numerous studies of reading achievement have shown that the mean reading scores of children who are deaf are well below those of hearing children; there is a lag of two to eight years. According to data published by the Center for Assessment and Demographic Studies at Gallaudet University (1991), the average 18-year-old with a severe to profound hearing loss reads with the comprehension of a normally hearing child in the early months of third grade. This is below or barely at literacy level. Only three percent of deaf 18-year-olds read at the same level as the average hearing reader of the same age.

There is some evidence that readers who are deaf use many of the same metacognitive strategies to comprehend print as do hearing readers (Andrews and Mason, 1991). For example, case studies of the reading process show that children who are deaf use contextual information to reconstruct the text using their semantic knowledge. But many of these students have very restricted vocabularies (LaSasso and Davey, 1987). Most can't comprehend even the most commonly used words, and children with limited vocabularies are likely to experience great difficulties in language and reading. These will be especially noticeable if reading words are removed from context, creating an unnaturally difficult situation. To add to the language and semantic difficulties, many readers with deafness lack background knowledge or prior experience of many of the topics found in commercial texts.

Children who are deaf are less educationally behind in more mechanical skills such as arithmetic and spelling. But while they seem to achieve well in mathematical computation, they are less successful at mathematical problem solving, which is predicated on a language base.

Social and Emotional Development

Because severe hearing loss so dramatically affects language and communication, it may produce barriers to normal social interaction that appear impossible to overcome (Warren and Hasenstab, 1986). The severity of social maladjustment patterns often depends on the depth of the hearing loss and the type of impairment. Severe hearing losses are more likely to result in social isolation.

In the case of hard-of-hearing students, the hearing impairment may be misdiagnosed and a child's inappropriate responses may be erroneously seen as behaviour problems or learning disorders. When this happens, the child's self-sufficiency, social maturity, and personality development are placed at risk, as we see in the profile of Ramon, a lad with an unidentified hearing loss.

Deaf children show a higher degree of emotional instability, neurosis, and maladjustment than hearing children. Estimates of the rates of emotional disturbance among hearing-impaired students range from 8 to 22 percent (Adams and Tidwell, 1989; Meadow, 1980). Although the range is broad, there is sufficient evidence to conclude that the frequency of behavioural disorders is higher than for the general population of school-age children (Adams and Tidwell, 1989).

Abnormal social development in children who are hearing impaired is often manifested by impulsive, irresponsible, and dependent behaviour. Frequently, children seem to disregard the feelings and misunderstand the actions of others. They typically exhibit a high degree of egocentricity and a low frustration threshold. These traits cause them to make inordinate demands and to act out their frustrations if demands are not met (Meadow, 1980).

Co-occurring Disabilities

With the multiple etiologies that can lead to hearing impairment, it is little wonder that many children suffer co-occurring disabilities. It is estimated that 33 percent of children with hearing impairments suffer additional disabilities, of which emotional disorders, mental retardation, and learning disabilities are the most common (Meadow, 1980). All studies on vision screening also indicate a higher incidence of visual deficits than among normally hearing children (Silberman, 1981).

Family Variables

The way in which the parents and the family react to and accept a disabling condition profoundly influences the development of the child with the disability. This is even more true in the area of hearing impairment, where the hearing status of the parents is a significant variable and where parental child-rearing attitudes appear to be the best predictors of the self-concept of children who are severely to profoundly hearing impaired (Warren and Hasenstab, 1986).

Approximately 10 percent of babies who are hearing impaired are born to deaf parents. These children form a distinct subgroup within the hearing-impaired population. Children

Profile

Ramon

At seven-and-a-half, Ramon already had a reputation for being disruptive in the classroom and difficult to manage. He was inattentive and restless, aggressive with other children, and poor in academic work. His speech was slurred and he had a lisp.

When Ramon was in kindergarten and grade one, his teachers had considered him immature and somewhat slow to learn. As he approached his eighth birthday, however, his learning problems were increasing. He was having particular trouble with language arts. Although Ramon had a small vocabulary of sight words, he was defeated by their use in context and any comprehension or sequencing exercises that were presented.

After a teacher initiated referral for an in-depth psycho-educational diagnosis, Ramon was labelled as learning disabled. However, even in a one-to-one situation in a resource room, he made little progress, and his parents blamed the school for his increasing frustration and unhappiness.

When Ramon saw a speech/language pathologist, the root of his learning difficulties was finally discovered. The pathologist found that Ramon had trouble recognizing and enunciating high-pitched speech sounds, and this inevitably led her to suspect hearing impairment. Audiological assessment diagnosed Ramon as suffering a 55 dB bilateral hearing loss. Because this loss occurred in the high frequencies between 4 000 and 8 000 Hz, it had been missed in regular school screening tests.

Ramon's audiologist did not suggest amplification for him. However, the classroom environment and curriculum have been modified. Ramon has been moved to a seat at the front of the room. His teacher is concentrating on building a strong sight word vocabulary and using a whole-word-family approach to improve his reading skills. Most importantly, Ramon now understands his problem and his sense of frustration and alienation is beginning to fade.

deafened by genetic factors tend to have far more positive outcomes than do children who are deaf and born to hearing parents.

Emotional and behavioural disturbance is about half as prevalent among deaf children with deaf parents as among children who are deaf with hearing parents (Stokoe and Battiston, 1975). Children with deafness who have deaf parents outperform children with deafness who have hearing parents on measures of language skills. In school, these youngsters consistently perform at a higher level on tests of academic achievement than do deaf children of hearing parents, achieving at about two-thirds the rate of hearing students (Vernon, 1969).

The reasons that underlie the differences between children who are deaf who have hearing parents and those who have deaf parents are not difficult to pinpoint. First of all, deaf children who have deaf parents are born into families that already have experience with deafness. Parents who are deaf understand the child's condition and seem better able to cope with any negative feelings that accompany diagnosis. Second, parents who are deaf are fluent in sign language, so their children usually experience language acquisition and family interaction earlier and at a greater rate than other children who are deaf. Mothers who are deaf help their infants acquire language in the same way that hearing mothers do with hearing babies. Deaf mothers of infants who are deaf seem to sign more slowly and modify the location of the sign so that the child can see it more easily, and use more repetitions (Erting, Prezioso, and Hynes, 1990).

As well, children who are deaf with parents who are also deaf have closer exposure to other deaf people and to the discrete culture of the **deaf community**. (See the Profile on Christopher.) Finally, deaf children of deaf parents rarely suffer additional injuries to the nervous system before birth. As a result, their incidence of secondary disabilities is no greater than for the population at large.

Hearing Children of Deaf Parents

We cannot close this section without a passing glance at another subgroup with potential language, speech, and social and emotional difficulties. Although not hearing impaired, the communication and emotional prognosis for hearing children of deaf parents is often problematic.

Research in this area is fairly scattered. One study (Schiff and Ventry, 1976) of 52 hearing children of parents who were deaf found that only 23 had developed normal language. The other 29 showed speech and language problems, including defective articulation, deviant stress and intonational patterns, and fluency disorders, problems that did not disappear after the children entered school. In another study of six preschool hearing children of deaf parents (Murphy and Slorach, 1983), three of the children showed delayed and deviant language development and three had other language problems. Finally, a British study (Flaxbeard and Toomey, 1987) of ten hearing children of parents who were deaf found that the children exhibited conversational difficulties, memory problems, reasoning difficulties, and poor language comprehension.

Socially, young children may take on unexpected burdens simply because of the parents' deafness. Hearing children feel a strong responsibility to help parents make decisions, to explain deafness to hearing people, and to be an advocate for the deaf community.

Intervention with Children Who Are Hearing Impaired

Children and youth who are deaf or hard of hearing require considerable intervention to provide health care, rehabilitation, therapy, and education. Generally, intervention involves two major components. The first is medical intervention to try to correct the physical causes of hearing loss and to provide amplification. The second form of intervention focuses on minimizing the educational and psychological consequences of hearing loss through counselling, special education, and related services.

Medical Intervention

Most conductive hearing losses can be medically corrected. Chronic otitis media is alleviated by antibiotics in the early stages or by a *myringotomy*, a puncturing of the ear drum to drain off fluid.

Otological surgeons can free the stapes in the case of otosclerosis; surgically reconstruct

Profile

Christopher

Increasingly, teachers complained about the behaviour and attitudes of 13-year-old Christopher. In his home room and in the other classes, Chris showed acting-out behaviour and, if reprimanded, would sulk and not participate in the lesson at all. When the teacher spoke to him, he would reach up and turn off his aid and close his eyes. At first, Chris's peers seemed to admire his audacious defiance of the teachers, but eventually they seemed bored with his constant disruptions of the class.

Christopher's parents are both deaf, and a younger sibling has a profound hearing impairment. Chris himself has been diagnosed as severely hard of hearing. He has a flat loss in both ears of 80 dB. He wears aids in both ears and had an interpreter in some classes (English, math, science, and social studies) to translate the teacher's message into sign language and to translate back the comments that Chris made and questions he answered. The interpreter was rather at a loss; she never knew how many of Chris's "off the cuff" and rude remarks to interpret for the teacher and was therefore playing the role of mediator.

This was only the second year that Chris has been integrated into a classroom with normally hearing peers. For all of elementary school, he was in a residential school for deaf students. His parents agreed, with some trepidation, when the residential school suggested that Chris could be integrated.

Chris uses sign as his main mode of communication but has developed quite acceptable speech. Both his language and reading were well below grade level, however, and he had great difficulty in keeping up with the work of the classroom.

As Chris's behaviour became worse and worse, team meetings were called with the classroom teachers, the special education teacher, the principal of the school for the deaf, Chris's parents, and a psychologist. Although most people in the room believed that integration is the most effective educational setting for hearing-impaired students, they considered whether Chris should return to the residential school.

Before the next meeting, both the school counsellor and the psychologist met with Chris at different times. They later reported that the residential setting was indeed where Chris wanted to be. He found the competition with his peers too difficult, did not feel that he was accepted in the class, often could not understand what was going on, even with an interpreter, and missed his deaf friends. Most especially, Chris stressed that he was a "deaf boy" and wanted to use sign, not speech, and to identify more closely with the deaf community. If his parents wanted him to go to university, then he would choose Gallaudet.

the middle ear (tympanoplasty); rebuild the three tiny bones of the ossicular chain; repair, shift, or rebuild an ear drum; and construct new membranous windows into the inner ear. When infants are born with an atresia, surgeons make a bony canal into the middle ear ("Hearing loss," 1982).

Cochlear Implants

Although there are no prosthetic devices capable of restoring normal hearing, the possibility does exist of replacing some lost function of the cochlea through the use of a prosthesis called a **cochlear implant**. These devices are designed for persons over age two with a profound loss in both ears, who receive little or no benefit from hearing aids or vibrotactile devices, and who are motivated to persevere through the necessary auditory training (Clark, Tong and Patrick, 1990). Not all people who are deaf are suitable recipients for implants; those with tinnitus, for example, may actually suffer an increase of head noises with the devices. Nevertheless, for many people who are hearing impaired, cochlear implants bring sound into a world that was previously silent.

Cochlear implants were developed in Australia in the late 1970s. They have become much more sophisticated since then, and an enormous range of rehabilitative devices are now available. There are intra- and extra-cochlear implants, and single and multichannel systems used with pre- and post-lingually deafened individuals. In 1993, implants were approved by the Ontario Ministry of Health.

The term *cochlear implant* is somewhat misleading, as it implies surgical reconstruction of the cochlea by repair or transplant. In actual fact, the implant is a device that converts sound into mild electrical currents to stimulate the cochlea and allow for some recognition of speech. In persons with profound deafness, the specialized hair cells in the cochlea that stimulate the nerve endings no longer work. In essence, the cochlear implants replace the function of these hair cells.

All cochlear implants consist of basically the same components and work essentially the same way. The device picks up sound, creates the sensation of sound in the inner ear, then sends it to the brain for interpretation. Specifically, each implant has a microphone that looks like a behind-the-ear hearing aid and is connected to the speech processor and transmitter by two cords. An encoder (speech processor), which is a tiny computer that changes the sound to electrical impulses, is worn on the person's belt. It looks like a pocket calculator and weighs about 3.5 ounces. There is an electrode driver that transmits the signal to the electrode either across the skin or by direct connection; and an electrode that transmits the impulses to the nerve through the cochlea (Burgio, 1986). The entire process takes milliseconds; there is virtually no delay between the presence of sound and its coding by the processor and interpretation by the brain.

Implants provide more and better sound cues to the person than do hearing aids (Cunningham, Eisenberg, Kirk, Luxford, and Thielmeir, 1986). Individuals who, prior to the implantation, relied entirely on speech reading, can carry on a conversation more adequately because they can hear at least some of their own voice and are able to recognize the words of others.

Technical Aids

In the classroom, it is seldom necessary to find special materials or equipment for the child with a hearing impairment other than their particular prosthetic equipment. Such equipment involves amplification or tactile methods to improve auditory comprehension. In addition, computer technology holds promise for the education of children who are hearing impaired. (See Chapter 2.)

Amplification

Hearing aids are primarily sound amplifiers. As such, they can help children to develop residual hearing, to improve the audition of their own voices, to use speech in a purposeful way, and to expand their vocabulary and language abilities. Even for those who are pro-

With sufficient amplification, reading a story while listening to it on headphones can help hearing-impaired students associate vocalizations with written language.

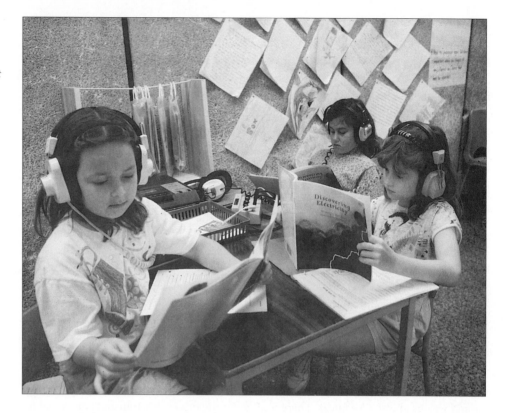

foundly deaf, the few distorted fragments of amplified sound that reach them may assist in the development of speech and language.

Aids differ in size, cost, and efficiency. While the various types can provide equivalent amounts of amplification (technically called *gain*), certain aids are designed to provide more amplification than others. This means that there can be a close match between the type of aid and the user's unique needs.

Despite the proven effectiveness of hearing aids, only one hearing impaired person in three or four actually owns and uses one (see Schein, 1994). A review of the literature (Stone and Adam, 1986) indicates that most children who are hearing impaired are wearing inadequate aids. Of the many reasons for non-use and incorrect use, the most important are

- Many children resist wearing a hearing aid because the awkwardness of the strange appliance outweighs their awareness of any benefits. After children are fitted with hearing aids, they still have much work to do before they can use or understand speech. They must learn to interpret the sounds they hear and to duplicate the sounds of speech.

- There is a widespread belief that persons with sensorineural hearing losses cannot benefit at all from an aid.

- Another belief holds that hearing aids are not appropriate for persons with mild hearing losses. However, some mild losses can be alleviated successfully with amplification.

- A particularly misleading fallacy claims that high frequency losses cannot be corrected with a hearing aid. That may have been true of body aids that rubbed against clothing and drowned out the high frequencies with low frequency sounds, but modern behind-the-ear models create no such problems. Hearing aids can also be programmed to amplify certain frequencies more than others.

- Some people cannot get used to the noise of the hearing aid. Amplification is indiscriminate, and hearing aids pick up extraneous reverberations (Blair, 1990). This can distort what is heard and may flood the individual with disconcerting auditory stimulation.

- Some people refuse to wear a hearing aid out of vanity or self-consciousness.

- Economic considerations are a factor. Not only are the aids expensive, but batteries, ear moulds, and receivers need to be replaced periodically.

In classroom situations, group amplification systems may be used. The FM (frequency modulation) system is the most popular. With a classroom FM system, the carrier wave is transmitted through the air via frequency modulation from a teacher-worn microphone to a student-worn FM receiver. FM transmission allows students who are hearing impaired to hear the teacher clearly from any location in the classroom, whereas an individual hearing aid has a restricted range of about six feet.

One of the biggest difficulties facing all hearing aid users is background noise. When the signal-to-noise ratio is poor, an auditory signal may be audible to the child who is hearing impaired but may not be intelligible. With direct audio input systems, an FM system is joined to the child's individual aid. This means that the hearing aid can be adapted for a wide variety of difficult listening situations and can cut out at least some extraneous classroom noise.

Vibrotactile Devices

Vibrotactile devices are tactile aids that help individuals to feel sound using the tactile/kinesthetic senses. They aid in speech development by vibrating to sounds so that users can feel and imitate the differences in duration, intensity, rhythmic pattern, pitch, and voice control. They also differentiate look-alike consonants, such as *p/b/m*, *t/d/n/l/* and *sh/ch*. Children hold the device in their hands or strap it to an arm.

Telephone Devices

The telecommunication device (TTD), sometimes called the TTY (tele-typewriter), offers persons who are deaf direct telephone access to each other and to community services. Instead of listening to a message and responding orally, the person with a TTD communicates by reading and typing. Typed messages are changed to electrical signals and then translated back to print on a TTD at the other end of the telephone connection.

Household Devices

To aid deaf adults in the home, a number of tools have been developed. These devices visually signal through flashing lights when, for example, the baby is crying, the telephone or door bell is ringing, or a wake-up alarm, smoke alarm, or fire alarm has sounded.

Captioned Films

Captioned television shows have been a boon to the hearing-impaired population. Closed captioning is an electronic process that converts the audio portion of a television program into written words that appear at the bottom of the TV screen. In some programs, captioned messages also describe sound effects or off-screen nuances that are vital to the storyline (Hysert, 1993b).

Educational Intervention

Students who are seriously hearing impaired may require extensive curricular modifications to compensate for the educational handicaps that accompany severe and profound hearing impairments. Modification of educational objectives may also be necessary to address the child's actual functional level rather than chronological age or grade placement.

Various educational settings are available for students with hearing impairments. Approximately one-third of students who are deaf attend residential schools, the most traditional setting for the education of students who are deaf ("Children with communication …," 1995).

An estimated two-thirds of students with severe hearing impairments attend programs in schools for students who are deaf or day classes located in regular schools ("Children with communication …," 1995). Day schools are similar to residential schools except that all students live at home. Self-contained special classes, located within regular elementary or secondary schools, offer separate programs for students who are hearing impaired. A number of students are included in regular classrooms supported by interpreters, resource rooms, or itinerant teachers.

Resource rooms offer hearing-impaired students from regular classes a chance to obtain tutorial assistance in a special class from a trained teacher of the deaf. Itinerant programs provide specialist teachers who offer tutorial assistance to hearing-impaired students who are included into regular classrooms. The itinerant teacher assists the child and the regular classroom teacher, and also acts as a facilitator or liaison with other support personnel, parents, and school administrators.

Inclusion

Many people disagree with schools for the deaf and special class placements; they tend to equate them with settings for mainstreaming failures, not as appropriate settings catering to the individual needs of many students who are deaf. On the other hand, many deaf people and professionals working with students who are deaf do not accept educational integration as it is now conceptualized. They describe the integration of students who are deaf as "forced assimilation"—an "unnatural attempt to make deaf persons hearing" (Elliott, 1993, p. 11).

Those opposed to integration marshall arguments that centre on deafness defined as a distinct culture—a deaf community. They argue that deaf persons "constitute a legitimate cultural and linguistic group and that they are entitled to educational programs which take this into account" (Reagan, 1988, p. 1). Viewing themselves in this fashion, people who are deaf tend to see the residential schools as a cultural component vital in creating group solidarity.

Michael Rodda and his colleagues (1986) found that only about 10 to 15 percent of all deaf children can be successfully included. Advocates for students who are deaf such as the Commission on the Education of the Deaf have issued statements supporting a strong separate special education system (Fuchs and Fuchs, 1994). Further, concerns are mounting about the full inclusion of students who are deaf without adequate communication and social supports (see Jones, Clark, and Salz, 1997).

Those in favour of integration argue that regular classroom placement exposes students to excellent language models and that there they must learn to use speech in order to interact with teachers and peers. In the psycho-social domain, students' perceptions of themselves are based on comparisons with hearing peers, preparing them to cope in an integrated society. Some studies have found that integrated students who are hearing impaired are more successful academically than those not integrated (Bunch, 1994; Holt, 1994; Kluwin and Moores, 1985). Further, Aplin (1987), who studied 42 children aged seven to sixteen with sensorineural losses attending ordinary schools, found them significantly better adjusted than their peers in special schools.

The findings on whether or not inadequate communication affects peer interaction are equivocal. They do, however, lean toward the conclusion that social integration may be more difficult to achieve than academic inclusion, since students who are deaf are frequently on their own when trying to initiate or sustain friendships with peers (Foster, 1988). This stretches right across the school years and into college.

For example, in very young children who are hearing impaired, communication deficits interfere with normal play development (Higginbotham, Baker, and Neill, 1980) and therefore with peer interactions. Children who are hearing impaired tend to engage in less complex and less social play than do normally hearing children (Esposito and Koorland, 1989). One study (Higginbotham and Baker, 1981) found that preschoolers with hearing impairment between 47 and 66 months of age preferred solitary constructive play, whereas hearing children of the same age preferred co-operative dramatic play.

Once in formal schooling, students may be isolated, lonely, or socially rejected. An Alberta survey (Alberta Response, 1989a), showed that 79.3 percent of schools had only one or two students with hearing impairments. In general, students who are hearing impaired demonstrate only minimal self-initiated interaction with normally hearing teachers and peers; many are permanent outsiders and never really become an integral part of their mainstream classes (Jaussi, 1991; Raimondo and Maxwell, 1987). Graduates of residential high school programs have described their social experiences more positively than graduates of mainstream programs.

Successful inclusion also depends on the classroom teacher and the availability of appropriate supports. How do teachers respond to the complex, difficult, and often frustrating task of including students with severe hearing losses? It is not unusual for teachers to express anxiety about working with a student with hearing impairment in a regular setting (Chorost, 1988). For one thing, many regular classroom teachers are not very knowledgeable about hearing impairment and related considerations (Martin, Daly, and Cody, 1988). Rittenhouse (1987), for example, found that only about 25 percent of the high school teachers he sampled felt that the information made available to them equipped them adequately for the task of developing IEPs. In Nova Scotia and New Brunswick, surveys reveal that the primary areas of concern for teachers are information on hearing loss in general, techniques for attaining comprehension, expectation levels for students with hearing impairment, effective techniques for teaching and managing behaviour, and the effective use of amplification (French and MacDonnell, 1985).

Although teachers may feel daunted by the task of integrating and educating children with hearing impairments in their classrooms, Chorost (1988) found that many teachers became more positive after having worked with a child during the school year. Teachers who did not express positive feelings had two major concerns—the child took too much time away from other students and the child was academically too far below the other students to be truly mainstreamed. Another study in the United States (Martin, Daly, and Cody, 1988) found that while regular classroom teachers did not reject the notion of accepting hearing impaired students, they would prefer substantial support and in-service training.

Educational Interpreters

The great majority of classroom teachers do not have proficiency in sign language and finger spelling. Enabling students to attend regular classes requires special assistance, and teachers may have to work with an interpreter in the classroom. The **interpreter**, sometimes called a *transliterator*, is a normally hearing person who facilitates the transmission of information between individuals who do not communicate with a common language or code. Educational interpreters translate directions, content, and assignments presented orally by teachers and the comments of peers, and share the student's responses and questions with teachers and peers (Salend and Longo, 1994).

There are different types of interpreters. A signed system interpreter makes speech visible and, in turn, converts manual communication to speech. The interpreter translates spoken language directed toward a student with a hearing impairment into a signed system such as ASL or a school-based system. An oral interpreter facilitates the student's understanding of verbal messages by subtly mouthing the complete verbal message or its paraphrased equivalent (Castle, 1988).

There is little extant research on educational interpreting in kindergarten to grade twelve classrooms. We do know that interpreters can function most effectively as an instructional resource in the classroom only when they carefully co-ordinate their efforts with teachers (Salend and Longo, 1994)

In general, the interpreter should be seated in a glare-free, well-lit location with a solid coloured background free of visual and auditory distractions. Interpreters should sit in front of the student without blocking the view of the chalkboard, overhead projector, or the teacher. However, the positioning of the interpreter depends on the nature of the instructional activity. When the teacher is using a lecture format, it may be desirable for the interpreter to stand or sit to the side and slightly in front of the teacher, with the student's desk located three to five feet from the interpreter. In a one-to-one instruction setting, the interpreter should be placed facing the student from a distance of about four to six feet. During group activities, the group should be seated in a circular fashion with the interpreter located across from the student (Salend and Longo, 1994).

Educational Approaches

Authenticated evidence of the education of deaf students can be traced back to the late sixteenth century. Almost since that time, teachers have divided themselves into two irreconcilable camps. The "oralists" have viewed deafness as a human handicap to be overcome through the development of speech and speech reading. The "manualists" have argued that deafness is a human difference that requires its own language, the language of signs.

Rampant conflicts in expert opinion about the use of sense modalities in the education of hearing-impaired children still exist. The stances are not as irreconcilable as they once were, but educators still hold quite different philosophies about the most effective means to impart language and promote speech. Many modes are possible, the most important of which are described below, moving from unisensory to multi-sensory approaches.

- *Acoupedic methods.* The acoupedic or unisensory approach is an oral method that aims to develop intelligible speech through the maximum development of listening skills (Pollack, 1970). It is founded on the belief that children in the first year of life have hearing abilities that, if activated sufficiently, play a functional role in determining speech development. On the other hand, auditory deprivation during this time diminishes these abilities and obstructs speech development. Evidence suggests that the process is irreversible (Brokx, 1987).

  The acoupedic approach requires early intervention, early amplification, unisensory stimulation, a normal listening environment, the use of auditory feedback mechanisms, and the preparation of parents to act as first models of communication (Pollack, 1980). This method excludes all visual clues, such as speech reading, and encourages the child to use residual hearing to the greatest extent possible. With major advances in hearing aid technology, acoupedic approaches have gained in popularity.

- *The oral/aural method.* Like other processes in special education, the oral/aural method used with children who are deaf today evolved through a number of stages. Beginning about 1867, teachers employed a pure oral method that placed stress on speech reading and writing but forbade the natural gestures that we all use as part of our communication. The pure oral method evolved into the oral method of speech and speech reading along with amplification through hearing aids, which were invented in the 1920s. This method downplayed the importance of writing and permitted natural gestures. From this grew the current oral method, more correctly called the oral/aural approach. It places stress on speech and speech reading and uses amplification and auditory training as integral components of speech and language development.

- *Cued speech.* Originated by Orin Cornett at Gallaudet University, cued speech is another primarily oral method of communication. The system uses eight hand configurations and four hand positions to supplement the visible manifestations of speech (Cornett, 1984). The hand cues add information to the speech reading process so that all single sounds can be identified by the child with a hearing impairment.

- *The Rochester Method.* This method was named after the Rochester School for the Deaf in New York, where it was first used in 1877. It employs finger spelling in conjunction with speech, speech reading, and amplification. Finger spelling adds a visible supplement to oral/aural language to provide children who are deaf with more complete visible language patterns. Ontario schools experimented with this method in the 1980s but today there are no programs that use finger spelling alone (Luetke-Stahlman and Luckner, 1991).

- *Total Communication.* By the early 1970s the benefits of using some manual components in the education of children with hearing impairments was apparent, and many educators turned from an oral emphasis to one that stresses a combination of methods. Total communication uses speech, speech reading, and amplification, along with a school-based manual system.

The school-based manual systems of Total Communication are a marriage of necessity between American Sign Language (ASL) and English. The systems, such as Signing Essential English or Manual English, incorporate the necessity of English and the utility of sign. Signs are presented in the order of English with correct morphological structures.

- *American Sign Language.* Unlike school-based manual systems, American Sign Language (ASL or Ameslan) does not follow the semantic and syntactic structure of spoken language. ASL has its own rule-governed syntactic system, a rich system of morphological processes, and a large lexicon of vocabulary.

Since the 1960s there has been a veritable explosion of research into ASL from the fields of linguistics, psycholinguistics, and sociolinguistics (Reagan, 1997). This led to a recognition that ASL is a true language; it is not related to or in any way derived from spoken English but is more accurately viewed as a distinct and genetically unrelated language (Reagan, 1988). Deaf people see ASL as their natural mode of expression and show great attachment to their "beloved language" (Schein, 1989, p. 29). In 1988 Manitoba recognized ASL as a heritage language of the deaf; Alberta followed in 1990.

ASL is founded on a combination of symbolic gestures produced by the shape, the location, and the movement of the hands. Many of the signs symbolize concepts rather than individual words. Most have an arbitrary tie to the referent. Some are iconic in that they represent an object or action for which they stand; some are metonymic—they take a relatively small aspect or feature of the referent and use that as the basis of the sign. For example, the sign for *dog* is snapping the fingers. ASL has no signs for the grammatical markers, such as *-ed* or *-ing* endings, that express verb tense and condition. Rather, users depend on facial expressions and body language to replace voice intonation and enhance meaning (Meadow, 1980; Odgen and Lipsett, 1982).

Although sign language is typically associated with people who are deaf, some has crept into everyday usage. For example, the football huddle was invented by a deaf player in the 1890s. Similarly, a deaf athlete was responsible for the ball and strike hand signals used in baseball. These were devised in 1888 by a deaf baseball player in Washington (Pirro, 1993).

Sign systems around the world essentially evolved from the sign language systemized by de l'Épée in France in the mid-1700s. However, these systems are no longer universal. They were quickly adapted to local needs and, like spoken language, each country has its own unique version. In North America ASL is used as an almost generic term. There is also CSL (Canadian Sign Language) and LSQ (Langue de Signes Québécoise).

Bilingual Programs in the Education of Deaf Students

Among deaf adults, the common mode of communication is American Sign Language (ASL or Ameslan). Because they hold that ASL is the natural language of the deaf community throughout anglophone North America, deaf adults favour **bilingualism** for all children who are deaf. They argue that young deaf children who are taught a conventional sign system develop language in sign that is comparable in both content and form to the child language that young hearing children develop in speech (Goldwin-Meadow and Morford,

ASL has its own semantic and syntactic structure. This deaf sign-language user is talking about his work. Literally, the signs translate as (a) boring,(b) work,(c) a lot.

1985). As a strong language base in one language facilitates learning another language, children arrive in school with a firm linguistic base. Further, say deaf adults, the deaf child is a member of a unique linguistic and cultural group, so "Forcing deaf children to be part of the hearing world denies them the right to themselves" (Elliott, 1993, p. 11).

Traditional approaches do not serve well children who are deaf. Bilingual advocates marshall data to show that deaf children rarely develop functional oral communication skills (speech and speech reading) anyway, so little is lost by the absence of spoken language in their environments. Only about 17 percent of students taught by oral methods ever become orally fluent, but nearly 75 percent of children become fluent manually. See the Matter of Debate box for more on the pros and cons of bilingual education for deaf children.

Bilingual education for deaf students uses ASL and English. Children use ASL as the major medium of instruction in preschool through the primary grades, with a major focus on sign production and comprehension. Development of English literacy begins in third grade and from then on ASL and English are used fairly equally for instructional purposes (McAnally, Rose, and Quigley, 1987).

In 1993 Ontario became the first place to authorize the use of ASL as the language of instruction for students who are deaf (Carbin, 1993–94). Ontario schools for the deaf now use ASL and written English and allow students opportunities to develop their auditory and speech potential. There are five key principles to Ontario's bilingual/bicultural policy. These are child-centered education, development of literacy skills in ASL and English, understanding and appreciation of deaf culture, appreciation of cultural diversity, and the development of a positive self-image ("Statement ...," 1993, p. 1).

Many hold reservations about the Ontario experiment and about bilingual education for deaf students in general. The most compelling arguments contend that English is crucial for functioning in our society because the language of the majority culture is English, not ASL.

A Matter of Debate

Bilingual Education for Students Who Are Deaf

✓ ARGUMENTS FOR BILINGUAL EDUCATION

Language is commonly taken as central to group identity, as its most important marker. The deaf community stresses the role of deaf persons in determining their own destiny and denotes sign language as essential to their identity.

Cultural awareness and identity enhances the self-concept of children who are deaf (Innes, 1994).

The child who is deaf is a member of a unique linguistic and cultural group. "Forcing deaf children to be part of the hearing world denies them the right to themselves" (Elliott, 1993, p. 11).

The absence of meaningful, satisfying communication between young deaf children and their parents may result in disturbed and fragmented communication, isolation from the family, poor school achievement later, and higher rates of psychiatric disturbance (Greenberg and Calderon, 1984). In contrast, a common mode of communication prevents frustration for both parents and children, and assists the children's emotional development.

Adult communication is bilingual in that ASL is the common language of discourse, and English is the written language and the means of access to the hearing world

It now seems that early manual communication helps rather than hinders the development of oral language.

Young deaf children who are taught a conventional sign system, such as ASL or signed English, develop language in sign that is comparable in both content and form to the language that young hearing children develop in speech (Goldwin-Meadow and Morford, 1985).

It seems that communication in humans is a resistant phenomenon: when prevented from emanating from the mouth, it comes almost irrepressibly from the hands.

The similarities between the development of spoken language and sign suggest a biological foundation for language learning. Deaf children are "preprogrammed" to learn sign. Those without any contact with sign language invent their own "home sign," a kind of communication through pantomime. However, home signs progress from simple single signs to real "sentences" (see Mayberry, Woodlinger, Cohen, and Goldwin-Meadow, 1987).

A strong base in one language facilitates learning another language. With ASL, children who are deaf come to school with a firm linguistic base.

The mastery of a language system is of enormous benefit in problem solving and academic performance.

Deaf people point to a vast array of meaningful research that clearly shows ASL to be a viable, rich language, and to bilingual education programs in Canada and around the world as evidence that this approach can be feasible and beneficial to students (MacDougall, 1988).

The needs of deaf children to learn English must be carefully balanced with their need to develop intellectually (Erting, 1985)

Educationally, deaf parents prefer to see their children intellectually challenged rather than constantly taught language.

School-based systems are unpopular with deaf adults, and the claim that they improve English remains unproven (Reagan, 1988).

Deaf children rarely develop functional oral communication skills anyway, so little is lost by the absence of spoken language in their environments.

Accumulating research evidence indicates that children taught by oral methods use sign language with their peers even when punished for doing so.

Teaching speech "is a matter in which human ingenuity has simply not been able to triumph over human biology" (Lane, cited by Elliott, 1993).

(X) ARGUMENTS AGAINST BILINGUAL EDUCATION

Children who use signs will not be motivated to learn to speak, use their residual hearing, or speech read.

Sign may be more natural for deaf children, but a sign system does not have to be ASL—it can be an English-based system.

English is crucial for functioning in our society.

English should be signed as it is spoken so that the linguistic input results in mastery of English.

Speech is important to deaf students in their efforts to negotiate the hearing world.

Under bilingualism, only some children may benefit from auditory and speech training.

Whatever aptitude the child may have to develop

Only about 17 percent of students taught by oral methods ever become orally fluent, but nearly 75 percent of deaf children become fluent manually.

Canadians are extremely sensitive to language issues, and acceptance of sign language will assist them in relating to a small group of people with very special language needs.

speech might be jeopardized by a practice that fosters ASL to the exclusion of speech.

Speech proficiency is of undeniable value to the individual who is deaf (see Stuckless, 1991).

The language of the majority culture is English, not ASL.

Children who are deaf are often learning to read at the same time they are learning English. Sign language use may impact on reading. Forms of sign language are structurally different from English and deaf readers must recode print into their own language (Andrews and Mason, 1991).

Ninety percent of deaf children are born to hearing parents who are not part of the deaf community. Hearing parents use spoken language as their primary mode of communication, and therefore must learn some form of sign (Sacks, 1990).

Speech is important for students who are deaf in their efforts to negotiate the hearing world and whatever aptitude a child may have to develop speech may be jeopardized by a practice that fosters ASL to the exclusion of speech.

A number of fascinating and provocative studies support the use of signed systems with children who are deaf. In acquiring language, for example, deaf infants pass through the same stages as hearing children. That is, deaf babies usually begin by babbling in sign—forming rough approximations of the signs that their parents use. They then proceed to one-word signs, and the kinds of signs that they first use are virtually identical to the categories of words that hearing children first acquire. They then use a type of telegraphic sign (Bonvillian, Orlansky and Novack, 1983).

Children exposed to ASL show an earlier onset of the first sign than would normally be expected for a child's first spoken word, and they typically acquire a sign language vocabulary more rapidly than a hearing child does a spoken one (Bonvillian, Orlansky, and Novack, 1983). First signs tend to emerge earlier than first words because human infants, whether deaf or hearing, typically initiate their symbolic communication in the gestural mode rather than the vocal mode because control of the hands matures more rapidly than the speech areas of the brain. According to Bay (1975), the visual cortex matures prior to the auditory cortex, facilitating the onset of a visual language system before an oral/aural system.

Curriculum

In the education of students with hearing impairments, the content is similar to that presented to hearing children. Differences are chiefly a matter of degree. For hearing students, teachers build a mastery of reading and written language upon a child's intact linguistic base of listening and speaking. In contrast, schools and classes for students who are hearing impaired must teach an entire language system. For example, to learn the single word *mother*, a child who is deaf must:

- Learn the concept.
- Learn to say the word.
- Learn to speech read the word.
- Learn the sound of the word through the hearing aid.
- Learn to recognize the printed word.
- Learn to recognize the written word.
- Learn to spell the word.
- Learn to print or write the word.
- Learn to sign the word.
- Learn to read the sign.
- Learn to finger spell the word.
- Learn to read the finger spelled word.
- Learn to use the word in context.
- Learn to use the word in different contexts. (After Levine, 1981, p. 100.)

As you can see, the process of developing language skills is long, arduous, and often tedious. Two major strategies for the teaching of language have evolved—the formal or grammatical approach and the informal or natural approach. All other methods essentially hark back to these two traditional approaches.

The grammatical approach focuses the student's attention on the structural aspects of language. (In Chapter 4, variations of this approach were described as diagnostic-prescriptive and syntax-based.) Armed with structural information, students learn to generate language deductively. The natural approach (performance) attempts to parallel the ways in which hearing children acquire language. The content and sequence of instruction are determined by the needs of individual children. This is illustrated in the In the Classroom section at the end of this chapter.

The Deaf Community

The deaf population is extremely heterogeneous, comprising people of varying levels of auditory capabilities, linguistic skills, cognitive abilities, social skills, and emotional development (Bullis and Reiman, 1992), as well as varying ethnicity, socio-economic status, geographic location, and so on. People in this heterogeneous population who use sign language find that their lives are defined by unique experiences and communication modalities that differ from those of an English-based hearing society. This leads inevitably to the strength of the *deaf community*, those hearing-mpaired people who share common attitudes, experiences, language, and participate in social institutions run for and by the deaf.

Although the deaf community in Canada can be traced back to the formation of the first residential schools, it is only in recent decades that political and social activism has characterized the community. This development paralleled the increased acceptance of ASL as a discrete language.

Today, many deaf adults describe themselves as a cultural or minority group and use the term *deaf* to designate cultural group membership (Brubacher, 1994; Dolnick, 1993). "The cultural view of the deaf community ... views deaf people as a group that shares a common language and a common means of communication" (Stewart and Ahamatsu, 1988, p. 238).

Today's deaf community is growing. In the past few decades, the fertility of deaf adults has rapidly approached that of the general population. Moreover, a deaf person typically marries someone else with a hearing handicap. Today, in-group marriages are estimated at between 86 and 90 percent of all marriages involving deaf people (see Reagan, 1988).

SUMMARY

1. *Hearing loss* (or *hearing impairment*) is a generic term that encompasses two major groups—those who are deaf and those who are hard of hearing. The difference lies in the intensity of the hearing loss and the amount of auditory input that the individual can use. People who are deaf cannot, even with the use of a hearing aid, hear speech. On the other hand, people who are hard of hearing can hear speech with or without amplification (hearing aids).

2. A hearing impairment is not the deprivation of sound but the deprivation of language. Because hearing loss interferes with both the reception and the production of language, the greatest single handicap of defective hearing is its effect on the development of communication skills. Children who are hearing impaired are isolated from the human voice and therefore isolated from language. As teaching is essentially a linguistic activity, hearing impairment poses a serious threat to children's learning.

3. Children who are deaf are likely to be identified during the preschool years. In contrast, the auditory problems of hard-of-hearing children may not be detected until they undergo a routine school screening, and perhaps not even then. Apart from the immediate problems for children, non-identification means that incidence and prevalence rates are extremely difficult to determine.

4. As long as the sounds of conversational speech remain audible, effective communication skills are possible. However, even mild losses can be educationally devastating.

5. Individuals who are hearing impaired are usually deficient in the language of the majority culture even when expert in the language of signs. Although they possess the same intellectual potential as the rest of the population, their deprivation in language can cause problems in every aspect of functioning. Academically, most deaf graduates today can barely read the daily newspaper. Emotionally, deaf students are prone to a greater number of emotional and psychological problems. Socially, many deaf persons turn for acceptance to the deaf community, where sign language is the accepted mode of communication.

6. Many of the etiologies responsible for hearing losses—rubella, meningitis, and Rh factor in particular—affect many domains of development and cause multiple disabilities.

7. Once a child's medical and audiological data have been gathered, he or she should receive and wear a personal hearing aid as soon as possible. All infants, children, and adults who are hearing impaired can benefit from an aid.

   Cochlear implants are now considered viable alternatives to hearing aids for some children to improve speech perception abilities.

8. In recent decades, the education of students who are deaf has undergone major changes. There has been a movement toward inclusion, a widespread adoption of total communication, and the initiation of bilingual education.

9. Setting is more than a matter of location. For students who are deaf, setting makes differences in the communication mode used, the type and amount of support services, the stress of the curriculum, and the possibility of identification with the deaf community and deaf culture.

10. Over the years, many approaches to teach communication have evolved. Today, all communication modes attempt to overcome the spoken language communication barrier with hearing aids, auditory trainers, and the like.

11. Many deaf parents and educators support the idea of bilingual education for students who are deaf. In this approach, very young children first learn sign language and then build English onto this linguistic base. Although the deaf community wants children to use what they see as their natural language and wants educators to accept bilingual education that includes ASL, bilingual education for students who are deaf is founded as much on philosophical arguments as it is on educational considerations, and the idea is far from universally accepted.

12. In the past, incorrect assumptions about the cognitive abilities of persons who were hearing-impaired led researchers to conclude that educational programming should concentrate on developing motor and mechanical skills rather than intellectual abilities. Today, the curriculum matches that presented to hearing students, but with a far greater emphasis on speech and language development.

13. One essential service that many students with hearing impairments attending regular classes may need is an educational interpreter. The importance of classroom interpreters is obvious as a support service for students to allow access to the same curriculum that is afforded hearing students.

14. Many deaf adults see themselves as a distinct culture, a deaf community.

In the Classroom

Profile: Steven

Steven is the third child in a family of four. He was an easy baby who smiled and cooed at everyone. He began to babble early but at about ten or eleven months of age stopped making many sounds at all.

His mother was aware quite early that something was amiss with Steven. When he was only six months of age, she took him to a pediatrician, who simply told her that the child would grow out of whatever she thought was ailing him—or alternatively, she was simply an overprotective parent. When Steven was twelve months of age, another doctor suggested that perhaps he was developmentally delayed or even mentally retarded. Steven's mother knew that neither diagnosis suited her outgoing little toddler, but it was not until Steven was almost a year and a half old that a diagnosis of profound hearing impairment was made.

Almost immediately, Steven was fitted with hearing aids which, to everyone's surprise, he readily accepted. He was placed on a home visiting program where a teacher came to the family's home weekly and taught him language, including sign language, and promoted speech. When he was three, his mother enrolled Steven in a local nursery school.

When Steven reached age five, his mother went to enroll him in the local kindergarten. The principal listened to her explanation of Steven's problem and agreed to place the child in a regular classroom for kindergarten, although no special aide or interpreter would be available. The principal did not seem to think this would be a problem, as she said that "Socialization was far more important than learning at this age, especially for a handicapped child." How surprised she was when Steven's mother explained carefully that she was placing Steven in the regular classroom not for socialization but for learning. She expected him to learn everything that other children did, and she also expected the school to provide assistance to ensure that he could.

What finally happened was that Steven remained in nursery school for the kindergarten year and then went to the local school for grade one. He was provided with an interpreter in the classroom. The home visiting teacher and later an itinerant teacher collaborated with the regular classroom teacher on his IEP, although the teacher was somewhat reluctant to make special adaptations. She felt that having an interpreter in the classroom was the only change that would be needed for Steven.

* * *

Steven's story is not unusual. Many young children with hearing impairments are initially misdiagnosed, and many teachers do not believe that children who are deaf can learn as adequately as their normally developing peers. As well, some programs that include deaf students assume that once an interpreter is assigned, all of the problems associated with deafness are solved and all services are provided. They overlook aspects such as reading and social skills.

Once Steven's needs were explained to the classroom teacher, she readily met with the school's special education consultant, the interpreter, and Steven's mother to plan an IEP. While the curriculum would parallel that taught to the other children, there would be a greater stress on speech and language using a natural approach. For example, Steven would receive extra classroom assistance in learning new vocabulary, and would be provided with many opportunities to interact in small groups with other children. Reading would be taught through a whole-word method rather than through a phonics approach, although Steven would participate in all of the many literacy activities offered, with an emphasis on storytelling and language experience approaches.

A speech therapist would work with Steven weekly and, as new sounds or words were acquired, the teacher would stress these in classroom activities and reinforce correct usage. As well, the ongoing assessment of communication development would be a feature of Steven's program.

During the IEP planning process, the special education consultant provided the teacher with many teaching tips and techniques, as outlined below. Throughout the school year, the two teachers collaborated closely. The teacher also used a few signs, such as "Good morning," and "Nice work, Steven."

Extract from Steven's IEP

Child: Steven
Teacher: Ms. Smith
School: Sunny Heights
Grade: 1
DOB: 12 June, 1995

MEDICAL INFORMATION	ADAPTIVE EQUIPMENT
Audiological assessment shows Steven to have a bilateral hearing loss in the severe to profound range.	Individual hearing aid Special seating—middle row, front Interpreter

AREAS OF NEED	AREAS OF STRENGTH
Speech training, auditory training, language, and reading skills	Normal cognitive functioning, good motivation, strong social skills

ASSESSMENT/PERFORMANCE INFORMATION

Date	Test	Result
October, 1999	Informal observations	Restricted receptive and expressive language; limited vocabulary; little speech use with many deviations. Uses sign for most communication; also speech reads to some extent
October, 1999	Test of Early Reading Ability (TERA)	Developing very basic literacy skills; understands the use of print and conventions of language such as reading from left to right. Barely started on formal reading. Only a small sight vocabulary—logos, own name, McDonald's, and so on
September, 1999	WISC-III Performance Scale only	Normal cognitive functioning

PERSONS RESPONSIBLE

Teacher, Ms. Smith	Stress oral skills; include in all activities; work with interpreter. Reinforce therapy sessions
Interpreter, Peer tutors, Speech therapist (weekly)	Auditory training, speech acquisition, language

LONG-RANGE GOALS

Steven's program will target speech and language development within the regular curriculum and with specialized assistance from an interpreter to assist classroom interactions. In the classroom, the teacher will stimulate language and communication skills through promoting interaction with other children; incidental teaching that includes expansions, paraphrasing, and open-ended questions (see Chapter 4); specific language intervention such as stressing therapy goals and correction where appropriate; and co-operative learning.

A second long-term goal is to begin to teach literacy skills. The teacher will use a word-recognition approach to circumvent the problems caused by the hearing loss, joined to the more holistic, experience-based method that is in place for other class members.

SHORT-TERM OBJECTIVES

1. When presented with words on flashcards, Steven will say the word, say it in a sentence, and write the word.
2. Steven will read short sentences containing new words.
3. Steven will write/draw in his journal daily with encouragement to use new reading words.
4. Steven will be placed in small learning groups as much as possible for socialization and language development.
5. To further promote peer interaction, peer tutoring (20 minutes daily) will be arranged for oral reading. Cross-age tutoring will also be arranged.

EFFECTS OF HEARING IMPAIRMENT	TIPS FOR TEACHERS
THE CHILD CANNOT LEARN THROUGH AUDITION	Allow students to make full use of the visual clues they rely on so heavily.
THE CHILD CANNOT HEAR CLASSROOM DIALOGUE	Allow children to turn in their seats when other students are talking or to move their seats when they need a better view.
	Point or move your head to cue children in to the person who is talking or the object under discussion.
	Use speech reading to understand messages and information.
	Seat the child near the front of the room and a little to one side. The second seat from the front allows an optimal distance of about two metres for speech reading and the detection of visual clues.
	Ensure good lighting, especially on the speaker's face. Teacher should face the light source. Natural light is better than fluorescent lighting.
	Speak naturally. Do not overenunciate, as this makes speech reading more difficult.
	Try not to smile or whisper while speaking, as this distorts the shape of the lips.
	Try to stand still while talking.
	Children cannot speech read if the teacher talks to the chalkboard or speaks in the dark during a movie or film strip.

EFFECTS OF HEARING IMPAIRMENT	TIPS FOR TEACHERS
	Keep the book low while reading aloud to allow children a good view of your face.
	Be in close proximity when speaking. Speech reading is best at about two metres, and aids function best within the same distance.
THE CHILD HAS POOR LANGUAGE KNOWLEDGE	
	Repeat and rephrase information and directions.
	Encourage children to ask questions if they are not sure.
	Use many visual aids. These are helpful for hearing children as well.
THE CHILD WEARS A HEARING AID OR USES AN FM SYSTEM	Provide an environment as quiet as possible so the child can listen to the best auditory message.
	Environmental noises are a problem for children with hearing aids because all sounds are amplified. Keep the auditory and visual distractions in the classroom to a minimum.
	Check daily that hearing aids are working.
	Keep a supply of extra batteries.
THE CHILD NEEDS AN INTERPRETER	For older students, provide interpreter with class routines, projects, and long-term assignments to help students understand and prepare for assignments.
	The child experiences social isolation
	Especially for older students, use techniques such as co-operative learning to promote peer interaction and communication skills.

WEBLINKS

The Canadian Hearing Society **http://www.chs.ca/**

Deaf Canada Web **http://dww.deafworldweb.org/int/ca/**

The Deaf Education Option Web **http://www2.pair.com/options/**

Students with Hearing Loss **http://www.educ.gov.bc.ca/.specialed/www/hearimpair/ cover.html**

Cochlear Implant Information **http://www.hearusa.com/cochlear.htm**

CHAPTER 10

Children with Visual Impairments

Historical Notes

Over the centuries, the history of visual impairment has been surrounded by fear, myth, and superstition, all interwoven into two contradictory themes. One common thread has blindness associated with darkness, despair, loneliness, and punishment—"one of those instruments by which a mysterious Providence has chosen to afflict man" ("Address...," 1836). The opposing theme held that blind persons were compensated for their lack of sight by both psychological and physical factors. Their condition was associated with superhuman and spiritual powers, uncanny memory ability, and musicality (Koestler, 1976).

Perhaps because blindness is such an obvious disability and one that is so feared by many people, blind persons were early granted special privileges, albeit ones that confirmed their deviant and different status in society. In ancient Rome, only those who were blind were allowed to beg on the steps of the temples, and throughout the centuries this privilege extended to the steps of churches in many places. Beginning in the fourth century, hospices for the blind were established. In the thirteenth century, one of the first hospitals was founded in Paris for blinded soldiers returning from the crusades.

Formal schooling for persons who were blind began in Paris in 1784, in Boston in 1832, and in Halifax in 1870. As well, many positive changes were wrought by dedicated educators such as Samuel Gridley Howe, by slowly evolving legislation, and by advocacy groups such as the Canadian National Institute for the Blind (CNIB), which was formed by blinded veterans after the First World War.

John Barrett McGann was the first person in Canada to undertake the education of students who were blind. Beginning in 1861, he admitted blind children to his Toronto school where they were taught by his fifteen-year-old daughter, Effie. In 1866, the Grey Nuns founded the Nazareth Institution in Montreal. Publicly supported institutions for the blind opened in Halifax in 1870 and in Ontario in 1872. By 1875 there were three institutions in Canada, which gathered pupils from all across the Dominion. It was common practice, for example, for Alberta students with visual disabilities to be sent to the Ontario institution as late as the 1970s (Conn-Blowers and McLeod, 1989).

Educational integration came quickly for students with severe visual impairments. As early as 1839 Samuel Gridley Howe (1801–1876) argued that blind children deserved "an equal participation in the blessing of education with seeing children" (Perkins Inst., 1839, p. 80). Chicago in 1900 witnessed the establishment of the first special class for blind students. After that, classes for children who were blind and sight-saving classes for those with visual impairments who were able to read print opened in most urban school districts. In sight-saving classes, children with poor sight were encouraged to "save" or reduce demands on their vision.

As early as 1911 there are reports of children who were blind being integrated into regular classrooms, and some educators were wont to argue that children with visual impairments were easily assimilated and taught in regular classrooms. In 1949, the year that the first children with retrolental fibroplasia reached school, the total number of visually impaired students in the public schools began to increase, and their population grew faster than that of the residential schools. By 1956, 25 percent of children with visual impairments attended regular schools; by 1980, the numbers had risen to 95 percent.

It is difficult for most of us to imagine life without sight. Vision and hearing are the senses that most connect us with our world. Well over half of the information our brains receive about the world comes through our eyes (Immen, 1995). In fact, the visual system is so dominant that many of us close our eyes to think more clearly and concentrate.

To many people, a world without images would seem bleak, frightening, and virtually impossible to navigate. It would seem socially cold; through expression and eye contact, our eyes play a crucial role in social interaction. Sight also affects our other senses; seeing something good to eat, for example, can trigger hunger pangs.

Most of us have a special fear of blindness (Conant and Budoff, 1982). A 1988 survey found that blindness was the most feared disability for 42 percent of the 1 072 adults surveyed. In the same survey, blindness was listed the fourth most feared disease, after AIDS, cancer, and Alzheimer's disease (Augusto and McGraw, 1990).

Sighted people tend to react to blindness on an emotional level (Kaplan, 1996) and see persons who are blind as either dependent or heroic. These long-standing perceptions are documented in the Historical Notes. Despite these common images, visual disabilities are not as daunting as they first seem. Many persons who are blind have contributed significantly to our culture and many other thousands who did not achieve fame lived normal and successful lives in spite of their disability.

Of course, this is not to deny that visual impairments can be among the most severe of all physical disabilities. In any individual, severe visual impairment can interfere with learning, social growth, adjustment, and mobility. In children, visual impairments cause complex developmental problems that make special education a necessity. Unique education needs include, but are not restricted to, early intervention; concept development; listening, study, and research skills; alternative methods for reading, writing, and mathematical computation; sensory training; daily living, socialization, and recreational skills; sexuality, career, and vocational training; utilization of low vision; accessibility to technology; orientation and mobility training; and meaningful transition programs (Huebner, 1985).

In recent years, many changes have occurred in the education of students who are visually impaired. Among the most dramatic is the inclusion of many children into public school classes. As well, greater attention is directed toward the functional rather than the legal definitions of sight handicaps, which has broadened the category of students who can benefit from special education. Children with borderline problems now qualify for services, as do children with visual impairments and co-occurring disabilities. Educators have also learned a great

Many individuals overcome visual impairments.

deal more about the effects of visual handicaps on learning, and there is increased emphasis on the development of residual vision. It is now realized that residual sight is enhanced, rather than diminished, with use, and children who were formerly classified as blind are now classified as low vision or visually impaired. At the same time, braille literacy is being reaffirmed by many in the field as an educational priority for children with severely limited vision (Schroeder, 1989; Stephens, 1989). The ability to read and write braille maximizes students' chances of educational and vocational success and lays the foundation they need to benefit from many new technological advances (Stephens, 1989).

New advances have also occurred in the diagnosis and treatment of visual disorders, particularly in the fields of ophthalmology and optometry. Vastly improved optical aids have been developed to enable children with severe sight impairments to read print materials. Advanced computer technology has brought many sophisticated devices that compensate for the lack of vision.

The Visual System

The visual system consists of the eye, which receives the light image; the nerve pathways, which transmit the image to the optical centres of the brain; and the brain itself, which interprets the image. Visual impairments can result from any interference with the passage of light as it travels from the outer surface of the eye along the nerve pathways to the brain.

The Eye

The eye is probably the most precious square inch in the human body. It is only 2.5 centimetres in diameter but its functions are extraordinarily complex and precise. It is composed of the eyeball and the accessory structures, such as the eyelids and muscles, that protect and move it. The eyeball is held in place by connective tissue in the orbit and is protected in front by the upper and lower eyelids. Figure 10-1 shows the structure of the eyeball.

The eyeball is a sphere wrapped in three layers of tissue. The outermost layer consists of the sclera and the cornea. The middle layer contains the iris and the lens, the muscles that support them, and the fluids that fill the eye's two chambers. The inner layer is the retina, the actual seeing part of the eye (Havener, 1979).

Light is essential for sight. A close look at the eye reveals that behind the black pupil and coloured iris there is a clear lens that serves to focus light gathered from the environment onto the retina. On reaching the cornea, the rays of light are refracted to pass through the anterior chamber of the eye. As the rays pass through the crystalline lens, they are further refracted. The lens is capable of changing its shape to accommodate light from objects at various distances. From the lens, the light makes its way through the vitreous humour and comes to focus on the **fovea**, the most sensitive spot of the retina. Images received by the fovea are here inverted, making the bottom appear like the top and vice versa (Abang 1980). The refraction and inversion of an object are illustrated in Figure 10-2.

The fovea possesses a rich supply of light-sensitive nerve cells, the rods and cones, which convert the light into electrochemical impulses. These impulses are transmitted to the brain

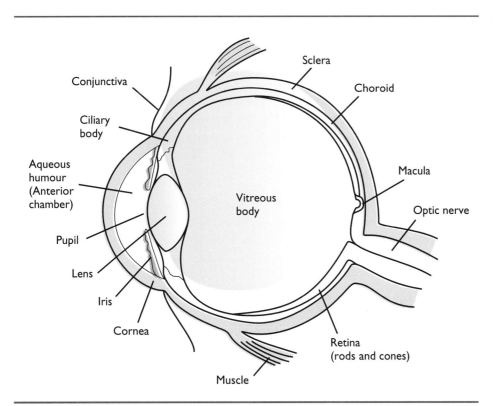

Figure 10-1
Anatomy of the eye

Figure 10-2

Refraction and inversion of an object

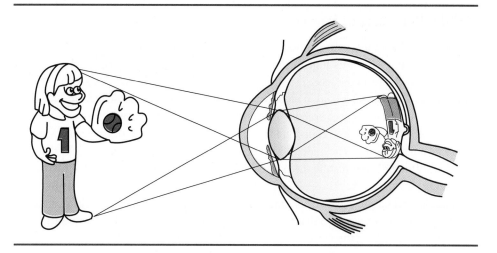

from the back of the eye through the bundles of nerve fibres that form the optic nerve. Immen (1995) describes the nerves that connect the eye to the brain as "the original information highway." The data are sent digitally, in a steady stream of electrical impulses, along a chain of nerve endings. Images are received and interpreted in the occipital lobe of the brain. Hence, vision is a function of the brain, not the eye. Table 10-1 outlines the important parts of the eye. The sequence of vision is shown in Table 10-2.

Definitions of Visual Impairment

People categorized as visually impaired range from individuals with mild visual losses to those with low vision to those who are totally blind. To cover this wide range, a number of terms and definitions are used.

Visual impairment, the most generic term, is often reported in terms of severity—mild, moderate, or severe. Many people reading this text will have mild or even moderate impairments that are correctable through prescription glasses. People with *severe visual impairments* would be unable to read the print. Severe visual impairment refers to serious visual problems ranging from an inability to read newsprint with the use of ordinary glasses to total blindness.

Apart from the generic *visual impairment,* two different types of definitions are used—medical/legal definitions and functional/educational definitions. For educational purposes, medical/legal definitions are not as appropriate as the latter because they do not adequately describe a child's visual functioning.

Legal Definitions

Legal definitions are founded on **visual acuity**, the measure of the smallest image distinguishable by the eye, and on visual field, reported in degrees, the entire area that can be seen when staring straight ahead. Normal individuals can see 180 degrees. Acuity measures begin with the 20/20 normal vision with which we are all familiar. This derives from the Snellen chart

Table 10-1 Parts of the eye

Sclera	Tough, flexible, white outer covering of the posterior portion of the eye. Its front part is commonly recognized as the white of the eye.
Cornea	A transparent window covering the front of the eye, continuous with the sclera.
Lacrimal apparatus	Glands that provide the tear film essential to the health of the cornea.
Iris	A circle of muscles that gives the eye its colour and adapts the size of the pupil aperture in response to light intensity.
Lens	A crystalline lens held in suspension by the iris.
Choroid	A vascular layer in which the blood supply to the retina is embedded.
Retina	A tissue-thin, intricate, and sensitive layer that consists of up to a quarter of a billion photo receptors and other nerve cells. Lines the back of the eye.
Ocular muscles	The six muscles connected to the outside of the eyeball that allow the eye to focus on an object, follow a moving target, and rotate. The muscles of one eye work in perfect synchrony with one another and with those of the other eye to enable the two eyes to co-ordinate. They are among the most rapidly responding muscles in the body.
Fovea	The most sensitive spot on the retina.
Macula	A crater-shaped yellow area of the retina in the centre of our focus. The point of clearest vision even though it represents only one-thousandth of our field of vision.
Cones	Photoreceptors that collect bright light.
Rods	Photoreceptors that work in teams to collect low light.

(often seen hanging on the back of your doctor's door), which consists of a series of letters, numbers, or symbols that must be read from a distance of twenty feet. Each line is a different size that corresponds to a standard distance at which it can be distinguished by a person with normal vision. This gives the measure 20/20 vision, which should not be read as a fraction. Snellen's equation was $V = d/D$ when V is visual acuity, d is distance, and D is the distance at which letters are clearly read.

Normal vision is 20/20; in Canada, **legal blindness** is defined as an acuity measure of

---

Table 10-2 The sequence of vision

---

1. When light reflected from an object hits our eye, the light rays pass through the cornea where they are refracted.

2. From the cornea, the light rays pass through the aqueous humour and proceed on their journey to the lens and the vitreous humour.

3. The rays are then directed to the central part of the retina. This contains rods and cones, which are light receptor cells. These are then stimulated by the light rays and consequently converted to electro-chemical energy.

4. The energy is further transmitted through the optic nerve to the visual centre of the brain, where the visual information is interpreted (Abang, 1980).

20/200 (6/600) or less in the better eye with the best correction; or visual acuity of more than 20/200 if the widest diameter of the field of vision subtends an angle of no greater than 20 degrees (CNIB, 1980). Visual acuity of 20/200 means that a normally sighted person can see at 200 feet (approximately 60 metres) what the visually impaired person can see at 20 feet (6 metres).

There is also a legal definition of partial sight, which includes those who have a visual acuity greater than 20/200 but not greater than 20/70 in the better eye after correction (CNIB, 1980).

Educational Definitions

Visual functioning (visual efficiency) refers to what a visually impaired person does with his or her residual vision. There is no correlation between the amount of residual vision a person has and the way in which vision is used. Two children with the same etiology and visual acuity may be very different in the way they use their residual vision. As well, fatigue, lighting, and emotions may affect the manner in which residual vision is utilized.

For these reasons, functional/educational definitions that indicate how well the child can use vision for learning are more useful than legal ones for educational purposes. Under a functional definition, a child with a visual impairment would be described as one "whose visual impairment interferes with his or her optimal learning and achievement, unless adaptations are made in the methods of presenting learning experiences, the nature of the materials used and/or in the learning environment" (Barraga, 1977).

Classification of Visual Impairments

There are many kinds of visual disabilities attributable to diverse causes. As a result, there are a number of ways to classify the conditions. One classification system is not necessarily better than another; they just describe different things and are used for different purposes.

Classification by Degree

Individuals with visual impairments may be classified in terms of the type and degree of disability as follows:

- *Near-normal vision.* Individuals are able to function without special training regardless of the strength of corrective lenses or reading aids they may need.

- *Moderate visual disability (moderate functional impairment).* People in this group have a moderate reduction of acuity, but no significant visual field loss. Specialized aids and lighting are needed, but sight is comparable to normal vision with correction.

- *Reduction in central vision.* These people have a moderate field loss and a possible inability to cope physically or psychologically with impaired vision. They may qualify for special services as legally blind individuals.

- *Low vision (severe visual disability).* Most persons who are visually disabled have low vision—their corrected vision is lower than normal. According to Corn (1980), a person with low vision is "one who is still severely visually impaired after correction, but who may increase visual functioning through the use of optical aids, non-optical aids, environmental modifications and/or techniques" (p. 3). That is, a person with low vision can read with special aids such as magnifying glasses or large-print books.

- *Poor functional vision and possible poor central vision.* These people show marked field loss and psychological or physical adaptation problems. For them, standard refraction is of little or no benefit; they usually require strong reading aids.

- *Blindness (profound visual disability).* Individuals in this group are the most visually impaired; they require education, habilitation, or rehabilitation to function at an independent level (Barraga, 1976; Faye, 1976).

Classification by Age of Onset

Children with visual impairments are often classified by age of onset of the problems. **Congenital low vision** refers to conditions that are diagnosable at birth or shortly thereafter. **Adventitious low vision** refers to conditions caused by accident or disease some time after birth.

Because many eye conditions change over time, age of onset can be critical in adjustment and learning, particularly in the development of concepts such as colour. Teresa Abang (1980) tells of a congenitally blind man who, when asked what he saw, said, "I see nothing." An adventitiously blind man responded to the same question with "I see darkness all around me." While the first man did not realize that he was experiencing darkness, the other had a memory of light and darkness.

Prevalence of Visual Impairments

Severe visual impairment, including total blindness, is a low-incidence condition. It is primarily an adult disability, probably one-tenth as prevalent in children as in adults (Hallahan and Kauffman, 1991). Only about one in one thousand children under the age of 18 have severe visual impairments (Hatton, Bailey, Burchinal, and Ferrell, 1997).

People with low vision far outnumber totally or functionally blind people who have no usable sight at all. In fact, students with low vision comprise between 75 and 80 percent of the school-aged population that is visually impaired (Bryan and Jeffrey, 1982).

In 1986, Statistics Canada conducted a special post-census disability survey. While this survey provided only estimates, it did indicate that the prevalence of visual impairment in the general population was 2.6 percent. Among the disabled population, the prevalence of visual impairment was 15.9 percent (Naeyaert and Grace, 1990).

It should be noted that although severe visual impairment is a low-incidence condition in the western world it is of particularly high prevalence in many countries of the Third World, where blindness affects millions of children and adults. In Asia, Africa, and South America, poverty and lack of sanitation create conditions in which severe visual impairment thrives. There are probably ten million blind people living in the world today (Mazurek and Winzer, 1994).

Etiology of Visual Impairments

Visual problems arise from any interference with the formation of images on the retina or the transmission of retinal images to the brain. Optical errors, defects of the eyes, diseases, syndromes, and associated conditions all affect vision to a greater or lesser extent. An outline of some conditions, their consequences, and their etiologies is shown in Table 10-3.

In the last century, the major causes of visual impairment included such things as *ophthalmia neonatorum* (inflammation of the eyes of the newborn); syphilis and smallpox; and massive epidemics of meningitis and scarlet fever. Measures such as washing the eyes of the newborn, vaccinations, and vastly improved sanitary conditions have eliminated most of these causes. During the past decade, retinopathy of prematurity, optic nerve hypoplasia, and cortical visual impairment have been among the most prevalent types of eye disorders in young children (Hatton, 1991, 1992; Teplin, 1995). Heredity is another leading cause of blindness in children under one year of age, with cataracts and retinoblastoma significant causes in terms of the number of children affected (Suran and Rizzo, 1983). Metabolic and vascular diseases, which include diabetes in the mother and disturbances in the metabolism of the infant, form an additional etiology.

In general, the etiologies and consequent conditions in visual impairments may be grouped as follows:

- Refractive errors, caused by irregularities in the shape or size of the eyeball, the cornea, or the lens. Errors of refraction may also occur in association with diseases of the eye or with oculomotor disturbances.
- Oculomotor problems, caused by disturbances in eye movement.
- Eye pathologies, caused by damage or disease before or after birth to one or more of the structures of the eye.
- Additional causes such as abnormalities of the central nervous system, which may result in faulty eye–muscle co-ordination.

Refractive Errors

Many people reading this book probably have minor visual losses caused by one of the four common types of refractive errors—myopia, hyperopia, astigmatism, and presbyopia.

Table 10-3 Examples of types of visual impairment and their etiologies

Category	Example	Manifestation	Etiology
Refractive errors	myopia	near-sightedness	
	hyperopia	long-sightedness	
	astigmatism	distorted or blurred vision	
	cataracts	growth over lens	aging, heredity, disease, and infection
Eye pathologies	glaucoma	impaired outflow of vitreous fluid causes pressure on eyeball	congenital heredity, aging
	retinopathy of prematurity	fibrous mass that destroys the retina	results from prematurity; oxygen in incubator
	retinoblastoma	malignant tumour on the retina	genetic
	albinism	lack of skin pigmentation	genetic, error of metabolism
	optic nerve atrophy	nerve degeneration	damage to the optic nerve
	retinitis pigmentosa	narrowing of field of vision	hereditary condition
Ocular-motor problems	strabismus	seeing double	
	nystagmus	rapidly moving eyeballs	
	amblyopia	lazy-eye blindness; lack of depth perception	arises from strabismus
Other problems	colour blindness	deficient in colour vision	genetic
	photophobia	extreme sensitivity to light	

Myopia (nearsightedness) is the greatest single cause of defective vision in children and young adults. The myopic eye is unable to focus the image precisely on the retina; the length of the eye or the shape of the cornea cause light rays to focus in front of the retina. In most cases, myopia can be corrected with concave optical lenses.

Hyperopia (farsightedness) is caused by too short an eye or too flat a corneal surface. The image is focused behind the retina. Corrective lenses aid hyperopic people. **Astigmatism** is the result of an irregularity in the curvature of the cornea or lens of the eye. The rays of light are refracted unevenly so that horizontal and vertical rays are focused at different points on the retina. In most cases, astigmatism is correctable (Harley and Lawrence, 1977).

With advancing age, numerous body changes occur. Some of these natural developments relate to changes in the eye's muscle tone and other tissues. **Presbyopia**, from the Greek word meaning "sight of age," is a condition in which the lens of the eye loses its ability to accommodate to near objects.

In the eye, the lens changes shape and lets us concentrate on a particular spot. To focus on distant objects, it flattens somewhat; when moving in close, it gets rounder. As we get older, the lens loses some of its adaptability and up-close focus becomes more difficult. In addition to blurring and difficulty with reading at normal distances, persons with presbyopia will usually experience "tired eyes" or headaches while doing close work. Most people at the age of forty or thereabouts develop some degree of presbyopia and need glasses for close work.

Disturbance of Ocular Motility

Normal vision requires the co-ordinated use of two eyes. Images from each eye are fused in the vision centres of the brain so that only one image is perceived. To achieve a synchronized image, the ocular muscles in both eyes must work in perfect harmony. Oculomotor disturbances occur when the eyes cannot control their direction of focus.

Strabismus, one of the most common oculomotor problems, results from inefficient ocular motor mobility. It can affect one or both eyes. Strabismus may be evident at birth or may not appear until the child begins to look at objects close up. Divergent strabismus causes what is called a "wall eye." *Amblyopia*, sometimes called lazy-eye blindness, results from strabismus. The brain will not tolerate double vision and eventually suppresses the image coming from the weaker eye.

Surgery, eye exercises, patches, or prescription lenses are used for strabismus. Treatment becomes less effective the longer it is postponed, and the longer suppression goes untreated, the more difficult it becomes to restore normal visual functioning.

Diplopia, or double vision, is another result of lack of co-ordination between the two eyes. **Nystagmus**, a rhythmic involuntary movement of the eyes, is often found in conjunction with other disabilities, such as Down syndrome. Ocular motility problems are common in children with cerebral palsy and other neurological disorders.

Diseases of the Eye

The most common eye diseases found in children cause clouding of the cornea and lens and dysfunctions of the retina and optic nerves. These diseases may be congenital or adventitious.

A **cataract** is an opacity of the lens or its capsule that restricts the eye's ability to receive light and therefore interferes with central and peripheral visual acuity. If the lens becomes cloudy, the light rays are blocked or distorted when they reach the retina, making things look hazy or dull, or dazzlingly bright.

Cataracts are caused by a chemical change in the lens itself. The exact reasons for the change are not understood, although there may be a hereditary tendency to develop cataracts. For the most part, cataracts are associated with aging and almost half the population over the age of sixty-five will suffer some degree of cataract formation ("Cataracts...," 1990). Younger people may be affected in association with conditions such as diabetes. Some babies are born with cataracts, often the result of maternal rubella. In rare cases, cataracts result from a blow to the eye or from exposure to radiation, toxic chemicals, or intense heat ("Cataracts...," 1990).

Glaucoma, a condition responsible for 12 percent of the blindness in Canada and the United States, has been called "the sneak-thief of sight" because its onset is slow and insidious. Glaucoma is caused by the increased intra-ocular pressure that occurs when the eye fluid that should be continually drained backs up along the outflow route. The increased pressure destroys intricate, sensitive structures in the retina, which then loses its ability to transmit pictures to the brain.

Congenital glaucoma is a baffling and mysterious hereditary condition that is a major cause of severe visual defects in children. Untreated glaucoma can cause total blindness in both children and adults.

Retinopathy of prematurity (ROP), until recently called retrolental fibroplasia (RLF), describes a condition affecting the retina and the vitreous humour. ROP was first described in 1942. It was seen in low-birth-weight (under 1.5 kg) babies and was soon attributed to high levels of oxygen in incubators. After its cause was discovered, there was a drop in the incidence of ROP. Since the mid-sixties, the incidence of milder ROP has been rising, and the 1980s saw a further resurgence of ROP as babies with even lower birth-weights survived (Trief, Duckman, Morse, and Silberman, 1989).

Current research indicates that oxygen alone does not account for all cases of ROP, and ROP is not always restricted to premature infants (Teplin, 1995). Birth-weight, gestation age, and duration of administration of oxygen are the most important factors in the development of ROP (Trief et al., 1989). Today, ROP primarily affects babies with a birth weight of less than 1 000 grams. About 20 percent of infants born weighing less than 1 500 grams also show evidence of ROP (Trief et al., 1989).

The problems of ROP begin as a distortion and outgrowth of the blood vessels of the retina. This is followed by the separation of the retina and the formation of an opaque mass behind the lens composed of detached retina, blood vessels, and fibrous tissue. There is bleeding, scarring, and detachment of the retina; the extent of visual impairment depends on the amount of scarring.

Retinitis pigmentosa is a hereditary condition that causes degeneration of retinal tissues and loss of peripheral vision. The age of onset of retinitis pigmentosa may vary from childhood to early adulthood. Other abnormalities, such as cataracts and glaucoma, may also be present.

When deafness is associated with retinitis pigmentosa, the condition is known as Usher's syndrome, named after the British ophthalmologist who in 1918 stressed the link between visual and auditory impairments. Usher's syndrome is a leading cause of deaf-blindness. (See Chapter 14.)

Damage to the blood vessels that supply the retina can cause macular retinal degeneration. The macula is the small area in the central portion of the retina that is responsible for fine or distinct vision, such as is required for reading. Macular degeneration may be inherited, but it is also associated with injuries such as contusions and concussions (Harley and Lawrence, 1977). The condition results in extremely poor central vision and may be undetected in young children.

Another type of retinal degeneration is associated with a high degree of myopia. Abnormal growth in the length of the eye causes a thinning of the retina and destruction of the retinal cells.

Diabetes is a major cause of retinal disease in young adults. **Diabetic retinopathy** is a disease of the retina's blood vessels. Not all diabetics develop retinopathy; generally, however, the longer the diabetes has been present, the more likely that changes in the retina will occur. People who have had diabetes for more than fifteen years are at greatest risk, and as medical technology and synthetic insulin prolong the life expectancies of diabetics, retinopathy is becoming more common. The type of diabetes a person has does not seem to determine whether he or she will be affected; some people with mild diabetes that is completely controlled by diet lose their sight, while others with severe forms of the disease do not experience any visual loss ("Diabetic...," 1990).

In the early stages of diabetic retinopathy, the blood vessels in the retina start to weaken and break. The leaked fluid distorts the light rays entering the eyes, and the person's vision blurs and fluctuates; or the person may see floating spots and a reddish haze. In the later stages, the blood vessels may shut down completely, which causes the retinal nerves that transmit sight images to the brain to die from loss of nourishment.

This kind of vision loss is gradual but permanent. New abnormal blood vessels may replace the old ones but they are unable to nourish the retina properly. They may start to grow into the normally transparent inner chamber of the eye, further interfering with the person's vision. If scar tissue forms, it can pull on the retina, tearing or detaching it completely, and the result is total blindness ("Diabetic...," 1990).

Retinal detachment occurs when a hole or rip in the retina allows the inner retina layer to separate from the back portion. Eye fluid can then enter through the break, seep between the layers, and further pressure the inner layer to peel or detach. Total blindness may result if the detached retina is not promptly reattached (Harley and Lawrence, 1977).

Optic nerve atrophy occurs when there has been damage to the fibres of the optic nerve. Degeneration of the nerve may be partial or complete, and its onset may be gradual or abrupt. Optic nerve atrophy may result from inadequate blood supply to the nerve or from optical diseases such as glaucoma or retinal degeneration.

Optic nerve hypoplasia (ONH) seems to be a relatively new type of visual impairment in which the optic nerve fails to develop fully during fetal development. Vision can range from normal to total blindness. ONH is associated with other neurological and endocrine abnormalities (Hatton et al., 1997).

Retinoblastoma results from a malignant tumour on the retina that may spread to the optic nerve and other areas. The condition usually arises in infancy or early childhood. It can be inherited as a Mendelian dominant trait with incomplete penetrance, which means that the person carrying the condition may not manifest the lesion but can still pass it on to offspring. In the past, surgical removal of the eyes was necessary. Today, the malignancy can be arrested without removal of the eyes. Still, blindness inevitably ensues and even a cured patient can transmit the condition to offspring.

Other Defects

Colour blindness is a rare, sex-linked, hereditary disorder found almost always in males. Defects of colour vision arise from the absence or malfunctioning of the cone cells of the retina. Cones come in three varieties, sensitive to the wavelengths of either blue, green, or red light. In some people, one of the three types of cones is missing, making them colour blind for that range of the spectrum (Immen, 1995). Persons with colour defects are likely to confuse colours, most commonly red and green. True colour blindness (seeing everything in shades of grey) is very rare. Although colour blindness is common among those with central vision problems, the condition is not necessarily associated with visual impairments.

Albinism is a condition carried as an inherited autosomal recessive trait. It is not sex-linked and the gene must be inherited from both parents, each of whom either has albinism or is a carrier of the trait. Albinism affects the production of melanin, the pigment contained in hair and skin. A pigment deficiency in the retina, iris, and choroid causes the pupil to take on a deep reddish colour and the iris to appear greyish, light blue, or pink. In visual terms, albinism is characterized by decreased acuity, astigmatism, nystagmus, and *photophobia*, a condition in which very bright light blinds the individual and thus decreases acuity (Abang, 1980; Vander Kolk and Bright, 1983).

Some central nervous system disorders may manifest as a lack of response to light stimulus in the cortex. Cortical blindness sometimes refers to blindness caused by swelling in the brain tissue due to trauma or congenital malformations (Hammer, 1984). At other times, the term describes blindness that cannot be medically explained. Most often, children who are congenitally cortically blind have other problems that are serious enough to affect several body systems. The visual functioning of children with cortical visual impairment has been shown to fluctuate from day to day and may improve in some cases (Good, 1992).

Prevention of Visual Impairments

Prenatal care, which includes genetic counselling, proper nutrition, and avoidance of alcohol and other drugs, is the most important form of prevention of visual impairment. Immediately after birth, the eyes of newborns are routinely washed with a one-percent silver nitrate solution to prevent infection. Later, children are given inoculations to prevent diseases that may result in visual impairments.

Total blindness in older children can often be prevented with immediate medical and surgical intervention in cases of retinal detachment, cataracts, and other forms of treatable eye diseases.

Identification and Measurement of Visual Impairments

Most children with visual impairments either are born with the disability or acquire it at an early age. Therefore, it is important that children be assessed early so that intervention can begin. If detected soon enough, at least some visual impairments can be corrected through the use of lenses, medication, and surgery.

A comprehensive assessment of a child with a visual impairment takes into account two areas—medical diagnosis and treatment of the problem, and psycho-educational assessment that leads to efficient educational planning.

Screening

Screening procedures assess large numbers of children in order to identify those needing additional diagnosis. In Manitoba, Rathegerber (1981) reported on screening procedures that identified 21 to 34 percent of children on the first screening and 11 to 24 percent on the second. When the identified children were sent for professional examinations, more than two-thirds required some care, either as an immediate prescription or for some incipient condition noted by the eye practitioner.

The most common screening procedure used in the measurement of central vision acuity is the Snellen chart, developed in 1862 by Herman Snellen, a Dutch ophthalmologist. This standard letter chart, familiar to most adults, may not suit young children and those who cannot read. Children are screened with the symbol E chart, which has Es pointing in different directions. Or the chart may have an outline of common objects rather than letters.

Screening tests to supplement the Snellen chart include measurements of visual fields and muscle-balance tests. One of the most common screening tests used with very young children is the Flash-Card Vision Test, which uses three symbols (apple, house, umbrella) that can be either verbally or manually matched.

Many children with visual problems are not identified until after they are enrolled in school and expected to read. In the identification of milder visual disorders, teachers are often on the front line when they observe children who have no outward appearance of anything wrong with the eyes but who exhibit abnormal behaviour. This includes frequent rubbing of the eyes, excessive blinking, crossing one eye when reading, or holding a book abnormally close or far away. Children who are suspected to have a visual problem should be referred for comprehensive eye examinations. Signs of visual problems that teachers can observe are presented in Table 10-4 below.

Diagnosis

In infants, diagnosis relies on observations of the child's responses to visual stimuli, such as a light or a moving object. Clinical observation includes reactions of the pupils of the eyes to light, blinking in response to light presentation, eye movements in response to objects moving in the visual field, and eye fixation on stationary objects (Rogow, 1987b).

Eye examinations, used with older children, consider both physical and functional aspects. The physical aspect involves measuring visual ability, which includes visual acuity, visual field, oculomotor control, and the effects of specific diseases or injuries and prenatal factors (Abang, 1980).

Visual functioning refers to the ways in which a child uses vision for purposeful behaviour in the various activities of daily life (Hall, Orel-Bixler, and Haegerstom-Portnoy, 1991). In diagnosis, functional aspects include the extent to which residual vision is being utilized and whether the child has opportunity, incentive, or optical aids to enable him or her to use residual vision (Abang, 1980). An eye examination should also determine a child's max-

Table 10-4 Some signs of visual problems

One eye turns in or out.

In near work, the child squints, closes, or covers one eye.

The child rubs the eyes, squints, or shakes the head while looking at near or far objects.

The child tilts the head or closes one eye.

The child is fearful of walking down stairs or running freely.

The child frequently falls or bumps into objects.

The child holds objects very close to—or far away from—the eyes.

The child appears to have abnormal eye movements.

The child complains of fuzzy vision.

The child has frequent eye infections, swollen eyelids, watery eyes, or reddened eyes or lids.

The eyes tear excessively.

The child has encrusted eyelids or frequent styes on the lids.

The child is poor or slow in reading.

The child is inattentive during reading class.

The child often loses the place when reading or persistently skips lines and confuses letters.

The child often stops to rest after brief periods of reading.

The head turns when the child is reading.

Pages in notebooks are poorly organized.

The child misaligns both horizontal and vertical series of numbers.

The child has difficulty in focusing on the blackboard.

The child can't remember things he or she has seen.

imum potential for achieving acuity and the type of optical aids the child needs to reach the maximum acuity level (Abang, 1980).

A number of specialized procedures used with children with multiple disabilities are addressed in Chapter 14.

Psycho-educational Assessment

When a child is deficient in a sense modality, assessment is fraught with problems. For students with visual impairments, many interlocking factors contribute to the difficulties met in the assessment process. First of all, the intelligence levels of blind and sighted children cannot be easily compared (Warren, 1984) and we do not have intelligence tests that are equally meaningful for both sighted and visually impaired children. And while IQ tests for individuals who are blind do not evaluate them in a way comparable to the evaluation of sighted children (Warren, 1984), so there is also a lack of viable effective or standardized procedures for testing both the totally and partially blind populations (Johnson, 1989).

Second, the test formats may disadvantage pupils with visual impairments since most existing tests depend to a large extent on printed stimuli (Johnson, 1989). To circumvent the visual disabilities, much IQ testing of children who are blind has been conducted using the non-visual verbal portions of common IQ tests. For children who are blind, tests use tactile or auditory modes; for those partially sighted, aural modes, large type, or magnified materials are used.

Several tools have been designed for visually impaired populations or specially adapted from other measures. Samuel Hayes, a psychologist involved with the Perkins School for the Blind, reasoned that children who are blind would be disadvantaged in using tests developed for sighted children. His modification of the Stanford-Binet Individual Intelligence Test, the Interim Hayes Stanford-Binet, eliminated items requiring sight. Following Hayes, various versions of the Binet tests, such as the Perkins-Binet, and the verbal scales of the WISC-R have been commonly used with children who are blind (Warren, 1984).

The Stanford Achievement Tests have been adapted and are available in both braille and large print for levels from second grade to college. The Maxfield-Buchholz Social Maturity Scale, an adaptation of the original Vineland Social Maturity Scale (Doll, 1941), screens the social maturity of children who are blind from birth to seventy-two months in the areas of general motor development, dressing, eating, locomotion, and occupation. Similarly, the Boehm Test of Basic Concepts has been adapted for students who are blind. Checklists or developmental scales such as the Developmental Activities Screening Inventory (Dubose and Langley, 1977) are useful indicators of social, physical, and communicative development.

Developmental Consequences of Visual Impairments

Obviously, the developmental consequences of total blindness differ from those related to low vision. Reading, other academic areas, socialization, life skills, and orientation and mobility will all be affected by the severity of the visual loss. The correlation is certainly not clear-cut, but as a broad generalization, we can say that the greater the degree of visual impairment, the more sharply reduced will be the range and variety of a child's experiences and the greater will be the restrictions placed on the child's ability to move freely within an environment. We can also say that visual impairment is linked to altered developmental pathways in young children. The global development of young children who are visually impaired tends to be delayed when compared to the development of sighted children. In part, development is determined by the type of eye condition.

Motor Development

Social, exploratory, and manipulative experiences lay the foundation for competence in communication, concept development, motor development, and self-reliance. Vision plays a leading role in an infant's first efforts to independently explore the environment. As the new world comes into sharper visual focus, the developing neuromuscular system sparks a push toward motor exploration and the infant reaches out to touch, feel, taste, and probe. Without vision, infants find it more difficult to explore their environment, to reach out into space, and to become aware of their bodies in space. Very young children who are blind have no natural motivation to lift their heads or roll, and they are less able to orient themselves to the external environment through such skills as reaching, crawling, and walking (Warren, 1984).

Restricted experiences mean that congenitally blind children may be delayed in motor development. While infants who are blind acquire early motor skills such as sitting and standing at about the same time as other children, they may be slower in crawling and walking. Delays in walking until sixteen to nineteen months are common, and even children with sufficient vision for orientation and mobility purposes may show a lack of confidence and a delay in ambulation.

Early play behaviour differs from that of sighted children. Of all disabilities, infantile autism and blindness seem to be the ones that affect the development of sensorimotor and symbolic play the most significantly. Children with severe visual impairments may be substantially delayed in sensorimotor play and exhibit delays or deficiencies in symbolic and social play. Abnormalities in symbolic play seem to be related to the limitations imposed by visual impairments.

Cognitive Development

The intelligence levels of persons who are visually impaired parallel those of the general population. How children learn and whether lags in learning are attributable to visual impairment is, however, a subject of intense debate.

Researchers debate whether or not children who are blind do more poorly on tasks involving abstract thinking and whether they are much more likely to deal with their environment in concrete terms. Because children who are blind rely far more on non-visual perceptions, the notions they form may differ from the notions of sighted children. However, many current researchers argue that the assumption that children who are blind experience problems of sensory reference has little basis in truth (Landau, 1983).

Another area of contention revolves around whether or not children with severe visual impairments lag significantly behind their sighted peers in the development of Piagetian tasks such as classification and conservation. Research is equivocal because much traditional testing of classification and conservation is based on visual information, and even when traditional visual tasks are adapted into a tactual mode, they cannot be considered comparable.

Perceptual Development

For children who are blind, the world is one of smells, sounds, and textures uninformed by the visual information that offers such a rich variety of colour, shape, and size detail to sighted persons. Hearing is the only distance sense available to individuals who are blind, and they must build their knowledge from auditory experiences joined to those that are olfactory, tactile, and kinesthetic.

It takes effort and concentration to learn to use the touch and auditory senses to compensate for lack of sight. There is no magical sensory compensation of the remaining senses;

blind persons must learn to pay more attention to auditory and tactual clues that sighted people can afford to ignore.

For the person who is blind, texture, weight, temperature, shape, and size merge into a sequence of touch sensations to permit identification of an object (Scott, 1969). Persons who are blind use synthetic touch—the tactual exploration of objects small enough to be enclosed by one or both hands. For larger objects, the person employs analytic touch, exploring the various parts of an object and then mentally reconstructing the parts (Hallahan and Kauffman, 1991).

Communication

Verbal language is critical in information-gathering functions for children who are blind. Even before they develop speech, infants with visual impairments use vocalizations to achieve and maintain social contact. They also learn a great deal about people in their environment from voices. They learn to measure personal attention by the nearness of the speaker and the touch gestures that accompany speech, and they become adept at interpreting meaning from nuances or variations in voice tone.

Studies of the speech and language development of children who are visually impaired have provoked controversy in the research literature. Whether language development parallels that of sighted children or whether it is delayed or different is not certain (Elstner, 1983; Matsuda, 1984). There seem to be language differences in the types of words acquired and in reciprocity and pragmatics (see Hatton et al., 1997). Bigelow (1987) found that very young blind children acquire vocabulary in the same way as sighted children, although some differences emerged in the percentage of words in each classification.

Others have studied verbalisms where a child uses words inappropriately and without an experiential base. For example, "a shirt as red as an apple" is a verbalism. A different line of research has looked at the increased numbers of questions that children who are visually impaired tend to ask as part of their information gathering. As sight decreases, so questioning increases (Erin, 1986), and children who are blind tend to ask fewer open-ended questions than do sighted children (Fichten, Judd, Tagalikis, Amsel, Robillard, 1991).

It may very well be that any speech and language difficulties in children who are visually impaired are more closely related to social and emotional factors than to low vision or blindness. Delays in speech and language development may result from restricted interaction with the people around them.

Academic Achievement

The educational achievement of children who are visually impaired is as variable as the population itself. In general, however, students who are visually impaired tend to achieve more highly in some areas than others. In a review of studies, Weiss and Weiss (1981) found that students who are blind do not perform as well in arithmetic: they tend to be from 8 to 27 percent below average-sighted children in basic arithmetic performance. On the other hand, the work of students who are blind in literary subjects was about the same as that of their sighted peers. Reading may be a problem, primarily because of the slower rate of reading large print or braille. As well, students who use braille often have problems with spelling because the contractions in braille do not conform to English spelling usage.

Social and Emotional Development

From infancy, parent–child relationships may be harmed if the child has a visual impairment (Dote-Kwan, 1995). Vision has a neuron growth spurt at the age of two to four months that corresponds with the time that babies really begin to notice the world, and peaks at eight months (Begley, 1996). During this period, sighted infants typically respond to attentive social initiations from their parents by visually focusing on their parents' eyes, smiling, and occasionally shifting their gaze to scan their parents' faces and the environment. In contrast, infants who are visually impaired demonstrate a flat, solemn affect characterized by bland facial expressions and the absence of expressive behaviour. Smiling is difficult to elicit (Baird, Mayfield, and Baker, 1997). This, in itself, can adversely affect parent–child relationships.

As they grow, children who are blind often demonstrate special needs in relation to self-awareness, self-esteem, and social skills. This happens because severe visual impairments tend to interfere with spontaneous social activity and with social interaction and communication. The visual impairment affects the child's ability to utilize visual clues which are needed for the modelling and feedback that underlie social skill acquisition.

Therefore, children who are blind face obstacles in obtaining the full benefits of peer interaction and may have trouble in acquiring an adequate repertoire of interpersonal skills (Farkas, Sherick, Matson, and Loebig, 1981). They often behave in ways that decrease their effective interaction with peers: research indicates that children with visual impairments initiate interactions less frequently than do their peers, have difficulty extending appropriate conversation, and are more likely to be rejected by peers (Mar and Sall, 1995).

Because of their visual limitations, these children miss many important non-verbal cues given by their teachers and peers through facial expressions, gestures, and body language (Scott, 1982). Children with severe visual impairments may fail to make expected eye contact with peers and typically will not smile. Communication may be impaired with sighted people by lack of eye contact (Fichter et al., 1991). Their failure to look at people may be interpreted as disinterest rather than as a manifestation of the disability itself. As well, children do not possess built-in feedback for appropriate head and facial movements once they are engaged in conversation.

Co-occurring Disabilities

Between 33 percent and 70 percent of children with visual impairments have co-occurring disabilities, the most frequent being mental retardation (Hatton et al., 1997) followed by emotional disorders and learning disabilities. The existing literature also points to a relatively high incidence of autism among congenitally blind children.

Intervention with Students Who Are Visually Impaired

Intervention with the population of students who are visually impaired serves different purposes, depending on the nature and degree of the visual loss, as well as the unique goals of differing professional disciplines. Generally, the major areas of intervention are habilitation (therapy) and education, which includes reading and optical enhancement, learning to use alternate modalities, and orientation and mobility training.

Medical Intervention

Medical intervention is provided by an ophthalmologist (a medical doctor); an optometrist (a specialist in vision problems); and an optician (a technician who makes lenses). Medical intervention takes the form of medication, surgery, technical aids, and prescriptive lenses to control and maximize visual function.

In the surgical area, laser beam techniques are used to re-attach damaged retinas, and there are sophisticated techniques for corneal transplants, artificial lens transplants, and the removal of cataracts. Various types of drug therapies and medications reduce the risk of blindness from glaucoma and diabetes.

Technical

There is not another field of special education that has benefited as much from technological advances as has the field of visual impairment. A range of sophisticated technical aids and devices exist for reading, mobility and orientation, and magnification. We explain some of them later in this chapter under the relevant headings.

For everyday living, an example of an exciting innovation is Voiceprint, a 24-hour reading service telecast specifically for persons who are blind, which is broadcast on TV to an estimated five million Canadian households that have cable systems. Supported mainly by Communications Canada and Rogers Communications, Voiceprint is a non-profit organization providing time-sensitive news, current affairs, and topical information from all major English daily newspapers, plus over one hundred Canadian and international newspapers, magazines, and periodicals (Hysert, 1993a).

Therapy

When children have severe visual impairments, special attention must be directed toward the efficient use of residual vision, gross motor skills for mobility, and fine motor skills for independent functioning, including compensatory hand skills. These children tend to use their hands in broad, sweeping motions and fail to acquire precise search and grasp skills.

Occupational therapists evaluate the effect of a child's visual impairment on daily living, play, and motor skills, and then design programs to improve these. For example, because young children with visual impairments may have weak hands and fingers, the program may incorporate manipulation of clay and plasticine, squeeze toys, pegboards, and puzzles.

Educational Intervention

Although residential schools still play a role in Canada, the emphasis on inclusion has meant a shift from segregated residential school education for students with severe visual disabilities to education in neighbourhood schools. Today, totally blind and other visually impaired students are enrolled in regular schools in all grades from kindergarten to secondary school.

A variety of technical aids have been developed to assist children with visual impairments.

Successful integration of students who are visually impaired depends on five components—the availability of specialist teachers; access to special equipment and optical aids; a braille transcription service; co-operation among principals, regular teachers, and special education teachers; and access to alternative programs for students who need them. Classroom needs include a flexible teacher and peer acceptance and interaction. Personal student characteristics include social skills, a positive self-image, independence, family acceptance, and inner motivation (Bishop, 1986).

In providing educational options for students who are visually impaired, school districts often make available a continuum of placement options. The resource room functions as a part-time classroom staffed by a specialist teacher who provides individual instruction as required, administers special tests, and adapts regular classroom materials. Itinerant programs make it possible for most children with visual disabilities to be integrated into regular classes. On itinerant programs, the specialist teacher travels from school to school within a district to offer special instruction to children at all school levels, including those in special programs. Specialist teachers work closely with school personnel who are involved with students who are visually impaired. Self-contained programs are designed mainly for younger children or students with special learning difficulties. The special class permits intensive individualization of instruction and concentrated attention to a child's problems.

Inclusion

A great many students with severe visual impairments can be included into regular classrooms, provided there are appropriate supports for both the student and the classroom teacher. To assist classroom teachers, specialists in the area of visual impairment collaborate in assessing and developing instructional programs for children who are visually impaired and

Learning braille is complex and time-consuming.

those with co-occurring disabilities. Specialists can work with teachers to adapt learning materials and interpret the medical, educational, and social implications of visual impairments to others involved with the child. They design and provide instructional programs in braille reading, braille math, and other academic subjects.

Specialists also provide supports to students. They may assess braille-reading readiness, visual perception, mobility, and social development. They also teach the use of visual aids and electronic reading devices, and design and provide instruction in self-help skills.

Do be aware that inclusive education is not universally accepted for students with visual impairments. Some educators and advocates of persons who are blind chide that "To many in the field of blindness, inclusion seems to have become embroiled in form without regard to substance—the if, when, why, and how of students' learning" (Bassett, Jackson, Ferrel, Luckner, Hagerty, Bussen, and MacIsan, 1996, p. 372). They point out that inclusion means far more than environmental modifications or minor lesson adaptations.

As children are given opportunities to learn more skills associated with general educational expectations, they are likewise restricted in the attainment of special skills such as braille and orientation and mobility. That is, for students who are blind, social interaction, the activities of daily living, and incidental learning are difficult in inclusive settings (Bassett et al., 1996). Skeptics specifically address the need for appropriate curriculum and instructional supports, training in such areas as orientation and mobility, and additional resources (Bassett et al., 1996).

Other critics worry about social isolation. During the adolescent period, many students who are visually impaired encounter difficulties in establishing relationships with peers. Even in integrated settings, they often do not interact (Hoben, Lindstrom, Gish, Shapiro, and Chalberg, 1979). Also, competition with sighted peers can cause difficulty, even with training and education.

Educational Approaches

Education for students who are visually impaired can be clustered into seven major areas to form a curriculum that combines the general curriculum goals of the child's grade level with specialized instruction. Areas of focus are the regular curriculum; personal competence, such as self-help skills and daily living skills; orientation and mobility; communication skills; vocational guidance and career education; use of special aids and equipment; and visual stimulation.

Curriculum

Students who are visually impaired can participate in practically all aspects of school activities. Reading is one potential area of difficulty, often because of slower reading speeds. For students who use braille, extra attention must be also paid to English spelling forms. Mathematics may be problematic. To master mathematical concepts, students need to explore the dimensions of shape and build up a vocabulary of meaningful mathematical terms.

Physical education and creative activities are a particular focus in a well-rounded curriculum. Students who are visually impaired need daily opportunities for vigorous exercise. Older children may need to correct body posture and movement. They may hold their heads down, droop their shoulders forward, or walk with a shuffling gait.

Reading Aids

For the majority of students classified as severely visually impaired, large print materials form the major reading medium. In large print, 18-point is the most popular type size. Large print readers will generally use normal handwriting in their work; the size of the writing is likely to conform to their type-size preference.

For blind persons, braille is the traditional medium of literacy. After its acceptance in North America in the 1890s, braille was widely used with persons who were blind. Then, during the 1960s and much of the '70s, there was a strong emphasis on the use of vision for individuals with visual impairments. The use of braille declined dramatically. Some people even felt that the new high-tech advances would eliminate the need for braille completely.

The percentages of braille users are telling. In 1955, more than 50 percent of all persons with visual impairments used braille. In 1963, about 55 percent of legally blind children used braille. By 1978, the rate dropped to 18 percent, and in 1989 only 12 percent used braille. By 1994, only 9.45 percent were braille users; in 1995, the number was 9.62 percent (De Witt, 1991; Schroeder, 1996).

Today there is an increased emphasis on braille as both educators and adult blind persons recognize that it is important for individuals who are severely visually impaired to have more than one literacy medium. Data suggest that braille is not only a tool of literacy but an identity mechanism for blind adults, a symbol of independence and competence, even group identity (Schroeder, 1996).

The braille alphabet uses six dots arranged in two rows of three dots each. Each dot is numbered. (Figure 10-3 shows the braille alphabet.) Numbers and punctuation signs are also represented in braille; numbers use dots 3 to 6, and the use of dot 6 just before a letter indicates a capital.

Braille has been adapted to many written languages, including those that do not use Roman letters. As well, a scientific and mathematical code has been developed. For liter-

Research Notes

Braille

Braille originally arose from the work of Charles Barbier, engineer, inventor, philanthropist, and officer in Napoleon's army, who devised a code which he called *criture nocturne*—night writing. These were not tracings of the ordinary alphabet but a secret code based on a twelve-dot unit, or cell, two dots wide and six high. Each dot or combination of dots stood for a letter or a phonetic sound. In 1808, when Barbier's system was presented to the French Academy of Sciences, it was hailed as a brilliant invention. Various adaptations of the system were undertaken by Barbier and duly submitted to the Academy. One report found its way to the school for the blind in Paris, where the twelve-dot system was tried but rejected in 1820 as impractical: the cells were simply too large to be read by a single finger tip (Winzer, 1993).

Louis Braille (1809–1852), the son of a harness maker, was born in Coupvray, a French town about forty-five kilometres from Paris. He had slit an eye at age three while playing with a sharp knife in his father's workshop and the resulting infection destroyed the vision in his other eye. Louis first attended the village school where he did very well even without the advantage of school books. Then, in 1819, his father sent him to the Paris Institute for the Blind. Louis proved an outstanding student and eventually became a teacher at the school.

Frustrated with the raised print method of teaching reading to blind pupils, Braille embarked on a search for a more efficient means and soon discovered Barbier's military code. When Braille undertook the adaptation of the Barbier system, he first solved the problem of the size of the cell by cutting the number of dots in half. He then devised a new code, alphabetic rather than phonetic, employing combinations of six dots. Because the new code was arbitrary, the symbols could stand for anything the users wanted to code. With his new system, Braille taught his students to read with more efficiency than was possible with embossed letters.

Braille's alphabetic code was published in 1834, his music notations in 1839. The braille system for reading and writing was officially adopted at the Paris School for the Blind in 1854. Dr. Simon Pollak, one of the founders of the Missouri School for the Blind, brought braille from Europe in the 1850s, but the braille code failed for many decades to find a niche in North America (Winzer, 1993).

In North America, educators preferred systems closer to regular written language. Schools for the blind used type faces such as Moon print, New York print, and raised print. It was not until 1892 that resistance to braille was finally overcome. Once accepted as a system to assist blind persons with reading and writing, braille evolved into a well-established system that employs many abbreviated signs and symbols.

acy, there are two braille alphabets. Grade 1, or alphabetic braille, is referred to as the simplified braille code. Grade 2, or abbreviated braille, is more common and much faster. There is also a Grade 3 braille.

Because of the complex rules underlying Grade 2 braille structure and the many abbreviations, teaching braille reading is more complex and time-consuming than teaching print reading. For the reader, the process is slower than reading print because the reading range of the fingers is much narrower than that of the eye. Reading efficiency is more difficult to achieve: readers must develop tactile tracking skills, a light touch, good reading posture, and smooth co-ordination of both hands (Mangold, 1982).

A skilled two-handed reader begins by placing both hands at the beginning of a line. When the middle of the line is reached, the right hand continues across the line while the left hand lo-

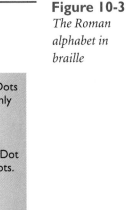

Figure 10-3
The Roman alphabet in braille

cates the beginning of the next line. The left hand begins to read the first several words of the new line while the right hand moves to its new reading position (Mangold, 1982).

Blind braille-reading students require braille textbooks. Traditional braille transcription was expensive and facilities were sparse. Computerized braille has almost superseded the slow and tedious manual versions and made the process both rapid and compact. Today, computer braille transcription centres are available in both Canada and the United States (Cox, 1984).

The Optacon (Optic to Tactile Converter), which converts printed material to braille, is the most widely used reading device. By passing a scanning device over the printed material, the microprocessor converts the words to braille via a small electronic braille-writing device that permits a blind person to "read along" as the viewer passes over the written words. Young children as well as adults can use the Optacon to gain immediate access to print materials. Reading with the Optacon is not analogous to reading with braille. With the Optacon, the user holds a small camera in one hand to read printed material and convert it into impulses. With the index finger of the other hand, the user can feel the letters and numbers through a tactile array of 144 small vibrating rods contained in a portable battery-operated electronic section about the size and weight of a portable cassette tape recorder. For example, if the camera moves across the letter H, the user of the Optacon feels two vertical lines and one horizontal line moving beneath his or her fingers and tries to recognize the letter shape (Abang, 1980). Recognition of letter shapes requires a great deal of skill and practice. Raymond Kurzweil's reading machine, first introduced in 1976 (Kurzweil, 1990), is designed to convert printed materials to an audio output. Its camera picks up printed letters which are then converted into synthesized speech.

Closed circuit television reading aids resemble regular television sets. They have a camera that scans reading material and conveys it to a monitor for enlargement. Users can regulate the size of the image to their own needs. Some machines are powerful enough to use with microfiche. Variable speech tape recorders are the most commonly used speech compressors (Rogow, 1987b).

Writing

For writing, the slate and stylus are the braille version of pen and paper. The user presses the stylus through openings in the slate that holds the paper. Since the material must be read from the underside of the paper, it must be written in reverse by starting at the right margin and moving toward the left.

In the first decade of this century, Frank Hall invented a machine, the brailler, that allowed the visually impaired person to type braille. Although less portable than a slate and stylus, the brailler is easier to use. Paperless braillers, such as the Cranmer Modified Perkins Brailler, allow students to feed information into a computer and receive a braille printout. The user can also write in braille, store material, and correct or amend material as on a standard computer (Mellor, 1981).

Visual Stimulation

Until the 1960s it was believed that children should conserve their vision so as not to "wear it out." Today's educators believe that if residual sight is used rather than saved, most children with visual disabilities can actually improve their visual functioning. The more children use their vision, particularly at close range, the more they stimulate the pathways to the brain. The brain accumulates a variety of visual images and stores them as memories. This process enables children to function more as visual learners (Barraga, 1976).

The visual skills targeted are diverse. They include attention to lights and objects; tracing and scanning; and figure–ground discrimination. Visual perception takes in object discrimination, the use of pictures, sorting and classification, and sequencing.

Vision is stimulated with the use of prescription devices and low-vision aids, which can considerably increase a child's ability to maximize near-vision potential. Children do not naturally use this equipment; they need training in how to use special aids and equipment, including aids for magnification. There are three main types of magnification and telescopic aids: hand-held magnifiers and telescopes; stand magnifiers, fixed focus or focusable; and headband aids—spectacles, clip-on loupes, and telescopes (Kelleher, 1979).

Personal Competence

Very young children who are visually impaired often need help in acquiring self-help skills such as dressing, feeding, and toileting. In older children, personal competence revolves around social skills. Students often need assistance to balance their interests, to tackle new areas of learning, to take risks, and to overcome a fear of failure. (See Chapter 16.)

Orientation and Mobility

To move freely and confidently, individuals who are visually impaired must know where they want to go, how, and in what direction. They must be able to move at a reasonable rate

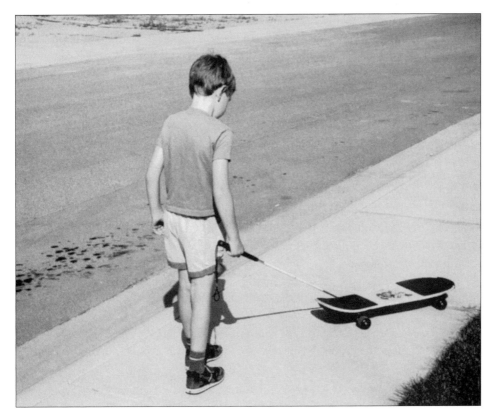

The prescription cane is the most commonly used travel aid for blind children and adults.

and with grace, comfort, and safety along existing routes between an origin and a destination.

Teaching independent travel is referred to as orientation and mobility (O and M) training. Orientation refers to an individual's knowledge of his or her position in space; mobility refers to negotiating that space. Training means learning to use a travel aid, such as a cane or a dog. Also stressed are the use of auditory, tactual, and kinesthetic senses together with any residual vision.

An orientation and mobility instructor (pripatologist) teaches mobility skills. Although O and M has been traditionally reserved for persons who are blind, today some experts recommend it also for individuals with low vision (Smith, Del'aunne, and Geruschat, 1992).

Orientation (cognitive mapping) involves knowing the spatial relations among objects or landmarks and one's own position in relation to the relevant objects or landmarks (Bigelow, 1991). Sighted persons use their visual system for orientation. Vision provides information as to where a seen object is in relation to the body, stimulating other senses so that they can determine whether or not the object is moving. Vision also maintains accurate functioning and position in space in spite of changes in the position of the eyes, head, and body, and judges relative direction (Howard and Templeton, 1966). These orientation tasks involve the retina, eye movements, visual direction, kinesthetic judgments, the vestibular apparatus, and auditory location.

Persons who are blind have little or no access to the visual information needed to construct cognitive maps. They acquire knowledge of the spatial relations among objects through tactile, proprioceptive, or auditory modes (Bigelow, 1991). Whereas a sighted person relies on visual representation and visual angle of perspective, a person who is blind must rely on sound distance to judge their relationship to an object. The person learns to detect subtle changes in the pitch of high frequency echoes as he or she moves toward objects. This is the Doppler effect, a physical principle that says the pitch of a sound rises as a person moves toward the source (Hallahan and Kauffman, 1991).

When guides are used, human guides are probably the most efficient (called the sighted guide technique). But human guides are not always available, and a constant human guide would inevitably lead to a decrease in independence.

Teaming a properly trained dog with a person who is blind helps in the achievement of independent mobility. Only a small proportion of the blind population actually use a dog guide. To qualify, the individual must be over sixteen, emotionally mature, and responsible. Children do not use guide dogs. The most usual breeds used for guiding are German shepherds, Labradors, retrievers, and sometimes setters, and these dogs are too big for young children to handle. As well, the dogs are not pets and need constant grooming and care, and children are not mature enough to keep from playing with the animal or to competently care for its needs.

Ideally, all guide dogs are placid, steady, precise animals of constant concentration, oblivious to people around them as they work with their blind owner to whom their responses are exclusively directed. But such dogs are rare, and all have idiosyncrasies that must be taken into account when matching a dog with a master. Some dogs are too fast for the owner; others are too slow. The profile of Pete tells of one man's experiences with his dogs.

Profile

Pete

Pete is now twenty-seven years old. He lost his vision as the result of an accident when he was only three years of age. Pete was sent to a residential school for the elementary years but attended the local high school near his home. He is now taking his master's degree at university.

At school, Pete was taught to use the Hoover cane and developed excellent mobility and orientation skills. But he wanted a guide dog and as soon as he was old enough applied to a centre for one. When Pete's application was accepted, he went to the centre and worked for nearly a month with the dog selected for him, under the guidance of a highly qualified trainer. Not only did Pete learn about how the dog could assist his own mobility, but he learned how to care for the dog—to feed it properly, to groom it regularly, and to provide it with lots of exercise. After

Pete brought his dog home, workers checked on both his progress and the dog's care and health.

Pete's first dog eventually grew too old to work and Pete keeps him as a beloved pet. He now has a second dog, a young Irish setter. He is, however, finding this experience a little different. The dog is young and more skittish than the first one. When people, not realizing that the dog is working, play with and pet it, the dog responds.

The dog loves the snow and, as they live in St. John's, has plenty of opportunity to go bounding over snowbanks and icy sidewalks. When this happens, the dog seems to be in control of Pete, rather than Pete being in control of the dog. Pete is not sure he can overcome these problems and is thinking that the white cane may be more suitable for him at the moment.

The prescription cane, also called the long cane, the white cane, and the Hoover cane, is the most common travel aid used by children and adults. It essentially came from the long staff that has been the symbol of blindness at least since Roman times. The cane is made of aluminum or fibreglass; its length is determined by the user's height and comfort level. The traveller holds the cane in front, swinging it in small arcs to detect obstacles.

A wide variety of other travel aids exist. Many work on a radar principle, sending out beams of ultrasound which cannot be heard by the human ear. If the beam hits an object, some of the ultrasound is reflected back to the device and converted into audible tones. For example, the Sonicguide supplies three kinds of information about an object—direction, distance, and general characteristics. The Sonicguide may be used with a long cane or a dog guide, and can be fitted into eyeglass frames. Another device is the laser cane, which transmits invisible infrared light. When it detects an obstacle, some of the light beam is reflected back to the cane, vibrating a pin beneath the user's index finger. The Mowat Sensor is a small hand-held device, light enough to be carried in a pocket or purse. It can be used to locate fallen objects, doorways, or even mailboxes (Mellor, 1981).

The age of onset of a visual impairment does not predict an individual's ability with mobility skills (McLinden, 1988). Canes are used with young blind children to increase mobility, early exploration of the environment, and self-confidence, and to decrease dependence on others (Pogrund and Rosen, 1988). Young blind children can also be taught to use specially adapted sensing devices. These can improve the locomotion and mobility of children as young as one year (Harris, Humphrey, Muir, and Dodwell, 1985).

The infant's Sonicguide uses a headband mounting and permits obstacle detection as close as fifty centimetres. The Canterbury Child's Aid is a binaural spatial sensor that reflects objects sensed from two receiving trandsductors mounted a small distance apart on an adjustable headband. Echoes are transduced into audible sounds that are presented to the ears through small speakers or earphones. The distance of an object is coded primarily in frequency; high frequencies signify far-away objects. The lower the frequency, the nearer the object (Harris et al., 1985).

A tactual map is a raised map that is used by blind persons as a supplemental aid for travel and navigation. Maps portray immediate indoor and outdoor environments, providing just enough information to support the specific movement requirements of the person who is visually impaired (Golledge, 1991).

Social

The care and training of persons who were blind made rapid advances with the return of blinded soldiers from Europe after the First World War. In 1917, a representative group of blinded soldiers and civilians met with women's organizations and businessmen and set about forming the Canadian National Institute for the Blind (CNIB) ("Canadian war blinded," 1942). Since that time, the CNIB has developed as a national voluntary service that serves more than 39 000 blind and visually impaired Canadians. The CNIB has two major objectives: to foster the integration of visually impaired Canadians into the mainstream of society and to prevent visual handicaps.

The Canadian Council of the Blind is a national organization made up of and run entirely by blind people. It is concerned with the welfare of individuals who are blind and maintains active committees on legislation, recreation, employment and other matters of concern to blind Canadians. The Council works in close liaison with the CNIB.

SUMMARY

1. Visual impairments vary widely in both degree and type. At one end of the spectrum are people who are totally blind and have no sight at all. At the other end are those with near-normal vision.

2. Mild visual impairments are a high-incidence condition, while the incidence of severe visual impairment and blindness is very low. Severe visual impairment accounts for only about one percent of all children who are disabled.

3. At the simplest level, the human eye can be seen as consisting of three parts—the eye itself, which picks up visual messages; the optic nerve, which transfers the messages; and the brain, which interprets the messages. Images are passed through the eye and along the optic nerve to the brain by light. If anything stops or hinders the correct passage of the light, visual problems occur.

4. A huge range of causes account for visual impairment. Some impairments are the result of villains such as rubella that cause many childhood disabilities. Others are unique to the etiology of visual impairment.

5. All children should be screened and observed in the classroom for behavioural and physical symptoms of visual impairment. Complete eye examinations are necessary to diagnose visual acuity and functioning and to determine optical needs. In psycho-educational assessment, children with severe visual impairments are particularly difficult to assess using standard measures and procedures.

6. A severe impairment in one of the most important of the human senses affects many other areas of a child's functioning, most particularly motor and mobility skills. Children also miss imitation and social reciprocity.

7. Surgery and correction are the most common forms of medical intervention.

8. The majority of children who are visually impaired or blind are educated in the regular school system. For a special curriculum such as mobility and orientation, they may receive additional assistance in a resource room from an itinerant teacher, or in a segregated classroom. Inclusionary practices have not been universally accepted by educators of students with severe visual impairments.

9. Training in orientation and mobility enables children who are blind to move with confidence and independence within their environment. Along with travel aids, children learn to gauge distance and direction from variations in sound.

In the Classroom

Profile: Gretchen

Name: Gretchen
Grade: 10
School: Point West

Gretchen is severely visually impaired and has low vision, even with the use of strong correction. She has always been included in regular classrooms and has learned orientation and mobility from a special teacher. Gretchen reads large print but has only very recently started to learn braille and does not use it for classroom work.

In elementary school, and even into junior high, Gretchen was an average student. She needed, and received, much extra assistance with reading and math, and adaptations of assignments and tests. High school, however, is proving very arduous for Gretchen. She is falling far behind her peers, chiefly because she can't keep up with the reading in the content area textbooks and with the homework. All her subjects are suffering, but in English she is failing badly. Her reading is slow, written language is poor, and her spelling shows gross deficits.

Gretchen is well aware that she is not doing well, but is reacting with defiance. She tells the teacher that there is too much homework and at home storms to her parents about the load. Adding to her academic deficits are developing social problems. Gretchen appears to be finding it difficult to accept her impairment and her moodiness has seen her more and more ignored by her peers.

* * *

Given the many types of visual impairment, the range of severity levels, and the unique ways that individuals use residual vision, it is not surprising that children with visual impairments form an extremely heterogeneous population. In a classroom, teachers may meet students with restricted vision who cannot see at a distance; those who are unable to see near images clearly; and those who need special lighting and optical aids to learn visually.

Gretchen has severe impairments and needs specialized aids. Her developing problems are consonant with those of some other students with severe visual impairments who have difficulty in matching the reading pace of their sighted peers. Nor is Gretchen very different in her reaction. Often, adolescents with severe visual disabilities react negatively to the disability, the needed optical aids, and the restraints on life style. (See also Chapter 16.)

Gretchen's teacher, the school counsellor, and a specialist teacher of the blind met to discuss Gretchen's program and possible adaptations in the classroom. The specialist explained that simply allowing Gretchen to use large print was not enough. The teacher must be aware, for example, of how to provide materials, make tactual maps, and teach using sensory modalities. She also stressed that the teachers should expect the same quality of work from Gretchen as from other class members, and behavioural expectations should be the same. Gretchen should also care for her own materials but be given a particular place for them that provides secure and safe storage.

When the team had a second meeting to discuss Gretchen's plan, they invited her to the meeting. Her complaints about the homework load were taken seriously and more oral work was suggested. The IEP also listed classroom adaptations and accommodations rather than any special education services outside the classroom.

Extract from Gretchen's IEP

ASSESSMENT RESULTS

An assessment of mental ability (verbal scale only) showed a student of average ability. Achievement testing indicated that Gretchen reads at age level, except that speed is constrained by the large print she must use. Math lags behind her peers by about two years; spelling is extremely poor.

TEACHER OBSERVATIONS

Almost daily, Gretchen seems to fall further and further behind others in the class. This is most noticeable in content areas, where she rarely completes assigned reading or homework. She almost never volunteers in class, and seems to resent being called upon.

STUDENT OBSERVATIONS

"School is much harder than it used to be. There is too much homework and the teachers do not understand how hard it is for me to keep up. In class, I need someone to help me with taking notes."

PERSONAL SUPPORTS

Glasses, large print, computer

SUGGESTED CLASSROOM ACCOMMODATIONS

Preferential seating among peers; a special place for storage of materials; selected homework assignments to be done orally on tape; adaptations to in-class tests to allow more time; note taker assigned for some subjects.

COUNSELLING

Assistance in dealing with the implications of the visual loss and using optical aids. May help with use of cosmetics and clothes selection.

EFFECTS OF VISUAL IMPAIRMENT	TIPS FOR TEACHERS
THE STUDENT LACKS A MAJOR DISTANCE SENSE	Provide direct learning experiences through a multi-sensory approach. Especially in the elementary years, students need concrete experiences, unifying experiences, and to learn by doing.
THE STUDENT LEARNS AUDITORILY	Language arts, conversational practice, social skill instruction, and role playing are only some of the ways that communication skills can be enhanced.
	Use words such as "look" and "see" but avoid "this," "that" and other intangibles.
	Take care with statements that require visualization, such as "Pick up the papers" (Fichten et al., 1991).
	When using the chalkboard, give much verbal information.
	Don't raise your voice.
	Explain, using concrete terms.

EFFECTS OF VISUAL IMPAIRMENT	TIPS FOR TEACHERS
THE STUDENT HAS A SLOWER READING RATE WITH BRAILLE OR LARGE PRINT	Allow longer time for tasks that require reading. In teaching reading, a phonics approach may prove helpful for students who cannot see whole words. Tapes or records can be helpful teaching devices, giving the student a break from visual fatigue. Low-vision students write in a size compatible with their own visual capacity. Stress legibility, not size. Scores on standardized achievement tests may be depressed by slow responses due to a slower reading or writing rate, or even to the fear of making errors. Allow more time for tests. A low vision student works under extra pressure and will be tired at the end of the day. Large amounts of homework should not be assigned.
THE STUDENT NEEDS LARGE PRINT AND ADAPTED MATERIALS	On application work sheets, blacken the print. Use buff rather than white paper. Never use purple spirit master copies. Assign the student a variety of types of seatwork. For older students, use graphs made of sandpaper, yarn, spaghetti, and other materials.
THE STUDENT NEEDS SOCIAL SKILL ASSISTANCE	Point out classroom rules to which the student must adhere. Expect the same quality of work as from other students. Try to emphasize the strengths of children who are blind without denying their special needs.
THE STUDENT NEEDS ORIENTATION AND MOBILITY TRAINING	If necessary, use a buddy at first but do not allow the student to grow too dependent. Don't move furniture in the classroom without informing the student.
THE STUDENT USES ADAPTED/ADAPTIVE EQUIPMENT	Cut down glare on glass, desks, and chalkboards in the classroom. Provide tilt-top desks. Try to have classroom displays at the student's eye level. Provide adequate storage space for materials while still keeping the student physically integrated.
THE STUDENT HAS DIFFERENT LIGHTING NEEDS	Check the lighting needs of the child. In children who are sensitive to light, for example, acuity increases with decreasing illumination.

EFFECTS OF VISUAL IMPAIRMENT	TIPS FOR TEACHERS
THE STUDENT NEEDS VISUAL STIMULATION	If glasses are worn, be sure that they are clean.
THE STUDENT NEEDS TO STRESS VISUAL FUNCTIONING	Know how, when, and under what circumstances students can use their vision most effectively. Students with central field defects may benefit from eccentric viewing techniques. Those who have nystagmus need to discover the best posture for reading. Those with poor peripheral vision can turn their heads, rather than move their eyes for scanning. Become familiar with the optical aids, large print, and reading aids.

WEBLINKS

Students with Visual Impairments **http://www.educ.gov.bc.ca/.specialed/www/ visimpair/contents.html**

The Canadian National Institute for the Blind **http://www.cnib.ca/**

Materials Resource Centre for the Visually Impaired **http://gonzo.lrdc.edc.gov.ab.ca/ mrc/homepage.htm**

The Basic Workings of Braille **http://www.chem.purdue.edu/facilities/sightlab/ structur.html**

Retinopathy of Prematurity **http://www.bethwood.com/billp71/ROP.html**

SECTION 6

Children with Low-incidence Disabilities

Nowhere in the study of exceptionality or special education is the spectrum of possible disorders more apparent than in the area of children with special health care needs, neurological disabilities, and orthopedic and physical disabilities. Of youngsters with these disabilities, almost half have cerebral palsy. Children with asthma and allergies make up almost all the remainder of the population. Children with other conditions, such as cystic fibrosis or spina bifida, form only a tiny percentage of those with physical and health disabilities.

Given such a diverse population, the medical, social, technical, and educational needs of these children vary dramatically. Some students require intense intervention; others need only minor adjustments to classroom physical layout or scheduling. Some children use adaptive equipment, including orthotic and prosthetic devices, to assist their functioning. Much adaptive equipment is used for support, for mobility, and for positioning.

Although the range of physical, neurological, and health disorders is vast, we are actually discussing low-incidence conditions. Pervasive developmental disorders and multiple disabilities are conditions of even lower incidence, but ones that have devastating effects on children's development and potential.

Pervasive developmental disorders, severe qualitative subnormalities that are not normal for any stage of development, have been the subject of intense research activity that has spawned a variety of treatment approaches. These children present a tremendous challenge to the school system and test the ingenuity of teachers and diagnosticians.

Subsumed within the broad category of pervasive developmental disorders are childhood psychoses that affect many basic areas of psychological development at the same time and to a severe degree. Children with psychoses display severe qualitative abnormalities and disturbances that are seen as distortions of development. Children with infantile autism differ markedly from those whose psychoses begin later, and most researchers today hold that autism is a developmental disorder that is distinct from childhood psychoses such as schizophrenia. Children who are autistic present a shifting array of behaviours that seem to defy analysis; they indulge in repetitive, ritualistic, and solitary activities, responding to those in the environment with aloofness and indifference.

Children with multiple disabilities have a range of impairments. While innumerable combinations of disabilities are possible, some appear more often than others and some are more difficult to cope with than others. Within the population with multiple disabilities, children who are deaf-blind are among the most studied.

In discussing children with multiple impairments, it must be remembered that conditions are not additive. In other words, a child who is both deaf and blind represents an entirely new category of exceptionality. The needs of these children are varied and complex; interventions involve a wide range of techniques and personnel.

In the fields of health disorders and physical disabilities definitions are particularly untidy, and there are many ways of categorizing the conditions for purposes of discussion. We arbitrarily discuss children with specific health care needs in one chapter and then look at children with neurological difficulties in Chapter 12.

Under pervasive developmental disorders, we discuss children with childhood schizophrenia and those with infantile autism. A chapter is reserved for children with multiple disabilities. The reader must remain aware that much overlap exists in all the conditions mentioned in this section. Many children with autism, for example, are actually multiply disabled and many children with multiple disabilities exhibit autistic behaviours. Pediatric AIDS can be discussed as a health problem, as a neurological difficulty or, depending on the course of the disease, as a multiply disabling condition.

Children with Special Health Care Needs

Historical Notes

It is reasonable to assume that health disorders have plagued humanity from its beginnings. For example, archeology provides evidence that the ancient Egyptians were aware of asthma and its effects. They treated it by "administering camel or crocodile dung, or by burning herbs on hot bricks and having the asthma patient inhale the fumes" (Isabell and Barber, 1993, p. 247). In ancient Greece, Hippocrates (ca. 460–377 B.C.) intervened with a variety of conditions. Ancient Rome saw physicians such as Aulus Cornelius Celsus (25 B.C.–A.D. 50) and Galen (A.D. 130–200), an anatomist, physiologist, and neurologist, produce a body of writing that influenced medical progress until the Renaissance. With the Renaissance came the development of more sophisticated surgery and medical practices. An age-old fear of dissecting the human body dissolved, and a huge spurt in anatomy and physiology was witnessed.

In the following centuries, medical advances continued apace. Franz Gall's discovery of the hemispheres of the brain, the discovery of vaccination and anesthesia, and the first glimmerings of the hereditary aspects of certain conditions lent light to medical diagnosis and prognosis. Amputation became feasible and safe in the nineteenth century with the use of anesthetic (Lowey, 1993). However, the conditions we discuss in this chapter were often lethal—and indeed, still are. Before the very recent advent of sophisticated medical intervention and technical assistance and devices, affected individuals could anticipate only an abbreviated life span.

Causes, prevention, and cures are still, to a greater or lesser extent, baffling. While, for example, cystic fibrosis and muscular dystrophy are known to result from defective genes, cures are not yet available. Since the discovery of insulin in the early 1920s, diabetes is controlled, but not yet prevented or cured. Intense medical research has not yet established precise causes and cures for cancer and AIDS.

In this chapter we discuss special health care needs. These diseases and conditions that affect the lives and functioning of children and adults include a huge range including cancer, diabetes, asthma and allergies, and genetic problems such as cystic fibrosis and muscular dystrophy.

Many health problems result from a variety of genetic and environmental causes; others are associated with prenatal problems, prematurity, and problems of gestation. Some conditions are transient, others are lifelong; some occur more frequently in children than in adults. When found in children, the majority of chronic illnesses manifest themselves during the first three years of life.

Essentially, special health care needs are medical problems that are handled within medical parameters. Because medical concerns are the major factors affecting learning for these children, their medical needs and technological dependence must be met before they can benefit from the classroom experience. Some children are technologically dependent; a child who in the recent past would never have left the hospital may now attend a neighbourhood school in a wheelchair with a ventilator and gastrotomy tube (Sirvis, 1988). Many students need pharmacological management; others may require supplemental assistance from support personnel such as physical and occupational therapists, nurses, and teachers aides.

Children with health care needs present educational challenges that differ in many ways from those presented by children with other disabilities. First, children with special health needs are often on a roller coaster of changing needs that is unlike any other disability. Teachers must be aware that children are subject to unpredictable ups and downs due to the changing course of some illnesses, and new medications and treatment regimens and their accompanying side effects. Other conditions result in a different sort of roller coaster of changing needs as children are in remission or in acute periods or are recovering from surgery or serious bouts. This entails changing treatment and different side effects.

All educational personnel must be familiar with the appropriate medical procedures and interventions that are part of the regular care of students with special health care needs as well as those required in emergency situations. Educators must also be aware of the factors that put students at risk for learning difficulties. These include fatigue, limited vitality, short attention span, and limited mobility.

Regardless of the diagnostic category, children with special health care needs have the same wants as other youngsters, and the basic goals of education are the same for these youngsters as they are for all other students. Children need to learn civic responsibilities, human relationships, self-realization, and economic efficiency, and they must be helped toward maximum self-sufficiency. Not all, or even most, children with special health care needs will require special education, but most will need some type of additional monitoring by school personnel.

Almost all children with health difficulties will be placed in regular classrooms. Special education may be warranted only because the condition or illness resulted in loss of school time and the child is consequently falling behind in school work. Note too that there may be psychological and emotional correlates of a number of physical and health problems, a concern of professionals within the discipline of pediatric psychology.

While the number of health problems involving other body systems is staggering, in this chapter we restrict discussion to a few specific and sometimes life-threatening conditions most often seen in our classrooms. We also discuss musculoskeletal impairments and child abuse or neglect.

Definitions

One of the major difficulties in discussing health care needs (and neurological disorders) is the diversity of conditions and their sequelae. This leads to a range of overlapping descriptors.

For example, orthopedic and neurological impairments, while two distinct types of disabilities, may nevertheless cause similar limitations in movement (Shivers and Fait, 1985). This means that a single child can be described in a number of ways. A child with muscular dystrophy, for example, can be said to have a health disorder, a musculoskeletal impairment, a physical disability, an orthopedic problem, or a motor impairment. Similarly, cerebral palsy can be categorized as a neurological impairment, a significant motor disability, a physical disability, and an orthopedic disability. The conditions discussed in this chapter and in Chapter 12 (excluding child abuse) are shown in Table 11-1 with their possible descriptors. Commonly used descriptors are discussed below.:

- The term **chronic health problems** is used when the presence of a disease or medical condition interferes with school attendance and learning and hinders the ability to lead a normal life. This category includes such conditions as sickle cell anemia, arthritis, cancer, and asthma.

Table 11-1 Conditions and possible descriptors

	Chronic health problems	Neurological dysfunction	Musculoskeletal impairment	Orthopedic impairment	Physical/motor disability	Technology dependent/ medically fragile
allergies	x					
arthritis	x			x		x
asthma	x					
cancer	x					
cerebral palsy		x		x	x	x
clubfoot				x	x	x
cystic fibrosis	x					
diabetes	x					
epilepsy	x	x				
hydrocephelus						x
limb deficiencies				x	x	x
multiple sclerosis	x	x			x	x
muscular dystrophy				x	x	x
pediatric AIDS	x	x				
scoliosis			x	x	x	x
sickle cell anemia	x					
spina bifida with myelomening-ocele			x	x	x	x
traumatic brain injury		x				

- *Physical disabilities* are those that affect body systems; they include health disorders and problems related to mobility and motor skills. Physical disabilities that have associated motor disabilities and deviations include cerebral palsy, muscular dystrophy, and spina bifida.

- *Orthopedic conditions* are those that arise from any cause and affect mobility. Specifically, the term refers to disabilities that relate primarily to disorders of the skeleton, joints, and muscles including clubfoot, the absence of some members, or other congenital anomalies; impairments caused by diseases such as poliomyelitis or bone tuberculosis; impairments caused by cerebral palsy; amputations; and contractures caused by fractures or burns (Federal Register, 1977)

- *Musculoskeletal impairments* are specific disorders involving bones or muscles. **Musculoskeletal impairments** are those conditions that impede bodily movements in the absence of damage to the central nervous system. Causes range from inherited diseases and congenital malformations to infections and accidents.

- *Neurological dysfunctions* occur before, during, or after birth and include cerebral palsy and head traumas.

- *Technology dependent* refers to conditions that require technological intervention. Children need "a medical device to compensate for the loss of vital bodily function and substantial ongoing nursing care to avert death or further disability" (OTA, 1987, p. 3). For example, a child may be ventilator dependent, oxygen dependent, or nutritional supplement dependent. Or a child may need heart monitoring, apnea monitoring, or kidney dialysis.

- *Medically fragile* is a term that overlaps the above category. According to the Council for Exceptional Children (1988), "medically fragile children require specialized technological health care procedures for life support during the school day. These students may or may not require special education."

In this chapter we restrict our discussion to health problems and musculoskeletal impairments that do not have neurological involvement. Impairments directly related to damage of the central nervous system are discussed in Chapter 12.

Prevalence of Health Problems

The prevalence of chronic health problems is very difficult to determine, primarily because

- there is such a variety of conditions, and there exist inconsistencies in defining various disabilities;

- different provinces use different methods for gathering data, producing very different results;

- nation-wide health statistics tend to rely on a limited number of categories, which means that many health problems go uncounted;

- in both provincial and national surveys, individuals with multiple disabilities may be counted twice;

- there are reported increases in certain physical disabilities over the past three decades (Batshaw and Perrett, 1986), especially allergies and asthma;

- physical disabilities are often found with other disabling conditions.

Although it is difficult to obtain exact prevalence and incidence figures for specific conditions, we can say that most (though not all) are very low-incidence problems. The major exceptions are asthma and allergies.

Allergies are the most common chronic disease in pediatrics. Allergic conditions are estimated to occur in 6.6 to 33 percent of children and adolescents (Crawford, 1982). In Canada, recent studies have shown that one in every five school children has a major allergy (Alberta Response, 1989b). Asthma is both a high-incidence and an increasing condition in most developed nations. Asthma severe enough to restrict childhood activities has risen approximately 65 percent since the 1970s (Newacheck and Taylor, 1992). This increased prevalence of asthma now makes it the most common chronic disease in children (Weitzman, Gortmaker, Sobol, and Perrin, 1992).

Within Canada, the prevalence of asthma in children is slightly higher than in the United States (Pfeurti, 1997). It affects about 7 to 10 percent of the Canadian pediatric population, as opposed to 5 to 10 percent of children in most industrialized countries (Canadian Lung Association, 1997).

Special Health Care Needs

Health disorders are essentially medical conditions requiring a complex and sophisticated range of interventions that include surgical procedures, prosthetic devices, drug therapy, diet management, and ongoing medical treatment. There is no necessary correlation between health disorders and impairments in other domains of functioning.

Generally, children with health problems show normal development in cognitive, communication, and socio-emotional skills. However, there may be disruptions attributable to the condition, such as long periods of illness, hospitalization, and missed school and peer interactions. These mean that special accommodations and programs are sometimes required.

It is not unusual for a teacher to have a student in the classroom who has a terminal illness. When this occurs, the inevitability of death has to be faced by the teacher and the other children on some level. Teachers may need special training in managing their own and other students' attitudes toward death and dying (Shell, 1981). When a child with AIDS is in the classroom, for example, children fare best when honest discussions about terminal illness occur right from the beginning (Weiner and Septimus, 1991). Children need to know they had no part in causing the illness and that it is not catching.

Cystic Fibrosis

Cystic fibrosis (CF) is a genetically determined inborn error of metabolism characterized by pervasive dysfunction of the exocrine glands (glands in which secretions are passed through ducts).

The condition seems to be both ethnically and geographically variable—it is very rare among Swedes and among African Americans and virtually non-existent among Asians. Among Caucasians, cystic fibrosis is the most frequently occurring genetic disorder in North America and many European countries (Brinthaupt, 1991). One out of every 20 Caucasians is a carrier of the gene for cystic fibrosis, and approximately one birth in every 1 600 to 2 000 among North American Caucasians is affected (Brinthaupt, 1991). In a family with an affected child, two out of three siblings are likely to be carriers, and one out of five is likely to have the disease.

Cystic fibrosis is transmitted through an autosomal recessive gene, but it appears that more than one genetic defect can cause the disease. The main malformation in the CF gene's twisted double chain of DNA is the absence of a few chemicals. However, some 15 000 DNA samples taken from patients around the world with cystic fibrosis indicate that there are at least 60 and probably a good many more additional malformations that produce the symptoms that were classically lumped together as cystic fibrosis.

Cystic fibrosis is therefore an extremely complex and involved disorder, quite variable in its manifestation. The condition primarily affects the respiratory and digestive systems, although there are varied degrees of system involvement. Fully manifested cases present a triad of chronic pulmonary disease, pancreatic enzyme deficiency, and inordinately high sweat electrolytes. Symptoms include high salt concentration in the sweat glands and the production of thick sticky mucus that clogs breathing and digestion. The mucus obstruction disrupts the functions of the lungs and other vital organs. In the lungs it creates pockets of infection and pulmonary dysfunction which frequently result in chronic episodes of pneumonia and bronchitis. With repeated infection, the lungs are gradually destroyed. As lung deterioration occurs the heart is also burdened, and heart failure is a common by-product of cystic fibrosis.

Excessive mucous secretions also interfere with or prevent digestion and other intestinal processes. Cystic fibrosis affects virtually every part of the digestive system. The pancreas, gall bladder, liver, and intestines often function abnormally and show changes in the tissues. Children often fail to gain weight despite increased appetite. They grow very slowly and never appear to thrive (Holsclaw, 1978).

Intervention for cystic fibrosis is as varied and complex as the disease, requiring diet management, therapy and management of respiratory disorders, and various regimes of drug therapy. Before antibiotics were available, approximately 75 percent of children with cystic fibrosis died before age 10. Life expectancy has been greatly extended and at present many older patients are being treated. Recently, surgical transplants have become an option.

Today's primary treatment procedures are medication and therapy. Antibiotics are prescribed when lung infections are present. With medication, percussion therapy serves to dislodge mucus as the chest is vigorously clapped and vibrated. In addition, diet can be quite effective in the management of disorders of the digestive system. The special diet is high in protein, high in calories, and low in fat. This is combined with dosages of an enzyme needed to compensate for the insufficiency of the pancreas.

Developmental Consequences

Children with cystic fibrosis do not suffer any form of intellectual impairment and should be educated in regular classrooms. However, they will probably miss many days of school because of respiratory infections or intestinal disorders. They may have a chronic cough and may need extra snacks during the day.

It is on the family that a child with cystic fibrosis seems to have the greatest impact. For many families, everyday activities are dependent on the current health status of the ill child. Regimens of treatment, medication, feeding, positioning, and medical care can take up most of the day. Parents must learn the therapeutic techniques to assist in their child's treatment. This usually consists of twice daily half-hour sessions involving chest percussion and postural

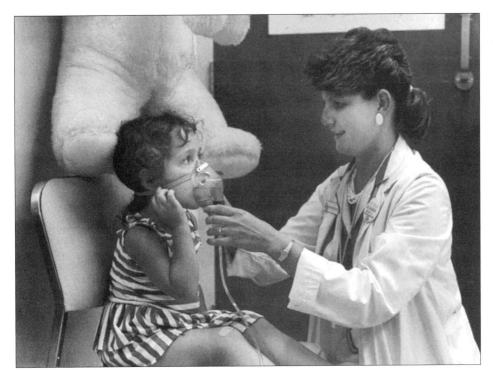

Treatment for cystic fibrosis is extensive. It involves diet management, respiratory disease management, and drug therapy.

draining. The purpose of pounding the chest is to elicit coughing, which encourages the elimination of mucus. The changes in posture also aid in the draining process.

When the child is young, meal times can be a recurrent problem, with hours spent feeding the child. As well, medical decisions become an ongoing part of family life. Parents spend much time searching out information and becoming fluent in the medical terms related to their child's illness.

Diabetes Mellitus

Diabetes mellitus is a disorder of sugar metabolism caused by a pancreatic disorder in the production of insulin, a hormone needed to metabolize glucose. Unlike many chronic health disorders, diabetes is a high-incidence condition. In Canada, it affects one in every 600 children under the age of 10.

Diabetes is divided into two major types. Type I, or insulin-dependent diabetes, is usually associated with early onset (under 25 years of age) and includes juvenile diabetes. Type II, non-insulin-dependent diabetes, ordinarily occurs after age 40 (Krupp and Chatton, 1983). Type II diabetics produce quantities of insulin but they do not use it efficiently.

Type I diabetes brews silently for several years. The onset of the disease is signalled by thirst, hunger, weight loss, fatigue or weakness, excessive urination, and sometimes blurred vision. Onset may occur several months after the outbreak of specific viruses (Rodger and Hunt, 1980). For example, there may be sequelae resulting from maternal rubella. One study of rubella-deafened children discovered that 2 percent had overt diabetes and a total of 20 percent had abnormalities of glucose metabolism (Shaver, Boughman, and Nance, 1985).

Young people stricken with insulin-dependent (Type I) diabetes once faced certain death within a year of diagnosis. As the pancreas lost its ability to make the insulin required for normal metabolism, glucose accumulated in the blood stream and urine. The body then drew on other sources of energy until it literally starved, and death ensued.

Isolation of the insulin hormone from animals in 1921 made it possible to control diabetes with daily insulin injections and has since meant survival for millions of diabetics. Note that neither animal insulin nor the more modern human form offer a cure. Injections must be taken once or more a day for life. Many diabetics eventually suffer from devastating complications. As the disease persists, blood vessels can be damaged, leading to heart disease, stroke, blindness, or kidney failure. Nerve damage is also common (Atkinson and MacLaren, 1990).

The treatment of Type I diabetes involves a diet low in carbohydrates and fats accompanied by regular injections of insulin. Food intake, insulin, and exercise must be carefully balanced and monitored throughout the diabetic's life.

Insulin intake, diet, and exercise can prevent immediate and long-term complications associated with hyperglycemia (high blood sugar) or hypoglycemia (low blood sugar). Hyperglycemia leads to ketoacidosis, a chemical imbalance that produces acute and serious illness, unconsciousness, coma, and ultimately death. Although moderate but chronic hyperglycemia is thought to cause the long-term complications associated with diabetes in adulthood (such as retinopathy and microvascular disease), the specific effects of a moderate elevation of blood glucose on children's brain functioning is not known. Severe hypoglycemia, caused by an excess of insulin intake, produces unconsciousness and seizures. Both hypoglycemic convulsions and ketoacidosis have been associated with abnormalities in brain functioning (Rovet, Erlich, and Hoppe, 1988).

The symptoms of non-insulin-dependent diabetes, a disease caused by an entirely different mechanism that is not fully understood, are more subtle than Type I diabetes. Type II diabetics are usually older than 40 and overweight; susceptibility may be genetically transmitted (Berkow, 1982). These patients produce various quantities of insulin but they typically use it inefficiently. Some are treated with insulin to control blood glucose levels, but they do not require the drug for day-to-day survival (Atkinson and Maclaren, 1990).

Developmental Consequences

Children who are diabetic can participate in all school activities unless otherwise advised by a physician. In addition to regular education, children must be taught to manage their condition. Parents and medical personnel teach older children to inject their own insulin, monitor their blood sugar and urine sugar levels, and maintain a balance among nutrition, exercise, and insulin levels.

In young children, the balance of diet, exercise, and insulin is often difficult to maintain, particularly in the presence of illness or infection. School personnel must always be informed when a student is diabetic. Teachers should understand the child's condition and recognize signs of imbalance. Health personnel should provide appropriate guidelines regarding the timing of school meals and school exercise.

Children with diabetes have an average range of intelligence, although those who develop their diabetes early in life are at risk for subsequent neuro-cognitive impairments and often show specific skill deficits. The earlier the onset, the more difficulties are experienced. Researchers who explored the effects on children's cognitive development of insulin-dependent diabetes mellitus concluded that those who develop diabetes before the age of four are at greatest risk for subsequent intellectual impairment (Rovet, Erlich, and Hoppe, 1988). Particularly affected are skills in the visuo-spatial area of cognitive functioning and mathematical ability. These findings correlate with a poorer academic history and a greater need for special education. Girls appear to be somewhat more affected than boys.

Diabetes is more than simply a matter of diet, insulin, and urine testing. It also involves an individual's emotional and physical development, which largely depend upon the reaction of others to the condition. The environment affects diabetic control, and diabetic control, in turn, affects the environment. This is particularly true of the school environment since children spend so much time in school.

Students who are diabetic may experience embarrassment over their unusual diets, the urine testing, and any symptoms of diabetic shock that may be displayed. Peers may ridicule them and treat them differently. An understanding and tactful teacher can minimize any potentially uncomfortable situations and model accepting attitudes for other students. The teacher may also wish to explain diabetes so that the other children in the class can understand the condition.

The child who is diabetic often experiences feelings of being punished (injections and no sweets) and of being different and inadequate. The child is likely to lack in self-confidence and self-esteem and may avoid activities for fear of failure. Additional praise and encouragement for accomplishments may be necessary. The Profile below describes some of the issues an adolescent with diabetes might experience.

Profile

Bob

Bob is entering his first year of high school this year. While many students worry about the move to a large somewhat impersonal school plant with many teachers and different responsibilities, Bob's reactions are far beyond the usual. He has told his parents over and over that he does not wish to attend high school and that if they force him to go he'll run away from home. His parents, deeply concerned, nevertheless understand Bob's reluctance.

Two years ago Bob was stricken with juvenile diabetes. For a healthy, active, and outgoing child, the effects were devastating. Bob was old enough to understand the chronic nature of the disease and to realize the restraints it would place on his life in terms of insulin injections and diet. He abandoned many of his usual pursuits, ignored his friends, and began to fall seriously behind in school work.

Although Bob is old enough to administer his own insulin, monitor his urine, and adapt his diet, he tacitly refused to do any of these things. It took a psychologist many months to help Bob to realize the necessity of attending to his own health care needs.

Even though he now looks after his own needs, Bob is resentful of the disease and embarrassed about it in front of his friends. His reluctance to attend high school centres on his fear of acute embarrassment in the case of an insulin coma (of which he has suffered a few) as well as his dislike of anyone knowing of his condition. To help Bob, his parents have again contacted the psychologist and hope that counselling will help overcome some of his deep-seated resentment about the diabetes.

Cancer

Cancer is a general term used to describe about a hundred conditions characterized by abnormal and uncontrolled cell growth. Cancer is the chief cause of death by disease in children aged three to fourteen. More children recover from cancer than do adults.

In adults, the most common cancers are lung, colon, and skin cancers. The most common cancers in children are of the blood, bone, brain, nervous system, and kidney. Acute lymphocytic leukemia is the most common of the childhood cancers. Approximately one-third of all cancers diagnosed in children are leukemias (Peckham, 1993), and leukemia is responsible for two-thirds of the deaths of children with cancer.

Survival rates for children with cancer have increased dramatically in the past two decades. For example, Wilms' tumour (a kidney cancer) has a survival rate of over 90 percent. Long-term survival rates of children with brain tumours is approaching 50 percent. Leukemia now has a survival rate of 70 percent or better (Peckham, 1993).

Major treatments for cancer are surgery, chemotherapy, and/or radiation, which may result in short- and long-term effects. Children respond in a variety of ways to current radiotherapy and chemotherapy. After diagnosis, a four-week treatment period begins with intensive therapy. When remission is confirmed, oral drugs are introduced.

Developmental Consequences

Apart from the condition itself, one of the major outcomes of cancer is the physical and emotional problems arising from treatment. Each child will have a unique experience at the hospital and in the diagnosis and treatment of a particular kind of childhood cancer. Children are told of the problem to enlist their help in treatment.

For many children, chemotherapy drugs cause plumpness and hair loss. Other physical results include amputation, disturbances in normal growth patterns, mood swings, difficulties in concentration, muscle weakness, fatigue, nausea, and dramatic weight gain or weight loss.

School is a major part of each child's life and children with cancer gain special benefits from education at all stages of their illness. They need the satisfaction of being normal productive learners and should attend school even in the terminal stages of the illness, if possible. School attendance provides peer contact and opportunities for maintaining self-esteem and competence by completing short-term goals. School helps in distracting children from their physical concerns, assists in their long-term emotional and physical rehabilitation, and helps them reach optimal social and psychological development.

It is important that teachers understand the illness and how it affects the child at each maturational stage. Teachers must be aware that after a period of hospitalization a youngster may be less energetic and very likely to hold deep concerns about the nature of the illness. Anger about forced dependency on parents and frustration at having to submit to the disruptions of therapy can cause withdrawal and regression. All this can result in decreased educational motivation, poor self-concept, social isolation, and an abnormally close relationship with one parent.

The teacher is a valuable link in the total care of the child. Teachers help by communicating with and supporting parents, by being a liaison between them and other professionals, and by helping the child to interact with others. Other class members should be prepared for their classmate's physical changes—loss of hair, weight gain, and the like.

Acquired Immunodeficiency Syndrome (AIDS)

Acquired Immunodeficiency Syndrome (AIDS) is caused by the virus HIV (human immunodeficiency virus) that attacks and seriously disrupts the body's immune system, its defence against disease. Without the protection of the immune system, AIDS sufferers are prone to fatal infections and cancers.

Today there are really only two major populations of children with HIV infection. The first is children with congenital or birth-acquired infection. About 30 percent of infants of HIV-infected mothers will acquire the virus. Almost all of these infected children will develop AIDS before the age of two. The second group of HIV-infected students is adolescents who acquire the virus sexually or through intravenous drug use. A very small third group are those infected by transfusions.

The typical course of AIDS depends upon how the infection was transmitted. For children who are affected before birth, the median incubation period is twelve months. For children infected as a result of transfusion, the median incubation period is three to five years (Simonds and Rogers, 1992). This means that many young children who have transfusion-transmitted AIDS will be in the school system.

Developmental Consequences

Pediatric AIDS is a severe medical condition as well as a potential neurological disability—symptomatic pediatric HIV cases involve central nervous system (cns) damage in as many as 78 to 93 percent of cases (Diamond and Cohen, 1987). As well, the disease carries a heavy weight of social and ethical concerns. Public ignorance and fear, coupled with sensationalist media reporting, have combined to create an atmosphere of fear and misunderstanding. Because AIDS is fatal and incurable, and because it has been linked in the public consciousness to homosexuality and drug use, it evokes passionately held opinions and deep fears (Kirp and Epstein, 1989).

Schools have been among the key North American institutions in which the meaning of AIDS has been debated and deciphered. Schools are facing problems in trying to accommodate children with AIDS while coming to grips with the fears and misunderstandings circulating in the community. Scientists may have demonstrated that HIV is not transmitted by casual contact, but parents and teachers concerned about the devastating nature of AIDS are not going to give up the myths easily (Dodds, Volker, and Vivand, 1989).

For parents, AIDS balances their interest in protecting the health and safety of their children against the public's interest in providing non-discriminatory schooling for all children. At the same time, AIDS poses a number of special challenges to teachers who are being forced to confront the issues of risk, relationships, and education and to deal with personal uncertainties, fear, and prejudices (Gilliss, 1990; Sloane and Sloane, 1990).

Having a child in the classroom who has AIDS means facing many unknowns. Teachers ask, "How will the other students react?" "What will parents say?" "Can I handle it?" "What type of support can I expect?" and "What should I be concerned about?"

First and foremost, anyone working with or planning for children with AIDS must understand the nature and course of HIV infection in children. They should realize that affected children show typical associated symptoms that include attention difficulties; cardiac disease; cognitive deficits; cold sores; coughing; diarrhea that can be acute and chronic; emotional problems; fine and gross motor difficulties; hearing problems; infections that include frequent bacterial and viral infections and middle ear, eye, and joint infections; seizures; shortness of breath; speech and language delays; visual problems; weakness; and weight loss (Le Roy, Powell, and Kelber, 1994). There will be progressive neurological defects, including speech, motor, and cognitive regressions. Children may also have to cope with social isolation, long-term hospitalization, parental illness and death, family problems, and lack of understanding.

School transmission of HIV is unlikely. The major health risk is to the child who has the virus, because that child will be more susceptible to and seriously affected by common childhood illnesses or may develop life-threatening complications.

The second challenge for teachers is to be consistently sympathetic and compassionate toward students and colleagues who may be infected with HIV. Excluding a child with AIDS teaches all children the wrong lessons about tolerance and about community.

Third, teachers must help other class members to understand and tolerate the condition. Children need accurate information. For example, a study (Schvaneveldt, Lindauer, and Young, 1990) showed that some third graders believed that AIDS could be contracted from toilet seats or people's clothing, and many held that cigarettes caused the disease.

While children with pediatric AIDS are not necessarily special education candidates, many qualify because of limited strength and vitality and acute health problems. When they are placed in special education, the most successful programs for them parallel those for other special learners. Instruction should be designed for success, based on concrete experiences, and broken down into small, manageable steps.

Sickle Cell Anemia

The defective recessive gene involved in sickle cell anemia results in the production of defective haemoglobin. Affected individuals produce abnormal haemoglobin, which then causes distortions in blood cells; under certain conditions, the red blood cells "sickle" (change shape). Sickle-shaped cells tend to clot together; the shape causes the cells to pile up and block small blood vessels, causing pain and tissue destruction (Pierce, 1990). However, the intensity of the effects varies widely.

Because the sickle cell trait protects against death from malaria, it is common in populations from malaria-prone parts of the world, which include areas of Africa and the Mediterranean countries. Sickle cell anemia is carried by about two million African Americans (about one in ten). Among Hispanic Americans, about one in twenty is a carrier. Sickle cell is therefore thought to affect about 500 000 people in the United States. Of the 10 percent of African Americans with sickle cell, most are heterozygous (one normal and one abnormal gene). Only about 0.25 percent are homozygous (two defective genes).

Individuals who are homozygous often have long bouts of illness and die in childhood. Because sickle cell impairs circulation, sufferers experience severe pains in their abdomen, back, head, and limbs. The deformed blood cells rupture easily. The disease also causes the heart to enlarge and deprives the brain cells of blood. People with severe cases may suffer heart and kidney problems and pneumonia, which can be fatal.

Those who are heterozygous (carriers) suffer fewer effects; intensity varies widely. Sickling occurs under certain conditions such as exposure to low oxygen levels. In carriers, 40 percent of the red blood cells may assume a sickle shape when the supply of oxygen to the blood is reduced. Treatment of a crisis usually involves rest, medication for pain, blood transfusions, and oxygen inhalation therapy.

In older children and adults, it appears that the sickle cell trait is generally benign and does not shorten life, although it may bring danger with exercise and increased altitude. The situation seems to be more serious for infants. In the United States, investigators have reported a mortality rate of 13 to 14 percent among sickle cell children under the age of two (Grover, Shahidi, Fisher, Goldberg, and Wethers, 1983). The spleen, the most efficient blood filter in the body, is vulnerable (Eichner, 1986).

Allergies

Allergy, a term coined by Clemens von Pirquet in 1906, means "altered reaction" (Hay, 1990). The term is used interchangeably with *hypersensitivity*, and is defined as "an abnormal and varied reaction which occurs following a contact with substances or agents which normally do not cause symptoms in other individuals" (Kuzemko, 1978).

There are two major categories of allergies. *Atopic allergies* are associated with hereditary and/or familial factors. The risk to children when both parents have a positive history of allergy is 30 to 40 percent, while the risk to children when one parent has a positive history is 20 to 30 percent (Kuzemko, 1978). *Non-atopic allergies* do not have a hereditary component but result from antibodies produced in response to allergens in the environment.

A huge range of substances create allergic reactions in humans. Generally, substances are divided into four categories: inhalants, contactants, ingestants, and injectants. Inhalants include dust, pollen, mould, aerosol sprays, and strong odours. Contactants are substances that come into contact with the skin, including fabrics, metals, cosmetics, and chemicals. Ingestants are foods and drugs; injectants are agents or substances that enter the body through the skin, including insect bites, bee stings, and some drugs (Voignier and Bridgewater, 1980).

There are a number of types of allergic reaction. One of the most common is allergic rhinitis, which may be either seasonal or perennial. The seasonal type—hay fever—is induced by windborne pollens; the perennial form is present throughout the year. Both forms involve nasal congestion, itching of the nose, or repetitive sneezing. Allergic pulmonary disease is usually referred to as bronchial asthma. The major symptom is narrowing of the bronchial tubes resulting in diminished air flow. Urticaria and eczema are skin reactions resulting in rashes, itching, swelling, and seeping of body fluids through the skin. Physical allergy is a response to cold, heat, or sunlight. Allergic conjunctivitis involves itching of the eyes and excessive tears. Gastro-intestinal allergy is a response to specific foods or drugs.

Asthma

The word **asthma** derives from the Greek meaning panting or difficulty in breathing. The condition is defined as a "variable, reversible obstruction of the airways characterized by the narrowing of bronchial tubes, swelling of tissues, and clogging of mucus" (Smith, 1978, p. 48).

Asthma should never be considered anything less than a serious condition. Approximately 20 children and 500 adults die as a result of asthma each year in Canada (Canadian Lung Association, 1997). Of all provinces, Alberta has the highest asthma mortality rate; compared to Saskatchewan and Manitoba, for example, Alberta's death rate is three times higher (Alberta Lung Association, nd; Canadian Lung Association, 1997).

An individual's asthma can be a continuous state of frequent attacks ranging in severity, or an intermittent state consisting of occasional attacks ranging from mild to severe (Howse, 1988). In young children, boys are twice as likely as girls to exhibit the condition. Many children improve or go into remission in adolescence. At the same time, a levelling occurs so that the male–female ratio is one to one after the age of 15.

Asthmatic attacks are characterized by wheezing, paroxysmal coughing, and shortness of breath. While a wide variety of stimuli are associated with bronchospasms, there may also be an inherited susceptibility. Many modern researchers believe that asthma is caused by "the interactions of heredity and environment" (Isabell and Barber, 1993, p. 245).

Different stimuli account for asthmatic attacks. The first group, known factors, include allergens, drugs, exercise, industrial exposure, infections, and reflexes. A second category, probable causes, includes things such as air pollutants, chemical irritants, sinusitis, and vasculitis. A final group, classed as possible triggers, include emotions, hormonal imbalance, and weather (Young, 1980). Nevertheless, it is extremely difficult to pinpoint exactly which factor or factors trigger an individual asthma attack since the same factors are not always responsible for subsequent attacks (Howse, 1988).

Various medications, of which drugs are the most common, are employed in the treatment of asthma. Since Adrenalin, the first drug treatment of asthma, was introduced, a wide number of drugs have emerged. These include drugs that act on the airways directly, drugs that halt the production of antigens, and corticosteroids which also hinder antigen production (Howse, 1988).

Bronchodilators are used to relieve obstruction of airflow. In severe cases, corticosteroids are useful. Both have side effects. Bronchodilators may overstimulate the child and cause hyperactive behaviour; excessive use of corticosteroids may result in abnormal hair growth, excessive appetite, and slowed growth. Common sense factors in treatment, other than medications, include rest, sufficient fluids, play and work to tolerance, avoidance of the allergens that cause attacks, and regular exercise to improve postural drainage, strengthen the diaphragm muscles, and expand lung capacity (Butts, 1980; Pilecka, 1995).

Developmental Consequences

Among children with asthma, school absenteeism is a major problem, especially in the first three years of school. Asthma is estimated to account for as much as 20 to 25 percent of all school absences (Pituch and Bruggeman, 1982).

Despite the fact that children who are asthmatic tend to have IQs slightly higher than average, they are likely to be underachievers and to be behind in school work, especially as adolescents. Children with asthma also have more emotional difficulties, but the nature of the relationship between psychological problems and asthmatic episodes is poorly understood (Pilecka, 1995).

Children Who Are Abused and Neglected

The history of humanity is rife with examples of cruelty to children, ranging from infanticide in early societies to child factory labour in the nineteenth and twentieth centuries. (This is discussed in the Research Notes on child abuse.) So although some researchers feel that child abuse is on the increase, it is more likely that abuse, under modern definitional constructs, is simply more open to identification and reporting.

It is not possible to assess the exact dimensions of child abuse and neglect because there remains widespread under-reporting. Many factors contribute; these include the social

Research Notes

Child Abuse

Child abuse is not new in our modern Western society. As Lloyd de Mause points out, "The human track record of child raising is bloody, dirty and mean" (1975, p. 85). For many centuries, maltreatment was justified in the belief that severe physical punishment was necessary to maintain discipline, to transmit educational ideas, to please certain gods, or to expel evil spirits (Radbill, 1974).

In tracing the history of child abuse, de Mause (1974) placed common societal reactions to children within six major, though overlapping and intertwined, stages: infanticidal, abandoning, ambivalent, intrusive, socializing, and helping. Infanticide existed in very early societies. It was not until the fourth century that the Church halted the practice. After that, many children were abandoned to wander, beg, or die by the wayside. The ambivalent mode appeared first in the late Middle Ages. Parents still displayed aggressive tendencies toward their children but generally kept them at home. Intrusive parenting, characterized by draconian authoritarianism, arose in the early eighteenth century.

The need for children to be socialized and helped paralleled the full blossoming of the notion of childhood as a discrete stage of development and children as separate beings, not miniature adults. Children were then provided with special environments, such as schools, and child labour laws brought them out of the mines and the factories.

Overt forms of child abuse prominent in earlier periods may have disappeared. Nevertheless, child abuse remains an endemic problem in modern society. In its modern garb, the problems of child abuse were first brought to the forefront by Caffey (1946), who suggested that ill treatment of children might be an intentional act on the part of parents. This caused a wave of concern, and throughout the 1950s research increased. In the early 1960s, a seminar on child abuse led to the identification of what became known as the Battered Child Syndrome (Kempe, Silverman, Steele, Droegemueller, and Silver, 1962). Following this, there was a flurry of articles, books, and research papers reflecting a heightened interest on the part of educators, social workers, welfare agencies, and politicians. By the 1970s, policies were established and laws enacted that recognized and protected abused children.

In Canada the awareness of child neglect and abuse has increased dramatically. A plethora of child protection laws have led to the development of policies and programs for intervention, education, and prevention. The law now requires the reporting of possible instances of abuse to the authorities. Teachers, neighbours, physicians, and anyone else who suspects child abuse are required to seek assistance for the child.

stigma attached to child beating, cultural variations in expectations concerning the roles of parents and children, and the fact that only a portion of children are taken for medical intervention. As well, parents make up believable stories, children are too young or too frightened to disclose what actually happened, and some physicians would rather attribute the symptoms to an accident than confront the awful truth (Fontana and Besharov, 1979).

Scientific studies of the prevalence of sexual abuse are rare, but there is a general consensus that the actual rate is underestimated by official reports because of the severe consequences of disclosure—public retribution, family disruption, unemployment and subsequent economic disaster, loss of friends, and incarceration (Csapo, 1988).

Child abuse exists regardless of occupation, educational attainment, religion, marital status, or family configuration. Abuse occurs at every socio-economic level, though it is more frequently reported among poorer families (Harris, 1986); the frequency of child abuse appears to vary across cultures (Korbin, 1987).

Essentially, abuse is not a fixed single incident but an ongoing interaction between parents and children associated with dysfunctional parent–child relations (Youngblade and Bibby, 1989). When looked at in this way, abuse becomes a complex combination of parent variables and child behaviours.

Definitions

There have been many thoughtful discussions about appropriate definitions of child abuse and neglect, psychological maltreatment of children, child sexual abuse, and spouse abuse; however, no consensus has been reached (Emery, 1989). In a general sense, child abuse is defined as "any interaction or lack of interaction...which results in non-accidental harm to the individual's physical and/or emotional state" (Helfer, 1987, p. 61).

Within the broad definition, subcategories have developed to describe specific aspects of abuse and neglect. Physical abuse is a non-accidental physical injury to a child. Overt and consistent signs indicate physical abuse. For example, children acquire many strange bruises in the course of normal activities; it is the frequency of such bruising that arouses the suspicion of abuse (Tower, 1984). Further indications of physical abuse include bald spots, burns from cigarettes or hot water, and marks from a strap or rope (Harrison, 1985). Behavioural indicators of physical abuse may include intolerance of physical contact and wearing inappropriate clothing that covers the body. Abused children may arrive at school early and stay late, suggesting a fear of going home.

Sexual abuse is one of the most studied areas. Sexual abuse is defined as "the sexual exploitation of a child who is not developmentally capable of understanding or resisting the contact, and a child or adolescent who may be psychologically and socially dependent upon the perpetrator" (Csapo, 1988, p. 121).

Sexual involvement imposed upon a child by an adult includes pedophilia, rape, and all forms of incest. Incest, the most common type of sexual abuse, refers to any kind of sexual activity between a child and relatives, either blood or legal, including fathers, mothers, stepparents, siblings, and so on (Mouzakitis and Vachese, 1985).

Victims of sexual abuse display a number of manifestations. Children may have difficulty walking or sitting, or may cry without provocation. They may show sudden drops in school performance or sudden non-participation in school activities accompanied by unusually infantile or withdrawn behaviour (Broadhurst, Edmunds, and MacDicker, 1979).

Neglect is the failure to provide adequate supervision, hygiene, nutrition, medical care, or the basic love and nurturing that children need to grow and develop. Emotional neglect refers to the failure of caretakers to provide the loving positive emotional atmosphere necessary to the development of self-esteem in a child.

Physical neglect can be as damaging psychologically as overt physical or sexual abuse. Experts now believe that strong and recurrent psychological abuse and neglect may prove to be even more harmful to children in the long run (Emery, 1989; Hart and Brassard, 1987). Neglect has been cited as the most common form of abuse as well as the most destructive, causing more deaths, injuries, and long-term problems than other types.

Neglected children tend to be ill-clothed and poorly fed. They may have untreated physical or medical problems and appear to be tired and listless. Possible behavioural responses include stealing food, falling asleep in class, frequent school absences, and pugnacious and destructive activity.

Indicators of emotional maltreatment are varied. Many children develop emotional or behavioural disorders for no apparent reason. Many of these cases could be the result of the caregiver failing to meet the child's basic emotional needs. In these children, observers may note delayed development, neurotic traits, or antisocial behaviour.

Prevalence of Child Abuse

Studies attempting to define the typical abusive family or parent provide inconsistent results. Abusive parents have been described as immature, impulsive, self-centred, hypersensitive, quick to react with poorly controlled aggression, and tending to show extremely inconsistent patterns of interaction with the child (Steele, 1986). Abusive parents have little knowledge of good parenting and tend to hold unrealistic expectations; they ascribe adult functions to children and cannot understand that children possess limited control, capabilities, and comprehension. They expect children to be good, loving, and obedient at all times, and when their child's disobedience or inattention threatens their perceptions of themselves as good parents, they use excessive discipline because they see it as their duty to make children behave. Many abusing parents are unable to cope with the complex problems of life. They tend to be isolated or their lifestyle may be chaotic. There seems to be a significant over-representation of alcoholism in severe cases of child maltreatment (Famularo, Stone, Barnum, and Wharton, 1986).

Consistently, the literature points to a cycle of abuse theory. That is, abusive parents were abused children themselves, and often patterns of maltreatment can be traced back three or four generations (Steele, 1986). Some researchers feel that the assumptions underlying a cyclical theory are not supported by available data, and that the majority of abused parents do not abuse their own children (e.g. Benjamin, 1980; Widom, 1989). Anywhere between 25 and 33 percent of all children who are abused grow up and abuse their own children (Kaufman and Zigler, 1989; Widom, 1989), and whether parents continue the cycle of abuse is influenced by many aspects of their developmental history, not just the abuse.

Just as strongly, other investigators believe in a cycle of abuse. Not only do parents who were abused mistreat their own children, but they tend to repeat the same types of abuse to which they were subjected, be it physical, sexual, or neglect (Steele, 1986).

Children learn parenting techniques from their own experiences in the family. A loving, cared-for child learns to become a good parent. A child who is unloved, neglected, and abused learns poor parenting behaviours. If a parent who was abused has a healthy, docile child, abusive tendencies may be held in check. However, if the child is ill or difficult to manage or if other stresses occur, the parent may well harm the child. Abuse and neglect may occur from conception (alcoholic mothers) to adolescence.

In some families, only one of several children in the family is abused. This child may be different by virtue of sex, by resembling a disliked family member, or by failing to meet the parent's expectations. There is a correlation between excessive crying and child abuse, although which is the cause and which is the effect is a matter of debate. Children can be more open to abuse because of the mental, physical, and behavioural anomalies that increase their vulnerability to abuse, or because they have developed characteristics that increase the likelihood of abuse (Frodi, 1981).

Children with disabilities, sick children, and premature and low-birth-weight children who require special attention or costly treatment and who fail to respond to the caregivers' efforts in ways the parents can appreciate appear to be at greater risk for abuse (Augoustinos, 1987; Frodi, 1981; Zirpoli, Snell, and Lloyd, 1987). Abuse seems very common among children with behavioural disorders (Zirpoli, 1990).

Developmental Consequences

There is sufficient empirical evidence to support the widely held assumption that child abuse and neglect have developmental effects on the physical, neurological, intellectual, and emotional development of children (Augoustinos, 1987). The data strongly suggest that systematic abuse causes significant dysfunction in intellectual, emotional, developmental, and motoric ability. Among adolescents in particular, systematic abuse creates substantial at-risk conditions for psychological, interpersonal, academic, medical, and legal problems. Self-image, motivation, personal satisfaction, and success in the workplace are negatively affected (Fink and Janssen, 1992).

Child abuse directly affects the amount of time children are in the classroom and their ability and interest in learning while in school. Intellectual development has been found to be delayed among some abused and neglected children with no evidence of neurological impairment (Augoustinos, 1987). One major study (Lynch and Roberts, 1982) found verbal scores to be more depressed than performance scores.

Social and emotional difficulties are endemic. Abused toddlers, for example, often respond to agemates' distress with fear, anger, or physical attacks (Main and George, 1985). Older children tend to show more aggressive behaviour than their peers. Abused elementary-aged children tend to be highly aggressive and are often rejected by their peers (Downey and Walker, 1989). Adolescents frequently respond to abuse through depression, suicide attempts, explosive anger, alcohol, drug abuse, self-mutilation, running away, or prostitution (see Destad, 1987).

Child maltreatment is destructive to the child who experiences it, to the caregiver who commits it, and to the society that allows it. Teachers hold both a moral and a legal responsibility for reporting suspected cases of abuse. They must know how to recognize the signs of abuse, how and where to report it, and what the school can do to offer support. When considering the significance of symptoms or behaviours, consultation with a public health nurse will prove to be very helpful.

Musculoskeletal Impairments

Musculoskeletal impairments are those that affect body movement and functioning but are not caused by neurological damage. These include a wide range of impairments; some are listed in Table 11-2 and a few are discussed in more detail below. Depending on the type and severity of the conditions, physical and motor development is affected.

When discussing *physical development*, we are referring to the acquisition of postural control and the necessary movement patterns to produce functional motor acts. **Motor** is a

Table 11-2 Some examples of orthopedic conditions that affect children

Clubfoot	Congenital malpositioning of one or both feet
Osteomyelitis	Bacterial infection of the bones
Osteogenesis imperfecta	Congenital abnormality of the bony cells resulting in frequent fractures causing deformities
Scoliosis	Congenital or acquired curvature of the spine, often caused by muscle weakness, dystrophy, or atrophy
Hip dislocation	Congenital misplacement of the thigh bone in the hip socket
Legg-Calvé-Perthes	Flattening of the head of a long bone, usually the thigh
Muscular atrophy	Degeneration of muscle tissue due to neural damage

Source: David, 1987

term used to denote muscular movement; motor development is the process through which a child acquires movement patterns and skills.

Limb Deficiencies

Limb deficiencies include the loss or absence of entire limbs or parts of limbs. A child born with such a condition is said to have a congenital amputation.

Congenital amputations of unusually large proportions occurred in the late 1950s and early 1960s due to Thalidomide, an anti-nausea drug prescribed to pregnant women for morning sickness. In Canada, the United States, and Europe, thousands of children were born with missing or deformed limbs. This specific condition is called *phocomelia*, a congenital deformity in which parts of limbs or entire limbs are missing or very short.

Congenital amputations are much less prevalent than acquired amputations. Many children lose limbs in mishaps involving vehicles, contact with high voltage lines, burns, and other accidents. In some instances, surgical amputations may be performed to prevent the spread of bone cancer or massive infections. Defective limbs or parts of limbs may also be amputated to permit the use of **prostheses**, functional devices that substitute for missing body parts.

Abnormalities of the bony structures include a number of conditions other than limb deficiencies. Some are congenital, such as spina bifida, cleft palate, clubfoot, hip dislocation, and osteogenesis imperfecta.

Spinal Problems

There are three types of curvature of the spine—scoliosis, lordosis, and kyphosis. *Lordosis* is an anterior (forward) curvature when viewed from the side. *Kyphosis* is a posterior (backward) curvature when viewed from the side. *Scoliosis*, which refers to a lateral (side to side) curve in the spine that is absent in normal spines, is the most common form of curvature. It is associated with prominent shoulder blades, poor posture, uneven shoulders, and a flattening of the back (Bauer and Shea, 1989). Scoliosis can impair motor functions.

Muscular Dystrophy

A number of conditions are characterized by a weakening and wasting away of muscular tissue. If there has been neurological damage or if the muscles are weakened due to nerve degeneration, the condition is known as **atrophy**. *Myopathy* occurs when there is no evidence of neurological disease or impairment. When the myopathy is progressive and hereditary, the condition is referred to as dystrophy (Hallahan and Kauffman, 1991).

Muscular dystrophy refers to a group of inherited conditions characterized by degeneration of muscle fibres without neurological deficit. The condition occurs in different forms, all characterized by progressive muscle weakness. The different types differ with regard to age of onset, the site of initial muscle involvement, and the kinds of hereditary transmission.

The most common type of the disorder is Duchenne's muscular dystrophy, often called pseudohypertonic muscular dystrophy. The term *pseudohypertonic*, meaning "false growth," describes an enlargement of the calves and sometimes other muscles. This enlargement occurs as a result of fatty deposits in the muscle along with degeneration of the muscle fibres.

As Duchenne's muscular dystrophy is inherited through a sex-linked recessive gene, this form typically occurs in boys. At birth, the child appears normal. In the early stages, the condition is painless and the symptoms unnoticeable. But onset is early and may be evident when the child is learning to walk. Gradually muscle fibres waste away to be replaced by fatty tissue. The child's pelvic area is affected first and then the shoulder girdle. By the age of four to seven years, the child exhibits a waddling gait and frequent falls, and has difficulty in climbing stairs and in standing up from a sitting position (Berkow, 1982). In the second stage of the condition, the child suffers difficulty in muscle movement; by the age of five, many affected children require ambulation aids. The condition worsens so that by the third stage, somewhere about eight years of age, the child is confined to a wheelchair. Finally, the individual is bedridden and totally dependent.

For children with Duchenne's muscular dystrophy, the progressive muscle weakness equates with an abbreviated life span. Before the advent of antibiotics, the life expectancy for children with Duchenne's was even shorter than today's twenty to thirty years. Death usually occurred in adolescence as a result of exhaustion, respiratory infection, heart failure, or, most often, pneumonia. Although life expectancy has been extended and recent studies have located the gene for muscular dystrophy, no treatment has yet been found to halt muscle decline.

Another form of the condition is Landouzy-Dejerine muscular dystrophy, also known as facioscapulohumeral muscular dystrophy, reflecting the fact that the facial and shoulder girdle muscles are the areas first affected. The shoulder girdle is weakened but the forearms are spared. As well, the facial features of affected children show drooping of the eyelids and thickening of the lips. Landouzy-Dejerine muscular dystrophy is inherited through dominant genes but is not sex-linked (Berkow, 1982) and is therefore found in both sexes. The condition commonly manifests itself in adolescence, although onset may occur any time between childhood and late adulthood. The progression of the condition alternates with prolonged periods of apparent arrest. Landouzy-Dejerine muscular dystrophy is not life threatening; life expectancy for affected individuals is normal (Krupp and Chatton, 1983).

Although these are the most common forms of muscular dystrophy, several others exist. For example, Charot-Marie-Tooth (CMT) is considered to be a form of muscular dystrophy. There are also related neuro-muscular disorders such as Friedreich's ataxia. Many forms are characterized by progressive muscle weakness and tissue change but the predicted life span varies from one type to another.

Some rather scattered evidence indicates a decrease in intellectual function associated with muscular dystrophy. It has been found that about 50 percent of patients with Duchenne's have a lower IQ than genetic expectations would suggest (Berkow, 1982), and these children tend to have lower than average verbal IQs (Karagan and Zellweger, 1978).

Arthritis

Arthritis is a common term for a variety of chronic systemic conditions involving inflammation of the joints. Many people assume that arthritis is a condition exclusive to adults, especially the aged. In reality, it occurs frequently in children and is then called juvenile arthritis or Still's disease.

Juvenile arthritis is similar in some respects to the adult type. It affects the large joints, sometimes to the extent of interfering with growth in the bony structures. Joint pain is a common feature and destruction of the joints may ensue. Other complications of juvenile arthritis include eye and respiratory infections, enlarged spleen, and inflammation of the tissue covering the heart.

The most severe form is juvenile rheumatoid arthritis, which affects the heart muscles and can be fatal. More girls than boys suffer from this condition. Among children with other disabilities, osteoarthritis is the most common form of arthritis. The cartilage around the joint is damaged, the space between the bones becomes smaller and loses its lubrication, and movement becomes painful or impossible. Osteoarthritis is especially likely to occur when the child has a condition in which a joint has been dislocated. Children with cerebral palsy, for example, may have recurring dislocation and suffer from painful arthritis (Hallahan and Kauffman, 1991).

The causes of both adult and juvenile arthritis are unknown and there is no cure. Aspirin seems to be the most effective medication. In children the prognosis is more favourable than it is for adults; about 75 percent of children with arthritis experience remission of the disease (Berkow, 1982).

Prevention of Physical and Health Disabilities

Although many physical and health disabilities are unpreventable, some precautions can be taken. Good prenatal health and appropriate nutrition reduce the risk to the developing fetus.

Sickle cell carriers can be detected by a simple blood test. Early medical screening can prevent early mortality by referring infants to programs structured for their care. Life-threatening complications of the disease can be diagnosed and treated early, while counselling can be provided to parents.

Genetic counselling is valuable in cases of inherited conditions. With counselling, parents become aware of the risks and are able to make informed decisions.

Massive research continues to try to find means to identify cystic fibrosis and muscular dystrophy carriers and to alleviate the conditions in affected children. Recent medical discoveries in Canada and elsewhere have located the genes responsible for both conditions.

Identification and Assessment

Given the enormous range of conditions, malformations, and diseases encompassed in this category, it is well nigh impossible to make definitive statements regarding assessment. Generally, health disorders and skeletal malformations do not impinge on cognitive and intellectual development, and diagnosticians can therefore use the same range of tools and tests as would be used with regular class children.

With the chronic nature of these conditions, however, special attention must be directed toward social and emotional growth and adaptive behaviour. As well, adaptations in test materials and procedures may be necessary to circumvent a physical disability such as muscular dystrophy. (See Chapters 12 and 14.)

Intervention for Children with Special Health Care Needs

Health disorders and physical disabilities affect children's learning and progress in a number of ways. Learning will be hindered when a child has experienced a great many medical procedures which lead to long periods of recuperation as well as missed time in the classroom. Once in school, children may tire easily, have limited vitality, short attention spans, and limited mobility. A physical impairment can affect a child's range of motion, physical strength, communication, interaction with materials, independence, and daily living skills.

The children discussed in this chapter require a variety of medical, psychological, and ed-

Medical management for health problems can be significant part of a child's daily life.

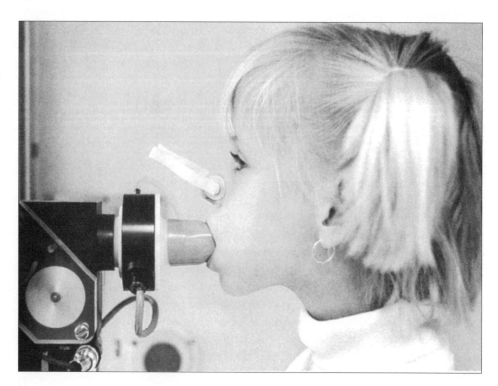

ucational interventions. Social service agencies frequently become involved with them and their families. As they grow older, students may require counselling and other support for independent living.

Medical

As they are essentially medical conditions, health disabilities require a complex and sophisticated range of interventions which include surgical procedures, prosthetic devices, drug therapy, diet management, and ongoing medical treatment. The medical management of these children is intensive, far beyond the scope of this text.

When a child with a health impairment is in the classroom, teachers should keep an emergency protocol that contains information on emergency practices and strategies developed by parents, school personnel, and medical personnel (Campbell, Cohen, and Rich, 1987). The protocol includes names, addresses, and telephone numbers of parents or guardians, emergency contacts, and family physicians.

Therapy

Students may need rehabilitation training and therapy from a range of therapists—physical, occupational, and speech and language. Counselling assumes importance to help students understand and deal with the stresses of the disability and the treatment. The level of knowledge children have about their own orthopedic disabilities is related to age. Generally, children move from a broad understanding of the disability at age six to a more acute realization of the implications by age eight (Dunn, McCartan, and Fugura, 1988). By adolescence, most students will have gained a realistic appreciation of their health condition and the manner in which it affects their lives. (See also Chapter 16.)

Technical

Many technical devices are designed to increase personal independence. Compensatory (assistive, adaptive, prosthetic, and orthotic) devices and equipment allow individuals to compensate for or minimize the effects of a disability. These devices are addressed in Chapter 12.

Educational Intervention

Education is a social norm in the lives of children, and the presence of a physical or health problem should not be seen as a reason to halt schooling. Educational intervention for children with special health care needs represents a critical aspect of the child's total health planning. Lacking school experiences, the child's psychosocial development would be seriously jeopardized. Special education assistance may be necessary simply because students are likely to be absent from school often.

Inclusion

Historically, educational services for children with chronic illnesses were developed to address specific diseases such as polio and tuberculosis. These services typically followed a medical model and were offered in special schools or centres that segregated students from their peers (Brady, 1988). In almost all cases today, children attend the regular public school.

The needs of children who are technology dependent and/or medically fragile present greater challenges to the school system. They may be placed in a variety of educational settings, depending upon the type and severity of the condition, the related services available, and the prognosis of the disability (see also Chapter 14).

Hospital schools are found today in facilities that specialize in providing long-term care for chronically ill children. In these, the classroom setting is designed to provide the children with familiar surroundings and continued interaction with other students. Academic involvement helps the child to keep abreast of school work and aids in self-development. Special education teachers provide regular organized instruction in a classroom setting where possible or on a tutorial basis.

For the child no longer hospitalized but still unready for school attendance, homebound instruction is a valuable option. A home-visiting or itinerant teacher provides individual tutorials on a regular basis, following the curriculum of the child's classroom.

Curriculum

No special curricula exist or are really necessary for students with health problems. They follow the regular curriculum.

SUMMARY

1. Special health care needs and physical impairments encompass an enormous variety of conditions and diseases. Some, such as cancer, are life threatening; others, such as muscular dystrophy, bring an abbreviated life span; still others mean that the child must carefully monitor activities, diet, or drugs.

2. Health disorders are so heterogeneous that no commonality can be found in students' behavioural, intellectual, and psychological functioning. Even with the same conditions, no two youngsters are affected in exactly the same way. The impact of a health or physical disorder depends upon a number of variables: the age of onset of the condition, the degree of disability, the visibility of the condition, family and social support, the attitudes toward the individual, and the individual's social status with peers.

3. Because the conditions are primarily medical, there is no reason that children should require special intervention. Nearly all children with health and musculoskeletal conditions will be educated within regular classrooms. Special education should be available to accommodate lags resulting from lost school time.

4. As increasing numbers of children are being infected with pediatric AIDS, schools must accommodate their special health and learning problems. Children with AIDS have periods of weakness and intermittent bouts of illness. They suffer chronic and frequent illnesses, failure to thrive, and a range of neurological and developmental problems.

5. Child abuse occurs at every socio-economic level. Parents often feel overwhelmed by stress, isolated, incapable of coping, and lacking in resources. More often than not, high stress is the common denominator in abusive families. Preschoolers, boys, children with disabilities, sick children, and premature and low-birth-weight children appear to be at greater risk for abuse.

6. Child abuse actually consists of two problems—the abused child and the abusive parents. Among parents, child abuse and neglect cannot be attributed to any single cause or to any particular class of people. Child abuse and neglect have developmental effects on the physical, neurological, intellectual, and emotional development of children. Sexually abused children often carry emotional scars for life, while the experiential deprivation that is part of neglect affects every aspect of a child's development.

In the Classroom

Profile: Czeslov

When Ms. Day, a psychologist in private practice, was asked by the local school board to test Czeslov, she was somewhat reluctant. The school described the child as suffering from cystic fibrosis, a chronic and life-threatening disorder. Ms. Day was unfamiliar with the condition and its consequences and did not quite know what types of educational and psychological tests to use with such a child.

However, when Ms. Day started into the testing session, she found that Czeslov performed well on the WISC-III. All his scores were within the average range and he presented a Full Scale IQ score of 124. It was when Ms. Day began to present some educational measures that problems emerged. Although this child obviously had good potential to learn in school, he was now nine years old and showed little progress beyond beginning-level in reading and the other language arts. He had developed some basic numeracy skills but his arithmetic was very poor in computation and in using basic addition, subtraction, and multiplication. Division problems were completely beyond him.

Ms. Day could see the school's dilemma. Here was a child with good intellectual potential who was lagging far behind his peers simply because he had missed so many days of school due to illness. Yet the school was loath to designate the child as a special education candidate without some sort of classification that would assure funding. Nor did anyone really believe that special education was truly necessary for Czeslov, and he certainly did not need a paraprofessional in the classroom.

* * *

Ms. Day, the classroom teacher, the school principal, and the mother met to discuss Czeslov's performance. Ms. Day explained that she found a child of average or above-average ability who was functioning academically two or three years below his classmates. The reasons were easy to discern. The principal found that Czeslov had missed about 50 days of school each year; that is, about one third of classroom time. His medical needs and the intense therapy, plus the changing nature of his condition, meant that on many days he simply could not handle school.

Special education, per se, was not necessary for this child. What was necessary was intense remediation in core areas, always taking into account his limited vitality and current health status. The main focus is to develop a support system that provides assistance to Czeslov in the classroom and adapts the curriculum and instructional environment to his specific needs.

Reading skills are the first and most important area to consider. To assist Czeslov, the teacher will use direct instruction techniques. She or a paraprofessional will work with Czeslov in a small group of five or six students for half an hour each day. During the session, all instruction will be focused on reading, writing, and print. The process will generally follow the following scheme: give the children some easy reading; teach new skills with a stress on phonological awareness and phonics; present some challenging reading. Children will also do some writing to focus their attention on print.

A second important area is the social domain. When a child has a serious health disorder and is absent a great deal the attitudes of other class members are critical. It is the teacher's task to ensure that a child is accepted by peers. As well, an understanding and tactful teacher can minimize potentially uncomfortable situations and model accepting attitudes for students.

EFFECTS OF HEALTH DISABILITIES	TIPS FOR TEACHERS
THE DISABILITY REQUIRES MONITORING OF MEDICAL CONDITIONS	Establish a building team, a kind of SWAT team to address the complex health needs.
	Keep an emergency list of personnel and telephone numbers close at hand.
	All children with special medical needs must have an emergency protocol that contains information on emergency procedures and strategies developed by parents, school personnel, and medical personnel (Campbell, Cohen, and Rich, 1987).
	List and display special needs for substitute teachers.
	Be aware of the child's schedule for drug dosages and for special diet considerations.
	Check your school district's procedures for drug administration.
	Guard against common asthma triggers. These include cold air; chalk dust; dust in the classroom or gymnasium; photocopy toner fumes; science class chemicals; perfumes, cosmetics, and hairspray; cleaning fluids; paint fumes; and viral infections such as colds.
	Constantly be alert for crisis situations. For example, be aware of how to monitor the status of the diabetic child, know the symptoms of insulin reaction, and have a remedy immediately ready.
THE CONDITION REQUIRES IMMEDIATE INTERVENTION FOR HEALTH CONCERNS	Ensure a hygienically safe learning environment.
	Especially if a child has AIDS, immediately clean up blood and bodily fluids. Wear latex gloves. Use paper towels to clean up and rinse spill area. Disinfect spill area with bleach solution (1/4 cup regular household bleach to one gallon of water). Wash hands well and carefully.
	Be aware of the signs and symptoms of an asthma attack. The child may wheeze; show retractions where the tissue of the chest wall is sucked in as the child breathes; prolonged exhalation; rapid breathing; or cold symptoms.
	If a child has an asthma attack, remove the child from the trigger area if it is known. Try to relax the child by sitting with him or her while you model deep breathing exercises. Then have the child use the inhaler. If the child is not responding to medication, seek medical advice immediately.

EFFECTS OF HEALTH DISABILITIES	TIPS FOR TEACHERS
THE CHILD HAS LIMITED VITALITY	Provide frequent rest periods (Whitworth, 1993). Adjust classroom schedules for students with limited vitality to create maximum on-task learning time. Encourage students to be as independent as possible in completing all self-help activities.
THE CHILD NEEDS ADAPTIVE EQUIPMENT	Become familiar with any special equipment that the student uses in the classroom. This includes wheelchairs and other mobility devices, visual and travel aids, amplification systems, catheterization equipment, ventilators, and so on.
THERE ARE ISSUES CONCERNING PEERS AND SOCIAL ACCEPTANCE	One way to increase positive attitudes is to answer accurately questions asked by other children about the differences in appearance and behaviour of the special child. This should be done at the time questions are asked, whether or not the special child is present. Provide time for children to talk about the disease and its treatment. The questions children ask most often are: What is cancer? Can our friend die from it? What does it feel like to have cancer? (Peckham, 1993, p. 28). Make children feel a part of the class even if illness keeps them absent for long periods.
THE CONDITION REQUIRES A TEACHER KNOWLEDGE BASE	Learn as much as you can about the condition, including the etiology, developmental consequences, and the prognosis. Be aware of the treatment procedures being used, the potential side effects of certain medical treatments on appearance and behaviour, and the approximate schedule of upcoming treatments. Be sympathetic to the child's feelings about hospital and separation.

WEBLINKS

Canadian Cystic Fibrosis Foundation **http://www.ccff.ca/~cfwww/index.html**

Canadian Diabetes Association **http://www.diabetes.ca/**

Pediatric AIDS Canada **http://www.cgocable.net/~pac/**

Calgary Anaphylactic Allergy Support Group **http://www.cadvision.com/aaiacgy/**

Canadian Society for the Investigation of Child Abuse (CSICA) **http://www.csica.zener.com/**

CHAPTER 12

Children with Neurological Disabilities

Historical Notes

When institutional settings for students with special needs were first established in the nineteenth century, they served discrete categories of students, specifically those who were deaf, blind, and mentally retarded. Children who were seriously crippled, not toilet-trained, or considered to be uneducable were not provided with schooling in the institutions or in the public system. Those with significant disabilities were seen as potential hindrances to programs because of the individual care they needed.

The one major exception was epilepsy. Probably no other nineteenth-century exceptional group was as misunderstood and inappropriately handled as those with epilepsy. In that period, no drugs to control the condition or technical devices to assess its etiology existed, and seizures engendered such fear in beholders that they held that epilepsy and insanity were inextricably joined. Institutionalization was imperative, either with those mentally retarded or with those mentally ill.

There are reports of a class in Boston in 1866 for crippled children. But compared to schooling for deaf or blind children, intervention for children described as crippled was a very late development. In Montreal,

the world's first organized movement on behalf of crippled children was started in 1906 by a group of educators at the Children's Memorial Hospital. However, facilities for these youngsters were generally not within the purview of the school system.

Even when classes opened, segregation was the mode. In spite of the fact that these students presented a wide range of abilities, potential, and educational need, and that there is little or no difference between their classroom performance and that of non-disabled students, the majority of pupils who were physically disabled were restricted to special schools or special classes. Among other reasons, teachers felt that youngsters with physical disabilities would be too difficult to handle and would take a disproportionate amount of time (Brulle, Barton, Wharton, and Brulle, 1983). There was also the traditional predisposition that stereotyped these children and focused on their disabilities while ignoring their strengths. In addition, many school plants were not equipped with the physical structures, the modifications, the technical equipment, and the support personnel to handle and teach such students. It was seen as more economical to transport children to one central location and to bring the therapists, the teachers, and the other intervenors to the students. Given the difficulties these children often have with mobility, it was more economical to construct one barrier-free building than to alter all the plants in a school district.

The history of another entire field feeds into the development of education for students with physical disabilities. Prosthetics is the field of science concerned with the artificial replacement of body parts, and includes designing, manufacturing, and fitting artificial limbs (Tiessen, 1996).

Prostheses have been used probably since the beginning of humankind. Artificial limbs and braces appear in ancient frescoes, mosaics, and pottery. The first written account is 2 200 years old and concerns one Marcus Sergius, a Roman general who lost his right hand in battle and had it replaced with a metal one.

Ambroise Paré, the surgeon general from the French army in the sixteenth century, is considered to be the modern father of prosthetics and orthotics. He made advances in surgical techniques and had many devices made for wounded soldiers. Many other people, from pirates to panhandlers, were leg amputees who used crude peg legs to replace a limb severed by sword or saw. These were fashioned out of forked sticks or tree branches, and fit was forsaken for function (Tiessen, 1996).

Artificial limbs have come a long way. With miniaturized power sources such as motors with sophisticated sensory control and hydraulic and pneumatic components, artificial limbs and braces are extremely functional today. Child amputees, whose residual limbs continue to grow, are the most susceptible to poor fit (Lowey, 1993).

Normal development of the central nervous system is the outcome of a carefully timed and precisely regulated combination of structural and chemical events. Something amiss in these events can lead to damage to, or deterioration of, the central nervous system which, in turn, is one of the most common causes of physical and neurological disabilities in children.

As in the case of health and musculoskeletal impairments, there exists a huge range of neurological disorders. Some are associated with impairments of the nervous system; others result from diseases and accidents. For many children, the decreased range of motion, the reduced strength of movement, or the addition of unwanted or uncontrolled movement can dramatically affect the way they perform. Many youngsters in this category also suffer co-occurring disabilities such as seizures or diabetes, and can therefore be viewed as multiply disabled.

Depending on the severity of the condition, the related services available, and the prognosis, students with neurological disabilities are served in regular classrooms, regular classroom and resource room combinations, or occasionally in special classes. But as the conditions are not in themselves inherently intellectually disabling, we should soon see almost all children with physical and neurological impairments integrated into regular classrooms.

Definitions

Neurological impairments are one of the subcategories of physical disabilities that we describe in Chapter 11. Essentially, we can say that neurological impairments result from damage or dysfunction of the brain and/or the spinal cord. Such damage may occur before, during, or after birth. Potential risks include severe deprivation of oxygen before birth, especially dur-

Children with physical disabilities can benefit from the same instructional practices as their non-disabled peers.

ing the first trimester when various important neural structures and interconnections between the brain cells are developing. Other risks are damage incurred during the birth process and damage directly caused by diseases, especially those that attack the central nervous system.

The effects of the damage vary greatly and wide differences are seen in the onset of symptoms, the parts of the body involved, the nature of the symptoms, the degree of severity, and the possible multiplicity of impairments. Injury to the brain may result in a relatively limited specific disorder. For example, one of the traditional etiologies of learning disabilities is minimal brain dysfunction. On the other hand, generalized and diffuse brain damage may cause very wide-ranging effects, including motor disturbances, sensory loss, speech and language disorders, and emotional and behavioural disorders. Diffuse damage will result in mental retardation; damage to the motor areas will cause cerebral palsy.

Injury to the spinal cord alone tends to result in motor and sensory disabilities without affecting intellectual function and special sensory functions (vision, hearing, and speech). Damage to the motor cells of the spinal cord results in *flaccid paralysis*, an inability to move the muscles because the neural impulses needed for muscle contractions are lacking.

How physical and neurological disabilities affect an individual's development and life style also varies dramatically. Some people are devastated by the condition and never achieve their optimal development. On the other hand, Canadians remember with special pride young people like Rick Hanson and Terry Fox, who worked through their physical disabilities in efforts to help others.

The majority of chronic illnesses occur during the first three years of life. Many illnesses that are chronic were fatal in the past; with current medical intervention, they are no longer life-threatening. As these children enter the school system, they bring with them a range of challenges that extend from simply monitoring drug usage, to watching for fatigue, to classroom adaptations that accommodate neurological dysfunctions, to adaptive equipment for mobility and communication. Probably the greatest challenge for teachers is handling a terminally ill child in the classroom (see Chapter 11).

Prevalence of Neurological Disorders

While neurological conditions are extremely varied, they are low-incidence disabilities. The prevalence is only about 0.2 to 1.5 percent of the school-age population, although rates vary from locale to locale and from decade to decade.

Cerebral Palsy

Cerebral palsy is a condition characterized by damage to the brain before, during, or after birth. The condition is present at birth in more than two-thirds of cases (Verhaaren and Connor, 1981).

Cerebral palsy is chiefly a motor disorder, though it is often accompanied by other disabilities. It is one of the most common crippling conditions in children. The most commonly cited incidence of cerebral palsy is 1.5 to 2 cases per 1 000 live births (Pope and Tarlov, 1991). More boys than girls are affected, and the condition occurs more often among children born to mothers in poor socio-economic circumstances (Hallahan and Kauffman, 1991). An extensive study of children with cerebral palsy (Nelson and Ellenberg, 1986) found that the most likely associated factors were mental retardation of the mother, premature birth, low birth-weight, and a delay of five minutes or more before the baby's first cry.

Cerebral palsy is sometimes referred to as Little's disease, after the surgeon who first described it. Another alternative label is *significant developmental motor disability*.

Classification of Cerebral Palsy

Cerebral palsy may be classified by topography or by type. The topographical classification system, as shown in Table 12-1, refers to parts of the body and is not limited to cerebral

Table 12-1 Topographical classification of cerebral palsy

Monoplegia	One limb impaired
Diplegia	Four limbs involved, with legs most impaired
Hemiplegia	One side of the body impaired
Paraplegia	Lower limbs of the body impaired
Triplegia	Three limbs impaired
Double hemiplegia	Both sides of the body impaired, with each side affected differently
Quadriplegia	All four limbs impaired

palsy. In the topographical system, the suffix *plegia* refers to paralysis. When classified by the type of brain damage and consequent motor disability, cerebral palsy can be differentiated according to specific motor patterns, as outlined in Table 12-2.

Spastic or pyramidal cerebral palsy affects approximately 50 percent of children with cerebral palsy. Individuals have suffered damage to the motor cortex or to the pyramidal tracts of the brain (Batshaw and Perret, 1986). Pyramidal cerebral palsy results in problems with voluntary movements. Spasticity, therefore, refers to slow, laborious, poorly co-ordinated voluntary movements. Children with spastic cerebral palsy also demonstrate the continued presence of a number of primitive reflexes.

Cerebral palsy is involved with **reflexes**—automatic, involuntary motor patterns that are triggered by specific stimuli. Most of the primitive reflexes present in all newborns disappear by about six months of age (see the Research Notes in this chapter). If these reflexes persist, they act as impediments to the development of smooth, co-ordinated movement.

Simple reflexes (stretch or spinal reflexes) involve the spinal cord. Above the spinal cord is the brain stem, the seat of tonic reflexes. Spinal and tonic reflexes contribute to muscle tone, posture, and allow the child to prepare for movement. Types of abnormal reflex movements seen in children with cerebral palsy include the rooting reflex, startle reaction, stretch reflex, asymmetrical and symmetrical tonic neck reflex, protective extensive reactions, and righting reactions. In the presence of the stretch reflex, for example, a muscle contracts involuntarily when suddenly stretched. Thus, when the arm is bent suddenly, the biceps contract but the reflex causes contractions in the opposing triceps as well. A mini-war results, rendering movements impossible to control. This means that children with spastic cerebral palsy cannot move when and how they choose.

Extrapyramidal cerebral palsy includes athetosis, hypotonia, rigidity, and ataxia. In these

Table 12-2 Classification of cerebral palsy

	Pyramidal cerebral palsy (spasticity)	Extrapyramidal cerebral palsy dyskinesia (five types)				
		Athetosis	Rigidity	Hypotonia	Tremor	Ataxia
movement	slow and difficult	consistent, involuntary, writhing	more severe than spasticity	may develop into spastic or athetoid type	involuntary, rhythmic	clumsy
co-ordination	poor	poor	poor	varied	depends upon affected limbs	poor
muscle tone	weak, hypertonic	fluctuating	continuous tension	low	varied	varied

Research Notes

Reflexes in Infants

Newborns are unable to control their motor behaviour smoothly and voluntarily. Instead, behaviour consists of twitches, jerks, and random movements, most of which involve reflexes—natural responses with which children are born. They are stereotyped movements produced in response to a particular sensory input.

Some reflexes are necessary for survival; others are interesting because they are controlled by the midbrain, that part of the brain that develops first. As the more advanced parts of the brain develop, these primitive reflexes disappear. The various feeding reflexes are necessary for survival. Infants also come equipped with a rooting reflex. If babies are touched on the cheek anywhere near the mouth, they will turn their heads and root around to put their mouths on the object that touched them. There is also the Moro reflex, described by Ernst Moro in 1918. If a loud noise is made near an infant, or if the infant's position is changed suddenly, the baby will throw both arms outwards and then bring them into the body. This reflex disappears at about three months of age as the neurological system matures. With the Babinski reflex, babies splay out their toes and then curl them in if stroked on the bottom of the foot. In an adult or older child, only the curling occurs.

The reflex actions of babies allow them to react to things in their world as they are learning to control their own bodies. Reflexes also help to ensure survival by protecting vital systems. As well, the presence of reflexes in infants and their eventual disappearance offers insights into the process of neurological development and organization, as well as information about the results of damage to discrete areas of the brain. A number of reactions appear to be the precursors of later development and can be used to diagnose certain kinds of brain damage

cases, damage is outside the pyramidal tracts and results in abrupt involuntary movements and difficulty in maintaining posture (Batshaw and Perret, 1986). When there is damage to both the pyramidal and the extrapyramidal regions of the brain, the child may show mixed effects, such as spasticity of the legs and rigidity of the arms. About 25 percent of cases are classified as mixed cerebral palsy (Batshaw and Perret, 1986).

Athetoid cerebral palsy is found in approximately 25 percent of individuals with cerebral palsy. *Athetosis* is characterized by constant, involuntary writhing movements, especially in the hands and wrists. Contractions occur in successive groups of muscles, creating extraneous movement that interferes with purposive action. Children with athetoid cerebral palsy are unable to stop moving when they want to. Athetosis stops during sleep.

Rigidity occurs when there is a low level of motor stiffness that never relaxes. The condition is rare, as is *tremor*, an involuntary movement in one extremity, usually one hand or arm. In constant tremor, the movement is continuous; in intention tremor, the involuntary movement happens only when the child undertakes to do something.

Ataxic cerebral palsy occurs in approximately 15 percent of individuals with cerebral palsy. *Ataxia* is characterized by poor co-ordination of the movements associated with balance, posture, and spatial orientation. Children with ataxia tend to walk with a wide gait, their legs well apart to compensate for poor equilibrium. They also exhibit a generalized lack of co-ordination of both fine and gross motor movements. The eyes are often unco-ordinated (Jones, 1987).

Developmental Consequences

The consequences of cerebral palsy vary in relation to many factors. These relate chiefly to the type of cerebral palsy, the severity of the condition, and the presence or absence of co-occurring conditions. While no two children with cerebral palsy develop in exactly the same way, the presence of extensive motor disorders alone is sufficient to interfere with normal development.

In normally developing children, each stage of motor development causes a shift in the child's interaction with the environment. Within 12 to 14 weeks of birth, for example, normally developing children achieve control of head movements. Within six months, they pull to a sitting position. At about 12 months they begin to walk unaided. These milestones offer children increased opportunities to make better use of sensory experience, to gain greater perceptual awareness, and to learn to manipulate objects and their own bodies. Damage to the motor system impedes this normal developmental course. Children with cerebral palsy have little control of the musculature necessary to reach developmental milestones.

Early diagnosis is difficult, and cerebral palsy is generally not diagnosed right at birth because there are few abnormal neurological signs at this time. In fact, a brain-damaged neonate may appear to be perfectly normal for the first several weeks of life. Clues to neuromotor disturbance in infants include irritability, excessive listlessness, pallor, stiffening, arching, excessive startle, *nystagmus*, and jaundice. In addition, infants with cerebral palsy behave differently. They tend to sleep excessively, have a weak cry, a poor suck, and show little interest in their surroundings. They rest differently, lying in a floppy extended position instead of a semi-flexed one (Batshaw and Perret, 1986; Cruickshank, 1976). Note that not all of these signs are found in all infants with cerebral palsy, and not all infants who manifest these signs have cerebral palsy.

As the child develops, predictions can be made on overall progress. If the child can sit by two years of age, for example, he or she will probably walk. About 80 percent of children with cerebral palsy are capable of learning to walk, although many need to use braces and other assistive devices (Bleck, 1979). If the child is able to utter recognizable sounds by age two, that child will probably learn to speak (Bleck and Nagel, 1982).

The brain damage that results in cerebral palsy is not always limited to motor areas. Indeed, cerebral palsy can generally be seen as a multi-disabling condition. A high percentage of children exhibit one or more additional impairments. These include mental retardation, learning disabilities, sensory loss, epilepsy, and emotional and behavioural disorders. As well, disorders of posture, listening, breathing, voice, articulation, and language are all found in association with cerebral palsy.

Many people assume, given the external appearance of the condition, that all children with cerebral palsy are intellectually disabled. As a blanket assumption, this is incorrect. However, it is true that the incidence of intellectual disability is significantly higher than average. Estimates of the number of children who are cerebral palsied who have some degree of intellectual impairment range from 25 to 75 percent (Gersh, 199b; Lefebrue, 1983; Nelson and Ellenberg, 1986). Little evidence exists to link the severity of intellectual impairment with any particular type of cerebral palsy, although hemiplegia seems to be associated with the best mental development (Batshaw and Perret, 1986).

The speech and language problems of children with cerebral palsy reflect the complexity of the condition. Estimates of co-occurring speech and language problems range from 50 to 83 percent (Cruickshank, 1976). In some cases, damage, usually to certain areas of the left cerebral hemisphere, results in language delays and disorders. Language problems are less common than speech disorders.

Motor dysfunctions that affect the organs of speech may make intelligible speech impossible (see Jones, 1987). The errors of articulation that accompany cerebral palsy are known as dysarthria, a condition discussed in Chapter 4. The speech characteristics of children with spastic forms of cerebral palsy may include articulatory defects, laboured speech with distortions of sound, uncontrolled pitch changes, and husky voice quality.

Visual and auditory problems are the most prevalent and serious of the associated sensory difficulties. It is estimated that more than 50 percent of children with cerebral palsy have visual defects of some type (Lefebrue, 1983); often these are related to loss of control of the ocular muscles. There is also a high incidence of middle ear problems; approximately 25 to 30 percent of individuals with cerebral palsy have hearing defects (Jones, 1983).

Other sensory problems include deficits in tactile sensation and the determination of pain, pressure, and temperature. Children with cerebral palsy may also show disorders such as short attention span and distractibility. Given these problems, it is estimated that from 15 to 20 percent are likely to have some type of specific learning disability (Telford and Sawrey, 1981).

An additional problem is some form of convulsive disorder. It is estimated that 25 to 50 percent suffer epileptic seizures (Gersh, 1991a; Jones, 1987). These are most common in hemiplegics and quadriplegics. As well, children who are cerebral palsied with normal IQs are three times more prone to psychiatric disorders (Seidel, Chadwick, and Rutter, 1975).

As the number of accompanying disorders indicates, cerebral palsy is a very complex multi-disabling condition. However, not every affected child faces all or even most of these disorders. Usually children with limited and localized brain injuries face fewer limitations than children with diffuse, extensive brain damage. The Profile below illustrates some special requirements of a young girl with cerebral palsy.

Spina Bifida

Midline defects, often referred to as clefts, result from the failure of parts of the embryo to fuse completely. Such defects may occur in many parts of the body, including the lip, the palate, the eye, and the spine. *Spina bifida* is a congenital midline defect of the spinal column.

Technically, the term spina bifida refers to a defect in the bony arch of the vertebrae protecting the spinal cord (Mitchell, Fewell, and Davy, 1983). In the early weeks of pregnancy, the neural tube of the embryo fails to develop normally. The bony arches of one or more spinal vertebrae do not fuse to protect the spinal cord, which leaves part of the nerve fibres of the cord exposed. The spinal defect may be found anywhere between the skull and the lowest segments of the vertebrae. Generally, spina bifida is evident by the end of the fourth week of gestation and the severity of the problem is apparent at birth (Myers, Cerone, and Olson, 1981).

Although the process is fairly well understood, the actual cause of spina bifida is unknown. Etiologically, it is believed that both heredity and environment are interweaving fac-

Profile

Karen

Karen is nine years old, functioning in a regular grade three classroom at her local public school. She has cerebral palsy and walks with leg braces, but is more affected on the left than the right side. The motor impairment has affected her speech, and she has a constant drool. She also has a mild to moderate bilateral, sensorineural hearing loss. She uses amplification in both ears.

In most curriculum areas, Karen is an average student. She reads at level and her arithmetic skills are adequate. She prints with her right hand in a slow and laboured manner, and the school is planning to use a special large-print typewriter with her. Although her articulation is poor, she has good receptive language skills and supplements the auditory message with speech reading.

An itinerant teacher of the hearing impaired works with Karen individually for four hours weekly, focusing primarily on enhancing the regular classroom curriculum. The itinerant teacher helps with homework and classroom assignments in order to maintain Karen's average grades. Some problems have also surfaced in the area of reading comprehension and social studies concepts, so an individual program has been devised in these areas. These gaps in Karen's learning are due to the expanded amount of auditory information she is expected to process. The itinerant teacher is therefore concentrating on the vocabulary and language structures inherent in reading and social studies. Karen tries to use her voice at all times. In addition to her individual work with the itinerant teacher, she receives special help from a visiting speech therapist for her articulatory difficulties.

---

tors. In Newfoundland, which has the highest rate of spina bifida in Canada, most affected children are conceived between May and August (Fraser, Frecker, and Allerdice, 1986).

Spina bifida can be initially detected prenatally by a test that looks at the level of alpha-fetoprotein in the mother's blood. Higher concentrations than usual indicate the necessity for ultrasound or fetoscopy.

The prevalence of spina bifida varies widely from country to country, from area to area, and even within the limits of a particular city. Worldwide, spina bifida occurs in from 0.1 to 4.13 live births per 1 000 (Bleck and Nagel, 1982). The incidence in Ireland is about 4 or 5 children per 1 000 live births, while in parts of Nigeria it is 0.2 per 1 000 live births. In Canada, as mentioned, the highest rate of spina bifida is found in Newfoundland.

There is a slight tendency for the condition to run in families. If one baby is born with spina bifida, there is a 4 to 5 percent chance of siblings having the same defect (Myers, Cerone, and Olson, 1981). Spina bifida is found more often in lower socio-economic groups and occurs more frequently in males (Bowley and Gardner, 1980).

Classification of Spina Bifida

Spina bifida includes a group of defects that range from those with few or no adverse effects to those that manifest as severely disabling. Spina bifida is divided into two main forms: spina bifida occulta and spina bifida cystica.

Of the affected population, about 40 percent suffer from spina bifida occulta and the remainder from cystica. This latter form is divided into two types—spina bifida with meningocele and spina bifida with myelomeningocele. The former accounts for 4 percent of individuals suffering the cystica form; the latter for 96 percent. (See Figure 12-1.)

Spina bifida occulta is the mildest form of the condition and has few or no negative effects. The only visible sign of the condition, if any, is a clump of hair on the skin covering the area of the cleft. In fact, this variety of spina bifida may affect up to 20 percent of North Americans; because symptoms are rare, people may not even know they have it (Moore and Persaud, 1993).

The two forms of spina bifida cystica—with meningocele and with myelomeningocele—have different results. In spina bifida with meningocele, the meninges, the membranes surrounding the spinal cord, protrude from the plane of the spine and form a sac containing cerebrospinal fluid. Surgery is usually performed in the first days of life to restore the sac within the spinal column. Following treatment, this condition does not usually create any major difficulties, although children must be wary of being hit directly on the area.

Spina bifida with myelomeningocele, the most severe type, results in a protruding sac that contains parts of the spinal cord as well as cerebrospinal fluid. The spinal cord not only enters the sac but is itself abnormal. Surgical treatment is necessary to deal with the sac, but the neurological damage is irreversible.

The effects of myelomeningocele vary considerably depending on the location of the cleft. The higher the cleft, the greater the damage. Clefts in the lower part of the spine may

Figure 12-1

Types of spina bifida

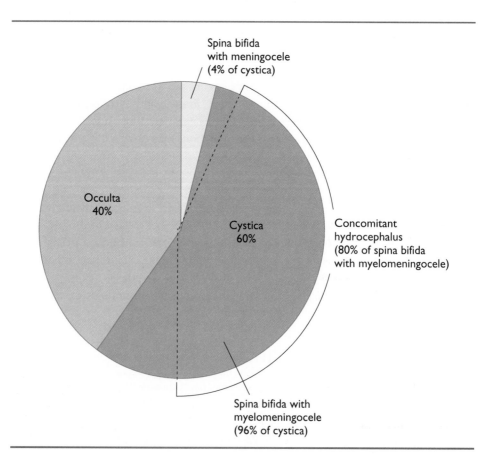

result in incontinence without paralysis. Clefts in the higher spinal regions produce paralysis and loss of sensation in the lower limbs, incontinence, and kidney problems. In addition to the cleft of the vertebral arches associated with spina bifida, other vertebrae unusual in slope or connection can occur, resulting in an uneven growth of the spine (Myers, Cerone, and Olson, 1981).

Twenty-five years ago, more than 90 percent of children with spina bifida died within a few years of birth (Kaplan, 1996), from urinary infection or infection of the sac. Today, 90 percent live an average life span.

Developmental Consequences

Children with spina bifida occulta or with meningocele are likely to develop normally. In the absence of co-occurring conditions, spina bifida does not preclude adequate learning ability. Children with spina bifida occulta exhibit a normal range of intelligence; those with meningocele are also likely to have normal intelligence.

Children with myelomeningocele suffer neurological damage that interferes with growth and development. The most obvious neurological damage is the flaccid paralysis of the lower part of the body, which makes braces, crutches, walkers, or wheelchairs necessary.

Children with myelomeningocele lack sensation and control of their bladders and bowel sphincters. Incontinence in itself does not create learning difficulties, but it may create social and psychological barriers for children in school. Non-disabled children usually view incontinence as a sign of immaturity or infantile behaviour and react accordingly. As incontinent children mature, they learn to cope with their condition. Using a procedure called clean intermittent catheterization, they catheterize themselves every three or four hours (Myers, Cerone, and Olson, 1981). Although it may not create problems, it has been found that children with spina bifida experience very early puberty, with menstruation occurring as early as eight years of age (Allum, 1975). Researchers are uncertain of the cause of this phenomenon.

Children with spina bifida with myelomenigocele generally have IQs in the low average to mildly retarded range (Calhoun and Hawisher, 1979). Perceptual and cognitive dysfunction is prevalent, especially in children with accompanying hydrocephalus (Anderson, 1973). While children show poorer general performance in reading, spelling, and arithmetic (Tew and Lawrence, 1975), most have good verbal ability, which may tend to mask the cognitive defects.

Although spina bifida may occur as a solitary condition, nearly 80 percent of children who have spina bifida with myelomeningocele have accompanying hydrocephalus. The combination of the two conditions dramatically increases the number of disabilities. The damage to the brain from hydrocephalus and to the spinal cord from spina bifida is likely to produce a child who is multiply disabled.

Hydrocephalus

Hydrocephalus is a condition characterized by an excessive accumulation in the brain of cerebrospinal fluid due to an obstruction of its flow. Normally, cerebrospinal fluid is constantly manufactured in the ventricles of the brain, circulates through the ventricles and the space between the two layers of meninges, and is absorbed into the circulatory system. Since fluids are largely non-compressible, a blockage of the flow results in the accumulation of cerebrospinal fluid in an enclosed area, placing pressure on the brain and the skull. The pressure against the skull creates thinning of the bone and separation of the sutures (the seams between the plates of the skull). The fluid also presses on the brain tissue, causing distortion of brain substance and damage and death to the neurons.

In some instances, hydrocephalus arrests itself spontaneously. In other cases, the condition progresses and creates increasing pressure on the skull. The progressive accumulation of cerebrospinal fluid results in a range of disorders. Because mental retardation is a primary result, hydrocephalus is included among the clinical forms of mental retardation. Other sequelae include motor disorders, seizures, and even death.

Before the 1950s, no effective treatment existed for hydrocephalus. Children developed marked symptoms; by the age of three months, their heads became too large and heavy for them to lift, and their condition often ended in death. In 1952 an engineer named Holter developed an effective shunt (tube) to drain off excess cerebrospinal fluid and reduce the pressure on the brain. Since Holter's invention, many children with hydrocephalus have been spared extensive impairments.

Developmental Consequences

In persons affected by hydrocephalus, consequences vary with the degree of severity of the conditions, the presence or absence of co-occurring conditions, and the success or failure of treatment. Evidence about cognitive functioning is contradictory. Some researchers have found no correlation between the degree of severity of hydrocephalus and IQ levels (Soare and Raimondi, 1977); others note that the average IQ of shunted children is 70 to 83 (Tew and Lawrence, 1975).

Beyond the rather undescriptive intelligence scores, it has also been found that many children who are hydrocephalic have particular learning problems that result in uneven intellectual functioning. Aspects of verbal ability, such as syntax and vocabulary, may be well developed, while comprehension and language usage are defective (Spain, 1972).

Epilepsy

The word *epilepsy* is derived from the Greek meaning "to be seized," and we still describe epilepsy in terms of seizures. During the 1800s Hughlings Jackson, a pioneer neurologist, defined epilepsy as a condition produced by a sudden violent electrical discharge of brain cells. Echoing Jackson's definition, epilepsy is today defined as "a convulsive disorder [that] is the expression of a sudden, excessive, disorderly discharge of neurons in either a structurally normal or diseased cortex. The discharge results in an almost instantaneous disturbance of sensation, loss of consciousness, convulsive movement, or some combination thereof" (Harrison, 1980, p. 131).

Implicit in this definition is the idea that epilepsy is not a disease but a symptom of a brain disorder which may be caused by any condition that results in damage to the brain. This does not imply that brain damage necessarily results in epileptic seizures, although it may. The definition further stresses the chronic and recurring nature of epilepsy. Chronicity is important because it is estimated that between two and three percent of the population have had, or will have, some form of epileptic seizure in their lifetime (B.C. Ministry of Health, 1978). However, such a single symptom might reflect some transient event, such as a high fever, heat exhaustion, ingestion of certain chemicals, or interference with the normal supply of oxygen to the brain.

The causes of epilepsy are varied and often unclear. Perinatal conditions, early childhood infection, and head trauma are identified as known causative factors. Heredity rarely plays a role: unless both parents have a strong family history of epilepsy, the chances that their children will inherit a tendency to have seizures is very slight.

If an individual shows strong evidence of brain damage, the condition is known as symptomatic epilepsy. The most common causes are brain tumour and stroke; head trauma of any type; injury, infection, or systemic illness of the mother during pregnancy that affects fetal brain growth; brain injury to the infant during delivery; the aftermath of an infection such as meningitis; and poisoning from substance abuse or alcoholism (Epilepsy [1994]). For about 75 percent of epileptics, a specific cause cannot be found. In this case, the condition is referred to as idiopathic epilepsy, or epilepsy of unknown origin.

The recognized incidence of epilepsy is greater today than in the past due to a higher survival rate among infants and persons with brain injuries and illnesses, and the increased willingness of people to seek treatment. More than 280 000 Canadians, or over one percent of the population, are affected.

No one is immune; epilepsy can strike anyone at any age. However, from 70 to 80 percent of patients develop epilepsy before the age of 18. About 55 percent develop epilepsy before the age of 10, and 44 percent before the age of 5. One of every 2 000 people is diagnosed with epilepsy each year; about 14 000 new cases are reported annually (Epilepsy [1994]).

Classification of Epilepsy

As a term, epilepsy describes two things—the conditions of seizure and the convulsions accompanying some types of seizures. Seizures occur as a result of a temporary breakdown in the brain's communication system caused by disorderly cell activity. There are many types of seizures, some fairly well understood and some still confusing to researchers. The type of seizure depends on the region of the brain where it originates. It also depends, to some extent, on the brain's maturation and its ability to spread the electrical discharge to other parts of the body (Robb, 1981).

The three main classifications of epilepsy are generalized seizures, partial seizures, and unclassified seizures. Seizure types and their progress are described in the Research Notes in this chapter.

Developmental Consequences

The effects on learning resulting from epilepsy can be chronic, with permanent impairment in the ability to process information. In other cases, the influence on learning is relatively short-lived, and includes brief transient disturbances in attention and short-term deficits in cognitive functioning (Binnie, Channon, and Marston, 1990; Huberty, Austin, Risinger, and McNelis, 1992). Effects chiefly depend on factors such as the nature of the seizure disorders and the medications used. Even with varied effects, however, a recent study found that retention in grade and placement in special education was twice as frequent for children with epilepsy as for normally developing children (see Williams, Sharp, Bates, Griebel, Lange, Spence, and Thomas, 1996).

Research Notes

Types of Seizures

Generalized seizures are bilateral and symmetrical without local onset in the brain. They are often accompanied by loss of consciousness and most have motor components. Generalized seizures include petit mal (absence seizures), myoclonic seizures, grand mal (tonic-clonic seizures), and atonic seizures, which include infantile spasm convulsions. The most common forms of generalized seizures are grand mal and petit mal. Many individuals experience both these forms, which may be either idiopathic or symptomatic.

The grand mal seizure proceeds through relatively distinct stages. Some epileptics consistently experience an aura just before the seizure's onset. This aura may be a subjective sensory or memory experience, such as an odour that is not present in reality. It may take the form of an odd internal sensation, or even a memory phenomenon in which the person actually experiences a scene from the past (Krupp and Chatton, 1983). Shortly after the aura appears, the individual loses consciousness, falls, and develops generalized stiffness of the body. During this tonic phase, the arms are flexed (bent) and the legs extended. The trunk muscles are also in spasm so that breathing ceases. After a short but varying period of tonic activity, the clonic stage follows. In this phase, the person exhibits alternate relaxations and contractions of the skeletal musculature which produce what is often referred to as thrashing movements. In the throes of the clonic state, the person may lose bladder and bowel control, bite the tongue, and froth at the mouth. After two to five minutes, convulsive movements diminish and finally stop. This is followed by a gradual regaining of consciousness. During this time, the person may experience confusion, headache, or other symptoms. A period of deep sleep marks the end of the seizure. If a child suffers a grand mal seizure and then immediately passes into another seizure, the condition is known as *status epilepticus*. This is potentially life-threatening and medical aid should be sought immediately.

Grand mal seizures can occur at any time and in a school setting can be frightening for the beholders and distressing for the victim. Teachers can ease the situation by trying to provide privacy during and after a seizure. If a child begins to have a seizure, the teacher should allow or help the child to lie down, move away furniture, loosen restrictive clothing, and tilt the head to one side to drain saliva. Teachers should never try to hold the child, stop the seizure, or force anything into the mouth.

The petit mal or absence seizure is most frequently seen in children. Some children suffer up to two hundred absence seizures a day. These often occur when the child is sedentary, and infrequently during exercise (Berkow, 1982). In more than 70 percent of all cases, petit mal seizures cease altogether by age 18 (Nealis, 1983).

Petit mal is considerably less dramatic than grand mal; the classic absence seizure lasts only 15 to 30 seconds and is so brief that it is often overlooked or misinterpreted. The child ceases all activity and appears to stare vacantly, as though daydreaming. During this period, there is a loss or clouding of consciousness. The return of consciousness is abrupt and the child immediately resumes interrupted activities.

There are other forms of petit mal seizures. During these, the child's eyes may blink or shift and the hands move aimlessly. On some occasions, the seizure may be prolonged, lasting for minutes or hours. During these long seizures, the child may simply appear confused and dazed.

Minor motor seizures, often called Lennox-Gastaug seizures, are similar to petit mal. They can be characterized by loss of muscle tone for a moment. Myoclonic seizures are so called because they are characterized by a single repetitive contracture of a muscle or group of muscles.

Partial seizures are characterized as simple or complex. Partial seizures begin locally (in a specific area of the brain) and may or may not cause loss of consciousness. They occur in many forms, but the common feature in all is the localized origin of brain irritability. Because they affect very local motor or sensory areas, partial seizures are sometimes referred to as focal seizures.

One form of partial seizure is the *Jacksonian seizure*, which only occurs in cases of symptomatic epilepsy. This type of seizure is characterized by motor symptoms without impaired consciousness. In a Jacksonian seizure, spasmodic (clonic) movements might start in the peripheral portion of a limb, such as the left thumb. These movements might then progress in an orderly fashion toward the central portion of the body and down into the left leg. Sometimes the violent electrical discharge that begins in one hemisphere of the brain spreads to the other. If this happens, the individual loses consciousness and undergoes a grand mal convulsion.

Another type of partial seizure is the psychomotor seizure, sometimes called the psychomotor equivalent or temporal lobe seizure because it is most characteristically associated with lesions of the temporal lobe of the brain.

Psychomotor seizures are poorly understood. They often include a clouding of consciousness and amnesia (loss of memory of the event). Along with altered consciousness, other manifestations include a change of body position or limbs, confused activity, a dazed expression, nausea, vomiting, drooling, muttering, mumbling, wandering, pallor or flushing, incoherent or irrelevant speech, and inappropriate emotional disturbances. Sometimes these symptoms are accompanied by relatively complex, well-organized movements, such as plucking clothing, or any other patterned activity. The category of *unclassified seizures* includes all other types.

Children with idiopathic epilepsy are more likely to develop normally than those with symptomatic epilepsy. Most children with idiopathic epilepsy function normally between attacks, and approximately 70 percent have normal or higher intelligence (Dikmen, Matthews, and Harley, 1975).

Symptomatic epilepsy is often seen in children who experience seizures before age two. The early onset of seizures that are unremitting or persistent for several years are more likely to be related to learning problems than is later onset or lower seizure frequency (Rodin, 1989). These children are usually suffering the effects of developmental defects, birth injuries, or a metabolic disease affecting the brain, and are more likely to exhibit multiple disorders that can include mental retardation, sensory loss, or motor disability.

As well, generalized seizures are more likely than partial epilepsy to be associated with learning problems. Individuals with more generalized seizures are usually expected to suffer greater disability than those whose seizures are more focused and partial.

Together with possible learning problems, a range of psychological and social adjustment difficulties have been associated with epilepsy, with boys consistently showing problem outcomes with greater frequency than girls (Williams et al., 1996). Students show, for example, increased psychiatric and behavioural disturbances, poor self-esteem, and excessive dependency.

In many ways, epilepsy is unique among chronic illnesses (see Pianta and Lothman, 1994). For the individual child, the chronic nature of the disorder and the unpredictability of seizures are disturbing.

Although the majority of children with epilepsy are well controlled with medication, and although some may outgrow seizures, none can look forward to a cure and must learn to live with the possibility of lifelong seizures. In addition, no one can predict when a seizure will occur; for this reason, there is little chance to adjust to epilepsy. Children may feel powerless at the prospect of losing control: the ambiguous nature of epilepsy can increase a child's apprehension at not knowing when and under what circumstances his or her behaviour will become visible to others.

Society's reaction to epilepsy remains problematic. Despite the success of modern treatment, confusion and misunderstanding still surround the condition. Some people continue to equate epilepsy with mental retardation or mental illness. This is not correct. Some persons with symptomatic epilepsy may exhibit mental retardation, but they are a minority in the population with epilepsy. Among persons with idiopathic epilepsy, mental illness or intellectual disability do not occur more frequently than in the general population.

Tourette Syndrome

Tourette syndrome is a condition characterized by multiple, involuntary muscular and cerebral tics which wax and wane, remit, and change. The onset is between the ages of two and fifteen, with six to seven years of age the most common time. The disorder results from a chemical imbalance in the brain. About 50 percent of those affected show hyperactivity, short attention spans, restlessness, and poor impulse control (Lemon and Barber, 1991).

Probably 1.6 percent of the entire population is affected with Tourette syndrome. There are about three times as many males as females affected. Only about 30 to 50 percent of persons with Tourette syndrome have *caprolia*, the verbal tic that results in uncontrollable uttering of obscenities (Lemon and Barber, 1991).

Head Trauma

In the United States, injuries, usually accidents, are the leading cause of death among children aged one to fourteen; almost half of these deaths occur among children aged one to four. Boys are involved in injuries twice as often as girls. The same is true in Canada, where injuries are the leading cause of death for children and youth after the age of one. For example, in 1990 injuries accounted for 40 percent of all preschool deaths; 50 percent of deaths among five to nine year olds; and almost 66 percent among 10 to 14 year olds ("Injuries...," 1994).

Rates vary greatly across the country and among groups. The preschool rates of injury in the territories are generally much higher than the national average. Injuries are more likely to occur among poor children, boys, and among aboriginal children and youth ("Injuries ...," 1994).

Among injuries in general, head injuries are on the rise. Traumatic Brain Injury (TBI) is defined as

> an insult to the brain, not of a degenerative or congenital nature but caused by an external physical force, that may produce a diminished or altered state of consciousness, which results in impairment of cognitive abilities or physical functioning. It can also result in the disturbance of behaviour or emotional functioning. These impairments may be either temporary or cause potential or total functional disability or psychosocial maladjustment (Savage, 1988, p. 13).

While head injuries occur most often in the 15 to 24 age range, Traumatic Brain Injury is becoming almost as frequent in children under age 15. In the United States, it is estimated that one out of every 500 school-aged children will be hospitalized for traumatic head injuries (Kraus, Fife, and Conroy, 1987). Among adolescents, vehicle accidents, involving either pedestrian or passenger vehicles including automobiles, motorcycles, and bicycles, are the most common cause of head injuries. Among young children, head injuries result from falls (the most frequent cause), bicycle accidents, other recreational activities, assaults, and child abuse.

TBI is unique in several ways, some of which are explained below.

· TBI is characterized by sudden onset (usually from motor vehicle accidents).

· TBI is not selective in its damage. It can cause diffuse cerebral swelling due to increased cerebral blood volume, and several areas of the brain can therefore be affected. Because of this, children and adolescents who suffer head injuries can be expected to present concomitant physical and perceptual-motor defects and organically based behaviour and emotional disorders (De Pompei and Blosser, 1987).

· Each child with a traumatic brain injury progresses through the recovery process in a unique way. Recovery is influenced by the site and extent of the injuries to the brain, the child's age, and other injuries or complications. Children are often in a coma and may at first show a state of confusion, as well as memory, attention, or speech and language impairments.

· TBI results in a loss of previous levels of personal, academic, and social functioning. Changes in behaviour and self-management can affect a student's performance, self-esteem, and social relationships (Berglund and Hoffbauer, 1996).

· Behaviour may be different than before the accident. In one study (Scarangi, 1994) parents reported that, in general, their children's behaviour tended to be more volatile; they were more short tempered and their tolerance level with frustrating tasks was lower. In addition, they had become quite stubborn. These children would often adamantly refuse to perform chores at home, complete homework assignments, and so on. During therapy sessions, they were highly distractible. They played with pencils, erasers, and tried to engage the reporting clinician in conversation that had nothing to do with the task at hand.

· Frontal lobe damage is the most common form of injury and ensures diminished cognitive capacity. Other insults to the brain also compromise cognitive functioning. Associated cognitive or information-processing deficits, particularly memory losses, impair a student's ability to learn new information and, consequently, can compromise academic performance.

· Language difficulties, the aphasia we discussed in Chapter 4, are common. In acquired aphasia, the age of onset is a critical factor. In children as young as four, evidence exists that the hemispheres of the brain process symbolic communication differently, with left hemisphere dominance in speech and language. With age, the brain becomes fixed and the various functions cannot be easily assumed by the other related segment of the brain. It is assumed that by about school age the brain has lost much of the organic plasticity found in young children. In adults, functional locational phenomena are even more pronounced, and adults are less able to recover functions lost through brain injury than are children. Nevertheless, many adults recover completely when they suffer serious brain damage of the left hemisphere (Snow, 1987).

Children who sustain injuries before the age of three may become temporarily mute and show a general inability to respond to the speech of others. However, very young children often make rapid improvement. They seem to relearn language in the same sequence as children acquiring language for the first time. In children over three years, symptoms of aphasia are usually different. These children may find it hard to retrieve words they have used only moments earlier. Recovery is slower and residual problems are likely to remain.

• Although TBI can result in learning disabilities of varying degrees, students show more variability in performance than do those with learning disabilities (Smith and Luckasson, 1995).

Developmental Consequences

Teachers familiar with students with TBI often report classroom difficulties (Savage and Wolcott, 1994). Children who have suffered a head injury may show chronic fatigue for up to a year. Whereas obvious motor problems may be resolved relatively quickly, problems with the execution of refined and complex psychomotor movements, particularly when speed is involved, may persist. Children may show problems in attention, retention, and auditory and recent memory. These deficits have implications for the child in the classroom because they influence the degree to which the child can keep up with class procedures such as copying, organizing material, and producing significant amounts of work.

Continuing language problems may also influence how the child functions in the classroom. When deficits such as lack of speech, restricted expressive output, and problems of breath control are present right after a trauma, they may subside rapidly, but as part of a global disorganization process, more subtle and long-standing difficulties with language comprehension and expression may persist. These include problems of word finding, organization of sequenced utterances, and comprehension breakdown as instructional complexity increases (Mira and Tyler, 1991; Ylvisaker, 1986).

It is estimated that among children with mild head injuries, about 25 percent will require special classes; of children with serious injuries, about 50 percent will need special education (see Tyler and Mira, 1993). For special education intervention, however, there are no special tested techniques or educational modifications in place (Tyler and Mira, 1993). The Profile below shows how one young man has been affected by a traumatic brain injury.

Drug-exposed Children

In Chapter 3 of this text, we pointed to the possible range of physical and behavioural difficulties that can affect a child exposed to drugs. It is important to keep in mind that there is a continuum of casualty risk. That is, the popular notion that all crack babies are severely affected is a myth; the effects vary dramatically and are moderated or exacerbated by other factors.

Children who do suffer effects perceive as stressful some events that teachers view as normal or routine (Evans, Tickle, Toppel, and Nichols, 1997). They are often overwhelmed by the ordinary experiences of a classroom—the classroom and environmental noises, the instructions, questions, interactions, and general business. Some children may withdraw; others may become wild and difficult to control (Rest, 1990).

Profile

Christopher

Christopher is now twenty-six years of age. He walks slowly, favouring his left side, writes painfully and slowly, slurs and stumbles over his speech when he is tired, and is subject to depression and sometimes violent temper outbursts.

Casual observers may think that Christopher suffers from some form of mental disability. In reality, he is suffering from permanent brain damage caused by an automobile accident when he was 15.

Christopher was out with a group of friends when their car hit some black ice and skidded into a lamp post. Even in his seat belt, Christopher was badly jarred and hit his head against the side window. He was in a coma for 11 days. When he finally awoke, he required intense physical and occupational therapy. The therapist began by helping him to walk with rails, to stop and roll a ball, and to move his tongue to produce articulate speech.

Recovery was slow. It was more than a year before Christopher could return to school. By then, he was far behind his peers, and his trouble with learning, processing, and retaining information presented him with almost insurmountable problems. He finished school in a special class where he received additional help to overcome his learning difficulties.

Fetal Alcohol Syndrome (FAS)

The disabilities resulting from FAS or FAE may be the least diagnosed and most misunderstood of all those affecting students today ("Fetal Alcohol...," 1997). Students with FAS experience multiple behavioural difficulties. They have problems communicating their needs, are easily frustrated, and have little control over their impulses. In the classroom, they often find it difficult to stay on task, refrain from constant motion, be non-disruptive, and work independently for long periods. Children often do not use good judgment and do not learn from their mistakes.

Multiple Sclerosis

Multiple sclerosis is a progressive disease of the central nervous system characterized by patchy scarring or hardening of the myelin sheath of the nerve cells in the brain and the spinal cord. The cause is unknown, although it is believed that the body's immune system engages in a self-destructive attack against its own myelin. There is no specific treatment for multiple sclerosis at present.

Demyelination results in various neurological symptoms—sensory problems, tremours, muscle weakness, spasticity, speech difficulties, dizziness, mild emotional disturbance, difficulty in walking, and other problems (Hallahan and Kauffman, 1991). These difficulties intensify as the condition progresses. Sufferers have periods of remission of various lengths, followed by recurrence of symptoms.

Typically, multiple sclerosis does not affect young children. The destruction of the myelin sheath often begins in the young adult and lasts for the remainder of the patient's life.

Multiple sclerosis affects females more frequently than males and is more common in temperate climates than in the tropics. The incidence in temperate zones is approximately 1 per 1 000 people, while the rate of occurrence in the tropics is 1 per 10 000 (Berkow, 1982).

Identification and Assessment

Many of the conditions characterized as neurological disabilities require intensive medical diagnosis and management. Vision and hearing assessment are crucial; specific measures are discussed in Chapters 9, 10, and 14. Some children may meet a neuropsychologist—a specialist in understanding and treating the problems that occur following damage to the brain.

With psycho-educational assessment, no consensus exists as to the types of measures to use. There is general agreement that testing for many children who are neurologically impaired is beset with difficulties that relate to the depth of physical and mental disabilities. Educators also agree that the information gathered in the screening and diagnostic processes must allow the formulation of a hypothesis that will take into account all the relevant factors and that will enable intelligent decisions to be made regarding placement and academic planning.

As means must be found to circumvent the disabilities in order to provide accurate assessment results, diagnosticians cannot rely on standardized tests. Instead, they must incorporate a battery of measures that range from developmental scales and ecological assessment, through communication and language tools, to tests of mental ability. They must also be willing to use different test procedures and must be flexible enough to incorporate various adaptations to tests and to responses.

The problems associated with the use of standardized tests with this population are well nigh insurmountable. Using standardized tests as the sole measure with children with physical or neurological disabilities places serious limitations on the child and may result in depressed scores that simply confirm the impairment without providing any functional information regarding potential for achievement.

If standardized tests are used at all, they must be used with a high degree of sophistication and form only one component of a test battery. Norm-referenced tests are largely standardized on the physically normal population; measures have generally not been specifically developed for those with physical and neurological disabilities. Many of the tasks that are used in such tests must be eliminated because of motor difficulties, sensory impairments, and special problems. It is appropriate for testers to modify administrative procedures. For example, eliminate verbal tests from a battery; adapt the way a test is presented, such as holding a picture closer to the child's eyes; or modify procedures, allowing more time for timed tasks. Or testers can alter the test stimuli by providing larger pictures or speaking more slowly. As well, a physical or occupational therapist may be on hand to assist in handling and positioning techniques so as to maximize a child's performance.

When altering response requirements, there are three general techniques. First, a support adaptation is used when the child must be placed in a certain position or provided some general form of support before being able to pass an item. A prosthetic adaptation is provided for the child who needs a specific piece of equipment, such as braces or a hearing aid, to demonstrate a skill. A general adaptation is one that does not require support or a piece of equipment but still represents a change in the basic requirements of the task or that changes the utility of the skill. For example, a child who is hearing impaired may need to perform communication tasks with sign language. Or a child with a physical disability may be allowed to look toward the response rather than pointing manually.

For children with physical or neurological disabilities, data regarding communication skills (see Chapters 4 and 14), adaptive behaviour (see Chapter 6), and mobility (see Chapters 11 and 14) are particularly important. Regular and periodic assessment of development in communication and motor movement provides data about how many skills a child has developed, what type of skills they are, and how they are used.

To conduct motor assessments teachers should rely on the expertise of physical or occupational therapists who have in-depth knowledge of the neurobiological system and can recognize the impact of specific impairments on movement and stability. The therapist will conduct an assessment of the physical domains that considers physical status, mobility, and functional aspects (how the child uses motor skills).

Developmental Consequences

Because of the diverse nature of physical and neurological disabilities, their varied severity, and co-occurring conditions, it is impossible to draw a profile of a typical affected child.

For children with orthopedic and motor disabilities, the key factor is the extent to which the disability affects movement potential. Motor skills are integral to almost everything that a child does or wants to do in the environment, and physical and motor problems affect educational and social progress in other ways than mobility. Deficient motor skills can affect cognitive development because they hinder a child's manipulation and exploration. Children with motor impairments have different first-hand knowledge and experiences than their peers because they cannot explore the environment as other children can. At the sensorimotor stage, for example, children with cerebral palsy have been found to include more visual exploration and less tactile exploration of toys than is seen among children developing normally (see Rogers, 1988).

Similarly, social skills may suffer because efficient motor skills are necessary for many forms of play with peers. Play depends on experience and opportunity, and this alone places restraints on children with severe physical disabilities. Children with motor disorders cannot manipulate toys and other objects, join in dramatic and pretend play or rough and tumble play, or engage in games in which children run or jump or skip.

Intervention with Students Who Have Physical and Neurological Disabilities

Physical and neurological disabilities are primarily medical and therapeutic conditions, and intervention stretches far beyond the academic and educational. No single professional can effectively fill the multiple needs of children who are physically and neurologically disabled; they receive help from educators, physicians and medical specialists, occupational and physical therapists, speech and language pathologists, counsellors, and others. It is the secondary difficulties in such areas as communication, mobility, and cognitive functioning that are of most concern to educators in the classroom.

Medical Intervention

Medical interventions cover a broad spectrum of treatments. For example, the hip dislocations, contractures, spinal defects, fractures, and osteoporosis that are common among children with spina bifida require medical assistance.

Although cerebral palsy is neither progressive nor curable, various medical techniques improve functioning. Children with cerebral palsy (and spina bifida) often suffer from contractures—a permanent shortening of the muscles, tendons, and ligaments that results in postural distortion and decreased joint mobility. Surgery can ease contractures and correct dislocations, and may also involve repair of the joints to reduce the risk of arthritis (Batshaw and Perret, 1986).

Another medical procedure—selective position rhizotomy—sees the surgeon cut selected nerve roots below the spinal cord that cause plasticity in the leg muscles (Hallahan and Kauffman, 1991). The treatment allows some spastic persons better control of certain muscles, lets some non-ambulatory children walk, and helps others to move more normally.

Medical treatment for epilepsy focuses primarily on seizure control. Drug therapy can control about 50 percent of grand mal, 40 percent of petit mal, and 35 percent of psychomotor seizures. Drugs can also reduce the frequency of grand mal and petit mal seizures in 35 percent of cases, and of psychomotor attacks in 50 percent of cases (Berkow, 1982). The choice of drugs is related to the type of seizure pattern and the presence of side effects from other drugs. The primary goal of anticonvulsant therapy is to achieve maximum control with the fewest possible drugs and side effects.

In the case of head trauma injuries (TBI), immediate medical attention may help to reduce the extent of damage. Trauma medicine has made a great deal of progress in recent years; new brain scan techniques can pinpoint sites of injury in the brain.

Therapy

Physical, occupational, and speech and language therapies are indicated for many children with neurological and orthopedic disabilities. Spina bifida children with myelomeningocele, for example, frequently have other orthopedic complications and problems requiring extensive physical and occupational therapies. In children with cerebral palsy, physical therapy can ease contractures.

For children with orthopedic and neurological impairments, therapies are most commonly associated with sensorimotor development, postural control, activities for daily living, and environmental adaptations. The need for occupational or physical therapy is determined by an absence of robust righting, protective extension, and equilibrium reactions; inefficient sitting and standing posture; limited ability to perform sensorimotor tasks; and inadequate physical fitness for daily living activities (Dunner, Connor-Kuntz, and Goodway, 1995).

Occupational therapists focus on motor development, attention to aspects of the sensory environment, and the achievement of functional daily tasks. They work to enhance a child's potential for learning and try to develop vestibular balance; tactile, kinesthetic, and perceptual motor co-ordination; and self-help skills.

Physical therapists work with children needing prosthetic management training, wheelchair mobility training, and gross-motor-skill exercises. Physical therapy is directed toward preventing disability; for example, developing, improving, or restoring more efficient muscular functioning and maintaining maximum motor functioning for each child. The physical therapist also provides information concerning positioning and handling of students and the use of adaptive equipment.

Promoting optimal postures and movement patterns for functional activities is an important objective for children with physical and motor disabilities. Areas of special concern are positioning and carrying. Carrying refers to the way that a child with a physical or motor disability is moved; positioning refers to how the child is seated or otherwise positioned.

Children must be handled in ways that normalize muscle tone and prevent the development of secondary muscular and structural disorders. Proper positioning can facilitate normal muscle tone and symmetry, provide stable and aligned posture, inhibit primitive reflexes, facilitate normal movement patterns, stabilize head and trunk control, and compensate for the lack of sitting balance (Bailey and Wolery, 1984; Clark and Allen, 1985; Copeland and Kimmel, 1989). Individual positioning is prescribed for each child.

Conductive Education

Conductive education is a type of therapy that was developed in Hungary by Dr. Andras Peto in 1945. The aim is to promote personal development and educational and social fulfillment for children with motor difficulties related to brain and spinal problems.

Physically disabled children can participate in many activities with their non-disabled classmates.

Care and education of an individual child rests with one person, a conductor, who is with the child 24 hours a day. He or she aims to challenge the child. Mobility is stressed and challenges consistently heighten. Children learn through games and music, which strengthen limbs and posture. (For more on conductive education, see Beattie, 1993.)

Technical Intervention

A range of equipment is now available for children with disabilities and is making a significant difference in the quality of their lives by allowing them more control of events in their environment. Devices and equipment range from the very simple, such as adapted spoons and switch-adapted battery-operated toys, to the very complex, such as computerized environmental control systems (Parette, Hofmann, and Van Biervliet, 1994).

Adaptive equipment is an umbrella term for these devices. The term refers to any device designed or modified to lead individuals with disabilities to independence (Raschke, Dedrick, and Hanus, 1991, p. 25). Within the broad category of adaptive equipment are prosthetic, orthotic, and adaptive devices, chiefly used to assist children with physical and motor disabilities and those with sensory impairments. There is quite a lot of overlap in these categories.

Much adaptive equipment is individualized for a child. When individually adapted equipment is used, children demonstrate improved motor, self-care, and social skills (see Dunn, 1989). In 1986, 26 percent of non-institutionalized children with disabilities used some form of assistive device, the majority of which assisted mobility and/or agility. That year, eight percent of children with disabilities used medically prescribed footwear; five percent had some type of braces (other than teeth braces); three percent used a wheelchair; two percent had crutches or other types of walking aids. Fewer than one percent had an artificial limb (Nessner, 1990).

Prosthetic Devices

Prosthetic devices are used to replace lost functions and/or provide support. They duplicate normal body movements as nearly as possible while restraining normal functions as little as possible. For example, an artificial leg is a prosthesis for a child missing a leg.

Much special equipment is used for mobility. Equipment for mobility and standing includes leg casts and braces, ankle–foot equipment, crutches, walkers, and wheelchairs. The most common mobility devices are braces, crutches, and wheelchairs.

Wheelchairs are designed for people who are unable to ambulate or whose ambulation is unsafe and unsteady, or for those for whom ambulation is too strenuous. Wheelchairs are almost as varied as the people who use them. A good wheelchair is tailored to the individual's needs. The main types are self-propelled wheelchairs, attendant-operated chairs, transit chairs, and electric or battery-powered chairs. An electronically controlled wheelchair can provide movement through voice activated commands for a person who is severely disabled; it is programmed to respond to the owner's voice and requires no muscle control.

Orthopedic braces are for the lower extremities. Braces do not prevent contractures or develop walking skills but serve to control and support. There are three main types—short leg braces, long leg braces, and hip braces. A short brace would be used on the ankle joint; a long leg brace from the knee to the ankle. For children with cerebral palsy, braces are used chiefly for control. They help in ambulation, control involuntary movements, and serve to prevent or correct deformities. In spina bifida and muscular dystrophy, the braces are used chiefly for support. Support braces weigh less than control braces.

Crutches are used during periods of temporary disability to help with balance and locomotion, and to reduce weight on the lower extremities. When the disability is of long duration or permanent, crutches have to be designed to reduce the weight the legs must bear and provide stability and support. The surface on which the crutch may operate is important. If it is slippery, rubber-tipped ends, spiked ends, or tripod legs should be provided.

Walkers are upright devices used to provide support and movement. Supported standing forces weight-bearing that is necessary for the normal formation of the hip joints. There are various types of walkers that can be modified in various ways to assist the individual. All provide standing support with forward inclined standing.

Prosthetic equipment may assist in the therapeutic techniques of positioning and carrying. Positioning equipment and strategies allow children with motor problems to achieve postures and movement that might otherwise be impossible or non-functional. Some children need support in a lying position and use adaptive boards, wedges, and bolsters. Positioning equipment is typically designed to place the child in one or more basic postures in as normal a body alignment as possible.

Sitting may be difficult for children with motor disorders. Because children spend a lot of time sitting, it is important that they sit in the most beneficial position. They need to find positions that allow the best hand use, that are easiest for eye–hand co-ordination, and that present the least difficulties for balance. Modified chairs are for children who have difficulty sitting well or those who have abnormal hip and leg patterns. A special chair aligns the body, limbs, and head; flexes the hips, knees, and ankles; and brings the head and shoulders slightly forward.

Adapted chairs include corner chairs and bolster chairs. Both usually have removable trays. Dangling feet are harmful to children with motor problems, so an abduction block—a chunk of something that the child's legs can straddle—is usually used to prevent the child from sliding to the floor, while a footstool ensures that the child's feet reach a flat solid surface. Straps and other props are sometimes used to improve posture.

Orthotic Devices

Orthotic devices assist a limb's action. For example, special utensils (spoons, forks, and dishes) make eating and drinking easier for a child with a movement dysfunction. Some eating implements have Velcro straps to make them easier for the child to handle and control. Adapted spoons have a built-up handle or swivel so that gravity can right the spoon and prevent spillage. A hand splint to support wrist extension can also be used to allow greater finger movements for manipulative tasks.

In the classroom, children may require specialized equipment. Page turners and book stands assist in reading. Magnetized pencils and equipment are helpful for writing and drawing; there are specially adapted scissors for cutting.

Adaptive Devices

Much of the current technology requires pre-academic readiness skills, and most of today's technological devices operate through one dominant modality (for example, touch for key-

Teachers should know how to position children in wheelchairs.

boards, vision for monitors). However, devices are increasingly allowing for alternative modalities such as voice activated computers and television captioning (Sawyer and Zantal-Wiener, 1993), and the availability of instrumentation that permits persons with disabilities whose cognitive level is less than two years to control devices in their environment is also increasing. As well, many technologies are becoming more transparent (less noticeable and obtrusive). This is because of miniaturization, the use of lighter materials, and higher capacities for information processing.

Some children with physical disabilities have difficult or unintelligible speech. However, their receptive language is probably far ahead of their expressive language, and they may know and understand far more words than they can express. These students require devices that act as substitutes for speech (see Chapters 4 and 14). Teachers need to be aware of methods of communication such as Blissymbolics and other pictographic systems as a substitute for speech.

Educational Intervention

In the past, non-educational considerations would have taken priority when considering placements for students with physical and neurological disabilities, and many students would have been taught in separate classrooms or special schools. Progress in medical science, improved technology, and changing attitudes have dramatically altered service delivery for these students, and today most are placed in regular classrooms.

Special class placement may still be provided for students who have additional severe problems with perception, cognition, or language. Other children may miss numerous days in school for surgery, medical appointments, and therapy. If school-time lost is extensive, students may be provided with hospital or home instruction.

Inclusion

Educators realize that students with physical and neurological disabilities have the same educational needs as non-disabled children. They may need special help from some apparatus to make a response, but they can benefit from the same instructional practices and curriculum as their peers.

Inclusion may not be appropriate for the full range of students with neurological disabilities. Rempel (1992) points out that "Except for a few isolated cases...this process as practised is generally a counterproductive experience for the student who has sustained an injury to the brain" (p. 46). He goes on to say that "Frequently the experience is in fact destructive" (p. 46). Rempel further notes that unless major accommodations are made in the regular classroom, the environment is hostile to the injured student. This happens because these students require a particularly structured and quiet environment (see this chapter's In the Classroom).

Curriculum

There is no special curriculum for students with physical and neurological disabilities. Children learn the same things as their peers. Children with physical and neurological disabilities should be presented with the regular curriculum to the greatest extent possible. Sound teaching principles are the same for all children and there do not need to be differences in strategies and techniques.

SUMMARY

1. Physical and neurological disabilities include a huge range of conditions. Of the many physical disabilities, the conditions described in this chapter all stem from some form of neurological damage. In this sense, the conditions are not curable, although they can be ameliorated by medical intervention, therapy, drugs, and education.

2. Cerebral palsy is the most common neurological difficulty seen in children. It takes a number of forms. Over half the children with cerebral palsy have spasticity in which the muscles don't work in harmony—some muscles are too tight, some too loose. Children with athetosis show jerky, uncontrolled, and writhing movements; those with ataxia show unco-ordinated movement and difficulties with positions in space. Together with motor problems, cerebral palsy can include any number of intellectual, sensory, and behavioural disorders.

3. Spina bifida comes in a number of forms and may be the precursor of multiple disabilities. Damage to the developing nervous system will leave varying degrees of paralysis, sensory loss, bowel and bladder incontinence, and hydrocephalus.

4. Epilepsy is a condition in which the smooth functioning of the brain's electrical system is briefly disturbed, causing a seizure, an electrical storm in the brain. Epilepsy af-

fects more than one percent of the population—more than 280 000 Canadians. The condition can be acquired at any time in life. Eighty percent of new cases are children under the age of 18, and half of these are affected before the age of five.

5. In epilepsy, manifestations depend upon the location, severity, and type of short circuit coming from the brain. The most frightening for the observer is the grand mal seizure, in which a child loses consciousness. Children may also suffer from petit mal— an extremely brief loss of consciousness. Other seizure types include Jacksonian and psychomotor. The developmental consequences of epilepsy are extremely varied; children have more learning and behavioral problems than their peers, and have higher rates of psychiatric disorders.

6. Traumatic Brain Injury (TBI) is an insult to the brain caused by an external physical force. Associated problems include cognitive, behavioural/psychological, sensory/motor, and language disorders. Students may experience problems with physical, cognitive, or psychosocial functioning well past their initial physical recovery and rehabilitation.

7. Physical problems may limit mobility, socialization, independence, learning, and educational opportunities. Children may be further handicapped by their lack of ability to explore the environment adequately.

8. Depending on the extent and nature of a condition, a child may require the services of many disciplines, including psychology, physiotherapy, occupational therapy, speech pathology, audiology, and medicine. For example, children with cerebral palsy have restricted movement and the retention of primitive reflexes. Occupational and physical therapists work in close collaboration with teachers and parents to assist the child in different functions.

9. Adaptive devices serve to make living easier. Students with physical disabilities require technical aids and adaptive equipment for mobility and ambulation, for seating, for classroom use, and for daily living.

10. For most children, special needs are not synonymous with a special education requirement. A physical or neurological disability, by itself, is no reason for special class placement.

In the Classroom

Profile: Kent

Kent suffers from a number of disabilities that affect every aspect of his life and development. He has cerebral palsy and needs leg braces and a walker for mobility. Psycho-educational assessment has shown Kent to be functioning in the low area of the mildly retarded range, so he needs a modified school program based on his unique strengths and weaknesses. Kent also suffers from a moderate to severe bilateral hearing loss and the audiologist has fitted him with two hearing aids.

At eight years of age, Kent has developed very little communication. He is included in a regular classroom primarily to stimulate his social functioning. This has improved, but he still has minimal linguistic skills.

A language therapist works with Kent in a one-to-one situation. After consultation with the teacher and the parents, she decided to introduce Kent to a new language system. In the past, both Blissymbolics and American Sign Language were tried, but these seemed to be too conceptually difficult for Kent. Because Kent's hand use is quite good, the therapist suggested that the teacher introduce some basic signs from the Amerind system and also teach these to the children in the class. Once Kent learns some simple signs and combinations, he may advance to American Sign Language.

* * *

With his cerebral palsy, hearing loss, and low intellectual ability, Kent can be categorized as a child with multiple disabilities. The combination of disabilities makes his condition unique.

For all children with cerebral palsy and other severe motor impairments, additions to the regular curriculum may be necessary to provide ambulation training and to teach certain self-help skills, leisure skills, prevocational skills, and articulation. Teachers may need to provide special help with a wheelchair, with toileting, and with dressing. Program planning must consider stamina levels; present levels of academic achievement; intellectual ability; independence in mobility and ambulation; and personal motivation (Gearheart, Weishahn, and Gearheart, 1992).

For Kent particularly, the individual program must include a potential mode of communication. The development of a system by which to communicate at some level with those in the environment is a first priority.

The language taught using the system and other related activities will build on what have been identified as Kent's interests. He is, for example, very interested in his classmates, so his language will stress names and simple actions such as "See Joe," or "Peter draws." Kent also enjoys books—both being read to and turning the pages himself—so much exposure to highly coloured print materials will be important. He also seems to enjoy music, so he will learn to listen to simple songs on a tape recorder that he will operate himself.

Extract from Kent's IEP

Name: Kent
Age: 8

PRESENT LEVELS OF FUNCTIONING

Kent has cerebral palsy. There may be some language, but so far there is no speech development.

PLACEMENT

Kent is in a regular setting. The object is to expose him to language and social models.

ADAPTIVE EQUIPMENT

Wheelchair, behind-the-ear aids in both ears; magnetized equipment for writing; large implements.

ADDITIONAL ASSISTANCE

Physical therapy, speech therapy, individual aide in regular classroom.

LONG-RANGE GOALS

- During therapy, Kent will learn a simple manual communication system, Amerind. Signs will be used in the regular classroom by the aide.
- Kent will be provided many opportunities to read books either alone or with a peer.
- Kent will operate a tape recorder to listen to simple songs.

SHORT-TERM OBJECTIVES

- Within classroom activities, the aide will sign to Kent and prompt him to use known signs.
- Kent will join in small groups with assigned tasks to improve language and social skills.
- Kent will use greeting behaviour—waving—when requested.
- Kent will maintain a supported sitting position in the carpeted reading area.
- Kent will use page turners, with support.
- Kent will look at the book as a peer reads a story.
- When given a tape recorder, Kent will depress the special switch to turn the recorder on and off.

EFFECTS OF NEUROLOGICAL DISORDERS

THE CHILD HAS DIFFICULTY IN DEALING WITH MANY DIFFERENT STIMULI AT ONCE (ESPECIALLY CHILDREN WITH TBI, FAS, AND THOSE WHO HAVE BEEN DRUG-EXPOSED)

TIPS FOR TEACHERS

Children need stability, routine, and sameness in the classroom to feel secure enough to learn (Walker, 1992/93). Give only one specific task at a time.

Keep change to a minimum—establish stable routines in the classroom. Provide a lot of structure. Explain ahead of time what will happen, when it will happen, and what is expected. If there is to be a change in the schedule of the class or in an activity, the child should be warned in advance ("Fetal Alcohol," 1997).

Some of the most common stressors for drug-exposed children are transitions, classroom interruptions, and

EFFECTS OF NEUROLOGICAL DISORDERS	TIPS FOR TEACHERS
	school disruptions such as field trips and fire drills. A serene classroom with a stress on routine is critical.
	Avoid overload and stress social skills, communication, and stable, consistent discipline.
THE CHILD HAS A SHORT ATTENTION SPAN (ESPECIALLY THOSE WITH TBI AND FAS)	Break assignments into small pieces and provide extra time to complete tasks.
	Provide many concrete examples.
THE CHILD NEEDS MUCH REPETITION FOR MEMORY	Overteach. In addition to direct instruction, use a lot of repetition to teach new skills and concepts. Use identical language when explaining ideas or rules.
	Use many diagrams, charts, and other graphic cues.
	Where possible, use concrete objects.
THE CHILD HAS DIFFICULTIES WITH PROBLEM SOLVING	Use advance organizers for older students.
	Give the child preferential seating
	Provide a personal work space free from distractions.
	Teach note taking skills. Provide a note taker, if necessary.
THE CHILD HAS LIMITED LANGUAGE SKILLS	Use assistive technology
	Provide appropriate wait time in questioning.
	Teach metacognitive skills
THE CHILD NEEDS A RANGE OF ADAPTIVE EQUIPMENT	Use magnetized rulers and instruments on the chair table.
	Use holders. To assist children who have motor problems with grip, use a pencil grip made of a piece of clay or foam material wrapped around the pencil or pen.
	Make paintbrushes out of roll-on deodorant bottles by removing the tops, filling the bottle with tempera paint, and snapping the top back in place.
	Use large chunks of sponge for painting.
	Use marking pens for free flow.
	Anchor paper by taping it to the table or easel.
THE CHILD'S PHYSICAL CONDITION MUST BE MONITORED	Lack of progress or deterioration of motor skills is a cause for concern. Observe children carefully.
	A shunt malfunction can be seen in a child's behaviour and physical functioning. For example, the child has a headache or pain in the neck area.
	Keep an emergency protocol (see Chapter 11).

EFFECTS OF NEUROLOGICAL DISORDERS	TIPS FOR TEACHERS
THE CHILD HAS SPECIAL MOBILITY NEEDS	Many children have difficulty moving from one place to another in the school. Within the entire school, attention must be paid to modifications such as widened doorways.
	When moving the child in a wheelchair, always ensure that the child's feet are on the footrest.
	Wear rubber-soled shoes.
THE CHILD NEEDS SPECIAL HANDLING	Learn about handling—how the child is picked up, carried, held, and assisted.
	Do not pull the child by the arms; lift the child under the arms.
	When helping a child dress, put clothes on the more affected side first.
	To straighten a limb, push it out at shoulder and elbow or hip and knee first.
	Don't try to pull a hand or foot through clothing—the limb will only bend tighter.
THE CHILD NEEDS REGULAR POSITIONING	Be constantly aware of positioning and know how to position children in wheelchairs. This refers to providing support for the child's body, changing the child's sitting position in the chair, and arranging instructional or play materials in certain ways.
	Constantly check on sitting position; reposition the child at least every half hour.
	Tell the child what you are going to do at all times, whether in positioning or moving.
THE CHILD HAS A LOSS OF TACTILE SENSE	Do not place the wheelchair too close to heaters.
	When children are wearing braces, be alert to circulation problems that may show up as swelling, coldness, change of colour, evidence of infection, or other skin problems.
THE CHILD NEEDS SPECIAL SEATING	At a desk, make sure that the child's heels touch the floor, knees are bent, and back is supported.
	Use an abduction block; don't let feet dangle.
THE CHILD MAY BE ISOLATED	Children should be expected to learn what their peers do and to join in all relevant classroom activities.
	Allow the child as much opportunity for success as possible.
	Establish realistic goals and expectations.

THE CHILD NEEDS ASSISTANCE IN SOCIAL INTERACTIONS	Use direct instruction, modelling, role playing, and scripting to teach specific social skills. Teach social skills in small groups
THE CHILD NEEDS TOLERANCE AND UNDERSTANDING	It is important for teachers to know and understand the precise nature of a child's problems, including the characteristics and the limitations imposed. Guard against overprotection and against the child's developing a dependency upon the teacher or a non-disabled peer.

WEBLINKS

Cerebral Palsy and Multiple Sclerosis **http://www.healthtouch.com/level1/leaflets/104947/105077.htm**

Epilepsy Canada **http://www.Generation.NET/~epilepsy/**

Spina Bifida and Hydrocephalus Association of Nova Scotia **http://www.chebucto.ns.ca/Health/SBANS/**

An Encounter with Tourette Syndrome **http://cec.wustl.edu/~jpk1/tourettes.html**

The Arc's Fetal Alcohol Syndrome Resource and Materials Guide **http://thearc.org/misc/faslist.html**

The Association for the Neurologically Disabled of Canada **http://www.AND.ca/**

FAS/FAE Information Service **http://www.ccsa.ca/fasgen.htm**

CHAPTER 13

Children with Pervasive Developmental Disorders

It was not until the closing decades of the nineteenth century that the psychotic child became an object of study. Psychiatrists and others initiated careful efforts to observe, describe, and classify the disordered behaviours demonstrated by child patients, and collected and organized the existing material in monographs on psychic disorders, mental diseases, and insanity in children. By 1900, there was an assortment of data demonstrating that children displayed psychotic disorders (see Winzer, 1993).

In 1906, Sante de Sanctus named the psychotic problems observed in youngsters *dementia praecoxissima* (dementia of childhood). Then in 1911, Eugen Blueler, a Swiss psychiatrist, renamed *dementia praecox* as *schizophrenia*. The work of de Sanctus, Blueler, and others contributed to the identification of a distinct condition known as childhood schizophrenia. By 1935 schizophrenia in children was well documented and distinguished, although not clearly, from the adult condition.

Credit for first identifying autistic behaviours in children and adults also goes to Eugen Blueler, who isolated specific non-verbal and non-relating behaviours in 1906. Blueler used the word *autistic* as an adjective; it was not until Leo Kanner's major study in 1943 that an autistic syndrome, with autism as a noun, was identified in children.

Early authorities viewed childhood psychoses as one inclusive category, ignoring distinctions among specific syndromes. Research was simply generalized from one population to another. This became seriously evident in the disproportionate number of studies that focused on infantile autism and led to generalization of data that had little direct relevance to the schizophrenic group.

Even after recognition of psychoses in children and the formulation of methods for identification, diagnosis, and intervention, the problems remained largely the bailiwick of psychiatrists and psychologists, and not the school system. Well into the twentieth century, children with severe and multiple disabilities were excluded from public school segregated classes and often not accepted into residential settings. When treatment was given, institutionalization was the common mode, as many psychiatrists and other professionals believed that children who were autistic and psychotic could most effectively be treated away from their homes.

In the 1960s, interest in returning many previously institutionalized children to the community mounted and education began to assume responsibility for children with serious disturbances. For example, children with autism were integrated into classes in Toronto as early as 1956 (Lovatt, 1962).

By the 1970s, the education of children with developmental disorders was firmly entrenched in the school system, and professionals began to encourage parents to keep their children at home. Today, many children with severe developmental disabilities are taught in special day schools or residential settings, but increasing numbers of these youngsters are attending classes in their neighbourhood schools.

Different types of conditions, including childhood psychoses, childhood schizophrenia, infantile autism, and severe and profound mental retardation are found under the developmental disorder umbrella. As children with pervasive developmental disorders very often exhibit co-occurring disabilities such as epilepsy, perceptual motor dysfunctions, and communication disorders, these conditions can also often be viewed as multiple disabilities.

Childhood psychoses and infantile autism represent the most extreme forms of emotional and behavioural disorders. Probably no other conditions are so hard to understand and so far removed from the range of normal experience. They strike at the very essence of human relatedness and human communication, and must therefore be considered the most devastating disorders that affect a child's learning and behaviour. Every aspect of functioning is affected.

Children who are psychotic and autistic frequently exhibit strange and inappropriate behaviour. They may display bizarre body movements and sometimes suffer inordinate fears. Or they may indulge in repetitive motor activity, self-stimulation, and self-mutilation. Many children are completely withdrawn; they never speak at all but pirouette in a silent internal dance, impervious to all around them. Their world may consist of touch sensations, of familiar routines, and rigidly obsessive behaviour. Still, such children may fly into tantrums at the smallest change in their surroundings, from a parent's new hair style to a door left slightly ajar.

Autism is a rare, severely and permanently disabling developmental disorder with a suspected but poorly understood neurological basis. It reveals itself in fleeting eye contact, the failure to form attachments, and disrupted relationships. Children who are autistic have difficulty developing language skills, learning to communicate, and relating. Many function at pre-academic levels and fail to develop basic self-care skills and language. Schizophrenia is a condition characterized by qualitative changes in functioning such as association disturbances, delusions, hallucinations, attention deficits, and inappropriate social interaction.

Because childhood psychoses and infantile autism are so spectacular and bizarre, they have recently elicited an enormous amount of interest, concern, and research. The importance of the study of pervasive developmental disorders is not related to the incidence and prevalence of the conditions; childhood schizophrenia and autism are rare. However, researchers believe that if they can develop an understanding of psychoses and autism, they will have made a giant step in the direction of unravelling the triple helix of brain, behaviour, and environment.

A number of forms of psychoses, due to multiple etiologies, affect children. Heller's disease, for example, is due to disintegrative brain disease. Psychiatric disorders subsequent to brain injuries in older children have also been reported (see Chapter 12).

In this chapter we restrict our discussion of childhood psychoses to schizophrenia. We also delve into the complexities of infantile autism. The manifestations of autism are similar enough to those of childhood psychoses to discuss them together. Children who are psychotic or autistic show a pattern of behaviour characterized by a failure to recognize, understand, or respond appropriately to people in their environment. They demonstrate withdrawal and a high frequency of problematic and bizarre behaviour. Keep in mind, though, that etiology, treatment, and prognosis for autism and for schizophrenia differ quite radically.

Definitions of Pervasive Developmental Disorders

Children with pervasive developmental disorders suffer from conditions that affect every aspect of their present and probably future functioning. The adjective *pervasive* means that the conditions affect all developmental domains and will probably be extremely long-lasting, if not lifelong. To reiterate the definitions given in Chapter 1, a developmental delay (pervasive developmental disorder) is a condition that represents a significant delay in the process of development. As the process of development is significantly affected, the term does not refer to a maturational lag or an at-risk child.

Individuals who are **developmentally disabled** are those who suffer from chronic disabilities, attributable to mental or physical impairments, or a combination of these, that are manifested before age 22 and that result in functional limitations in major life activities requiring special services and treatment that are of extended duration or lifelong. Childhood psychoses and infantile autism fit under the broad category of pervasive developmental disorders.

Childhood Schizophrenia

In general terms, psychoses are serious mental disorders in which the behavioural and thought processes of an individual become so disturbed that the person is out of touch with reality. The more specific term, **childhood psychoses**, refers to

> a heterogeneous group of clinical syndromes characterized by any number of maladaptive behaviours or clusters of behaviours including severe disturbances in ego functioning. Such disturbances affect various aspects of adaptive behaviour, including the perception and ordering of experience, the assessment of reality, the control and channeling of impulses, and the success of interpersonal relations (Cummings and Finger, 1980).

Childhood schizophrenia is one of the childhood psychoses. To many people, schizophrenia brings to mind the condition of split personalities depicted in movies such as *The Three Faces of Eve*. In reality, adult schizophrenia is not commensurate with split personality. Nor are adult schizophrenia and childhood schizophrenia parallel conditions with only developmentally determined variations in symptomology. Early findings that equated the childhood condition with the adult disorder have been replaced by research that sees childhood schizophrenia as a discrete, identifiable condition. Today, childhood schizophrenia is defined as a pervasive psychotic disorder involving a decline or arrest of ego development following a period of relatively normal development, occurring in children who demonstrate some degree of useful language and relatedness to others. Among children characterized as schizophrenic, there are wide variations in personality organization, clinical course, intellectual functioning, and identifiable etiological conditions (Cummings and Finger, 1980, p. 510).

This definition points out that childhood schizophrenia occurs late in childhood, often around the beginning of puberty. Before its onset, the child has usually developed according to normal patterns. It stresses the wide range of behaviours seen in children characterized as schizophrenic and focuses on particular domains of deviation.

Infantile Autism

The word *autism* comes from the Greek *autos*, meaning "self." It is fitting, because the most prominent feature of children with infantile autism is their apparent self-absorption and socially withdrawn behaviour. But despite being the subject of more research than any other child psychiatric disorder, autism remains difficult to understand. A precise definition does not exist, the boundaries of autism remain vague and undifferentiated, and much remains unknown about the condition. According to recent American legislation (IDEA, 1990),

Autism means a developmental disability significantly affecting verbal and non-verbal communication and social interaction, generally evident before age three, that adversely affects educational performance. Characteristics of autism include irregularities and impairments in communication, engagement in repetitive activities and stereotyped movements, resistance to environmental change or change in daily routines, and unusual responses to sensory experiences. The term does not include children with characteristics of the disability serious emotional disturbance (National Association, 1991, p. 2).

Autistic children demonstrate severe self-isolation.

This definition is both inclusive and specific. It stresses that infantile autism is a developmental disability, not an emotional disturbance. Note that this is a recent classification. The first changes in classification came when autism was removed from the area of severe emotional disturbance to the area of "other health impaired." With IDEA (1990) it again moved to become a separate category.

The definition also stresses that in autism, manifestation is before age three, hence the common adjective *infantile*. Behaviours that affect educational performance are emphasized.

Classification of Pervasive Developmental Disorders

Dissension and controversy surround the classification of pervasive developmental disorders and the subcategories of psychoses and infantile autism. Many of these problems stem from the historical antecedents of the field (see Historical Notes) as well as the rapid alterations brought to the field by new genetic, psychological, and educational research.

Currently, the most commonly cited classification system is that appearing in the *Diagnostic and Statistical Manual of Mental Disorders* (DSM IV) (American Psychiatric Association, 1994), which identifies several categories of adult, adolescent, and childhood severe and profound disorders. In DSM, the category of pervasive developmental disorders refers directly to childhood conditions and includes four subcategories: infantile autism; disintegrative psychoses; other specific early childhood psychoses, including childhood schizophrenia; and unspecified psychoses.

Of these four groupings, we will only discuss infantile autism and childhood schizophrenia. When these two conditions are compared, infantile autism is clearly distinguishable from childhood schizophrenia on a number of variables. These include

- *etiology*, which we discuss later in this chapter.
- *age of onset*. This is one of the primary characteristics that distinguishes autism from psychoses. Infantile autism occurs before thirty months of age and is usually preceded by markedly abnormal behaviour patterns. Childhood schizophrenia is of later onset; children show a normal early pattern of development, followed by severe regression as the condition takes hold.
- *behavioural manifestations*. Behavioural patterns in autism are pervasive; those in schizophrenia may be episodic. Children with schizophrenia exhibit a wide variety of symptoms and send very mixed messages to the outside world: their extremes of activity, sudden mood changes, and verbal disturbances bewilder observers. In this, schizophrenic children are unlike those affected by infantile autism, who tend to exhibit repetitive behaviour. As well, children with schizophrenia may develop delusions and experience hallucinations, whereas those with autism do not. One child with schizophrenia, for example, reported that a kitchen light said to do things and said to "Shut up" (Russell, Bott, and Sammons, 1989).
- *prognosis*. Researchers in the area of childhood pervasive developmental disorders agree on only one thing—the dismal prognosis. In terms of future functioning, children who are autistic differ markedly from those whose difficulties begin later. Depending on the

age of onset, the course of the condition, and the intensity of intervention, children who are schizophrenic may be returned to somewhat normal functioning. Encouraging results are certainly emerging in the area of autism, but the prognosis for the whole population remains poor.

Table 13-1 shows the major behavioural symptoms of infantile autism and childhood schizophrenia.

Table 13-1 Behavioural characteristics of psychotic and autistic children

Behavioural symptoms	Infantile autism	Childhood schizophrenia
Social development		
emotional responsiveness	−	x
lack of anticipatory response	+	−
social imitation	−	+
looks and walks "through" people	+	−
extreme aloneness	+	−
talks to, not with	+	−
strong attachment to inanimate objects	+	−
insistence on sameness	+	−
delusions and hallucinations	−	+
Motor and sensory functions		
not physically pliable	+	−
overly sensitive to stimuli	+	−
often graceful motor performance	+	x
unusual motor behaviours, such as repetitive movements	+	+
self-stimulation	+	+
self-mutilation	+	x
odd movements and grimaces	+	+
Language and communication		
delayed acquisition	+	−
deficient, deviant babble	+	−
sometimes thought to be deaf	+	−
overly sensitive to sound	+	−
non-verbal communication	−	+
echolalia	+	−
pronominal reversal	+	−
spontaneous speech	−	+
expressive-intonational features	−	+

   − seldom occurs   x may occur   + commonly occurs

Prevalence of Pervasive Developmental Disorders

Although pervasive developmental disorders are extremely low-incidence conditions, the changing terminology and classification make prevalence figures precarious. Most estimates allow five cases of pervasive developmental disorders per 10 000 children (Treffert, 1970). Infantile autism occurs less frequently than childhood schizophrenia, but prevalence figures for autism tend to vary more widely.

There are an estimated 3.1 cases of childhood schizophrenia per 10 000 children (Treffert, 1970). Among children, twice as many boys as girls are schizophrenic. By adolescence, the ratio is equal between boys and girls (Wicks-Nelson and Israel, 1991).

Prevalence estimates for autism range from 0.7 per 10 000 to 4.8 per 10 000 school-aged children. Among the population of people who are autistic, the condition is three to four times more common in males (Bryson, 1996).

Etiology of Pervasive Developmental Disorders

The etiology of pervasive developmental disorders is a broadly researched area. It is also widely disputed, and etiological data are best described as inconclusive.

Many of the theories concerning the causes of developmental disorders can be categorized as either nature or nurture. Nature theories stress biological dysfunction; in contrast, the nurture approach views the environment as the vital developmental factor. Until the late 1960s, theoretical constructs of childhood psychoses and autism focused on psychosocial (nurture) origins. Compelling recent research increasingly leans toward biological interpretations.

The best approach may be multifactorial, viewing these disorders not as a single entity but rather as the final common pathway of multiple etiologies: that is, attributing developmental disorders to a combination of biological and environmental factors. Infantile autism, for example, is probably a final expression of multiple determinants and may be the result of metabolic, infectious, developmental, environmental, and genetic insults.

Childhood Schizophrenia

If a multifactorial etiology is indeed the best approach to the etiology of childhood schizophrenia, then it is hardly surprising that its causes are the subject of considerable debate. Children who are schizophrenic display such a wide variety of symptom patterns and respond to so many different treatment modes that no one etiology seems sufficient to account for the disorder (Cummings and Finger, 1980).

Early investigations pinpointed environmental factors—maternal overprotection, maternal rejection, stimulus deprivation during infancy, inconsistent parenting, and severe and repeated emotional trauma (Cummings and Finger, 1980). However, many children exposed to these factors do not develop schizophrenia, and it is moot whether family forces alone are enough to produce such a devastating condition.

While the significance of environmental factors has not been completely discounted, the weight of accumulating evidence points toward biology as the primary factor in childhood schizophrenia. One consistent finding in support of biological factors is the high frequency of prenatal and perinatal complications among infants later diagnosed as schizophrenic (White, 1974). Pregnancy and birth complications include toxemias, vaginal bleeding, and maternal illness during pregnancy (Gittelman and Birch, 1967).

Investigators have also found a higher incidence of neurological symptoms in children who are schizophrenic, which leads to the suspicion that the condition may be a manifestation of subtle neurological damage, similar in origin to such disorders as minimal brain dysfunction (White, 1974). Moreover, neurological dysfunction is highly correlated with birth and pregnancy complications, further evidence that biological factors are responsible, at least to some degree, for childhood schizophrenia.

There is also convincing evidence for a hereditary predisposition (Plomin, 1989). Studies of monozygotic twins (e.g. Gottesman and Shields, 1976) have found that if one twin is affected, the other, regardless of environmental variables, is more prone to the condition. Because fraternal twins do not correlate nearly as highly, a genetic determinant is indicated. But along with a genetic component in schizophrenia, the evidence also indicates a strong environmental effect. What appears to be transmitted is not the disorder itself but a predisposition to acquire the disorder.

Infantile Autism

In 1906, Eugen Blueler, a Swiss psychiatrist, used the term *autistic* to describe the withdrawn behaviours he observed among adult schizophrenics. As a discrete syndrome, autism was first identified by Leo Kanner in 1943. Kanner described a number of symptoms that he found among a group of eleven children. In particular, he stressed the subjects' profound withdrawal from human contact and their obsessive desire for sameness in their environment. Kanner also identified similarities in the families of the eleven children. He found the parents to be highly intelligent and unusually high achievers, but also emotionally cold, aloof, and reserved in their interaction with their children.

Kanner himself did not reject biological factors as contributive causes of infantile autism. However, the researchers who followed him chose to focus almost exclusively on psychogenic properties. They speculated that lack of adequate parenting was the primary factor in the onset of autism. Infants with autism were seen as withdrawing into isolation to escape a hostile world, deeply lacking in warmth, love, and nurturance.

Bruno Bettelheim, who established the Sonja Shankman Orthogenic School for severely emotionally disturbed children in 1944, adopted this line of thought. He interpreted autistic behaviour as a defence against a world perceived as hostile and rejecting. Bettelheim argued that children become autistic when their parents reject them or fail to respond to their attempts to influence their environment. Because children feel unable to exert any control over the external world, they withdraw into a private fantasy world and try to impose some order and consistency through an obsessive insistence on sameness.

Bettelheim used the term "refrigerator mother" to characterize the mothers of autistic children (Csapo, 1981b). An even more devastating term, "the schizophregenic mother" laid direct responsibility for the child's condition on the mother's failure to provide love and nurturance. All the same, Bettelheim did not deny the possibility that genetic or organic causes might also contribute to infantile autism. In fact, although researchers tended to agree that parents created a climate that encouraged autism, few investigators attributed the condition exclusively to parental behaviour.

During the 1970s, environmental theories were largely abandoned as emerging evidence indicated that children from emotionally deprived settings were not at higher risk for autism and that mothers of children with autism also had non-disabled offspring. With little to support environmental theories, autism emerged as an ideal candidate for biological study.

Researchers turned their attention to investigating a range of biochemical, sensorimotor, neurological, and cognitive defects. Today the evidence for biological causes is accumulating. A multifactorial neurobiological etiology has been posited (Goodman, 1987); however, this etiological diversity tends to cloud the issue simply because so many causes have been suggested.

Neurobiological investigations indicate that factors critical to the normal development of the central nervous system seem to have gone awry in autism. Among children who are autistic, 83 percent have been found to have brain lesions or pathological enlargement of the left temporal horn (Hauser, De Long, and Rosman, 1975). Some investigators (e.g. Gillberg, Rosenhall, and Johansson, 1983) have attemped to account for autism on the basis of dysfunction in the vestibular area of the brain, the area thought to modulate the interaction of sensory and motor functions.

As in the case of childhood schizophrenia, there is solid evidence to connect obstetrical problems and subsequent autism in children. On average, children with autism experience more pre- and perinatal complications than their siblings (Links, Stockwell, Abichandani, and Simeon, 1980). In one study (Kolvin, Ounsted, and Roth, 1971), 54 percent of children with infantile autism had demonstrable neonatal and perinatal abnormalities when given neurological examinations.

It may be that both maternal and paternal age is a factor (Tsai and Stewart, 1983). In a small-sample study, Gillberg (1980) found the risk of having a child with autism to be nine times greater for mothers 35 or older than for mothers under 30. Although Gillberg stresses that his small sample size makes generalizations difficult, the findings bolster earlier research on maternal age in the United States (Treffert, 1970), in Finland (Allanan, Arajar, and Vitamaki, 1964), and in Canada (Finnegan and Quarrington, 1979).

The importance of hereditary factors in the etiology of autism is well established (Folstein and Rutter, 1988). A number of researchers (e.g. Links et al., 1980) suggest a genetic factor; others point to the possibility of a genetic predisposition (see Gerdtz and Bergman, 1990). Some support is lent to genetic factors because autism is often accompanied by minor physical anomalies, such as fine hair, large head circumference, and malformed ears (Links et al., 1980).

Twin studies and the increasing number of reports on multiple incidence in siblings and second-degree relatives give further credence to the genetic hypothesis. The prevalence of infantile autism is far higher in siblings and second-degree relatives of children with the disorder than in the general population (Folstein and Rutter, 1988; Ritvo, Ritvo, and Brothers, 1982).

In family studies (e.g. Folstein and Rutter, 1988), only about two percent of the siblings of children who are autistic display the condition, but this is 50 times greater than the expectation for the general population. The incidence of autism in the identical twin of a child who is autistic is around 50 percent (Folstein and Rutter, 1988). In one study (Steffenburg,

Gillberg, Hellgren, Andersson, Gillberg, Jakonsson, and Bohman, 1989), nine of ten identical twin pairs were autistic, as were all three children in a set of identical triplets.

Infantile autism has also been associated with various X-linked chromosomal abnormalities, and in particular with the genetic subtype fragile X, which has the highest incidence of autism of any documented syndrome or chromosomal abnormality. Of the entire population diagnosed with infantile autism, it is estimated that 10 to 14 percent have fragile X syndrome (Brown, Jenkins, Cohen, et al., 1986). In studies of the fragile X population, autism has been reported in from 16 to 69 percent of fragile X males (Hagerman, Jackson, Levitas, Rimland, and Braden, 1986; Levitas, McBogg, and Hagerman, 1983). This makes fragile X syndrome the most commonly known organic cause of autism (Hagerman, 1988).

Other investigators are attempting to correlate the autistic syndrome with neurochemical measures. Measurement of blood serotonin levels has been a source of both optimism and frustration. Elevated platelet serotonin is the most consistently replicated biological abnormality found in subjects, occurring in roughly 30 percent of all cases (Piven, Tsai, Nehme, Coyle, Chase, and Folstein, 1991), but its origin and significance are unclear. In addition, autism is associated with PKU, an example of aberrant biochemistry (see Chapter 3 on PKU).

Identification and Assessment

Treatment programs for children with developmental disabilities relate to the accuracy and specificity with which the problems and deficits are initially identified. Without clear and precise information about the nature of disabilities and a child's current level of functioning, an effective treatment strategy cannot be developed. But even when the conditions can be readily diagnosed, their causes often remain a mystery, and the most efficient identification may not lead directly to the most effective programming.

In the diagnosis of childhood psychoses and infantile autism, we find interwoven currents of research and investigation. We also find that diagnosis has provoked unresolved controversy. Clinicians vary in their theoretical conceptions of the conditions and emphasize different aspects as essential for specific diagnostic labels. The presence of co-occurring conditions further muddies clear identification. Children with autism, for example, display a wide range of behaviours, many of them similar to those found in children with other disorders. Before they are correctly diagnosed, children who are autistic may be falsely labelled as blind or deaf. Mental retardation is often the initial diagnosis; however, this is not an either-or category, as a high percentage of children with autism are also retarded. As well, clinicians try to determine whether a child is classically autistic, mildly autistic, or shows autistic features (Eaves, 1988).

For students who are developmentally disabled, the actual assessment procedures are replete with difficulties. So much so that in the past children with developmental disabilities, especially those with infantile autism, were considered untestable through standardized intelligence tests. The complex and varied disabilities made such children exceptions to many of the rules by which psycho-educational tests are designed and administered and, as a result, standardized tests were seldom administered. When tests were given, incomplete results were often interpreted on the basis of the examiner's intuitive sense of a child's peak skills.

Testing of students who are psychotic and autistic is particularly difficult because

• children often show a deficient ability to establish relationships;

- regular systems of reinforcement may be inadequate for these children;

- most of these children suffer impaired communication skills;

- sensory abnormalities may result in unusual responses to sensory stimuli;

- children have attention differences;

- children may show abnormal motor behaviour;

- clinicians must take into account the frequent co-existence of developmental disabilities, mental retardation, and neurological deficits;

- children who are autistic especially have a need for sameness and often demonstrate an inability to switch tasks;

- children with autism demonstrate marked variability on test performance. They may do poorly on tasks requiring abstract thought, symbolism, and sequential logic, but perform well on tasks that demand manual and visual spatial skills.

There is now a growing recognition that broad and thorough assessment of children who are psychotic and autistic is both possible and essential to provide the basis for educational and behavioural programming. Evaluation must be multidisciplinary and incorporate a variety of procedures, tools, and adaptations. Procedures require flexibility in administration, appropriate means of communication, alternation of free and structured time, motivation and reinforcers, predictable routines, and tools that limit the use of language to tasks that measure language skills.

Functional Assessment

Many assessors adopt a functional approach to testing, which examines a child's performance within the context of naturalistic environments. Interviewing the parents and others who know the child is the functional assessment method most commonly used by practitioners (Horner and Carr, 1997).

Systematic observation is also important. Teachers would attempt to collect performance data; identify the factors that affect performance, particularly those under teacher control; present and examine the effect of repeated teaching trials; and closely assess the success of teaching (Suigai and Maheady, 1988). For example, in assessing language the teacher would first identify the child's specific communication needs and interests. This includes the settings (when and where communication interactions occur); the people in them (with whom the most appropriate interactions occur); the purposes for communication (the reasons for the child to communicate); and why a child communicates (the objects and activities that the child prefers). Such an assessment allows a teacher to pinpoint specific communication needs as well as the vocabulary that the teacher and parents should include in instructional activities.

Psycho-educational Assessment

Psychologists administer both formal and informal assessment measures to students who are developmentally disabled. Commonly used measures of mental ability include the Bayley Scales of Infant Development, the Hiskey Nebraska Test of Learning Aptitude, the McCarthy Scales, the Wechsler Preschool and Primary Scale of Intelligence, and the Wechsler Intelligence

Scale for Children-III. The Leiter International Performance Scale has been found useful for children who have poor verbal skills (Shah and Holmes, 1985).

Specialized instruments are often needed to explore particular diagnostic and treatment questions. Tests used to determine receptive and expressive language skills, for example, include language questionnaires that are completed by parents and clinicians.

Specially designed measures are also used to accommodate the variation typical of the profiles of children who are autistic. For example, The Behaviour Rating Scale for Autism and Atypical Children (Ruttenberg, Kalish, Wenar, and Wolf, 1977) observes children on eight scales that measure relationship to an adult, communication, drive for mastery, vocalization, expressive speech, sound and speech reception, social responsiveness, body movement, and psychobiological development. The Behaviour Observation Scale for Autism (Freeman, Ritvo, Guthrie, Schroth, and Ball, 1978) has 67 behaviours on a checklist. The Childhood Autism Scale (Schopler, Reichler, De Vellis, and Daly, 1980) has 15 separate subscales on a seven-point continuum, ranging from normal to severely abnormal. Similarly, The Autism Screening Instrument for Educational Planning (Krug, Arick, and Almond, 1979, 1980) has five components—sensory relating, body and object use, language, social skills, and self-help skills.

Developmental Consequences

Pervasive developmental disorders affect almost every domain of a child's development and seriously hinder all aspects of progress. Affected individuals exhibit a range of disordered behaviour and may appear to be severely retarded. While much research has been directed toward autism, there is far less on childhood schizophrenia. Many behaviours and devel-

Bizarre behaviour is characteristic of children with childhood psychoses and infantile autism.

opmental consequences are similar in the two conditions, although the prognosis for children who are schizophrenic is somewhat more optimistic.

Children who are psychotic and autistic show extreme variability in intellectual functioning; many, however, function at pre-academic levels. Especially in children with autism, language development is often so poor as to render verbal communication impossible; language is either non-existent or bizarre in nature. Deficits range from phonological to syntactic and pragmatic defects. Many children do not speak at all, nor do they appear to comprehend language. Others show echolalia, parroting, meaningless jargon, and the incessant repetition of questions and statements.

Typically, these children live in their own isolated worlds, barely relating to others in the environment. Social development is minimal; even at their most developed, social interactions are limited in their quality and scope. Children with autism respond to other humans with aloofness and indifference, often becoming upset when interaction is demanded. Some severely disabled children throw massive temper tantrums, during which they bite, kick, scratch, and strike out at others.

Children with autism or schizophrenia demonstrate maladaptive behaviours which fall largely within two classes. The first is aggressive behaviour, either self-directed (self-injurious behaviour) or directed toward others (Lovaas and Favell, 1987). Many children inflict serious injury upon themselves—they bang their heads against sharp corners, bite themselves, and gouge their own eyes. Some children hurt themselves so often they must be kept in restraints for their own safety. Aggressive behaviour can also sometimes cause serious physical harm to peers, parents, and teachers. Such aggressive behaviour may result in the child's being medicated and/or moved to a more restrictive environment (Lovaas and Favell, 1987).

The second class of maladaptive behaviour is **self-stimulation**, a persistent, stereotypic, repetitive mannerism. One of the defining characteristics of autism, it involves activities such as prolonged and repetitive body rocking, spinning, jumping, pacing, gazing at lights, twirling objects, excessive and repetitive vocalization, finger playing, flapping the hands, swishing saliva, patting the cheeks, and humming for hours on end. These behaviours do not possess the physical risks associated with aggressive behaviour, but they are socially stigmatizing and decrease a child's responsiveness to educational instruction (Lovaas, Newson, and Hickman, 1987).

Childhood Schizophrenia

Schizophrenia is a psychiatric illness characterized by serious loss of contact with reality and a marked deterioration in the ability to function. Children show delusions and hallucinations, emotional disturbance, apathy, and withdrawal.

Schizophrenia is extremely rare before the age of six, becomes more common in middle childhood, and is even more prevalent during adolescence. Because childhood schizophrenia typically does not take hold until early puberty, those affected escape early impairments of development in the realms of cognition, perception, and sensation. When the condition does take hold, however, affected children regress dramatically in their behaviour and demonstrate extreme withdrawal from the real world. Their close relationships are severely disrupted and they experience an overall deterioration in work, social relations, and self-care. They often lack or lose daily living skills, including such basic self-care as grooming, dressing, using the toilet, and feeding.

The behaviour of children with schizophrenia is extremely variable. According to Cantor (1989) the four characteristics most often found in children with schizophrenia are:

- Sleep disturbance—a common symptom by the third year of life.
- Variable rather than short attention span. A child who is schizophrenic may attend for long periods of time to activities that are repetitive or perseverative.
- Variable behaviour—can vary from hyperactive to lethargic.
- Disturbances in thought processes.

Physical and Motor Development

Children who are schizophrenic tend to lag in physical and motor development. Individuals show serious deficits in gross motor areas but milder problems in the fine motor areas. As children with schizophrenia regress, acquired toilet and grooming skills may disappear.

Cognitive Development

Youngsters who are schizophrenic show great variability in cognitive functioning. On the Weschler scales, most achieve higher scores on the Performance than the Verbal subscales (Cantor, 1988).

Language is intimately related to cognition and to social development, and therefore the properties of language usage vary considerably as a function of the general level of language and cognitive development. As children regress, their speech becomes limited and may reveal incoherent thinking.

Social and Emotional Development

Schizophrenia in childhood has its most devastating effects on a child's ability to monitor and test reality and on the ability to initiate and sustain interactions with others in the environment. Schizophrenia results in extreme withdrawal from the real world: affected children display a wide variety of disturbances in mood, thought, and behaviour. Children who are schizophrenic show a marked reduction in interests and human attachments. They appear to live in a fantasy world and show emotional apathy, indifference, and withdrawal. Yet apathy can quickly give way to uncontrollable excitement or an enraged temper tantrum.

Social relationships are invariably disturbed. The profile of Mark describes a youngster with schizophrenia demonstrating a marked increase in tantrum-throwing behaviour.

Infantile Autism

Autism is found in a heterogeneous group of individuals who show wide variability in the type, number, and severity of observed deficits in cognitive functioning, communication, social interaction, and overt behaviour (Soucy and Andrews, 1997). While children show a core group of symptoms, a further cluster of traits may not all be present in any given child. Children with autism demonstrate severe self-isolation, lack of appropriate use of language, stereotypical and inappropriate use of objects, a preoccupation with music, and

Profile

Mark

Mark had always been a difficult child. As a baby, he cried incessantly; as a toddler, he was so afraid of strangers he would not let his mother out of his sight. During his preschool years, he was a whining, clinging child. By the time he was 12, he had become totally withdrawn and seemed to survive in a fantasy world of his own making.

When Mark ventured out of his fantasy world, it was to kick, bite, scream, and throw tantrums. In Mark's special class in a large Toronto school, an incident occurred that illustrates his aberrant behaviour. Another child borrowed Mark's bottle of white-out fluid. Mark reacted by grabbing a nearby baseball bat, swinging it wildly, and threatening to kill the other child. When the teacher tried to restrain Mark by holding his arms, she was badly kicked, punched, and bitten. Following his tirade, Mark sat for the rest of the day in his cubby. With his thumb in his mouth, he slowly rocked back and forth. All efforts to draw him out failed.

Mark has been diagnosed as suffering from childhood schizophrenia. He is in therapy and a special class, but he continues to withdraw more and more. His outbursts are becoming more violent and prolonged, and he treats other children with calculated cruelty. His parents find him almost impossible to handle at home and are seriously considering institutionalization.

abnormal motility patterns such as toe walking, body rocking, and bizarre choreoathetotic posturings. The most common behavioural problems are tantrums and non-compliance (Olley, 1992). These and other behaviours that appear as the child develops are presented in Table 13-2.

Affected children never begin to establish normal human attachments. They are extremely alone from earliest infancy, and are unresponsive to other people. As infants, children who are autistic show far less mutual gaze and facial responsiveness than other children. These children may be indifferent to physical contact, or may even show aversion to it. Parents report that their children do not respond in normal ways to being held. Infants fail to make the usual anticipatory movements prior to being picked up and fail to make the usual body adjustment to adapt to the person carrying or holding (Rimland, 1964).

Between the fourteenth and eighteenth months, several disturbing symptoms begin to appear. These include prolonged rocking and head banging in the crib, apathy and disinterest in the surroundings, unusual fear of strangers, obsessive interest in certain toys or mechanical appliances, highly repetitive and ritualistic play, insistence on being left alone, demands that the physical environment remain unchanged, and very unusual language behaviour (Rimland, 1964).

In older children, autism reveals itself in fleeting eye contact, the failure to develop any relationships, and insistence on rituals and routines. Children fail to form attachments to other people. They seldom initiate contact and sometimes seem to look or walk through others. They appear distant, aloof, or in a shell, and are extremely alone. They have severely impaired communication skills and show an obsessive insistence on sameness.

Objects are preferred to people; children's only strong attachments are toward inanimate things. Children who are autistic, for example, are fascinated by things that spin. They

Table 13-2 Symptoms of infantile autism in the preschool child

Birth to eighteen months

- No mutual gazing
- Feeding problems, such as poor sucking
- Lack of smile response
- Apathy and unresponsiveness
- Rigidity and stiffness or limpness and hypotonia when held
- Constant crying or an unusual absence of crying
- Repetitive motor movements
- Obsessive interest in certain objects
- Great resistance to change

Eighteen months to two years

- Continued poor eye contact
- Withdrawal and isolation
- Difficulties in toilet-training
- Odd eating habits and food preferences
- Feeding problems, such as refusal to hold food in mouth, refusal to chew or swallow, or gagging
- Little or no development of speech
- Little or no receptive language skills
- Lack of interest in toys, but obsessive play with some items

After two years

- Continued withdrawal and isolation
- No development of co-operative play
- Continued problems with feeding, sleeping, and using the toilet
- Slow or precocious motor development
- Obsessive desire for sameness
- Development of repetitive habits, gestures, and mannerisms
- Tantrums at change or restriction of activities

can sit for hours with a toy car upside down, endlessly spinning the wheels. Unlike other children, they are virtually impossible to distract from this behaviour.

Physical and Motor Development

Children with autism tend to be healthier than other children with pervasive disorders (Schreibman and Charlop, 1989). Motorically, they may show grace and normal motor skill development; however, it is not unusual to find ten-year-olds who are not yet toilet-trained or capable of dressing themselves.

Cognitive Development

Although there is no common theoretical base, conceptions of autism share the assumption that it stems from some deficient cognitive structure. Poor cognitive development affects children's ability to learn, while behaviour problems interfere with attention and motivation.

Some degree of mental handicap is present in most individuals with infantile autism; 50 to 75 percent of individuals are mentally retarded (Bryson, Clark, and Smith, 1988; Goodman, 1987; Sigelman and Shaffer, 1991), and they often display an extremely low level of cognitive functioning. Co-occuring conditions that further deflate cognitive functioning are very common. In a British Columbia survey of 152 children with autism, Marg Csapo (1979) found 85 percent to have additional conditions which included mental retardation (51.1 percent), speech dysfunction and retardation (14 percent) and epilepsy and retardation (9.6 percent). Of children showing autistic symptoms before age six, 21 percent have been found to develop seizure disorders by age 18 (Deykin and MacMahon, 1979). For one in three children who are autistic, problems worsen with the onset of puberty.

Cognitive development appears to differ from that observed in typical retardation; in youngsters with autism, IQ scores become stable over time, predictive of later functioning, and fail to rise with age-related improvements in clinical symptoms (Rutter, 1983). Evidence suggests that females with autism tend to be more seriously affected, with lower intelligence scores and greater problems in cognition and language (Konstentareas, Hamatidis, and Busch, 1989).

Perceptual Development and Sensory Response

Children with pervasive developmental disorders, especially those diagnosed as autistic, may display abnormal responses to visual stimuli. They seem to suffer from constraints in attending to relevant cues and may exhibit a generalized over- or under-responsiveness to incoming stimuli. While fixating on an object or lights, they may flutter their hands, cross their eyes, glance to the side, or unfocus their eyes. They may try to smell new objects, or run their hands and tongues over rough and smooth surfaces. Sound may elicit indifference, distress, or intense fascination.

Faulty modulation of sensory input is an intrinsic feature of the pattern of autistic behaviour. To try to explain the disturbances of sensory input, a number of models have emerged. Some investigators believe that the child is overwhelmed by sensory input and unable to attend to pertinent environmental stimulation. Others see the child as showing overselectivity: he or she seems to select a part of a stimulus and maintain attention to that part. Once fixated on relatively few stimuli, the child becomes incapable of scanning the environment.

Language Development

Professionals have long been intrigued by children who are autistic and psychotic, especially their language patterns or, more often, lack of language. The central roles of deficits in language and cognitive factors in autism are well documented.

Research data indicate fairly conclusively that children with autism have incurred some damage to the brain which may particularly affect the language centres. If this is the case, children with autism have a neurologically-based language dysfunction that seriously interferes with their learning of expressive speech and abstract language.

It is the deviance in the quality and pattern of language usage, rather than language delay, that differentiates autism from other developmental disorders. Many children with autism seem to lack the awareness, intentionality, or competence to use language as a tool to convey messages to others. From infancy, children show little or no ability to analyze or make sense of sounds. As they mature, their language and communication skills remain impaired. Attempts to communicate are characterized by immaturity and abnormalities in grammatical constructions.

Many children fail to speak at all. Those who do speak show atypical language features—delayed echolalia, metaphorical language, pronoun reversals, and stereotypic utterances. Children with autism often use unusual words, with curious metaphors and odd expressions. They use neologisms, defined as non-words or words that are obviously peculiar (Le Coutuer, Rutter, Lord, Rios, Robertson, Holdgrafer, and McLennon, 1989).

There are frequent pragmatic oddities, with language used in ways that are socially or contextually inappropriate (Hobson, 1988). Children typically perseverate on topics and fail to recognize turn-taking rules. Pronoun usage is unusual. A child may say "You want ride," when he means "I want to ride."

Facial and gestural expression of emotions can also be abnormal. Children with autism are thought to have a visual motor imitation deficiency akin to dyspraxia, which interferes with the learning of normal body language and the understanding of non-verbal communication, so important during the pre-verbal stage of development (Cummings and Finger, 1980). Affected children fail to use gestures appropriately, and do not interpret such gestural clues as eye contact, body posture, tone of voice, and facial expression (Hobson, 1988).

If language is impaired, speech problems almost inevitably ensue. In their use of speech, children who are autistic are almost always delayed. Almost 50 percent of these children fail to develop speech (Cummings and Finger, 1980), especially those who are also mentally retarded. In the other 50 percent, speech is severely delayed and, if present, frequently consists of meaningless repetitive and stereotypical utterances.

When learning speech, the process is abnormal and different from that seen in, say, children who are mentally retarded. Acquisition of first words is often delayed and, after that, vocabulary often doesn't grow the way it does in other children. New words may appear but old ones are forgotten, resulting in a plateau (DeMyer, 1979). Some children with autism begin to speak and then lose all speech. Some then regain speech; others do not.

In children with speech, prosody is often peculiar (Rutter, 1985); for instance, everything may be said staccato or in a monotonous drone. In spontaneous speech usage, children with autism display a lack of expressive intonational features, such as stress and pitch, although echolalic children can repeat sentences and phrases with uncanny accuracy of intonation.

Echolalia is the most frequently cited language characteristic of individuals with autism who are verbal. It is estimated that 50 to 60 percent of persons with autism are verbal, and of this group, 75 percent are echolalic (Rydell and Mirenda, 1991). Echolalic children may repeat whole sentences in parrot-like fashion as if the sentence were unanalyzable into smaller components—as if they had learned the behaviour and stored it in memory ever since. Children who use echolalia seem able to attend to a linguistic string. They may even use a response to a consistent stimulus, but fail to relate it enough to the content to associate it with anything but a vague and general meaning.

Language problems weaken the capacity of children with autism for symbolic thought and abstract reasoning. In discussions of their behavioural deviations, for example, play disorders are consistently cited. Children with autism demonstrate significant delays in the development of all forms of play, especially symbolic play. Evidence indicates that their play is quite different from that of mentally retarded and other exceptional children. For children with autism, it is not delayed play, but play that differs in topography, pleasure, and complexity.

Even when intellectual level is allowed for, play is often obsessional, mechanical, and repetitive, with a marked absence of both co-operative play and innovative pretend play. Play as a vehicle for learning about objects and events and especially for engaging in make-believe does not appear to be intrinsically motivating (Lifter, Sulzer-Azaroff, Anderson, and Cowdery, 1993). Perhaps because of the language deficits that invariably characterize infantile autism, the play is striking in its lack of fantasy and its sterile, repetitive, ritualistic, and solitary nature.

These children do not seem to know how to use play forms. In a room full of toys, a child who is autistic is more likely to ignore the toys and engage in stereotypic self-stimulating body movements. If the child does play, toys are used in a deviant fashion. Unusual pre-occupations (such as memorizing timetables) are characteristically pursued single-mindedly to the detriment of other activities (Rutter, 1985).

Social and Emotional Development

Impairments in social relatedness are increasingly considered to constitute some of the core symptoms of autism. Children with autism and other developmental disorders exhibit severe social interaction deficits. They demonstrate severely impaired relationships with parents, family members, and others in the environment. They do not attempt to gratify their needs through meaningful personal relationships; rather, they behave toward people as if they were inanimate objects. Children who are autistic often resent parents and others who try to show affection. They demonstrate both aggressive and stereotypical behaviours that further interfere with social interactions.

Prognosis

The outlook for children with infantile autism seems bleak. For many, there is little likelihood of attaining normal functioning within the context of currently available treatment and educational techniques. Even after years of the most effective treatment, many children are likely to remain at the retarded level, requiring close supervision and care. Speech and language development is related to general prognosis; the outcome appears to depend on the child's intellectual functioning at diagnosis and communicative speech development prior to the age of six (Gillberg and Steffenberg, 1987). Unless children achieve some use of spontaneous language by age five or six, the outlook is likely to be poor even for those with a relatively high level of non-verbal skills.

Many children with autism require close supervision and care. About 50 percent are eventually placed in institutions and remain there into adulthood. Among the remaining 50 percent are some children who eventually achieve a degree of independence and a large number who show moderate levels of disability (Lotter, 1978). One child in six makes an adequate social adjustment to perform some kind of regular work in adulthood. Another one in six develops a modest degree of self-sufficiency.

Intervention with Pervasive Developmental Disorders

Children with pervasive developmental disorders present many challenges to those who attempt to help them develop more meaningful lives (Lovaas and Favell, 1987). At present, no specific treatment exists to help children who are psychotic or autistic reduce their anxiety and cope more effectively with reality. No one treatment method has proven notably effective with these children, and the prognosis remains poor.

Medical Intervention

A wide variety of medications have proven useful in the treatment of youngsters with schizophrenia. Of these, stimulants and tranquillizers are the most commonly administered. In contrast, drug therapy has shown inconclusive but unpromising results in the treatment of autism. There is little evidence that stimulants or tranquillizers significantly enhance the functioning of children who are autistic.

Therapy

Over the years, many different methods and approaches to therapy for children who are psychotic and autistic have been tried. These include psychotherapy, family therapy, speech therapy, residential treatment, psychiatric hospitalization, medication, megavitamin therapy, sensory stimulation, and sensory isolation. However, despite strong claims by individual researchers, no one method has been conclusively shown to substantially alleviate pervasive developmental disorders.

Increasing the depth and intensity of treatment may produce more encouraging results. Some recent research has indicated that if intensive treatment (40 hours or more of one-to-one treatment weekly) is begun before three-and-a-half years of age, about 50 percent of children with autism may recover completely. They become indistinguishable from other children by the time they are in the first or second grade (Lovaas, 1982).

Technical

For children who are not often interested in other people or comfortable with them, a computer may serve as a catalyst for social interaction. If children work in pairs, studies show that they spontaneously teach, help, and praise one another in computer environments, asking more questions of one another than of their teachers (Borgh and Dickson, 1986).

Educational Intervention

Although the precise causes of pervasive development disorders remain shrouded in confusion, various conceptual models have been used to treat them in different settings, ranging from special schools, to clinics, to regular classrooms.

Today, the majority of children live at home with their families. If the strain on the family becomes too great, they may be placed in foster homes, group homes, residential training centres, or institutions. Children are only enrolled in residential programs when they are seriously delayed in feeding, toilet use, or other self-help skills; when their families badly need relief; or when they must be placed under extensive observation for assessment purposes.

Inclusion

Historically, students presenting intensive educational challenges to our schools have been served outside the regular classroom and, in many cases, outside the community school (Thousand, Fox, Reid, Godek, Williams, and Fox, 1986). At the moment, a growing number of parents and educators are calling for the inclusion of all students within the mainstream of regular education, including those with severe disabilities (Stainback and Stainback, 1984).

Nevertheless, there is acute disagreement within the field as to whether students with intensive educational needs belong in general education classrooms. In fact, the major placement issue of the day is whether such students should be based in regular or special education classrooms or in home schools. Some argue for regular school placement; others that children who show extreme symptoms are probably not suitable for integration. Some researchers contend that children with severe and multiple disabilities may be at odds with a system that has few resources and little inclination to meet their needs. Link (1991), for example, argues that there is a population of students—those with severe and multiple disabilities—who, despite any currently popular instruction, will not be capable of functioning in the general classroom, will not be completely self-sufficient, and will not live independently within our society. Arguments from both sides are shown in the Matter of Debate box.

A Matter of Debate

The Inclusion of Students with Severe Disabilities

✓ Arguments for inclusion

Perceived advantages include removing the stigma associated with segregated placements, facilitating the modelling of appropriate social behaviour, and enhancing the peer status of children with disabilities.

Inclusion in regular classrooms increases the social and communicative interactions of students with severe disabilities.

In specialized, segregated classrooms, children have few opportunities to associate with non-disabled peers. Students have fewer opportunities to practise, refine, and expand their skill repertoires, thereby reducing the likelihood that they will develop friend-

ships (Hendrickson, Shookoohi-Yekta, Hamre-Nietupski, and Gable, 1996).

Social benefits accrue to students with severe disabilities in inclusive settings (Fryxell and Kennedy, 1995; Kennedy, Shukla, and Fryxell, 1997).

Anecdotal reports of successful inclusion of children with severe and profound disabilities are emerging consistently in the literature (e.g. Giangreco, Denis, Cloninger, Edelman, and Schattman, 1993; Janney, Snell, Beers, and Raynes, 1995; Kozleski and Jackson, 1993; Ruiter, 1997; Salisbury, Palambaro, and Hollowood, 1993).

Studies (e.g. Giangreco et al., 1993; Janney et al., 1995; Kozleski and Jackson, 1993; Salisbury et al., 1993) find increases in positive teacher attitudes following the experience of including children with severe disabilities.

ⓧ Arguments against inclusion

Schools and districts will likely have trouble finding enough teachers and specialists who are specifically trained to work with these students. They are low-incidence disabilities with sparse geographic dispersal. There is limited availability of trained personnel as well as budgetary constraints.

The needs of students with intensive educational needs extend beyond the normal developmental curriculum that a classroom teacher is responsible for delivering and adapting for individual learners.

Teachers who are asked to include students with severe or profound disabilities may feel that they have limited resources, are not properly trained, and may not believe that these students really belong in regular classrooms (see ATA, 1993; Dahl, 1986; Winzer, 1995).

In a survey of special educators (Izen and Brown, 1991), researchers found that many teachers did not feel adequately trained by university teacher training programs to work with children with severe disabilities.

The intense needs of children with severe disabilities challenge the boundaries of practitioner knowledge and organizational supports and, for some, their commitment to integration and inclusion.

The regular school may inhibit children's development by imposing educational models and social demands which do not meet their needs. In regular classrooms, they may not receive the special services they need to become self-sustaining adults.

Students for whom traditional task requirements are not relevant can still learn social skills and see that they are full class members, not inferior to others.

The academic competencies of general education are not within the purview of children with severe and profound disabilities.

Natural supports may mean that some important aspects of education are lost because of lack of specialization.

Deviant behaviours such as resistance to change, an inability to generalize from one situation to another, and stereotypical and aggressive behaviour seriously jeopardize a child's functioning in a normalized environment.

Training often emphasizes early developmental skills usually thought of as too routine or too basic to be part of a regular instructional program.

The curricula proposed for students with significant disabilities is are often vague, inconsistent, and show wide swings in emphasis (Fuchs and Fuchs, 1995).

These students may take an inordinate amount of time away from their peers without disabilities because of the traditionally required high learner/teacher ratios (Schaffner and Buswell, 1991).

Inclusive settings are potentially harmful. Not only may the physical environment of the public school present barriers, but there is also a lack of medical intervention.

A general model for inclusion is the Autism Mainstream Collaboration Model (Simpson and Myles, 1993), which is designed to support general educators. It stresses collaboration and shared responsibility among special and regular educators and support personnel. It includes additional planning time for teachers and paraprofessionals.

Although the tide is flowing very strongly toward inclusion, the norm within most North American schools is still for students who are intensively challenged to be educated in schools or classrooms other than those of their neighbours' children. In both Canada and the United States, the full integration of students with severe disabilities has not been realized in many school districts. Two major barriers are a lack of trained classroom teachers and physical barriers in the schools.

Educational Approaches

Regardless of setting, three major approaches tend to be applied in the education and training of children with developmental disorders. The psychodynamic and behavioural approaches are the most popular of these, but a psycho-educational approach is also widely employed.

Psychodynamic Approaches

Before the 1960s, almost all intervention with children who were psychotic or autistic was founded on psychodynamic principles; today, this approach is still widely used though not as popular. Psychodynamic treatment is usually conducted in a residential setting away from the parents and typically lasts several years. Children are given individual therapy within a therapeutic placement designed to promote and sustain emotional growth. Treatment may also be given through outpatient clinics or day treatment centres.

The psychodynamic approach tries to help children understand the inner forces that guide their behaviour. By responding to the child in ways that are consistent, positive, and accepting, the therapist builds the child's confidence and trust. At the same time, the therapist helps the child to understand the sources of conflicting ambivalent emotions. Art, play, pet, and music therapy may be part of the psychodynamic approach. (See Chapter 9.)

Behavioural Approaches

Autism and schizophrenia are extremely difficult to treat; children with these conditions pose a variety of complex management problems. Although very resistant to psychotherapy, many children do respond to behaviour modification techniques, and the recent research literature has been flooded with positive reports of the use of behaviour therapy and highly structured learning procedures with children categorized as psychotic or autistic. For children with autism, behavioural approaches have been used to teach children to focus attention, to imitate actions, to develop basic speech skills such as vocalizing and word imitation, to label objects and pictures, and to extinguish temper tantrums (Block, Gersten, and Kromblum 1980; Forehand and Atkeson, 1981; Howlin, 1981; Lovaas, Schreibman, and Koegel, 1974).

Behaviour therapists do not claim to cure autism and give no promise of normalization or intellectual improvement. Rather, they attempt to modify deficits and excesses in behaviour patterns. However, "the long-term effectiveness of behavioural therapy for autism remains much in question, at times sparking intense debate even among investigators using it" (Bower, 1989, p. 312).

Behaviourists claim that behaviour modification trains children who are autistic to lead a more useful existence. Critics respond that behavioural techniques program children to perform like robots, unable to generalize their training to other situations. These critics claim that the child's trained responses are much too closely linked to the original training situation. Light (1983) found that a child trained to answer "Fine, thank you," to one trainer's

"How are you?" does not necessarily respond the same way when the question is asked by another trainer. Despite these criticisms, the general evaluation of behaviour therapy has been cautiously optimistic. But even with behaviour modification, most children with autism still need supervision.

Curriculum

The major goals of any intervention with children with pervasive developmental disorders are to decrease the behavioural symptoms that interfere with the individual's functioning and to promote the development of skills in language, adaptive behaviour, and social interaction, self-care, and independent living.

The 1980s saw many new curriculum developments that built on longitudinal, age-appropriate skills taught in domestic, recreational, vocational, and social contexts, and in integrated educational programs (Udvani-Solner, Jorgessen, and Guchrane, 1992). But with their unresponsiveness and lack of communication skills, children with psychoses and infantile autism are very hard to train. Few receive academic training beyond basic levels.

At the outset, curriculum reflects all areas of development. Training may begin with the sensorimotor levels. (It clearly matches the curriculum we describe in Chapter 14 for children with multiple disabilities.) Many students need to be taught a wide range of basic daily living skills such as independent eating, dressing, and using the toilet. They must also learn how to relate effectively to others through training in social interaction and communication. Some students will need help to decrease inappropriate behaviours such as severe aggression or strong and persistent ritualistic and stereotyped behaviours (Lovaas and Favell, 1987).

Communication is a focus. In some children, echolalic speech is decreased by non-attention, and normal speech is gradually shaped by food rewards for imitation of the therapist's vocalizations (Lovaas and Smith, 1988). Some behavioural methods to stimulate communication focus on reinforcing the utterances and demanding closer and closer approximations to real words to obtain a reinforcer (Kaplan, 1996). But as we pointed out earlier, doubts have been raised about the effectiveness of speech training with all children with autism.

An alternative approach, relying on the simultaneous use of speech and sign language, has been attempted with some success (Konstantereas, Webster, and Oxman, 1979). One study (Konstantereas, 1984) found that sign and speech produced better results than speech alone, possibly because sign language relies primarily on visual and kinesthetic modalities and circumvents the auditory.

Another approach, facilitated communication, was introduced to North America in 1990. Since then, its use has become an area of intense controversy, with confirmations and rebuttals abounding. We outline the issues surrounding facilitated communication in the Research Notes.

Research Notes

Facilitated Communication

Perhaps because special education concerns itself with individuals who can often not advocate for themselves, and with parents who are often desperate for guidance, if not cures, the field has long been the arena for fads, untried methods, and questionable treatments for which it is not uncommon for developers to overstate the efficacy. The penchant to promise more than can be delivered has a long history and we often embrace untried treatments, "only to find out subsequently that they were ineffectual, and in some cases, actually fraudulent" (MacMillan, Gresham, and Forness, 1996, p. 145).

This is not to suggest that facilitated communication is fraudulent. What it does suggest is that there is enormous discord in the professional literature on the subject. Some research results are negative; most are ambiguous; only a few are clear.

Facilitated communication was developed by Rosemary Crossley, an Australian educator, originally for persons with cerebral palsy. It soon came to be used with those with developmental disabilities and mental retardation. The technique was pioneered in the United States by Douglas Biklen in 1990.

Facilitated communication is a technique for some children and adults with autism who cannot talk and who do not point independently and reliably (Molnar, 1993). In this method of augmentative communication, someone physically assists an individual who is disabled to communicate through typing. The assistant enables the person to speak by physically supporting his or her arm, wrist, or hand while the individual hunts and pecks for letters, words, or pictures on a keyboard (Molnar, 1993).

Facilitated communication has been widely disseminated and promoted as a breakthrough for autistic and other communication-impaired individuals. But the method has generated a storm of controversy around the central issue: Whose words are they? Those of the person with the disability or those of the facilitator?

Advocates herald facilitated communication as a kind of key that has unlocked the imposed silence of autism. However, detractors say that it is far too easy for the assisted person to be led by the facilitator, that the method virtually puts words into his or her mouth whether it be intentional or not (Molnar, 1993).

Testimonies of parents and facilitators and some observational work show effectiveness (Kaplan, 1996). One study (Salomon Weiss, Wagner, and Bauman, 1996) offered evidence of valid facilitated communication from a 13-year-old boy diagnosed with autism. Others (e.g. Simon, Toll, and Whitehair, 1994; Vasquez, 1994) demonstrate that individuals can produce their own messages.

However, in controlled studies it has often been difficult to confirm that successful independent communication was indeed happening (Molnar, 1993). Careful empirical studies (e.g. Mulick, Jacobson, and Kobe, 1993; Thompson, cited in Kauffman, 1993) indicate that the facilitator, not the disabled individual, is the communicator in all but a very small number of cases.

SUMMARY

1. Pervasive developmental disorders are exceedingly complex conditions. To many people, children who are psychotic and autistic are beyond comprehension. Their behaviour is bizarre, their emotions intense, and their isolation total. These children usually have difficulty developing language skills, learning to communicate, and learning to relate to others. They display unusual bodily movements, inordinate fears, and extreme resis-

tance to change. Many children function at pre-academic levels and fail to develop, or lose, basic self-care skills or language.

2. Although infantile autism is generally considered the most devastating of developmental disorders, childhood schizophrenia is also extremely incapacitating. Schizophrenia is variously characterized by qualitative changes in functioning such as association disturbances, delusions, hallucinations, attention deficits, and inappropriate social interaction. Autism is a pervasive developmental disorder stemming from biophysical impairment.

3. The behaviour of children with psychoses and autism has traditionally placed them in the category of the uneducable. Even with structured intervention procedures, the prognosis is poor. Many children continue to exhibit disordered behaviour as adults. Instead of becoming self-sufficient, they require institutionalization or continuous care.

4. Even after intense research efforts, the etiology of childhood psychoses and infantile autism remains vague, the symptoms severe and complex, the diagnosis difficult, the treatments unclear, and the prognosis uncertain at best. At the moment, the stress is on medical causality; serious biomedical research on autism is ongoing. While there is no irrefutable proof of causation, efforts have led to a much clearer understanding of the diagnosis of autism; today the condition is generally viewed not as a psychosis but as a developmental disability of neurological origin.

5. For children with autism, poverty of language is a major factor that interferes with adjustment. Some children fail to develop speech; others have great difficulty following the conventions of conversation and interpreting linguistic and non-linguistic contextual rules. Poor language development spills over to affect many other areas, such as play and imaginative skills. Instead of language, children with autism turn to less problematic, more predictable, inanimate objects. They may sit for hours spinning or twirling an object, such as a shiny ashtray.

6. Children who are psychotic or autistic pose a variety of complex management problems. Of all the interventions that have been attempted, most children have responded best to behaviour modification techniques. Nevertheless, these and other current educational treatments are unlikely to cure the disorders, although they alleviate the symptoms. Children can learn to make small gains and develop basic skills.

7. The educational prognosis for children with pervasive developmental disorders improves as they learn social skills. Children must first learn basic social behaviours, such as communication, and be trained to refrain from socially unacceptable actions.

8. Controversy still surrounds the placement of children who are psychotic or autistic in regular schools. Some contend that children with severe and multiple disabilities may be at odds with a system that has few resources and little inclination to meet their needs. Today, however, children are placed in a range of settings, with inclusion in general classrooms becoming much more common.

In the Classroom

Profile: David

"David is our third child. Although the pregnancy was uneventful, he was born nearly a month early after a prolonged and arduous labour. When we brought David home he was fussy and distractible, and he cried almost constantly. He had feeding problems with breast and bottle, and he could not be comforted by holding or rocking. Even with his feeding problems, David gained weight and developed into a beautiful child. However, his crying continued and worried the entire family. By the time David was a year old, we were sure he had some problem or disorder.

"Most of the time, David lay in his crib. He never seemed to notice when anyone walked into the room. He never smiled and never liked to be picked up and held. Except for crying, he made almost no sounds, especially not the babbling sounds his two older sisters had made.

"At first, we suspected David was deaf. For nearly a year, we went from doctor to doctor seeking help. One doctor said David might be hearing-impaired, and told us to come back in six months. Another suggested he was severely mentally retarded, and another said he was simply slow in developing.

"One evening, a friend who taught special children was visiting the house. He tried to play with David, but could garner no responses. We discussed our frustration and growing sense of hopelessness. The teacher suggested we get in touch with a local society that helped the parents of troubled children. At this time, the word *autism* had still never been mentioned.

"Within a month of being directed to the right facilities, David had been diagnosed as autistic. In a way, the diagnosis was a relief. Although we had hoped that David was only slow to mature, we knew in our hearts that something was truly amiss. Professionals may rail against labels, but we badly needed a starting point, a direction in which to find help.

"As soon as David was diagnosed, we contacted a local facility for autistic children. A therapist from the centre immediately began working with David in our home. When David was old enough, he attended a special preschool on a daily basis. At school age, David first went to a special school. When he was nine years old, David moved from the special school into a special class in his local school. We did not feel that he was ready at that time for full inclusion but kept that as a hope.

"At school, the team developed a number of integration strategies for David to give him more opportunities to interact with his peers. So far, his progress has been disappointing and we have seen few changes in David's responsiveness. The prognosis still is not very good.

"As a family, we now understand David's problems, although we sometimes find it very difficult to cope with them. He has developed only a few words of speech. His baby crying has given way to a high-pitched whine that goes on and on. David is extremely rigid in his attitudes. He has massive temper tantrums that frighten his sisters at home and embarrass us all in public. He is just beginning to be toilet-trained, and still has eating problems. He has great difficulty dressing himself, although he is better at taking his clothes off.

"Another worry is the continuing effect of David's behaviour on his older sisters. Teenagers have their own wants and needs. We cannot let David disrupt their lives too seriously. Nor can we impose too heavily on them for babysitting."

* * *

For children with pervasive disorders such as David's, education transcends its traditional boundaries. To provide David with many opportunities, he needs a curriculum consisting of:

- Social skills training. A primary goal is to help children get in touch and keep in touch with their environments. Training begins with establishing self-concept; children must learn who, what, and where they are in order to realize that they are separate from others. Once they are aware of themselves as separate beings, they are ready to establish basic relationships. Their prognosis improves, and they are ready to learn new tasks.

- Independent behaviour. Independent behaviour is behaviour performed without the assistance of others (Bailey, Harms, and Clifford, 1983). It includes self-help skills, those abilities needed for independent functioning in relation to such basic needs as food and warmth.

- Communication skills. Relatedness to others in the environment depends on some basic communication. For young children, language allows them to initiate contact and to act positively on the environment. For adolescents, there are two primary goals in communication—participation in age-appropriate social relationships outside the family and development of the ability to use language to pursue personal interests (Lord, 1988).

- Appropriate behaviours. Children with autism and psychoses show both aggressive and stereotypic behaviours. The most frequently observed inappropriate behaviours are non-compliance, physical aggression, self-stimulation, and self-injury. Other behaviours include destruction of materials, temper tantrums, and a host of actions ranging from teeth grinding to throwing toys.

In the special classroom, intervention for David will be a very structured behavioural program. When included in the regular classroom, the major aim is social interaction and opportunities to hear and respond to normal language. The IEP below focuses on goals for the regular classroom.

Extract from David's IEP

Name: David
School: John Brown
Grade: 4

PRESENT LEVELS OF FUNCTIONING

David has been diagnosed as autistic. No IQ levels have been estimated, but he is functioning at pre-academic levels. David has not developed any language or speech.

PLACEMENT

David is in a special class but there is to be increasing integration into the regular classroom for social purposes.

ANNUAL GOAL (REGULAR CLASSROOM)

To increase interactions with others in the environment and awareness of environmental stimulation.

LONG-RANGE GOALS

- David will develop gaze-to-gaze behaviour.
- David will respond to others in the environment.
- David will use simple speech when it is modelled for him.
- David will participate in art classes with his peers on a daily basis.

OBJECTIVES

- When assisted to the correct hallway, David will locate and enter the art room independently.
- When given a visual cue by the teacher, he will sit in his assigned place.

- At the beginning of the class, he will respond to communication by waving or saying "Hi" to a peer.
- When presented with a choice of paints and a gestural cue for each option, David will select the colours he wishes to use.
- At the end of the class before clean-up, he will tap the arm of a peer at the table and will point to his own artwork to show it to the peer.
- When prompted by other students, he will look at their art work.
- When cued, David will place the finished work in his own folder.
- David will return to his own classroom with a peer.

EFFECTS OF AUTISM/PSYCHOSES	TIPS FOR TEACHERS
THE CHILD IS INSISTENT ON SAMENESS AND ROUTINE	Provide a structured day.
THE CHILD HAS DIFFICULTIES WITH CONCEPTS, ABSTRACTIONS, GENERALIZATIONS	Use many concrete materials.
THE CHILD HAS DEFICIENT OR ABSENT LANGUAGE	Avoid long verbal instructions. Encourage art and computer activities. Use much music and rhythm.
THE CHILD IS DISTRACTIBLE	Provide an environment with little visual and auditory stimulation. Speak using whispers.
THE CHILD NEEDS HELP TO DEVELOP PEER INTERACTIONS	Circle of Friends. Modify teacher roles so that the student belongs to the classroom teacher but receives support. Treat the student the same as the group as much as possible. Modify classroom routines and physical environment to keep the student situated near peers in similar seating.

WEBLINKS

Center for the Study of Autism **http://www.autism.org/**

Schizophrenia: Youth's Greatest Disabler **http://www.mentalhealth.com/book/p40-sc02.html**

Autism Society Manitoba **http://www.enable.aroundmanitoba.com/orgs/asm/index.html**

Ontario Association of Children's Mental Health Centres **http://www.oacmhc.org/**

CHAPTER 14

Children with Multiple Disabilities

Historical Notes

History tells us very little about persons with multiple disabilities. In the middle of the eighteenth century, the Scots philosopher Dugald Stewart told of a deaf-blind lad named James Mitchell who responded to educational intervention. In Paris in the 1760s the Abbé de l'Épée experimented with a system of raised print blocks to use with individuals who were deaf-blind. In 1789 in Paris Victorine Morriseau was the first deaf-blind woman to receive education (Collins, 1995).

In 1837 Laura Bridgman was admitted to the Perkins Institution for the Blind in Boston, where Samuel Gridley Howe undertook her education. Laura had lost her sight, hearing, taste, and smell to scarlet fever at the age of two. Howe taught her the manual alphabet and eventually Laura read embossed books, did simple arithmetic, and mastered needlework and other kinds of handicrafts.

Howe's extensive reports of Laura Bridgman's education and development left an outstanding legacy to the entire field of special education, and to teachers of the deaf-blind in particular (Hallahan and Kauffman,

1991). His son-in-law, Michael Aganos, used Howe's directives when Helen Keller became a pupil at the Perkins Institution (Winzer, 1993).

Between 1900 and 1950, only a few programs opened. Most children with multiple disabilities were excluded from the residential schools because they had handicaps that cut across several categories of impairment. They therefore tended to fall between the cracks. Public schools did not take the responsibility for providing education on the assumption that these people were uneducable, that they could not learn.

The world-wide rubella epidemic between 1962 and 1964 left thousands upon thousands of children multiply disabled. With the impetus of huge numbers, many programs were established. Since the 1970s, there has been an explosion of research and demonstration projects which have shown the learning potential of children with multiple disabilities. Researchers continue to compile dramatic evidence that shows that even the most severely disabled youngsters can become productive members of society.

Children with multiple disabilities show evidence of independent and interdependent deficits in two or more areas of functioning. But this definition is so broad and people with multiple disabilities form such an extremely heterogeneous population that we cannot paint a general portrait of students with severe and multiple disabilities.

Innumerable combinations of impairments are possible, although some appear more often than others, and some are more difficult to cope with. Individuals may suffer multisensory impairments such as deaf-blindness, or they may have conditions that combine sensory disorders with physical, neurological, or mental disabilities. Impairments of vision or hearing occur much more frequently among children with multiple disabilities than among other children. It has been estimated that one in five can be expected to have impaired hearing and two in five impaired vision (Orelove and Sobsey, 1987).

Children's development is integrated and organized across the various developmental domains—cognitive, language, physical, social, and emotional. Therefore, with multiple disabilities, we cannot look at the impact of a single disability in isolation, but must instead realize that the interaction of disabilities results in the appearance of unique developmental and behavioural patterns. The conditions are not additive but cumulative and present a completely unique condition that may affect all the mind/body systems in different ways and to different degrees. For example, a deaf child with severe mental retardation may have independent deficits in cognitive functioning, producing language, understanding language, and in social interaction, as well as deficits resulting from a combination of these individual impairments.

Students with multiple disabilities present a range of special educational and psychosocial needs. To an even greater degree than for children with single disabilities, each child must be considered individually. Because of their complex conditions, children who are multiply disabled require the services of many disciplines, most importantly education, psychology, physiotherapy, occupational therapy, speech pathology, audiology, and medicine. As a result, a transdisciplinary approach to their treatment and education is essential.

Many of the children that we have already encountered in this text could be considered multiply disabled. The child with Down syndrome who has a speech disability, the youngster who is deaf and also emotionally disturbed, the child who is cerebral palsied with language disorders, the child who is profoundly retarded, and the child with autism, for example, have conditions that, taken together, severely disrupt their learning. And, while multiple disabilities are usually conceptualized as severe disabilities, it should be remembered that children can suffer from combinations of minor disabilities that can be devastating to their learning and behaviour. In this chapter, however, we focus on children with severe and debilitating multiple impairments. Particular attention is paid to children who combine visual and hearing impairments.

Definitions of Multiple Disabilities

In the area of multiple disabilities, the differences among students are greater than the similarities. This makes the formulation of precise definitions a complex and virtually impossible task. The heterogeneous nature of the population and the combinations of disabilities mean that we would not have one but dozens of definitions.

To overcome the problem, broad and encompassing generic definitions that attempt to include the entire range of possible combinations of conditions have evolved. One generic

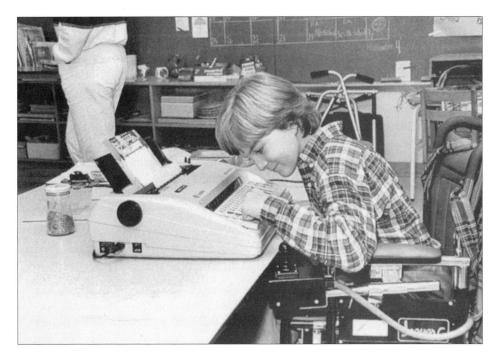

Students with multiple disabilities usually have a range of special educational and psychosocial needs.

category refers to multiple disabilities as those in which children suffer two or more impairments that hinder their attainment of their full potential. The category includes those children who,

> because of the intensity of their physical, mental or emotional problems, or a combination of such problems, need educational, social, psychological, and medical services which will make it possible for them to maximize their full potential for meaningful participation in society and for self-fulfillment (Thompson, 1976, p. 41).

This definition includes children who are severely and profoundly retarded; deaf-blind; mentally retarded and deaf-blind; physically disabled; and severely emotionally disturbed (Van Osdol and Shane, 1982). It focuses on the combinations of problems possibly present as well as the range of interventions and allied disciplines necessary if children are to achieve their potential.

A second generic definition refers to students who are severely handicapped. These are "school-aged students who function intellectually within the lowest one percent of the particular age-groups" (Brown, Nisbet, Ford, Sweet, Shirga, York, and Loomis, 1983, p. 77). These students within the generic *severely handicapped* may also be labelled as physically handicapped; multiply handicapped; dual sensory impaired; autistic or psychotic; and moderately, severely, or profoundly mentally retarded.

There have been many criticisms of generic definitions, specifically because they tend to use very broad parameters which may obscure the effects of particular disabilities, making it harder to clinically interpret the needs of an individual child. Moreover, generic definitions do not lead to precise programming. For example, children with visual or hearing impairments who are enrolled in generic programs do not have access to specialist services, such as orientation and mobility training, low vision services, or communication training.

Critics of generic definitions argue that definitions should be worded in terms of children's behaviours and needs. When individuals who are multiply disabled are defined by their service needs, they are people "who require ongoing support in several major life areas in order to participate in the mainstream of community life and who are expected to require such support throughout life" (Bellamy, 1985, p. 6).

Some educators avoid generic definitions, preferring more specific definitions for particular broad groupings of individuals who are multiply disabled. *Multisensory impaired* is a term used to describe children with sight and hearing handicaps. It includes children who may also be developmentally delayed or have neurological impairments. *Multiple dependent handicapped* refers to children who are severely mentally handicapped and who also have sensory and/or other physical handicaps (see Orelove and Sobsky, 1987). Children described as multiple dependent handicapped display a wide variety of visual, auditory, and physical/neurological handicaps.

Deaf-blind children are those whose disabilities are a complex of auditory, visual, communication, and language factors, often accompanied by other conditions that interfere with their learning. A individual who is deaf-blind is described as having

> both auditory and visual impairments, the combination of which causes severe communication and other developmental and educational problems that cannot be properly accommodated in special education programs either for the hearing handicapped child or for the visually handicapped child (Kirk and Gallagher, 1979, p. 437).

This definition stresses that because children who are deaf-blind suffer impairments in both vision and hearing, they will not have their needs met if they are placed in special education programs for students who are only deaf or only visually impaired. Programs for students who are deaf rely heavily on the use of vision, while instruction for students with visual impairment depends on auditory instruction; but children who are deaf-blind suffer deficits in both these modalities. For many of these children, the sensory impairments co-exist with other challenging cognitive, physical, health, and behavioural characteristics.

Classification of Multiple Disabilities

The complexity and variety of multiple disabilities has spawned a number of definitions and descriptions; it also means that classification systems and service delivery are beset with confusion. Generally, services have been administered on the basis of labels and discrete categories, and this tendency has resulted in the creation of a number of overlapping classification systems.

The most common way to classify multiple disabilities is in primary and secondary terms. The major condition that causes a child to differ in learning or behaviour is referred to as the primary disability; other conditions that arise or are present are known as secondary disabilities. A child who is both visually impaired and mentally retarded may be judged to suffer visual disabilities as the primary disabling condition, with mental retardation being the secondary disability.

Approaches that focus on presumed primary and secondary disabilities have their own built-in set of problems. For one thing, many children have more than one set of pertinent characteristics, and the primary disability is often impossible to identify. Children who are both blind and retarded, for example, may be visually inattentive because they do not see or because they are intellectually unaware of the visual environment.

Second, and perhaps more importantly, viewing multiple disabilities as primary and secondary overlooks the cumulative nature of the conditions. Children cannot be appropriately classified under the category of a single impairment because the combination of conditions creates an entirely new disability that requires access to special services for all the child's impairments, whether sensory, physical, mental, or behavioural. Children who suffer from visual impairments as well as mental disabilities, for example, cannot be appropriately accommodated in programs for mentally disabled children who don't have sight problems.

Sometimes children are classified and counted according to the agency that serves them. This also leads to problems, as the same child may be identified within the service delivery system of a number of agencies. Sometimes, too, children are simply classified by the type of educational program they attend.

Prevalence of Multiple Disabilities

Estimating the true incidence and prevalence of almost any disability is an onerous if not impossible task. In the case of multiple disabilities, a number of factors combine to hamper prevalence estimates. Difficulties arise for several reasons:

- Prevalence figures tend to be influenced by changes in technology, demographic trends, and social factors (Hayden and Beck, 1981).

- Interpretations of the definition of certain populations have changed dramatically. For example, the number of persons with deaf-blindness has not increased substantially since 1974. Today, however, individuals categorized as deaf-blind can represent those with moderate to profound auditory and visual impairments with or without other educationally disabling conditions, who need services to increase independence; those with central processing problems that result in cortical blindness or central auditory dysfunctions; or those with progressive sensory impairments such as Usher's syndrome (Michael and Paul, 1991)

- As we mentioned earlier, children with combined disabilities may be registered for services with a variety of agencies so that the same child might be identified within the service delivery systems of any of these agencies.

- Probably the greatest difficulty in obtaining prevalence figures arises as children are counted in terms of their primary handicap. In school districts where special programs for children who are multiply disabled are unavailable, children may be entered into classes designed for mentally retarded, hearing impaired, or visually impaired children, and are then defined and counted by what is presumed to be the primary disability.

Etiology of Multiple Disabilities

The major causes of childhood disabilities that we have outlined throughout this text are also causes of multiple disabilities in children. In fact, with the exception of rubella, the etiology of multiple disabilities almost parallels that of physical impairments. This is especially true for central nervous system damage that results in severe motor impairment.

Rubella is the culprit in many childhood conditions. At its most devastating, rubella causes deaf-blindness and severe multiple disabilities. Studies of deaf-blind rubella children reveal great differences between this group and other children with deaf-blindness, primarily due to the gross effects of the rubella virus on many body parts. Most children who have combined sight and hearing problems due to rubella are neither totally blind nor profoundly deaf; however, the combination of sensory impairments creates severe learning difficulties (Van Dijk, 1982). The following profile tells of James, a child affected by rubella.

Chromosomal and genetic disorders account for only a tiny number of multiple disabilities. When they do appear, children often have complex multiple disorders affecting several different body systems. On the other hand, injuries to the central nervous system account for significant numbers of multiple disabilities. Neurological impairments result from damage or dysfunction of the brain and/or the spinal cord incurred before, during,

Profile

James

Mrs. J. did not know that she had contracted the rubella virus early in her third pregnancy. She felt healthy throughout and was not overly concerned when her infant arrived nearly a month before term. Labour was normal, lasting about 14 hours. The infant cried lustily, and Mrs. J. readily accepted the explanation that he was in neonatal intensive care only because he was of slightly low birth-weight.

Information about the true nature of the child's condition came quickly. Within 24 hours, the physician explained to both parents that the child, now named James, was suffering serious defects as a result of the rubella virus. Examination had shown a defective heart and serious visual problems. The physician explained that other anomalies could emerge, possibly deafness and mental retardation, and urged the parents to think about institutional placement for James if he survived the first month.

The parents' shock was soon displaced by grief and the necessity for making decisions about care. Mr. J. urged institutionalization. Their oldest son had already been identified as learning disabled, and Mr. J. perceived a seriously handicapped infant as potentially very disruptive to the family climate. Mrs. J., on the other hand, was determined not to accept the rather hopeless prognosis of the physician. She wanted to raise the child at home, to treat him, as far as possible, like the other children, and to seek support to assist in his development.

James spent nearly three months in the neonatal unit. Once at home, he proved a fairly easy baby to handle. In fact, he was so docile and passive that this concerned his mother and spurred her to seek outside help. By the time James was nine months old, a visiting teacher was coming once a week. She worked with James on various developmental tasks, especially in the motor area. Because language was a concern, she showed Mrs. J. how to stimulate vocalizations, and gave her some tips on receptive language development.

By the time James was 16 months old, a severe to profound hearing loss was confirmed. His vision was poor, with a restricted visual field. However, with some complaint, he accepted both a hearing aid and glasses. He also reached some major developmental milestones—he walked and began to eat solid foods.

Throughout James's preschool years, Mrs. J. behaved toward him and disciplined him just as she did the older children. She accepted his multiple disabilities but held appropriate expectations for his development. He became an integral part of the family circle. Sibling resentment was not directed at any special treatment James received; it surfaced only when he got into the same type of mischief that any preschooler does. For both siblings, their proudest day was when James marched off with them to his first day at the local public school.

or after birth. Other nervous system disorders resulting in multiple disabilities stem from trauma, accident, or child abuse. Hydrocephalus is frequently associated; if treatment is unsuccessful or only partly successful, the child may have damage to the optic nerve as well as motor impairments (see Chapter 12).

New medical technology, intensive care nurseries, and lifesaving techniques are saving many infants who would have perished just a few years ago. Children who are premature, especially those with birth-weights less than 1 500 grams, are particularly vulnerable to insults of the central nervous system (Fenichel, 1980).

Meningitis contracted immediately after birth is a major cause of multiple disabilities. Fifty percent of infants who survive the disease suffer significant neurological impairments that include cerebral palsy, hydrocephalus, convulsive disorders, and hearing and visual handicaps (Fenichel, 1980).

Syndromes

Usher's syndrome is a condition of familial nerve deafness associated with pigment degeneration of the retina (Harley and Lawrence, 1977). The incidence of Usher's syndrome in the general population is no greater than one in 15 000 to 30 000 births. Nevertheless, Usher's syndrome is the most common etiology of deaf-blindness, accounting for more than half of the deaf-blindness found in adults. It also accounts for three to six percent of all the profound prelingually deaf population, almost always born to hearing parents (Miller, 1985; Miner, 1995).

Usher's syndrome is transmitted through an autosomal recessive trait. The child is born deaf and gradually loses sight due to retinitis pigmentosa, which is most often diagnosed in the early teen years (Miner, 1995). As well as hearing loss and retinitis pigmentosa, a significant number of persons with Usher's syndrome show other symptoms, such as abnormal vestibular functioning, seizures, mental retardation, abnormal EEGs, schizophrenia, and autism (Davenport, O'Nuallian, Omenn, and Wilkus, 1978).

Not all individuals who are genetically deaf-blind suffer from Usher's syndrome. The single conditions may be caused by different genes or infections. There are other syndromes, such as Refsum's and Laurence-Moon, that involve both deafness and visual impairment; however, additional pathology such as obesity, retardation, diabetes, or scaly skin clearly distinguishes these from Usher's.

Identification and Assessment

Whether diagnosis is medical or psycho-educational, the assessment of children with multiple disabilities taxes the ingenuity of clinicians. Because data generation is so difficult, a diverse range of measures are used. All attempt to assess the child's disabilities, as well as the impact of the combination of disabilities, the possible etiology, the prognosis, and the strengths a child possesses.

Medical Assessment

A medical examination, a routine part of the diagnostic process, is undertaken with the child who is multiply disabled as early as possible. Several diagnostic procedures are used to determine the exact nature and sometimes the underlying causes of multiple disabilities. These include a careful medical history; psychological and psychiatric assessment; laboratory tests to detect metabolic disorders; cytogenetic studies to identify possible causes; clinical neurophysiological investigation through electroencephalogram (EEG) tests of auditory and visual potential and electromyograms to test nerve conduction; and neuroradiology, which involves skull x-rays, echoencephalography, radio-isotope brain scans, and PET and CAT scans that can pinpoint the presence of brain lesions (Rogow, 1987a).

Assessment of Hearing

It is often difficult to distinguish whether children fail to respond to an auditory stimulus because they do not hear it or because they are simply inattentive. This is particularly true of children with multiple disabilities who require a wide range of sophisticated techniques for the assessment of auditory status. For these children, audiological assessment is divided into two major methods—electrophysiological and behavioural (see also Chapter 9).

Electrophysiological procedures often provide the most reliable information about a child's ability to receive sound stimuli, because the techniques do not rely on a child's behaviour or responses. But although these tests help to detect whether a child in fact hears sound, they do not provide information about the child's ability to interpret the auditory stimuli. As we explained in Chapter 9, electrophysiological measures include impedance audiometry (the drum and the middle ear) and electroencephalography-evoked response audiometry. The latter refers to the measurement of various evoked electrical potentials that are responses to auditory stimuli.

Behavioural testing includes observations and play audiometry. In behaviour observation, a sound is presented to a child in a sound-proofed room. The tester observes any behavioural responses, such as a blink or head turning. Play audiometry involves teaching the child to respond to a sound when it is presented by performing some action, such as putting beads in a bowl. Another method used with very young and multiply disabled children is tangible reinforcer operant conditioning audiometry, which uses tactile rather than visual cues.

Assessment of Vision

It is often difficult to determine whether a child with multiple disabilities has usable vision. This is particularly true of children with neurological impairments who seem unable to establish normal visual contacts. A child who does not respond to conventional testing may be a candidate for several physiological tests that are administered by qualified clinical or medical personnel. Diagnosticians use electrophysiological procedures, functional tests, and behavioural measures.

Electrodiagnostic procedures assess the electrical activity of the optic pathway and occipital cortex of the brain. The presence of electrical activity indicates that an active pathway exists. Tests include Visually Evoked Response (VER), also known as the Electroretinogram (ERG). This sophisticated technique measures the chain of electrical nerve responses created by a flashing light and thus allows the examiner to assess the functional state of the retina. The ERG has been used extensively to determine the visual acuity of infants and children with neurological handicaps (Harley, 1983; Mohn and Van Hall-Van Duin, 1983).

The electro-oculogram, which measures the ability of visual nerve cells to respond to light, can be performed under general anesthetic on infants and children who are multiply disabled.

Visual Evoked Potential (VEP) is a technique for measuring visual acuity that uses a bioelectrical signal generated in the visual cortex of the brain in response to visual stimulation. These generated bioelectrical signals are measured by recording electrodes placed over the occipital regions of the cortex (Hall, Orel-Bixler, and Haegerstrom-Portnoy, 1991). VEP can be used with anyone who can maintain fixation on a TV monitor on which black and white stripes of different widths are presented. Because the VEP technique permits the examiner to record the reception of light images by the visual cortex, it is a particularly valuable test for infants and children who are multiply disabled (Ikeda, 1976). Other methods for assessing vision are discussed in Chapter 10.

Behavioural measures include field tests that use gross objects or lights. In one test, the child is held over the parent's shoulder facing the examiner while a toy or other familiar object is moved into the temporal field. The child is tested for each eye separately and for both eyes together and the child's reaction is observed (Faye, 1976).

The Bailey-Hall Cereal Test for visual acuity (Bailey and Hall, 1983) is a behavioural technique that uses picture cards including one of cereal; if the child selects the correct picture, he or she is rewarded with praise and a piece of cereal (Bailey and Hall, 1983). For estimating the visual acuity of children with very limited cognitive abilities, diagnosticians may use the UC-Berkeley Preferential Looking Test (Bailey and Hall, 1984). This test consists of six grey rectangular cards, each of which has one grey square and a second square with black and white stripes. The brightness of the grey background, the grey square, and the striped square are about equal. The procedure is based on the premise that if children see the striped square they will prefer to look at it rather than the less interesting grey square or grey background. As each square is presented, the examiner determines where the child prefers to look by observing his or her eye movements.

Functional tests assess the visual behaviour of an individual rather than just the physiological condition of the eyes. Assessed are the ability to track objects, use visual fields, develop eye–hand co-ordination, and perform other functions that reflect visual development. The tests are portable and can be administered by trained personnel, such as teachers.

Psycho-educational Assessment

With their obvious disabilities, most students with severe and multiple problems are not screened; assessment begins with diagnostic testing. Assessment is never a one-time affair; administration is on a regular basis, usually once or twice a year.

The psycho-educational assessment of children who are multiply disabled has a number of separate but equally important goals which include measurement of the overall level of intellectual function and exploration of the individual child's impairments and abilities. Assessment data are used to decide on the most appropriate educational placement and to formulate an individual educational plan. Specifically, the assessment of students with multiple disabilities attempts to answer some critical questions:

- Is the child attentive to auditory language and symbolic code systems?
- Does the child respond to communication? This includes receptive language comprehension to determine if the child responds appropriately to gestures, words, and short and

complex sentences, as well as expressive language and vocabulary to check whether the child uses gestures, noises, jargon, baby talk, and concrete and abstract words.

- How are the child's hands used? Are they limp, like wet sponges, or are they actively employed for exploration and manipulation?

- How does the child respond to training?

- Does the child refuse to learn because of poor motivation or is the material too complex and confusing?

- Does the child use vision and hearing fully?

- Does the child indulge in stereotypical behaviours? These may serve as indicators of ability. For example, light gazing or hand flapping in front of a light indicates that the child has some vision (Ficociello, 1977; Hammer, 1984).

The assessment of children who are multiply disabled is an arduous and challenging task requiring skilled practitioners, input from care providers, and many hours of observation and testing. Even so, results are always tenuous not only because of a child's complex disabilities but due to untrained personnel and a lack of appropriate tools. In a comprehensive study of assessment practices of special education staff serving students with severe disabilities in five school districts (Sigafoos, Cole, and McQuarter, 1987), for example, researchers reported that special educators lacked training in the assessment of students with severe disabilities, were limited by the unavailability of appropriate assessment tools, and were dependent on norm-referenced instruments.

The standard diagnostic and evaluation tools currently used with children who are mildly disabled will generally be of little use to those involved with individuals with severe and multiple disabilities. Problems most frequently occur when a child's performance on a particular item is inappropriately influenced by the disabling condition (Bailey and Wolery, 1989).

We point out in Chapter 13 that in the assessment of children with pervasive developmental disorders many of the tasks that are used in tests must be eliminated because of motor difficulties, sensory impairments, and special problems present in the children being assessed. Similar concerns surround assessment for children with multiple disabilities. Before even beginning an assessment, diagnosticians must work out how they can provide special procedures for children with limited or absent expressive and/or receptive language or for those who withdraw from social interaction. There are also problems that concern children's inability to name letters or pictures; their short attention spans and limited cooperation in testing situations; and their limited hand use in conjunction with limited expressive language so that sign language use is affected. Children may also have severe cognitive delays; may perform certain behaviours in one milieu but not during testing; and may perform tasks for a known person but not an unknown tester.

Some or all of the following adaptations enhance the assessment situation for both the child and the tester:

- A natural environment is an advantage to children. Psychological and educational assessments of children with multiple disabilities are best made in familiar surroundings using familiar tasks and materials.

- A number of adaptations to standard routines may need to be considered, as we discuss in Chapter 12.

- No single assessment tool can meet all the needs of a population as diverse as that of children with multiple disabilities. Specific instruments should vary according to the needs of the individual and to the areas being assessed. It is now common practice to use a combination of direct observation; informant interviews; adaptive behaviour scales; measures of prelinguistic communication behaviour and alternate methods of communication; developmental scales, observational checklists, and formal intelligence tests.

- The foundation of an accurate and appropriate assessment is the establishment of rapport with the child and the family. Having parents present may add to a child's feeling of security. Parents should also be involved during the assessment process as sources of information.

- Interdisciplinary assessments should be conducted. The size and nature of the team involved will vary according to the child's disabilities. Arena testing can be used. This is an observational assessment approach in which people from several disciplines focus on their particular domains such as motor skills or language within the context of play.

- Findings must be frequently monitored to reflect and encourage changes in the child's competency (see Bailey and Wolery, 1989; Langley, 1991).

To assess mental ability, diagnosticians usually select scales of infant development because the sensorimotor behaviours tapped are often in the repertoires of these children. Although infant scales are known to be poor predictors of later development in non-disabled children, these measures with children who are severely disabled give IQs that have proven to be good predictors of later development (Fewell and Cone, 1983). Perhaps the most widely used test of cognition for children functioning in the sensorimotor period is the Ugiris and Hunt Scale of Infant Psychological Development or its adaptations (Dunst, 1980).

Psychometric tests are not suitable for a large proportion of children who are multiply disabled. Nor are norm-referenced developmental scales that compare the exceptional child with normally developing peers in order to determine the extent of deviation from the norm. A variety of other tools are needed to measure a child's ability to perform in the areas of motor skills, language and communication, social behaviour, and self-help skills. Most instruments permit comparisons of each child's performance at a different point in time rather than trying to establish a child's relative standing on a normative scale (Liepman 1981).

The Callier-Azusa Scale (Stillman 1978), for example, is designed to assess children from birth to six years of age who are deaf-blind and severely and profoundly disabled. It covers motor development, perceptual development, daily living skills, communication, and social development. The scale is used in classroom settings by someone familiar with the child so that typical behaviour can be observed in natural contexts. This links assessment to curriculum so that teachers can synthesize developmentally appropriate activities for the child.

The Developmental Activities Screening Inventory 2, a screening test of functioning for children from birth to five years, has adaptations for blind and deaf children (Fewell and Langley, 1984). Motor scales include the Peabody Developmental Motor Scales and Activity Cards (Folio and Fewell, 1983).

Language assessment is both crucial and complex. Standardized measures include the Preschool Language Scale (Zimmerman, Sheener, and Pond, 1979) and the Sequenced Inventory of Communication Development (Hedrick, Pratter, and Tobin, 1975). Both provide individual scores for receptive and expressive language and both are standardized on very young children.

Children with significant disabilities meet problems in responding to interactions, in imitating, and in using basic communication. Many children are either prelinguistic or minimally linguistic. Informal language assessment for this group largely focuses on measures of prelinguistic communication behaviour. It attempts to determine a child's understanding of sounds and gestures, and includes observation of the child's response to environmental sounds, speech sounds, and response to gestures, names, and requests. Assessment also examines communication use, which includes how the child gains the attention of others; how he or she initiates play with caregivers and peers; whether the child anticipates and takes turns; and how the child interacts in routine communication events. Important to note are the settings, people, and purposes for communication. Needs and interests are assessed by looking at the reasons for the child to communicate, the objects and activities that the child prefers, and when and with whom the most appropriate interactions occur.

Observational data and parent interviews are strong indicators of a child's level of skills and awareness. Direct observation techniques permit assessment of children's behaviour and achievements in their normal daily routine. A number of questionnaires and interview schedules have been constructed for use with parents, teachers, and other key informants who can provide important information about aspects of a child's progress.

Educational assessment focuses on functional areas of competence in the domains of communication, social behaviour, self-help, and independence skills. For some children, educational assessment also measures areas of academic competence, such as reading, writing, and mathematics.

Prevention of Multiple Disabilities

Adequate prenatal care, good nutrition, and avoidance of alcohol and drugs improve the health of mothers and babies. Maternal rubella is effectively prevented by the rubella vaccine; meningitis is also prevented by immunization. Research is ongoing for ways to prevent and cure other congenital birth defects. Recent advances in genetics have increased our understanding of genetically linked disorders, and genetic counselling is available to help decrease the frequency of genetic conditions.

The most extreme consequences of severe physical, sensory, and mental disabilities can often be prevented by early intervention programs undertaken simultaneously with ongoing medical care and treatment. Some conditions of the eye and ear can be treated medically or surgically. Cosmetic or plastic surgery can, in some cases, correct skeletal anomalies that cause visual or hearing problems. Cosmetic surgery may also help a child with social acceptance.

Developmental Consequences of Multiple Disabilities

Children with multiple disabilities are those who have two or more exceptional conditions that hinder the attainment of their full potential. The variety and combinations of disorders presented by children who are multiply disabled make generalizations about developmental consequences virtually impossible. These students may have orthopedic or health impairments, or hearing or speech disabilities. They may use unconventional behaviour to communicate a basic need or they may exhibit a combination of behaviours (Jones and Carlier, 1995).

Physical Development

Many domains of learning depend upon a child's ability to interact with the environment. As a result, many children with multiple disabilities are very late in reaching developmental milestones. Walking, using first words, and toilet training may be severely delayed.

During the period when normal children are developing most rapidly, the multiple deficits of these children prevent them from interacting with the environment in ways that are critical for the subsequent development of social, motor, cognitive, and communication skills. They are then doubly limited by their delayed physical development and by their limited ability to engage with the environment in ways that can stimulate development (Warren, Alpert, and Kaiser, 1988).

Cognitive Development

Depressed cognitive development is not a necessary concomitant of multiple disabilities. Nevertheless, the disabilities can be so severe that many children function in very low ranges. For example, although 94 percent of children who are deaf-blind have some usable vision and usable hearing (Chen and Haney, 1995), many of these children function in the severe to profound ranges of mental retardation as a result of their inability to perform basic skills (Orlansky, 1981).

Communication

Most children with multiple disabilities are deprived of orienting movements of the head and body, as well as of purposive gaze. This leaves them with no available modality through which to communicate. They are unable to clearly co-ordinate actions of looking, searching, reaching, and touching, which operate as functional units of communication. Such children find it very difficult to acquire the complex symbol system of language without enough sensory data to make language meaningful. They tend to remain at early stages of communication development for long periods of time (Rogow, 1987a).

Children lacking efficient communication are often divided into two groups. The first group comprises presymbolic children who do not use signs, words, or pictures for communication. They may not possess a recognizable communication system or may use gestures such as pointing or touching or moving objects. The second group is made up of minimally symbolic children who use some visual, verbal, or tactile symbols alone or in combinations (Owens, 1991).

Social and Emotional Development

From the very beginning of life, the onset of attachment behaviours and social interactions may be severely delayed as the child's physical and behavioural deficits disrupt the natural interchange between caregiver and child that is essential to early interactions. In addition, the baby's first months may be dominated by periods of hospitalization, feeding problems, and an inability to maintain a wakeful state.

Young children may appear not to recognize other family members, or they may be obsessively engaged in such self-stimulating behaviours as light gazing or hand flapping. In older children, emotional difficulties may be manifested in any or all of the following personality traits: frequent panic reactions, hyperkinesis, autism, withdrawal, and frequent tantrums (Van Dijk, 1982).

Behaviour

Problem behaviours may reflect the intense frustration caused by a child's inability to communicate. In some cases, the cause of problem behaviours is unknown, although such behaviours often seem related to the type of brain damage a child has sustained.

Academic Achievement

The learning and educational attainments of children who are multiply disabled depend upon a matrix of factors. Not the least of these are the quality of education, the age at which education begins, the age of onset of the conditions, the nature of the combination of handicaps, and the severity of each condition. Also important are factors such as the family's response to the child, the educational setting, the amount of integration with non-disabled peers, the related services available for both the child and the family, and the amount of acceptance by the community.

Some children who are multiply disabled achieve well in school. For most, however, functioning is at pre-academic levels. Because their perception of events is impaired, they find it hard to develop awareness, attention, anticipation and purpose—all skills needed for efficient learning.

Intervention with Children Who Have Multiple Disabilities

In the past, persons with severe and multiple disabilities were excluded from educational services. Over the last 40 years, the education and treatment of children who are multiply disabled has undergone considerable revision and expansion.

Treatment generally hinges on two major factors—etiology and the specific combination of disabilities. Although etiology is of less overall significance for educators, critical program modifications must be made for such secondary spin-offs as rubella-induced sensory aberrations and the psychological adjustments precipitated by Usher's syndrome.

Medical Intervention

Medical and paramedical personnel can provide information about many aspects of a child's functioning to teachers and parents. Those intervening with a child who is multiply disabled require information concerning

- special arrangements that may be needed to accommodate seizure activity, medications, allergies, susceptibility to illness, poor muscle strength, and special feeding problems;
- physical deformities that may require special equipment or prosthetic devices;
- alterations that may be needed in work, play, and rest schedules;
- special positioning or handling techniques or special feeding techniques (Rogow, 1987a).

Therapy

Children with multiple disabilities require the services of a range of therapists, most specifically physical, occupational, and speech and language therapists. Physical and occupational therapists can help children to develop hand skills, body co-ordination, and other physical skills, and aid in gross motor development, muscle relaxation, and fine motor control (see Chapter 13).

Speech and language therapy assists the child's development of speech and language. This form of therapy may also be used with children who have difficulty in controlling the fine motor muscles needed for eating. Therapists may also develop appropriate augmentative communication for children who cannot talk.

Technical

Improved equipment and adaptive devices have been developed to enrich education and improve the quality of life for individuals of all ages. (See Chapter 13.) Computer applications have been successfully used to enhance functioning and assist in the learning of a specific task. Garner and Campbell (1987), for example, used computers to develop specific cognitive skills in order to provide more opportunities for individuals to perform a wide variety of functional activities independently in integrated environments.

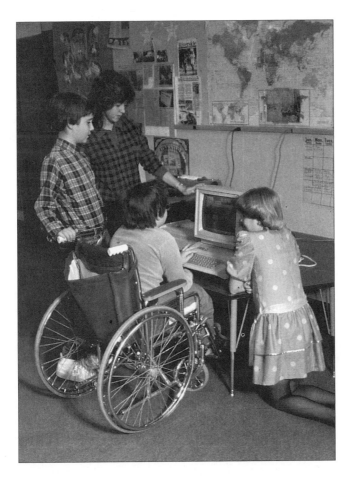

Technical aids continue to be developed to improve the quality of life for severely disabled children and assist in their education.

Educational Intervention

Children who are multiply disabled take education beyond its traditional boundaries. These children may show different learning characteristics and developmental patterns. The instructional process may be hindered by maladaptive behaviour, the need to adapt technology and materials, and the difficulty in identifying appropriate reinforcers (Sisson, Van Hasselt, and Hersen, 1987).

Children's development is predicated on such factors as alteration of the physical environment, sensory stimulation, and well-planned, consistent habilitative and educational programs. Training begins with basic developmental skills and, for some, may never proceed beyond pre-academic levels. Multiple treatment modalities are employed.

Children who are multiply disabled need an extensive network of services to enable them to thrive and learn; they also need a responsive environment capable of providing appropriate stimulation and opportunities for interaction. The difficulties and potentialities resulting from each unique combination of disabilities represents the decision point in placement and programming, so we find that students with multiple disabilities are educated in a variety of settings. Some may attend regular school or special classrooms in the local school. Others may learn in special schools, residential placements, hospitals, or clinics.

If children with visual and hearing impairments see well enough to learn in classes with deaf children, they may be enrolled in special classes or schools for the hearing impaired. These children require additional help from specialist teachers of the visually impaired to develop maximum use of their remaining vision. Children with moderate to severe sensory impairments may require programs specifically designed for deaf-blind children. Some school boards in large urban areas accommodate these children within special classes in regular schools. In hospital-based day schools, children attend school in hospital classrooms, where medical treatment and physiotherapy are readily available.

Although the numbers are decreasing, some Canadian children with multiple disabilities are still educated in residential settings. Such placements have both their advocates and their opponents. Some professionals (e.g. Silverstein, 1985) feel that residential placements are appropriate not only for sensorially impaired children with severe intellectual dysfunction, but also for those with average or above average IQs. Others actively promote less restrictive environments.

With the current stress on integration and inclusion, there has been a movement away from the traditional residential model. Policy in the United States is instructive in this regard. American courts have decided that residential programming is necessary when more than six hours of instruction are required to meet the child's educational needs; when the severity of the child's language deficiency precludes meaningful benefit from peer group learning and interaction with non-disabled peers in a mainstream setting; or when social and emotional adjustment are poor in the normal setting.

Inclusion

The historical legacy of special education means that students with intense needs are often served in some form of special services. Increasingly, however, children who are deaf-blind or who have other severe or multiple disabilities are being educated in regular classes.

To a large extent, the full inclusive position justifies the integration of students who are disabled by arguments based on the potential social and emotional benefits to the child with a disability. Defensible reasons for placing children with severe and profound disabilities in regular classrooms are access to social relationships with peers and access to normalized learning environments.

While there is increasing availability and growing support for the placement of students with severe disabilities in general education classes, there is still disagreement within the field as to whether students with intensive educational needs belong in general education classrooms. In fact, the major placement issue of the day is whether students with severe intellectual disabilities and multiple disabilities should be based in regular or special education classrooms or in home schools. The pros and cons echo those we presented in Chapter 13 on whether children with pervasive developmental disorders should be candidates for inclusion.

Children with mild physical or sensory impairments can learn well in the regular classroom, provided they receive additional support. These children are able to participate in academic programs, and benefit from interaction with non-disabled peers. In addition to regular instruction, they may need the services of speech therapists, physical therapists, audiologists, mobility and orientation specialists, and specialist teachers of the hearing or visually impaired.

When the placement of children with severe or multiple disabilities is considered, three critical questions must be addressed:

- How are educational programs for individual students in inclusive settings designed?
- How can it be determined which services are needed to support the students in these settings?
- How can individual lesson accommodations be developed to include the students in typical classroom activities? (Cloninger and Giangreco, 1995, p. 262).

Placing a child with a multiple disability in an inclusive setting means a stress on natural supports; that is, supports in the environment the person would have access to if he or she did not have a disability (home, neighbourhood, local school, regular classroom, job site) and relying on persons in the environment (family members, classmates, general education teachers) (see Giangreco, Edelman, MacFarland, and Luiselli, 1997). For example, classmates can help students to feel welcome, accepted, and secure. As well, schools may elect one person, often a special education teacher, to act as a support facilitator. This person not only works with the severely disabled students but helps regular classroom teachers adapt instruction and aids in facilitating peer acceptance (Stainback and Stainback, 1988). For the child who is deaf-blind, there may be an interpreter-tutor who acts as interpreter and facilitator. He or she needs skills in orientation and mobility, communication, and sign language if necessary (Ford and Fredericks, 1995).

When a child is in a regular classroom, some skills can be taught incidentally and students who require opportunities to learn practical living, working, and social skills can be provided guidance and opportunities to do so at natural times throughout the day. Susan Stainback and colleagues suggest that lunch and snack times and home economics can provide opportunities to learn about food preparation and eating and dining skills; dressing and grooming skills are learned when students do this before and after school or for gym class; and bus riding skills can be taught when students need to travel back and forth to school. Additionally, functional and vocational skills can be learned at natural times such as in after-school jobs and on weekend shopping trips with family and friends and in integrated, general education work-study programs and home economics and other such classes (Stainback, Stainback, and Stefanich, 1996).

Educational Approaches

While the learning characteristics and needs of children who are multiply handicapped vary widely, the following components are essential to a comprehensive system of education:

- Early and continuous intervention. Early intervention can prevent the consequences of sensory deprivation and emotional withdrawal.

- Transdisciplinary models that rest on consultation and collaboration.

- Systematic instructional procedures. As students who are multiply disabled miss so much incidental learning, they must be helped to develop a foundation for later and more complex learning.

- Appropriate curricula. Children require both educational and psychosocial development founded on a carefully task-analyzed individual education plan. The more disabled the child, the more detailed and precise the task analysis and the goals and objectives need to be. Each child's educational plan (which will probably span five years) should include ongoing assessment of the child's progress and a detailed evaluation of the educational program. Curriculum materials should then be developed to meet the individualized educational goals of each child.

- Critical program modifications. These must be made because children suffer from combinations of conditions that interact in such a way as to depress or block the emergence of normal patterns of interaction with the environment (Rogow and Rodrigues, 1977). As well, accommodations provide for co-occurring disabilities.

- Adjunctive services. These include the provision of medical and therapeutic services to individual children. Associated professionals may also provide specific training and instruction to parents.

Team Approaches

The training and education of children with multiple disabilities cannot rely on one person. Different disciplines bring unique skills and knowledge to intervention, and the nature of the child necessitates a partial blending of roles, skills, and knowledge across disciplines (McCollum and Thorp, 1988; Thorp and McCollum, 1988). When professionals in diverse roles function co-operatively to help students achieve their goals, this may be framed in the context of a transdisciplinary model.

A transdisciplinary model is a team approach in which it is assured that the team members will perform the various services together. This means that the expertise of different types of agencies serving children with disabilities can be shared so that services are enriched, expanded, and made more comprehensive. A team approach enables everyone involved to see the child as a total being rather than concentrating on one aspect of that child's development. On a team, roles and expectations are shared by more than one member and experts on the team train other members (see Landerholm, 1990).

Teamwork demands *collaboration*, which is a "generic (umbrella) term used to describe a style of interacting in which persons with diverse backgrounds voluntarily agree to work together to generate creative solutions to mutually defined problems" (CEC, 1991). Collaboration "depends inherently on the voluntary efforts of professional educators to improve their schools and their own skills through teamwork" (Smith and Scott, 1990, p. 2). In collaboration, the ownership of a problem is always shared and the consulting relationship is characterized by a sense of parity demonstrated through two-way communication and the sharing of knowledge and skills. The key hypothesis behind the process is that the group, functioning together, is greater than the sum of its individual parts.

Typically, the transdisciplinary team is composed of the family and professionals from a variety of disciplines who collaborate in assessment and program planning. One individual, in consultation with other team members, works to carry out the individual program so that the case manager is both primary provider and service co-ordinator. Generally, in school settings, the teacher assumes the role of service provider (Orelove and Sobsey, 1987).

Although simple in concept, the implementation of a trandisciplinary model can initially be difficult because it represents a significant departure from most models of service delivery to which professionals are accustomed (Orelove and Sobsey, 1987). Certain attributes seem important to efficient team functioning:

- Each team must have a leader who may involve himself or herself in specific tasks related to team functioning.
- The size of the team will vary according to the child's disabilities.
- While the composition of a team will differ from case to case, certain core people are usually involved. These include teachers, therapists, aides, and other paraprofessionals such as an audiologist. Family members should be encouraged to join the team; not only do they have the right to be included, but they are the people most familiar with the child.
- On a team, each team member has a role and each role has a set of skills and certain expectations associated with it.
- Effective teams develop over time and they need nurturance. When the membership of the team changes frequently, implementation and maintenance of child and family goals are jeopardized.
- The way people respond to others' communication directly determines the extent to which people on the team can continue the interchanges and initiate further dialogue. Personal characteristics that can assist in developing good communication and collaboration on the team include being empathetic and open, being able to establish good rapport, respecting different points of view, and being positive and enthusiastic (West and Cannon, 1987).

Curricula

Curricula designed for children who are multiply disabled must reflect all areas of development. Educational needs include language development, visual and auditory training, mobility training, and self-care skills. For children who are deaf-blind, stress must be placed on visual stimulation and visual perception skills as a basis for cognitive and academic tasks. The development of communication skills is a simultaneous activity. Language is the product of all aspects of development—physical, sensory, social, and neurological. Therefore, in the education of children who are deaf-blind, and indeed all children with multiple disabilities, no aspect of language development can be ignored. Psychosocial needs include adaptive behaviour, group activities, life skills, and a range of socialization experiences (Hammer, 1984).

For many children with multiple disabilities, training emphasizes early developmental skills usually thought of as too routine or too basic to be part of a regular instructional program. Most curricula for children with severe disorders have tended to adhere to a biological-developmental or cognitive-developmental approach. That is, developmental milestones are emphasized and skills must be developed in a specific hierarchical order regardless of the ages of the children. The developmental order of skills corresponds to what has been observed in younger children without disabilities (Bailey, Jens, and Johnson, 1983).

While popular, there are problems associated with an approach based on the attainment of developmental milestones. For one thing, the sequences of behaviour typical for non-disabled students may not be relevant for a child with severe problems because such children may not develop or acquire skills in a normal sequence. When a pathology of the central nervous system exists, or when there are severe sensory losses, the organization of behaviour is disturbed and a child's early development is often uneven. Children who are severely handicapped may learn in a different sequence and the relationship between skills may be different (Snell, 1987). For example, a child with multiple disabilities may walk at a relatively early age, but be severely delayed in the acquisition of language.

Apart from the uneven development seen in students with multiple disabilities, a curriculum based on developmental sequences is likely to have little impact upon the ultimate attainment of self-sufficiency because the skills taught are not functional enough. When teaching students with multiple disabilities, a better approach is to focus on **functional skills**, skills that are useful to a student in many current and future environments. These are skills that have a high probability of being required at home, in school, at work, or in the community, and that will increase self-sufficiency in those environments.

The functional skill approach improves the child's functioning in present environments and facilitates transition to and participation in age-appropriate future environments. For example, sorting shapes to corresponding pictures of shapes is not a skill that a child is likely to use during daily activities, whereas the child is likely to use the skill of matching various shaped lids to corresponding containers. While both skills involve matching, recognizing, and sorting shapes, the use of functional objects such as containers and lids enables the child to learn a necessary skill that will foster independence in real-life situations (Notari-Syverson and Shuster, 1995). Similarly, placing pegs in a board may aid in fine motor development, but it is not really related to future needs. On the other hand, putting coins in a vending machine will develop the same motor areas and also provide a living skill.

The actual methodology for teaching skills (whether developmental or functional) is usually based on ecological and applied behavioural practices. This can lead to significant gains in language, self-care, socialization, and independent living skills (Lane, 1996).

Communication Training

Of all the needs of children with multiple disabilities, the acquisition of communication skills is one of the greatest. Children require training in all aspects of understanding and expression. Training may take place in one-to-one, highly structured environments, but more generally in natural contexts such as the classroom. In a milieu (natural environment) approach to communication intervention, teachers use incidental teaching and structured behavioural approaches such as time delay and mand models (Reickle, 1997; see Winzer, 1997, on models).

The major goal of language intervention is the initiation of effective communication. Two general strategies are used in communication training programs for presymbolic and minimally symbolic children, often in tandem. These are presymbolic training and communication-first approaches (Owens, 1991).

Presymbolic training is based on the belief that there are cognitive prerequisites for language acquisition. Teaching programs are organized around initial assessment and subsequent training related to cognitive, perceptual, social and/or communication targets identified as significant in the acquisition of symbol use in non-handicapped children. The skills that make up presymbolic training are those that are identified as characteristic of the sensorimotor stage of development. Training begins with the development of basic sensorimotor skills such as object permanence, causality, means–end behaviour, spatial relationships, schemas for relating to objects, and imitation.

A communication-first approach is a functional approach to language which stresses nurturant and naturalistic language. Communication-first approaches place the initial emphasis on the establishment of a communication system that can later be expanded to symbol use. Elaborated forms of communication are built on simpler forms. The progression of communication moves from signals (cries, for example), to the use of sign (systematic, consistent gesturing to indicate wants, for example), to the use of increasingly complex linguistic forms, to the metalinguistic uses of language.

The major skills taught are initial communication; turn-taking skills; generalized imitation skills; lexical growth and establishment of a basic vocabulary; early symbol communication rules; and participation in interactions that occur outside the training context (see Owens, 1991).

Alternative Methods of Communication

Relatedness to others in the environment depends on some basic communication. When speech is delayed, or when there is reason to think that it may be delayed or not develop at all (for example, when the child has multiple disabilities including a significant hearing loss), alternative means of communication are considered.

Anything that augments speech or accomplishes communication function is grouped under the term *augmentative communication*. **Augmentative communication** refers to a general group of procedures designed to support, enhance, or augment the communication of non-speaking individuals or utilize and supplement whatever vocal skills an individual possesses. The various procedures that make up augmentative communication are used chiefly by individuals whose speech communication is impaired by hearing impairments; individuals with severe language deficits; individuals with severe neuromuscular or physical disabilities; and those with severe and multiple disabilities.

Augmentative communication devices receive and transmit messages and include communication boards, charts, mechanical or electrical devices, and computers. There are two main types of augmentation—unaided and aided approaches. Unaided approaches rely on gestural communication; aided approaches depend on a device of some kind or a pictorial or symbolic communication system. Figure 14-1 shows examples of Bliss symbols.

Communication mode refers to "the form in which the content of a message is expressed"

Figure 14-1
Bliss symbols

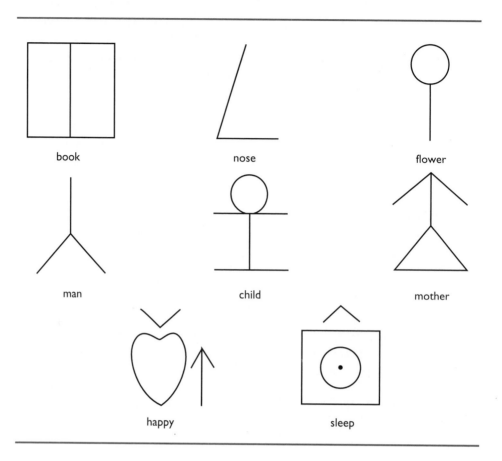

(Sailor, Guess, Goetz, Schuler, Utley, and Baldwin, 1980, p. 72). The selection of a communication mode and the strategies for teaching its use should be an interdisciplinary task. The choice of an adjunct to communication is ideally made in conjunction with family and therapists. Factors such as long-term linguistic needs, people with whom the child needs to communicate, and the most appropriate mode of communication must be considered. The mental ability, motivation, visual perception, motor control, and behavioural problems of the child are further considerations in selecting a mode of communication. Table 14-1 outlines some alternative methods of communication.

Unaided Approaches

The major types of unaided approaches in augmentative communication are

- Signal communication, which includes the use of a simple yes/no system and audio-signalling. Yes and no signals may be indicated by movements of head, hands, face, or eye (Mysak, 1982). A portable audio-oscillator that emits a loud tone has been used to teach four simple signals *(need, help, yes, no).*

- Code communication uses Morse code as a method of communication.

- Natural gestures are simple movements of one or both hands used to convey meaning to the child. For example, the word *eat* is indicated by tapping the lips with the fingertips of

Table 14-1 Alternative methods of augmentative communication

Signal/code	Symbol	Manual
yes/no	rebus systems	idiosyncratic gesturing
audio-signalling	Blissymbolics	Amerind
gesturing	Pictorial Ideographic Communication (PIC)	American Sign Language (ASL)
Morse code		school-based manual systems

one hand. Although natural gestures are often used with children who are deaf-blind, they may also be part of communication training for children with multiple disabilities who are not hearing impaired. Natural gestures vary from child to child. If a child consistently points to the mouth to indicate hunger, then everyone working with that child should use the same gesture.

•   Sign language is typically associated with deaf children; however, studies suggest that manual communication may be beneficial to a much larger population in improving communication skills. Its use may potentially offer unlimited opportunities for language development and may facilitate the onset and development of spoken language in prelinguistic children (Kouri, 1989).

•   Amerind is a simpler system and more suitable for low-functioning individuals for whom sign language may prove too difficult. Amerind was adapted by Madge Skelly (1979), a speech and language pathologist and full-blooded Indian, from the system she learned from her grandfather. Amerind is built on the hand signals used by Native Americans and contains about 250 hand signals that may be arranged in any combination.

Aided Approaches

Augmentative devices are operated by the individual to communicate basic needs. They can be easily activated by movement of the head or hand, or even by an eye blink. The Vocaid is an example of an augmentative device suitable for functional needs, such as a call for assistance. Some augmentative devices make use of speech synthesis. Children with good intellectual ability might use a system where the child spells a message on a grid using row-column scanning with an electronic device.

Blissymbolics has been successful with children with severe motor disabilities. Charles Bliss, a refugee from Hitler's concentration camps, went to Shanghai where he learned the Chinese writing system in which each symbol stands for an idea rather than a sound. Based on this, Bliss developed an ideographic universal writing system. It was not popular until discovered by Shirley McNaughton at the Ontario Crippled Children's Centre in Toronto. Today Blissymbolics is a complete language system. Even though it can be used for general conversation, the symbols are simple enough to be learned by children too young to read alphabetic writing (Archer, 1977). Bliss is used by 25 000 people in Canada, of whom one-quarter have cerebral palsy (Reich, 1986). Depending on a child's abilities, vocabularies of up to four hundred terms may be learned (Mysak, 1982).

Pictorial systems were designed to enhance oral communication among intellectually impaired non-verbal and limited-verbal individuals. They use pictures rather than the stylized symbols of Blissymbolics. For example, Pictorial Ideographic Communication (PIC) is presented on a communication board and consists of pictures and symbols that represent objects and actions.

The idea of using real pictures is based on normal child development, which demonstrates that in the typical child, representational skills emerge early in development. Children as young as 24 months of age recognize photographs as symbols of the objects they represent (Daehler, Perlmutter, and Myers, 1976).

Bliss or picture systems are displayed on communication boards. Picture communication boards have clear pictures or photographs depicting basic needs and activities. The board may display pictures of an item of food, a cup, a toilet or pot, a bed, and a toy. The child communicates by pointing to the appropriate pictures.

Studies have compared Blissymbolics and picture symbols (Mezriko, 1987). They report that non-disabled preschoolers find picture symbols to be more transparent and more learnable than Blissymbolics.

Skills for Independence

A curricular approach that encourages students to exercise their own initiative requires both systematic teaching of choice-making and provision of opportunities to practice choosing. But providing choice-making opportunities for students with the most severe disabilities, who often do not communicate independently, presents a major challenge to educators.

Mealtime is ideal for such instruction because it naturally occurs on a consistent, daily basis in school, at home, and in community environments. Instruction centres on providing the student with structured opportunities for selecting foods, by offering a series of choices among familiar, meaningful, and disparate options (Gothelf, Crimmmins, Mercer, and Finocchiaro, 1994).

Students Who Are Deaf-Blind

Deprivation in one distance sense tends to increase reliance on the other. Deprivations in the senses of both vision and hearing place reliance on the near senses of taste, touch, and smell. Children who are deaf and blind therefore have an infinitely more complex task in gaining information about their environments.

Education for children who are deaf-blind begins with self-care skills such as feeding, grooming, toilet-training, dressing and undressing. Associated with this is motor development, which includes body awareness, relaxation and muscle stimulation, sitting, attaining a standing position, and standing. Other areas then include movement through space, first non-ambulatory movement and then ambulation. Light stimulation, eye control, and visual tracking are used for visual training. Auditory training exercises encompass vibration, music, and receptive language.

A primary goal in working with children who are deaf-blind is to teach them to communicate in the easiest possible way. Such children often need training in the use of specific communication systems (Heller, Alberto, and Bowdin, 1995). When a system is chosen, it must be familiar to all those working with the child and to the parents.

All children who are capable of speech should undergo intensive speech training. Many children who are deaf-blind have learned to perceive speech through the vibration method. With this method, the deaf-blind person places a thumb on the speaker's lips, an index finger on the speaker's jaw, and three fingers on the speaker's neck. This allows the learner to manually perceive the vibrations of the speaker's voice, the tension of the speaker's face, and the shape of the speaker's lips.

A number of commercial programs have been developed for youngsters who are deaf-blind; for example, the Assessment-Intervention Model for Deaf-Blind Students (AIM) (Schein, Kates, Wolf, and Theil, 1983) is a curriculum consisting of specific self-care and independence skills: drinking and pouring; dressing and undressing; using the toilet; personal care; kitchen preparation and cleanup; and housekeeping. It provides very low starting points and tiny steps in the sequence of reaching behavioural objectives.

Orientation and Mobility Training

Orientation and mobility training teaches individuals who have multiple disabilities that include blindness a basic knowledge of the environment and how to find their way to specific locations, such as the schoolroom or the workshop.

Although the goals of orientation and mobility training for children with multiple disabilities that include visual loss are the same as for other children who are visually impaired, some of the teaching techniques may differ. Children who are multiply disabled often need alternative methods that provide safety and information and yet are within their capabilities. Some specialists introduce cane travel before the child is technically ready in the hope of developing greater confidence. This has proved very successful with low-functioning blind children.

SUMMARY

1. A number of useful definitions of multiple disabilities have evolved. Some attempt to offer comprehensive generic descriptions; others describe the parameters of types of disabling conditions. More specific definitions have developed for particular combinations of disabling conditions.

2. Medical assessment includes auditory and visual status. A variety of clinical and functional hearing tests should be administered to children with dual sensory impairments over a period of time.

3. The assessment of children who are multiply disabled is difficult for even the most experienced clinicians. Because the value of IQ scores for diagnosis is relatively limited for this population and no one measure or battery of measures is suitable for all, a range of assessment measures must be employed. Assessment serves to generate data for program and placement decisions.

4. The special and diverse needs caused by the unique combinations of conditions challenge all those charged with training and educating multiply disabled children.

5. Education may take place in public schools in regular or special class settings, residential schools, or through school programs in hospitals. In regular classrooms, curricular items

such as daily life and vocational skills, which were traditionally addressed because of their practical utility for students who were in segregated learning settings, need not be eliminated.

6. Many students who are multiply disabled require the expertise of specially trained staff, more intensive staffing allocations, community referenced curricula, and/or prosthetic techniques.

7. Although a developmental curriculum approach for children with multiple disabilities is popular, there are two major criticisms. The first revolves around the contention that all children, regardless of disability, follow a logical progression of development. The second has to do with the functional value of the skills taught. A functional approach where the selection of objectives is based on their future usefulness is more appropriate.

8. There are cognitive prerequisites for language acquisition. Some researchers suggest organizing a teaching program around the initial assessment of and subsequent training in cognitive skills such as object permanence, classification, imitation, and representational play with objects. Others stress a communication-first approach.

9. Children who are unable to acquire oral language may learn other communication methods. Several systems of augmentative communication may be used in place of speech.

In the Classroom

Profile: Juanita

Very early in her pregnancy, Juanita's mother contracted rubella. She was warned by medical personnel that her child might suffer some type of disability but was stunned and frightened to find that the infant was both deaf and blind and also suffered a host of other problems.

Throughout Juanita's infant and preschool years, home-visiting teachers came to show her mother a range of activities to stimulate Juanita's mobility, communication, and interpersonal interactions. Consistent medical assessment demonstrated that although the child suffered serious visual and hearing difficulties, she was not totally deaf or completely blind. Juanita had quite a lot of usable vision and, although her hearing loss was in the severe to profound range, amplification seemed to help. Not that Juanita took kindly to either a hearing aid or glasses. Despite the intensity of her disabilities, she had a mind of her own, and it took many months of perseverance on the part of her mother and the intervenors and many types of primary reinforcers before she would tolerate either appliance.

Juanita attended the local preschool classes on a part-time basis. When she was ready for school, her mother enrolled her in the neighbourhood school, which had a special class for children with severe and multiple disabilities. For the first little while, Juanita remained in her special class, but soon the teacher worked to integrate her into a regular classroom for increasingly longer periods of the day. The teacher facilitated a "Circle of Friends" to assist Juanita's integration and worked co-operatively with the classroom teacher on planning specific activities that Juanita could accomplish in a small group setting. Juanita is now nine years old. She still spends part of her time learning specific skills in the special class, but she is also comfortable and welcome in the regular classroom and has a small group of friends who share with her both in and out of school.

* * *

Including children with severe or multiple disabilities into regular classrooms poses enormous challenges. While many parents support inclusion on the presumption that primary placement in general education facilitates socialization, children must still acquire basic living and communication skills.

Juanita's regular classroom teacher looked at both formal and informal ways to provide multiple interactions daily in the classroom. She helped to develop informal peer supports and friendships for Juanita by fostering respect for individual differences and by providing a positive model. She stressed proximity through peer tutoring, co-operative learning, buddy systems, and involvement in extra-curricular activities. Juanita's modified program kept her with the class but at her own developmental level.

In one lesson, for example, the teacher read a book to the class. Juanita's objective was to sit on the floor in an assigned spot and direct her attention to the teacher. The second part of the lesson was to colour a picture from the story. The other children chose their colours, but a peer handed Juanita a marker and instructed her where to colour. As the other children then wrote a story about their pictures, they read them aloud to Juanita and, using signs and natural gestures, prompted her to point to the pictures.

Extract from Juanita's IEP

PRESENT LEVELS

Deaf, visually impaired, low cognitive functioning. Pre- to minimally linguistic. No intelligible speech and a few gestures for wants. Very interested in other children in the class.

PLACEMENT

Regular classroom with paraprofessional assistance.

CURRENT PROGRESS

Growing awareness of classmates. Will wave with assistance. Interest in signing as used by other class members.

STRATEGIES FOR INCLUSION

Paraprofessional; simple signs used by all in environment; modified program stressing communication and life skills; out-of-class daily therapy.

PERSONNEL

Classroom teacher, paraprofessional, therapist.

GOALS AND OBJECTIVES

- co-operating with others
- following classroom directions
- adhering to the rules and routines of the classroom
- waving on command
- using basic sign communication
- developing life skills (special class)

EFFECTS OF MULTIPLE DISABILITIES	TIPS FOR TEACHERS
THE CHILD NEEDS TRAINING IN A NATURAL ENVIRONMENT	Most training efforts should be conducted in natural environments. For children with more severe deficits in speech and language, formal language training may involve lessons a few brief times daily. However, communication training with children who are severely impaired need not, and should not, be confined to one-to-one therapy sessions.
THE CHILD BENEFITS FROM MULTI-SENSORY APPROACHES	Activities should contain multiple components. Multiple components provide numerous opportunities within a single activity. Painting, for example, would provide at least three opportunities for communication: obtaining access to the paint, the water, and the brush.
THE CHILD BENEFITS FROM REPETITIVE APPROACHES	Activities should lend themselves to repetitive action. If the child desires repeated actions by a caregiver, repeated opportunities exist for language use. Examples

EFFECTS OF MULTIPLE DISABILITIES	TIPS FOR TEACHERS
	of these activities include playing catch and being pushed on a swing.
THE CHILD NEEDS TO DEVELOP SKILLS FOR COMMUNICATION	Reinforce vocalizations as consistently and frequently as possible.
	Provide vocal reinforcement for a short time after the child stops vocalizing. This offers a model dialogue and ensures that the child is not interrupted. It also reinforces turn-taking patterns. Vocal reinforcement should include imitation of the child's sounds, whether verbal or preverbal.
	Place your mouth on the child's cheek or hand when speaking so that the child can feel your speech. Continue to hold your mouth against the child's cheek or hand between vocalizations so the child can feel the silence.
	Do not treat children who are visually impaired as if they were totally blind. However, make sure to accompany communication with rhythmic body actions, touch sensations, or actions that engage a number of senses simultaneously.
	Improve the quality of language stimulation by interspersing short bursts of speech with short periods of silence.
	Use playful social routines, rhyming verses, and other communication games that are enjoyable for you and the child. For older students, try using rock and roll and other rhythmic patterns.
	Children who are multiply disabled are often able to comprehend far more than they indicate; keep sentences short and use an expressive voice.
	For most deaf–blind children with other impairments, natural gestures offer the best foundation for communication. Natural gestures can be easily individualized.
THE CHILD NEEDS TO DEVELOP SOCIAL SKILLS	Develop short- and long-range goals that stress the child's self-help capabilities.
THE CHILD NEEDS TO LEARN APPROPRIATE BEHAVIOURS	Model the behaviours you want the child to learn.
THE CHILD NEEDS ROUTINE BEHAVIOUR	Children feel anxious and frustrated when confronted with unfamiliar experiences and variations in their routine.
	Encourage spontaneity by rewarding spontaneous behaviour.

EFFECTS OF MULTIPLE DISABILITIES	TIPS FOR TEACHERS
THE CHILD USES ADAPTIVE EQUIPMENT	Children with Usher's syndrome need exposure to O and M training, braille, and tactile sign language.
	Use prosthetic aids to enhance active involvement.

WEBLINKS

Usher's Syndrome **http://www.educ.kent.edu/deafed/laurie.htm**

Meningitis Research Foundation **http://www.meningitis.org/**

A Home of Blissymbolics **http://members.tripod.com/~jorj/sebliho.html**

Laurence-Moon-Bardet-Biedl Syndrome **http://www.avalon.nf.ca/~merbland/ LMBB/home.html**

SECTION 7

Intervention with Infants, Preschoolers, and Young Adults

Educators sometimes think of the critical years for learning as those between about five and eighteen, the time when children and adolescents are within the formal school system. Of course, learning is a life-long experience but an enormous amount takes place before children even reach school. By the time children are six years old, almost two-thirds of their ultimate cognitive ability is formed. After the age of six, the child's potential for further intellectual growth is slowed (Bloom, 1964).

Educators must be aware of the experiences of the preschool years, as this period of development lays the groundwork for what we see in formal classrooms. They must also be knowledgeable about the special requirements of students at the other end of the age spectrum—young adults who are leaving the school system.

For very young children, the family is the central focus. All families face stresses and strains, which are only multiplied when a child has a disability. Families may differ greatly in structure, cultural values, and economic status, but most families with a child who is disabled have to cope with additional emotional adjustments and caregiving demands.

Early childhood special education (ECSE) is a new discipline designed to ameliorate the effects of a disability in a very young child and to assist the parents and family in dealing with the associated stress. Early identification and early intervention are essential elements of ECSE.

Just as ECSE is a new discipline, so interest in the needs of students nearing the end of their school careers is a relatively new development. Essentially, initiatives arose from data that showed that youths with disabling conditions are not faring well in the adult world, especially in the work force.

Discussions of very young children with disabilities focus on the manner in which a child affects the family, the influence the family has on the child's development and progress, types of early intervention that are available to help parents cope with and enhance prospects for optimal development for their exceptional child, and parent involvement and parent training. Especially important is the concept and practice of transition.

Transition is an umbrella term for all activities and opportunities that prepare students for significant changes in their lives ("Transition programs...," 1997). For young children and their parents, transition is the movement from preschool to school. In older students, transition means the movement from elementary to junior high school, or to secondary school. The most important meaning relates to secondary school students moving to new environments, most often from school to work. More and more, schools are becoming involved in assisting adolescents to negotiate the transition to independent adult living.

Although transition is the major focus of programs for older students with disabilities and only a part of those for very young children, many commonalities are apparent. These are in curriculum, the location of services, futures planning, multiagency collaboration, and family and student focus (Repetto and Correa, 1996).

This section addresses students with disabilities at both ends of the age spectrum. For those who are in the preschool years, we emphasize the family and early childhood special education, and only mention transition. For students at the end of their school careers, the concepts and practices of transition form the major focus of the chapter.

CHAPTER 15

Early Intervention

For most of the nineteenth century, educators saw early adolescence, not early childhood, as the formative years for both normal and exceptional populations. Most agreed that a commitment to mental discipline was incompatible with children under the ages of six or seven years and that school was physically, psychologically, and intellectually harmful to children younger than five or six years of age. The public schools catered to children from seven or eight years of age and up. Youngsters who were disabled went to institutional settings where they were admitted much later, at ten or twelve years of age.

In the final three decades of the nineteenth century, the view of the incapacity of young children was revised as part of the emerging child study movement. Infancy was distinguished from childhood as a discrete period of development. Children from birth to about six years of age were now seen to be active beings who required play rather than formal lessons, but this could be presented within the confines of educational settings. Kindergarten care, together with day care and nursery education, become a feature of American education in the 1880s.

Programs for young children with special needs were boosted early in the 1900s when Maria Montessori (1870–1962) began to work with retarded children in Italy. Montessori drew heavily on the sense training methods developed by Itard in his work with Victor. (See Chapter 4.)

Nineteenth-century parents had little say in their children's education; they deferred to educational experts. Throughout this century, there has been a rather slow but growing trend for parents to become more involved in the educational progress of their children.

Parent–teacher groups sprang up in the opening decades of this century. The first parent group was the National Society for Crippled Children, formed in the United States in 1921. In 1933, an Ohio group of parents of children with mental disabilities established a parents' group to advocate the legal and educational rights of disabled children. The United Cerebral Palsy Association began in 1948.

Largely because of inadequate public and professional response to their children's educational and other needs, parents began to organize more formally on a local level in the 1940s and 1950s and on a national level in the 1960s. Often in uneasy alliance with professionals, they lobbied for more effective education and more humane treatment of persons with disabilities.

Since then, parent organizations have had a tremendous impact on special education. Across Canada today, parent organizations exist at the local, provincial, and national level. Some of these groups are small, local, and casual; others are affiliated with professional organizations. Parent organizations have lobbied successfully for improved educational, social, recreational, and vocational services for their children. Parent advocacy has altered the standards of treatment in institutions, the development of community-based living facilities, personnel training, and research in prevention and amelioration of disabling conditions. Parent and professional activism has also brought to the courts the plight of children who are exceptional.

However, in the actual delivery of services, parents tended to be ignored; they were not invited to participate to any degree. Until the early 1970s, parents remained passive recipients of professional advice. Professionals made the major decisions about a child's needs and educational placement and then worked with the family and other agencies to attain the prescribed goals.

During the 1970s, professionals began to agree that parents could have a constructive impact, but involvement was typically limited to carrying out specific activities directed by the school. By the early 1980s, the traditional notion of professional expertise, which denied that parents are competent to take the initiative in regard to their child, began to change. Today, family-centred approaches emphasize that parents are chief intervenors and advocates for their own children.

All parents want their children to be born healthy, normal, and perfect, with sturdy bones, good vision, working organs and the promise of growing into a normal, intelligent, and happy person. For most parents, the wish is fulfilled; the chances are huge that a child will be born in superlative condition.

While most children are born healthy and well-formed, some parents must reduce the expectations they hold for their new infant. For them, the not-so-perfect child has been born. Their children are not like other children; they have problems that potentially threaten their physical, intellectual, social, or emotional functioning. When this happens, parents face frustrations stemming from broken dreams; the goals and hopes for the child are no longer clear and the entire family functioning is affected.

No family, regardless of wealth, education, religious persuasion, race, or physical and mental health, is immune. About three percent of newborn infants have a handicap that can be considered a developmental delay or developmental disability. Another three percent are born with significant conditions capable of causing medical or social disabilities (Berlin, 1983). For other children, problems appear later as a result of disease or accident.

The child with a disability has a major impact on the family, which usually requires modifications in family structure and roles. It is only during the past few decades that professionals have begun to fully appreciate the parental pain and stress that accompany the diagnosis of a disabling condition in a child and the degree of courage and external support that parents need to retain their equilibrium. They now realize that family problems arising from the presence of a child with a disability require as much professional attention as the educational and medical treatment of the child. Parents require assistance in understanding the nature and prognosis of the condition; in handling the child; in stimulating mobility, locomotion and communication; and in responding appropriately to different or unexpected behaviours.

In the broadest terms, work with very young children and their families is referred to as *early childhood special education*. It takes in two main processes. Early identification is designed to find the childhood disability as soon as possible. Early intervention includes a variety of educational, psychological, or therapeutic procedures aimed at infants and preschoolers. Generally, the children who benefit from early intervention are those between birth and age eight in three groups:

- disabled or developmentally delayed children who have known congenital disorders, sensory impairments, neurological dysfunctions, or significant delays in major areas of functioning;

- medically or biologically at-risk children who have a history of health factors, such as prematurity, known to be a potential threat to development;

- environmentally at-risk children who are biologically sound but whose physical or social circumstances (such as poverty, neglect, abuse) may indicate a high probability of delayed development ("CEC Position ...," 1993; Dunlap, 1989; Zeitlin and Williamson, 1986).

Parents and Families

Parenting should be counted among the most esteemed professions. But while there are many apprenticeships available for professions and careers, none exist for that most difficult job—parenting. Few study the art—or craft—and there are no courses to teach really practical methods of child-rearing, or to teach parents how to weather the crises, frustrated ambitions, and periods of high stress that are common to most families. Nonetheless, most parents manage to raise their children remarkably well. They willingly endure many trials, problems, and moments of despair, secure in the hope that one day their children will become self-sufficient adults.

Expecting parents have great dreams for their unborn child. They hope for intelligence and physical beauty and plan ahead for later accomplishments and successes. By the time the baby is born, parents are ready to provide for the infant's physical needs and have probably consulted one of the hundreds of volumes on child care and child rearing.

Typically, the birth of a child brings joy and excitement. When a parent holds a newborn close for the first time, feelings of belonging, togetherness, and attachment are cemented. The birth ends the period of expectations about the child and brings new challenges and responsibilities for parents as they adjust to the new family member (Brooks, 1987).

The diagnosis of a disabling condition in a child shatters parental aspirations. The perfect child has died and in its place is a baby with apparent and frightening problems and unknown prospects for the future. When a disability is found, a void is created that is only bridged as the family reformulates its expectations to accommodate reality. The entire family undergoes a crisis, the resolution of which determines whether they will live together in relative peace and contentment or in frustration, anger, and guilt.

The characteristics of the family—cultural background, socio-economic status, size, even religion—shape its ability to cope with a child who is exceptional. Each family's unique combination of strengths, stressors, vulnerabilities, and coping styles comes into play as the discovery of a disability in a child creates intense and conflicting feelings among the members of a family.

Looking at Families

There are a number of ways to look at families and to conceptualize the relationship of family members, the child with a disability, the care and treatment of the disabled member, the extended family, and the wider culture. Each of the theoretical frames used to view families is a little different, although they should be seen as a continuum with a different emphasis on certain factors and components of family functioning rather than different variables. Moreover, each of these ways of looking at families is important because these frameworks undergird the manner in which professionals present early intervention programs and interact with parents. Table 15-1 outlines ways of looking at families.

Stage Theories

Stage theories represent the most traditional way of examining a family that includes a member with a disability. Stage theories hold that parents pass through discrete stages before they can fully accept the child's condition (see Table 15-2). Not all parents pass through all

Table 15-1 Looking at families

Model	Principles	Major focus
Stage theory	Parents pass through discrete stages from grief to acceptance	Parent counselling
		Parent therapy
		Parent self-help groups
		Information about the condition
Life-cycle theory	Families pass through cycles in which there may be crises transition points	Transition support
		Liaison with other agencies
		Family support
		Intervention with the child
Systems theory	The family is a system within the larger social context	Priorities set by the family
		Stress on all family members
		Functional skills for the child
		Improved functioning within family needs
Social support theory	Families are systems of themselves	Families helping themselves
		Families setting priorities
		Advocating for child

Table 15-2 Parental reactions to the diagnosis of a disability

Acute initial reaction	Chronic adaptive reaction	Mature adaptation
shock	withdrawal and isolation	refashioning expectations
denial and disbelief	depression	coping with everyday practical problems
anger	ambivalence	
bitterness and shame	rejection	maximizing the child's potential
loss of self-esteem	overprotectiveness; self-sacrifice; defensiveness	protecting the interests of the whole family
inappropriate guilt, projection of blame	"doctor shopping"	
disappointment, sadness, grief, and bargaining		interaction with others

of these stages, and each person works through them at a different rate (Eden-Piercy, Blacher, and Eyman, 1986); however, most pass through similar stages before they accept the reality of their child's condition (Chinn, Winn, and Walters, 1978).

Acute initial (crisis) reactions accompany the diagnosis of a child's condition. These are mediated by the severity of the disability, the parents' socio-economic status, their religious orientation, and the quality of external and intrafamily support systems (Ormerod and Huebner, 1988).

When first confronted with their child's condition, most parents react with shock, often accompanied by denial and disbelief. The period of shock is usually brief because of the necessity for making decisions regarding treatment. Parents must be concerned with the provision of daily care for their child. They may have to arrange transportation to treatment, alter methods of scheduling time, meet new financial costs, and assimilate technical information about the disability. Parents may also have to provide support for other family members (Fortier and Wanless, 1984).

In instances of clear-cut organic damage or with conditions such as Down syndrome, the child will probably be diagnosed at birth or shortly afterwards and the parents will learn about the problem immediately. Other parents may discover a problem more slowly as the child matures and tends to lag behind others of the same age. When the problem is not detected at birth, parents may start to suspect some disability when their child is too slow in reaching developmental milestones. Parents of children with severe disabilities may not deny the handicap, especially if they themselves were the first to recognize the child's disability, as in the case of deafness (Kroth, 1987). They may even respond positively when they find that they were not imagining problems. Some mothers have described feelings of relief on the confirmation of their suspicions, not defensive reactions (Faerstein, 1986). Once the problem is verbalized and labelled, some parents find that they can mobilize both the defensive and coping mechanisms available to them. For other parents, the confirmation of a diagnosis results in a compelling need for knowledge (Hobbs, Perrin, and Ireys, 1985).

Parents' initial grief may be more intense when the diagnosis is made well after the birth of the child. By this time, their hopes for the child have lasted longer and their bonds of affection have grown stronger (Fortier and Wanless, 1984). The period of denial may be more protracted, especially if the condition is not readily obvious to the parents.

Denial may operate as a protective device, giving parents additional time to adjust to the pain and disappointment of lost expectations. Denial becomes maladaptive when it results in the withholding of treatment necessary to ensure a child's optimal development. Unwittingly, family, friends, and even professionals may support parental denial. Anxious to relieve the parents' worries, they may suggest that the child will "grow out" of the condition, and parents may delay proper treatment as a result.

Parents may also feel anger when they learn of their child's condition. In fact, anger can be the most enduring emotion among parents of children with disabilities (Hall and Richmond, 1984). Some come to believe that the world is against them, as health practitioners, teachers, neighbours, and relatives confront them with the reality they do not want to accept. Initially parents may direct their anger at the child as the obvious source of frustration. When parents turn the anger inward, they can react with fear, guilt, and shame.

Fear arises when parents hold unfounded apprehensions and incorrect information about the disability, the implications, and the prognosis. Some parents feel that the condition might be of a genetic nature and worry about their future children; others view the disability as a defect in themselves. Many parents develop understandable apprehensions about their child's future life. Major concerns are sexual, social, and occupational exploitation of their offspring.

Parents who feel shame see their child who is disabled as a threat to the family's prestige. They worry about social stigma and anticipate social rejection. Some parents feel guilt because they think the condition could have been avoided if they had done something differently. Others believe the disability serves as retribution for some misdeed. Parents ask, "Why us?" and seek answers in factors such as marital discord, prenuptial pregnancy, unusual sex practices, use of drugs, and unusual events during pregnancy.

Sometimes parents project guilt on others. They direct resentment and hostility at their spouses, their other children, the doctor, the counsellor, society in general, even God. Some parents question their religious beliefs; others find solace in them. Studies have found parents with a strong religious affiliation to be more accepting; their religious beliefs seem to sustain them through difficult situations in raising a child with an impairment (Erin, Rudin, and Njoroge, 1991; Zuk, 1962).

For other parents, having a child with a disability destabilizes their religious beliefs; they begin to question a previously held belief in God (Erin, Rudin, and Njoroge, 1991). Preconceived notions about God, fate, a just world and their implications for personal existence are often challenged (Chester and Barbarin, 1987).

Feelings of isolation are common. Gill (1994) notes that parents may be subjected to rude questions, crude comments, and withdrawal, even from formerly close friends. Once the initial sympathy fades, friends sometimes reveal a lack of understanding or interest.

Mourning or grief is a natural reaction to the disappointment of having a child with a disability. Like anger, denial, and guilt, grief follows the initial diagnosis and takes on different forms in different families. For some parents, grief results in withdrawal and depression. Others take recourse in bargaining—trying to make a deal with God, science, or society to cure their child. Grief may continue to some extent throughout the parent's life, never disappearing completely (Wikler, Wasow, and Hatfield, 1981).

With a severe disability, the family's adjustment to the idea of future dependency can be made fairly easily (Turnbull, Summers, and Brotherston, 1983). But with a milder disability, the family may find itself on a roller coaster of expectations, with hopes for the future alternately dashed and raised as the child progresses or falls back.

Some parents are never able to completely accept their child's condition. They may accept the diagnosis but reject the prognostic implications. Such parents are vulnerable to even the most unsubstantiated claims for cures or relief. They may embark on a trek from doctor to doctor and clinic to clinic in search of a more promising prognosis, miracle drugs, a new operation, a novel form of psychotherapy, or a radically new diet. Probably as many parents seek other opinions not because they reject or cannot handle their child but because they are simply seeking clarity about the problem (O'Hara and Levy, 1984). If a parent visits five professionals and obtains five different diagnoses, the ensuing confusion and need for clarification become obvious.

Some parents may reject the child as well as the condition. They may treat the child with open hostility, or use more subtle ploys, such as setting unrealistic goals or failing to praise positive behaviour. Other parents may develop positive and accepting attitudes, but nevertheless harbour resentment toward the child. Every parent must occasionally feel ambivalent about restricted activities, additional responsibilities, disappointments, and anxieties. If parents feel guilty about their ambivalent feelings, they may become overprotective and oversolicitous and try to compensate for their negative feelings with a life of martyrdom and self-sacrifice.

Such attitudes can foster an overdependency in the child, which will eventually become circuitous. In the course of investing themselves emotionally in the child, these parents exaggerate the child's needs and promote an overly dependent attitude. Then, to prove their worth as parents, they allow their whole lives to become centred on the child. Such parents may actually resist attempts by others to ease the burden.

Most parents reach a stage of mature adaptation which is the end of the crisis period. However, acceptance does not come all at once; it begins fleetingly and goes on to fluctuate at different levels in different situations. Parental sadness may resurface at critical junctures in the life of the child and the family. A re-occurrence of sorrow and frustration may be triggered by milestones such as reaching school age, attaining puberty, and watching other children graduate from school or marry.

When parents have reached this stage, they can accept the child, the disability, and themselves. They become reconciled to the fact that their child's condition deeply affects, and will continue to affect, the entire family. As one mother explains,

> The whole process of having a handicapped child hurts. It's not the greatest thing on the face of the earth, but life throws these little curves at us and we can make our adjustments if we have good supports. Then, having a handicapped child becomes just like having any other child in the family. You deal with the problems that come along just as for any child (Wilgosh, 1990, p. 302).

Parents do not differ significantly in their level of acceptance (McLinden, 1990). Some earlier studies indicated lack of involvement with and acceptance of the child by the father (e.g. Farber and Ryckman, 1965). Investigators found that fathers, more than mothers, were affected in the social domain. Fathers had more difficulty coping with the child, were more vulnerable to social stigma, and encountered more difficulty living with the uncertainty of the child's impairment and discussing the problem with friends (Erickson, 1976). Later, Moran (1982) reported fathers to be positively involved with the child with a disability, playing and helping with their daily care. However, it still seems that fathers are more likely to show extreme patterns of great involvement or withdrawal than mothers; such extreme patterns are found more often when a son rather than a daughter has a disability (Lamb and Meyer, 1991).

Life-cycle Approach

Instead of adopting a stage approach, some researchers tend to view the family and the impact of a member with a disability through a life-cycle or life-span approach. A life-cycle perspective sees the family as a unit that is moving through time and experiencing a series of events, tasks, and transitions. By looking at the family life cycle, it can be seen that the impact of the child with a disability on the family changes over time.

Life-cycle transitions are experienced by all families, and there seem to be specific periods which result in increased stress (Wikler, Wasow, and Hatfield, 1981). For all families with children, these are the age at which the child should begin to walk; the age at which the child should begin to talk; entry into the public school system; onset of puberty; and the twenty-first birthday. When a child with a disability is a member of the family, transitions may also include events such as first encountering the disability; early childhood; school entry; when the development of a younger sibling surpasses that of the disabled child; when placement outside the home is considered; when a child-management crisis occurs; adolescence; beginning adult life; maintaining adult life; and when guardianship issues are discussed. These events can serve to magnify a child's special needs and create heightened stress in the family.

Systems Approach

Currently, a systems approach is seen as the most appropriate way to view families with a disabled member. A systems theory or perspective sees a family as more than individuals bound by a biological relationship. It recognizes that actions in any part of the system affect the other parts and that solutions to problems can only be found when the problem is properly defined in its larger environmental context.

Under a systems model, influences are seen as multidirectional. Each adult and child influences every member of the household and each family relationship affects all the other family members. Therefore, whether the family is nuclear, single-parent, or extended, it plays a powerful role in the child's social, emotional, behavioural, and academic development and progress. The outcomes of any child-rearing patterns on any child depend on many factors that interact with each other. These include the child's age, sex, and temperament; the parents' personality characteristics, personal history, economic circumstances, and so on; the needs of family members; and the values of the culture.

The relationship between the child who is exceptional and the family is reciprocal; the child deeply affects the family climate, while the family, in turn, affects the child. Interaction with family members deeply influences the child's opportunities and barriers, challenges and expectations, ambitions and frustrations, and general quality of life.

Social Support Approach

In many ways, the social support approach overlaps the systems approach; the difference is mainly one of emphasis. Whereas a systems approach focuses chiefly on the social context of the family, a social support approach focuses on a family's functioning in four family sub-systems—marital, sibling, parental, and extra-familial (Carter and McGoldrick, 1980). It stresses families helping themselves and sees informal supports such as the extended family and church as more important than formal support.

Family support approaches include two major concepts—embeddedness and social networks influence. Embeddedness refers to the way that a developing child is enveloped within the family system and its members, and the way that the family unit is embedded in broader social units consisting of relatives, friends, neighbours, church members, and so on. These people—the family's social network—directly and indirectly influence both the family and the child (Dunst, Trivette, Hamby, and Pollock, 1990).

Support networks may be more important for mothers than fathers. A study investigated the differences between mothers and fathers in the areas of social support and family satisfaction, and in their reported frequency-of-occurrence and degree-of-problem of events and feelings related to the presence of a child with special needs. It found that mothers had a higher frequency of demands placed on their lives than did fathers and also experienced more negative physical and emotional states (McLinden, 1990).

The Condition

Another way to look at families is on the basis of the type of condition. This is not a theoretical model or approach, but it does recognize that the nature of a child's disability can have a substantial impact on parental stress and levels of acceptance. Researchers (Frey, Greenberg, and Fewell, 1989) have found that a child's characteristics predict the amount of stress that parents report and the amount of psychological stress reported by fathers.

Most observers conclude that raising a child with a disability is often burdensome, tiresome, and frustrating. High levels of family stress may be created by a particular child's slower progress, more difficult temperament, lack of social responsiveness, stereotypical behaviour patterns, or additional or unusual caregiving needs. Research in families with infants indicates that role confusion, social isolation, fatigue, financial worries, and lack of information on child development are cited by new mothers as primary causes of stress (Salisbury, 1987). Behaviours that parents of disabled infants have identified as most difficult, stressful, or uncomfortable are crying, resisting being held, being hard to soothe, passive non-responsiveness, tuning out, and emitting atypical motor responses.

Symptoms of stress are more evident among parents of children with delayed rather than prompt diagnoses and with unknown rather than specified etiologies (Goldberg, Marcovitch, MacGregor, and Lojkasek, 1986). Stress is also more evident among families when the child has a severe or profound rather than a mild or moderate condition (Frey, Greenberg, and Fewell, 1989). Studies have found greater stress reported by parents of boys and of children with limited communication skills (Frey, Greenburg, and Fewell, 1989).

Stress may occur from the outset if the attachment process between infants with disabilities and their parents is disrupted. Premature and disabled infants may be kept in neonatal intensive care for up to twelve weeks, depending on birth weight, gestational age, physical anomalies, respiration, and weight gain. Later, children who show disturbed interactions include preterm, Down syndrome, blind, autistic, and failure-to-thrive infants (Field, 1983). Such infants are less responsive than others, and parents need to work harder to focus their attention and generate smiles and contented vocalizations.

Children with problems such as Fetal Alcohol Syndrome, Down syndrome, and cleft palate may have feeding problems and limited abilities to suck, bite, chew, or swallow. Feeding problems are common among infants who are autistic, beginning with poor nursing habits and continuing through infancy and childhood.

Some disruption may arise from the medical needs of a child. Children with chronic conditions such as cystic fibrosis require intense medical and therapeutic intervention.

The age of the child may also be related to the stress felt by the family. One mother pointed out that "the stress level of women with handicapped children increases as the child gets older" (Wilgosh, 1990, p. 302). If a child who is severely disabled does not develop sufficient independence and autonomy, that child may permanently occupy the social position of the youngest in the family—the perpetual baby who never emerges from infantile status. This can easily become elevated to a source of conflict and difficulty. As well, as they grow older, children become harder to manage. At the same time, the gap between the progress of children who are exceptional and their peers becomes more noticeable.

Parents with exceptional children must also take on new roles—educator, lobbyist, advocate, therapist and, of course, chauffeur. In addition, financial burdens can cause parents constant concern and frustration. The need for special equipment, special medical care, and special programs often brings financial hardship. Economic pressures can distort the family's emotional response to their child, particularly in families with limited financial resources.

Specific Conditions

The discovery that a child is severely intellectually disabled causes great stress for the parents and other family members. Across all socio-economic levels, mothers of children who are mentally retarded report depression (Breslau and Davis, 1986). Parents must eventually confront three critical issues. They must decide how to train and educate the child, accept that the child may never be self-sufficient, and plan for the child's future.

Parents of children with learning disabilities may seem, at first glance, much more fortunate than parents of children with more severe disabilities. In fact, when a child is identified as learning disabled, parents may feel relieved, hoping this identification will lead to solutions that will eliminate the child's learning or behaviour problem (Bos and Vaughn, 1988). However, learning disabilities create much confusion within a family. Families may experience increased parental stress, family routines may be altered, and sibling interactions may be disrupted to some extent (Dyson, 1996; Waggoner and Wilgosh, 1990). In particular, a lack of clear diagnosis causes great concern and anxiety, resulting in high levels of stress for parents. Faerstein (1986), for example, found that a gap of 3.5 years elapsed between the time a learning disability was suspected and its diagnosis. This gap was not due to the mother's lack of responsibility, but more often to others who denied the child's problem and averred that he or she would outgrow it.

The receptive and expressive language problems of children who are learning disabled may cause them to appear slow, confused, impulsive, inattentive, or even obstinate. Parents may react to these problems with guilt, overprotection, rejection, or concern. Some parents react by placing too much responsibility on the child; others deny the gravity of the problem. Still others place responsibility on themselves and accept failure.

Deafness is often suspected when children are about twelve months of age and expected to say their first words. Ross (1990) found that many mothers, especially of children with profound deafness, suspected a loss before the child was one year old. Deaf children with hearing parents comprise more than 90 percent of the deaf population. Hearing parents are much more likely than deaf parents to view their child's diagnosis as a tragic crisis. Hearing parents often express feelings of incompetence, self-doubt, and sorrow. In some cases, the birth of a child with a hearing impairment threatens family integration and destroys the balance of family relationships (Meadow, 1980). The profile of Diana shows how the parents of a hearing-impaired child coped.

Parents of children with clefts often worry about the physical manifestations and social stigma, while emotional and social development are harmed by parents' feelings of guilt that the deformity is their fault. Of particular concern to parents are the child's appearance; the need for immediate surgery and regular and protracted contact with physicians; speech development; fears that the child may choke during feeding; reaction of the spouse, siblings, family and friends; intellectual development; financial considerations; and a recurrence of the defect in

Profile

Diana

Diana is three years old and attends a preschool for hearing-impaired children five mornings a week. Diana's profound sensorineural hearing loss was diagnosed at 20 months. Since that time, she has been fitted with a hearing aid that she tolerates but does not yet appreciate.

Diana was two months premature and spent her early weeks in an incubator. Her mother suspected a hearing impairment by about eight months when Diana seemed impervious to cleaning, vacuuming, or telephone sounds. As Diana grew, she reached all the physical developmental milestones and became a sociable, gregarious child.

At age two-and-a-half, Diana's expressive language was restricted to two words—*ma* for all her wants, and *moo* for a special doll. Receptively, she responded consistently to her own name and *no*. Diana also began to develop her own unique set of gestures and actions to convey meaning to her listeners.

Diana's parents decided to enroll her in a total communication preschool program. This decision had more to do with geography than to adherence to any one philosophy of communication. Although the parents would desperately like Diana to speak and not sign, a total communication program was in the area. As well, the parents now realize that language acquisition is the important goal, whatever the mode.

Diana's preschool teachers have set her several long-range goals. These include the introduction of simple nouns, verbs and colour signs; some awareness of gross sounds through play activities and listening exercises; and increased vocalizations. They have also structured many activities to expose Diana to language, such as story telling, "dress up," and art and craft activities. Diana's teachers will show her parents how to stimulate home communication and use home-making activities to present language. Diana's parents will be encouraged to learn sign language so that they can communicate more effectively with their daughter.

future children. Very often, parents are anxious about possible mental retardation in the child as well as the physical defect (Vanpoerlvoorde and Shaughnessy, 1991).

Many parents of infants with severe visual impairments feel anxious and apprehensive, even grief-stricken, when they learn of their child's disability. Parents may be worried and frustrated by the infant's responses, or seeming lack of responses.

Maternal interaction behaviour has been an important focus of research with children with visual impairments. Attachment behaviours between infants and parents are facilitated by the infant's ability to elicit parental responses, but very young visually impaired children do not always react to their parents in the same way that sighted children do (Ferrell, 1985). For example, babies who are blind do not reach out in the "Pick me up" gesture seen in sighted babies at about five months. The facial expressions of babies who are blind are less varied and less frequently seen; they smile significantly less frequently than sighted ones, and the mother's voice does not automatically and consistently evoke smiling. Babies who are blind vocalize much less frequently than do sighted babies, and their vocalizations to initiate contact with parents appear much later, even when families encourage such interaction and reward it (Fraiberg, 1977).

Of all caretaking demands, none seems to have more impact than the demands of coping with a child who has a behavioural problem. When parents cannot handle or control the child fully, the integrity of the family is threatened. Parents can become physically and emotionally exhausted. Preschoolers with behavioural disorders may be somewhat more fussy and irritable than normal. They may exhibit irregular patterns of eating and sleeping and abusive, destructive, cantankerous behaviour that causes disruption and disharmony in the home.

Parents of children with special health care needs suffer many traumas and stresses. Family reactions include depression, denial, anxiety, resentment, and anger. Moreover, illnesses such as cystic fibrosis are an affront to an assumed developmental order for the family life cycle; parents must confront the abbreviated life expectancy of the child; some must handle the additional stress of a dying child.

When conventional medical treatment fails, parents of children with serious health disabilities sometimes hunt for miracle cures and faith healers. They may focus normal feelings of anger upon medical personnel, other family members, or any other available target. They may experience feelings of guilt, believing they should have noticed symptoms sooner or been more lenient in their discipline. Parents often transmit their anxiety to the child. They may also create conflict and jealousy among siblings by spending a disproportionate amount of time with the special child.

Raising and training a psychotic or autistic child can cause enormous stress for parents and family. Caregivers must contend with the bizarre withdrawn attitudes of autism or the clinging behaviours of schizophrenia. Children who are autistic are likely to ignore the presence of their mother or other family members, and the parents are continually faced with their children's failure to respond to interaction. The deviant gaze pattern, known as *gaze aversion* (the failure to look directly at another individual) is a conspicuous characteristic of children who are autistic and severely hinders parent–child interaction. As well, children tend to show little response to their mother's voice, do not anticipate being picked up, and do not adapt their body postures to the people holding them. These behaviours inevitably have a deep effect on parental interaction and are compounded in later years by the children's lack of verbal responsiveness and bizarre and inappropriate behaviours.

For the parents, the child who is gifted may be both a blessing and a burden. Although giftedness is socially acceptable, giftedness is not without stigma and other potentially troublesome psychosocial correlates (Kauffman, 1997). Many parents of children who are gifted are bewildered and frustrated about issues related to both home and school. We can see a little of this in the father's letter about his young son.

The advent of a child who is gifted can alter normal parental roles. Ross (1979) hypothesized that the degree of a gifted child's impact on traditional family roles is directly related to the degree of discrepancy between the child's intellectual capacity and that of other family members. Parents sometimes have difficulty clarifying the differences between parent and child roles. They wonder whether they should treat their offspring as a child or as an adult.

Parents may treat the child differently. The family of a gifted child may wish to make special adaptations that can include costly and time-consuming measures, such as special schools and extra equipment. When special adaptations are made for the child, sibling competition and jealousy may result. Siblings may resent the extra money and attention spent by their parents. Moreover, if parents give the preschooler who is gifted too much attention, that child may later meet difficulties in coping with sibling and peer competition (Rimm and

Profile

Gerry

Dear Gerry,

Sorry that I haven't written for a while but you know how it is; have been busy with the boys, especially Gerry the Younger. In fact, it's because of Gerry that I'm writing to you tonight. The boys got your package today. John really liked the whip. Made of elephant hair, eh? The African headgear that you sent Gerry, though! Now that was really something else.

The interesting thing was that he knows all about the thing, how it was made, history, symbolism, the works. I gather he saw a picture of one of them in one of those books you left at the house and read up on it. It's downright disturbing what that kid knows. After all, he's only eight years old and in grade three but he reads better than John, who's two years older. Now, I'm not saying that the kid can read a university book on Africa and extract all the information, but he did read some of it and understood a whole lot more. He remembers all of it, too. And he never shuts up about it. Question, question, question, talk, talk, talk! The kid is really something special.

I know that all parents say that but in this case it's true. He's a ball of energy, always poking into things, always doing or saying something weird. Always asking "Why?" Makes me feel like a jerk sometimes. Most of the stuff he asks I don't know "why." You know what the young Mr. Spock's latest interest is? My computer. He and John are playing games on it. I've had the thing for three years and I can't get it to do that. Gerry said he learned how to do it in school. He's in grade three. I was in grade eleven before I learned to use a slide rule. I take that back—I never learned how to use a slide rule.

Mixed feeling time, old buddy. I feel kind of not up to the job of raising the kid. I know he'll be more on the ball than his old man ever was. But on the other hand, I'm proud of him. Another thing is that I sometimes think I'm spending too much time and money on Gerry at the expense of Number One Son. I know John sometimes resents his kid brother, but then again he won't let anyone kick sand in the kid's face.
So long, buddy, John.

Lowe, 1988). Finally, parents of children who are gifted often have to choose between regular class placement and special programming—and even experts cannot agree on which is the best option.

Siblings

Brothers and sisters play important parts in the entire family drama; indeed, "The fabric of the family is hard to imagine without the complex, frustrating, joy-inducing realities of siblings" (Cramer, Erzkus, Mayweather, Pope, Roeder, and Tone, 47).

Siblings have a profound influence on each other's social and emotional development. Of the huge host of variables that affect sibling relationships, some of the most important are family size, birth order, gender, responsibilities and roles of all family members, temperaments, feelings and perceptions of self, personalities and their match, personal values and attitudes, and style. Further, there is style and effectiveness of communication, expression or lack of expression of feelings, time management, perceived and actual favouritism, type of control exerted in the household, economic and marital status, marital harmony, competition and rivalry, outside stress and coping mechanisms, parenting and caregiving styles, and parents' attitudes toward themselves, one another, and their children (Atkins, 1987).

Parent roles change with the advent of a child with a disability, and it is obvious that sibling relationships will also change and take on special significance when one sibling is disabled. However, although the points of view of parents have been investigated in depth,

Gifted children are advantaged in many ways, but they may cause disruption within the family.

research has largely overlooked the possible consequences to children of having a sibling with a disability. The general picture of sibling interaction is bland; it simply tells us that the outcomes for the other children can range from very little effect to very positive or very negative ones (Yura, 1987).

Some research has looked at more specific interactions and finds differences in the following groupings:

- Role confusion. The relationship between siblings is special and intimate, particularly during childhood when siblings serve each other as playmates, models for identification, caretakers, and socializing agents. When a child has a disability, the roles a sibling normally assumes are somehow altered. A child with a disability may not function as a playmate, a caretaker, or a socializing agent for his or her siblings.

- The kind and amount of attention the child who is disabled requires of parents and siblings. The parents' attempts to protect the child with a disability may result in various degrees of neglect for the other children in the family and may interfere with their normal child–parent relationship, with family activity, and with social life outside the home. Researchers (Cantwell, Baker, and Rutter, 1979) found that mothers spent twice as much time in concentrated interaction with the child with a disability as they did with normally developing siblings.

- Disappointment at not having a normal sibling. Children share their parents' anticipation and excitement about a new addition to the family; they also share the grief, stress, and pain that accompanies the birth of a brother or sister who is disabled (Milstead, 1988; Seligman, 1991).

- The embarrassment of relating to the disabled sibling in the company of peers or in public. The presence of a sibling with a physical disability, for example, may lead to "de-identification" (see Neal and MacLean, 1995). Children may feel that they are viewed as flawed or weird by others because there is a disability in their family (Gill, 1994).

- The heavy demands on normal siblings to care for the child. In some families, the child who is disabled may generate caretaking responsibilities and siblings may become overworked caretakers. Females, especially older sisters, are more likely to be adversely affected. Older sisters with siblings who are intellectually disabled, for example, assume multiple caretaking responsibilities and frequently assume a teacher role (Brody, Stoneman, Davis, and Crapps, 1991; Stoneman, Brody, Davis, and Crapps, 1988).

  When normally developing siblings are required to supervise, care for, defend, and protect the child with a disability, resentment often develops. Excessive responsibility for caretaking by siblings is related to anger, guilt, increased sibling conflict, decreased opportunities for peer contacts and out-of-home activities and, quite possibly, subsequent psychological damage (Seligman, 1991; Stoneman et al., 1988).

- The pressure on the normal child to "make up for" the deficits in the child who is disabled. Siblings may find themselves recipients of uneven expectation standards as compensation for parental disappointment. Sometimes, children are made to bear unrealistically high parental expectations. Or they may be expected to repress their abilities so that they do not perform better than the child who is special.

- Some parents have different ways of treating the normally developing children and the child with a disability. Because parents feel uncertainty regarding the care and management of a child who is disabled, they may subject that child to patterns of socialization that are significantly different from those that operate in the case of the other children. They may allow two quite different disciplinary systems to run side by side—one for the siblings and a more lenient, permissive one for the child who is disabled. Some parents treat their children with disabilities as though they were ill; they give them fewer responsibilities, place fewer restrictions on behaviour, and are more tolerant of undesirable behaviour, often at the expense of other siblings. Two different sets of rules intensify sibling rivalry. A twelve-year-old sister of a child with a hearing impairment complained, "I have to clean up my room and Mom cleans up Sherry's. That's just not fair. Her ears don't work, but her hands do" (Atkins, 1987, p. 38).

- Resentment is aggravated when additional care expenses deprive the others of educational and recreational opportunities. Siblings share family resources and the sibling relationship may be negatively affected by the additional resources required by the special child (Dyson and Fewell, 1989).

- There are only a few empirical studies on the self-concept of the siblings of children with disabilities, and their results are conflicting. Some research has found that children who have siblings with disabilities scored more poorly than children with non-disabled siblings on almost every measure of internalized adjustment problems. Others have found lower than average self-concept in siblings of children with physical disabilities (Harvey and Greenway, 1984) and with diabetes (Ferrari, 1987). In contrast, a study of 74 American and Canadian children with disabilities and normal siblings (Dyson and Fewell, 1989) showed no differences in level of self-concept. Other research finds no difference in the self-concept of siblings of chronically ill (Ferrari, 1984) and developmentally disabled (Lobato, Barbour, Hall, and Miller, 1987) children. One study (Gayton, Friedman, Tavormina, and Tucker, 1977) found higher than average self-concept in the siblings of children with cystic fibrosis.

The Extended Family

Children with disabilities have a considerable influence on the extended family. At the same time, the extended family may influence the development of children who are disabled through direct interactions and through the nature of the support provided to their parents.

There exists relatively little research on the grandparents of normal children, much less the grandparents of children with disabilities. However, in many ways, grandchildren provide a new lease on life for their grandparents. The sense of surviving through the grandchild may help soothe the increasing infirmities of advancing age and the approaching reality of death. Grandchildren also allow grandparents to relive the joys of their own early parenthood. Playing with and caring for young grandchildren supplies grandparents with a revitalized feeling of importance and purpose in life (Gabel and Kotsch, 1981).

Like parents, grandparents hope for a healthy, normal baby. When a child is diagnosed as exceptional, they too may experience a death of expectations (Berns, 1980) that can leave them with a diminished capacity to provide support for the child's parents.

Generally, more support is provided by the maternal than the paternal grandmother (Harris, Handleman, and Palmer, 1985). Such support is consistent with the maternal grandmother's understanding of her daughter's distress. On the other hand, some paternal grand-

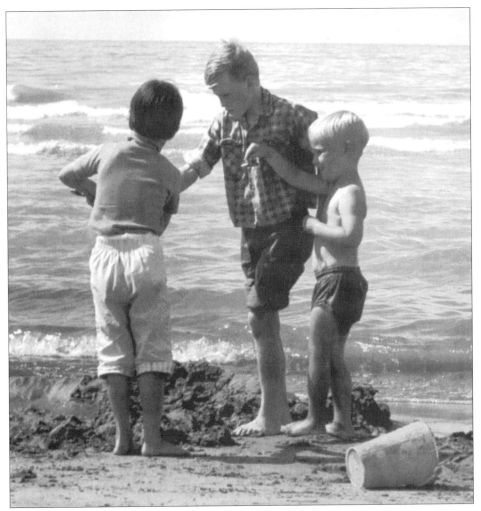

The relationship between siblings is particularly close during childhood, a time when children serve each other as playmates, role models, and caregivers.

mothers express their resentment toward their daughters-in-law. Pieper (1976) described how her mother-in-law lashed out in anger when presented with a grandchild with a disability. The grandmother blamed the daughter-in-law for having bad blood and burdening her husband with such a child.

Early Childhood Special Education

We use the phrase early childhood special education (ECSE) to encompass two major processes—early identification and early intervention. These processes are not exclusive but natural corollaries. Early identification serves no purpose if it is not followed by early intervention, and appropriate early intervention rests on accurate identification.

ECSE is a relatively new field. Although efforts to intervene early actually date from preschool programs for children who were deaf in the 1880s, the term and concept were only formalized in 1986. This is explained in the Research Notes.

Research Notes

The Formalization of Early Intervention

In the late 1960s, the disciplines of regular early childhood education, special education, and ameliorative programs such as Head Start began to draw together. The result was an entirely new field, early childhood special education, formalized by federal legislation in the United States in 1986.

Public Law 99-457, the Handicapped Children's Protection Act, an amendment of PL94-142, and IDEA of 1990, underlie the rights afforded parents of preschoolers with disabilities. IDEA contains three critical sections: Part H; Part B, section 619; and the Early Education Program for Children with Disabilities (EEPCD). These deal specifically with children with disabilities under the age of five and their families.

Of the many provisions in PL 99-452 and IDEA, one of the most important is the mandate for the full inclusion of families in any decisions relating to the preschool child or infant with a disability. To ac-complish this, all intervenors must complete and comply with an Individual Family Services Plan (IFSP), which is akin to the IEP used for school-aged children.

PL 99-457 has been described as "the most important legislation ever enacted for developmentally vulnerable young children" (Shonkoff and Meisels, 1990, p. 19) and has intensified concerns and interest about early intervention in the United States, in Canada, and elsewhere. Canada does not have comprehensive legislation on service provision for children under the age of five with special needs. In Canada, programs for preschoolers generally fall under provincial departments of social services or health and are covered by provincial legislation in these areas. Nevertheless, the influence of PL 99-457 has seen ECSE become an important component of special education in this country.

Given the field's newness and rapid expansion, the education and training of infants and preschoolers with disabilities is an area characterized by innovation and creativity. It also encompasses a variety of program models, many trends and movements, and not a little controversy. Studies of early intervention programs cannot conclusively document positive effects for a range of problems and disability groups. Although the integration of children with exceptionalities with their normally developing peers is clearly the most appropriate option for many children, controversy and discussion still cloud the issue. However, the major issues today do not revolve around the question of whether or not to provide early intervention programs but rather focus on the most effective and efficient types of intervention. We present some of the arguments in the Matter of Debate feature below.

Early Identification

Early identification is the practice of screening infants and young children in an attempt to identify those likely to experience problems in learning or behaviour. Assessing very young children with disabilities is a necessary and fundamental activity for teachers, therapists, and other professionals in early intervention (Bailey and Wolery, 1989). However, early identifi-

A Matter of Debate

Early Intervention

✔ Arguments in favour of early intervention

In 52 reviews of early intervention efficacy studies, 92 percent of the reviews concluded that early intervention provided significant immediate effects for children who are disabled, at risk, or disadvantaged (White, Bush, and Casto, 1986).

Outcomes for children are better in integrated rather than segregated programs. Children in segregated programs often miss the potential social and cognitive benefits of integration.

Language abilities improve in integrated programs. Studies, for example, document substantial changes in language abilities of preschool children with autism exposed to an intensive language stimulation program (Harris, Handleman, Kristoff, Bass, and Gordon, 1990).

Segregated early intervention programs may make young children with disabilities overly dependent on adults and make their transition to school or kindergarten more difficult (Hamachek and Kauffman, 1994).

Increased hours of programming are associated with greater gains.

Earlier is better. That is, children seem to do better if intervention is begun before 36 months of age.

When Shonkoff and Hauser-Cram (1987) studied a group of newborn to three-year-old children, they indicated that more mildly handicapped children had better outcomes if they were enrolled in early intervention programs before six months of age.

✘ Arguments against early intervention

Critics of early intervention complain that too much has been claimed and too little proven concerning the efficacy of early intervention.

Studies have failed to find adequate relationships between the intensity of intervention and the age of start and effect size. There are no conclusive data to indicate that intense and very early intervention is truly beneficial to a child.

Casto and Mastropieri (1986) provided no support to the principle that "earlier is better" and found that children's progress did not differ given the time that intervention was initiated.

Children in specialized settings obtain assistance for their specific disabilities.

Edmister and Ekstrand (1987) point out that "generally, the only documented benefit from integration of handicapped and non-handicapped preschool-

aged children seems to be in the social domain" (p. 133).

The major difference between regular and special education deals with the extent to which a teacher directs learning activities. Children with special needs require more intentional instruction to optimize their growth and development. Sustained social outcomes in integrated settings have been found only when interaction is frequent, planned, and carefully orchestrated by teachers. In and of itself, regular early childhood education is not designed to intervene with young children with special needs.

The successful teaching of children with disabilities demands that trained professionals be equipped with skills for dealing with their unique characteristics and needs. But early childhood education is not designed to handle children with special needs.

Most teachers in general, and preschool and day-care teachers in particular, are not trained to serve children with disabilities (Rule, Killoran, Stowitschek, Innocenti, Striefel, and Biswell, 1985).

Research clearly indicates that personnel who are well-trained are more effective than those who are not (Tingey-Michaelis, 1985). But most typical preschools do not have the rich training and staffing resources that might facilitate inclusion of children with special needs (Peck, Palyo, Bettencourt, Cooke, and Apolloni, 1988).

cation is even broader than the practices seen with school-aged children. Personnel must be acquainted with procedures for assessing infants, toddlers, and preschoolers across a variety of domains and also for assessing family functioning and the child's environment.

Why assess so early? The early assessment of young children serves to collect data and target skills that will increase options for the child's participation in present and future environments. It is based on the assumption that early identification will lead to an individual program plan that will either prevent or diminish the effects of an inappropriate education. Lacking early assessment, a child may experience years of failure before a diagnosis is reached. Children may also develop secondary conditions, such as behavioural disorders.

Infant Identification

The identification of atypical or high-risk infants and their needs is critical to the provision of appropriate early intervention. The chief purpose of infant assessment is to provide information regarding an infant's strengths and weaknesses in order to plan intervention.

Observation is a primary assessment strategy. A trained observer may be able to distinguish signs of sensory or neurological problems, for example. Observation also provides an assessment of the child's strengths and needs related to a particular home and/or community activity that is identified as a concern to families; for example, feeding behaviours or behaviour while shopping.

There are no tests available that adequately assess intelligence in the newborn or reliably predict later intellectual development. Measures designed to assess an infant's developmental state make use of sensorimotor tasks—gross motor behaviour, vocalization, and language behaviour. Generally, a six-month-old would be assessed on recognition of people and objects, motor co-ordination, alertness, awareness of the environment, and vocalization.

Preschool Assessment

In infants and preschoolers, screening is used to look for maturational lags and problems that can be improved through early intervention. Before examiners can assess a child, they must know what behaviours they expect to observe. To test a three-year-old, they must focus on behaviour usually exhibited by two- to four-year-olds. These might include speaking in sentences of four to six words, building three-block pyramids, matching similar pictures, or buttoning. Problem behaviours might include poor attention span or failure to respond to oral language and visual symbols. A child who is out of touch with the environment may manifest poor motor control, low body image, and poor visual and auditory discrimination.

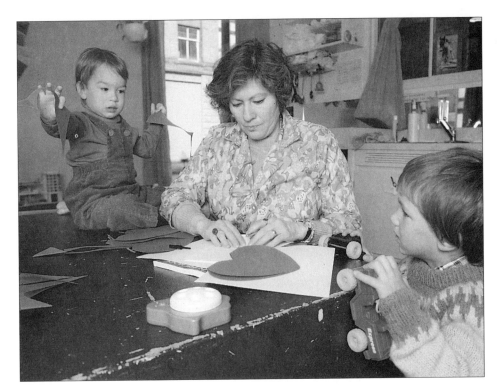

Very young exceptional children usually receive their education in regular classes.

Observations of how a child functions in a setting such as a nursery school provides essential information about the child's progress and the effectiveness of the program. As well, it gives information to others involved with the child. An audiologist, for example, needs data on how a child is responding with specific amplification.

Together with observations, early childhood personnel may use a variety of standardized measures. Diagnosticians involved in early identification frequently use developmental checklists, rating scales, readiness measures, and basic concept inventories. They also use such scales as the Denver Developmental Screening Test (Frankenberg, Dodds, Archer, Bresnick, Maschka, Edelman, and Shapiro, 1990), the Boehm Test of Basic Concepts (Boehm, 1986), or the Metropolitan Readiness Test (Nurss and McGauvren, 1976).

Kindergarten Assessment

In kindergarten, as at the preschool level, the observation of behaviour serves as a valuable indicator of potential learning problems. Screening is used to identify children who do not possess the readiness skills needed to perform well in a structured school environment.

Readiness tests attempt to assess a child's readiness for academic learning in specific areas of school achievement as well as potential academic difficulties. For example, reading readiness tests typically include subtests of letter recognition, shape perception, sound–symbol correspondences, and oral vocabulary.

Do remember our warning from Chapter 5 about children with maturational lags. Kindergarten screening procedures may identify maturational lags but they should not be used to inappropriately label children early in their school careers.

Family Needs Assessment

Family needs refers to a family's expressed desire for services to be obtained or outcomes to be achieved (Bailey and Blanco, 1990, p. 196). Family needs are determined by a needs assessment, a process that helps to identify and examine both values and information. A needs assessment evaluates current conditions and needs in a family and provides information on what the parents' goals are for their child and for potential parent involvement in the early intervention program.

A parent interview is one mechanism used to determine family needs. In interviews, intervenors can explore child-rearing methods, discipline, the opportunities for learning in the home, and parental attitudes and perceptions about the child's behaviour and skills. Professionals and family members can then discuss questions such as: Are there specific home and/or community activities that are concerns for family members? What skills would family members like the child to learn or to do more often? What behaviours would family members like the child to do less often? Which of these concerns are priorities for family members? (Cordesco and Laus, 1993).

Few formal instruments are available to use with families, and tools from other fields may be applicable. For example, the Impact on Family Scale (IFS) (Stein and Riessman, 1978) was developed to assess the impact of a child's illness on a family. The IFS can be used because of the similarities between parents of ill children and those of children with disabilities. The tool assesses negative effects (strain) and positive effects (coping).

Early Intervention

Early intervention occurs at much the same time as early identification. There are many types of intervention provided by different people in different settings.

Why Early?

The first issue in early intervention is overarching. The question is, "Why intervene early?" The answer is complex and includes the following:

- Research in child development clearly demonstrates that the early years are a time of rapid learning. Benjamin Bloom (1964), for example, summarized a plethora of studies on intellectual growth and suggested that a stimulating environment is critical to optimal cognitive growth. He proposed that intellectual development can be seen as following a negative growth curve; as the child grows older, a rich and diverse environment has a decreasingly positive effect. Thus, children at the age of three will benefit more from enrichment activities than children aged eight to ten.

- Early intervention can "help ensure that all young children reach their full developmental potential; that they can become valued and full participants in their families, schools and communities; and that their families benefit from consistent and supportive collaboration with service providers" (see CEC Position, 1993b).

- Early services can maximize skill development and reduce or alleviate the need for special services when a child enters school (Guralnick, 1989). Both developmental and educational intervention are likely to be more effective if they occur before the child's deficiencies become massive and are compounded by the numbing effects of extended school failure. In fact, the earlier intervention is started, the higher the rate of later educational attainment (Bloom, 1991).

- Intervention sustains growth. Among preschoolers, for example, Down syndrome is the most frequent specific diagnosis in the population of delayed children (Lojkasek, Goldberg, Marcovitch, and MacGregor, 1990). For children with Down syndrome, early and sustained intervention halts the decline in cognitive development that typically occurs during the first twelve to eighteen months of life (see Guralnick and Bricker, 1987) and appears to prevent further decreases throughout the remaining early childhood years. Similar outcomes have been observed for the motor development of children with cerebral palsy (Palmer, Shapiro, Wachtel, Allen, Hiller, Harryman, Master, Meinert, and Capute, 1988).

- For the family, early intervention serves as a support that enhances family functioning, provides crucial information for parents, and makes parents the primary players in their child's developmental progress. Activities are designed to support families to the greatest extent possible. These family-centred activities optimally include the siblings and the extended family as well as the parents. In one study of the parents of children with disabilities (Winton and Turnbull, 1981), approximately two-thirds of the parents surveyed felt that the major value of early intervention was to provide a break from their continuous responsibility for the child.

- For the school-age child, the prime time for intervention is before the end of grade three. Young children learn inappropriate strategies that soon become habitual and which can present an almost insurmountable obstacle to remediation. Teachers are well aware, for example, of how difficult it is to change the way children form letters once they have internalized incorrect formations.

Achievement levels in third grade seem to have particular predictive value. If reading is still poor at the end of the third grade, then the prognosis for subsequent rapid gains is bleak (Badian, 1988). Indeed, it has been estimated that only 10 to 15 percent of children who first receive remediation in grades five to seven can be brought up to regular classroom work (Strag, 1972).

Where Should Intervention Take Place?

Infants and preschoolers with disabilities may be served in the home, in clinic settings, in separate specialized programs, or within the regular complex of childcare facilities. Those in the five to eight years of age range will be in regular schools and classrooms.

Infant Programs

Infants and toddlers are often served in centre-based (or clinic-based) programs which are typically specialized, serving only children with disabilities and their families. In centre-based programs, families bring their infant or toddler to a program or an agency setting where appropriate services are provided by professionals and paraprofessionals. Regular intervention sessions are scheduled either on an individual basis for infants or in small groups for toddlers. Most programs tend to follow developmental and therapeutic models in their curricula. A professional related to a discipline in the child's area of most significant need is the primary intervenor.

While many infant programs are clinic-based, educators more often support the idea that early intervention for infants and toddlers takes place in the home and/or uses the home as a basis for curricular objectives. They argue that the home is the natural environment for infants and toddlers and therefore home-based programs are more normalized options. As well, methods used in restrictive clinical settings are neither as effective nor as practical as those used in the home, and the transfer and generalization of skills from a clinic setting to other situations is problematic.

Home-based programs are often referred to as *home visiting*—a process whereby a professional or paraprofessional provides help over an extended period of time to a family in its own home (Wasik, Bryant, and Lyons, 1990). In general, home-based early intervention involves a consistent contact in the client's home between the child and the family and a representative of a formal agency.

The appeal of home visiting is based on the opportunity to work with individuals within the family context. This enables professionals to learn firsthand about the conditions of life for children and parents (Powell, 1990) and means that instructional recommendations are practical and realistic because the teacher has the opportunity to observe the family's life style and available resources.

Preschool Programs

At three years of age, the child can generally be admitted to an early childhood education program, a program that is concerned with the development and special needs of young children and their families with particular emphasis on the preschool years (Alberta Education, 1982).

Although segregated preschool programs are still to be found right across Canada, the current philosophy is that early childhood special education should generally not take place in settings separate from early childhood education. The integration of children with disabilities into natural settings is predicated on the development of social interaction and friendship among children, the improvement in self-concept in children with disabilities, and observation and imitation of the language, behaviour, and skills of normally developing youngsters.

Children with mild disabilities need the same skills as their peers and they usually acquire the same skills in the same sequence. Therefore, it makes sense that the normal developmental processes of children provide the most critical reference for teachers of preschool children with mild disabilities. The regular early childhood curriculum includes communication, social and emotional development, self-care and physical development, the demands of the current environment, and the skills needed in the next environment.

These curriculum objectives will be the same for young children with disabilities. Exceptions will probably be a somewhat expanded program to include early assessment, the development of an individualized program, the intervention of professionals and paraprofessionals, a range of teaching approaches and techniques, and adaptations to the environment.

Who Is Involved?

Parents' discovery of their child's disability brings them into the orbit of a number of professional disciplines. Learning about the exceptionality is only the first of a lifelong series of interactions; many families are plunged into the world of infant stimulation, early intervention, preschools, respite services, medical intervention, and so on.

A wide range of professionals and paraprofessionals are available to support the parents and to help the child through various stages of development. Families will interact in some way with professionals from the disciplines of education, psychology, medicine, therapy, counselling, and allied public health and social work (Bailey, Simeonsson, Yoder, and Huntington, 1990). Few children who are exceptional will require all, or even most, of these professional services. However, the child certainly will need some of these services at some time. A child diagnosed in infancy, for example, would encounter many of the medical personnel in hospital. Once the child is in the home, visiting personnel might provide infant stimulation, information for the parents, and the first steps for educational intervention.

Parents as Intervenors

Apart from teachers and other professionals, the primary intervenors in the early years are a child's own parents. Parent involvement does not mean that parents should do the job of professionals. Nor is parent involvement a specific set of activities such as parents' groups or teaching activities. Rather, parent involvement implies shared responsibility for a child's progress. As one worker said, "Effective parent involvement programs acknowledge the fact that parents are a child's earliest and most influential teachers. Trying to educate the young child without help and support from the home is akin to trying to rake leaves in a high wind" (Gough, 1991, p. 339).

Parents are trained to assist in program planning and/or teaching activities either at home or in a centre. They learn strategies for imparting specific skills and competencies to their own child in the belief that with instruction, modelling, and reinforcement, they can become more effective teachers of their own children. Some specific areas of parent training include physical management; managing self-care and daily living activities; guidance and behaviour management; understanding the nature and prognosis of the condition; handling the child; stimulating mobility, locomotion, and communication; and responding appropriately to different or unexpected behaviours.

Treatment regimes depend on the special needs of a child. For example, parents of children with autism can learn how to manage their child and how to stimulate social, motor, and communicative development. Howlin (1981) trained parents of children with autism to use behavioural techniques to stimulate language at home and to deal with obsessions, rituals, phobias, temper tantrums, and hyperactivity. The parents also learned to teach constructive play and social skills. After a six-month period, the children spoke more than previously and used appropriate communicative language.

For a child with a hearing impairment, parents may be instructed as to the nature of hearing impairment, the stages of normal language development, the use of the hearing aid, and the various available modes of communication. Parents can be taught to reinforce their child's early vocalizations by responding with pleasure and attention through smiling, talking, and touching so that the child is encouraged to continue vocalization as a means of receiving positive reinforcement.

In the early months of the life of an infant with severe visual impairment, sound without vision does not provide adequate information. Infants with visual impairments have specific developmental needs that require the specialized services of infant/visual impairment specialists working simultaneously with the infant and the parents (Friedman, 1989).

The developmental progress of children with Down syndrome appears to be best when parents and other regular companions are persistent in their attempts to stimulate the child while providing ample emotional support (Mundy, Sigman, Kasari, and Yirmira, 1988). With early support, children with Down syndrome can make remarkable progress. In the University of Washington Early Intervention Program for Down syndrome children, studies of experimental and control groups demonstrated that children lacking early intervention showed progressive declines in their performance compared to normally developing peers. In contrast, those children with early intervention showed positive developmental patterns. Initially they were able to perform only 62 percent of the tasks expected of their normal peers; those who participated in the program and were between three and four years of age typically performed approximately 95 percent of the tasks (Peterson, 1987).

For children with physical and health disorders, parents must be educated to promote their children's independence. This involves an acceptance of the disability as well as a recognition of the child's individual strengths and abilities. Early intervention allows treatment to begin; draws parents into the intervention process; may prevent the development of secondary conditions; and increases the chances that the child will achieve the greatest possible degree of independence.

Even though parent participation is highly valued, many difficulties remain. In fact, studies (e.g. Bricker, 1986) have found that only 20 to 40 percent of parents were actively involved in their child's early intervention program. The factors that influence parent involvement are diverse and often difficult to document. Some parents simply choose not to play an active role. The greater the number of unmet needs the parents have in their own lives, the less time, energy, and commitment they have to carry out educational and therapeutic interventions with their child (Dunst and Leet, 1987).

In other cases, collaboration between parents and professionals is hindered by limited knowledge bases, skill deficits, lack of self-confidence, impaired objectivity, economic considerations, and the needs of other family members. The cultural background of the family is a major factor that can alter the intervention process, the role of professionals, and the amount of active parent participation. Culturally-based beliefs affect the manner in which families adapt to the child, the family's willingness and ability to seek help, their communication styles with professionals, the level of trust given to caregivers and caregiving agencies, the amount and type of participation, the goals and outcomes they select for the child, and the family members who will participate in intervention activities (Hansen, Lynch, and Wayman, 1990; Schorr-Ribera, 1987).

Other parents may be resentful if intervenors fail to take into consideration different family types and changing roles within families. Even though the traditional family is not as represented in today's society, infant and preschool programs are often directed toward the two-parent, one-mother, middle-class family. Some programs have assumed that mothers are the primary caregivers, that children are raised by two biological parents, and that fathers show their concern for their children through participation in organized efforts such as fund raising, meeting with legislators, and so forth. These assumptions are not based on data (Atkins, 1987). Intervention should not become the sole concern of the mother.

Even for those parents eager for involvement, the process may be neither cheap nor convenient. Parents enter programs with the expectation of getting help for their child. When the assistance carries with it high explicit or implicit expectations of parent participation and time-consuming commitments by the parents, to not participate fully may make parents feel guilty. They feel that they are open to criticism for appearing not to have their child's interests at heart (Akerley, 1975).

Transition

One common experience for each child and each family is the transition from a setting serving very young children to the formal school system. In early childhood special education, transition is as the process of moving from one program to another, or from one service delivery mode to another (Chandler, 1992). When a transition is carefully planned and undertaken, it becomes one of the processes through which continuity of services is assured for young children and their families.

The child's transition from a preschool to a public school program is a time of change for both the child and the family. Preschool and public school programs differ on a number of dimensions, including location, personnel, transportation options, schedules, family support services, and methods of communication between home and teacher.

Changing programs, systems, and personnel can be stressful for both child and parents. For the parents, the public school brings changing roles and expectations. For example, in public school the child is often labelled officially for the first time as being different.

For the child, the separation from a child-care or preschool program may be the most abrupt and permanent break with the past that he or she experiences before leaving home as a young adult. Transition means severing bonds with preschool staff, making new friends, generalizing old skills to new situations, acquiring new routines, and exploring new environments. Children face a group of strange people and inevitably experience separation fears along with the daunting tasks of learning the rules and consequences of an unfamiliar environment and learning their place in a new hierarchy.

The factors contributing to the success or failure of transitions are multiple and complex. They involve not only the child but the quality of the sending and receiving programs, and the behaviour of the teachers, families, and communities. Especially important are the preparation, implementation, and follow-up that underlie the entire transition process. Preparing for transition involves a number of components:

• preparing children and family members for the move to a new program;

• minimizing the disruption caused by necessary changes in services;

• supporting children and family members as they adjust to the new program;

• making subsequent adjustments to new experiences for the child and the child's family;

• providing the child with the skills to succeed in the new placement.

Preparation of the child focuses on the demands of the public school environment. These differ from those of the preschool, as do the skills that are needed for the child to function in a kindergarten program. In kindergarten classrooms, there is a predictable and consistent schedule of activities. Kindergarten teachers require children to respond to directions given once to a large group; preschool teachers often give children repeated individual directions in small groups or on a one-to-one basis. There are provisions for free play in kindergarten, but these differ from programs for younger children as does the stress on academic subjects or academic readiness. Literacy behaviour is stressed.

In a kindergarten or grade one classroom, children must learn to follow group instructions, respond to group-directed teaching activities, follow rules and routines, work and play independently in close proximity to others, work and play co-operatively with peers, take turns, share, and wait. They are expected to develop the ability to attend to tasks, to complete tasks successfully with a minimum of adult assistance, to initiate interactions appropriately, and to go along with simple classroom rules and routines. They must also understand how to ask for, offer, accept, and refuse appropriate help.

The success of transition is influenced by the skills and behaviours a child has and the match between the child's skills and the expectations and requirements of the receiving program. Children who make the transition to kindergarten armed with the necessary survival skills and who use those skills in appropriate contexts are more likely to succeed in the regular classrooms than peers without these skills (Fowler, Schwartz, and Atwater, 1991). However, there can never be a universal list of transition skills because classroom and teacher expectations differ too much.

The research does indicate that in kindergarten the skills most crucial for success are not naming colours or recognizing the letters of the alphabet, but social skills. These are generally self-help skills, social interaction, play, the ability to function independently, and responding to group instruction.

Parent Support

Before parents can effectively assist in the care and progress of their child with an exceptionality, they need to overcome their own emotional reactions. Many parents seek counselling or join self-help groups, especially in the period immediately following the initial diagnosis.

Counselling

Many parents require counselling because they continue to experience periods of grief (Kratochvil and Devereux, 1988). While parent counselling offers a range of approaches, it differs from the usual conception of adult counselling, which is structured to facilitate changes in the client's behaviour. Parent counselling is not intended to change the personalities of family members and is really closer to social work than to psychotherapy. The major aims are to help the family handle the special problems and environmental adjustments that having a child with a disability entails, to help parents understand the meaning of a child's diagnosis, and to aid them in developing realistic expectations for the child.

Counselling focuses on information about the child, the nature and degree of the handicap, educational planning, and future prognosis. Sessions also provide a forum in which parents can openly express and work through their feelings of anger, fear, and anxiety. They offer coping self-help skills, group relaxation, self-praise and self-instruction, and opportunities to favourably contrast participants with each other.

As siblings are an important aspect of family-centred practice, in many cases the counselling sessions will actively involve siblings. Problems are explained simply and honestly to siblings, with a fair assessment of how the problems will affect family life.

Parent Self-Help Groups

Social supports complement personal coping skills for parents. These groups promote understanding and offer parents therapeutic involvement with people with similar problems. Groups provide a forum in which parents can discuss their concerns and exchange ideas with each other. It helps parents to talk about role changes, exhaustion, money problems, isolation, and so on with people who are going through the same experiences (Gill, 1994). Parents can channel their frustrations and anxieties into positive action for their children while gaining more realistic hopes for the future. Groups also help parents to develop a more positive sense of their parenting roles.

Information Networks

With the enormous geographical distances in Canada, parents in rural areas may be disadvantaged in receiving services for their children with exceptional conditions. To partly overcome this difficulty, computerized information networks have evolved to provide parents and others with up-to-date information about specific conditions, additional resources, and special education programs and practices.

SUMMARY

1. One of the major changes in early childhood education, whether it be for normally developing children or those with special needs, is a new focus on the family and the role of family members.

2. Having a child with a disability in the family has been acknowledged for many years to be a difficult situation for all family members. However, the emphasis on the family as the critical factor in the development of a child with a disability is a fairly new thrust in early childhood special education. Today there is a greater commitment to provide comprehensive, co-ordinated, and family-focused services to children with disabilities and their families.

3. The effects of stress on the families of very young disabled or at-risk children are pervasive, multiple, and sometimes unsuspected. Families are as individual and unique as their children. With a child who is disabled, some families cope effectively and adaptively; others tend to feel helpless and experience less personal gratification and more child-related problems.

4. Over the years, families, family functioning, the impact of a member with a disability, and the provision of treatment and services have been looked at in different ways. Researchers examine family functioning in terms of a stage-theory approach, a life-cycle approach, a systems approach, or its first cousin, a social-support approach. Each

of these ways of viewing families translates into practical models for actually intervening and working with families.

5. The most common and traditional way of looking at families with a disabled member is through a stage-theory approach. This suggests that the parents of children with disabilities pass through orderly stages before they accept the reality of their child's condition. Shock, denial, blame, guilt, depression, anger, and bargaining are all responses to the disabled family member. Several authorities have questioned the validity of the stage theory in understanding parents' reactions to a child with a disability and prefer other approaches.

6. The life-cycle approach sees families moving through time experiencing a series of events and tasks which include transitions. The currently favoured way of viewing families is through a systems approach or perspective that sees the family as a system and any event involving a change in the life of a family that has a disabled child can cause stress to the whole system. A family support system approach stresses how the family fits into the broader social context.

7. Each parent, each sibling, and each member of the extended family may reveal different reactions to the presence of a handicapped child in the family. However, studies on sibling relationships are contradictory and inconsistent.

8. Early intervention is based on research evidence in child development, models of successful performance, the general observations of lay persons and experts, and the impetus from the American legislation, PL 99-452. Early intervention activities are directed toward ameliorating problems in children with established disabilities and toward intervention with children who are at risk in order to prevent or hinder the development of conditions that impair learning or behaviour.

9. Programs in which workers visit the home are a promising mechanism used to provide for a growing population of children under the age of three receiving special services.

10. Infant and toddler programs offer parents intensive participation and usually continue until the child is about three years of age. Programs try to enhance a child's development by helping the parents to become effective intervenors. The goal of training is to enable family members to achieve desired outcomes and to deal effectively with future concerns. For the child, the goal is optimal development in the motor, cognitive, language and communication, social, and self-help skill domains.

11. Today, many young children with disabilities are placed in normalized preschool settings (day-care or nursery school) under naturalistic curricula.

12. Transition is more than simply transferring records or relocating a child. It is a complex process as it relates to both the family and the child. For the child, moving from preschool involves a movement to a larger program with more children and new expectations. Children must learn to understand co-operation, interdependence, sharing, teamwork, and group membership.

In the Classroom

Profile: Abu

Abu's parents were very excited about their first child. They talked and planned and organized as they got ready for the arrival. When Abu was born, his disability was almost immediately noticeable to the attending physicians. Within twenty-four hours the parents were informed that their new baby was severely visually impaired. The grandparents did not live in Canada, so mother and father had almost no one to turn to for support.

The infant years were particularly difficult for Abu's mother. Many of her expectations for the child did not materialize. Certainly, he seemed to reach developmental milestones almost on target and by two years of age was developing language and some intelligible speech. Abu's mother tried to hide her fears, and played and talked with her child as much as possible.

When he was three she asked, with little optimism, if he could attend the local nursery school. To her surprise, the school personnel willingly accepted Abu and were pleased to allow her to work as a volunteer on the condition that she intervene with all the children, not just Abu.

The nursery school experience has proved an enormous success for Abu and for his mother. The teachers modify activities where necessary for Abu. For example, they add sand to the finger paints so that he has greater tactile experiences. An extract from Abu's IEP is shown later in this section.

Abu's mother is enthusiastic about integration and holds more positive attitudes about his future. She knows that his inability to perceive through the use of his eyes changes the way he learns, understands, and relates to the world, and that he will require additional assistance to overcome the deficits imposed by severe visual impairment. But she now realizes that Abu can learn and interact, and that he may achieve some of the goals his parents so hopefully set for him. Early intervention is important for very young children with visual impairments and their families. From infancy on, children may be trained in motor skills, locomotion and mobility, self-help skills, and communication. When they are integrated into nursery schools or day-care centres, adaptations to the environment and modifications to the program enhance their progress.

Researchers have identified specific program variables likely to influence intervention outcomes significantly and positively. These include the physical and cognitive adaptation of the classroom to accommodate children with disabilities; the provision of multi-sensory learning stimuli and experiences; incorporation of the child's strengths and weaknesses in the development of curricula; promotion of peer tolerance; a focus on independence and exploration of the environment; and the promotion of social interaction (see Guralnick, 1988).

Extract from Abu's IEP

Name: Abu
Age: 4
Centre: Daycrest
Supervisor: Ms. Teacher
Report number: 2

Abu has been going to the centre for almost a year. During this time, he has been working on individual goals and objectives embedded within the daily routines and activities of the centre. A specialist teacher assists with orientation and mobility training (white cane) on a biweekly basis.

ADAPTATIONS

No particular environmental adaptations are necessary. Additional lighting is provided in the reading corner. Some special materials are provided; for example, large and sturdy toys. There are books that provide alternative sensory information and pictures that are clear and uncluttered. Some toys are adapted. For example, some have bases that are covered in textures such as sandpaper. Abu wears his glasses quite readily.

ASSESSMENT

At the outset, an assessment of Abu's potential and progress was undertaken. The full assessment included a psychological report as well as observations and informal checklists used by the teachers.

PRESENT LEVELS OF FUNCTIONING

Cognitive: The report of the psychologist confirms the teachers' observations that Abu is a child functioning at the norm. His language, problem-solving skills, and the activities he undertakes in the centre are normal for a child of his chronological age, taking into account the visual disability. Play behaviour lags somewhat. Abu is still into the stage of constructive activities and is not yet involved in symbolic play alone or with peers.

Language: Abu shows good language skills although he requires more experience in some areas. He asks many questions and shows a natural curiosity.

Behaviour: At first Abu was very shy with his peers. As he becomes more confident, he is increasingly accepted by the other children. He is beginning to participate in group work.

Motor: Abu's gross motor skills are developing. Fine motor skills are lagging a little, probably the result of the visual impairment.

LONG-RANGE GOALS

- To develop security in the environment and in moving about in it.
- To strengthen the other sense modalities, especially audition and touch.
- To stimulate peer interactions.

OBJECTIVES

- Improve auditory skills through identification and localization of sound.
- Improve tactile discrimination.
- Improve taste and smell awareness.
- Encourage the use of residual vision.
- Improve social interaction through teaching appropriate smiling behaviour.

WEBLINKS

The Canadian Association of Family Resource Programs **http://www.cfc-efc.ca/frpc/htmle/home.htm**

Family Village **http://www.familyvillage.wisc.edu/**

Parent Pals Gifted and Special Education Guide **http://parentpals.com/index2.html**

Canadian Parents Online **http://www.canadianparents.com/**

Canadian Early Childhood Care and Education Research and Policy **http://www.inforamp.net/~zsonia/**

CHAPTER 16

Adolescents and Young Adults

For most of the nineteenth century, special education catered to discrete age groups. Schooling was not designed for young children, although a high proportion of older students were instructed within the institutional complex. The Ontario Institution for the Deaf, for example, was established in 1870; by 1879 about 7 percent of the student population was between the ages of 21 and 40. In the schools for the blind, students were allowed to remain up to their thirtieth birthdays (Best, 1930).

Adult attendance at school was voluntary and indicated the imperative need of disabled lads—getting a job and keeping it. Some adults were early school leavers who wanted more skills for the work force; others had never before been offered the opportunity for education and training. When students were admitted for upgrading in trades they received no wages for their work but were given free room and board (Winzer, 1993).

The adult experiences of persons with disabilities have not been of great interest to historians. The formation of deaf communities is probably the most widely studied. It seems that wherever there were schools for the deaf, a community flourished with deaf adults tending to marry other deaf people, send their children to residential schools for the deaf, and confine their social relations to their community.

There are some scattered indications of blind communities in the late nineteenth century, but they seem to have been short-lived. When persons with intellectual disabilities were institutionalized, it was usually for life. However, in the early 1920s, Walter Fernald conducted a study of the later lives of persons who had left his institution at Waverley. His findings on their occupational status and independent living were generally pessimistic (see Winzer, 1993).

In all of special education, secondary-level students have tended to be overlooked. Although the field has had access to well-articulated models of high school programs for students with mild disabilities for more than two decades, adolescents and young adults with mild disabilities have received less than their share of special education services (Halpern and Benz, 1987). There continues to be limited emphasis on vocational goals despite the fact that successful community transition depends on successful vocational experiences and the fact that vocational teachers appear willing to accept them. Only low numbers of disabled students receive vocational education in high school (Sitlington and Okolo, 1987). As well, there is much that we still do not know about educational and counselling needs and transition planning at secondary levels and the needs of young adults with disabilities.

Most programs occur at elementary levels.

Contemporary educators are attempting to close the gap with the new thrust on transition. The idea is not new. Historically the secondary transition movement is grounded in the co-operative work/study programs of the 1960s and the career education initiative of the 1970s. However, its implementation on today's special education is a new advance for the field.

It is only very recently that special education has begun to focus on early childhood and late adolescence. Currently, intense research is being directed toward very young children with special needs, and interest has grown dramatically in secondary-level students who are disabled and the schools' responsibilities to this population. Nevertheless, there remains a relative vacuum; research in the area of adolescents with learning or behavioural disorders is strikingly deficient compared to the childhood groups. While there is a far greater focus on the post-school experiences of young adults than there was even ten years ago, not enough is known about effective secondary-level programming, the experiences of young adults, and how schools can assist them as they enter the work force or tertiary education.

In one sense, adolescence officially ends at the age of eighteen or so with graduation from high school. Graduation is the point at which young people make decisions about their futures and begin in earnest to join the adult community. Students get ready for employment, continuing education, moving out of the family home, increased independence, and marriage.

In concert with their non-disabled counterparts, students with disabilities experience a wide variety of post-secondary outcomes. Young people with disabilities may enroll in university or community college; they may enter competitive employment or military service; or they may be supported in more restrictive employment and sheltered workshops.

For many young people with disabilities, the school experience, though tainted with frustration and failure, still offers some predictability. But the adult world does not have this predictability, and many tend to flounder in both occupations and independent living. As adults, "the vast majority of students with disabilities never attain a satisfactory level of career development consistent with their capabilities" (Brolin and Gysbers, 1989, p. 155). Moreover, these students are not as adept in general independent living skills and may show deficits in areas such as knowledge about sexual conventions and behaviour.

As educators have begun to appreciate that the needs of students with disabilities do not stop at the school door, various means of assisting young adults are being implemented. Three main areas are stressed: academic achievement, social and personal adjustment, and post-school adjustment.

In the school, counselling and sex education stand out as important elements contributing to adult life skills. There is also a greater focus on remedial education and a stress on programming designed to help students to obtain training, gain employment, and live productive, self-sufficient lives (Stodden and Boone, 1987).

All of these—counselling, sex education, and remedial programs—together with community-based programs and access to support services, can be grouped under the rubric of transition services. For adolescents at the close of their school careers, transition focuses on the school-to-community scenario. Transition services are intended to provide young people with disabilities access to relevant post-secondary education opportunities, employment in competitive settings, residential independence, and future self-sufficiency (Johnson, Thompson, Sinclair, Krantz, Evelo, Stolte, and Thompson, 1993).

In this final chapter we discuss the needs of adolescents and young adults with disabilities. We focus particularly on the need for transition planning and specific transition programming. This chapter also considers various types of post-secondary and employment options available to persons with disabilities.

Adolescents

The teenage years are characterized by major biological, psychological, and social changes. Adolescence is a time of confusion, uncertainty and anxiety, of rapid physiological change and acute self-awareness. It is a period of identity crisis and of intense peer-group relationships, a time of rebellion against established order, and a time of social anxiety. Adolescent students are developing their own identities and their own expectations of the future. As they begin to think of themselves as independent individuals, not their parents' children, adolescents become less compliant with teachers and parents and prone to question and criticize more than younger children.

Every contemporary adolescent faces a daunting task in learning to become a competent adult, and the task is made more difficult if overlaid by an exceptional condition. Adolescence is a bad time to feel incompetent and unconfident. Small children can still feel comfortable being helped by adults; adults learn the limits of their abilities. But daily tests of personal competence against one's peers are the stuff of adolescence, and those who compete poorly meet a variety of problems in self-concept and interpersonal relationships.

Fulfilling the multiple tasks of adolescence is more difficult when a student has a disability because the characteristics specific to adolescents with mild disabilities exacerbate the normal difficulties of adolescence (Dossetor and Nicol, 1989). Students with intellectual disabilities, for example, do not have the cognitive ability to cope with the new developments within themselves and the new demands of the environment (Drew, Logan, and Hardman, 1988).

There is more to high school success than competency in academics. Most middle and high schools are organized on a departmental or subject-matter basis and secondary schools are generally large places in which students are expected to function independently. As student bodies become larger, schedules become more complex and the system's ability to differentiate and individualize is compromised.

Students need a plethora of survival skills that include going to class every day; arriving at school on time; bringing pencils and other supplies to class; turning in work on time; talking to teachers politely; and reading and following directions (Zigmond, Kerr, Brown, and Harris, 1984). Students with disabilities often have problems adjusting to the school and its expectations, classroom routines, the pressures of daily life, peer groups, and a range of different teachers. Students who have been successful in elementary school where there is some continuity between instructional areas and teachers often have difficulty in high school dealing with several different teachers and with compartmentalized instruction. They meet problems with schedules and routines. For example, school attendance is a problem for adolescents who are learning disabled: more secondary students with learning disabilities fail regular courses because of attendance than for any other reason (Kaplan, 1996).

In adolescents, social competence and peer acceptance become increasingly important. Peers, being popular with peers, and belonging to the right crowd are a critical part of growing up. Between the ages of six and twelve, children spend an average of 40 percent of their waking hours in the company of peers, children of their own age and status (Cole and Cole, 1989). By adolescence, students spend far more time with friends and place special emphasis on the qualities of intimacy, mutual understanding, and loyalty.

Adolescents are particularly vulnerable to the negative impact of having few or no friends, a situation that may be common for students with disabilities. One report (Polloway, Epstein, Patton, Cullinan, and Lueble, 1986) found that teacher ratings indicated that more than 20 percent of older students with mild intellectual disabilities were rejected by their peers.

For normally developing students, self-esteem increases steadily during adolescence and early adulthood; on the average, eighteen-year-olds have higher self-esteem than thirteen-year-olds. Social, physical, and cognitive deficits hinder this process in adolescents with disabilities. Physical disabilities, for example, reduce the rate of self-concept formation (Lawrence, 1991). Low-achieving students are frequently judged in relation to high achievers, and feelings of inferiority, lack of motivation, and interpersonal hostility often result (Levine, 1983). Students may become caught in a spiral of failure, dissatisfaction, and frustration, and lose their self-esteem and motivation.

Of course, adolescents with disabilities share many of the same worries and anxieties as their non-disabled peers. A survey of the concerns and interests of visually impaired and sighted adolescents (Tobin and Hill, 1988), for example, found them to be similar. However, the gap between students with disabilities and their peers continues to widen the further they progress in school. Teenagers who are disabled often become frustrated with their lack of progress and resign themselves to a poor view of their intelligence and their ability as a whole.

For teachers at the secondary level, the world of the adolescent raises issues that are far broader than those raised for the elementary school child. These include the adolescent's emerging sexuality, vocational interests and talents, future expectations, range of leisure activities, and independent living skills (C. R. Smith, 1991). Teachers are also faced with negative attitudes toward school and academic learning that many adolescents have developed, the manifestations of disabilities, and the need for remedial programming.

The Concept of Transition

Definitions of the term *transition* have in common the concept that a transition is a passage or an evolution, not simply a "here today gone tomorrow" phenomenon. In other words, transitions are not a fleeting proposition but rather represent recurrent, life-long processes that all individuals experience (Shea and Baeur, 1991).

As used in relation to the needs of adolescents with disabilities, *transition* has a number of meanings and foci.

- Transition as an ongoing experience. For all students, the high school experience represents a period of transition between the security of school and the complexity associated with the opportunities and risks of adult life. For adolescents, the quality of the secondary school experience and the decisions made during this time have significant implications for the quality of life experienced after they leave school.

- Transition as a movement. The general concept of transition has recently become a

Training in social skills is particularly important for adolescents with disabilities.

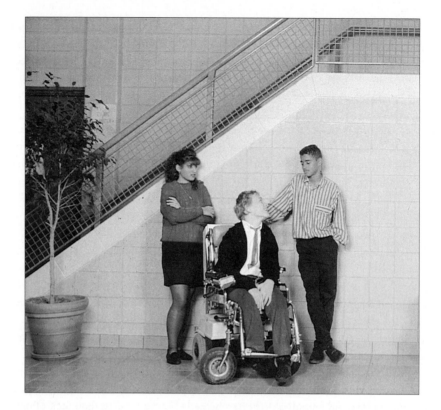

thrust in special education in the sense that transition is the movement from one service delivery system to another. For the adolescent with disabilities, this means the school with its services in education and counselling to an adult world with community services and advocacy and self-help groups such as the Canadian Association for Community Living.

• Transition as a school program focus. Transition programs focus on both job preparation and job finding and maintenance. It implies the maximum development of intellectual, personal, social, and vocational skills necessary for independent functioning. Programs place emphasis on the acquisition of life and vocational skills with the focus on the local community.

An emphasis on transition in the adolescent years is rather new in special education. It essentially developed from a number of interlinked thrusts. First, if normalization is to succeed, adults with disabilities must achieve independent living, occupational stability, and status within their communities. Follow-up studies of graduates of public school programs indicate that most do not utilize community services and resources effectively, and they tend to be isolated from peers both disabled and non-disabled (see Hardman and McDonald, 1987).

Second, as students near the end of their school careers, some families feel abandoned—they realize that special education services are ending but hold little certainty that community services will begin and provide needed support. Parents are also aware that, unlike special education systems, community and work environments may not provide the support needed by the individual to ensure success.

Far more telling are data indicating that, despite special education programs, many students with special needs still experience major difficulties in bridging the gap from school to community work and living. Something has to be done about the poor post-school performance of many young adults with disabilities, and transition is an appropriate response.

In the early 1980s, the American government made commitments to transition services in terms of both policy and federal discretionary grants. First, amendments to PL 94-142 (PL 98-199) included a Secondary Education and Transition Services section in which Section 626 authorized funds to be spent on research, training, and demonstration in the transition area (Lee and Csapo, 1989). A later amendment, the Individuals with Disabilities Education Act (IDEA, 1990, PL 101-476) provided a clear definition along with transition mandates and programming. According to IDEA, transition is

> a co-ordinated set of activities for a student, designed with an outcome-oriented process, which promotes movement from school to post-school activities, including post-secondary education, vocational training, integrated employment (including supported employment), continuing and adult education, adult services, independent living, or community participation. The co-ordinated set of activities shall be based upon the individual student's preferences and interests, and shall include instruction, community experiences, and development of employment and other post-school adult living objectives, and, when appropriate, acquisition of daily living skills and functional vocational evaluation (PL101-476, Sec. 602 (a)(19)).

The American definition makes a number of points that are relevant to the Canadian situation:

- The transition process is a vehicle for alleviating the problems of youth with various disabilities and need levels through integrating planning, instruction, placement, and provision of ongoing support as they leave school (Newbert, Tilson, and Ianacone, 1989).

- Transition initiatives enhance the prospects for economic stability for persons who are exceptional.

- Transition is founded on the premise that all persons with disabilities can perform meaningful tasks and assume valued roles within normal community settings.

- Effective transition planning is much more than the mere physical transfer of administrative responsibility for an individual's service program from the school to adult service agencies. Successfully negotiating the transition through and out of high school is a process that requires varying degrees of assistance from family and school personnel.

- Although community employment is the goal of transition planning and secondary level vocational instruction, the placement of a graduating student into a job should not be considered an outcome in and of itself. It is also important to identify the quality of life outcomes that the student wishes to obtain through employment (Steere, Wood, Panscofar, and Rucker, 1993). Quality of life outcomes are the tangible and intangible results of employment that contribute to the enhancement of students' lifestyles.

- A basic objective during the transition period is to arrange for individuals with disabilities those services needed to support successful adult living. There may be many different agencies, depending on the nature and severity of the disability.

- Transition involves collaboration and co-ordination. In order for a program to be truly successful, there must be a firm alliance forged between special education, regular education, and vocational education.

- In transition, the school has two primary roles. First, it is the school's responsibility to develop and implement an effective program that will prepare students for life in their local communities. Second, the school must take the lead in co-ordinating the transition planning process (see Figure 16-1). This involves secondary programs for transition, linkages to post-secondary environments, and post-secondary services.

- Transition planning must be incorporated into the IEP planning process. The transition component, to be developed not later than the student's sixteenth birthday, is designed to provide instruction and community experiences that lead to post-school outcomes in a variety of areas, including post-secondary education, training, employment, independent living, and community participation (Furney, Hasazi, and De Stefano, 1997).

- Student participation. Self-evaluation, self-determination, student-identified post-school goals, and self-selected educational experiences are important.

- Encouragement of parent involvement. The involvement of parents in secondary programs has been traditionally underemphasized (Haring, Lovett, and Saren, 1991). For transition to be successful, parents must be involved.

- Co-ordinated services. A transition team should include all those providing services in both school and community. That is, special educators, family members, general and vocational educators, adult service providers, employers, community leaders, and consumers (Smith, Edelen-Smith, and Stodden, 1995). The team should target skills that the student may need to be successful after he or she leaves school. It should also address the student's strengths, the family's critical concerns, transition, and other needs as

Figure 16-1

The transition process

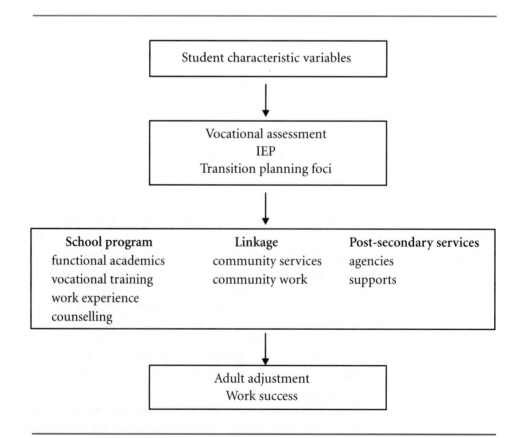

related to broad skill domains (e.g. non-verbal communication, language, social relationships, self-management, academics, personal care, community living, homeliving, vocational skills, and recreational interests and skills).

Transition services for young adults with disabilities are in their infancy; problems abound and there remain many barriers to the implementation of programs (Mithaug, Martin, and Agran, 1987). There is a lack of a systematic approach to providing transition services and there is much that we still do not know about educational and counselling needs and transition planning at secondary levels and the needs of young adults with disabilities. It does appear that the goals to ensure a successful transition from high school to adult life will require major changes in schools, adult services, and communities (De Stefano and Wermuth, 1992).

In the following section, we examine various facets of the transition process. The focus is on the school's responsibilities; also mentioned are student participation, parent involvement, and post-school options.

The School's Responsibilities in Transition

At the school level, transition involves the provision of school experiences that will assist in locating and maintaining employment together with training in skills for successful adulthood. The school should also identify community resources to assist students and involve students and parents.

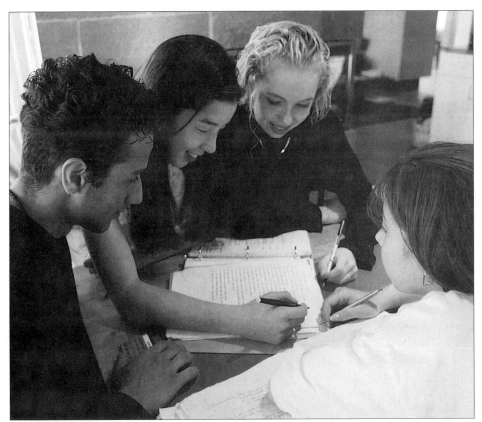

Planned and systematic opportunities to interact with disabled peers help prepare young people with disabilities to function independently in the general community.

Preparation for Transition

Schools must provide preparation for transitions. Transition planning should start much earlier than high school; it should begin in the elementary grades. Career awareness can begin as early as the primary grades with discussions about what it means to work in a particular job (Bounds, 1997). Students also begin to learn the rudiments of community and vocational living skills in upper elementary school (Hasazi and Clark, 1988; MacMillan, 1988).

This preparation should include systematic and planned opportunities for students' interactions with normal peers. In a study of 106 graduates of a school for students with severe physical disabilities, for example, investigators (Liebert, Lutsky, and Gottlieb, 1990) found that many graduates felt they would have benefited from a less sheltered environment as well as more exposure to peers without disabilities.

Formal Transition Plan

For secondary students with mild disabilities, there are three essential components in senior programming—work preparation skills, functional academics, and life-skills training, which includes counselling and sex education. For students with severe disabilities the curriculum should expose them to job options in the community in which they live; teach specific work skills such as using tools and equipment; and teach work-related skills, such as transportation and personal hygiene (McDonnell, Ferguson, and Mathot-Buckner, 1992).

Adolescents with disabilities need a comprehensive curriculum that leads to successful, satisfying employment. A variety of generic curriculum domains have been proposed during recent years as important components of secondary special education. The major areas of instruction are:

- academic skills, specifically functional academics, to remediate deficient basic skills;
- vocational skills that include career exploration and occupational knowledge and skills, such as job finding skills, work experience, and job maintenance;
- personal management skills that include independent living knowledge and skills such as budgeting, home management, and social skills;
- leisure skills (Halpern and Benz, 1987; Wilcox and Bellamy, 1982).

Within these domains, instruction should occur throughout the school years, with the relative emphasis on the vocational domain increasing at secondary levels. Training in this area helps students to develop stronger self-concepts and to engage in self-supporting productive work.

Preparation should include an individual transition plan as part of a student's IEP. The plan will include goals and objectives, timelines, and designations of responsible persons and agencies (Moon, Diambra, and Hill, 1990).

Educationally, the IEP will focus on a comprehensive curriculum that is functional in nature and that includes community-based vocational instruction (Moon, Diambra, and Hill, 1990). It will identify and teach activities that will maximize the individual's participation in community settings, such as vocational training, personal management, and recreation/leisure activities. The plan will also identify the types of community services that will be necessary to support the individual's participation, and complete the steps required to access community services (Hardman and McDonald, 1987).

Inclusion

Integration at the secondary levels is harder to implement than it is for very young children. Various factors account for this:

- Younger children acclimatize more rapidly to integrated settings than older students.

- The mental gap between non-disabled students and those with disabilities continuously widens with age.

- The instructional emphasis at the secondary levels is different from that of the elementary school. Curriculum in secondary schools is no longer focused on the acquisition of basic skills but on the use of skills to acquire content knowledge (Espin and Foegin, 1996).

- The needs of adolescents are quite different from those of younger children and, when the adolescent has a disability, the needs become even more intense.

- The grade level of the class is a proxy for a number of variables. For example, primary grade students are more tolerant than are those of junior high school age, who are more likely to ostracize a child.

- Teachers at the elementary level are more student oriented than subject-matter-oriented, and the opposite goes for most high school teachers (MacMillan, Gresham, and Forness, 1996).

- The current needs and ultimate goals of students at the end of their school careers are different from those of younger children. As Figure 16-2 shows, the needs that must be addressed by secondary programming meld into after-school needs.

In many ways, inclusive practices are in direct conflict with what we know works for adolescent students with disabilities in terms of functional skill instruction and vocational training in the community. It is not surprising that there is skepticism about whether inclusion is feasible or desirable for secondary students (Fox and Ysseldyke, 1997). Some researchers go so far as to contend that at the secondary level, the full integration of all students is simply not appropriate; it is an invitation to failure (Braaten, Kauffman, Braaten, Polsgrove, 1988; Edgar, 1987; Schumaker and Deshler, 1988). Wayne Nesbit (1990) points out that for senior students with special needs, a case can be made for special programming because it is the special aspects of the senior program that will do much to facilitate long-term normalization. The argument circles around three interrelated themes—the characteristics of adolescent students with disabilities, the content of the regular curriculum, and the future needs of students.

If we examine the characteristics of students, we find that adolescents do not outgrow their learning difficulties, nor is simple maturation matched with an increase in motivation and achievement. On the contrary. Factors correlated with students with mild disabilities include physiological and neurological problems, deficits in cognitive processes such as memory and metacognitive awareness, disorders of attention, social behaviour problems, communication problems, and perceptual problems.

Secondary students classified as learning disabled, for example, often retain subtle manifestations of childhood traits such as lack of co-ordination and hyperactivity. Academically, adolescents with learning disabilities tend to plateau at fourth or fifth grade. The result: almost all adolescents with learning disabilities lack functional proficiency in language, reading, handwriting, spelling, and arithmetic. Adolescents who are learning disabled tend to demonstrate a high degree of anxiety, low expectations of future success, poor adaptive strategies

Figure 16-2
Needs of secondary students

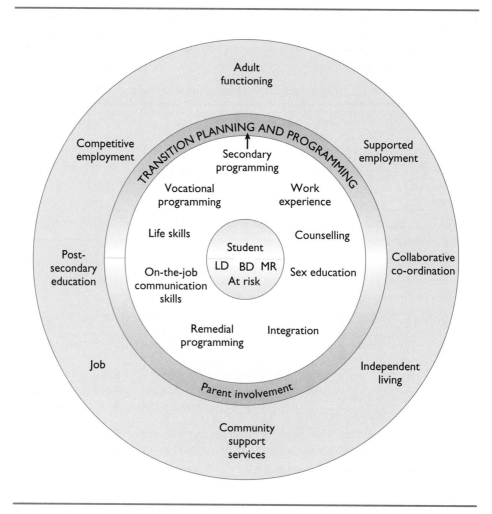

for coping with normal stress and solving everyday personal problems, reduced motivation, and poor self-concept. These students are then characterized as passive learners, lacking in motivation, underachieving in academic skills, lacking social skills, without the ability to comprehend the varied demands of secondary school, and lacking organizational skills.

While an estimated 50 percent of individuals classified as having Attention Deficit Hyperactivity Disorder experience a brain maturational spurt of unknown etiology and do outgrow the condition, the other 50 percent have difficulties that persist into adulthood and cause concentration and attention problems. In a longitudinal study, Lambert (1988) identified more than 100 hyperactive children in elementary school, tracked them until they were seventeen or eighteen years old, and then compared them with non-hyperactive peers. He found that the hyperactive group were less likely to have graduated from high school and more likely to have run away from home or become delinquent. They were more aggressive than their peers and more likely to be receiving treatment for psychological problems. Long-term prospects for students who are both hyperactive and aggressive are even more bleak (Whalen, 1989).

The second argument against universal inclusion stresses the content of the secondary school curriculum. Adolescents with mild disabilities who spend the majority of their school day in general education classes are expected to meet the same demands as their non-disabled peers. Students must be able to listen to lectures and take notes; complete many written assignments; read content-area information, often from poorly organized textbooks; and take tests that frequently do not facilitate students' responding.

In the general education classroom, students can experience success only when the teacher is able to meet their individual learning needs through appropriate curriculum adaptations and modifications (Haman, Issacson, and Powell, 1985). But curriculum adaptations are not a part of secondary classroom life. In general, regular educators teach to single large groups and incorporate little or no differentiation based on student need (Baker and Zigmond, 1990). Few teachers make adaptations and, when they do, it is more often than not lowering their expectations of students rather than attempting to improve their programs (Fuchs, Fuchs, Hamlett, Phillips, and Karns, 1995). For example, a study of 60 social studies and science teachers who were seen as effective with students with learning disabilities by peers, principals, and self found that the teachers made few adaptations to meet special learning needs (McIntosh, Vaughn, Schumm, Haager, and Lee, 1994).

Even the special education curriculum, as it now stands, may be inappropriate. Researchers (Kaiser and Abell, 1997) observe that: "The traditional special education curriculum at the secondary level, driven by both graduation requirements and deficits in the students' present levels of performance, often does not meet the transitional needs of youth with mild disabilities" (p. 70). For example, students with learning disabilities enter secondary school severely deficient in basic reading and written expression skills; three or four years later they leave with little or no improvement in these areas (Espin and Foegen, 1996).

Finally, there are the future needs of students. In the educational mainstream, some of the necessary curricular elements are simply not present (Nesbit, 1990). The overall secondary curriculum is not congruent with the present needs of many senior students with disabilities; they do not have either the interest or the reading ability required for academic credit courses (Nesbit, 1990). Traditional secondary school subjects are generally not related to the future needs of students; preparation for independent living requires much more than academic goals for adolescents who are disabled. Their hope is to work, not to continue schooling, and there is less likelihood that their career development needs will be met in regular classrooms (Izzo, 1987).

By this stage, the major goal of education should not be to compensate for intellectual and physical deficiencies per se. Rather, instruction must be directed toward the development of critical skills necessary for adulthood, for success in daily life, for citizenship, and for a future career.

Counselling

The needs of adolescents are quite different from those of younger children and, when the adolescent has a disability, the needs become even more intense. Both guidance and vocational/career counselling are important.

Guidance Counselling

Guidance counselling assists students in selecting courses, in adapting to their disability, and in personal concerns. It may also slip over into the area of career plans, occupational choice, and job placement.

Adaptation to the disability is a major thrust. Children with physical disabilities, for example, reach an awareness of their disability and its implications at different ages. Generally, they move from a broad understanding of the disability at age six to a more acute realization of the implications by age eight (Dunn, McCartan, and Fugura, 1988). By the time they reach the adolescent years, students with physical disabilities hold deep concerns regarding social acceptance, sexuality, and career choices. Students may need instruction in social skills as they mature and may also have to deal with sexual needs.

Learning how to dress and use makeup to improve personal appearance can prove tricky for students who are blind. The problem is intensified if the appearance of the eyes is abnormal, while the unattractive appearance of optical aids may cause adolescents to reject them. Students often need to be made aware of dress codes and the use of cosmetics. Many adolescents with visual impairments try to mask their disabilities because they perceive visual impairments as a negative attribute (Sacks and Corn, 1996). Personal counselling services and sex education may help them to develop greater social awareness.

For adolescents with hearing impairments, the problems of deciding on communication modes and on a cultural identity complicate life (Garbe and Rodda, 1988). Deafness is an invisible handicap, and students with hearing impairments do not receive much sympathy (Coryell, Holcomb, and Scherer, 1992). Counselling can assist in improving relations between students who are hearing impaired and their hearing peers.

The needs of students who are gifted cannot be overlooked in the counselling process. Some, but certainly not all, students who are gifted in high school consider their giftedness a social liability, and may need assistance in course selection and understanding the implications of potential.

The increases in antisocial and law-breaking behaviour, in truancy, the emotional conflicts, personal disturbances, and learning problems characteristic of students with behavioural disorders suggest the need for intervention in the areas of vocation and career, sexuality, and drug abuse (Cullinan, Epstein, and Lloyd, 1983). Counselling must be a long-term process: it needs an extended time frame to deal with students' affect, to increase their understanding of why they behave as they do, and to explore the possibility of change.

Vocational/Career Counselling

For all of us, career choices are limited by such factors as individual preferences, aptitude, and temperament. Career and vocational education are particularly important for students with disabilities who need to critically assess the competencies required in specific occupations and identify realistic vocational goals that match their maximum vocational potential.

Few adolescents, disabled or not, know about available occupations in their geographic area, the content of people's work, or their earnings. Students with congenital disabilities often have even fewer and less diverse career-related experiences and learning opportunities than do their peers without disabilities (Turner and Szymaski, 1990). Individuals who are deaf, for example, know less than their hearing peers about different types of occupations (Schroedel, 1992).

Data suggest that students are aware of their lack of preparedness. A study of 106 students with severe physical disabilities (Liebert, Lutsky, and Gottlieb, 1990), for example, found that graduates expressed a desire for more intensive guidance counselling (especially in the area of job placement), additional training in upgrading job skills, more help with transportation, and more access to social and recreational programs. In another study of students with and without learning disabilities, the learning-disabled group had a far greater desire for more information about how to find a job, keep a job, and live independently than did their non-disabled peers (Dowdy, Carter, and Smith, 1990).

For adolescents who are visually impaired, realistic career choices can be difficult. Those who are deaf need help in vocational training and counselling to assess their strengths, weaknesses, and interests. Counsellors can encourage students to consider a broad array of options and to take a major role in decision making.

Multipotential can be a mixed blessing; many youngsters who are gifted share a feeling of ambivalence about the future and their place in it. By ages thirteen or fourteen, some students are already conditioned to avoid failure at all costs. They are willing to pursue career choices far below their potential (Willings, 1983). Others cannot focus on career plans.

For average learners, career plans can change between seventeen and nineteen years of age. For those who are gifted, changes in career plans can occur between thirteen and fourteen, sixteen and eighteen, and twenty-one and twenty-three. A radical change in careers for the gifted develops between ages twenty-eight and thirty-two. (Talented children, on the other hand, often have fixed career goals prior to adolescence.) Gifted students need personal and career counselling, a networking system that links students to school and community resources (Clifford, Runions, and Smyth, 1986), and appropriate role models.

For all students who are exceptional, a major aim of career counselling is a careful assessment and analysis of students' strengths and weaknesses, motivations and preferences, and performance in training programs (Fonosh, Avony, Lee, and Loving, 1982). Counsellors need to establish students' present levels with regard to readiness for adult settings (Smith, 1992).

For this, a vocational evaluation is required. A vocational evaluation is a comprehensive and systematic process that utilizes work (real or simulated) to assess the vocational potential of people with disabilities. The process incorporates data such as test scores, medical data, information on education and work experience, and the needs and interests of the individual in setting vocational goals and service requirements (Pruitt, 1986).

Vocational evaluation helps students identify their functional capacities and limitations, formulate realistic vocational goals, and determine their needs for rehabilitation programming (Power, 1984). Sometimes the results of a vocational evaluation will suggest that the goals of the students (and sometimes their parents) are unrealistic. At other times, job choices may be below a student's capacity.

Counsellors may use instruments such as Becker's (1981) Vocational Interest Inventory, which requires no reading. Individuals select the jobs they would prefer from 55 black and white outline drawings depicting 11 categories of unskilled, semi-skilled, and skilled jobs. Students who are deaf can use the Transition Competence Battery (Bullis and Reiman, 1992) or the Self-Help Inter Personal Skills Assessment (Loeding and Crittenden, 1993).

Sex Education

Adolescents with disabilities are less likely to have accurate information about sex, are more subject to fears and myths, and are more likely to be sexually exploited than are their normally developing peers. Studies indicate that children with disabilities are 150 times more at risk than others for being sexually abused ("Increased ... ," 1993). The problems are particularly acute for individuals with intellectual disabilities in the community who are exposed to all the contingencies of sexuality, including situations that involve sexual coercion (Podell, Kastner, and Kastner, 1996). It is reported that as many as 89 percent of persons with intellectual disabilities say they have been sexually abused ("Increased...," 1993). A study using structured interviews (Stromsness, 1993) found that just under 80 percent of the subjects had been sexually abused.

It is imperative that these students be provided with sex education that includes instruction in social behaviour and self-protection. Participation in society has increased the risk of unwanted pregnancies, venereal diseases, and abuse (McCabe, 1993). And, since most persons with mild and moderate retardation now live in the community and do not learn easily from non-directed observations, books, or friends, instruction in appropriate sexual behaviour is particularly important today.

Equally compelling are the principles of normalization. The major goal of normalization is a normal family and community life for all individuals, and sexual activity is a normal part of human life. It is a myth that individuals who are physically disabled do not have sexual needs or that persons with intellectual disabilities are asexual or oversexed. People with mental and physical disabilities have the same range of sexual needs and drives as everyone else.

Persons who are intellectually disabled are just as likely to develop a strong and normal interest in the opposite sex as anyone else. But as with non-disabled people, some seem to have little need for physical contact, some express more need than the average, and the majority fall in the middle range (McClennen, 1988).

If physical development is normal, sexual development follows chronological rather than cognitive development, although psychosocial development may be reached at a later chronological age (Martin and Forchuk, 1987). Because of this, some individuals who are disabled are more likely to express experimentation overtly. They may also have trouble figuring out where the boundaries are and when they should say no.

To understand sexuality, an individual must be educated (Romaneck and Kuehl, 1992). Adolescent students may need to be made aware that their own sexuality is acceptable and that they have the same rights to sexual expression as do their peers. Sex education programs for adolescents who are physically and mentally disabled should include explanations of bodily functions, the mechanics of reproduction, social behaviour, dating skills, and preparation for marriage and family.

AIDS is also an issue for adolescents because adolescence is often a time of sexual confusion and experimentation (Sloane and Sloane, 1990). Effective AIDS education means talking about topics such as homosexuality, drugs, and condoms (although this makes many parents uneasy) (Kirp and Epstein, 1989).

Functional Academics

Despite special education programming often offered throughout their school careers, many adolescent students with disabilities continue to function far below grade level. Rather than focusing solely on the traditional three Rs, teachers of secondary students with disabilities must be concerned with targeting useful learning objectives. Students require functional academics; that is, academics that have meaning and are relevant to the learner soon to enter community work and life. This may include intense remedial instruction for skill deficits, such as basic knowledge and skills in reading, computation, study skills, and strategy training to enable older students to gain the knowledge of how to use skills to meet demands of the academic, occupational, and social environment. Also incorporated may be skills in self-care, mobility training, communication, social interaction, health and safety, leisure time, and vocational pursuits.

Vocational Education and Work Study Experiences

Transition should focus on work personality (self-concept and motivation); work competencies (habits, physical and mental skills, and interpersonal skills); and work goals (career objectives) (see Szymanski, 1994). It should facilitate students' access to and participation in the receiving environment through job preparation that includes skills such as locating job openings in newspapers and displaying correct behaviour during a job interview.

Students are given opportunities to learn a trade through high-school-sponsored vocational training and on-the-job training in the context of full or part-time work-study programs. Course content includes a multitude of job search, job maintenance, and work-related interpersonal skills lesson formats including the following: obtaining documentation necessary to become employed; preparing a résumé; completing a job application; identifying jobs of interest; finding job leads; organizing a job search; contacting employers by telephone, in person, and in writing; interviewing for a job; and handling work-related paperwork such as timecards, paycheque stubs, work schedule, and tax returns. Students are taught about being a good employee and getting along with others on the job. This includes skills such as understanding instruction; asking a question; asking for help; accepting criticism; ordering job responsibilities; accepting assistance; giving instruction; offering assistance; apologizing; convincing others; being punctual; and practising good attendance. They also need practice in getting to and from work, which includes telephoning for bus route information, reading bus maps and schedules, and practising appropriate and safe behaviour on public transit. There is also information on making positive job changes; setting realistic goals for the future; and being an effective self-advocate (Montague, 1988; Patton, Cronin, Polloway, Hutchinson, and Robinson, 1989).

Work-study experiences, founded on the premise that there should be some cross-coordination between school work and vocational experiences, play a major role in the secondary curriculum and link the preparatory employment to the receiving environment through community-based instruction. Instruction is referenced directly to activities and performance demands in the local community. Students are placed in work situations in the community, and their academic programs are oriented to supplement the work experience.

For youth who are disabled, part-time jobs during school and enrollment in vocational classes correlate with increases in employability (Siegel, Robert, and Gaylord-Ross, 1992). Students who have paid work as part of secondary school experiences are significantly more likely to have a competitive job than those without such experiences (62 percent versus 45 percent) (Bounds, 1997). Persons who are intellectually disabled, for example, who have been in school work experience programs tend to respond better to occupational demands and are more employable than those not in programs (Patton et al., 1989).

The reasons are fairly obvious. Work experiences allow individuals to try new things in an atmosphere that allows for a second chance (Nesbit, 1990). Students learn how to adapt to changes in the work environment and how to maintain acceptable levels of work performance. As well, training often gives students the boost they need to succeed in the work world. Not only do they learn specific job skills, they also learn how to conduct themselves on the job, the responsibilities that accompany employment, and a better idea of what it takes to succeed in a particular field (Bounds, 1997). Holding a paid job allows youth to hone their work skills and demonstrate their reliability to potential employers. Also, paid work experiences provide students an opportunity to apply classroom learning in the real world, gives meaning to their learning, and can be a great motivator (Bounds, 1997).

For students with severe disabilities, the school's vocational curriculum cannot be divorced from the community in which the child lives. Schools need to identify potential employment in early training conducted in the home community (Moon and Inge, 1993).

Social Skills Instruction

The existence of social skill deficits among populations of students who are disabled has been well documented in the professional literature. Adaptive behaviour is predictive of certain aspects of future vocational performance (Harrison, 1987), and the absence of effective social skills is considered to be a major cause of the less than successful adjustment of students who are disabled to the regular competitive work force. Wayne Nesbit notes that when senior students finish school, their personalities must be marketable. "The reality," observes Nesbit, "is that they will not receive an academic high school certificate nor will they earn a university degree. It is their personality and ability to work co-operatively which determines their acceptance and success in the work world" (1990, p. 5).

Programs provide training in the social skills needed for job success. For students with intellectual disabilities, for example, targeted social skills range from isolated non-verbal responses such as eye contact and gestures to complex skills involved in asking questions, expressing appreciation and praise, and carrying on a conversation (Misra, 1993). Students may also need training in aspects of speech such as loudness, intonation, and intelligibility.

Self-management

Self-management refers to a multiplicity of skills needed for independence in the adult world. For example, students learn about apartment living, marriage, family responsibilities, budgeting, and community resources. Students with severe disabilities need instruction in life skills, which include basic hygiene, grooming and dressing, as well as mobility, money handling, shopping, housekeeping, and leisure skills. Even for those who can never achieve full independence, life skills training contributes to feelings of confidence, self-reliance, and personal satisfaction.

Futures Planning

Upon completion of their public schooling, many young people with disabilities still need additional assistance and support to negotiate the transition process successfully.

Transition should ensure access to community support and continuity of services. The adult agency support component is designed to educate students and their family members about the procedures of becoming active clients of vocational rehabilitation, or other agencies, before graduation.

Parent Involvement

In a survey of special educators in secondary schools, the activities they considered most important were teaching social skills and job skills, involving parents, and matching skills to the job (Morgan, Morre, McSweyn, and Salzberg, 1992).

Nevertheless, parent involvement continues to be a major gap in successful transition services. The available evidence and collective experience of families suggest that current transition efforts are far from optimal. Rather, with a few exceptions, they are fragmented, disorganized, and largely ineffective (Johnson, Bruininks, and Thurlow, 1987).

The experiences of parents of students with blindness are illustrative. Researchers (Houser, Moses, and Kay, 1987) found that families are not actively involved in the transition process; are frequently isolated from information about available resources and possibilities for employment; are frequently isolated from emotional support that other families with similar needs can supply; in many cases, are unaware of their own resources; rely on professionals to plan and implement services for them; and may not understand the differences between education and rehabilitation services.

Post-school Experiences

Despite difficulties, many young people with disabilities move into post-secondary education or competitive employment with their non-disabled peers. Sadly, though, there remains a high proportion who are either underemployed or unemployed (Kamp, 1993).

Dropouts

From a sociological perspective, high school graduation may be seen as a rite of passage marking the successful movement of an individual from adolescence into adulthood. Dropouts voluntarily leave the system before completing their education. A general definition used by researchers identifies a dropout as any person who has left secondary school for any reason prior to graduation (Sullivan, 1988). There is a widespread belief that many students who drop out of school are capable of graduating (Neufeld and Stevens, 1992).

Local, provincial, and national studies show a multiplicity of definitions and methodologies for calculating dropout rates. Generally, Canadian estimates give the proportion of grade nine students who do not fulfill graduation requirements at 33 percent (Watt and Reossingh, 1994).

Factors correlated with dropping out include community type, single-parent family, attendance rate, low self-concept, low need for self-development, pregnancy, marriage, having a job, institutionalization or incarceration, delinquency, and drug use. Poverty, membership in a dysfunctional family, and poor mental and physical health serve to further disadvantage some youth and their expectations of high school graduation (Squires, 1992).

Students themselves give varied explanations for dropping out, although three major reasons surface in the dropout literature. First is a sense of alienation on the part of dropouts. Students' satisfaction with school, their sense that their classes are interesting and that teachers care, and teacher feedback and evaluation influence students' self-esteem (Hoge, Smit, and Hanson, 1990). School dropouts often feel that no one cares for them. Second is the belief that courses are irrelevant, which results in students being bored and unmotivated. Third is frustration born of poor academic concept, resulting in failure, grade retention, and poor self-concept (Can. CEC, 1992).

Predicting who will drop out is not easy, although poor reading performance and retention in a grade seem to be primary. According to Robert Slavin and his colleagues (1990):

> Reaching the third grade on time with adequate basic skills may not provide a guarantee that a student will complete his education, but it appears that children who do not reach third grade on time with adequate skills have little chance of educational success, regardless of the remedial or special education resources invested in them later in their school careers.

Only a small amount of literature deals specifically with dropping out by students identified as candidates for special education (Lichenstein, 1989). In the United States, approximately 30 percent of students who are disabled drop out (Edgar, 1987; Knight and Rieck, 1997). In Canada, there is evidence that the majority of students in two categories of special education (gifted and physically disabled) graduate from high school. In all other categories, non-completion rates are staggering (Can. CEC, 1992).

It is estimated that 47 percent of adolescents with learning disabilities drop out of school by age 16 (Gartner and Lipsky, 1987). In Calgary, researchers (Watt and Roessingh, 1993) tracked 388 ESL students and found a rate close to 74 percent of immigrant students dropping out of high school. Sylvia Rimm (1986) points out that almost invariably, gifted dropouts are underachievers, talented students who are unguided, uncounselled, and unchallenged.

The dropout percentage for students with disabilities has decreased steadily over the past five years, and the graduation percentage has shown a general upward trend (see Blackorby and Wagner, 1996). More students go to college and more have access to some form of vocational education that contributes significantly to the probability of competitive employment. Nevertheless, special education must still address the fact that an unacceptable percentage of students with disabilities drop out of school, and a significant number of those students who do graduate do not secure employment later or do not retain secured jobs.

Generally, high unemployment, low income, and low educational levels characterize school leavers with disabilities. When Lichenstein (1989) followed a population of students with mild disabilities beyond high school, he found that dropping out was a greater factor in unemployment than the disability itself. Other research findings consistently suggest that young adults at greatest risk for lifelong economic and social harm are those with disabilities who also dropped out of high school. These young people are seriously at risk because of their history of inadequate educational attainment, their chronic dependence on society, and their uncertain future in the job market (Edgar, Levine, and Maddox, 1985).

Competitive Employment

Competitive employment of persons with disabilities enhances feelings of self-worth and efficacy and increases the normalization of these persons, both in self-perception and the perception of society (Scott and Sarkee, 1982; Seyfarth, Hill, Orelone, McMillan, and Wehman, 1985). The mere observation of disabled individuals engaging in functional, integrated, and age-appropriate activities appears to have effects on the development of a more respectful and optimistic attitude toward them from the public, one factor which would contribute further to employment success (Bates, Morrow, Pancsafar, and Sedlak, 1984).

When young adults with disabilities enter the work force, they find many difficulties in obtaining and retaining employment. Secondary students with mild disabilities tend to be employed less often than their non-disabled peers (Edgar, 1988). Students with learning disabilities, intellectual disabilities, behavioural disorders, and other disabilities tend to be far less successful than peers. Follow-up studies have reported low levels of employment for those exiting special education; young people in virtually all disability groups are employed at a lower rate than the general population.

For individuals who are disabled, jobs found are often at entry level but with few employee benefits, and they are often obtained through a self-family-friend network (Lombard and Newbert, 1992). In Vermont, a study of 459 youths exiting special education (Hasazi, Gordon, and Roe, 1985) showed an employment rate of only 54 percent. In Colorado, researchers (Mithaug, Horiuchi, and Fanning, 1985) found employment rates of 69 percent, but almost half of those employed were earning less than $3 an hour.

It is difficult to pinpoint the factors that contribute to failure for students with disabilities. Some problems certainly stem from conditions in the labour market, inadequate or inappropriate vocational and educational preparation, lack of transition support services, or other related factors, such as employer attitudes. Others relate to individual traits, work habits, and attitudes. Exactly how a disability affects an adult depends on the adult's past academic, social, and emotional experiences and the expectations of the settings in which he or she works.

The research on learning disabilities in adulthood is fragmented. One study (see Sitlington, Frank, and Carson, 1992) found that only 54 percent of young adults with learning disabilities had achieved independent living and stable roles. When Zetlin and Hossenini (1989) studied six post-school case studies of young adults with mild disabilities, they found that the students were "at a loss to plan for the future, maintained an unrealistic appraisal of their skills, and expressed discontent with their present situation" (p. 406).

Some adults with learning disabilities learn to compensate for their attention problems and find occupations that allow them to utilize their strengths while minimizing their shortcomings. For others, the disabling aspects of learning disabilities may become more firmly established in adulthood. Adults with learning disabilities continue to have reading problems (Rogan and Hardman, 1990), difficulties with written expression, and need help with math skills (Hoffman, Shelson, Minskoff, Sautter, Steidle, Baker, Bailey, and Echols, 1987). Individuals may exhibit low motivation, distractibility, self-concept problems, and lack of organization (Buchanan and Wolf, 1986). They feel frustrated, have little self-confidence, and have difficulty controlling emotions and/or temper; depression often follows (Hoffman et al., 1987). The behaviours that characterize learning disabilities in some adults contribute to the problems they experience after school and may actually increase as the individual experiences new social and vocational expectations (Weller and Sipherd, 1982).

Adults who are learning disabled secure employment at nearly the same rate as their non-disabled peers. The jobs, however, have less social status, lower wages, and fewer regular hours than those of non-disabled groups (Okolo and Sitlington, 1986). When they find jobs, students with learning disabilities often cannot keep them. It seems to be the subtle invisible aspects of learning disabilities that impede success in the work world (Hursh, 1985).

Little information is available on adults with Attention Deficit Hyperactivity Disorder, and treatment programs are virtually nonexistent. It is estimated that up to 70 percent of children diagnosed with ADHD continue to have symptoms in adolescence and adulthood (Burt, Parks-Charney, and Schwean, 1996; Heiligenstrin and Keeling, 1995) although the prevalence in adults is unknown (Richard, 1995). It is known that the disorders manifest in different ways in adults and may vary considerably depending on task and content (Brown, 1995). While the hyperactivity component often dissipates in adults, it is replaced by inner feelings of restlessness.

Transition from school to work is particularly difficult for adolescents who are behaviourally disordered. Given the manner in which their problems manifest, it is not surprising that these are among the students most likely to drop out of school and among the most difficult individuals to train in transition programs (Edgar, 1987; Neel, Meadows, Levine, and Edgar, 1988). Many lack the basic skills needed for employment. Students with behavioural disorders often use inappropriate strategies to solve conflicts and cope with frustration; they often behave in ways that prevent them from being accepted, liked, and helped by employers and co-workers (Hallahan and Kauffman, 1991).

Many adults who are mildly retarded are able to merge into the community and work at a variety of semi-skilled and service positions. They have varying degrees of success in attaining and retaining employment, but most can partially or totally support themselves. However, students with intellectual disabilities do less well at getting employment than learning-disabled or emotionally disturbed subgroups (Edgar, 1988). If not underemployed or unemployed, they are often the last hired and tend to hold unskilled and semi-skilled jobs.

Adults who are intellectually disabled seem to be particularly susceptible to changes in the economy. Job success is a function of attitudes and personality, not IQ. On the job, persons with intellectual disabilities often have problems with job responsibility, task production competence, and/or social competence (Salzberg, Lignugaris-Kraft, and McCuller, 1988).

Having some work experience before graduation helps adolescents with the transition to adult life.

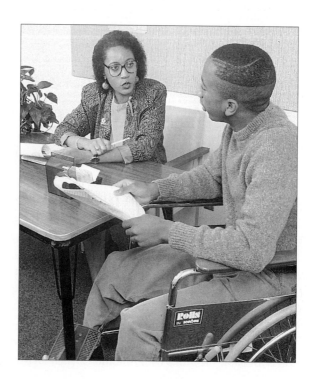

Supported Employment

Supported employment, sometimes referred to as sheltered workshops, offers more structure for persons with disabilities. Supported employment ensures that a person may receive continuous help managing the routines of living and working (see Kregel, 1997). Three essential features characterize supported employment: opportunities for paid productive work with ongoing support; training to ensure continued employment; and employment in a socially integrated environment (Sinnott-Oswald, Gliner, and Spencer, 1991).

In Canada, a workshop describes a wide variety of work situations and vocational rehabilitation programs that range from adult day programs to highly automated production factories. In their present form, sheltered workshops are commercial–industrial models of production. They provide long-term support in a controlled and protected work environment where they offer work experience for those who cannot be in competitive employment (Kaplan, 1996). They serve to assess, improve, and stabilize vocational functioning, thus assisting a person who is disabled to progress to employment in the competitive labour market. Within the workshop, expectations are adjusted to each individual's ability. The workers have constant input and supervision and their personal differences are tolerated.

Block (1993) reports that the field of vocational rehabilitation is undergoing change, and one facet is the move to new service models. It seems that sheltered workshops will continue to play a role in the field of vocational rehabilitation but their use may diminish.

Post-secondary Education

Of all disabled groups, those with learning disabilities represent the greatest number in post-secondary education. Indeed, in any Canadian college or university of 10 000 students, as many as 1 000 may have some type of learning disability (Cox and Klas, 1996). Keep in mind that these numbers are tenuous. Because students in post-secondary institutions are typically asked to self-identify, many disabilities remain hidden (Cox and Klas, 1996).

While students with learning disabilities represent the largest numbers, those who have suffered traumatic brain injuries represent the fastest-growing segment of the disabled population entering post-secondary institutions (Cook, 1991).

Special educators and vocational counsellors are often caught off guard by the hidden limitations of learning disabilities (Cox nd Klas, 1996). While they may assume that these students can go on to higher education without support, this is not valid. While an unprecedented number of individuals with learning disabilities have entered and succeeded in post-secondary education in the past few decades, the success of these students does not correlate as much as previously thought to a higher quality of life during the adult years (Kamp, 1993). As mentioned earlier, the adult population still has a high number of individuals who lack self-esteem, self-direction, and suffer from chronic depression and other coping problems (Kamp, 1993).

Nevertheless, students with learning disabilities can succeed in college and university if they are given reasonable accommodations. Cox and Klas (1996) mention that Ontario has been the most responsive to the needs of students with learning disabilities but also note that specially designed programs are found at St. Mary's University, Memorial University of Newfoundland, the University of British Columbia, the University of Alberta, the University of Western Ontario, and York University.

To assist students with learning disabilities, typical approaches include modified tests, more time to complete tests, many short rather than one long examination, alternate assignments, and assistive devices such as computer access. Generally, faculty members seem willing to make accommodations (Nelson et al., 1990).

Only three percent of Canadians who are deaf attend university (Schein, 1994). Qualified students with deafness can both succeed and compete in public post-secondary institutions if provided with adequate support services such as note taking and sign language interpreting (Jones, 1986). However, full integration, especially social integration, may not occur (Brown and Foster, 1991).

Students with visual impairments my have difficulties in college. In one study (cited by McBroom, 1997), 32 percent of these students dropped out. Matching the students' needs to the program is critical for students with visual impairments.

SUMMARY

1. Consistent and structured programming for adolescents with disabilities has not traditionally been a prominent feature of special education. Although the field has had access to well-articulated models of high school programs for students with mild disabilities for more than two decades, adolescents and young adults with mild disabilities have received less than their share of special education services.

2. In recent years, special educators have examined the needs of students with disabilities as they move from the school environment to the world of employment and found that these students are in obvious need of programs and services that will enable them to make a successful transition from school to adult community environments. Transition should be seen as serving the needs of parents and students and conforming to the principles of normalization. In the transition from school to work there are two related areas which must be considered—community adjustment and employment.

3. As both a concept and a process, transition is relatively new in special education. The need for transition services arose from data demonstrating less than complimentary outcomes from special education. Once out of school, youth with disabilities experience high rates of unemployment, and if they do find jobs they often cannot keep them. In addition to problems with job finding and retention, young adults with disabilities may not possess adequate functional skills.

4. For older adolescents with disabilities, school practices attempt to establish relationships between educational variables and better employment and independent living outcomes. Programs should match the skills needed by individuals in the community so as to better prepare students for post-school life.

5. Effective counselling plays an important role in guidance and career planning for students with disabilities and for gifted students. Counselling assists in making appropriate career plans and enhances an individual's ability to acquire a positive self-concept, self-understanding, and self-acceptance.

6. A major concern for those involved with adolescents who have intellectual or physical disabilities concerns sexual awareness.

7. Many adolescents with disabilities reach secondary school with severe deficits in the core areas of reading and math. There is often a mismatch between their abilities and the requirements of the system.

8. Some necessary skills can be taught in regular settings; some cannot. Therefore, where students should be educated is a matter of concern. As curriculum, expectations, and outcomes may not match the needs of older learners who are disabled, full academic inclusion may not be what is needed at the senior level. A number of educators argue that despite the current emphasis on inclusion, the regular classroom may not be the most suitable setting for late-secondary students. They contend that we need to pay more attention to bettering the lives of students than to their school address. The acquisition of requisite employment skills cannot be left to chance or viewed as a peripheral adjunct to mainstream curricula.

9. Students who are disabled need to function successfully in school, home, job, and community settings. If they are to live independently, to manage their affairs without supervision, and to be self-sufficient, they must develop marketable occupational skills.

10. Training in social skills is particularly important for adolescents with disabilities. However, the most critical needs area of disabled adults is in the realm of vocational competency, including the ability to find an appropriate job and the provision of rehabilitation services.

In the Classroom

Ben is in his last year of school. When he was only a preschooler, he was identified as being moderately mentally retarded. Throughout elementary school he was included in the regular classroom with modified programming. However, it was soon apparent that secondary programs are not consistent with Ben's future needs, and almost all of his secondary experience has been in a program that stresses life and occupational skills and functional academics.

Now in his final year in school, Ben's transition plan is more critical than ever. It includes functional academics, community services and agencies, vocational training and work experience, and opportunities to function independently in the community.

At the moment, the teacher is working on living and recreational skills in a thematic topic on communities. Ben and his classmates are learning about shopping, restaurants, and other community places. For example, under shopping the lesson areas and activities include making a shopping list; floor plans and aisle signs; the sequence of shopping and shopping in aisle order; locating items, prices, and sizes; and unpacking and storing groceries. The restaurants segment includes areas such as standing in line; selecting a seat; ordering; and table manners. In the section on the post office, Ben learns about buying stamps, addressing envelopes, and sending mail (see Beakley and Yoder, 1998).

Karen attends the same school as Ben, although they have never met. Karen is in a regular classroom although she has a serious learning disability that limits her reading and writing. Throughout her high school years, the teachers have all made various adaptations to help Karen remain in the regular classroom and to earn the grades she needs to pass on to college.

Examples of adaptations in various subject areas for Karen include adjusted length of assignments; extra time for classroom assignments; use of a word processor for homework; photocopied notes and marginal glosses; and advanced organizers for lectures. Karen has also been allowed test adaptations. These include extra time; a separate setting to write the test; oral questions and oral answers; and the use of a word processor.

As she approaches the end of her school career, Karen is finding that the teachers use more and more of a lecture mode, sometimes lecturing for up to half of the class period. She is allowed to tape some of the lectures, but is also working with her homeroom teacher to improve her note-taking skills. The teacher is helping her with strategic note taking. This procedure involves using special cued note paper in which Karen fills in the details during and after a lecture. The cues are:

1. Today's topic. Karen identifies the topic and briefly summarizes any knowledge she has of it before the class.

2. Major points of the lecture, given in clusters.

3. New points included in the lecture.

4. Later, Karen writes five main points from the lecture and describes each point (Weishaar and Boyle, 1997).

WEBLINKS

The Opportunity of Adolescence **http://www.winternet.com/~webpage/ adolescence.html**

Global Applied Disability Research and Information Network on Employment and Training **http://www.gladnet.org/**

The Canadian Vocational Association **http://www.cva.ca/**

Institute on Disability Culture Newsgroup Archive **http://www.dimenet.com/ cgi-bin/disculture/getindexdisculture?1R**

Glossary

Academic underachievers: those about whom we can make a reasonable prediction of academic potential that is not fulfilled.

Acquired aphasia: conditions (trauma) that occur after language has been developed.

Adaptive behaviour: how well a person is able to adapt to environmental demands. Differs according to the individual's age group and particular situation.

Adventitious hearing impairment: one acquired some time after birth, through accident or disease.

Adventitious low vision: conditions caused by accident or disease some time after birth.

Aggression: any form of behaviour designed to harm or injure another living being who is motivated to avoid such treatment.

Albinism: a condition carried as an inherited autosomal recessive trait.

Allergy (hypersensitivity): an abnormal and varied reaction that occurs following a contact with substances or agents that normally do not cause symptoms in other individuals.

Antisocial behaviour: overt, aggressive, disruptive behaviour, or covert antisocial acts which are repeated infractions of socially prescribed behaviour patterns that violate social norms and the rights of others.

Aphasia: child's primary impairment is the inability to communicate effectively with verbal language because of comprehension and/or production difficulties.

Apraxia: the inability to program, position, and sequence the muscle movements involved in speech.

Arthritis: a common term for a variety of chronic systemic conditions involving inflammation of the joints.

Assessment: the process of gathering valid evidence to guide decisions about curriculum and instruction, and to evaluate the outcomes of instruction.

Asthma: a variable, reversible obstruction of the airways characterized by the narrowing of bronchial tubes, swelling of tissues, and clogging of mucus.

Astigmatism: the result of an irregularity in the curvature of the cornea or lens of the eye.

At risk: one who is more vulnerable to biological or environmental insult.

Ataxia: a type of cerebral palsy characterized by poor co-ordination of the movements associated with balance, posture, and spatial orientation.

Athetosis: a type of cerebral palsy characterized by constant, involuntary writhing movements, especially in the hands and wrists.

Atrophy: when there is neurological damage or the muscles are weakened due to nerve degeneration.

Attention: the process of tuning in to sensory information with engagement or active participation.

Audiogram: in a hearing test, the data for each ear are plotted on this chart of hearing.

Augmentative communication: a general group of procedures designed to support, enhance, or augment the communication of nonspeaking individuals or to utilize and supplement whatever vocal skills an individual possesses.

Autosomal (identical) chromosomal pairs: the first 22 chromosomes that determine the thousands of traits that make up a human being.

Behaviour management: all the ways in which teachers control inappropriate and disruptive behaviour as well as ways in which children are taught discipline and to control their own behaviour.

Bilingual education: schooling provided fully or partly in the second language with the object of making students proficient in the second language while at the same time maintaining and developing their proficiency in the first language and fully guaranteeing their educational development.

Bilingual: describes individuals who speak two languages. In the education of deaf students, refers to ASL and English.

Biological risk: relates to infants and toddlers with a history of prenatal, perinatal, neonatal, or early developmental events resulting in biological insults to the developing nervous system.

Body image: a person's awareness of the body, its capabilities, the interrelationship of body parts, and the relationship of bodies to the environment.

Bound morphemes: sound units that are not words by themselves but units of meaning only when combined with words.

Cancer: a general term used to describe about a hundred conditions characterized by abnormal and uncontrolled cell growth.

Cataract: an opacity of the lens or its capsule that restricts the eye's ability to receive light and interferes with central and peripheral visual acuity.

Cerebral palsy: a condition characterized by damage to the brain before, during, or after birth.

Childhood psychoses: a heterogeneous group of clinical syndromes characterized by any number of maladaptive behaviours or clusters of behaviours that affect various aspects of adaptive behaviour and the success of interpersonal relations.

Children with exceptionalities: those who have difficulty in realizing their full human potential. Their intellectual, emotional, physical, or social performance falls below or rises above that of other children. The differences may be related to physical, psychological, cognitive, emotional, or social factors, or a combination of these.

Chronic health problems: occur when the presence of a disease or medical condition interferes with school attendance and learning and hinders the ability to lead a normal life.

Classroom management: the way in which teachers manipulate the classroom environment to minimize disruptions and give all children the optimum opportunity to engage in appropriate behaviour and reach learning and social goals.

Cochlea: a tiny, snail-shaped structure filled with a fluid similar to cerebral spinal fluid.

Cochlear implant: a prosthesis designed to replace some lost function of the cochlea.

Cognition: the process of recognizing, identifying, associating, and inferring meaning beyond the figural information provided by the environment that allows an understanding of a concept and application to new conditions.

Cognitive development: orderly changes that occur in the way children understand and cope with their world.

Colour blindness: a rare, sex-linked, hereditary disorder found almost always in males. Defects of colour vision arise from the absence or malfunctioning of the cone cells of the retina.

Communicative competence: when individuals know how to interact, how to communicate appropriately in various situations, and how to make sense of what others say and do in communicative interactions.

Conceptual definition: a statement that describes a condition theoretically.

Conduct disorders: describes hyper-aggressive and highly disruptive children who form the major por-

tion of those identified in the schools as behaviourally disordered

Conductive hearing loss: caused by problems in the mechanical transmission of sound waves through the outer and middle ear.

Congenital hearing impairment: one that is present at birth.

Congenital low vision: conditions that are diagnosable at birth or shortly thereafter.

Creativity: the process of bringing unusual and unexpected responses to bear on given situations; a capacity to restructure the world in unusual or useful conceptual terms.

Critical period: that part of the life cycle during which the developing organism is particularly sensitive or responsive to specific environmental forces.

Curriculum-based assessment: a standardized measurement system used to monitor a student's academic growth and to improve instructional programs.

Cystic fibrosis (CF): a genetically determined inborn error of metabolism characterized by pervasive dysfunction of the exocrine glands (glands in which secretions are passed through ducts).

Deaf community: describes social and other associations of persons who are deaf and bound together by a common language and culture.

Deaf person: one whose hearing disability precludes successful processing of linguistic information through audition, with or without a hearing aid.

Decibel: the smallest difference in loudness intensity that can be perceived.

Delinquency: a set of antisocial behaviours acquired over time.

Delinquent behaviour: any illegal act by a juvenile, regardless of whether the perpetrators are apprehended.

Developmental delay: a condition which represents a significant

delay in the process of development; an indication that the process of development is significantly affected and that without special intervention, it is likely that educational performance at school age will be affected.

Developmental disability: a significant lag in development.

Developmental risk factors: the wide range of biological and environmental conditions that are associated with increased probability for cognitive, social, affective, and physical problems.

Developmentally disabled individuals: those who suffer from chronic disabilities, attributable to mental or physical impairments, or a combination of these, that are manifested before age 22 and that result in functional limitations in major life activities, requiring special services and treatment that are of extended duration or are lifelong.

Diabetes mellitus: a disorder of sugar metabolism caused by a pancreatic disorder in the production of insulin, a hormone needed to metabolize glucose.

Diabetic retinopathy: a disease of the retina's blood vessels.

Diagnose: to determine the causes of a condition.

Differential diagnosis: the precise specification that a given set of symptoms is indicative of one disorder rather than another.

Directionality: an awareness of left and right in the environment outside the body.

Disabilities: reflect the consequences of impairments in terms of functional performance and activity by the individual.

Discipline: helping children to learn to guide their own behaviour in a way that shows respect and caring for themselves, other people, and the physical environment.

Dysarthria: refers to a group of speech disorders resulting from disturbed muscular control over the speech mechanisms.

Dyspedagogia (maleducation): poor learning brought about by inadequate teaching and other school variables.

Dyssynchrony: uneven development.

Early childhood education program: a program that is concerned with the development and special needs of young children and their families with particular emphasis on the preschool years.

Early identification: the practice of screening infants and young children in an attempt to identify those likely to experience problems in learning or behaviour.

Early intervention: a variety of educational, psychological, or therapeutic interventions provided for disabled, at-risk, or disadvantaged infants and preschoolers to prevent or ameliorate developmental delays of disabilities or to provide support to children and families in cases where disabilities exist.

Echolalic speech: speech that is an immediate imitation of some other speaker.

Elective mutism: seen in children who are emotionally disturbed who do not speak or speak only in certain circumstances.

Emotional overlay: an adverse reaction to learning problems and academic failure.

Enrichment: providing special activities in the regular classroom setting.

Environmental risk: applies to families and their infants and toddlers who are considered biologically sound but whose early life experiences (including maternal and family care, health care, nutrition, opportunities for expression of language, adaptive behaviour, and patterns of physical and social stimulation) are sufficiently limited that there is a high probability of delayed development.

Epidemiology: the study of the distribution and determinants of diseases and handicapping conditions in a population.

Established risk: a diagnosed medical disorder with a known etiology (cause) that bears relatively well-known expectancies for developmental outcomes within varying ranges of developmental disabilities.

Etiology: the process of finding causes to explain how a particular problem came into existence.

Eustachian tube: connects the middle ear to the nasopharynx.

Expressive disorders: those which affect the formulation of grammatical utterances.

External (outward) locus of control: when students view themselves as controlled by outer rather than inner forces.

Extra-familial influences: those agencies outside the family that influence a child's cognitive, social, and emotional development.

Family needs: a family's expressed desire for services to be obtained or outcomes to be achieved.

Fine motor skills: those skills that involve small body movements and refer to the muscles of the hand.

Fovea: the most sensitive spot of the retina.

Functional skills: those skills that help children to get along in their current and future environments.

Gaze aversion: the failure to look directly at another individual.

Generalized seizures: seizures that are bilateral and symmetrical without local onset in the brain.

Glaucoma: a condition caused by interocular pressure on the eyeball.

Grammar: the sum total of conventions that govern the communication of meaning of a particular language.

Gross motor skills: large body movements such as running, climbing, and throwing.

Habilitation: to restore to normal functioning.

Handicap: environmental or functional demands placed on a disabled person in a particular situation that are not met.

Haptic problems: these encompass touch, body movement, and position in space.

Hard-of-hearing person: one who, generally with the use of a hearing aid, has residual hearing sufficient to enable successful processing of linguistic information through audition.

Hearing impairment: a generic term indicating a hearing disability that may range in severity from mild to profound. It includes the subsets of deaf and hard of hearing.

Hemisphericity: a person's tendency to rely more on one cerebral hemisphere to process certain types of information.

Hereditary anomalies: genetic disorders present at birth.

Holophrasic speech: when a single word is used to express a more complex idea.

Hydrocephalus: a condition characterized by an excessive accumulation of cerebrospinal fluid in the brain due to an obstruction of its flow.

Hyperactive: children display rates of motor behaviour that are too high for their age groups.

Hyperopia: far sightedness caused by too short an eye or too flat a corneal surface.

Idiopathic epilepsy: epilepsy of unknown origin; the causes cannot be found.

Impairments: abnormalities of body structure and with system function resulting from any cause.

Incidence: the number of new cases of a particular condition ascertained over a given period of time, usually a year.

Incus: small bone in the middle ear.

Information processing: a psychological theory which holds that humans process information in different ways and at various levels of analysis.

Intelligence quotient (IQ): the relationship between a child's mental age (MA) and chronological age (CA).

Interpreter (sometimes called a transliterator): a normally hearing person who facilitates the transmission of information between individuals who do not communicate with a common language or code.

Intervention: a general term for the application of professional skills to maintain or improve a child's potential and functioning; care and education aimed at influencing the direction and scope of children's developmental processes.

Jacksonian seizure: one form of partial seizure which only occurs in cases of symptomatic epilepsy. Characterized by motor symptoms without impaired consciousness.

Labelling: the categorizing of children on the basis of their primary disability.

Language delays: seen in children who demonstrate significant lags but whose language is still progressing according to the stages of normal language development.

Language disorders: impairment of deviant development of comprehension or the use of a spoken, written, or other symbol system.

Language problems: a range of difficulties with the linguistic code, or with the rules and concentrations for linking the symbols and the symbol sequences.

Laterality: an internal knowledge of the differences between left and right.

Leadership: the ability to effect positive and productive changes that are self-enhancing or group-enhancing.

Legal blindness: an acuity measure of 20/200 or less in the better eye with the best correction or visual acuity of more than 20/200 if the widest diameter of the field of vision subtends an angle of no greater than 20 degrees.

Life cycle (lifespan) approach: this perspective sees the family as a unit that is moving through time and experiencing a series of events, tasks, and transitions.

Macular retinal degeneration: problems with macular, the small area in the central portion of the retina responsible for fine or distinct vision. May be inherited, but is also associated with injuries such as contusions and concussions.

Malleus: small bones in the middle ear.

Maturational lag: when a child is slow to reach some developmental milestones.

Meatus: external ear canal which runs obliquely from the pinna to the ear drum.

Medically fragile children: those with special health management needs; includes children who demonstrate a wide range of chronic and progressive illnesses and severe disabilities.

Meningitis: a disease that attacks the meninges, or coverings of the brain and spinal cord; it is accompanied by a high fever.

Metacognition: the awareness of basic learning strategies and one's own awareness of how one learns.

Metalinguistic skills: the ability to think about and talk about language.

Microcephalus: a rare phenomenon in which brain development is impaired by an abnormally small cranium.

Minimal brain dysfunction (MBD): a diagnostic classification for children who present a diverse variety of mildly disabling symptoms.

Morphology: the system of word building in the language.

Motherese: child–adult communicative interaction characterized by unique alterations in speech, meaning, form, and even language usage.

Motor development: the process through which a child acquires movement patterns and skills.

Motor skills: those skills related to the development and use of the muscles and limbs.

Motor: a term used to denote muscular movement.

Multifactorial inheritance: inheritance that results from the interaction of many genes with other genes or environmental factors.

Multiple disabilities: those in which children suffer two or more handicaps that hinder their attainment of their full potential.

Multiple sclerosis: a progressive disease of the central nervous system characterized by patchy scarring or hardening of the myelin sheath of the nerve cells in the brain and the spinal cord.

Multisensory impaired: a term used to describe children with sight and hearing handicaps.

Muscular dystrophy: a group of inherited conditions characterized by degeneration of muscle fibres without neurological deficit.

Musculoskeletal impairments: those conditions that impede bodily movements in the absence of damage to the central nervous system.

Mutism: the total absence of speech.

Myopia: nearsightedness; the greatest single cause of defective vision in children and young adults.

Neurological impairments: those that result from damage or dysfunction of the brain or the spinal cord.

Normalization: the philosophical belief that all exceptional individuals, no matter what their level and type of disability, should be provided with an education and living environment that is as close to normal as possible.

Norm-referenced test: when an individual child's performance is compared to the normative group consisting of other children of the same age.

Nystagmus: a rhythmic involuntary movement of the eyes.

Objective: a clear statement of exactly what a teacher wants a child to be able to do as a result of instruction.

Optic nerve atrophy: occurs when there has been damage to the fibers of the optic nerve.

Orthotic devices: those that assist a limb's action.

Otitis media: a condition in which the mucous lining of the middle ear becomes inflamed and the cavity filled with fluid.

Partial seizures: various types that may be characterized as simple or complex.

Pediatric AIDS: AIDS contracted by children under thirteen years of age.

Perception: the use of the senses to recognize, discriminate, and interpret stimuli; it forms a link between sensation and perception.

Perseverate: to purposelessly and sometimes disadvantageously repeat and activity.

Pervasive developmental disorder: a general term used to describe children and youth suffering from chronic and severe conditions that affect every aspect of their development.

Petit mal (absence seizure): this type is seen most frequently seen in children.

Phobia: an anxiety reaction that is specific to one stimulus, an intense fear with no rational basis.

Phonetics: the description of the speech sounds of a language.

Phonological awareness: the ability to blend, segment, rhyme, or in other ways manipulate the sounds of spoken words.

Phonology: the sound system of language; the rules for using the sounds of language.

Physical development: the acquisition of postural control and the necessary movement patterns to produce functional motor acts.

Pinna: the cartilage structure on the side of the head.

Post-lingual deafness: becoming deaf after the development of speech and language.

Postmature: infants born two weeks or more beyond the expected due date.

Pragmatics: the ways in which we use language, the role of context in communicative interactions.

Precocious: remarkable early development.

Prelingual deafness: those who are deaf prior to the development of speech and language.

Premature babies (preterm): those born before the completion of 37 weeks of gestation.

Presbyopia: a condition in which the lens of the eye loses its ability to accommodate to near objects.

Prevalence: the total number of existing cases, old and new.

Preventative discipline: strategies and procedures that militate against any discipline problems arising.

Primary disability: the first or chief disability.

Primary prevention: procedures concerned with removing the causative factors that account for the initial occurrence of the disorder or strengthening the well-being of individuals in the population as a form of inoculation against the causes of subsequent problems.

Prostheses: functional devices that substitute for missing body parts.

Prosthetic adaptation: a specific piece of equipment such as braces or a hearing aid.

Prosthetic devices: used to replace lost functions or provide support; they duplicate normal body movements as nearly as possible while restraining normal functions as little as possible.

Psycho-educational assessment: testing children across a variety of domains relevant to social and educational performance.

Psychological processing: how an individual processes sensory information and puts it to meaningful intellectual use.

Reflexes: automatic, involuntary motor patterns that are triggered by specific stimuli.

Rehabilitation: procedures that endeavour to restore an individual to normal or optimal functioning.

Remediation: helping a child to overcome, or compensate for, specific deficits in learning and development.

Retinal detachment: occurs when a hole or rip in the retina allows the inner retina layer to separate from the back portion.

Retinitis pigmentosa: a hereditary condition that causes degeneration of retinal tissues and loss of peripheral vision.

Retinoblastoma: results from a malignant tumour on the retina that may spread to the optic nerve and other areas.

Retinopathy of prematurity (retrolental fibroplasia): a condition affecting the retina and the vitreous humour.

Rigidity: a type of cerebral palsy that occurs when there is a low level of motor stiffness that never relaxes.

Risk factors: the causes of potential disabilities.

School law: the legislation, regulations, by-laws, and judicial decisions that apply primarily to all or part of the public school system.

Screening: developmental and health activities that are intended to identify those children who have a high probability of exhibiting delayed or abnormal development.

Secondary prevention: ascertaining, as early as possible, the evidence of disorders that may cause disabilities as well as allied attempts to reduce, remove, or reverse substantially complex aspects of disabilities.

Self-stimulation: a persistent, stereotypical, repetitive mannerism.

Semantics: word meaning.

Sensorineural hearing impairments: these interfere with the conversion of sound waves to neural impulses for the brain.

Severe visual impairment: serious visual problems ranging from an inability to read newsprint with the use of ordinary glasses to total blindness.

Sociability: a child's willingness to engage others in social interaction and to seek attention or approval.

Social cognition: the knowledge and cognitive activities employed by people in dealing with the social world.

Social competence: the ability of children to successfully and appropriately select and carry out their interpersonal goals.

Social skills: those responses that prove effective within a given situation.

Social support approach: focuses on a family's functioning; stresses families helping themselves and sees informal support as more important than formal support.

Socialization: the means by which individuals become reasonably acceptable and competent members of their society.

Spastic cerebral palsy (pyramidal): individuals with this type of cerebral palsy have suffered damage to the motor cortex or to the pyramidal track of the brain.

Special education: instruction that is specially designed to meet the unique needs of children and youth who are exceptional.

Special needs: an educational term used to designate pupils who require special education.

Speech disorders: problems encountered in the oral production of language; an impairment of verbal communication such that the intelligibility of spoken language is reduced.

Speech range: the range of pitch between 500 and 2 000 Hz.

Speech reading (lip reading): the skill of understanding speech through watching the lips and face.

Speech reception threshold (SRT): the level at which an individual actually understands speech.

Spina bifida occulta: the mildest form of the spinal bifida with few or no negative effects.

Spina bifida with meningecele: the meninges protrude from the plane of the spine and form a sac containing cerebrospinal fluid.

Spina bifida with myelomeningocele: there is a protruding sac which contains parts of the spinal cord as well as cerebrospinal fluid.

Spina bifida: a congenital midline defect of the spinal column.

Stapes: small bone in the middle ear.

Strabismus: a condition that results from inefficient ocular motor mobility; can affect one or both eyes.

Support services: services designed to assist a child with a disability and his or her teacher.

Symptomatic epilepsy: a condition where an individual shows strong evidence of brain damage.

Syndrome: a constellation of findings similar from patient to patient.

Syntax: the network of organizational principles underlying linguistic expression.

Systems theory: recognizes that actions in any part of the system affect the other parts, and that solutions to problems can only be found when the problem is properly defined in its larger environmental context.

Tactual map: a raised map used by blind persons as a supplemental aid for travel and navigation.

Talent: a specific dimension of a skill in areas such as music, visual arts, drama, athletics, and particular academic domains.

Task analysis: analyzing the behavioural components and prerequisite skills of a task; breaking skills down into their component parts.

Telegraphic speech: the reduced speech resembles a telegram in that only the essential aspects of the message, those possessing meaning, are included.

Teratogens: environmental agents that may harm the developing infant.

Tertiary prevention: intervention strategies used after a negative outcome has been attained.

Testing: explicit criteria for performance are established in advance.

Tests: controlled and structured procedures that attempt to elicit particular responses that the child might not demonstrate spontaneously.

Therapy: the treatment of an illness or disabling condition.

Threshold of hearing: the level at which a person can first detect a sound.

Transition services: intended to provide young people with disabilities access to relevant post-secondary education opportunities, employment in competitive settings, residential independence, and future self-sufficiency.

Transition: in early childhood special education is the process of moving from one program to another, or from one service delivery mode to another.

Traumatic Brain Injury: an insult to the brain caused by an external physical force which results in impairment of cognitive abilities or physical functioning and may result in disturbances of behaviour or emotional functioning.

Tremor: a rare type of cerebral palsy where there is an involuntary movement in one extremity, usually one hand or arm.

Tympanic membrane (ear drum): a tough, tightly stretched tissue that separates the outer from the middle ear.

Usher's syndrome: a condition of familial nerve deafness associated with pigment degeneration of the retina.

Vestibular mechanism: lies behind the cochlea; composed of three fluid-filled semi-circular canals.

Visual acuity: the measure of the smallest image distinguishable by the eye.

Visual functioning (visual efficiency): what the impaired person is doing with his or her residual vision.

Bibliography

Aase, J.M. (1979) Environmental causes of birth defects. In A. Lane (Ed.) *Human growth and development of exceptional individuals.* Connecticut: Special Learning Corporation.

Abang, T.B. (1980) *Teaching visually handicapped children in Nigeria.* Ibadan, Nigeria: Cleverianum Press.

Abroms, K.I. and Bennett, J.W. (1983) Current findings in Down's syndrome. *Exceptional Children,* 49, 449–450.

Achenbach, T.M. (1991) *Child Behavior Checklist and Revised Child Behavior Profile.* Burlington VT: University of Vermont.

Acredolo, L. and Goodwyn, S. (1988) Symbolic gesturing in normal infants. *Child Development,* 59, 450–466.

Action for integration: A guide to inclusive education. (1993, summer). *Abilities,* pp. 62–63.

Adams, J.W. and Tidwell, R. (1989) An instructional guide for reducing the stress of parents of hearing impaired children. *American Annals of the Deaf,* 134, 323–328.

Adams, K. and Markham, R. (1991) Recognition of affective facial expressions by children and adolescents with and without mental retardation. *American Journal on Mental Deficiency,* 96, 21–28.

Address of Trustees of the New England Institute for the Education of the Blind to the public (1836). In C. Dunscombe, *Report upon the subject of education made to the Parliament of Upper Canada 25 February 1836, through the Commissioners, Doctors Morrison and Bruce, appointed by a resolution of the House of Assembly in 1835 to obtain information upon the subject of education, etc.* (pp. 95–109) Upper Canada: M.C. Reynolds.

Agnew, J. (1986) Tinnitis: An overview. *Volta Review,* 88, 215–221.

Akerley, M.S. (1975) Parents speak. *Journal of Autism and Childhood Schizophrenia,* 5, 373–380.

Alberta Education (1982) *Early childhood services: Philosophy, goals, and dimensions.* Edmonton: Government of Alberta.

Alberta Education Response Centre (1989a) *Education of the deaf and hard of hearing.* Edmonton: Author.

Alberta Education Response Centre (1989b) *A teacher's guide to allergies in the classroom.* Edmonton: Alberta Education.

Alberta Lung Association (nd). *Asthma.* Edmonton: Author.

Alberta Teachers Association (1993) *Trying to teach.* Edmonton: Author.

Alberta Teachers Association (1994) *Trying to teach: Necessary conditions.* Edmonton: Author.

Alderson, D. (1993, February) Attention Deficit Disorder. *Keeping in Touch,* p. 2.

Aleman, S.R. (1991) *CRS report for Congress: Special education for children with attention deficit disorders: Current issues.* Washington, DC: Congressional Research Services.

Algozzine, B., Christenson, S., and Ysseldyke, J.E. (1982). Probabilities associated with the referral to placement process. *Teacher Education and Special Education,* 5, 19–23.

Algozzine, B., Maheady, L., Sacca, K.C., O'Shea L., and O'Shea D. (1990) Sometimes patent medicine works: A reply to Braaten, Kauffman, Polsgrove, and Nelson. *Exceptional Children,* 56, 552–557.

Algozzine, B., Morsink, C.V., and Algozzine, K.K. (1988) What's happening in self-contained special education classrooms? *Exceptional Children,* 55, 259–265.

Allanan, Y.O., Arajar, T., and Vitamaki, R.O. (1964) Psychoses in childhood. *Acta Psychiatrica Scandinavica,* Supp. 174.

Allen, R.E. and Wasserman G.A. (1985) Origins of language delay in abused infants. *Child Abuse and Neglect,* 9, 335–340.

Allen, R.M., Cortazzo, A.D., and Adams, C. (1970) Factors in an adaptive behavior checklist for use with retardates. *Training School Bulletin,* 67, 144–157.

Allum, N. (1975) *Spina bifida: The treatment and care of spina bifida children.* London: George Allen and Unwin.

Alper, S.K., Schloss, P.J., and Schloss, C.N. (1994) *Families of students with disabilities.* Boston, MA: Allyn and Bacon.

Ambrose, N.G., Cox, N.J., and Yairi, E. (1997) The genetic basis of persistence and recovery in stuttering. *Journal of Speech, Language and Hearing Research,* 40, 567–580.

American Association on Mental Retardation (1993) *Mental retardation: Definition, classification, and systems of support* (9th. ed.) Washington, DC: AAMR.

American Psychiatric Association (1994) *Diagnostic and statistical manual of mental disorders.* (4th. ed.) Washington, DC: American Psychiatric Association.

American Psychological Association (1993) *Commission on violence and youth.* Report, vol. 1. New York: Author.

American Speech-Language-Hearing Association (1982) Definitions: Communicative disorders and variations. *ASHA,* 24, 949–959.

Anderson, E.M. (1973) Cognitive defects in children with spina bifida and hydrocephalus: A review of the literature. *British Journal of Educational Psychology,* 43, 257–268.

Anderson, H., Barr, B., and Wedenberg, E. (1970) Genetic disposition: Prerequisite for maternal rubella deafness. *Archives of Otolarnygology,* 91, 141–147.

Anderson, R.M. and Greer, J.G. (Eds.) (1976) *Educating the severely and profoundly retarded.* Baltimore, MD: University Park Press.

Andrews, G.A., Craig, A., Feyer, A., Hoddinott, S., Howie, P., and Neilson, M. (1983) Stuttering: A review of research findings and theories. *Journal of Speech and Hearing Disorders*, 48, 226–246.

Andrews, J. and Violato, C. (1996) A structural equation model of learning approaches and strategies. *Canadian Journal of School Psychology*, 12, 60–73,

Andrews, J.W. and Mason, J.M. (1991) Strategy usage among deaf and hearing readers. *Exceptional Children*, 57, 536–545.

Anvar, B., Mencher, G.T., and Keet, S.J. (1984) Hearing loss and congenital rubella in Atlantic Canada. *Ear and Hearing*, 5, 346–348.

Aplin, D.Y. (1987) Social and emotional adjustment of hearing-impaired children in ordinary and special schools. *Educational Research*, 29, 56–64.

Archambault, F.X. and Hallmark B.W. (1992) Regular classroom practices: Results of a national survey. In J.S. Renzulli, Chair) Regular classroom practices with gifted students: Findings from the National Research Center on the Gifted and Talented Symposium conducted at the American Educational Research Association, San Francisco.

Archbald, D.A. and Newman, F.M. (1988) *Beyond standardized testing: Assessing authentic achievement in the secondary school.* Reston, VA: National Association of Secondary Principals.

Archer, L.A. (1977) Blissymbolics: A nonverbal communication system. *Journal of Speech and Hearing Disorders*, 42, 568–579.

Arnold, K.M. and Hornett, D. (1990) Teaching idioms to children who are deaf. *Teaching Exceptional Children*, 22, 14–17.

Astin, A.W., Green, K.C., and Korn, W.S. (1989) *The American freshman: National norms for fall 1989.* Los Angeles, CA: University of California Higher Education Research Institute.

Atkins, D.V. (1987) Siblings of the hearing impaired: Perspectives for parents. *Volta Review*, 89, 32–45.

Atkinson, M.A. and MacLaren, N.K. (1990) What causes diabetes? *Scientific American*, pp. 63–71.

Augoustinos, M (1987) Developmental effects of child abuse: Recent findings. *Child Abuse and Neglect*, 11, 15–26.

Augusto, C.R. and McGraw, J.M. (1990) Humanizing blindness through public education. *Journal of Visual Impairment and Blindness*, 84, 397–400.

Bacon, E.H. and Schulz, J.B. (1991) A survey of mainstreaming practices. *Teacher Education and Special Education*, 2, 144–149.

Badian, N.A. (1988) The prediction of good and poor reading before kindergarten entry: A nine–year follow up. *Journal of Learning Disabilities,* 21, 98–103.

Bagnato, S., Neisworth, J., and Mussen, S. (1989) *Linking developmental assessment and early intervention: Curricula-based prescriptions.* Rockville, MD: Aspen.

Bailey, D.B. and Brochin, H.A. (1989) Tests and test development. In D.B. Bailey and M. Wolery (Eds.) *Assessing infants and preschoolers with handicaps* (pp. 22–46) Columbus, OH: Merrill.

Bailey, D.B. and Wolery, M. (1989) *Assessing infants and preschoolers with handicaps.* Columbus, OH: Merrill.

Bailey, D.B. Jr. and Blanco, P.M. (1990) Parents' perspectives of a written survey of family needs. *Journal of Early Intervention*, 14, 196–203.

Bailey, D.B. Jr., Simeonsson, R.J., Yoder, D.E., and Huntington, G.S. (1990) Preparing professionals to serve infants and toddlers with handicaps and their families: An integrative analysis across eight disciplines. *Exceptional Children*, 57, 26–35.

Bailey, D.B., and Wolery, M. (1984) *Teaching infants and preschoolers with handicaps.* Columbus, OH: Merrill.

Bailey, D.B., Jens, K., and Johnson, N. (1983) Curricula for handicapped infants. In S. Garwood and R. Fewell (Eds.) *Educating handicapped infants: Issues in development and intervention.* (pp. 387–415). Rockville, MD: Aspen.

Bailey, I.L. and Hall, A. (1983) *Bailey–Hall Cereal Test for the Measurement of Visual Acuity in Children.* Berkley, CA: Multimedia Center, School of Optometry, University of California.

Bailey, I.L. and Hall, A. (1984) *U.C. Berkley Preferential Looking Test.* Berkley, CA: Multimedia Center, School of Optometry, University of California.

Bain, D.A. (1980) Gifted and enriched education in Canada. In M. Csapo and L. Goguen (Eds.) *Special education across Canada: Issues and concerns for the '80s.* Vancouver: Centre for Human Development and Research.

Baird, S.M., Mayfield, P., and Baker, P. (1997) Mothers' interpretations of the behavior of their infants with visual and other impairments during interactions. *Journal of Visual Impairment and Blindness*, 91, 467–483.

Bak, J.J., Cooper, E.M., Dobroth, K.M., and Siperstein, G.N. (1987) Special class placements as labels: Effects on children's attitudes toward learning handicapped peers. *Exceptional Children*, 54, 151–155.

Baker, D. (1983) Justin Clark: Legal implications of the Mental Incompetency Act for 'Citizens of the World.' *Canadian Journal on Mental Retardation*, 33, 14–20.

Baker, J.M. and Zigmond, N. (1990) Are regular education classes equipped to accommodate students with learning disabilities? *Exceptional Children*, 56, 515–526.

Baker, L. and Cantwell, D.P. (1982) Psychiatric disorders in children with different types of communication disorders. *Journal of Communication Disorders*, 15, 113–126.

Baker, L. and Cantwell, D.P. (1987) A prospective psychiatric follow–up of children with speech/language disorders. *Journal of the American Academy of Child and Adolescent Psychiatry*, 26, 546–553.

Balakrishnan, T.R. and Wolf, L.C. (1976) Life expectancy of mentally retarded persons in Canadian institutions. *Journal of Abnormal Psychology*, 80, 211–224.

Balthazar, E.E. (1973) *The Balthazar Scales of Adaptive Behavior: Scale 2, Scales of Social Adaptation.* Palo Alto, CA: Consulting Psychologists Press.

Balthazar, E.E. (1976) *The Balthazar Scales of Adaptive Behavior: Scale 1, Scale of Functional Independence.* Palo Alto, CA: Consulting Psychologists Press.

Banbury, M.M. and Wellington, B. (1989) Designing and using peer nomination forms. *Gifted Talented Creative*, 33, 161–164.

Bank–Mikkelson, N.E. (1969) A metropolitan area in Denmark: Copenhagen. In R. Kugel and W. Wolfsenberger (Eds.) *Changing patterns in residential services for the mentally retarded.* Washington, DC: President's Committee on Mental Retardation.

Barden, R.C., Ford, M.E., Jensen, A.G. Rogers-Salyer, M., and Salyer, K.E. (1989) Effects of craniofacial deformity in infancy on the quality of mother–infant interactions. *Child Development*, 60, 819–824.

Barkley, R.A. Fisher, M., Newby, R., and Breen, M. (1988) Development of multi–method clinical protocol for assessing stimulant drug responses in ADHD children. *Journal of Clinical Child Psychology*, 17, 14–24.

Barkley, R.A., Du Paul, G., and McMurray, M. (1990) Comprehensive evaluation of attention deficit disorder with and without hyperactivity as defined by research criteria. *Journal of Consulting and Clinical Psychology*, 58, 775–789.

Barnett, W.S. (1986) Definition and classification of mental retardation: A reply to Zigler, Balla and Hodapp. *American Journal on Mental Deficiency*, 91, 111–116.

Baron, R.A. and Byrne, D. (1981) *Social psychology: Understanding human interaction.* Boston, MA: Allyn and Bacon.

Barraga, N.C. (1976) *Increased visual behavior in low vision children.* New York: Belmont, CA: Wadsworth.

Barraga, N.C. (1977) *Teacher's guide for development of visual learning: Abilities and utilization of low vision.* Austin, TX: American Printing House for the Blind.

Barringer, D.C., Strong, C.J., Blair, J.C., Clark, T.C., and Watkins, S. (1993) Screening procedures used to identify children with hearing loss. *American Annals of the Deaf*, 138, 420–426.

Bassett, D.S., Jackson L., Ferrel, K., Luckner, J., Hagerty, P., Bussen T., and MacIsan, D. (1996) Multiple perspectives on inclusive education: Reflections of a university faculty. *Teacher Education and Special Education*, 19, 355–386.

Bates, J.E. (1987) Temperament in infancy. In J.D. Osofsky (Ed.) *Handbook of infant development* (pp. 1101–1149). New York: Wiley.

Bates, P. Morrow, S.A., Pancsafar, E., and Sedlak, R. (1984) The effect of functional vs nofunctional activities on the attitudes/expectations of nonhandicapped college students: What they see is what we get. *Journal of the Association for Persons with Severe Handicaps*, 9, 73–78.

Batshaw, M.L. and Perrett, Y.M. (1986) *Children with handicaps: A medical primer.* Baltimore, MD: Paul H. Brooks.

Bauer, A.M. and Shea, T.M. (1989) *Teaching exceptional students in your classroom.* Toronto: Allyn and Bacon.

Baum, C. (1989) Conduct disorders. In T.H. Ollendick and M. Hersen (Eds.) *Handbook of child psychopathology.* (2nd ed.) New York: Plenum.

Baum, S. (1995) Gifted but learning disabled: A puzzling paradox. *ERIC Digest, No 479.* Reston, VA: Council for Exceptional Children.

Baum, S. and Owen, S. (1988) Learning disabled students: How are they different? *Gifted Child Quarterly*, 32, 321–326.

Baumeister, A.A., Kupstas, F., and Klindworth, L.M. (1990) New morbidity: Implications for prevention of children's disabilities. *Exceptionality*, 1, 1–16.

Bauwens, J., Hourcade, J.J., and Friend, M. (1989) Cooperative teaching: A model for general and special education integration. *Remedial and Special Education*, 10, 17–22.

Bay, E. (1975) Ontogeny of stable speech areas in the human brain. In E.H. Lenneberg and E. Lenneberg (Eds.), *Foundations of language development: A multidisciplinary approach* (vol. 2). New York: Academic Press.

Beakley, B.A. and Yoder, S.L. (1998) Middle schoolers learn community skills. *Teaching Exceptional Children*, 30, 16–21.

Beare, P.L. (1991) Philosophy, instructional methodology, training and goals of teachers of the behaviorally disordered. *Behavioral Disorders*, 16, 211–218.

Beattie, L. (1993, summer) Conductive education: Renewing the integration vs segregation debate. *Disability Today*, pp. 51–53.

Becker, R. (1981) *Revised Reading–Free Inventory: Manual.* Columbus, OH: Erlbaum.

Beckman, P. J. and Lieber, J. (1994) The Social Strategy Rating Scale: An approach to evaluating social competence. *Journal of Early Intervention*, 18, 1–11.

Befring, E. (1997) The enrichment perspective: A special educational approach to an inclusive school. *Remedial and Special Education*, 18, 182–187.

Begley, S (1996, February 19) Your child's brain. *Newsweek*, pp. 55–62.

Belcostas, F.P. (1987) Elementary pull–out programs for the intellectually gifted: Boon or bane? *Roeper Review*, 9, 41–55.

Bell, L.M. (1986) Evaluation and implementation of innovation in gifted/enrichment programs. *Gifted Education International*, 4, 120–127.

Bell, R., Fisher, M., and Rodriguez, J. (1994, October 30) Ritalin use sparks concern. *Calgary Sun*, pp. 3, 16–17.

Bellamy, T. (1985). Severe disability in adulthood. *Newsletter for the Association for Persons with Severe Handicaps*, 11, 1–6.

Benbow, C.P. (1991) Meeting the needs of gifted students through use of acceleration. In M.C. Wang, M.C. Reynolds, and H.J. Walberg (Eds.) *Handbook of special education* (vol. 4, pp. 23–36). Elmsford, NY: Pergamon.

Bender, W.N. and Smith, J.K. (1990) Classroom behavior of children and adolescents with learning disabilities: A meta-analysis. *Journal of Learning Disabilities*, 23, 298–305.

Benedict, H. (1979) Early lexical development: Comprehension and production. *Journal of Child Language*, 6, 183–200.

Benjamin, M. (1980). Abused as a child, abusive as a parent. In R. Volpe, M. Breton, and J. Witten (Eds.) *The maltreatment of the school-aged child*. Toronto: Lexington.

Bentley, K.M. and Li, A.K.F. (1995) Bully and victim problems in elementary schools and students' beliefs about aggression. *Canadian Journal of School Psychology*, 11, 153–165.

Berg, F.S. (1986) Characteristics of the target population. In F.S. Berg, J.C. Blair, S.H. Viehweg, and A. Wilson–Vlotman, *Educational audiology for the hard of hearing child* (pp. 1–24) Orlando, FL: Grune and Stratton.

Berglund, M. and Hoffbauer, D. (1996) New opportunities for students with traumatic brain injuries. *Teaching Exceptional Children*, 28, 54–56.

Berkow, R. (Ed.) (1982) *The Merck manual of diagnosis and therapy*. Rahway, NJ: Merck, Sharp and Dohme.

Berlin, C.M. Jr. (1983) Biological causes of exceptionality. In R.M. Smith, J.T. Neisworth, and F.M. Hunt (Eds.) *The exceptional child: A functional approach*. New York: McGraw–Hill

Bernard, H. (1973) *Child development and learning*. Boston, MA: Allyn and Bacon.

Berns, J.H. (1980) Grandparents of handicapped children. *Social Work*, 15, 238–239.

Bernstein, D.K. and Tiegerman, E. (1989) *Language and communication disorders in children* (2nd. ed.) Columbus, OH: Merrill.

Bernthal, J. and Bankston, N. (1981) *Articulation disorders*. Englewood Cliffs, NJ: Prentice–Hall.

Best, H. (1930) Educational provisions for the deaf, the blind, and the feeble–minded compared. *American Annals of the Deaf*, 75, 239–240.

Betts, G.T.(1985) *Autonomous learner model for the gifted and talented*. Greeley, CO: Autonomous Learning Publications and Specialists.

Bhatara, V. (1980) Overlap of autism, mental retardation, and CNS dysfunction. *Psychiatric Annals*, 10, 298–304.

Bickett, L. and Milich, R. (1990) First impressions formed of boys with attention deficit disorders. *Journal of Learning Disabilities*, 23, 253–259.

Bierman, K.L., Miller, C.L., and Stabb, S.D. (1987) Improving the social behavior and peer acceptance of rejected boys: Effects of social skill training with instruction and prohibitions. *Journal of Consulting and Clinical Psychology*, 53, 194–200.

Bierne–Smith M. (1991) Peer tutoring in arithmetic for children with learning disabilities. *Exceptional Children*, 57, 330–337.

Bigelow, A. (1987) Early words of blind children. *Journal of Child Language*, 14, 47–56.

Bigelow, A. (1991) Spatial mapping of familar locations in blind children. *Journal of Visual Impairment and Blindness*, 85, 113–117.

Bingol, N., Schuster, C., Fuchs, M., Iosub, S., et al. (1987) The influence of socioeconomic factors in the occurrence of fetal alcohol syndrome. *Advances in Alcohol and Substance Abuse*, 6, 105–118.

Binnie, C.D., Channon, S, and Marston, D. (1990) Learning disabilities in epilepsy: Neurophysiological aspects. *Epilepsia*, 31 (supp. 4), 52–58.

Bishop, V. (1986) Identifying the components of success in mainstreaming. *Journal of Visual Impairment and Blindness*, 80, 939–946.

Bishop, W. (1968) Successful teachers of the gifted. *Exceptional Children*, 34, 317–325.

Blackhurst, A. E. (1997) Perspectives on technology in special education. *Teaching Exceptional Children*, 29, 40–47.

Blackorby, J. and Wagner, M. (1996) Longitudinal postschool outcomes of youth with disabilities: Findings from the national longitudinal transition study. *Exceptional Children*, 62, 399–413.

Blair, J.C. (1990) Front–row seating is not enough for classroom listening. In C. Flexner, D. Wray, and R. Leavitt (Eds.) *How the student with hearing loss can succeed in college: A handbook for students, families, and professionals*. Washington DC: A.G. Bell Association for the Deaf.

Bleck, E.E. (1979) Integrating the physically handicapped child. *Journal of School Health*, 49, 141–146.

Bleck, E.L. and Nagel, D.A. (1982) *Physically handicapped children: A medical atlas for teachers*. New York: Grune and Stratton.

Block, E.L. and Goodstein, L.D. (1971). Functional speech disorders and personality: A decade of research. *Journal of Speech and Hearing Disorders*, 31, 295–314.

Block, J.H., Gersten, E., and Kromblum, S. (1980) Evaluation of a language program for young autistic children. *Journal of Speech and Hearing Disorders*, 45, 76–89.

Block, L. (1993, spring) Out of the workshops and into the work force. *Abilities*, p. 61.

Blomquist, H., Gustavson, K.H. Holmgren, S. Nordenson, I., and Paslsson–Strade, U. (1983) Fragile x syndrome in mildly mentally retarded children in a northern Swedish county: A prevalence study. *Clinical Genetics*, 24, 393–398.

Bloodstein, O. (1975). *A handbook on stuttering* (rev. ed.) National Easter Seal Society for Crippled Children and Adults.

Bloom, B.S. (1964) *Stability and change in human characteristics.* New York: Wiley.

Bloom, B.S. (1985) *Developing talent in young people.* New York: Ballantine Books.

Bloom, B.S. (Ed.) (1956) *Taxonomy of educational objectives: Handbook 1: cognitive domain.* New York: David McKay.

Bloom, B.S. and Sosniak, L.A. (1981) Talent development vs schooling. *Educational Leadership*, 39, 86–94.

Bloom, D.T. (1991, winter) Mainstreaming remains the goal. *Day Care and Early Education*, 18, 44–45.

Bluestone, D.C. (1982) Otitis media in children: To treat or not to treat. *New England Journal of Medicine*, 306, 1399–1404.

Blumstein, A., Cohen J., and Farrington, D.P. (1988) Criminal career research: Its value for criminology. *Criminology*, 26, 1–35.

Boehm, E.A. (1986) *Boehm Test of Basic Concepts– Revised* New York: Psychological Corporation.

Bogie H. (1997, fall) Eaton versus Brant County Board of Education: The Supreme court of Canada decision, released Feb. 6, 1997. *Keeping in Touch*, p. 6.

Bond, G.G. (1987) An assessment of cognitive abilities in hearing and hearing impaired preschool children. *Journal of Speech and Hearing Disorders*, 52, 319–323.

Bonvillian, J.D., Orlansky, M.D., and Novack, L.L. (1983) Developmental milestones: Sign language acquisition and motor development. *Child Development*, 54, 1435–1445.

Borgh, K. and Dickson, W.P. (1986) Two preschools sharing one microcomputer: Creating prosocial behavior with hardware and software. In P.F. Campbell and G.G. Fein (Eds.) *Young children and microcomputers* (pp. 37–44). Reston, VA: Reston.

Borland, J.H. (1989) *Planning and implementing programs for the gifted.* New York: Teachers College Press.

Borthwick–Duffy, S.A., Palmer, D.S., and Lane, K.L. (1996) One size doesn't fit all: Full inclusion and individual differences. *Journal of Behavioral Education*, 6, 311–329.

Bos, C.S. and Vaughn, S. (1991) *Strategies for teaching students with learning and behavior problems.* Boston, MA: Allyn and Bacon.

Bouchard, T.J. Jr. and McGue, M. (1981) Familial studies of intelligence: A review. *Science,* 212, 1055–1059.

Bounds, B (1997, April/May) Should special education students be paid for vocational training? *CEC Today*, p. 14.

Bourque, J. and Li, A.K. (1987) Perceived competence, social adjustment and peer relations of intellectually gifted children in segregated versus regular–classroom settings. *Canadian Journal of Special Education*, 3, 191–200.

Bower, B, (1989) Remodeling the autistic child. *Science News*, 136, 312–313

Bowley, A. and Gardner, L. (1980) *The handicapped child.* London: Churchill Livingstone.

Boyle, R. and Yeager, N. (1997) Blueprints for learning: Using cognitive frameworks for understanding. *Teaching Exceptional Children*. 29, 26–31.

Braaten, S., Kauffman, J.M., Braaten, B., Polsgrove, L., and Nelson C.M. (1988) The regular education initiative: Patent medicine for behavioral disorders. *Exceptional Children*, 55, 21–28.

Bracken, B.A. and Newman, V.L. (1994) Child and adolescent interpersonal relations with parents, peers, and teachers: A factor analytic investigation. *Canadian Journal of School Psychology*, 10, 108–122.

Braden, J.P. (1987) An explanation of the superior performance IQs of deaf children of deaf parents. *American Annals of the Deaf*, 132, 263–266.

Braden, J.P. and Shaw, S.R. (1987) Computer assisted instruction with deaf children: Panacea, placebo or poison. *American Annals of the Deaf*, 132, 189–193.

Bradley, C. (1937) The behavior of children receiving Benzedrine. *American Journal of Psychiatry*, 94, 577–585.

Brady, M.P., Swank, P.R., Taylor, R.D., and Frieberg, J. (1992) Teacher interactions in mainstreamed social studies and science classes. *Exceptional Children*, 58, 530–540.

Brady, R.C. (1988). Physical and other health handicaps. In E.W. Lynch and R.B. Lewis (Eds.) *Exceptional children and adults: An introduction to special education* (pp. 136–179). Glenview, IL: Scott, Foresman.

Bransky, T. (1987) Specific program information: A key to attitudes about the gifted education program. *Gifted Child Quarterly*, 31, 20–24.

Brantlinger, E.A. and Guskin, S.L. (1987) Ethnocultural and social psychological effects of learning characteristics of handicapped children. In M.C. Wang, H.C. Reynolds, and H.J. Walberg (Eds.) *Handbook of special education: Research and practice (vol. 1) Learner characteristics and adaptive education* (pp. 7–34) New York: Pergamon.

Breslau, N. and Davis, G.C. (1986) Chronic stress and major depression. *Archives of General Psychiatry*, 43, 309–314.

Bricker, D. (1986) *Early education of at–risk and handicapped infants, toddlers and preschool children.* Glenville, IL: Scott, Foresman.

Bricker, D. and Squires, J. (1989) Low cost system using parents to monitor the development of at–risk infants. *Journal of Early Intervention*, 13, 50–60.

Bricker, D. D. (1982) *Intervention with at-risk handicapped infants.* Baltimore, MD: University Park Press.

Bricker, D.D. (1995) The challenge of inclusion. *Journal of Early Intervention, 19,* 179–194.

Brinthaupt, G.P. (1991) Cystic fibrosis and parental adjustment. In M. Seligman (Ed.) *The family with a handicapped child* (2nd. ed.) (pp. 295–336) Boston, MA: Allyn and Bacon.

British Columbia Ministry of Education, Special Education Services (1996) *Individual Education planning for students with special needs: A resource guide to support teachers.* Victoria, BC: Author.

British Columbia Ministry of Health, (1978) *Epilepsy: The causes, the treatment, the hope.* Victoria: B.C. Ministry of Health.

Broadhurst, D.D., Edmunds, M., and MacDicker, R.A. (1979) *Early childhood programs and the prevention and treatment of child abuse and neglect: The user manual series.* Washington, DC: U.S. Department of Health, Education and Welfare.

Brod, N. and Hamilton, D. (1973) Binocularity and reading. *Journal of Learning Disabilities, 6,* 574–576.

Brody, G.H., Stoneman, Z., Davis, C.H., and Crapps, J.M. (1991) Observations of the role relations and behavior between older children with mental retardation and their younger siblings. *American Journal on Mental Retardation, 95,* 527–536.

Brody, H. (1989) The great equalizer: PCs empower the disabled. *PC Computing, 2,* 82–93.

Brody, J. (1988, March 8) Cocaine: Litany of fetal risks grows. *New York Times.*

Brokx, J.P. (1987) The integration of hearing aid rehabilitation in the management of young hearing–impaired children. *Audiology in Practice, 4,* 7–8.

Brolin, D. and Gysbers, N. (1989) Career education for students with disabilities. *Journal of Counseling and Development, 68,* 155–159.

Brookhart, S.M. and Freeman, D.J. (1992) Characteristics of entering teacher candidates. *Review of Educational Research, 62,* 37–60.

Brooks, D.N. (1977) Auditory screening: Time for reappraisal. *Public Health, 91,* 282–288.

Brooks, J.B. (1987) *The process of parenting* (2nd. ed.) Palo Alto, CA: Mayfield Publishers.

Brown, A.L. and Palinscar, A.S. (1982) Inducing strategic learning from texts by means of informed, self–control training. *Topics in Learning and Learning Disabilities, 2,* 1–17.

Brown, L., Nisbet, J., Ford, A., Sweet, M., Shirga, B., York, J., and Loomis, R. (1983). The critical need for non-school instruction in educational programs for severly handicapped students. *Journal of The Association for the Severely Handicapped, 8,* 71–77.

Brown, L.L. and Hammill, D.D. (1990) *The Behavior Rating Profile–2.* Austin, TX: Pro–Ed.

Brown, P.M. and Foster, S.B. (1991) Integrating hearing and deaf students on a college campus: Successes and barriers as perceived by hearing students. *American Annals of the Deaf, 136,* 21–27.

Brown, T.E. (1995) Differential diagnosis of ADD versus ADHD in adults. In K.G. Nadeau (Ed.) *A comprehensive guide to attention deficit disorder in adults: Research, diagnosis, treatment* (pp. 93–108) New York: Bruner Mazel.

Brown, W.T., Jenkins, E.C., Cohen I.L., et al., (1986) Fragile X and autism: A multicenter survey. *American Journal of Medical Genetics, 13,* 341–352.

Brubacher, RG (1994) Acculturative stress: A useful framework for understanding the experiences of deaf Americans. *Journal of Rehabilitation of the Deaf, 28,* 1–15.

Bruininks, R.H. (1977) *Manual for the Bruininks–Osteresky Test of Motor Proficiency.* Circle Pines, MI: American Guidance Service.

Brulle, A.R., Barton, L.E., Wharton, D.L., and Brulle, C.L. (1983) A comparison of teacher time spent with physically handicapped and able–bodied students. *Exceptional Children, 49,* 543–547.

Bryan, T.H. and Pflaum, S. (1978) Social interactions of learning disabled children: A linguistic, social, and cognitive analysis. *Learning Disability Quarterly, 1,* 70–79.

Bryan, T.H. and Sullivan–Burstein, K. (1997) Homework how-to's. *Teaching Exceptional Children, 29,* 32–37.

Bryan, W.H. and Jeffrey, D.L. (1982) Education of visually handicapped students in the regular classroom. *Texas Teachers Journal of Education, 9,* 125–131.

Bryson, S. (1996) Brief report: Epidemiology of autism. *Journal of Autism and Developmental Disabilities, 26,* 165–167.

Bryson, S., Clark, B., and Smith, I. (1988) First report of a Canadian epidemiological study of autistic syndromes. *Journal of Child Psychology and Psychiatry, 29,* 433–446.

Buchanan, M. and Wolf, J.S. (1986) A comprehensive study of learning disabled adults. *Journal of Learning Disabilities, 19,* 34–38.

Buescher, T.M. (1991) Gifted adolescents. In N. Colangelo and G.A. Davis (Eds.) *Handbook of gifted education* (pp. 382–401). Boston, MA: Allyn and Bacon.

Bullis, M. and Reiman, J. (1992) Development and preliminary psychometric properties of the Transition Competence Battery for deaf adolescents and young adults. *Exceptional Children, 59,* 12–26.

Bullock, L.M., Ellis L.L., and Wilson N.J. (1994) Knowledge/skills needed by teachers who work wth students with severe emotional/behavioral disorders: A revisitation. *Behavioral Disorders, 19,* 108–125.

Bunch, G.O. (1994) Inclusion. *American Annals of the Deaf, 139,* 150–152.

Burgio, G.R., Fraccaro, M., and Tiepolo, L. (1981) *Trisomy 21*. Berlin: Springer–Verlag.

Burgio, P. (1986) Safety consideration of cochlean implantation. *Otolaryngologic Clinics of North America*, 19, 237–247.

Burt, K.L., Parks–Charney, R., and Schwean, V.L. (1996) The AD/HD skills and strategies program: A program for AD/HD adults in postsecondary education. *Canadian Journal of School Psychology*, 12, 122–134.

Buski, J. (1997, winter) Education reform— What you've told us. Part 2. *ATA Magazine*, pp. 34–35.

Busse, T.V.and Mansfield, R.S. (1980) Renzulli is right. *Gifted Child Quarterly*, 24, 132.

Butler, D.L. (1995) Promoting strategic learning by postsecondary students with learning disabilities. *Journal of Learning Disabilities*, 28, 170–190.

Butts, K.R. (1980) *Breathing exercises for asthma*. Springfield, IL: Thomas.

Byrne, M. E. and Shervanian, C.C. (1977) *Introduction to communication disorders*. New York: Harper and Row.

Caffey, J. (1946) Multiple fractures in the long bones of infants suffering from chronic subdural hematoma. *American Journal of Roentgenology*, 56, 163–173.

Cain, L.F., Levine, S., and Elzey, F.F. (1963) *Manual for the Cain-Levine Social Competency Scale*. Palo Alto, CA: Consulting Psychologists Press.

Calfee, R.C. (1977) Assessment of independent reading skills: Basic research and practical applications. In A.S. Reber and D.L. Scarborough (Eds.) *Toward a psychology of reading*. Hillsdale, NJ: Erlbaum.

Calfee, R.C. (1987) The school as a context for assessment of literacy. *The Reading Teacher*, 40, 738–743.

Calhoun, M.L. and Hawisher, M. (1979) *Teaching and learning strategies for physically handicapped students*. Baltimore, MD: University Park Press.

Camp, B. (1973) Psychiatric tests and learning tests in severely disabled readers. *Journal of Learning Disabilities*, 6, 512–517.

Campbell, M. (1997, August 9) A pill before lunch at Camp Ritalin. *Globe and Mail*, p. 30

Campbell, M., Grange, M., Cernetig, M., Ha, T.T., and Galt, V. (1997, October 4) Shakedowns in the schoolyard. *Globe and Mail*, pp. 1, 6,

Campbell, M.S., Cohen S.L., and Rich, M. (1987) *Guidelines for the management of health impaired students*. ERIC Doc No Ed 287 269.

Canadian Association for the Mentally Retarded [1980] *Questions and answers about mental retardation*. Pamphlet, n.p., CAMR.

Canadian Council for Exceptional Children (1989) Status of education service delivery to exceptional students: A provincial survey. *Keeping in Touch*.

Canadian Council for Exceptional Children (1992, March) *Monograph one: Staying in school initiatives*. Toronto:

Canadian Council for Exceptional Children.

Canadian Lung Association (1997) *Asthma*. Toronto: Author.

Canadian National Institute for the Blind (1980) Brochure. Toronto: CNIB.

Canadian Pediatric Society (1988) Hyperactivity in children. *Canadian Medical Association Journal*, 139, 211–212.

Canadian war blinded (1942) *Outlook for the Blind and the Teacher's Forum*, 36, 281–286.

Cantor, S. (1988) Childhood schizophrenia. *American Journal on Mental Retardation*, 94, 688–690.

Cantor, S. (1989) *Childhood schizophrenia*. New York: Guilford Press.

Cantwell, D.P., Baker, B.L., and Rutter, M. (1979) Families of autistic and dysphonic children: Family life and interaction patterns. *Archives of General Psychiatry*, 36, 682–687.

Carbin, C. (1993/94, winter) Ontario's new ASL/LSQ law–pah! *Gallaudet Today*, pp. 15–17.

Carey, S. T. (1978) The child as word learner. In M. Halle, J. Bresnan, and G. Miller (Eds.) *Linguistic theory and psychological reality*. Cambridge, MA: MIT Press.

Carlberg, C. and Kavale K. (1980) The efficacy of special versus regular class placement for exceptional children: A meta–analysis. *Journal of Special Education*, 14, 295–309.

Carnine, D. and Kameenui, E.J. (1990) The regular education initiative and children with special needs: A false dilemma in the face of true problems. *Journal of Learning Disabilities*, 23, 141–144.

Carpenter, D. (1985) Grading handicapped pupils: Review and position statement. *Remedial and Special Education*, 6, 54–59.

Carpenter, S.L. and McKee–Higgins, E. (1996) Behavior management in inclusive classrooms. *Remedial and Special Education*, 17, 195–203.

Carter, D.E. and Rogers, W.T. (1989) Diagnostic and placement practice for mildly educable mentally handicapped students. *Canadian Journal of Special Education*, 5, 15–23.

Carter, E.A. and McGoldrick, M. (Eds.) (1980) *The family life cycle: A framework for family therapy*. New York: Gardner Press.

Cartledge, G. and Kleefeld, J. (1989) Teaching social communication skills to elementary school students with handicaps. *Teaching Exceptional Children*, 22, 100–105.

Casby, H.W. (1997) Symbolic play of children with language impairment: A critical review. *Journal of Speech, Language and Hearing Research*, 40, 468–479.

Caspi, A., Elder, G.H., and Bern D.J. (1987) Moving against the world: Life–course patterns of explosive children. *Developmental Psychology*, 23, 308–313.

Casserly, P.L. (1979) Helping young women take math and science seriously in school. In N. Colangelo and R.T. Zaffran (Eds.) *New voices in counseling the gifted* (pp. 346–369).

Castle, D. (1988) *Oral interpreting: Selections from papers by Kirsten Gonzales.* Washington, DC: A.G. Bell Association for the Deaf.

Cataracts: Some facts you should know. (1990) Alberta: CNIB.

Cazden, C.B. (1988) *Classroom discourse: The language of teaching and learning.* Portsmouth, NH: Heinemann.

Center for Assessment and Demographic Studies (1991) *Stanford Achievement Test, eighth edition: Hearing–impaired norms booklet.* Washington, DC: Gallaudet University.

Chan, L.K. (1988) Comprehension monitoring in students with reading difficulties. *Australian Educational Researcher*, 15, 19–39.

Chandler, L.K. (1992) Promoting young children's social competence as a strategy for transition to main-streamed kindergarten programs. In S.L. Odom, S.R. McConnell, and M.A. McEvoy (Eds.) *Social competence of young children with disabilities* (pp. 245–276). Baltimore, MD: Brookes.

Chapman, L.J. and Wedell, K. (1972) Perceptual–motor disabilities and reversal errors in children's handwriting. *Journal of Learning Disabilities*, 5, 321–325.

Chasnoff, I. J. Burns, K.A., Burns, W.J., and Schnoll, S. (1988b) Prenatal drug exposure: Effects on neonatal and infant growth and development. *Neorobehavioral Toxicology and Teratology*, 8, 357–362.

Chasnoff, I.J. (1987, May) Prenatal effects of cocaine. *Contemporary OB/GYN*, pp. 163–179.

Chasnoff, I.J., Chisum. G., and Kaplan, W. (1988) Maternal cocaine use and genitourinary malformation. *Teratology*, 201–204.

Chen, D. and Haney, M. (1995) An early intervention model for infants who are deaf–blind. *Journal of Visual Impairment and Blindness*, 89, 213–221.

Biological features of HIV–1 that correlate with virulence in the host. *Science*, 240, 80–82.

Cheng–Meyer, C., Seto, D., Tateno, M., and Levy J. (1988) Biological features of HIV–1 that correlate with virulence in the host. *Science*, 240, 80–82.

Chester, M.A. and Barbarin, O.A. (1987) *Childhood cancer and the family.* New York: Brunner/Mazel.

Children should see more and more each day [1980] Toronto: National Retinitis Pigmentosa Foundation of Canada.

Children with communication disorders (1995). *ERIC Digest, H 470.* Reston, VA: Council for Exceptional Children.

Chinn, P.C., Winn, J., and Walters, R. (1978) *Two-way talking with parents of special children.* St. Lois, MO: C.V. Mosby.

Chomsky, N. (1965) *Aspects of the theory of syntax.* Cambridge, MA: MIT Press.

Chorost, S. (1988) The hearing–impaired child in the mainstream: A survey of the attitudes of regular classroom teachers. *Volta Review*, 90, 7–12.

Church, J.A., Allen, J.R., and Stiehen, E.R. (1986) New scar-let letter(s) pediatric AIDS. *Pediatrics*, 77, 423–427.

Clarizio, H.F and Klein, A.P. (1995) Assessing the severity of behavior disorders: Rankings based on clinical and empirical criteria. *Psychology in the Schools*, 32, 77–85.

Clark, B. (1988) *Growing up gifted* (3rd. ed.) Columbus OH: Merrill.

Clark, G.M. and Tong, Y.C. (1985) The engineering of future cochlean implants. In R.F. Gray (Ed.), *Cochlean implants* (pp.211–226). San Diego, CA: College Hill Press.

Clark, G.M., Tong, Y.C., and Patrick. J.F. (Eds.) (1990) *Cochlea prothesis.* New York: Churchill Livingtone.

Clark, P.N. and Allen, A.S. (1985) *Occupational therapy for children.* St. Louis, MO: Mosby.

Clarke, B.R. and Kendall, D.C.(1976) Communication for hearing–impaired people in Canada. In H.J. Oyer (Ed.) *Communication for the hearing handicapped: An international perspective.* Baltimore, MD: University Park Press.

Clements, D.H. (1985) *Computers in early childhood and primary education.* Englewood Cliffs, NJ: Prentice–Hall.

Clifford, J.A., Runions, T., and Smyth, E. (1986) The Learning Enrichment Service (LES): A participatory model for gifted adolescents. In J.S, Renzulli (Ed.) *Systems and models for developing programs for the gifted and talented.* Mansfield, CT: Creative Learning Press.

Cloninger, C.J. and Giangreco, M.F. (1995) Including students with deaf–blindness in general education classes. *Journal of Visual Impairment and Blindness*, 89, 262–271.

Coates, R.D. (1989) The Regular Education Initiative and opinions of regular classroom teachers. *Journal of Learning Disabilities*, 22, 532–536.

Coggins, T.E. and Morrison, J.A. (1981) Spontaneous imitations in Down's syndrome children: A lexical analysis. *Journal of Speech and Hearing Research,* 24, 303–308.

Coie, J. (1985) Fitting social skills intervention to the target group. In R.H. Schnider, K.H. Rubin, and J.E. Ledingham (Eds.) *Peer relationships and social skills in childhood: Issues in assessment and training.* New York: Springer–Verlag.

Colangelo, N. (1989) Moral dilemmas as formulated by gifted students. *Understanding Our gifted*, 1, 10–12.

Colangelo, N. and Dettman, D.F. (1983) A review of research on parents and families of gifted children. *Exceptional Children*, 50, 20–27.

Colangelo, N. and Fleuridas, C. (1986) The abduction of childhood. *Journal of Counseling and Development*, 64, 561–563.

Cole, C.K., Jones, M.K., and Sadofsky, G.S. (1990) Working with children at risk due to prenatal susbstance exposure. *PRISE Reporter—Issues in the Education of Students with Handicaps*, 21, 1–6.

Cole, E. (1992) Depression and the risk for suicide in children and adolescents. In S. Miezitis (Ed.) *Creating alternatives to depression in our schools.* Toronto: Hogrefe and Huber.

Cole, E. (1995) Responding to school violence: Understanding for today and tomorrow. *Canadian Journal of School Psychology*, 11, 108–116.

Cole, E. and Brown, R. (1996) Multidisciplinary school teams: A five–year follow–up study. *Canadian Journal of School Psychology*, 12, 155–168.

Cole, H. and Sarnoff, D. (1980, June) Interactive creativity: Explorations of basic meanings and their implications for teaching and counselling. Papers at the Twenty–sixth Annual Creative Problem Solving Institute, Buffalo.

Cole, K.N., Dale, P.S. Mills, P.E., and Jenkins, J.R. (1993) Interactions between early intervention curriculum and student characteristics. *Exceptional Children*, 60, 17–28.

Cole, M. and Cole, S.R. (1989) *The development of children*. San Diego, CA: Scientific American Books.

Coleman, J.M. and Minnett, A.M. (1992) Learning disabilities and social competence: A social ecological perspective. *Exceptional Children*, 59, 234–246.

Coleman, M.C. (1992) *Behavior disorders: Theory and practice* (2nd. ed.) Boston, MA: Allyn and Bacon.

Coles, G. (1978) The learning disabilities test battery: Empirical and social issues. *Harvard Educational Review*, 48, 313–340.

Collins, M.T. (1995) History of deaf–blind education. *Journal of Visual Impairment and Blindess*, 89, 210–212.

Comer, R.J. (1992) *Abnormal psychology*. New York: Freeman.

Conant, S. and Budoff, M. (1982) The development of sighted peoples' understanding of blindness. *Journal of Visual Impairment and Blindness*, 76, 86–90.

Conger, J.C. and Keane, S.P. (1981) Social skills intervention in the treatment of isolated or withdrawn children. *Psychological Bulletin*, 90, 478–495.

Conn–Blowers, E.A. and McLeod, H.J. (1989) Special education in Alberta. In M. Csapo amd L. Goguen (Eds.) *Special education across Canada* (pp. 19–27) Vancouver: Centre For Human Development and Research.

Conners, C.K. (1973) Rating scales for use in drug studies with children. *Psychopharmocology Bulletin*, 9, 24–81.

Conrad, R. (1979) *The deaf school child: Language and cognitive formation*. London: Harper and Row.

Conte, R., Andrews, J., Loomer, M., and Hutton, G. (1995) A classroom–based social skills inventory for children with learning disabilities. *Alberta Journal of Educational Research*, 41, 84–102.

Cook, J. (1991) Higher education: An attainable goal for students who have sustained head injuries. *Journal of Head Trauma Rehabilitation*, 6, 64–72.

Cooper, D.H. and Speece, D.L. (1990) Maintaining at–risk children in regular education settings: Initial effects of individual differences and classroom environment. *Exceptional Children*, 57, 117–126.

Copeland, L., Wolraich, M., Lindgren, S., Milich, R., and Woolson, R. (1987) Pediatricians reported practices in the assessment and treatment of attention deficit disorders. *Journal of Developmental and Behavioral Pediatrics*, 8, 191–197.

Copeland, M.E. and Kimmel, J.R. (1989) *Evaluation and management of infants and young children with developmental disabilities*. Baltimore, MD: Brookes.

Cordesco, L.K. and Laus, M.K. (1993) Individualized training in behavioral strategies for parents of preschool children with disabilities. *Teaching Exceptional Children*, 25, 43–47.

Corn, A.L. (1980) Optical aids in the classroom. *Education of the Visually Handicapped*, 12, 114–121.

Cornell, D. (1983) Gifted children: The impact of positive labelling on the family system. *American Journal of Orthopsychiatry*, 53, 322–355.

Cornell, D. (1984) *Families of gifted children*. Ann Arbor, MI: UMI Research Press.

Cornell, D.G., Callahan, C.M., and Loyd, B.H. (1991) Socioemotional adjustments of adolescent girls enrolled in a residential acceleration program. *Gifted Child Quarterly*, 35, 58–66.

Cornett, O.R. (1984, June) Cued speech: What and why. Paper available at the A.G. Bell Conference, Portland, Oregon.

Corno, L. and Mandinach, E. (1983) The role of cognitive engagement in classroom learning and motivation. *Educational Psychologist*, 18, 88–108.

Cornwell, A. and Bawden, H.N. (1992) Reading disabilities and aggression: A critical review. *Journal of Learning Disabilities*, 25, 281–289.

Corywell, J., Holcomb, T.K., and Scherer, M. (1992) Attitudes towards deafness: A collegiate perspective. *American Annals of the Deaf*, 137, 299–302.

Cosden, M.A., Gerber, M.M., Semmel, D.S., Goldman, S.R., and Semmel, M.L. (1987) Microcomputer use with micro–educational environments. *Exceptional Children*, 53, 399–409.

Cotler, S. (1986) Epidemiology and outcome. In J.M. Reisman (Ed.) *Behavior disorders in infants, children, and adolescents*. New york: Random House.

Council for Exceptional Children (1988) *Final report: CEC and ad hoc committee on medically fragile students*. Reston, VA: Council for Exceptional Children.

Council for Exceptional Children (1991) Code of ethics of the CEC. *Teaching Exceptional Children*, 23 (2).

Council for Exceptional Children (1993a) Policy on inclusive schools and community settings. *Teaching Exceptional Children*, 25, supplement.

Council for Exceptional Children (1993b) *Position paper*. Division for Early Childhood: Council for Exceptional Children.

Council for Learning disabilities (1993) Concerns about the full inclusion of students with learning disabilities in regular education classrooms. *Learning Disabilities Quarterly*, 16, 26.

Council of Administrators of Special Education (CASE) Inc. (1997, fall) Position paper on delivery of services to students with disabilities. *Keeping in Touch*, p. 3.

Cowan, W.M. (1979) *The brain*. San Francisco, CA: Freeman.

Cowen, E. (1980) The Primary Mental Health Project: A summary. *Journal of Special Education*, 14, 133–154.

Cox, B.J. (1984) Transcription of Braille textbooks by computer. *Journal of Visual Impairment and Blindness*, 78, 244–247.

Cox, D.H. and Klas, L.D. (1996) Students with learning disabilities in Canadian colleges and universities: A primer for service provision. *Journal of Learning Disabilities*, 29, 93–97.

Cox, J., Daniel, N., and Boston, B. (1985) *Educating able learners*. Austin, TX: University of Texas Press.

Cramer, S., Erzkus, A., Mayweather, K., Pope, K., Roeder, J. and Tone, T. (1997) Connecting with siblings. *Teaching Exceptional Children*, 30, 46–51.

Cramond, B. and Martin, C.E. (1987) Inservice and preservice teachers' attitudes toward the academically brilliant. *Gifted Child Quarterly*, 31, 15–19.

Cratty, B. (1986) *Perceptual and motor development in infants and children* (3rd. ed.) Englewood cliffs, NJ: Prentice–Hall.

Crawford, L.V. (Ed.) (1982) *Pediatric allergic diseases*. Garden City, NY: Medical Examination Publishing Company.

Crealock, C. (1983) Teacher and student behaviours in regular and special education settings. *B.C. Journal of Special Education*, 7, 321–330.

Crealock, C. (1984) *The JD/LD link: Causation or condition?* Report prepared for the Solicitor General of Canada. Ottawa: Solicitor General.

Crealock, C. (1986) *The learning disabilities/ juvenile delinquency link: Causation or correction*. Ottawa: Ministry of the Solicitor–General.

Crealock, C. (1989) The on–task and off–task behaviour of exceptional students in segregated and mainstreamed classrooms. *Canadian Journal of Special Education*, 5, 23–32.

Crisis for the newborn [1986] Videotape, National March of Dimes Foundation.

Crockenberg, S.R. and Litman, C. (1990) Autonomy as competence in two year olds: Maternal correlates of child defiance, compliance, and self–assertion. *Developmental Psychology*, 26, 961–971.

Cruickshank, D. (1983) Human rights and charter rights in special education. *B. C. Journal of Special Education*, 7, 205–220.

Cruickshank, W.M. (Ed.) (1976) *Cerebral palsy: A developmental disability*. New York: Syracuse University Press.

Crystal, D., Fletcher, P., and Garman, M.G. (1976) *The grammatical analysis of language disability: A process for assessment and remediation*. London: Edward Arnold.

Csapo, M. (1979) Prevalence and needs assessment study of autistic children in British Columbia. *B.C. Journal of Special Education*, 3, 159–191.

Csapo, M. (1981a) The emotionally disturbed child in Canada's schools. *Behavior Disorders*, 6, 139–149.

Csapo, M. (1981b) Educational provisions for emotionally disturbed children in British Columbia: A status report. *BC Journal of Special Education*, 5, 357–367.

Csapo, M. (1988) Sexual abuse of children. *BC Journal of Special Education*, 12, 121–159.

Cullen, B. and Pratt, T. (1992) Measuring and reporting student progress. In S. Stainback and W. Stainback (Eds.) *Curriculum considerations for inclusive classrooms* (pp. 171–196). Baltimore, MD: Brookes.

Cullinan, D. and Epstein, M.H. (1982) Behavior disorders. In N. Haring (Ed.), *Exceptional children and youth* (3rd ed.). Columbus, OH: Merrill.

Cullinan, D., Epstein, M.H., and Lloyd, J.(1983) *Behavior disorders of children and adolescents*. Englewood Cliffs, NJ: Prentice–Hall.

Cullinan, D., Epstein, M.H., and Lloyd, J.W. (1991) Evaluation of conceptual models of behavior disorders. *Behavioral Disorders*, 16, 148–157.

Culross, R.D. (1997) Concepts of inclusion in gifted education. *Teaching Exceptional Children*, 29, 24–26.

Cummings, E.M., Ionatti, R.J., and Zahn–Waxler, C. (1989) Aggression between peers in early childhood: Individual continuity and developmental change. *Child Development*, 60, 887–895.

Cummings, S.T. and Finger, D.C. (1980) Emotional disorders. In H.E. Rie and E.D. Rie (Eds.) *Handbook of minimal brain dysfunction*. New York: Wiley.

Cummins, J. (1984) *Bilingualism and special education: Issues in assessment and pedagogy*. Clevedon, England: Multilingual Matters.

Cummins, J. (1986) Empowering minority students: A framework for intervention. *Harvard Educational Review*, 56, 18–36.

Cummins, J. (1989) Institutionalized racism and the assessment of minority children. In R.J. Samuda and S.L. Kong (Eds.) *Assessment and placement of minority students* (pp. 95–98) Toronto: C.J. Hogrefe.

Cunningham, J.K., Eisenberg, L.S., Kirk, K.I., Luxford, W.M., and Thielmeir, M.A. (1986) Cochlean implants in children: Speech production and auditory discrimination. *Otolarynologic Clinics of North America*, 1992, 409–421.

Curci, R.A. and Gottlieb, J. (1990) Teachers' instruction of noncategorically grouped handicapped children. *Exceptionality*, 1, 239–248.

Daehler, M.W., Perlmutter, M., and Myers, N.A. (1976) Equivalence of pictures and objects for very young children. *Child Development*, 47, 96–102.

Dahl, M. (1986). *The Canadian symposium on special education issues. Proceedings*. Toronto: Canadian Council for Exceptional Children.

Daiute, C. (1989) Research currents: Play and learning to write. *Language Arts*, 66, 656–664.

Dao, M. (1991) Designing assessment procedures for educationally at–risk southeast Asian–American students. *Journal of Learning Disabilities*, 24, 594–601, 629.

Darnforth, M. (1984) Personal communication.

Dauber, S.L. and Benbow, C.P. (1990) Aspects of personality and peer relations of extremely talented adolescents. *Gifted Child Quarterly*, 34, 10–14.

Daurio, S.P. (1979) Educational enrichment versus acceleration: A review of the literature. In W.C. George, S.J. Cohn, and J.C. Stanley (Eds.) *Educating the gifted: Acceleration and enrichment* (pp. 13–63) Baltimore, MD: Johns Hopkins University Press.

Davenport, S.L., O'Nuallian, S., Omenn, G.S., and Wilkus, R.J. (1978) Usher's syndrome in four hard-of-hearing siblings. *British Journal of Opthalmology*, 7, 484–488.

David, C. (1987) Physically and health handicapped children. In M. Winzer, S. Rogow and C. David, *Exceptional children in Canada*, Toronto: Prentice-Hall.

Davis, G.A. and Rimm, S.B. (1985) *Education of the gifted and talented*. Englewood Cliffs. NJ: Prentice Hall.

Davis, G.A. and Rimm, S.B. (1994) *Education of the gifted and talented* (3rd. ed.) Boston, MA: Allyn and Bacon.

De Apodaca, R.F. Watson, J.D., Mueller, J. and Isaacson–Koiles, J. (1985) A sociometric comparison of mainstreamed orthopedically handicapped high school students and nonhandicapped classmates. *Psychology in the Schools*, 22, 95–101

de Bettencourt, L.U. (1987) Strategy training: A need for clarification. *Exceptional Children*, 54, 24–30.

De La Paz, S. and Graham, S. (1997) Strategy instruction in planning efforts on the writing performance and behavior of students with learning disabilities. *Exceptional Children*, 63, 167–181.

de Mause, L. (1974) *The history of childhood*. New York: Psychohistory Press.

de Mause, L. (1975) Our forefathers made childhood a nightmare. *Psychology Today*, 8, 85–88.

De Myer, M. (1979) *Parents and children in autism*. Washington, DC: V.H. Winston and Sons.

De Pompei, R. and Blosser, J. (1987) Strategies fo helping head–injured children successfully return to school. *Language, Speech and Hearing Services in the Schools*, 18, 292–300.

De Stefano, L. and Wermuth, T.R. (1992) IDEA (PL 101–476) Defining a second generation of transition services. In F.R. Rusch, L. De Stefano, J. Chadsey-Rusch, L.A. Phelps, and E. Szymanski (Eds) *Transition from school to adult life* (pp. 537–549) Sycamore, IL: Sycamore Press.

de Villiers, J.G. and de Villiers, P.A. (1978) *Language acquisition*. Cambridge, MA: Harvard University Press.

De Witt, K. (1991, May 12) How best to teach the blind: A growing battle over braille. *New York Times*, pp. 1, 18.

Decker, S.N. and DeFries, J.C. (1980) Cognitive abilities in families with reading disabled children. *Journal of Learning Disabilities*, 13, 517–522.

Deno, S. L. (1985) Curriculum–based assessment: The emerging alternative. *Exceptional Children*, 52, 219–232.

Derevensky, J. and Coleman, E. (1989) Gifted children's fears. *Gifted Child Quarterly*, 33, 65–68.

DeRuiter, J.A. and Wansart, W. (1982) *Psychology of learning disabilities*. Rockville, MD: Aspen Systems.

Destad, L. (1987) A personal legacy. *Phi Delta Kappan*, 68, 744–745.

Developmental delay: Questions and answers. (1991). *DEC Communicator. The Council for Exceptional Children*, 17, 1–4.

Deykin, E.Y. and MacMahon, B. (1979) The incidence of seizures among children with autistic symptoms. *American Journal of Psychiatry*, 116, 1310–1312.

Diabetic retinopathy (1990) Alberta: Canadian National Institute for the Blind.

Diamond, G.W. and Cohen, H.J. (1987, December) *AIDS and developmental disabilities: Prevention update of the National Coalition in Prevention on Mental Retardation*. Silver Spring, MD: American Association of University Affiliated Programs for Persons with Developmental Disabilities.

Dikmen, S., Matthews, C.G., and Harley, J.P. (1975) The effect of early versus late onset of major motor epilepsy upon cognition–intellectual performance. *Epilepsia*, 76, 73–81.

Directions: A report of the Canadian Organizing Committee for 1981, the International Year of Disabled Persons (1982) Ottawa: Department of Health and Welfare.

The discipline problem—and ways to deal with it (1996) *CEC Today*, 3, 1, 9, 14.

Dishart, M. (1981) Special education and personal needs of gifted and talented children. *Association of Educators of Gifted, Talented and Creative Children in B.C.*, 3, 6–12.

Dishion, T.J., Andrews, D.W., and Crosby, L. (1995) Antisocial boys and their friends in early adolescence: Relationship characteristics, quality, and interactional process. *Child Development,* 66, 139–151.

Dodds, S.E., Volker, M., and Vivand, H.F. (1989) Educating children and youth about AIDS. In J.M. Seibert and R.A. Olson (Eds.) *Children, adolescents, and AIDS.* (chapter 5). Lincoln, NB: University of Nebraska Press.

Dodge, K.A. and Frame, C.L.(1982) Social cognitive biases and deficits in aggressive boys. *Child Development*, 53, 620–635.

Dodge, K.A., Bates, J.E., and Pettit, G.S. (1990) Mechanisms in the cycle of violence. *Science*, 250, 1678–1683.

Dodge, K.A., Pettit, G.S., and Bates, J.E. (1994) Socialization mediators of the relation between socioeconomic status and child conduct problems. *Child Development*, 65, 649–665.

Dodge, K.A., Pettit, G.S., McCloskey, C.L., and Boron, M.M. (1986) Social competence in children. *Monographs of the Society for Research in Child Development*, 51, 2. Serial 213.

Dohrn, E.and Bryan, T. (1994) Attribution instruction. *Teaching Exceptional Children*, 26, 61–63.

Dokecki, F., Baumeister, A.A., and Kupstas, F.D. (1989) Biomedical and social aspects of pediatric AIDS.

Journal of Early Intervention, 13, 99–113.

Doll, E. (1941) The essentials of an inclusive concept of mental deficiency. *American Journal of Mental Deficiency*, 46, 214–219.

Dolnick, E. (1993) Deafness as culture. *Atlantic Monthly*, 272, 37–53.

Dossetor, D.R. and Nicol, A.R. (1989) Dilemmas of adolescents with developmental retardation: A review. *Journal of Adolescence*, 12, 167–185.

Dote–Kwan J (1995) Impact of mother's interactions on the development of their young visually impaired children. *Journal of Visual Impairment and Blindness*, 89, 46–58.

Douglas, V.I., Bari, R.G., Amin, K., O'Neill, M.E., and Button, B.G. (1988) Dosage effects and individual responsivity to methylphenidate in attention deficit children. *Journal of Child Psychology and Psychiatry*, 29, 453–475.

Dowdy, C.A., Carter, J., and Smith T.E.C. (1990) Differences in transitional needs of high school students with and without learning disabilities. *Journal of Learning Disabilities*, 23, 343–348.

Downey, G. and Walker, E. (1989) Spacial cognition and adjustment in children at risk for psychopathology. *Developmental Psychology*, 25, 835–845.

Downey, J., Elkin, E.J., Ehrhardt, A.A., Meyer–Bahlberg, H., Bell, J.J., and Morishima, A. (1991) Cognitive ability and every day functioning in women with Turner syndrome. *Journal of Learning Disabilities*, 24, 32–39.

Doxey, I.M. (1990) *Child care and education: Canadian dimensions*. Toronto: Nelson.

Drash, P.V., Raver, S.A., Murrin, M., and Tudor, R.M. (1989) Three procedures for increasing vocal response to therapist prompt in infants and children with Down syndrome. *American Journal on Mental Retardation*, 94, 64–73.

Drew, C.J., Logan, D.R., and Hardman M.L. (1988) *Mental retardation: A life cycle approach* (4th. ed.) Columbus, OH: Merrill

Drew, C.J., Logan, D.R., and Hardman M.L. (1992) *Mental retardation: A life cycle approach* (5th. ed.) New york: Macmilan.

Driscoll, M. (1994) *Psychology of learning for instruction* (2nd. ed.) Boston, MA: Allyn and Bacon.

Dubose, R. and Langley, (1977) *Developmental Activities Screening Inventory*. Austin, TX: Pro-Ed.

Dudley–Marling, C. (1985) Perceptions of the usefullness of the IEP by teachers of learning disabled and emotionally disturbed children. *Psychology in the Schools*, 22, 65–67.

Dunlap, W.R. (1989) A functional classification for early childhood education. *Journal of Early Intervention*, 13, 73–99.

Dunn, L. M. (1968) Special education for the mildly retarded— Is much of it justifiable? *Exceptional Children*, 35, 5–22.

Dunn, N.L. McCartan, K.W., and Fugura, R.W. (1988) Young children with orthopedic handicaps: Self–knowledge about their disability. *Exceptional Children*, 55, 249–252.

Dunn, W. (1989) Integrated related services for preschoolers with neurological impairments. *Remedial and Special Education*, 10, 31–39.

Dunner, G.M. Connor–Kuntz, F.J., and Goodway, J.D. (1995) A physical education curriculum for all preschool students. *Teaching Exceptional Children*, 27, 28–34.

Dunst, C.J. (1980) *A clinical and educational manual for use with the Ugiris and Hunt Scales of Infant Psychological Development.* Baltimore, MD: University Park Press.

Dunst, C.J. and Leet, H.E. (1987) Measuring the adequacy of resources in households with young children. *Child: Care, Health, and Development,* 13, 111–125.

Dunst, C.J., Trivette, C.M., Hamby, D., and Pollock, B. (1990) Family systems correlates of the behavior of children with handicaps. *Journal of Early Intervention*, 14, 204–218.

Dykens, E., Leckman, J., Paul, R., and Watson, M. (1988). Cognitive, behavioral and adaptive functioning in fragile X and non–fragile X retarded men. *Journal of Autism and Developmental Disorders,*18, 4l–52.

Dykens, E.M. (1996) DNA meets DSM: The growing importance of genetic syndromes in dual diagnoses. *Mental Retardation,* 34, 125–127.

Dyson L.L. (1996) The experiences of families of children with learning disabilities: Parental stress, family functioning, and sibling self–concept. *Journal of Learning Disabilities,* 29, 280–286.

Dyson, L.L. and Fewell, R.R. (1989) The self–concept of siblings of handicapped children: A comparison. *Journal of Early Intervention*, 13, 230–238.

Eaves, L.C. (1988) Prevalence and needs survey of autistic preschool children in the lower mainland of British Columbia. *B.C. Journal of Special Education, 12,* 29–39.

Eber, L., Nelson, C.M., and Miles, P. (1997) School–based wraparound for students with emotional and behavioral challenges. *Exceptional Children*, 63, 539–555.

Edelbrock, C. (1979) Empirical classifications of children's behavior disorders: Progress based on parent and teacher ratings. *School Psychology Digest*, 8, 355–369.

Eden–Piercy, G.V., Blacher, J.B., and Eyman, R.K. (1986) Explaining parents' reactions to their young child with severe handicaps. *Mental Retardation*, 24, 285–291.

Edgar, E. (1988) Employment as an outcome for mildly handicapped students: Current status and future directions. *Focus on Exceptional Children*, 21, 1–8.

Edgar, E., Levine, P., and Maddox, M. (1985) *Washingon State follow–up data of postsecondary special education students.* Seattle: Networking and Evaluation Team, University of Washington.

Edgar, E.B. (1987) Secondary programs in special education: Are many of them justifiable? *Exceptional Children*, 53, 555–561.

Edlind, E.P. and Heansly, P.A. (1985) Gifts of mentorship. *Gifted Child Quarterly*, 29, 55–60.

Edmister, P. and Ekstrand, R. (1987). Preschool programming: Legal and educational issues. *Exceptional Children*, 54, 130–136.

Eichner, E.R. (1986) Sickle cell trait, exercise, and altitude. *The Physician and Sports Medicine*, 14, 144–157.

Einfield, S.L. and Tonge, B.J. (1995) The Develomental Behavioral Checklist: The development and validation of an instrument to assess behavioral and emotional disturbance in children and adolescents with mental retardation. *Journal of Autism and Developmental Disabilities*, 25, 81–104.

Eisenberg, A.R. and Garvey, C. (1981) Children's use of verbal strategies in resolving conflicts. *Discourse Processes*, 4, 149–170.

Eisenson, J. and Ingram, D. (1972) Childhood aphasia: An updated concept based on recent research. *Acta Symbolica*, 3, 108–116.

Eisenson, J.J. (1971) Speech defects: Nature, causes, and psychological concomitants. In W. M. Cruickshank (Ed.) *Psychology of exceptional children and youth*. Englewood Cliffs, NJ: Prentice–Hall.

Elias, M.J. and Taylor, M.E. (1995) Building social and academic skills via problem solving videos. *Teaching Exceptional Children*, 27, 14–18.

Elksnin, L.K. and Elksnin, N. (1997) Issues in the assessment of children's social skills. *Diagnostique*, 22, 75–86.

Elksnin, L.K., and Elksnin, N. (1989). Facilitating successful vocational/special education programs for mildly handicapped adolescents through collaborative consultation with parents. In *Conference proceedings of the fifth international conference of the division of career development*, Atlanta. ERIC Doc. Ed. No. ED 320 363.

Elliot, A.J. (1981) *Child language*. Cambridge: Cambridge University Press.

Elliott, L. (1993, 18 May) Mainstreaming opposed by deaf community. *ATA News*, p. 11.

Elstner, W. (1983) Abnormalities in the verbal communication of visually impaired children. In A.E. Mills (Ed.) *Language acquisition in the blind child*. San Diego, CA: College Hill Press.

Emery, R. (1989) Family violence. *American Psychologist*, 44, 321–328.

Englemann, S.E. (1977) Sequencing cognitive and academic tasks. In R.D. Kneedler and S.G. Tarner (Eds.) *Changing perspectives in special education*. Columbus, OH: Merrill

Epanchin, B.C. and Paul, J.L. (1986) *Emotional problems of children and adolescents. A multidisciplinary perspective*. Columbus, OH: Merrill

Epilepsy Canada Scientific Council [1994] *Statistics*. Ottawa: Author.

Epstein, M.H., Polloway, E.A., Patton, R., and and Foley, R. (1989). Mild retardation: Student characteristics and services. *Education and Training in Mental Retardation*, 24, 7–16.

Erickson, G. (1976) The concept of personal network in clinical practice. *Family Process*, 14, 487–498.

Erickson, J.G. and Walker, C.L. (1983). Bilingual exceptional students: What are the issues? In D.R. Omark and J.G. Erickson (Eds.) *The bilingual exceptional child*. San Diego, CA: College Hill Press.

Erickson, M.T. (1992) *Behavior disorders in children and adolescents* (2nd. ed.) Englewood Cliffs, NJ: Prentice Hall.

Erin, J., Rudin, D., and Njoroge, M. (1991) Religious beliefs of parents of children with visual impairments. *Journal of Visual Impairment and Blindness*, 85, 157–162.

Erin, J.E. (1986) Frequencies and types of questions in the language of visually impaired children. *Journal of Visual Impairment and Blindness*, 80, 670–674.

Eron, L. (1982) Parent–child interaction, television violence and aggression of children. *American Psychologist*, 37, 197–211.

Eron, L., Heusmann, L.R., Brice, P., Fisher, P., and Mermelstein, R. (1983) Age trend in the development of aggression, sex–typing, and related television habits. *Developmental Psychology*, 19, 71–77.

Eron, L.D. and Huesmann, R.L. (1987) Television as a source of maltreatment of children. *School Psychology Review*, 16, 195–202.

Erting, C. (1985) Sociocultural dimensions of deaf education: Belief systems and communicative introduction. *Sign Language Studies*, 47, 111–125.

Erting, C.J., Prezioso, C., and Hynes, M. (1990) The interactional content of deaf mother–infant communication. In V. Volterra and C. Erting (Eds.) *From gesture to language in hearing and deaf children* (pp. 97–106). New York: Springer–Verlag.

Espin, C.A. and Foegen, A. (1996) Validity of general outcome measures for predicting secondary students' performance on content–area texts. *Exceptional Children*, 62, 497–514.

Esposito, B.G. and Koorland, M.A. (1989). Play behavior of hearing impaired children: Integrated and segregated settings. *Exceptional Children*, 55, 412–419.

Evans, S., Tickle, B., Toppel, C., and Nichols, A. (1997) Here's help for young children exposed to drugs. *Teaching Exceptional Children*, 29, 60–62.

Ewing–Cobbs, L.E., Fletcher, J.M., and Levin, H.S. (1985) Neuropsychological sequelae following pediatric head injury. In M. Ylvisaber (Ed.) *Head injury rehabilitation: Children and adolescents* (pp. 118–137). San Diego, CA: College Hill Press.

Eysenck, H.J. (1979) *The structure and measurement of intelligence.* New York: Springer-Verlag.

Faerstein, L.M. (1986) Coping and defence mechanisms of mothers of learning disabled children. *Journal of Learning Disabilities*, u19, 8–11.

Famularo, R., Stone, K., Barnum, R., and Wharton, R. (1986) Alcoholism and severe child maltreatment. *American Journal of Orthopsychiatry*, 56, 481–485.

Farber, B. and Ryckman, D.B. (1965) Effects of severely mentally retarded children on family relationships. *Mental Retardation Abstracts*, 2, 1–17.

Farber, S. (1981) *Identical twins reared apart: A re–analysis.* New York: Basic Books.

Farkas, G.M., Sherick, R.B., Matson, J., and Loebig, M. (1981) Social skills training of a blind child through differential reinforcement. *The Behavior Therapist*, 4, 24–26.

Farmer, T.W. and Farmer E.M. (1996). Social relationships of students with exceptionalities in mainstream classrooms: Social networks and homophily. *Exceptional Children*, 62, 431–450.

Farmer, T.W. and Hollowell, J.H. (1994) Social networks in mainstream classrooms: Social affiliations and behavioral characteristics of students with EBD. *Journal of Emotional and Behavioral Disorders*, 7, 143–155, 163.

Farrington, D.P. (1983) Offending from 10 to 25 years of age. In K.T. Van Dusen and S.A. Mednick (Eds.) *Prospective studies of crime and delinquency* (pp. 17–37). Boston, MA: Kluwer–Nijhoff.

Farrington, D.P. (1987) Early precursors of frequent offending. In J.Q. Wilson and G.C. Loury (Eds.) *From children to citizens (vol. 3) Families, schools, and delinquency prevention* (pp. 27–51) New York: Springer Verlag.

Farrington, D.P., Gallagher, B., Morley, L., St. Ledger, R., and West, D.J. (1986) *Cambridge study in delinquent development: Long term follow–up.* Cambridge, England: Cambridge Institute of Criminology.

Fausti, S.A. [1987] Pure tone audiology and high frequencies. *Audiology in Practice*, 4, 4–6.

Faye, E.E. (1976) Management of the child. In E. Faye (Ed.) *Clinical low vision.* Boston, MA: Little Brown.

Federal Register (1977), 41, 42. Washington, DC: US Government Printing Office.

Feingold, B.F. (1975) Hyperkinesis and learning disabilities linked to artificial food flavors and dyes. *American Journal of Nursing*, 75, 797–803.

Feingold, B.F. (1976) Hyperkenesis and learning disabilities linked to the ingestion of artificial food colors and flavors. *Journal of Learning Disabilities*, 9, 551–559.

Feitler, F. and Tokar, E. (1982) Getting a handle on teacher stress: How bad is the problem? *Educational Leadership*, 39, 456–458.

Feldhusen, F.F. Hoover, S.M., and Sayler, M.F. (1990) *Identification and education of gifted students at the sec-* ondary level. New York: Trillium.

Feldhusen, J., Proctor, T.B., and Black, K.N. (1986) Guidelines for grade advancement of precocious children. *Roeper Review*, 9, 25–27.

Feldhusen, J.F. (1989) Why the public schools will continue to neglect the gifted. *Gifted Child Today*, 12, 55–59.

Feldhusen, J.F. and Clinkenbeard, P.A. (1987) Creativity instructional materials: Review of research. *Journal of Creative Behavior*, 20 1153–1182.

Feldhusen, J.F. and Hoover, S.M. (1986) A conception of giftedness: Intelligence, self concept and motivation. *Roeper Review*, 8, 140–143.

Feldhusen, J.F. and Moon, S. (1992) Grouping gifted students: Issues and concerns. *Gifted Child Quarterly*, 36, 63–67.

Feldhusen, J.F., Van Winkle, L., and Ehle, D.A. (1996) Is it acceleration or simply appropriate instruction for precocious youth? *Teaching Exceptional Children*, 28, 48–51.

Feldman, D. (1993) Child prodigies: A distinctive form of gitedness. *Gifted Child Quarterly*, 37, 188–193.

Fencham, F.D., Hokada, A., and Sanders, R. Jr. (1989) Learned helplessness, test anxiety, and academic achievement: A longitudinal analysis. *Child Development*, 60, 138–145.

Feniak, C.A. (1988) Labelling in special education: A problematic issue in England and Wales. *International Journal of Special Education*, 3, 117–124.

Fenichel, G.H. (1980) *Neonatal neurology.* New York: Churchill Livingstone.

Fensler, M.A., Rosenberg, M.S., and Rosenberg, L.A. (1991) Concomitant learning disabilites and learning problems among students with behavioral/emotional disorders. *Behavioral Disorders*, 16, 97–106.

Ferrari, M. (1984) Chronic illness: Psychological effects on siblings:. 1, Chronicaly ill boys. *Journal of Child Psychology and Psychiatry*, 25, 459–476.

Ferrari, M. (1987) The diabetic child and well siblings: Risk to the well child's self-concept. *Children's Health Care*, 15, 141–147.

Ferrell, K.A. (1985) *Reach out and teach. Meeting the training needs of parents of visually impaired and multihandicapped children.* New York: American Foundation for the Blind.

Fetal Alcohol Syndrome: The misdiagnosed disability (1997, October) *CEC Today*, pp. 12–13, 15.

Feuerstein, R. (1980) *Instrumental enrichment.* Baltimore, MD: University Park Press.

Fewell, R.R. and Cone, J.D. (1983) Identification and placement of severely handicapped children. In M.Snell (Ed.) *A systematic approach for instruction of moderately, severely and profoundly handicapped children* (pp. 46–73). Columbus, OH: Merrill.

Fewell, R.R. and Langley, B. (1984) *Developmental Activities Screening Inventory, 11.* Austin, TX: Pro-Ed.

Fichten, C.S., Judd, D., Tagalikis, V., Amsel, R., and Robillard, K. (1991) Communication cues used by people with and without visual impairments in daily conversations and dating. *Journal of Visual Impairment and Blindness*, 85, 371–377.

Ficociello, C. (1977) Visual stimulation for low functioning deaf–blind rubella children. In M.S. Thomas (Ed.) *Developing skills in severely and profoundly handicapped children*. Reston, VA: Council for Exceptional Children.

Fiedler, C.R. and Simpson, R.I. (1987) Modifying the attitudes of nonhandicapped high school students toward handicapped peers. *Exceptional Children*, 53, 342–349.

Field, T. (1983) High risk infants 'have less fun' during early interactions. *Topics in Early Childhood Special Education*, 3, 77–87.

Figueroa, R.A, Fradd, S.H., and Correa, V.I. (1989) Bilingual special eucation and this special issue. *Exceptional Children*, 56, 174–178.

Fine, S. (1991, 5 October) Plan would send retarded home. *Globe and Mail*, p. A8.

Fink, A.H. and Janssen, K.N. (1992) The management of maltreated adolescents in school settings. *Preventing School Failure*, 36, 32–36.

Finkelstein, N.W., Gallagher, J.J., and Farran, D.C. (1980) Attentiveness and responsiveness to auditory stimuli of children at risk for mental retardation. *American Journal on Mental Deficiency*, 85, 135–144.

Finn, J.D., Pannozzo, G.M., and Voelkl, K.E. (1995) Disruptive and inattentive: Withdrawn behavior and achievement among fourth graders. *Elementary School Journal*, 95, 421–433.

Finnegan, J.A. and Quarrington, B. (1979) Pre-, peri- and neonatal factors and infantile autism. *Journal of Child Psychology and Psychiatry*, 20, 119–128.

Finnegan, L.P., Reeser, P.S., and Connaughton, J.F. (1977) The effects of maternal drug dependence on neonatal mortality. *Drug and Alcohol Dependence*, 3, 131–140.

Fiore, T.S., Becker, E.A., and Nero, R.C. (1993) Educational interventions for students with attention deficit disorder. *Exceptional Children*, 60, 163–173.

Fishburne, G.J. (1989) Stimulant drug therapy and children with attention deficit disorder: An ethical issue. *McGill Journal of Education*, 24, 55–68.

Flaxbeard, R. and Toomey, W. (1987) No longer deaf to their needs. *British Journal of Special Education*, 14, 103–105.

Flynn, P.T. and Byrne, M.C. (1970) Relationship between reading and selected auditory abilities of third grade children. *Journal of Speech and Hearing Research*, 13, 731–740.

Fokes, J. (1976) *Fokes Sentence Builder*. Boston, MA: Teaching Resources Corporation.

Folio, M.R. and Fewell, R.R. (1983) *Peabody Developmental Motor Scale and Activity Cards*. Hingham, MA: Teaching Resources Corporation.

Folstein, S.E. and Rutter, M.L. (1988) Autism: Familial progression and genetic implications. *Journal of Autism and Developmental Disorders*, 18, 3–29.

Fonosh, G.G., Avony, J., Lee, A., and Loving, S. (1982). Providing career planning and placement services for college students with disabilities. *Exceptional Education Quarterly*, 3, 67–74.

Fontana, V.J. and Besharov, D.R. (1979) *The maltreated child* (4th. ed.) Springfield, IL: Thomas.

Ford, A. and Davern, L. (1989) Moving forward with school integration: Strategies for involving students with severe handicaps in the life of the school. In R. Gaylord-Ross (Ed.) *Intervention strategies for students with severe handicaps* (pp. 11–32). Baltimore, MD: Brookes.

Ford, J. and Fredericks, B. (1995) Using interpreter-tutors in school programs for students who are deaf–blind. *Journal of Visual Impairment and Blindness*, 89, 229–234.

Forehand, R. and Atkeson, B.M. (1981) Behavior modification with severely disturbed children. In W.E. Craghead, A.E. Kazdin, and M.J. Mahoney (Eds.), *Behavior modification: Principles, issues, and applications*. Boston, MA: Houghton Mifflin.

Forness, S.R. and Kavale, K.A. (1994) The balkanization of special education: Proliferation of categories for 'new' behavioral disorders. *Education and Treatment of Children*, 17, 215–277.

Fortier, L.M. and Wanlass, R.L. (1984) Family crisis following the diagnosis of a handicapped child. *Family Relations*, 33, 13–24.

Foster, S. (1988) Life in the mainstream: Deaf college freshmen and their experiences in mainstreamed high school. *Journal of the American Deafness and Rehabilitation Association*, 22, 27–35.

Foster, S.L. and Ritchey, W.L. (1979) Issues in the assessment of social competence in children. *Journal of Applied Behavior Analysis*, 12, 625–638.

Fowler, S.A., Schwartz, I., and Atwater, J. (1991) Perspectives on the transition from preschool to kindergarten for children with disabilities and their families. *Exceptional Children*, 58, 136–145.

Fox, C.L. (1989) Peer acceptance of learning disabled children in the regular classroom. *Exceptional Children*, 56, 50–59.

Fox, L.H. (1977) Sex differences and program planning. In J.C. Stanley, W.C. George, and C.H. Solan (Eds.) *The gifted and the creative: A 50 year perspective*. Baltimore, MD : Johns Hopkins University Press.

Fox, N.E. and Ysseldyke, J.E. (1997) Implementing inclusion at the middle school level: Lessons from a negative example. *Exceptional Children*, 64, 81–98.

Fraiberg, S. (1977) *Insights from the blind*. New York: Basic Books.

Frankenberg, W.K., Dodds, J., Archer, P., Bresnick, B., Maschka, P., Edelman, N., and Shapiro, H., (1990) *Denver 11: Technical Manual*. Denver, CO: Denver Developmental Materials.

Fraser, F.C., Frecker, M., and Allderdice, P. (1986) Seasonal variation in neural tube defects in Newfoundland and elsewhere. *Teratology.*

Freedman, R. and Doyle, G. (1974) Depression in children. *Psychology in the Schools, 11,* 19–23.

Freeland, A. (1989) *Deafness: The facts.* Oxford: Oxford University Press.

Freeman, B.J., Ritvo, E.R., Guthrie, D., Schroth, P. and Ball, J. (1978) The Behavior Observation Scale for Autism (BOS): Initial results of factor analysis. *Journal of Autism and Developmental Disorders, 10,* 343–346.

French, D.B. and MacDonnell, B.M. (1985) A survey of questions posed by regular classroom teachers integrating hearing impaired students in Nova Scotia and New Brunswick. *ACEHI Journal, 11,* 12–33.

French, K.F. and Pickett, A.L. (1997) Paraprofessionals in special education: Issues for teacher education. *Teacher Education and Special Education, 20,* 61–73.

Freund, J., Casey, P.H., and Bradley, R.H. (1982) A special education course with pediatric components. *Exceptional Children, 48,* 348–351.

Frey, K.S., Greenberg, M.T., and Fewell, R.R. (1989) Stress and coping among parents of handicapped children: A multidimensional approach. *American Journal on Mental Retardation, 94,* 240–249.

Friedman, C. T. (1989). Integrating Infants. *Exceptional Parent,* pp. 52–57.

Friesen, J.W. (1997) The concept of giftedness in First Nations context. *Multicultural Education Journal, 15,* 26–35.

Frith, G.H. and Lindsey, J.D. (1980) Paraprofesional roles in mainstreaming multihandicapped students. *Education Unlimited, 2,* 17–21.

Frodi, A. M. (1981) Contributions of infant characteristics to child abuse. *American Journal on Mental Deficiency, 85,* 341–349.

Frymier, J. and Gansneder, B. (1989, October) The Phi Delta Kappa study of students at risk. *Phi Delta Kappan, 71,* 142–151.

Fryxell, D. and Kennedy, C.H. (1995) Placement along the continuum of services and its impact on students' social relationships. *Journal for the Association for Persons with Severe Handicaps, 20,* 259–269.

Fuchs, D. and Fuchs, L.S. (1994) Inclusive schools movement and radicalization of special education reform. *Exceptional Children, 60,* 294–309.

Fuchs, D. and Fuchs, L.S. (1995) Special education can work. In J.M. Kauffman, J.W. Lloyd, D.P. Hallahan, and T.A. Astuto (Eds.) *Issues in educational placement* (pp. 363–377) Hillsdale, NJ: Erlbaum.

Fuchs, L.S. and Deno, S.L. (1992) Effects of curriculum with curriculum-based measurement. *Exceptional Children, 58,* 232–242.

Fuchs, L.S., Fuchs, D., Hamlett, C.L., and Ferguson, C. (1992) Effects of expert system, consultation within curriculum-based measurement, using a reading maze task. *Exceptional Children, 58,* 436–450.

Fuchs, L.S., Fuchs, D., Hamlett, C.L., Phillips, N.B., and Karns, K. (1995) General educators' specialized adaptations for students with learning disabilities. *Exceptional Children, 61,* 440–459.

Fugate, D.J., Clarizio, H.E., and Phillips, S.E. (1993) Referral-to-placement ratio: A finding in need of reassessment? *Journal of Learning Disabilities, 26,* 413–416.

Furney, K.S., Hasazi, S.B., and De Stefano L. (1997) Transition policies, practices, and promises: Lessons from three states. *Exceptional Children, 63,* 343–355.

Furth, H.G. (1966) *Thinking without language: Psychological implications of deafness.* New York: The Free Press.

Furth, H.G. (1971) Linguistic deficiency and thinking: Research with deaf subjects, 1964–1969. *Psychological Bulletin, 76,* 58–72.

Gabel, H. and Kotsch, L.S. (1981) Extended families and young handicapped children. *Topics in Early Childhood Special Education, 1,* 29–35.

Gabor, T. (1995) *School violence and the zero tolerance alternative.* Ottawa: Solicitor General Canada.

Gadow, K. (1986) *Children on medication (vol 1.): Hyperactivity, learning disabilities, and mental retardation.* Boston, MA: College Hill.

Gadow, K.D. (1979) *Children on medication: A primer for school personnel.* Reston, VA: Council for Exceptional Children.

Gage, N.L. and Berliner, D.C. (1984) *Educational psychology* (3rd. ed.) Boston, MA: Houghton Mifflin.

Gagné, F. (1985) Giftedness and talent: Reexamining an examination of the definitions. *Gifted Child Quarterly, 29,* 103–112.

Gagné, F. (1989) Peer nominations as a psychometric instrument: Many questions asked but few answered. *Gifted Child Quarterly, 33,* 53–58.

Gagné, F. (1991) Toward a differential model of giftedness and talent. In N. Colangelo and G.A. Davis (Eds.) *Handbook of gifted education* (pp. 65–80). Needham Heights, MA: Allyn and Bacon.

Gallagher, J.J. (1972) *The search for an educational system that doesn't exist.* Reston, VA: Council for Exceptional Children.

Gallagher, J.J. (1975) *The gifted child in the elementary school.* Washington, DC: American Educational Research Foundation.

Gallagher, J.J. (1985) *Teaching the gifted child* (3rd. ed.) Boston: Allyn and Bacon.

Gallagher, J.J. (1991) Educational reform, values, and gifted students. *Gifted Child Quarterly, 35,* 12–19.

Gallagher, W.F. (1988) Categorical services in the age of integration: Paradox or contradiction. *Journal of Visual Impairment and Blindness, 82,* 226–229.

Galligan, B, (1990) Serving people who are dually diagnosed: A problem evaluation. *Mental Retardation*, 28, 353–358.

Galt, V. (1997, 28 August) Teachers support disabled in classes: Fiscal, social realities prevent student integration. *Globe and Mail*, pp. A1, A10.

Galton, F. (1869) *Hereditary genius: An enquiry into its laws and consequences*. London, New York: Appleton, 1870.

Garbe, B. and Rodda, M. (1988) Growing in silence: The deaf adolescent. *ACEHI Journal*, 14, 59–69.

Garcia, E.E. (1988) Attributes of effective schools for language minority students. *Education and Urban Society*, 20, 387–398.

Gardner, H. (1983) *Frames of mind: The theory of multiple intelligences*. New York: Basic Books.

Garner, J.B. and Campbell, P.H. (1987) Technology for persons with severe disabilities: Practical and ethical considerations. *Journal of Special Education*, 21, 122–132.

Gartner, A. and Lipsky, D.K. (1987) Beyond special education: Toward a quality system for all students. *Harvard Educational Review*, 57, 367–395.

Gaylord-Ross, R.J. and Holveot, J. (1985) *Strategies for educating students with severe handicaps*. Boston, MA: Little, Brown.

Gayton, W.F., Friedman, S.B., Tavormina, J.F., and Tucker, F. (1977) Children with cystic fibrosis: 1. Psychological test findings of patients, siblings, and parents. *Pediatrics*, 59, 888–894.

Gdowski, B.S., Sanger, D.D., and Decker, T.N. (1986) Otitis media: Effect on a child's learning. *Academic Therapy*, 21, 283–291.

Gearheart, B., Mullen, R. C., and Gearheart, C.J. (1993) *Exceptional individuals: An introduction*. Pacific Grove, CA: Brooks/Cole.

Gearheart, B., Weishahn, M. and Gearheart, C. (1992) *Exceptional students in the regular classroom* (5th. ed.) Columbus, OH: Merrill.

Gedye, A. (1989) Extreme self-injury attributed to frontal lobe seizure. *American Journal on Mental Retardation*, 94, 20–26.

Gelb, S.A. and Mikokawa, D.T. (1986) Special education and social structure: The commonality of 'exceptionality'. *American Educational Research Journal*, 23, 543–557.

George, N.L., George, M.P., Gersten, R., and Grasenick, J.K. (1995). To leave or to stay? An exploratory study of teachers of students with emotional and behavioral disorders. *Remedial and Special Education*, 16, 227–236.

Gerard, J.A. and Junkula, J. (1980) Task analysis, handwriting, and process based instruction. *Journal of Learning Disabilities*, 13, 49–58.

Gerber, M.M. (1988) Tolerance and technology of instruction: Implications for special education reform. *Exceptional Children*, 54, 309–314.

Gerbner, G., Gross, L., Morgan, M., and Signorelli, N., (1980) The `mainstreaming' of America: Violence pro-

file no. 11. *Journal of Communication*, 30, 10–29.

Gerdtz, J. and Bergman, J. (1990) *Autism: A practical guide for those who help others*. New York: Continuum.

Gersh, E.S. (1991a) What is cerebral palsy? In E. Geralis (Ed.) *Children with cerebral palsy*. New York: Woodbine.

Gersh, E.S. (1991b) Medical concerns and treatment. In E. Geralis (Ed.) *Children with cerebral palsy*. New York: Woodbine.

Gersten, R., Walker, H., and Darch, C. (1988) Relationship between teachers' effectiveness and their tolerance for handicapped students. *Exceptional Children*, 54, 433–438.

Geschwund, N. and Galaburda, A.M. (1978) *Cerebral lateralization*. Cambridge, MA: MIT Press.

Giangreco, M.F. Denis, R., Cloninger, C., Edelman, S., and Schattman, R. (1993) "I've counted Jon:" Transformational experiences of teachers educating students with disabilities. *Exceptional Children*, 59, 359–372.

Giangreco, M.F., Edelman, S.W., MacFarland, S., and Luiselli, T.C. (1997) Attitudes about educational and related service provisions for students with deaf–blindness and multiple disabilities. *Exceptional Children*, 63, 329–342.

Giddan J.J., Melling, L., and Campbell N.B. (1996) Unrecognized language and speech deficits in predolescent psychiatric patients. *American Journal of Orthopsychiatry*, 66, 85–92.

Gill, C. (1994, February) Disability and the family. *Mainstream*, pp. 30–35.

Gillberg, C. (1980). Maternal age and infantile autism. *Journal of Autism and Developmental Disorders*, 10, 293–297.

Gillberg, C. and Steffenburg, S. (1987) Outcomes and prognostic factors in infantile autism and similar conditions: A population based study of 45 cases followed through puberty. *Journal of Autism and Developmental Disorders*, 17, 273–287.

Gillberg, C., Rosenhall, U., and Johansson, E. (1983) Auditory brainstem responses in childhood psychoses. *Journal of Autism and Developmental Disorders*, 13, 181–195

Gillet, P. (1994) *Presidential points*. Reston, VA: Council for Exceptional Children.

Gilliss, G. (1990, March/April) Coming to terms with AIDS. *ATA Magazine*, pp. 6–8.

Gittelman, M. and Birch, H.G. (1967) Childhood schizophrenia: Intellectual, neurologic status, perinatal risk, prognosis, and family pathology. *Archives of General Psychiatry*, 17, 16–25.

Glassberg, L.A. (1994) Students with behavioral disorders: Determinants of placement outcomes. *Behavioural Disorders*, 19, 181–191.

Gleason, J.B. (1985) *The development of language*. Columbus, OH: Merrill.

Gogel, E.M., McCumsey, J., and Hewitt, G. (1985, November/December) What parents are saying. *Gifted Talented Creative*, pp. 7–9.

Goldberg, S., Marcovitch, S., MacGregor, D., and Lojkasek, M. (1986) Family responses to developmentally delayed preschoolers: Etiology and the father's role. *American Journal on Mental Deficiency*, 90, 610–617.

Goldring, E.B. (1990) Assessing the status of information on classroom organizational frameworks for gifted students. *Journal of Educational Research*, 83, 313–326.

Goldwin-Meadow, S. and Morford, M. (1985). Gestures in early child language: Studies of deaf and hearing children. *Merrill-Palmer Quarterly*, 31, 145–176.

Golledge, R.G. (1991) Tactual strip maps as navigational aids. *Journal of Visual Impairment and Blindness*, 85, 296–301.

Good, W.V. (1992, summer) Cortical visual insufficiency: *Awareness* (Newsletter of the National Association for Parents of the Visually Impaired).

Goodlad, J.I. and Field S. (1993) Teaching for renewing schools. In J.I. Goodlad and T.C. Lovitt (Eds.). *Integrating general and special education* (pp. 229–252). New York: Merrill Macmillan.

Goodman, G. (1990) Utilizing the paraprofessional in the mainstream. *Support for Learning*, 5, 199–204.

Goodman, R. (1987) Infantile autism: A syndrome of multiple primary deficits. *Journal of Autism and Developmental Disorders*, 19, 409–424.

Goodman, R. and Sevenson, J. (1989) A twin study of hyperactivity: 2, The etiological role of genes, family relationships, and perinatal adversity. *Journal of Child Psychology and Psychiatry*, 30, 691–709.

Gorman, T. and Rose, M. (1994) Inclusion: Taking a stand. *American Teacher*, 78, 9–12.

Gothelf, G.R., Crimmmins, D.B., Mercer, C.A., and Finocchiaro, P.L. (1994) Teaching choice-making skills to students who are deaf–blind. *Teaching Exceptional Children*, 26, 13–15,

Gottesman, I.I. and Shields, J. (1976) A critical review of recent adoption, twin, and family studies of schizophrenics: Behavioral genetic perspectives. *Schizophrenia Bulletin*, 2, 360–401.

Gottlieb, J. Leyser, Y., and Micheals, C. (1990) Parental attitudes toward mainstreaming: A new look at an old question. In R.A. Curci and J. Gottlieb (1990) Teachers' instruction of noncategorically grouped handicapped children. *Exceptionality*, 1, 239–248.

Gough, P.B. (1991) Tapping parent power. *Phi Delta Kappan*, 75, p. 339.

Gray, C.D. (1989) Opening comments on the conference on developmental disabilities and HIV infection. *Mental Retardation*, 27, 199–200.

Green, A.L. and Stoneman, Z. (1989) Attitudes of mothers and fathers of nonhandicapped children. *Journal of Early Intervention*, 13, 292–304.

Green, S.K. and Shinn, M.R. (1995) Parent attitudes about special education and reintegration: What is the role of student outcomes? *Exceptional Children*, 61, 269–280.

Greenberg, M.T. and Calderon, R. (1984) Early intervention: Outcomes and issues. *Topics in Early Childhood Special Education*, 3, 1–9.

Greer, J.V. (1990a) The drug babies. *Exceptional Children*, 56, 382–384.

Greer, J.V. (1990b) Shattering the monolith. *Exceptional Children*, 56, 286–289.

Grenwood, C.R., Carta, J.J., and Hall, R.V. (1988) The use of peer tutoring strategies in classroom management and educational instruction. *School Psychology Review*, 17, 258–275.

Gresham F. (1997, November/December) We need a better way to identify students with learning disabilities. *CEC Today*, p. 14.

Gresham F. and Elliott S. (1987) The relationship between adaptive behavior and social skills: Issues in definition and assessment. *Journal of Special Education*, 21, 167–181.

Gresham, F.M. (1986) Conceptual and definitional issues in the assessment of children's social needs: Implications for classification and training. *Journal of Clinical Child Psychology*, 15, 3–15.

Gresham, F.M., MacMillan, D.L., and Bocian K.M. (1996) Learning disabilities, low achievement, and mild mental retardation: More alike than different? *Journal of Learning Disabilities*, 29, 570–581.

Griffin, G.W. (1987) Childhood predictive characteristics of aggressive adolescents. *Exceptional Children*, 54, 246–252.

Griffiths, P., Smith, C., and Harvie, A. (1997) Transitory hyperphenylalaninaemia in children with continuously treated phenylketanoria. *American Journal on Mental Retardation*, 102, 27–36.

Grossberg, I.N. and Cornell, D.G. (1988) Relationship between personality adjustment and high intelligence: Terman versus Hollingsworth. *Exceptional Children*, 55, 266–272.

Grossman, H. (1995) *Special eduction in a diverse society*. Boston, MA: Allyn and Bacon.

Grossman, H. (Ed.) (1977) *Manual on terminology and classification in mental retardation*. Washington, D C: American Association on Mental Deficiency.

Grover, R., Shahidi, S., Fisher, B., Goldberg, D., and Wethers, D. (1983) Current sickle cell screening program for newborns in New York City, 1979–1980. *American Journal of Public Health*, 73, 249–252.

Groves, P.M. and Rebec, G.V. (1988) *Introduction to biological psychology* (3rd. ed.) Dubuque, IA: Brown.

Gualtieri, G.J., Koriath, U., Van Bourgondien, M., and Saleeby, N. (1983) Language disorders in children referred for psychiatric services. *Journal of the American Academy of Child Psychiatry*, 22, 165–171.

Gubbins, E.J. (1991, April) Research needs of gifted and talented through the year 2000. In J. Renzulli (Chair) The

National Research Center on the Gifted and Talented: Present activities, future plans, and an invitation for input and involvement. At American Educational Research Association, Chicago.

Guerra, N.G. and Slaby, R. (1990) Cognitive mediators of aggression in adolescent offenders. 2: Intervention, *Developmental Psychology*, 26, 269–277.

Guilford, J.P. (1988) Some changes in the Structure-of-Intellect model. *Educational and Psychological Measurement*, 48, 1–4.

Guralnick, M. (1988) Efficacy research in early childhood intervention programs. In S.L. Odom and M.B. Karnes (Eds.) *Early intervention for infants and children with handicaps: An empirical base* (pp. 75–88) Baltimore, MD: Brookes.

Guralnick, M. (1989) Recent developments in early intervention efficacy research: Implications for family involvement in PL 99-457. *Topics in Early Childhood Special Education*, 9, 1–17.

Guralnick, M.J. (1981) Programmatic factors affecting child–child social interactions in mainstreamed preschool programs. *Exceptional Education Quarterly*, 1, 71–91.

Guralnick, M.J. (1986) The peer relations of young handicapped and nonhandicapped children. In P.S. Stein, M.J. Guralnick, and H.M. Walter (Eds.) *Children's social behavior: Development, assessment, and modification* (pp. 93–140). New York: Academic Press.

Guralnick, M.J. (1990) Social competence and early intervention. *Journal of Early Intervention*, 14, 3–14.

Guralnick, M.J. and Bricker, D. (1987) The effectiveness of early intervention for children wih cognitive and general developmental delays, In M. J. Guralnick and C. Bennett (Eds.) *The effectiveness of early intervention for at-risk and handicapped children* (pp. 115–173). New York: Academic Press.

Gynderson, C.W., Maesch, C., and Rees, J.W. (1987) The gifted/learning disabled student. *Gifted Child Quarterly*, 31, 158–160.

Haager, D. and Vaughn, S. (1995) Parent, teacher, peer, and self-reports of social competence of students with learning disabilities. *Journal of Learning Disabilities*, 28, 205–215, 231.

Hagerman, R.J. (1988) Fragile x syndrome: An overview. *Early Childhood Update*, 4, pp. 1, 6.

Hagerman, R.J. and Sobesky, W.E. (1989). Psychopathology in fragile X syndrome. *American Journal of Orthopsychiatry*, 59, 142–152.

Hagerman, R.J., Jackson, A.W., Levitas, A., Rimland, B., and Braden, M. (1986) An analysis of autism in 50 males with the fragile x syndrome. *American Journal of Medical Genetics*, 23, 359–374.

Hall, A., Orel-Bixler, D., and Haegerstrom-Portnoy, G. (1991) Special visual assessment techniques for multiply handicapped persons. *Journal of Visual Impairment and Blindness*, 85, 23–28.

Hall, B.J.C. (1991) Attitudes of fourth and sixth graders toward peers with mild articulation disorders. *Language, Speech and Hearing Services in Schools*, 22, 334–340.

Hall, C.W. and Richmond, B.O. (1984) Consultation with parents of handicapped children. *Exceptional Children*, 31, 185–191.

Hall, M. and Dennis, L. (1968) *Living and learning: The report of the provincial committee on aims and objectives of education in the schools of Ontario.* Toronto: Newton Publishing.

Hallahan, D. P., Kauffman, J. M. and Lloyd, J. W. (1985) *Introduction to learning disabilities* (2nd. ed.) Englewood Cliffs, NJ: Prentice-Hall.

Hallahan, D.P. and Kauffman, J.M. (1991) *Exceptional children: Introduction to special education* (5th. ed.) Englewood Cliffs, NJ: Prentice-Hall.

Hallahan, D.P., Keller, C.E., McKinney, J.D., Lloyd, J.W., and Byron, Q. (1988) Examining the research base of the regular education initiative: Efficacy studies and the Adaptive Learning Environments model. *Journal of Learning Disabilities*, 21, 290–35.

Halpern, A.S. and Benz, M.R. (1987) A statewide examination of secondary special education for students with mild disabilities: Implications for the school curriculum. *Exceptional Children*, 54, 122–129.

Hamachek, B. and Kauffman, J. (1994) Special education in the United States. In K. Mazurek and M. Winzer (Eds.) *Comparative studies in special education.* Washington, DC: Gallaudet University Press.

Haman, T.A., Issacson, D.K., and Powell, O.H. (1985) Insuring classroom success for the learning disabled adolescent. *Academic Therapy*, 20, 517–524.

Hammer, E. (October, 1984) Quality of life for the multiply handicapped child. Paper prepared for the Helen Keller Seminar on the Multiply Handicapped, New York City.

Hammill, D.D. (1990) On defining learning disabilities: An emerging concensus. *Journal of Learning Disabilities*, 23, 74–84.

Hamre-Nietupski, S., Nietupski, J., Bates, P., and Maurer, S. (1982) Implementing a community-based educational model for moderately, severely handicapped students: Common problems and suggested solutions. *Journal of the Association for the Severely Handicapped*, 7, 38–42.

Handel, R.D. (1983) Teachers of gifted girls: Are there differences in classroom management? *Journal for the Education of the Gifted*, 6, 86–97.

Hansen, H. (1978) Decline of Down's syndrome after abortion reform in New York State. *American Journal on Mental Deficiency*, 83, 185–188.

Hansen, J.B and Feldhusen, J.F. (1994) Comparison of trained and untrained teachers of gifted children. *Gifted Child Quarterly*, 38, 115–123.

Hansen, M.J., Lynch E.W., and Wayman, L.I. (1990) Honoring the cultural diversity of families when gathering data. *Topics in Early Childhood Special Education*, 10, 112–131.

Hanson, L. (1996, October) Are special educators still struggling to gain respect? *CEC Today*, p. 14.

Harber, J.R. (1980) Issues in the assessment of language and reading disorders in learning disabled children. *Learning Disability Quarterly*, 3, 20–28.

Hardman, M. and McDonald, J. (1987) Implementing federal transition initiatives for youth with severe handicaps: The Utah Community-Based Transition Project. *Exceptional Children*, 53, 493–498.

Hardman, M.L. Drew, C.J., Egan, M.W., and Wolf, B. (1993) *Human exceptionalty: Society, school, and family* (4th. ed.) Boston, MA: Allyn and Bacon.

Hardy, W.G. and Bordley, J.E. (1973) Problems in diagnosis and management of multiply handicapped deaf children. *Archives of Otolaryngology*, 73, 269–274.

Haring, K.A., Lovett, D.L., and Saren, D. (1991) Parent perspectives of their adult offspring with disabilities. *Teaching Exceptional Children*, 23, 6–10.

Harley, R.D. (Ed.) (1983) *Pediatric optholomolgy* (2nd. ed.) Philadelphia, PA: Saunders.

Harley, R.K. and Lawrence, G.A. (1977) *Visual impairments in the schools*. Springfield, IL: Thomas.

Harris, A.C. (1986) *Child development*. St. Paul, MI: West.

Harris, D.B. (1963) *Goodenough-Harris Drawing Test Manual*. New York: Harcourt, Brace and World.

Harris, L., Humphrey, K., Muir, D.M., and Dodwell, P.C. (1985) Use of the Cantebury child's aid in infancy and early childhood: A case study. *Journal of Visual Impairment and Blindness*, 79, 4–11.

Harris, S.L., Handleman, J.S., and Palmer, C. (1985) Parents and grandparents view the autistic child. *Journal of Autism and Developmental Disorders*, 15, 127–137.

Harris, S.L., Handleman, J.S., Kristoff, B., Bass, L., and Gordon, R. (1990). Changes in language development among autistic and peer children in segregated and integrated preschool settings. *Journal of Autism and Developmental Disorders*, 20, 23–31.

Harrison R. and Philips, B. (1971) Observations on hearing levels of preschool cleft palate children. *Journal of Speech and Hearing Disorders*, 36, 252–256.

Harrison, P. (1987) Research with adaptive behavior scales. *Journal of Special Education*, 21, 37–61.

Harrison, R. (1985) How you can help the abused child. *Learning*, 74–78.

Harrison, T. R. (1980). *Harrison's principles of internal medicine* (9th. ed.). New York: McGraw-Hill.

Harry, B. (1992) Making sense of disability: Low-income, Puerto Rican parents' theories of the problem. *Exceptional Children*, 59, 27–40.

Hart, S.N. and Brassard, M.R. (1987) A major threat to children's mental health: Psychological maltreatment.

American Psychologist, 42, 160–165.

Harth, R. (1988) The Feuerstein perspective on the modification of cognitive performance. In E.L. Meyen, G.A. Vergason, and R.J. Whelan (Eds.) *Effective instructional strategies for exceptional children*. Denver, CO: Love.

Hartup, W.W.(1974) Aggression in childhood: Developmental perspectives. *American Psychologist*, 29, 336–341.

Harvey, D.H.P. and Greenway, A.P. (1984) The self-concept of physically handicapped children and their non-handicapped siblings: An empirical investigation. *Journal of Child Psychology and Psychiatry*, 25, 273–284.

Hasazi, S.B. and Clark, G.M. (1988) Vocational preparation for high school students labelled as mentally retarded: Employment as a graduation goal. *Mental Retardation*, 26, 343–349.

Hasazi, S.B., Gordon, L.R., and Roe, C.A. (1985) Factors associated with the employment status of handicapped youth exiting from high school from 1979–1983. *Exceptional Children*, 51, 455–469.

Hasenstab, M.S. (1985) Reading evaluation: A psycholinguistic approach. In C.S. Simon (Ed.) *Communication skills and classroom success: Assessment*. College Hill, CA: Little Brown.

Hatcher, P.J., Hanline, C., and Ellis A.W. (1994) Ameliorating early reading failure by integrating the teaching of reading and phonological skills: The phonological linkage hypothesis. *Child Development*, 65, 41–58.

Hatton, D.D. (1991) Leading causes of blindness in the infant–preschool population. *Journal of Visual Impairment and Blindness*, 85, 99.

Hatton, D.D. (1992) Service for young children with visual handicaps in North Carolina. *IN–TAC Tribune*, 5, 1–4.

Hatton, D.D., Bailey, D.B., Burchinal, M.R., and Ferrell, K.A. (1997) Developmental growth curves of preschool children with vision impairments. *Child Development*, 68, 788–806.

Hauser, S.L., De Long, G.R., and Rosman, N.P. (1975) Pneumographic findings in infantile autism syndrome: A correlation with temporal lobe disease. *Brain*, 98, 667–688.

Havener, W.H. (1979) *Synopsis of ophthalmology*. St Louis, MO: Mosby.

Hay, H. (1990) Allergies and the teacher. Unpublished paper, University of Lethbridge.

Hayden, A.M. and Beck, (1981) The epidemiology of high risk and handicapped infants. In C.T. Ramey and P.L. Trohanis (Eds.) *Finding and educating high-risk and handicapped infants*. Baltimore, MD: University Park Press.

Haywood Gear, G. (1976) Accuracy of teacher judgment in identifying intellectually gifted children: A review of the literature. *Gifted Child Quarterly*, 20, 478–487.

Hazel, J.S., Schumaker, J.B., Sherman, J.A., and Sheldon-

Wildgren, J. (1981) *ASSET: A social skills program for adolescents.* Champaign,IL: Research Press.

Hearing loss and surgery. (1982) *Lifeline Magazine,* 4, 8–10.

Heber, R.A. (1961) *A manual on terminology and classification in mental retardation* (Rev. ed.). *American Journal on Mental Deficiency,* monograph supplement.

Hedrick, D.L., Pratter, E.M., and Tobin, A.R. (1975) *Sequenced Inventory of Communication Development.* Seattle, WA: University of Washington Press.

Heiligenstrin, E. and Keeling, R.P. (1995) Prevention of unrecognized attention deficit hyperactivity disorder in college students. *Journal of American College Health,* 43, 226–228.

Helfer, R.E. (1987) The developmental basis of child abuse and neglect: An epidemiological approach. In R.E. Helfer and R.S. Kempe (Eds.) *The batttered child* (4th ed.) Chicago, IL: University of Chicago Press.

Heller, K., Alberto, P.A., and Bowdin, J. (1995) Interactions of communication partners and students who are deaf–blind: A model. *Journal of Visual Impairment and Blindness,* 89, 391–401.

Henderson, R.A. (1989) PKU and maternal PKU: The cure and the problem. *BC Journal of Special Education,* 13, 253–257.

Hendrickson, J.M., Shookoohi-Yekta, M., Hamre-Nietupski, S., and Gable R.A. (1996) Middle and high school students' perceptions of being friends with peers with severe disabilities. *Exceptional Children,* 63, 19–28.

Henig, R.M. (1982, February 28) Saving babies before birth. *New York Times Magazine,* pp.19–22.

Henker, B. and Whalen, B. (1980) The changing faces of hyperactivity: Retrospect and prospect. In C. K. Whalen and B. Henker (Eds.) *Hyperactive children: The social ecology of identification and treatment.* New York: Academic Press.

Henry, A. (1975). Specific difficulties in reading. *Remedial Education,* 10, 81–85.

Hepting, N.H. and Goldstein, H. (1996) What's natural about naturalistic language intervention? *Journal of Early Intervention,* 20, 249–265.

Herbst, D.S. and Baird, P.A. (1983) Non-specific mental retardation in British Columbia as ascertained through a registry. *American Journal on Mental Deficiency,* 87, 506–513.

Herronkohl, R.C., Egolf, B.P., Ellen, C., and Herrenkohl, E.C.(1997) Preschool antecedents of adolescent assaultive behavior: A longitudinal study. *American Journal of Orthopsychiatry,* 67, 422–432.

Hessler, G. and Kitchen, D. (1980) Language characteristics of a purposive sample of early elementary learning disabled students. *Learning Disability Quarterly,* 3, 36–41.

Hetherington, E.M. and Parke, R.D. (1986) *Child psychology: A contemporary viewpoint* (3rd. ed.) New York: McGraw Hill

Heumann, J. (1994, February). *A message for the Assistant Secretary.* Denver, CO: Strategies for Inclusive Eduction.

Heward, W.L. and Orlansky, M.D. (1992) *Exceptional children: An introductory survey of special education* (4th. ed.) Toronto: Maxwell Macmillan Canada.

Hicks, L. (1987) Unpublished paper, St. John's: Memorial University of Newfoundland.

Higginbotham, D.J., and Baker, B.M. (1981). Social participation and cognitive play differences in hearing-impaired and normally hearing preschoolers. *Volta Review,* 83, 135–149.

Higginbotham, D.J., Baker, B.M., and Neill, R.D. (1980). Assessing the social participation and cognitive play abilities of hearing-impaired preschoolers. *Volta Review,* 82, 261–270.

Higgins, A.T. and Turnure, J.E. (1984) Distractibility and concentration of attention in children's development. *Child Development,* 55, 1799–1810.

Hinshelwood, J. (1917) *Congenital word blindness.* London: H.K. Lewis.

Hobbs, N., Perrin, J.M., and Ireys, H.T. (1985) *Chronically ill children and their families.* San Francisco, CA: Jossey Bass.

Hoben, M., Lindstrom, V. Gish, S., Shapiro, S., and Chalberg, C. (1979) *Integration of vision impaired students and hearing impaired students in regular classrooms: A report of research.* Minneapolis, MN: Hennepin Technical Center.

Hobson, R.P. (1988) Beyond cognition: A theory of autism. In G. Dawson (Ed.) *Autism: New perspectives on diagnoses, nature and treatment.* New York: Guilford.

Hoff-Ginsberg, E. (1986) Function and structure in maternal speech: Their relation to the child's development of syntax. *Developmental Psychology,* 22, 155–163.

Hoffman, F.J., Shelson, K.L., Minskoff, E.M., Sautter, S.W., Steidle, E.F., Baker, D.P., Bailey, M.B., and Echols, L.D. (1987) Needs of learning disabled students. *Journal of Learning Disabilities,* 20, 43–53.

Hoge, R.D, Smit, E.K., and Hanson, S.L. (1990). School experiences predicting changes in self-esteem of sixth and seventh grade students. *Journal of Educational Psychology,* 82, 117–127.

Hoge, R.D. and Andrews, D.A. (1992) Assessing conduct problems in the classroom. *Canadian Psychology Review,* 1–20.

Hoge, R.D. and McSheffrey, R. (1991) An investigation of self-concept in gifted children. *Exceptional Children,* 57, 238–245.

Holahan, C. K. (1991) Lifetime achievement patterns, retirement and life satisfaction of gifted aged women. *Journal of Gerontology,* 36, 741–749.

Holder, H.B. and Kirkpatrick, S.W. (1991) Interpretation of emotion from facial expressions in children with and without learning disabilities. *Journal of Learning Disabilities,* 24, 170.

Holland, A.L., Swindell, C.S., and Ruinmuth, O.M. (1990) Aphasia and related adult disorders. In G.H. Shames and E.H. Wiig (Eds.) *Human communication disorders* (3rd. ed.) (pp. 424–462). Columbus, OH: Merrill

Hollinger, C.L. and Fleming, E.S. (1984) Internal barriers to the realization of potential: Correlates and interrelationships among gifted and talented female adolescents. *Gifted Child Quarterly*, 28, 135–139.

Hollinger, J.D. (1987) Social skills for behaviorally disordered children as preparation for mainstreaming: Theory, practice, and new directions. *Remedial and Special Education*, 8, 17–27.

Holsclaw, D.S. (1978) Recognition and management of patients with cystic fibrosis. *Pediatric Annals*, 7, 9–10.

Holt, J. (1994) Classroom attributes and achievement test scores of deaf and hard of hearing students. *American Annals of the Deaf*, 139, 430–437.

Horner, R.H. and Carr, E.G. (1997) Behavioral support for students with severe disabilities: Functional assessment and comprehensive intervention. *Journal of Special Education*, 31, 84–104.

Horowitz, E. (1981) Popularity, decentering ability, and role-taking skills in learning disabled and normal children. *Learning Disability Quarterly*, 4, 23–30.

Houser, L., Moses, E., and Kay J.L. (1987). A family orientation to transition. *Education of the Visually Handicapped*, 19, 109–119.

Howard, I. and Templeton, W. (1966) *Human spatial orientation*. New York: Wiley.

Howe, M.L. and O'Sullivan, J.T. (1990) The development of strategic memory: Coordinating knowledge, metamemory, and resources. In D. F. Bjorklund (Ed) *Children's strategies: Contemporary views of cognitive development*. Hillsdale, NJ: Erlbaum.

Howlin, P. (1981) The results of a homebound language training program with autistic children. *British Journal of Disorders of Communication*, 16, 73–87.

Howse, H. (1988) Asthma in children. Unpublished paper, St. John's: Memorial University.

Hoyme, H.E., Jones, K.L., Dixon, S.D., Jewett, T., Hanson J.W., Robinson, L.K., Masall, M.E., and Allanson, J.E. (1990) Prenatal cocaine exposure and fetal vascular disruption. *Pediatrics*, 85, 743–747.

Huberty, T.J., Austin, J.K., Risinger, M.W., and McNelis, A.M. (1992) Classroom performance and adaptive skills in children with epilepsy. *Journal of School Psychology*, 30, 331–342.

Huebner, K.M. (1985) The challenges in providing appropriate educational services to rural visually impaired children and their families. *Rural Special Education Quarterly*, 6, 2–4.

Huessman, L.R., Eron, L.D., and Yarmel, P.W. (1987) Intellectual functioning and aggression. *Journal of Personality and Social Psychology*, 52, 232–240.

Huessman, L.R., Eron, L.D., Lefkowitz, M., and Walder, L. (1984) Stability of aggression over time and generations. *Developmental Psychology*, 20, 1120–1134.

Hull, J., Phillips, R., and Polyzoi, E. (1995) Indian control and the delivery of special education services in band-operated schools in Manitoba. *Alberta Journal of Educational Research*, 39, 36–62.

Huntze, S. (1985) A position paper for the Council for Children with Behaviour Disorders. *Behavioral Disorders*, 10, 167–174.

Hursh, N. (1985) Vocational evaluation of learning disabled adults. *Journal of Rehabilitation*, 50, 45–52.

Hynd, G.W. and Semrud-Clikeman, M. (1989) Dyslexia and brain morphology. *Psychological Bulletin*, 106, 447–482.

Hysert, L. (1993a, fall) Read it on television. *Disability Today*, pp. 49, 59.

Hysert, L. (1993b, fall) Voiceprint presents the information age to the blind. *Disability Today*, pp. 41–42.

Iber, F.L. (1980) Fetal alcohol syndrome. *Nutrition Today*, pp.4–11.

Ikeda, M. (1976) Electrophysiology of the retina and visual pathway. In F. Ross (Ed.) *Medical Ophthalmology*. London: Chapman and Hall.

Illebrun, D. and Leong C.K. (1981) Evaluating the effectiveness of structured language teaching with developmentally delayed children. *The Exceptional Child*, 28, 31–42.

Ilott, H.G. (1990, June) Speech and language services. Whose responsibility? When we ask the wrong question. *Keeping in Touch*, pp. 4–5.

Immen, W. (1995, April 19) The truth about selective vision. *Globe and Mail*, p. A8.

Inclusion: Where are we today? (1996) *CEC Today* 1, pp. 1, 5, 15.

Increased threat of sexual abuse facing kids with disabilities (1993, summer) *Disability Today*, p. 8.

Injuries at a glance (1994, fall). *Disability Today*, pp. 73–74.

Innes, J.J. (1994) Full inclusion and the deaf student: A deaf consumer's review of the issue. *American Annals of the Deaf*, 139, 152–156.

International Association for the Evaluation of Educational Achievement (1988) *Science achievement in seventeen countries*. Oxford, UK: Pergamon.

Isabell, R.A. and Barber, W.H. (1993) Respiratory disorders: An update and status report for educators. *BC Journal of Special Education*, 17, 244–255.

Izen, C.L. and Brown, E. (1991) Education and treatment needs of students with profound multiple handicaps and medically fragile conditions: A survey of teachers' perceptions. *Journal of the Association for Persons with Severe Handicaps*, 16, 94–103.

Izzo, M.V. (1987) Career development of disabled youth: The parents' role. *Journal of Career Development*, 13, 47–55.

Jack, S.L., Shores, R.E., Denny, R.K., Gunter, P.L., DeBriere, T., and DePaepem, P. (1996) An analysis of the relationship of teachers' reported use of classroom management strategies and types of classroom interactions. *Journal of Behavioral Education*, 6, 67–87.

Jacobs, L. (1991) Assessment concerns: A study of cultural differences, teacher concepts, and inappropriate labelling. *Teacher Education and Special Education*, 14, 43–48.

Jacobs, P.A., Mayer, M., and Abruzzo, M.A. (1986) Studies of the fragile (x) syndrome in populations of mentally retarded individuals in Hawaii. *American Journal of Medical Genetics,* 23, 567–572.

Janney, R.E., Snell, M.E., Beers, M.K., and Raynes, M. (1995) Integrating students with moderate and severe disabilities into regular education classrooms. *Exceptional Children*, 61, 425–439.

Jarvelin, M.R., Laara, E., Rantakillio, P., Moilanen, I., and Isohanni, M. (1994) Juvenile delinquency, education, and mental disability. *Exceptional Children*, 61, 230–241.

Jaussi, K.R. (1991) Drawing the insiders in: Deaf students in the mainstream. *Perspectives in Education and Deafness*, 9, 12–15,

Jensema, C.J., Karchmer, M.A., and Trybus, R.J. (1978) *The rated speech intelligibility of hearing impaired children: Basic relationships and a detailed analysis.* Series R, No. 6. Washington, DC: Gallaudet College, Office of Demographic Studies.

Johnson, A.B. (1987) Attitudes toward mainstreaming: Implications for inservice training and teaching the handicapped. *Education*, 107, 229–233.

Johnson, D., Thompson, S., Sinclair, M. Krantz, G., Evelo, S., Stolte, K., and Thompson, J. (1993) Considerations and the design of follow–up and follow–along systems for improving transitional program and services. *Career Development for Exceptional Individuals*, 16, 225–238.

Johnson, D.G. (1989) An unassisted method of psychological testing for visually impaired individuals. *Journal of Visual Impairment and Blindness*, 83, 114–118.

Johnson, D.R., Bruininks, R.H., and Thurlow, M.L. (1987) Meeting the challenge of transition services planning through improved interagency cooperation. *Exceptional Children*, 53, 522–530.

Jones, B.E., Clark, G.M., and Soltz, D.F. (1997) Characteristics and practices of sign language interpreters in inclusive education programs. *Exceptional Children*, 63, 257–268.

Jones, C.S. (1987) Cerebral palsy. In C.E. Reynolds (Ed.) *Encyclopedia of special education* (pp. 293–296). New York: Wiley.

Jones, K.N. and Bender, W.N. (1993) Utilization of paraprofessionals in special education: A review of the literature. *Remedial and Special Education*, 14, 7–14.

Jones, M.H. (1983) Cerebral palsy. In J. Umbriel (Ed.) *Physical disabilities and health impairment: Assessment, treatment, education.* Baltimore, MD: University Park Press.

Jones, M.M. and Carlier, L.L.(1995) Creating inclusionary opportuniiities for learners with multiple disabilities: A team–teaching approach. *Teaching Exceptional Children*, 27, 23–27.

Jones, R.I. (1986) Can deaf students succeed in a public university? *ACEHI Journal*, 12, 43–49.

Jones, V.J. (1996) "In the face of predictable crisis:" Developing a comprehensive treatment plan for students with emotional or behavioral disorders. *Teaching Exceptional Children*, 29, 54–59.

Jordan, T.E. (1976) *The mentally retarded* (4th.ed) Columbus, OH: Merrill.

Kaiser, D. and Abell, M, (1997) Learning life management in the classroom. *Teaching Exceptional Children*, 30, 70–75.

Kalter, H. and Warkany, J. (1983) Congenital malformations: Etiologic factors and their role in prevention. *The New England Journal of Medicine*, 308, 424–431.

Kamp, J. (1993 spring) Project provides support to adults with learning disabilities. *Abilities*, p. 62

Kanner, L. (1943) Autistic disturbances of affective contact. *Nervous Child*, 2, 217–250.

Kaplan, P.S. (1996) *Pathways for exceptional children: School, home, and culture.* Minneapolis/St. Paul, MI: West Publishing.

Kaplan, R.M. and Saccuzzo, D.P.(1993) *Psychological testing: Principles, applications, and issues* (3rd. ed.) Pacific Grove, CA: Brooks/Cole.

Karagan, N. and Zellweger, H. (1978) Early verbal disability in children with Duchenne muscular dystrophy. *Developmental Medicine and Child Neurology*, 20, 435–441.

Karnes, M.B. and Strong, P.S. (1978) *Nurturing leadership talent in early childhood.* Urbana, IL: Institute for Child Behavior and Development, University of Illinois.

Kauffman J.M., Lloyd, J.W., Baker, J., and Riedel, T.M. (1995) Inclusion of all students with emotional or behavioral disorders? Let's think again. *Phi Delta Kappan*, 76, 542–546.

Kauffman, J. M., Gerber, M.M., and Semmel M.I. (1988) Arguable assumptions underlying the Regular Education Initiative. *Journal of Learning Disabilities*, 21, 6–11.

Kauffman, J.M. (1991) *Characteristics of children's behavior disorders* (3rd. ed.) Columbus, OH: Merrill.

Kauffman, J.M. (1993) How we might achieve the radical reform of special education. *Exceptional Children*, 60, 6–16.

Kauffman, J.M. (1997) Caricature, science, and exceptionality. *Remedial and Special Education*, 18, 130–132.

Kauffman, J.M. and Wong, K.L.H. (1991) Forum: Effective teachers of students with behavioral disorders: Are generic teaching skills enough? *Behavioral Disorders*, 16, 225–237.

Kaufman, F.A and Sexton, D. (1983, September) Some implications for home–school linkages. *Roeper Review,* pp. 49–51.

Kaufman, J. and Zigler, E. (1989) The intergenerational transmission of child abuse. In D. Cicchetti and V. Carlson (Eds.) *Child maltreatment: Theory and research on the causes and consequences of child abuse and neglect* (pp. 129–151). New York: Cambridge University Press.

Kaufman, M. J., Gottlieb, J., Agard, T. A. and Kukic, A. (1975) Mainstreaming: Toward an explication of the construct. *Focus on Exceptional Children*, 7, 1–13.

Kay, M. (1986) Overcoming passive behavior. *Academic Therapy*, 22, 35–39.

Kaye, K., Elkind, L., Goldberg, D., and Tytum, A. (1989) Birth outcomes for infants of drug abusing mothers. *New York State Journal of Medicine,* 89, 256–261.

Kazdin, A.E. (1987) Treatment of antisocial behavior in children: Current status and future directions. *Psychological Bulletin*, 102, 187–203.

Kazdin, A.E. (1989) *Behavior modification in applied settings* (4th. ed.) Pacific Grove, CA: Brooks/ Cole.

Kearney, C.A. and Durant, V.M. (1992) How prepared are our teachers for mainstreaming? A survey of postsecondary schools of education in New York state. *Exceptional Children, 59, 6–11*

Keating, D.P. (1980) Four faces of creativity: The continuing plight of the intellectually underserved. *Gifted Child Quarterly*, 24, 56–61.

Keilitz, L. and Dunivant, N. (1986) The relationship beween learning disabilities and juvenile delinquency: Current state of knowledge. *Remedial and Special Education*, 3, 18–26.

Kelleher, D.K. (1979) Orientation to low vision aids. *Journal of Visual Impairment and Blindness*, 73, —

Keller, H. (1933) *Helen Keller in Scotland*. London: Methuen.

Kempe, C., Silverman, F., Steele, B., Droegemueller, W., and Silver, H. (1962) The battered child syndrome. *Journal of the American Medical Association*, 181, 17–24.

Kennedy, C.H., Shukla, S., and Fryxell, D. (1997) Comparing the effects of educational placement on the social relationships of intermediate school students with severe disabilities. *Exceptional Children*, 64, 31–47.

Kerr, B.A. (1988) Raising career expectations of gifted girls. *Vocational Guidance Quarterly*, 32, 37–43.

Kershner, J.R. and Ledger, G. (1985) Effect of sex, intelligence, and style of thinking on creativity: A comparison of gifted and average IQ children. *Journal of Personality and Social Psychology*, 48, 1033–1040.

Kessler, J. (1977). Parenting the handicapped child. *Pediatric Annals*, 6, 654–661.

Key trends in Canada. (1996, September). *CEC Today*, p. 7.

Khatena, J. (1982) *Educational psychology of the gifted*. New York: John Wiley.

Khoury, J.T. and Appel, M.A. (1979) Gifted children: Current trends and issues. In A. Lane (Ed.) *Readings in human growth and development of the exceptional individua*l. Connecticut: Special Learning Corporation.

Kinsbourne, M. and Hiscock, M. (1978) Cerebral lateralization and cognitive development. In J. Chall and A. Mirsky (Eds.) *Education and the brain: The 77th. Yearbook of the National Society for the Study of Education, part 2*. Chicago, IL: University of Chicago Press.

Kirk, S. (1963, April 16) Behavioral diagnosis and remediation of learning disabilities. In *Proceedings of the conference on exploration into the problems of the perceptually handicapped child: First annual meeting,* (vol. 1) Chicago.

Kirk, S. and Gallagher, J.J. (1979) *Educating exceptional children.* Boston, MA: Houghton Mifflin.

Kirp, D.L. and Epstein, S. (1989) AIDS in American schoolhouses: Learning the hard lessons. *Phi Delta Kappan*, 70, 585–593.

Kittler, F.J. (1970) The effect of allergy on children with minimal brain damage. In F. Speer (Ed.) *Allergy of the nervous system*. Springfield, IL: Thomas.

Klapauszak, R. (1994, October) Parent teacher interviews: Walking the thin line between advocating and aggravating. *K–12 Canada*, 2, p. 4.

Klien, R.G. and Last, C.G. (1989) *Anxiety disorders in children*. Newbury Park, CA: Sage.

Kluwin, T.N. and Moores, D.F. (1985) The effects of integration on the mathematical achievement of hearing impaired adolescents. *Exceptional Children*, 52, 153–160.

Knight, D. and Rieck, W. (1997) Contracts for careers. *Teaching Exceptional Children*, 29, 42–46.

Koestler, F. (1976) *The unseen minority: A social history of blindness in the United States*. New York: David McKay.

Kolata, G. (1988, January 5) New treatments may aid women who have miscarriages. *New York Times*, p. C5

Kolvin, I., Ounsted, C., and Roth, M. (1971) Cerebral dysfunction and childhood psychoses. *British Journal of Psychiatry*, 118, 407–414.

Konstantareas, M.M. (1984) Sign language as a communication prosthesis with language–impaired children. *Journal of Autism and Developmental Disorders*, 14, 9–25.

Konstantareas, M.M., Hamatidis, S., and Busch, J. (1989) Cognition, communication, and social differences between autistic boys and girls. *Journal of Applied Developmental Psychology,* 10, 411–424.

Konstantareas, M.M., Webster, C.D., and Oxman, J, (1979) Manual language acquisition and its influence on other areas of functioning in autistic and autistic–like children. *Journal of Child Psychology and Psychiatry*, 20, 337–350.

Kopp, C.B. (1983) Risk factors in development. In P.H. Mussen (Series ed.), M.M. Haith, and J. Campos (vol.

eds.) *Handbook of child psychology. Vol. 2. Infancy and developmental psychobiology.* (pp. 1081–1088). New York: Wiley.

Korabek, C.A. and Cuvo, A.J. (1986) Children with spina bifida: Educational implications of their medical characteristics. *Education and Treatment of Children*, 9, 142–159.

Korbin, J.E. (1987) Child abuse and neglect: The cultural context. In R.E. Helfer and R.S. Kempe (Eds.) *The battered child* (4th. ed.) (pp. 23–41). Chicago, Il: University of Chicago Press.

Kouri, T. (1989) How manual sign acquisition relates to the development of spoken language: A case study. *Language, Speech and Hearing Services in the Schools*, 20, 50–62.

Kovacs, M. (1989) Affective disorders in children and adolescents. *American Psychologist*, 44, 209–215.

Kozleski, E.B. and Jackson, L. (1993) Taylor's story: Full inclusion in the neighborhood elementary school. *Exceptionality*, 4, 153–175.

Kratochvil, M.S. and Devereux, S.A. (1988) Counseling needs of parents of handicapped children. *Social Casework*, 69, 42–46.

Kraus, J.F., Fife, D., and Conroy, D. (1987) Pediatric brain injury: The nature, clinical course, and early outcomes in a defined United States population. *Pediatrics*, 79, 501–507.

Kregel, J. (1997) Supported employment. *Remedial and Special Education*, 19, 194–196.

Kroth, R.L. (1987) Mixed or missed messages between parents and professionals. *Volta Review*, 89, 1–10.

Krug, D.A., Arick, J.R., and Almond, P.J. (1979) Autism Screening Instrument for Educational Planning: Background and development. In J. Gilliam (Ed.) *Autism: Diagnosis, instruction, management, and research.* Texas: University of Texas and Austin Press.

Krupp, M.A. and Chatton, M.J. (1983) *Current medical diagnosis and treatment.* Los Altos, CA: Lange Medical Publications.

Kulik, J.A. (1992) *An anlaysis of the research on ability grouping: Historical and contemporary perspectives.* Storrs, CT: National Research Centre on the Gifted and Talented, University of Connecticut.

Kulik, J.A. and Kulik, C. (1991) Research on acceleration. In N. Colangelo and G.A. Davis (Eds.) *Handbook of gifted education* (pp. 190–191) Boston, MA: Allyn and Bacon.

Kulik, J.A. and Kulik, C.L. (1984) Effects of accelerated instruction on students. *Review of Educational Research*, 54, 409–425.

Kulik, J.A. Kulik, C.C. (1992) Meta–analytic findings on grouping. *Gifted Child Quarterly*, 36, 73–78.

Kurant, J.E. and Sever, J.L. (1977) Infectious diseases. In J.G. Wilson and F.C. Fraser (Eds.) *Handbook of teratology (vol. 1) General principles of etiology.* New York: Plenum Press.

Kurzweil, R. (1990) *The age of inteligent machines.* Cambridge, MA: MIT Press.

Kusserow, R.P. (1990, February) *Crack babies: A report of the office of Inspector General Department of Health and Human Services.* Washington, DC: Inspector General.

Kuzemko, J.A. (1978) *Allergy in children.* Kent, England: Pittman Medical.

La Pointe, L. (1982) Neurogenic disorders of speech. In G. Shames and E. Wiig (Eds.) *Human communication disorders.* Columbus, OH: Merrill.

Lagercrantz, H. and Slotkin, T.A. (1986, April) The 'stress' of being born. *Scientific American*, pp. 100–107.

Lahey, B. and Carlson, C. (1991) Validity of the diagnostic category of attention deficit disorder without hyperactivity: A review of the literature. *Journal of Learning Disabilities*, 24, 11–120.

Lahey, B.B. and Ciminero, A.R.(1980) *Maladaptive behavior: An introduction to abnormal psychology.* Glenview, IL: Scott Foresman.

Lahey, B.B., Hammer, D. Crumrine, P.L., and Forehand, R.L. (1980) Birth order x sex interactions in child development problems. *Developmental Psychology*, 16, 608–615.

Lahey, M. (1988) *Language disorders and language development.* New York: MacMillan.

Lamb, M.E. and Meyer, D.J. (1991) Fathers of children with special needs. In M. Seligman (Ed.) *The family with a handicapped child*, (2nd ed.) (pp. 151-180). Boston, MA: Allyn and Bacon.

Lambert, N. and Windmiller, M. (1981). *AAMD Adaptive Behavior Scale— School edition.* Washington, DC: American Association on Mental Deficiency.

Lambert, N.M. (1988) Adolescent outcomes for hyperactive children: Perspectives on general and specific patterns of childhood risk for adolescents' educational, social, and mental health problems. *American Psychologist*, 43, 786–799.

Lambert, N.M., Hartsough, C.S., Sassone, D., and Sandoval, J. (1987) Persistence of hyperactivity symptoms from childhood to adolescence and associated outcomes. *American Journal of Orthopsychiatry*, 57, 22–32.

Lamond, M.B. (1995) Should inclusion of children with emotional and physical disabilities in regular classrooms be a good idea even when teachers are given limited support? *Education Update*, 37,

Lamont, I.L. and Hill, J.L. (1991) Roles and responsibilities of paraprofessionals in the regular elementary classroom. *BC Journal of Special Education*, 15, 1–24.

Landau, B. (1983) Blind children's language is not `meaningless.' In A.E. Mills (Ed.) *Language acquisition in the blind child.* (pp. 62–76) San Diego, CA: College Hill Press.

Landerholm, E. (1990) The transdisciplinary team approach in infant intervention programs. *Teaching Exceptional Children*, 22, 66–70.

Landesman–Dwyer, S., Martin, J.C. Smith D.W., and

Streissguth, A.P. (1980) Teratogenic effects of alcohol in human and laboratory animals. *Science*, 209, 353.

Lane, G.M. (1996) The effectiveness of two strategies for teaching students with blindness and mental retardation. *Journal of Visual Impairment and Blindness,* 90, 125–133.

Lane, H. and Pillard, R. (1978) *The wild boy of Burindii.* New York: Random house.

Langley, M.B. (1991) Assessment: A multidimensional process. In M.B. Langley and L.J. Lombardino (Eds.) *Neurodevelopmental strategies for managing communication disorders in children with severe motor dysfunction* (pp. 199–250). Austin, TX: Pro–Ed.

LaSasso, C. and Davey, B. (1987) The relationship between lexical knowledge and reading comprehension for prelingually, profoundly hearing–impaired students. *Volta Review*, 89, 211–220.

Lavach, J.F. and Lanier, H.B. (1975) The motive to avoid success in 7th., 8th., 9th. and 10th. grade high–achieving girls. *Journal of Educational Research*, 68, 216–218.

Lawrence, B. (1991) Self–concept formation and physical handicap: Some educational implications for integration. *Disability, Handicap, and Society*, 6, 139–146.

Laycock, F. (1979) *Gifted children*. Glenview, IL: Scott, Foresman.

Le Coutuer, A., Rutter, M. Lord, C., Rios, P. Robertson, S., Holdgrafer, M., amd McLennon, J.D. (1989) Autism diagnostic interview: A semi–structured interview for parents and care givers of autistic persons. *Journal of Autism and Developmental Disorders*, 19, 363–387.

Le Roy, C.H., Powell, T.H., and Kelber, P.H. (1994) Meeting our responsibilities in special education. *Teaching Exceptional Children*, 26, 37–44.

Learning Disabilities Association (1993) Position paper on full inclusion of all students with learning disabilities in regular education classrooms. *LDA Newsbrief*, 28 (2).

Leavitt, A. and Ioannides, A. (1993) Using character development to improve story writing. *Teaching Exceptional Children*, 25, 41–45.

Lee, M.W.Y. and Csapo, M. (1989) Vocational transition of young people with mental handicap. *BC Journal of Special Education*, 13, 35–53.

Lefebrue, A. (1983) The child with physical handicaps. In P.D. Strenhauser and Z. Rae–Grant (Eds.) *Psychological problems of the child in the family* (2nd ed.). New York: Basic Books.

Leffert, J.S. and Siperstein, G.N. (1996) Assessment of social–cognitive processes in children with mental retardation. *American Journal on Mental Retardation*, 100, 441–455.

Leiter, R. (1948) *The Leiter International Performance Scale*. New York: Wiley.

Lemon, L.A. and Barber, W.H. (1991) Gilles de Tourette syndrome: A review and implications for educators. *BC Journal of Special Education*, 15, 146–158.

Leonard, L. B. (1981). Facilitating language skills in children with specific language impairment: A review. *Applied Psycholinguistics*, 2, 89–118.

Leonard, L.B. (1982) Early language development and language disorders. In G. Shames and E. Wiig (Eds.) *Human communication disorders*. Columbus, OH: Merrill.

Lepper, M.R. and Gurtner, J. (1989) Children and computers: Approaching the twenty–first century. *American Psychologist*, 44, 170–178.

Lerner, J., Mardell–Czudnowski, C. and Goldenberg, D. (1981) *Special education for the early childhood years.* Englewood Cliffs, NJ: Prentice–Hall.

Lessen, E., Dudzinski, M., Karsh, K., and Van Acker, R. (1989) A survey of ten years of academic intervention with learning disabled students: Implications for research and practice. *Learning Disabilities Forum*, 4, 106–122.

Leuenberger, J. and Morris, M. (1990) Analysis of spelling errors by learning disabled and normal college students. *Learning Disability Focus*, 5, 103–118.

Levin, M.E. and Levin, J.R. (1990) Scientific mnemonics: Methods for maximizing the memory. *American Educational Research Journal*, 27, 301–321.

Levine, E. (1981) *The ecology of early deafness: Guides to fashioning environments and psychological assessments.* New York: Columbia University Press.

Levine, J.M. (1983) Social comparisons and education. In J.M. Levine and M.C. Wang (Eds.) *Teacher and student perceptions: Implications for learning* (pp. 29–55) Hillsdale, NJ: Erlbaum.

Levine, M.D. (1982). The child with school problems: An analysis of physical participation. *Exceptional Children*, 49, 296–304.

Levitas, A., McBogg, P., and Hagerman, R. (1983) Behavioral dysfunction in the fragile X syndrome. In R. Hagerman and P. McBogg (Eds.) *The fragile X syndrome: Diagnosis, biochemistry and intervention*. Dillos, CO: Spectrum.

Lewis, J. and Samuda, R.J. (1989) Non–discriminatory assessment of culturally different students. *McGill Journal of Education*, 24, 253–266.

Lewis, R.B. and Doorlag, D.H. (1991) *Teaching special students in the mainstream*. New York: Macmillan.

Lewis, T.J., Chard, D., and Scott T.M. (1994) Full inclusion and the education of children and youth with emotional/ behavioral disorders. *Behavioral Disorders*, 19, 277–293.

Lewis, T.J., Heflin, J. and DiGangi, S. (1991) *Teaching students with behavioural disorders. Basic questions and answers.* Reston, VA: Council for Exceptional Children.

Leyser, L. and Gottlieb, J. (1996) Reactions of parents of nondisabled children to mainstreaming over time: Implications for education practitioners. *International Journal of Special Education*, 11, 73–87.

Li, A.K. and Adamson, G. (1992) Gifted secondary students' preferred learning style: Cooperative, competitive, or individualistic. *Journal for the Education of the Gifted,* 16, 46–54.

Li, A.K. (1985) Changing preservice teachers' attitudes toward emotionally disturbed children. *Canadian Journal of Special Education,* 1, 73–82.

Lichenstein, S. (1989) Post–school employment patterns of handicapped and nonhandicapped graduates and dropouts. *International Journal of Educational Research,* 15, 501–513.

Licht, B.A. and Kistner, J.A. (1986). Motivational problems of LD children. In J.K. Torgesen and B.Y.I. Wong (Eds.) *Psychological and educational perspectives on learning disabilities* (pp.225–255). New York: Academic Press.

Lieberman, L. (1991) REI revisited ... again. *Exceptional Children,* 56, 561–526.

Liebert, D., Lutsky, L., and Gottlieb, A. (1990) Postsecondary experiences of young adults with severe physical disabilities. *Exceptional Children,* 57, 56–63.

Liepman, M.C. (1981) Test procedures and other techniques for the assessment of handicaps: Problems of method. In B. Cooper (Ed.) *Assessing the handicaps and needs of mentally retarded children.* New York: Academic Press.

Lifter, K., Sulzer–Azaroff, B., Anderson, S.R., and Cowdery, G.E. (1993) Teaching play activities to preschool children with disabilities: The importance of developmental considerations. *Journal of Early Intervention,* 17, 139–159.

Light, J.C. (1983) Language intervention programs for autistic children. *Special Education in Canada,* 57, 11–14.

Lindfors, J. (1987) *Children's language and learning* (2nd. ed.) Englewood Cliffs, NJ: Prentice–Hall.

Lindsay, B. (1978) Leadership giftedness: Developing a profile. *Journal for the Education of the Gifted,* 1, 63–69.

Link, M.P. (1991) Is integration really the least restrictive environment? *Teaching Exceptional Children,* 23, 63–64.

Links, P.S., Stockwell, M., Abichandani, F., and Simeon, E. (1980) Minor physical anomalies in childhood autism. Part II: Their relationship to maternal age. *Journal of Autism and Development Disorders,* 10, 287–292.

Linn, R.J., Algozzine, B. Mann, L., and Schwartz, S.E. (1987) Communication skills of learning disabled adolescents. *BC Journal of Special Education,* 11, 301–312.

Linn, S., Schoenbaum, S., Manson, R., Rosner, B., Stubblefield, R., and Ryan, K. (1982) Coffee and pregnancy. *New England Journal of Medicine,* 306, 141–145.

Lipp, M. (1988, May) Educating gifted students. Paper presented at Canadian Education Association Meeting, Fredericton.

Little, D. M. (1980) Learning disabilities and the severely learning disabled— Status quo in B.C. *B.C. Journal of Special Education,* 4, 155–163.

Lloyd, J.W. (1975) The pedagogical orientation: An argument for improving instruction. *Journal of Learning Disabilities,* 8, 74–78.

Lloyd, J.W. (1988) Direct instruction. In M.C. Wang, M.C. Reynolds, and H.J. Walberg (Eds.) *Handbook of special education (vol. 2): Mildly handicapping conditions.* New York: Pergamon.

LLoyd, J.W., Keller, C.E.I., Kauffman, J.M., and Hallahan, D.P. (1988, Jan.) *What will the regular education initiative require of general education teachers?* Washington, DC: Office of Special Education Programs, Department of Education.

Lobato, D., Barbour, L., Hall, L.J., and Miller, C.T. (1987) Psychosocial characteristics of preschool siblings of handicapped and nonhandicapped children. *Journal of Abnormal Child Psychology,* 15, 329–338.

Loeber, R. (1982) The stability of antisocial and delinquent child behavior: A review. *Child Development,* 53, 1431–1446.

Loeber, R. (1985) Patterns and development of antisocial child behavior. *Annals of Child Development,* 2, 77–116.

Loeber, R. (1990) Developmental and risk factors of juvenile antisocial behavior and delinquency. *Clinical Psychlogy Review,* 10, 1–41.

Loeding, B.L. and Crittenden, J.B. (1993) *The Self–Help InterPersonal Skills Assessment (SHIPS).* Tampa, FL: University of South Florida.

Logan, K.R., Bakeman, R., and Keefe, E.B. (1997) Effects of instructional variables on engaged behavior of students with disabilities in general classrooms. *Exceptional Children,* 63, 481–497.

Lojkasek, M., Goldberg, S., Marcovitch, S., and MacGregor, D. (1990) Influences on maternal responsiveness to developmentally delayed preschoolers. *Journal of Early Intervention,* 14, 236–273.

Lombard, R.C. and Newbert, D. (1992) Collaborative transition planning: Federal mandates and local solutions. *International Journal of Special Education,* 7, 123–132.

Lord, C. (1988) Enhancing communication in adolescents with autism. *Topics in Language Disorders,* 9, 72–81.

Lotter, V. (1978) Follow–up studies. In M. Rutter and E. Schopler (Eds.) *Autism: A reappraisal of concepts and treatment.* New York: Plenum Press.

Louis, B. and Lewis, M. (1992) Parental beliefs about giftedness in young children ans their relationship to actual ability level. *Gifted Child Quarterly,* 36. 27–31.

Lourie, N.V. (1975) The many faces of advocacy. In I.N. Berlin (Ed.) *Advocacy for child mental health.* New York: Brunner\Mazel.

Lovaas, O.I. (1982, September) An overview of the Young Autism Project. Paper presented at the Annual Convention of the American Psychological Association, Washington, DC.

Lovaas, O.I. and Favell, J.E. (1987) Protection for clients undergoing aversive/restrictive intervention. *Education and Treatment of Children*, 10, 311–325.

Lovaas, O.I. and Smith, T. (1988) Intensive behavioral treatment for young autistic children. In B.B. Lahey and A.E. Kazdin (Eds.) *Advances in clinical child psychology* (vol. 2) New York: Plenum.

Lovaas, O.I., Newsom, C., and Hickman, C. (1987) Self–stimulating behavior and perceptual reinforcement. *Journal of Applied Behavior Analysis*, 20, 45–68.

Lovaas, O.I., Schreibman, L., and Koegel, R.L. (1974) A behavior modification approach to the treatment of autistic children. *Journal of Autism and Childhood Schizophrenia*, 4, 111–129.

Lovatt, M. (1962) Autistic children in a day nursery. *Exceptional Children*, 29, 103–108.

Lowenbraun, S. and Thompson, M.D. (1982) Hearing impairments. In N.G. Haring (Ed.) *Exceptional children and youth* (3rd. ed.). Columbus, OH: Merrill.

Lowenthal, B. (1986) Planning abilities and metacognition. *Academic Therapy*, 22, 199–203.

Lowey, M. (1993, summer) 3–D image and laser camera improving prostheses for amputees. *Disability Today*, pp. 7–9.

Lozoff, B. (1989) Nutrition and behavior. *American Psycholoigist*, 44, 231–236.

Luetke–Stahlman, B. and Luckner, J. (1991) *Effectively educating students with hearing impairments*. New York: Longman.

Luftig, R.L. (1988) Assessment of the perceived school loneliness and social isolation of mentally retarded and nonretarded students. *American Journal of Mental Retardation*, 92, 472–475.

Lundrum, T.J. (1992) Teachers as victims: An interactional analysis of the teacher's role in educating atypical learners. *Behavioral Disorders*, 17, 134–144.

Lynch, M.A. and Roberts, J (1982) *Consequences of child abuse*. London: Academic Press.

MacAnally, P., Rose, S., and Quigley, S. (1987) *Language learning practices with deaf children*. Boston, MA: College Hill Press.

Maccoby, E.E. (1980) *Social development: Psychological growth and the parent–child relationship*. New York: Harcourt Brace Javonavich.

MacDonald, I.M. (1997) Violence in schools: Multiple realities. *Alberta Journal of Educational Research*, 43, 142–156.

MacDougall, J.C. (1988, August 22) Deaf education: Time for change. *Globe and Mail*, p. A.7.

MacGregor, D.L. (1980) Mental retardation and medical services. *Mental Retardation/ Deficience mentale*, 30, 3–10.

MacGregor, K., Rosenbaum, S., and Skoutajan, K. (1982) *Putting the pieces together: A parent's guide to special education in Ontario*. Toronto: Association for Children with Learning Disabilities.

MacKay, A.W. (1987a) The Charter of rights and special education: Blessing or curse? *Canadian Journal for Exceptional Children*, 3, 118–127.

MacKay, A.W. (1987b) The Elwood case: Vindicating the educational rights of the disabled. *Canadian Journal of Special Education*, 3, 113–116.

MacMillan, D.L. (1988) Issues in mild mental retardation. *Education and Training in Mental Retardation*, 23, 273–284.

MacMillan, D.L., Gresham F.M., and Forness S.R. (1996) Full inclusion: An empirical perspective. *Behavioral Disorders*, 21, 145–159.

Madden, N. and Slavin, R. (1983) Mainstreaming students with mild handicaps: Academic and social outcomes. *Review of Educational Research*, 53, 519–659.

Magnusson, D. (1988) *Individual development from an international perspective: A longitudinal study*. Hillsdale, NJ: Erlbaum.

Main, M. and George, C. (1985) Responses of abused and disadvantaged toddlers to distress in agemates: A study in the day care setting. *Developmental Psychology*, 21, 407–412.

Maker, J.C., Nielson, A.B., and Rogers, J.A. (1994) Giftedness, diversity, and problem–solving. *Teaching Exceptional Children*, 27, 4–19.

Makin, K. (1997, February) Classroom exclusion acceptable, court days. *Globe and Mail*, p. A 7

Maloney, J. (1995) A call for placement options. *Educational Leadership*, p. 25.

Malouf, D.B. and Schiller, E.P. (1995) Practice and research in special education. *Exceptional Children*, 61, 414–424.

Manfredini, D. (1988) Down syndrome. *ERIC Digest, No. 457*. Reston, VA: Council for Exceptional Children.

Mangold, S.S. (1982) Teaching reading in Braille. In S.S. Mangold (Ed.) *A teacher's guide to the special educational needs of blind and visually handicapped children*. New York: American Foundation for the Blind.

Mar, H.H. and Sall, N. (1995) Enhancing social opportunities and relationships of children who are deaf–blind. *Journal of Visual Impairment and Blindness*, 89, 280–286.

Marland, S.P. Jr. (1972) *Education of the gifted and talented: Report to the Congress of the United States by the Commission of Education*. Washington, DC: US Government Printing Office.

Marston, D. (1996) A comparison of inclusive only, pull–out only, and combined service models for students with mild disabilities. *Journal of Special Education*, 30, 121–132.

Martin, F., Daly, J., and Cody, J. (1988) Classroom teachers' knowledge of hearing disorders and attitudes about mainstreaming hard–of–hearing children. *Language, Speech and Hearing Services in the Schools*, 19, 83–95.

Martin, M.L. and Forchuk, C. (1987) Sexuality and the developmentally handicapped: Health education strategies. *Canadian Journal of Special Education*, 3, 181–189.

Martinson, R.A. (1975) *The identification of the gifted and talented.* Reston, VA: Council for Exceptional Children.

Marvin, C. and Mirenda, P. (1993) Home literacy experiences of preschoolers enrolled in Head Start and special education programs. *Journal of Early Intervention,* 17, 351–367.

Matsuda, M.M. (1984) A comparative analysis of blind and sighted childrens' communication skills. *Journal of Visual Impairment and Blindness,* 78, 1–5.

Maurer, H. and Newbrough, J. (1987) Facial expressions of mentally retarded and nonretarded children: 1: Recognition by mentally retarded and nonretarded adults. *American Journal on Mental Deficiency,* 91, 505–510.

Mayberry, R., Woodlinger, Cohen, R., and Goldwin–Meadow, S. (1987) Symbolic development in deaf children. In D. Cicchetti and M. Beeghly (Eds.) *Symbolic development in atypical children* (pp. 109–126) San Francisco, CA: Jossey Bass.

Mazurek, K. and Winzer, M. (1994) *Comparative studies in special education.* Washington, DC: Gallaudet University Press.

McBride, S.L., Brotherson, M.J., Joanning, H., Widdon, D., and Demmitt, A. (1993) Implementation of family–centered services: Perceptions of families and professionals. *Journal of Early Intervention,* 17, 414–430.

McBroom, L.W. (1997) Making the grade: College students with visual impairments. *Journal of Visual Impairment and Blindness,* 91, 261–270.

McBurnett, K., Lahey, B.B., and Pfiffner, L.J. (1993) Diagnosis of attention deficit disorders in DSM–1V: Scientific basis and implications for education. *Exceptional Children,* 60, 108–117.

McCabe, M.P. (1993) Sex education programs for people with mental retardation. *Mental Retardation,* 31, 377–387.

McCarthy, M.M. (1994) Inclusion and the law: Recent judicial developments. *PDK Research Bulletin,* 13.

McClennen, S. (1988) Sexuality and students with mental retardation. *Teaching Exceptional Children,* 20, 58–61.

McCollum, J.A. and Thorp, E.K. (1988) Training of infant specialists: A look to the future. *Infants and Young Children,* 1, 55–65.

McCombs, B.G. and Manzano, R.J. (1990) Putting the self in self–regulated learning: The self as agent in integrating skill and will. *Educational Psychologist,* 25, 51–70.

McCormick, L. (1987) Comparison of the effects of a microcomputer activity and toy play on social and communication behaviors of young children. *Journal of the Division of Early Childhood,* 11, 195–205.

McCrindle, K. (1995, summer). War on words: Label vs euphemism. *Disability Today,* pp. 16–22.

McDonnell, J., Ferguson, B., and Mathot–Buckner, C. (1992) Transition from school to work for students with severe disabilities: The Utah comunity employ-ment placement project. In F. Rusch, L. De Stefano, J. Chadsey–Rusch, L.A Phelps, and E. Szymanski (Eds.) *Transition from school to adult life: Models, linkages, and policy* (pp. 33–50). Sycamore,Il: Sycamore Publishing,

McGee, L.M. and Richgels, D.J. (1990) *Literacy's beginings: Supporting young readers and writers.* Boston, MA: Allyn and Bacon.

McGrew, K.S., Bruininks, R.H., and Thurlow, M.L. (1992) Relationship between measures of adaptive functioning and community adjustment for adults with mental retardation. *Exceptional Children,* 58, 517–529.

McIntosh, K. (1984) Viral infections of the fetus and newborn. In M. Avery and H.W. Taeusch Jr. (Eds.) *Schaffer's diseases of the newborn* (5th. ed.) Philadelphia, PA: Saunders.

McIntosh, R., Vaughn, S., Schumm, J.S., Haager, D., and Lee, O. (1994) Observations of students with learning disabilities in general education classrooms. *Exceptional Children,* 60, 249–261.

McKinney, J. D. and Forman, S. G. (1982) Classroom behavior patterns of EMH, LD, and EH students. *Journal of School Psychology,* 20, 271–279.

McKinney, J.D., McLure, S., and Feagans, L. (1982) Classroom behavior of learning disabled children. *Learningw Disability Quarterly,* 5, 45–51.

McKinney, J.D., Montague, M., and Hocutt, A.M. (1993) Educational assessment of students with attention deficit disorders. *Exceptional Children,* 60, 125–131.

McLaren, J. and Bryson, S.E. (1987) Review of recent epidemiological studies of mental retardation: Prevalence, associated disorders, and etiology. *American Journal on Mental Retardation,* 92, 243–254.

McLean, L.K., Brady, N.C., and McLean, J.E. (1996) Reported communication abilities of individuals with severe mental retardation. *American Journal on Mental Retardation,* 100, 580–591.

McLeod, P. (1981) Fetal Alcohol Syndrome. *B.C. Medical Journal, 23,* 319–320.

McLeskey, J. and Pacchiano, D. (1994) Mainstreamed students with learning disabilities: Are we making progress? *Exceptional Children,* 60, 508–517.

McLinden, D.J. (1988) Spatial task performance: A meta–analysis. *Journal of Visual Impairment and Blindness,* 82, 231–236.

McLinden, S. (1990) Mothers' and fathers' reports of the effects of a young child with special needs on the family. *Journal of Early Intervention,* 14, 249–259.

McNeill J., and Fowler, S. (1996) Using story reading to encourage children's conversations. *Teaching Exceptional Children,* 28, 44–46.

McShane, D. (1982) Otitis media and American Indians: Prevalence, etiology, psychoeducational consequences, prevention, and intervention. In S. Manson (Ed.) *New directions in prevention among American Indian children and Alaska native communities.* Portland, OR: Oregon Health Sciences University.

McWilliams, B., Morris, H., and Shelton, R. (1990). *Cleft palate speech* (2nd ed.). Philadelphia, PA: B.C. Decker, Inc.

Meadow, K.P. (1980) *Deafness and child development.* Berkeley: University of California Press.

Meadows, N.B., Neel, R.S., Scott, C.M., and Parker, G. (1994) Academic performance, social competence, and mainstreaming: A look at mainstreamed and non–mainstreamed students with serious behavior disorders. *Behavioral Disorders,* 19, 170–180.

Meece, J.L., Parsons, J.E., Kaczada, C.M., Goff, S.B. and Futterman, R. (1982) Sex differences in math achievement: Toward a model of academic choice. *Psychological Bulletin,* 91, 324–348.

Meeker, M.N. (1979) *Teachers' guide to the Structure of Intellect Learning Abilities Test.* El Segundo, CA: SOI Systems.

Meents, C.K. (1989) Attention deficit disorder: A review of the literature. *Psychology in the Schools,* 26, 168–178.

Meikle, S. and Kilpatrick, D. (1971) Changes in perceptual, motor, and reading test scores in a remedial reading group. *The Canadian Psychologist,* 12, 254–269.

Mellor, M.C. (1981) *Aids for the 80s: What they are and what they do.* New York: American Foundation for the Blind.

Menolascino, F.J. and Stark, J.A. (1984) *The handbook of mental illness in the mentally retarded.* New York: Plenum Press.

Menser, M.A., Forrest, J.M., and Bransky, R.D. (1978) Rubella infection and diabetes mellitus. *Lancet,* 78, 57–60.

Mercer, C.D. (1979) *Children and adolescents with learning disabilities.* Columbus, OH: Merrill.

Mercer, C.D. (1987) *Students with learning disabilities* (3rd. ed.) Columbus OH: Merrill.

Mercer, J.R. (1973) *Labelling the mentally retarded: Clinical and social system perspectives on mental retardation.* Berkeley, CA: University of California Press.

Merrell, K.W. (1993) *School social behavior scales.* Brandon, VT: Clinical Psychological Publishing

Metcoff, J., Cristiloe, P., Crosby, W.M., Sandstread, H.H., and Milne, D. (1989) Smoking in pregnancy: Relation of birth weight to maternal plasma carotene and chlosterol levels. *Obsterics and Gynecology,* 102, 302–308.

Meyers, E. (1984) A study of concerns of classroom teachers regarding a resource room program for the gifted. *Roeper Review,* 7, 32–36.

Mezriko, M. (1987) Transparency and ease of learning of symbols represented by Blisssymbols, PCS and Picsyms. *Augmentative and Alternative Communication,* 3, 129–136.

Michael, M.G. and Paul, P.V. (1991) Early intervention for infants with deaf–blindness. *Exceptional Children,* 57, 200–210.

Milisen, R. (1971) The incidence of speech disorders. In L. Travis (Ed.) *Handbook of speech pathology and audiology.* New York: Appleton–Century–Crofts.

Miller, C.A. (1985) Infant mortality in the United States. *Scientific American,* 235, 31–37.

Miller, C.R. (1976) Subtypes of the PMR: Implications for placement and progress. In C.C. Cleland, J.S. Swartz, and L.W. Talkington, *The profoundly mentally retarded.* Austin, TX: Western Reserve Conference and Hogg Foundation.

Miller, L. (1990) The regular education initiative and school reform: Lessons from the mainstream. *Remedial and Special Education,* 11, 17–22.

Mills, J.R. and Jackson, N.E. (1990) Predictive significance of early giftedness: The case of precocious reading. *Journal of Educational Psychology,* 82, 410–419.

Mills, P.E., Dale, P.S, Cole, K.N., and Jenkins, J.R. (1995) Follow–up of children from academic and cognitive preschool curricula at age 9. *Exceptional Children,* 61, 378–393.

Milstead, S. (1988) Siblings are people, too! *Academic Therapy,* 23, 537–540.

Milunsky, A. (1975) The causes and prevention of mental retardation. In *The prevention of genetic disease and mental retardation.* Toronto: W.B. Saunders.

Miner, I.D. (1995) Psychosocial implications of Ushers Syndrome Type 1 throughout the life cycle. *Journal of Visual Impairment and Blindness,* 89, 287–296.

Minke, K.M., Bear, G.G., Deiner, S.A., and Griffin S.M. (1996) Teachers' experiences with inclusive classrooms: Implications for special education reform. *Journal of Special Education,* 30, 152–186.

Minner, S. (1989). The use of a paraprofessional to work with parents in a rural school. *Rural Special Education Quarterly,* 10, 38–43.

Mira, M. P. and Tyler, J. S. (1991) Students with Traumatic Brain Injury: Making the transition from hospital to school. *Focus on Exceptional Children,* 23, 1–6.

Misra, A. (1993) Generalization of social skills through self–monitoring by adults with mild mental retardation. *Exceptional Children,* 58, 495–507.

Mitchell, D., Fewell, E., and Davy, P. (1983) Spina bifida. In J. Umbriel (Ed.) *Physical disabilities and health impairments: An introduction.* Columbus, OH: Merrill.

Mithaug, D.E., Martin, J.E., and Agran, M. (1987) Adaptability instruction: The goal of transitional programming. *Exceptional Children,* 53, 500–505.

Mithaug, D.Z., Horiuchi, C.N., and Fanning P.N. (1985) A report on the Colorado statewide follow–up survey of special education students. *Exceptional Children,* 51, 397–404.

Mohn, G. and Van Hol–Van–Dwin, J. (1983) Behavioral and electrophysiological measures of visual functions in children with neurological disorders. *Behavioral Brain Research,* 10, 177–187.

Molnar, M. (1993, November) Whose words are they anyway? *Mainstream*, pp. 18–22.

Monroe, E. (1991) Who's the teacher? *ATA Magazine*, 71, 25–26.

Montagu, A. (1977) *Life before birth.* New York: Signet Books.

Montague, M. (1988) Job-related social skills training for adolescents with handicaps. *Career Development for Exceptional Individuals*, 11, 26–41.

Montague, M. and Graves, A. (1993) Improving students' story writing. *Teaching Exceptional Children*, 25, 36–37.

Montague, M., Maddux, C.D., and Dereshiwsky, M. (1988, April) Story grammar and learning disabled students' omprehension and production of narrative prose. Paper presented at American Educational Research Association Conference, New Orleans.

Montgomary, D. (1981) Do dyslexics have difficulty assessing auditory information? *Psychological Research*, 43, 235–245.

Montigny, G. (1990, winter) Reading skills. *Canadian social Trends*, 22–24.

Moon, M.S. and Inge, K. (993) Vocational preparation and transition. In M.E. Snell (Ed.) *Instruction of students with severe disabilities* (4th. ed.) (pp. 556–588) New York: Merrill.

Moon, M.S., Diambra, T., and Hill, M. (1990) An outcome–oriented vocational process. *Teaching Exceptional Children*, 23, 47–50.

Mooney, C. and Algozzine, B. (1978) A comparison of the disturbingness of behaviors relating to learning disabilities and emotional disturbance. *Journal of Abnormal Child Psychology*, 6, 401–406.

Moore, K.L. and Persaud, T.V.N. (1993) *Before we are born.* Philadephia, PA: Saunders.

Moore, P. (1986) Voice disorders. In G. Shames and E. Wiig (Eds.) *Human communication disorders* (2nd. ed.) (pp. 183–229). Columbus, OH: Merrill.

Moore, S.E. and Perkins, W.R. (1990) Validity and reliability of judgments of authentic and simulated stuttering. *Journal of Speech and Hearing Disorders*, 55, 383–391.

Moores, D. (1987) *Educating the deaf: Philosophy, principles and practices* (3rd. ed.) Boston, MA: Houghton Mifflin.

Moores, D.F. (1982) *Educating the deaf: Psychology, principles and practices* (2nd ed.). Boston, MA: Houghton Mifflin.

Moran, M. (1982, April) Living with a handicapped child: Findings on families and early intervention. Paper presented at CEC, Houston, Texas.

Moran, M.J. and Pentz, A.L. (1995) Helping the child with a cleft palate in your classroom. *Teaching Exceptional Children*, 27, 46–48.

Morgan, R.L., Morre, S.C., McSweyn, C.A., and Salzberg, C.L. (1992) Transition from school to work: Views of secondary special educators. *Education and Training in Mental Retardation*, 27, 315–323.

Morsink, C.V., Thomas, C.C., and Correa, V.I. (1991) *Interactive teaming: Consultation and collaboration in special programs.* New York: Merrill

Moskowitz, D.S. and Schwartzman A.E. (1989) Painting group portraits: Studying life outcomes for aggressive and withdrawn children. *Journal of Personality*, 57, 723–746.

Mossish, R. (1997) Gambling with discipline. *Keeping in Touch*, pp. 1,4.

Mouzakitis, C. and Vachese, R. (1985) *Social work treatment with abused and neglected children.* Springfield, IL: Thomas.

Mulick, J.A., Jacabson, J.W., and Kobe, F.H. (1993) Anguished silence and helping hands: Autism and facilitated communication. *Skeptical Enquiries*, 17, 270–287.

Mundy, P. Sigman, M., Kasari, C., and Yirmira, N. (1988) Nonverbal communication skills in Down syndrome children. *Child Development*, 59, 235–249.

Murphy, D. (1986) The prevalence of handicapping conditions among juvenile delinquents. *Remedial and Special Education*, 7, 7–17.

Murphy, J. and Slorach, N. (1983) The language development of pre–school hearing children of deaf parents. *British Journal of Disorders of Communication*, 18, 118–126.

Murphy, K.R. and Barkley R.A. (1996) Parents of children with attention deficit–hyperactivity disorder: Psychological and attentional impairment. *American Journal of Orthopsychiatry*, 66, 93–102.

Murray, A.D. (1988) Newborns and brainstem–evoked responses (BERs): Prenatal and contemporary correlates. *Child Development*, 52, 71–82,

Murray, M.E. (1981) Diagnostic psychological testing for reading/learning disorders in preschool children. *Reading Psychology*, 2, 146–157.

Musgrove, P. (1984, November 21) Struggling to survive. *Vancouver Sun*, pp.1–2.

Myers, G., Cerone, S., and Olson, A. (1981) *A guide for helping the child with spina bifida.* Springfield, IL: Charles C. Thomas.

Myers, J. (1976) The efficacy of the special day school for EMR pupils. *Mental Retardation*, 14, 3–11.

Myers, P. and Hammill, D.D. (1990) *Learning disabilities: Basic concepts, assessment practices and instructional strategies.* (4th ed.) Austin, TX: Pro–Ed.

Mykelbust, H.R. (1960). *The psychology of deafness.* New York: Grune and Stratton.

Mysak, E. (1982) Cerebral palsy. In G. Shames and E. Wiig (Eds.) *Human communication disorders.* Columbus, OH: Merrill.

Mysak, E.D. (1980). *Neurospeech therapy for the cerebral palsied.* New York: Teachers College, Columbia University.

Naeyaert, K.M. and Grace, G. (1990) Prevalence and causes of blindness and visual impairment in Canada. *Journal of Visual Impairment and Blindness*, 84, 361–363.

National Advisory Committee on Dyslexia and Related Reading Disorders (1969) *Reading disorders in the United States.* Washington, DC: Department of Health, Education and Welfare.

National Association (1991) *Liaison Bulletin,* 17, 2.

National Joint Committee on Learning Disabilities (1988) *Letter to NJCLD member organizations.*

National Joint Committee on Learning Disabilities (1993) Providing appropriate education for students with learning diabilies in regular education classrooms. *Journal of Learning Disabilities,* 26, 33–332.

National March of Dimes [1986] Crisis for the unborn. Videotape.

National Prevention Committee, Canadian Association for the Mentally Retarded (1982) *Final Report to the Minister of National Health and Welfare on the five regional symposia on the prevention of mental retardation in Canada.* Ottawa: Health and Welfare.

Neal, S. and MacLean, W. (1995) Disrupted lives: Siblings of disturbed adolescents. *American Journal of Orthpsychiatry,* 65, 274–281.

Nealis, J.T. (1983) Epilepsy: In J. Umbriel (Ed.) *Physical disabilities and health impairments: An introduction* (pp. 74–85). Columbus, OH: Merrill.

Neel, R. , Meadows, N., Levine. P., and Edgar, E.B. (1988) What happens after special education: A statewide follow-up study of secondary students who have behavioral disorders. *Behavioral Disorders,* 13, 209–216.

Nelkin, D., and Tancredi, L. (1989). *Dangerous diagnostics: The social power of biological information.* New York: Basic Books.

Nelkin, V. (1987) *Family–centred health care for medically fragile children: Principles and practices.* Washington, DC: Georgetown University Child Development Center. ERIC Doc Ed. 303 000

Nelson, C.M., Rutherford, R.B. Jr., Center, D.B., and Walker, H.M. (1991) Do public schools have an obligation to serve disabled children and youth? *Exceptional Children,* 57, 406–413.

Nelson, K.B. and Ellenberg, J.H. (1986) Antecedents of cerebral palsy: Multivariate analysis of risk. *New England Journal of Medicine,* 315, 81–86.

Nesbit, W. (1990, March) The efficacy of integrated senior programs. *Keeping in Touch,* pp. 3–4.

Nessner, K. (1990, winter) Children with disabilities. *Canadian Social Trends,* pp. 18–20.

Neufeld, G.R. and Stevens, A. (1992) *Stay in school initiatives— Book 1: A summary of research on school dropouts and implications for special education.* Kingston, Ont: Council for Exceptional Children.

New developments in ADD/ADHD (1997, September). *CEC Today,* pp. 12–13.

Newacheck, P.W. and Taylor, W.R. (1992) Childhood chronic illnesses: Prevalence, severity, and impact. *American Journal of Public Health,* 82, 364–371.

Newbert, D.A., Tilson, G.P., and Ianacone, R.N. (1989) Postsecondary transition needs and employment patterns of individuals with mild disabilities. *Exceptional Children,* 55, 494–500.

Newborg, J., Stock, J.R., and Wnek, L. (1984) *Battelle Developmental Inventory.* Allen, TX: DLM Teaching Resources.

Newcomb, M.D. and Bentler, P.M. (1989) Substance use and abuse among children and teenagers. *American Psychologist,* 44, 242–248.

Nicholls, A. C. and Martin, Y. M. (1983) Judicial decisions and the public schools. *Canadian Journal of Education/ Revue canadienne de l'education,* 8, 97–116.

Nihira, K., Foster, R., Shellhaas, M., and Leland, H. (1974) *AAMD Adaptive Behavior Scale, 1974 revision.* Washington, DC: American Association on Mental Deficiency.

Nirje, B. (1979) Changing patterns in residential services for the mentally retarded. In E. L. Meyen (Ed.) *Basic readings in the study of exceptional children and youth.* Denver, CO: Love Publishing.

Nixon, M. (1989) An old problem: Will new approaches come? *ATA Magazine,* 69, 41–43.

Nixon, N. (1990) Assessment issues in relation to experience–based learning on placement with courses. In C. Bell and D. Harris (Eds.) *World yearbook of education, 1990: Assessment and evaluation* (pp. 81–111). London: Kegan Paul.

Noel, M. (1980) Referential communication abilities of learning disabled children. *Learning Disability Quarterly,* 3, 70–87.

Northern, J.L. (1980) Acoustic impedance measures in the Down's population. *Seminars in Speech, Language and Hearing,* 1, 81–86.

Northern, J.L. and Lemme, M. (1982) Hearing and auditory disorders. In G.H. Shames and E.H. Wiig (Eds.) *Human communication disorders: An introduction.* Columbus, OH: Merrill.

Notari–Syverson, A.R. and Shuster, S.L. (1995) Putting real–life skills into IEPs? IPSPs for infants and young children. *Teaching Exceptional Children,* 27, 29–32.

Nurss, J.R. and McGauvren, M.E. (1976) *Metropolitan Readiness Tests.* New York: Harcourt Brace Jovanovich.

O'Hara, D.M. and Levy, S.M. (1984) Family adaptation to learning disability: A framework for understanding and treatment. *Learning Disabilities,* 3, 63–77.

O'Melia, M.C. and Rosenberg, M.S. (1994) Effects of cooperative homework teams on the acquisition of mathematics skills by secondary students with mild disabilities. *Exceptional Children,* 60, 538–548.

O'Tuel, F.S., et al. (1983). The SOI as an identification tool for the gifted: Windfall or washout? *Gifted Child Quarterly,* 27, 126–134.

Oderkirk, J. (1993, winter) Disabilities among children.

Canadian Social Trends, pp. 22–25.

Odgen, P.W. and Lipsett, S. (1982) *The silent garden: Understanding the hearing impaired child.* New York: St. Martin's Press.

Odom, S.L. Kohler, F.W. and Strain, P.S. (1987) *Teaching strategies for promoting social interaction skills.* Pittsburgh, PA: The Early Childhood Research Institute, Univerity of Pittsburgh.

Office of Technology Assessment, US Congress (1987) *Technology dependent children: Hospital vs home care– a technical memorandum.* OTA–TM–H–38. Washington, DC: Author.

Ohlsen, M.M. (1977) *Group counseling* (2nd ed.). New York: Holt, Rinehart and Winston.

Okolo, C.M. and Sitlington, P. (1986) The role of special education in LD adolescents' transition from school to work. *Learning Disability Quarterly,* 9, 141–155.

Oller, D.K. and Eilers, R.E. (1988) The role of audition in infant babbling. *Child Development,* 59, 441–449.

Olley, G. (1992) Autism: Historical overview, definition, and characteristics. In D.E. Berkell (Ed.) *Autism: Identification, education, and treatment* (pp. 3–21) Hillsdale, NJ: Erlbaum.

Olweus, D. (1987, fall) Schoolyard bullying: Grounds for intervention. *School Safety,* pp. 4–11.

Olweus, D.(1979) Stability of aggressive reaction patterns in males: A review. *Psychological Bulletin, 86,* 852–875.

Onslow, M. Costa, L. and Rue, S. (1990) Direct early intervention with stuttering: Some preliminary data. *Journal of Speech and Hearing Disorders,* 55, 405–416.

Ontario CEC develops a position paper on professional standards and competencies for educational assistants (1997, September) *CEC Today* p. 7.

Ontario Ministry of Health (1978) *You and your hearing.* Toronto: Ontario Ministry of Health.

Ontario, Ministry of Education (1981) *Special education handbook.* Ontario: Ministry of Education.

Orelove, F.P. and Sobsey, D. (1987) *Educating children with multiple disabilities: A transdisciplinary approach.* Baltimore, MD: Brookes.

Orlansky, M.C. (1981) The deaf–blind and the severe/profoundly handicapped: An emerging relationship. In S.R. Walsh and R. Holzberg (Eds.) *Understanding and educating the deaf–blind/ severely and profoundly handicapped* (pp. 5–23). Springfield, IL: Thomas.

Ormerod, J.J. and Huebner, E.S. (1988) Crisis intervention: Facilitating the parental acceptance of a child's handicap. *Psychology in the Schools,* 25, 422–428.

Ortiz, A. and Yates, J.R. (1989) Staffing and the development of individual education plans for the bilingual exceptional student. In L.M. Baca and H.T. Cervantes (Eds.) *The bilingual special education interface* (2nd. ed.) (pp. 183–193) Columbus OH: Merrill.

Orton, S. (1927) Studies in stuttering. *Archives of Neurology and Psychology,* 18, 671–672.

Otto, T.L. and Barber, W.H. (1992) Prader-Willi syndrome: Causes, characteristics, intervention, long–term consequences. *BC Journal of Special Education,* 16, 38–50.

Overton, T. (1992) *Assessment in special education: An applied approach.* Columbus, OH: Merrill.

Owens, R.J. Jr. (1991) *Language disorders: A functional approach to assessment and intervention.* New York: Merrill.

Owens, R.J.Jr. (1996) *Language development: An introduction.* (4th. ed.) Boston, MA: Allyn and Bacon.

Ozanne, A.E., Kaimmer, and Murdoch, (1990). Speech and language skills in children with early treated phenylketanoria. *American Journal on Mental Retardation,* 94, 625–632.

Paciorek, K.M. and Munro, J.H. (1995) *Early childhood education: Annual editions.* Guilford, CT: Dushkin.

Pagliaro, L.A. (1995) Adolescent depression and suicide: A review and analysis of the literature. *Canadian Journal of School Psychology,* 11, 191–201.

Painter, K. (1997, August 10) Tumor gene identified by scientists. *Calgary Sun,* p. 13.

Palinscar, A.S. and Brown, A.L (1984) Reciprocal teaching of comprehension: Fostering and comprehension monitoring activities. *Cognition and Instruction, 2,* 117–175.

Palmer D.S., Borthwick–Duffy, S.A., and Widaman, K. (1998) Parent perceptions of inclusive practices for their children with significant cognitive disabilities. *Exceptional Children,* 64, 271–282.

Palmer, F.B., Shapiro, B.F., Wachtel, R.C., Allen, M.C., Hiller, J.E., Harryman, S.E., Master, B.S., Meinert, C.L., and Capute, A.J. (1988) The effects of physical therapy on cerebral palsy. *New England Journal of Medicine,* 318, 803–808.

Pardeck, J.T. (1990) Children's literature and child abuse. *Child Welfare,* 69, 83–88.

Parette, H.P. Jr., Hofmann, A., and Van Biervliet, (1994) The professional's role in obtaining funding for assistive technology for infants and toddlers with disabilities. *Teaching Exceptional Children,* 26, 22–28.

Paris, S.G. and Cross, D.R. (1983) Ordinary learning: Pragmatic connections among children's beliefs, motives and actions. In J. Bisanz, G. Bisanz, and R. Kail (Eds.) *Learning in children.* New York: Springer/Verlag.

Parker, J.A. and Asher, S.R. (1987) Peer acceptance and later personal adjustment: Are low–accepted children 'at–risk?' *Psychological Bulletin,* 102, 357–389.

Parker, W.D. (1997) An empirical typology of perfectionism in academically talented children. *American Educational Research Journal,* 34, 545–562.

Patten, B.M.(1973). Visually mediated thinking: A report of the case of Albert Einstein. *Journal of Learning Disabilities,* 6, 415–420.

Patterson, D. (1987, August) The causes of Down syndrome. *Scientific American,* pp. 52–57, 60.

Patterson, G.R. (1982) *Coercive family process.* Eugene, OR: Castalia Press.

Patterson, G.R. and Banks, L. (1989) Some amplifying

mechanisms for pathological processes in families. In M.R. Gumar and E. Thalen (Eds.) *Systems and development: The Minnesota symposium on child psychology* (vol.22) (pp. 167–209) Hillsdale, NJ: Erlbaum.

Patterson, G.R., De Baryshe, B.D., and Ramsey, E. (1989) A developmental perspective on antisocial behavior. *American Psychologist, 44,* 322–335.

Patton, J.R., Cronin, M.E. Polloway, E.A., Hutchinson, D., and Robinson G.A. (1989) Curricula considerations: A life skills orientation. In G.A. Robinson, J.R. Patton, E.A. Polloway, and L.R. Sargent. *Best practices in mild mental disabilities.* Reston, VA: Council for Exceptional Children.

Paul, J.L. (1987) Defining behavior disorders in children. In B.C. Epanchin and J.L. Paul (Eds.) *Emotional problems of childhood and adolescence* (pp. 15–29). Columbus, OH: Merrill.

Paynter, E.J., Jordan, W.J., and French, D.L. (1990) Patient compliance with cleft palate team regimens. *Journal of Speech and Hearing Disorders, 55,* 740–752.

Pearl, R. (1987) Social cognitive factors in learning disabled children's social problems. In S.J. Ceci (Ed.) *Handbook of cognitive, social, and neurological aspects of learning disabilties* (vol. 2) Hillsdale, NJ: Erlbaum.

Peck, C.A., Palyo, W.J., Bettencourt, B., Cooke, T.P., and Apolloni, T. (1988). An observational study of "partial integration" of handicapped students in a regular preschool. *Journal of Research and Development in Education, 21,* 4–44

Peckham, V.C. (1993) Children with cancer in the classroom. *Teaching Exceptional Children, 26,* 26–32.

Pennington, B.F. (1990) *Diagnosing learning disorders: A neuropsychological framework.* New York: Guilford.

Perkins Institution for the Blind (1839) *Annual reports of the Trustees of the New England Institution for the Education of the Blind to the Corporation.* Boston, MA: J.T. Buckingham.

Perkins, W.H. (1978) *Human perspectives in speech and language disorders.* St.Louis, MO: Mosby.

Perkins, W.H. (1990) What is stuttering? *Journal of Speech and Hearing Disorders, 55,* 370–382.

Perks, B. (1984) Identification of gifted children. Ed.D. thesis, University of British Columbia.

Perl, J. (1995) Improving relationship skills for parent conferences. *Teaching Exceptional Children, 28,* 29–31.

Perlmutter, B. (1986) Personality variables and peer relations of children and adolescents with learning disabilities. In S.J. Ceci (Ed.) *Handbook of cognitive, social and neoropsycholigical aspects of learning disabilities* (vol. 1) (pp. 339–359) Hillsdale, NJ: Erlbaum.

Perry, D.G., Perry, L.C, and Boldezar, J.P. (1990) Learning of aggression. In M. Lewis and S. Miller (Eds.) *Handbook of developmental psychopathology.* New York: Plenum.

Perry, D.G., Perry, L.C., and Weiss, R.J. (1989) Sex differences in the consequences that children anticipate for aggressors. *Developmental Psychology, 25,* 312–319.

Perry, D.G., Williard, J.C., and Perry, L.C. (1990) Peers' perceptions of the consequences that victimized children provide aggressors. *Child Development, 61,* 1310–1325.

Peterson, J. (1925) *Early concepts of tests of intelligence.* Chicago, IL: World Book.

Peterson, K.L. (1992) Helping student teachers understand conflict among preschool children. *Journal of Early Childhood Teacher Education, 13,* 15–18.

Peterson, N. L. (1987) *Early intervention for handicapped and at–risk children.* Denver, CO: Love.

Pettito, L.A. and Marenette, P.F. (1991) Babbling in the manual mode: Evidence for the ontogeny of language. *Science, 251,* 1493–1495.

Pfeffer, C.R. (1986) *The suicidal child.* New York: Guilford.

Pfeuti, M. (1997) Asthma: A chronic illness in the classroom. Unpublished paper, University of Lethbridge.

Phillips, K. (1990) Why can't a man be more like a woman— and vice versa. *Omni,* 42–48, 68.

Phipps, (1982) The learning disabled learner is often a boy— Why? *Academic Therapy, 17,* 425–430.

Pianta, R.C. and Lothman, D.J. (1994) Predicting behavioral problems in children with epilepsy: Child factors, disease factors, family stress, and child–mother interaction. *Child Development, 65,* 1415–1428.

Pickett, A.L. (1989) *Restructuring the schools: The role of paraprofessionals: Results in education.* Washington, DC: National Governor's Association.

Piechowski, M.M. (1991) Emotional development and emotional giftedness. In N. Colangelo and G.A. Davis (Eds.) *Handbook of gifted education* (pp. 285–306). Needham Heights, MA: Allyn and Bacon.

Pieper, E. (1976) Grandparents can help. *Exceptional Parent, 6,* 7–10.

Pierce, B.A. (1990) *Family genetic sourcebook.* New York: Wiley.

Pihl, R.D. and McLarnon, L. (1984) Learning disabled children as adolescents. *Journal of Learning Disabilities, 11,* 96–100.

Piirto, J. (1994) *Talened children and adults: Their development and education.* New York: Merril.

Pilecka, A. (1995, July) Childhood allergies. Lecture presented at University of Lethbridge.

Pirro, J.F. (1993, September) Gallaudet football: "The difference is in the hear" for the up-and-down Bisons. *Mainstream,* p. 16.

Pituch, M. and Bruggeman, J. (1982). Lungs unlimited. *Children Today, 11,* 6–10.

Piven, J. Tsai, G., Nehme, E. Coyle, J.T. Chase, G.A., and Folstein, S.E. (1991) Platelet serotonin, a possible marker for familial autism. *Journal of Autism and Developmental Disorders, 21,* 51–54.

Planta, R.C. (1990) Widening the debate on educational reform: Prevention as a viable alternative. *Exceptional Children, 56,* 306–313.

Pledgie, T.K. (1982) Giftedness among handicapped children: Identification and programming development. *Journal of Special Education, 16,* 221–227.

Plomin, R. (1989) Environment and genes: Determinants of behavior. *American Psychologist, 44,* 105–111.

Plomin, R., De Fries, J.C., and McClearn, G.E. (1990) *Behavioral genetics: A primer* (2nd. ed.) New York: Freeman.

Plowman, P.D. (1981) Training extraordinary leaders. *Roeper Review,* 3, 13–16.

Podell, D.M., Kastner, J., and Kastner, S (1996) Adolescents with mental retardation: Perceptions of sexual abuse. *American Journal of Orthopsychiatry, 66,* 103–110.

Pogrund, R.L. and Rosen, S.J. (1989) The preschool blind child can be a cane user. *Journal of Visual Impairment and Blindness,* 83, 431–439.

Poirier, D. and Goguen, L. (1986) The Canadian Charter of Rights and the right to education for exceptional children. *Canadian Journal of Education/ Revue canadienne de l'education, 11,* 231–244.

Poirier, D., Goguen, L., and Leslie, P. (1988) *Education rights of exceptional children in Canada: A national study of multi–level commitments.* Toronto: Carsell.

Pollack, D. (1970) *Educational audiology for the limited hearing infant.* Springfield, IL: Thomas.

Pollack, D. (1980) Acoupedics: An approach to early management. In G.T. Mencher and S.E. Gerber (Eds.), *Early management of hearing loss.* New York: Grune and Stratton.

Pollins, L.D. (1983) The effects of acceleration on the social and emotional development of gifted students. In C. P. Benbow and J.C. Stanley, (Eds.) *Academic precocity: Aspects of its development* (pp. 160–179) Baltimore, MD: Johns Hopkins University Press.

Polloway, E.A. (1985) Identification and placement in mild retardation programs: Recommendations for professional practice. *Education and Training of the Mentally Retarded, 20,* 218–221.

Polloway, E.A. and Smith, J.E. (1982) *Teaching language skills to exceptional children.* Denver, CO: Love Publishing.

Polloway, E.A. Patton, J.R., Payne, J.S., and Payne, R.A. (1989) *Strategies for teaching learners with special needs* (4th. ed.) Toronto: Merrill.

Polloway, E.A., Epstein, M.H., Patton, J.R., Cullinan, D., and Lueble, J. (1986) Demographic, social, and behavioral characteristics of students with educable mental retardation: A survey of the field. *Education and Training of the Mentally Retarded, 21,* 27–34.

Pope, A.M. and Tarlov, A.R. (Eds.) *Disability in America: Toward a national agenda for prevention.* Washington DC: National Academy Press.

Potter, M.L. and Wamre, H.M. (1990) Curriculum–based measurement and developmental reading models: Opportunities for cross validation. *Exceptional Children,* 57, 16–25.

Powell, D.R. (1990) Home visiting in the early years: Policy and program design decisions. *Young Children,* 45, 65–73.

Power, P.W. (1984) *A guide to vocational assessment.* Austin, TX: Pro–Ed.

Powers, D.P. and Franks, C.M. (1988) Behavior therapy and the education process. In J.C. Witt, S.N. Elliott, and F.M. Gresham (Eds.) *Handbook of behavior therapy in education* (pp. 3–36) New York: Plenum.

Prasher, V.P., Chowdhury, T.A., Rowe, B., and Bain, S.C. (1997) ApoE genotype and Alzheimer's disease in adults with Down syndrome: Meta–analysis. *American Journal on Mental Retardation,* 102, 103–110.

Preece, M.A., Kearney, P.J., and Marshall, W.C. (1977) Growth–hormone deficiency in congenital rubella. *Lancet, 77,* 842–844.

Pre–natal care [1987]. Pamphlet, n.p. Available at Lethbridge Health Unit.

Prendergast, D.E. (1995) Preparing for children who are medically fragile in educational programs. *Teaching Exceptional Children,* 27, 37–41.

Pressly, N., Levin, J.R., and McDaniel, M.A. (1987) Remembering versus inferring what a word means: Mnemonic and contextual approaches. In M.G. McKeown and M.E. Curtis (Eds.) *The nature of vocabulary acquisition* (pp. 107–127) Hillsdale, NJ: Erlbaum.

Prevalence of disability in Canada rises. (1995, winter). *Disability Today,* p. 7.

Proctor, T.B., Black, K.N., and Feldhusen, J.F. (1984) Early admission of selected children to elementary school: A review of the research literature. *Journal of Educational Research,* 80, 70–76.

Projections of visible minority groups, 1991 to 2016 (1996, summer) *Canadian Social Trends,* p. 3.

Pruess, J.B., Vadazy, P.F., and Fewell, R.R. (1987) Language development in children with Down syndrome: An overview of recent research. *Education and Training in Mental Retardation,* 22, 44–55.

Pruitt, W. (1986) *Vocational evaluation* (2nd. ed.) Menomonie, WI: Walt Pruitt Associates.

Pugach, C. and Johnson. L. (1989) Prereferral interventions: Programs, problems, and challenges. *Exceptional Children,* 56, 217–226.

Quay, H.C. (1972) Patterns of aggression, withdrawal, and immaturity. In H.C. Quay and J.S. Werry (Eds.). *Psychopathological disorders of childhood.* New York: Wiley.

Quay, H.C. (1986) Classification. In H.C. Quay and J.S. Werry (Eds.) *Psychopathological disorders in childhood* (3rd. ed.) New York: Wiley.

Quay, H.C. and Peterson, D.R. (1987) *Manual for the Revised Behavior Problem Checklist.* Coral Gables, FL: Inviersity of Miami.

Quinsland, L.K. and Vanginkel, A. (1990) Cognitive processing and the development of concepts by deaf students. *American Annals of the Deaf*, 135, 280–284.

Radbill, S.X. (1974) A history of child abuse and infanticide. In R.E. Heifer and C.H. Kempe (Eds.) *The battered child* (2nd. ed.) Chicago, Il: University of Chicago Press.

Raimondo, D. and Maxwell, M. (1987) The modes of communiction used in junior and senior high school classrooms by hearing impaired students and their teachers. *Volta Review*, 89, 263–275.

Ramcharan, S. (1988) The role of education in multi–racial Canada. *Multiculturalism*, 11, 23–27.

Raschke, D.B., Dedrick, C., and Hanus, K. (1991) Adaptive playgrounds for all children. *Teaching Exceptional Children*, 24, 25–28.

Rathegerber, A.J. (1981). Manitoba vision screening study. *Journal of Visual Impairment and Blindness*, 75, 239–243.

Rathus, S. (1988) *Understanding child development*. New York: Holt, Rinehart and Winston.

Raven, J. (1948) *Progressive matrices*. New York: Psychological Corporation.

Reading difficulties versus learning disability. (1997, November/December) *CEC Today*, pp. 1, 9, 13.

Reagan, T. (1988) Multiculturalism and the deaf: An educational manifesto. *Journal of Research and Development in Education*, 22, 1–6.

Reagan, T. (1997) When is a language not a language? Challenges to 'linguistic legitimacy' in educational discourse. *Educational Foundations*, 11, 5–28.

Reardon, S.M. and Naglieri, J.A. (1992) PASS cognitive processing characteristics of normal and ADHD males. *Journal of School Psychology*, 30, 151–163.

Reich, P.A. (1986) *Language development*. Englewood Cliffs, NJ: Prentice–Hall.

Reickle, J. (1997) Communication intervention with persons with severe disabilities. *Journal of Special Education*, 31, 110–134.

Reid, R., Maag, J.W, and Vasa, S.F. (1993) Attention deficit hyperactivity disorder as a disability category: A Critique. *Exceptional Children*, 60, 198–214.

Reiff, H.B., Evans, E.D., and Cass, M. (1991) Special education requirements for general education certification: A national survey of current practices. *Remedial and Special Education*, 12, 56–60.

Reinert, H.B. and Huang, A. (1987) *Children in conflict*. Columbus, OH: Merrill.

Reinert, H.R. (1980) *Children in conflict* (2nd. ed.) St. Louis, MO: Mosley.

Reis, S. M. (1995). Curriculum compacting communicator. 28(2), 1, 27–32. Mansfield Center, CT: Creative Learning Press, Inc.

Reis, S., Levitan, G.W., and McNally, R.J. (1982) Emotionally disturbed mentally retarded people. *American Psychologist*, 37, 361–367.

Reis, S.M. (1989) Reflections on policy affecting the education of gifted and talented students: Past and future perspectives. *American Psychologist*, 44, 399–408.

Reis, S.M. and O'Shea, A.A. (1984) An innovative enrichment program: The Enrichment Triad/Revolving Door Model. *Special Education in Canada*, 58, 135–138.

Reis, S.M. and Westberg, K.L. (1994) The impact of staff development on teachers' ability to modify curriculum for gifted and talented students. *Gifted Child Quarterly*, 38, 127–135.

Reiss, A.L. and Freund, L. (1990) Fragile X syndrome. *Biological Psychiatry*, 27, 223–240.

Reist, M. (1991, March) The Young Offenders Act and how it impacts upon educators. *Keeping in Touch*, pp. 2–3.

Rempel, R.G. (1992, winter) Let the buyer beware: Integration is more than just a word. *Disability Today*, pp. 46–48.

Renaud, V. and Badets, J. (1993, autumn) Ethnic diversity in the 1990s. *Canadian Social Trends*, 17–22.

Renzulli, J. S. (1980) What we don't know about programming for the gifted and talented. *Phi Delta Kappan*, 61, 601–602

Renzulli, J.S. (1978) What makes giftedness? Reexamining a definition. *Phi Delta Kappan*, 60, 180–184, 261.

Renzulli, J.S. (1979) *What makes giftedness?* Los Angeles: National/State Leadership Training Institute on the Gifted and Talented, Brief no. 6.Report, (1981).

Renzulli, J.S. and Reis, S. (1991) The reform movement and the quiet crisis in education. *Gifted Child Quarterly*, 35, 26–35.

Renzulli, J.S. and Reis, S.M. (1991) The schoolwide enrichment model: A comprehensive plan for the development of creative productivity. In N. Colangelo and G. Davis (Eds.) *Handbook of gifted education* (pp. 111–141) Boston, MA: Allyn and Bacon.

Renzulli, J.S. and Smith, L.H. (1984) Revolving door: A truer turn for the gifted. *Learning*, 9, 91–93.

Renzulli, J.S., Hartman, R.K.,and Callahan, C.M. (1975) Scale for Rating the Behavioral Characteristics of Superior Students. In W.B. Barbe and J.S. Renzulli (Eds.) *Psychology and education of gifted children* (2nd. ed.) New York: Irvington.

Repetto, J.B. and Correa, V.I. (1996) Expanding views on transition. *Exceptional Children*, 69, 551–563.

Report of Task Force on the physical and emotional abuse of teachers (1990) Winnipeg: Manitoba Teachers' Society.

Report of the Blue Ribbon Panel on Special Education (1997). Edmonton: Alberta Teachers Association.

Reschley, D.J. (1989) Incorporating adaptive behavior deficits into instructional programs. In G.A. Robinson, J.R. Palton, E.A. Polloway, and L.R. Sargent (Eds.) *Best practices in mental retardation* (pp. 39–63). Reston, VA: Council for Exceptional Children.

Resistance and acceptance: Educator attitudes to inclusion

of students with disabilities (1997, fall) *Keeping in Touch*, pp. 1,4,

Rest, M.C. (1990, July) The shadow children: Preparing for the arrival of crack babies in school. *Phi Delta Kappan Research Bulletin*, pp. 1–6.

Reynolds, C.R. and Kamphaus, R.W. (1992) *Behavior Assessment System for Children.* Circle Pines MN: American Guidance Service.

Reynolds, M.C. and Birch, J.W. (1977) *Teaching exceptional children in all America's schools.* Reston, VA: Council for Exceptional Children.

Reynolds, M.C., Wang, M., and Walberg, H.J. (1987) The necessary restructuring of special and regular education. *Exceptional Children*, 53, 391–398.

Rich, L.H. (1982) *Disturbed students: Characteristics and educational strategies.* Baltimore, MD.: University Park Press.

Rich, Y. (1986) Curriculum development for co–operative learning in mixed ability classes. *Journal of Curriculum Studies*, 18, 339–341.

Richard, M.M. (1995) Students with attention deficit disorders in postsecondary education: Issues in identification and accommodation. In K.G. Nadeau (Ed.) *A comprehensive guide to attention deficit disorder in adults: Research, diagnosis, treatment* (pp. 284–307). New York: Brunner Mazel.

Richards, C.M., Symons, D.K., Greene, C.A., and Szuskiewicz, T. (1995) The bidirectional relationship between achievement and externalizing behavior problems and students with learning disabilities. *Journal of Learning Disabilities*, 28, 8–17.

Richert, E.S. (1991) Rampant problems and promising practices in identification. In N. Colangelo and G.A. Davis (Eds.) *Handbook of gifted education* (pp. 81–96). Needham Heights, MA: Allyn and Bacon.

Richert, E.S., Alvino, J.J., and McDonnel, R.C. (1982) *National report on identification: Assessment and recommendations for comprehensive identification of gifted and talented youth.* Sewell, NJ: Information Resource Center.

Richey, L. and Ysseldyke, J. (1983) Teacher expectations for the younger siblings of learning disabled students. *Journal of Learning Disabilities*, 16, 610–615.

Richey, L., Ysseldyke, J., Potter, M., Regan, R. and Greener, J. (1980) *Teachers' attitudes and expectations for siblings of learning disabled children.* St. Paul's MN: Institute for Research in Learning disabilities. ERIC Doc. No. ED 203–613.

Richley, D. (1991, spring) Emerging realities. *Abilities*, pp. 19–21.

Rimland, B. (1964) *Infantile autism.* New York: Appleton–Century–Crofts.

Rimland, B. (1983). The Fiengold diet: An assessment of the reviews by Mattes, by Kavale and Forness and others. *Journal of Learning Disabilities*, 16, 331–333.

Rimm, S. and Davis, G.A. (1976) GIFT: An instrument for the identification of creativity. *The Journal of Creative Behavior*, 10, 178–182.

Rimm, S. and Lowe, B. (1988) Family environments of underachieving gifted students. *Gifted Child Quarterly*, 32, 353–359.

Rimm, S.B. (1986) *Underachievement syndrome: Causes and cures.* Watertown, WI: Apple Publishers.

Ritchey, D. (1993, June) Frustration of a parent of gifted children. *Keeping in Touch,* pp. 3–4.

Rittenhouse, R.K. (1987) The attitudes of teachers toward mainstreaming of hearing impaired high schoolers. *Journal of Rehabilitation of the Deaf*, 20, 11–13.

Ritter, D.R. (1989) Teachers' perceptions of problem behavior in general and special education. *Exceptional Children*, 55, 559–564.

Ritvo, E.R., Ritvo, E.C., and Brothers, A.M. (1982) Genetic and immunhematologic factors in autism. *Journal of Autism and Developmental Disorders*, 12, 109–114.

Rivers, D. (1986) Labeling and learning disabled children: The implications of variability. In Smith, Finn, and Dowdy (1993)

Rizzo, J.V. and Zabel, R.H. (1988) *Educating children and adolescents with behavioral disorders: An integrative approach.* Boston, MA: Allyn and Bacon.

Robb, P. (1981). *Epilepsy: A manual for health workers.* Bethesda, MD: Department of Health and Human Services.

Roberts, C., Pratt, C., and Leach, D. (1991) Classroom amd playground interactions of students with and without disabilities. *Exceptional Children*, 57, 212–224.

Roberts, C.A., and Lazure, M.D. (1970) *One million children: A national study of Canadian children with emotional and learning disorders.* Toronto: Crainford.

Roberts, J.E., Burchind, M.R., Koch, M.A., Fodto, M.M., and Henderson, F.W. (1988, Nov.) Otitis media in early childhood and its relationship to later phonological development. *Journal of Speech and Hearing Disorders*, pp. 424–432.

Roberts, K. (1997) A preliminary account of the effects of otitis media on 15–month–olds' categorization and some implications for early language learning. *Journal of Speech, Language and Hearing Research*, 40, 508–518.

Robins, L.N. and Earls, F. (1985) A program for preventing antisocial behavior for high–risk infants and preschoolers: A research prospectus. In R.L. Hugh, P.A. Gongla, V.B. Brown, and S.E. Goldston (Eds.) *Psychiatric epidemiology and prevention: The possibilities* (pp. 73–84) Los Angeles, CA: Neuropsychiatric Institute.

Robinson, D.O., Allen, D.V., and Root, L.P. (1988) Infant tympanometry: Differential results by race. *Journal of Speech and Hearing Disorders*, 53, 341–346.

Robinson, G.A., Palton, J.R., Polloway, E.A, and Sargent,

L.R. (1989) (Eds.) *Best practices in mental retardation.* Reston, VA: Council for Exceptional Children.

Robinson, H.B. and Robinson, N.M. (1976) *The mentally retarded child: A physiological approach* (2nd. ed.) New York: McGraw Hill.

Robinson, H.B., Roedell, W.C., and Jackson, N.E. (1979) Early identification and intervention. In A.H. Passow (Ed.) *The gifted and talented: Seventy eighth yearbook of the National Society for the Study of Education.* Chicago, IL: University of Chicago Press.

Rock, E.E., Fessler, M.A., and Church, R.P. (1997) The concomitance of learning disabilities and emotional/behavioral disorders: A conceptual model. *Journal of Learning Disabilities,* 30, 245–263.

Rockefeller, N.A. (1976, October 16). Don't accept anyone's verdict that you are lazy, stupid or retarded. *TV Guide,* pp. 12–14.

Rodda, M., Grove, C., and Finch, B.M. (1986) Mainstreaming and the education of deaf students. *Alberta Journal of Educational Research, 32,* 140–153.

Rodger, N.W. and Hunt, J.A. (1980) *Research horizons.* Toronto: Canadian Diabetic Association.

Rodin, D. (1989) Prognisis of cognitive function in children with epilepsy. In B.P. Hermann and M. Seidenberg (Eds.) *Childhood epilepsies: Neurophysiological, psychosocial and intervention aspects* (pp. 33–50). New York: Wiley.

Rogan, L.L. and Hardman, L.D. (1990) Adult outcome of learning disabled students 10 years after initial follow–up. *Learning Disability Focus,* 5, 91–102.

Rogers, J. (1993, May) The inclusion revolution. *Research Bulletin of PDK,* pp. 1–6.

Rogers, S.J. (1988) Cognitive characteristics of handicapped children's play: A review. *Journal of the Division for Early Childhood,* 12, 161–168.

Rogers–Warren, A.K. and Warren, S. (1984) The social basis of language and communication in severely handicapped preschoolers. *Topics in Early Childhood Special Education,* 4, 57–72.

Rogow, S. (1987a) Children with multiple handicaps. In M. Winzer, S. Rogow, and C. David. *Exceptional children in Canada.* Toronto: Prentice–Hall.

Rogow, S. (1987b) Children with visual impairments. In M. Winzer, S. Rogow, and C. David, *Exceptional children in Canada.* Toronto: Prentice–Hall.

Rogow, S. and Rodrigues, M. (1977) *Their special needs.* Ontario: Ontario Ministry of Community and Social Services.

Romaneck, G.M. and Kuehl, R. (1992) Sex education for students with high–incidence special needs. *Teaching Exceptional Children,* 25, 22–25.

Rose, D. (1980) Some functional correlates of the maturation of neural systems. In D. Caplan (Ed.) *Biological studies of mental processes* (pp. 27–43). Cambridge, MA: MIT Press

Rosenblith, J.F. and Sims–Knight, J.E. (1985) *In the beginning: Development in the first two years.* Monterey, CA: Brooks\Cole.

Ross, D.M. and Ross, S.A. (1982) *Hyperactivity: Current issues, research, and theory* (2nd. ed.) New York: Wiley.

Ross, M. (1990) Implications of delay in detection and management of deafness. *Volta Review,* 92, 69–79.

Ross, R. (1979) A program model for altering children's consciousness. *Gifted Child Quarterly,* 23, 109–117.

Roth, M., McCaul, E., and Barnes, K. (1993) Who becomes an "at–risk" Student? The Predictive Value of a kindergarten screening battery. *Exceptional Children,* 59, 348–

Roug, L., Lundberg, I., and Lundberg, L.J. (1989) Phonetic development in early infancy: A study of four Swedish children during the first eighteen months of life. *Journal of Child Language,* 16, 19–40.

Routh, D.K. (1980) Developmental and social aspects of hyperactivity. In C.K. Whalen and B. Henker (Eds.) *Hyperactive children: The social ecology of identification and treatment.* New York: Academic Press.

Rovet, J.F., Erlich, R.M., and Hoppe, M. (1988). Specific intellectual deficits in childhood with early onset diabetes mellitus. *Child Development,* 59, 226–234.

Rueda, R. and Chan, K. (1979) Poverty and culture in special education: Separate but equal. *Exceptional Children,* 45, 422–431.

Ruiter, L. (1997, summer). Celebrating friendship. *ATA Magazine,* p. 31.

Rule, G.B. and Ferguson, T.J. (1986) *The effects of media violence on attitudes, emotions, and cognitions.* Society for the Psychological Study of Social Issues.

Rule, S., Killoran, J., Stowitschek, J.J., Innocenti, M., Striefel, S., and Biswell, C. (1985) Training and support for mainstream day care staff. *Early Child Development and Care,* 20, 99–113.

Ruppert, E.S. and Buhrer, K. (1992) Ohio's infant hearing screening and assessment program. *Clinical Pediatrics,* 31, 19–22.

Russell, A.T., Bott, L., and Sammons, C. (1989) The phenomonology of schizophrenia occurring in childhood. *Journal of the American Academy of Child and Adolescent Psychiatry,* 28, 399–407.

Rutherford, R.B. (1997, July) Why doesn't social skills training work? *CEC Today,* p. 14.

Ruttenberg, B.A., Kalish, B.I., Wenar, C., and Wolf, E.G. (1977). *Behavior Rating Instrument for Autistic and other Atypical Children* (Rev. ed.) Philadelphia, PA: Developmental Center for Autistic Children.

Rutter, M. (1983) Cognitive defects in the pathogenesis of autism. *Journal of Child Psychology and Psychiatry,* 24, 513–531.

Rutter, M. (1985) Infantile autism and other pervasive developmental disorders. In M. Rutter and L. Herson

(Eds.) *Child and adolescent psychiatry: Modern approaches* (pp. 545–566) Oxford: Blackwell.

Rutter, M. (1990) Psychosocial resilience and protective mechanisms. In J. Rolf, A.S. Masten, D. Cicchetti, K.H. Neuchterlein, and S. Weintraub (Eds.) *Risk and protective factors in the development of psychopathology.* (pp. 181–214). New York: Cambridge University Press.

Rydell, P.J. and Mirenda, P. (1991) The effects of two levels of linguistic constraint on echolalia and generative language production in children with autism. *Journal of Autism and Developmental Disorders*, 21,

Saad, M. (1997) Instilling confidence and competence: Anxiety–withdrawal among elementary aged children and what teachers can do about it. Unpublished paper, University of Lethbridge

Sacks S.Z. and Corn A.L. (1996) Students with visual impairments: Do they understand their disability? *Journal of Visual Impairment and Blindness*, 90, 412–422.

Sacks, O. (1990) *Seeing voices: A journey into the world of the deaf.* New York: Harper Perennial.

Safer, D.J. and Krager, J.M. (1988) A survey of medication treatment for hyperactive/inattentive students. *Journal of the American Medical Association*, 260, 2256–2258.

Safran, S.P. and Safran, J.S. (1984) Elementary teachers' tolerance of problem behaviors. *Elementary School Journal,* 85, 247–253.

Safran, S.P. and Safran, J.S. (1985) Classroom context and teachers' perceptions of problem behaviors. *Journal of Educational Psychology*, 77, 20–28.

Safran, S.P. and Safran, J.S. (1987) Teachers' judgment of problem behaviors. *Exceptional Children*, 54, 240–244.

Sagal, R., Rosenbaum, P., Stotskopf, B., and Milner, R. (1982) Follow–up of infants 501 to 1500 gm birth weight delivered to residents of a geographically defined region with perinatal intensive care facilities. *Journal of Pediatrics*, 100, 606–613.

Sailor, W., Guess, D., Goetz, L., Schuler, A., Utley, B., and Baldwin, M. (1980) Language and severely handicapped persons: Deciding what to teach to whom. In W. Sailor, B. Wilcox, and L. Brown (Eds). *Methods of instruction for severely handicapped students.* Baltimore, MD: Brookes.

Salend, S.J. and Longo, M. (1994) The roles of the educational interpreter in mainstreaming. *Teaching Exceptional Children*, 26, 22–28.

Salend, S.J., and Andress, M. (1984) Decreasing stuttering in an elementary level student. *Journal of Language, Speech and Hearing Services in the Schools, 15,* 133–140.

Salisbury C.L., Palambaro, M.M., and Hollowood, T.M. (1993) On the nature and change of an inclusive elementary school. *Journal of the Association for Persons with Severe Handicaps*, 18, 75–84.

Salisbury, C.L. (1987) Stressors of parents with young handicapped and nonhandicapped children. *Journal of*

the Division for Early Childhood, 11, 154–160.

Salisbury, C.L. (1991) Mainstreaming during the early childhood years. *Exceptional Children*, 58, 146–155.

Salkind, N. (1990) *Child Development* (6th ed.) Fort Worth, TX: Holt, Reinhart and Winston.

Salomon, —, Weiss, M.J., Wagner, S.H., and Bauman M.L. (1996) A validated case of facilitated communication. *Mental Retardation*, 34, 220–230.

Salt, P., Galler, J.R., and Ramsey, F.C. (1988) The influence of early malnutrition on subsequent behavioral development. *Developmental and Behavioral Pediatrics*, 9, 1–5.

Salzberg, C.L. and Morgan, J. (1995) Preparing teachers to work with paraeducators. *Teacher Education and Special Education*, 18, 49–55.

Salzberg, C.L., Lignugaris–Kraft, B., and McCuller, G.L. (1988) Reasons for job loss: A review of employment termination studies of mentally retarded workers. *Research in Developmental Disabilities*, 9, 153–170.

Sameroff, A.J., Seifer, R., Zax, M., et al. (1987) Early indicators of developmental risk: Longitudinal study. *Schizophrenia Bulletin*, 13, 383–394.

Samson, G.E. (1985) Effects of training in test–taking skills on achievement test performance: A quantatative synthesis. *Journal of Educational Research*, 78, 261–266.

Samuels, S.J. and Miller, N.L. (1985). Failure to find attention differences between learning disabled and normal children on classroom and laboratory tests. *Exceptional Children*, 51, 358–375.

Sancilio, M.F.M, Plumment, J.M., and Hartup, W.W. (1989) Friendships and aggressiveness as determiners of conflict outcomes in middle children. *Developmental Psychology*, 25, 812–819.

Sandberg, B. and Michaelson, C. (1993, October 18) This is a sham: Parents, educators speak out. *New York Teacher*, pp. 2–3.

Sanders, D. (1971) *Aural rehabilitation.* Englewood Cliffs, NJ: Prentice–Hall.

Sandor, G. (1981) Fetal alcohol syndrome: Cardiac malformations. *BC Medical Journal*, 23, 326–327.

Santos, K.E. (1992) Fragile X Syndrome: An educator's role in identification, prevention, and intervention. *Remedial and Special Education*, 13, 32–37.

Sapon–Shevin, H. (1984) The tug–of–war nobody wins: Allocations of educational resources for handicapped, gifted, and 'typical' students. *Curriculum Inquiry*, 14, 57–81.

Sapon–Shevin, M. (1995, January) Why gifed students belong in inclusive schools. *Educational Leadership*, pp. 64–69.

Sasso, G.M. and Rude, H.A. (1987) Unprogrammed effects of training high–status peers to interact with severely handicapped children. *Journal of Applied Behavior Analysis*, 20, 35–44.

Satz, P., Taylor, H.G., Friel, J., and Fletcher, J.M. (1978)

Some developmental and predictive precursors of reading disabilities: A six year follow–up. In A.L. Benton and D. Pearl (Eds.) *Dyslexia: An appraisal of current knowledge.* New York: Oxford University Press.

Savage, H. (1983) The Canadian Charter and the rights of handicapped persons: The moral imperative of blood, sweat and tears. *Canadian Journal on Mental Retardation, 33,* 28–31.

Savage, R.C. (1988) Introduction to educational issues for students who have suffered traumatic brain injury. In R.C. Savage and G.F. Wolcott (Eds.) *An educators' manual: What educators need to know about students with traumatic brain injury.* Scarborough MA: National Head Injury Foundation.

Savage, R.C. and Wolcott, G.F. (1994) Overview of acquired brain injury. In R.C. Savage and G.F. Wolcott (Eds.) *Educational dimensions of acquired brain injury* (pp 3–12). Austin TX: Pro–Ed.

Sawyer, R.J. and Zantal–Wiener, K. (1993) Emerging trends in technology for students with disabilities: Considerations for school personnel. *Teaching Exceptional Children, 26,* 70–72.

Scaldwell, W.A. and Frame, J.E. (1985) Prevalence of otitis media in Cree and Ojibway school children in six Ontario communities. *Journal of American Indian Education, 25,* 1–5.

Scarborough, H. (1989) Prediction of reading disability from familial and individual differences. *Journal of Educational Psychology, 81,* 101–108.

Scarborough, H. (1990) Very early language deficits in dyslexic children. *Child Development, 61,* 1728–1743.

Scaringi, M. (1994, fall) A study in pediatric brain injury. *Disability Today,* pp. 75–77.

Scarr–Salapatek, S. (1975) Genetics and the development of intelligence. In F.D. Horowitz (Ed.) *Review of child development research* (Vol. 4) Chicago, IL: University of Chicago Press.

Schaffner, B. and Buswell, B. (1991). *Opening doors: Strategies for including all students in regular education.* Colorado Springs, CO: Peak Parent Center, Inc.

Schein, J. (1994) Deafness in Canada and the United States. *Deaf American Monographs,* pp.93–99

Schein, J.D. (1989) *At home among strangers: Exploring the deaf community in the United States,* Washington, DC: Gallaudet University Press.

Schein, J.D., Kates, L., Wolf, E.G., and Theil, L. (1983) Assessing and developing communication abilities of deaf–blind children. *Journal of Visual Impairment and Blindness, 77,* 152–157.

Schiff, N.B. and Ventry, I.M. (1976) Communication problems in hearing children of deaf parents. *Journal of Speech and Hearing Disorders, 41,* 348–358.

Schildroth, A.N., Rawlings, B.W., and Allen, T.E. (1989) Hearing–impaired children under age 6: A demographic analysis. *American Annals of the Deaf, 134,* 63–69.

Schlesinger, H.S. and Meadow, K.P. (1972) *Sound and sign: Childhood deafness and mental health.* Berkeley, CA: University of California Press.

Schneider, B.H., Clegg, M.R., Byrne, B.M., Ledingham, J.E., and Crombie, G. (1992) Social relations of gifted children as a function of age and school program. In S. Towson (Ed.) *Educational psychology: Readings for the Canadian context.* Peterborough, Ont: Broadview.

Schneider, J.W. and Chasnoff, I.J. (1987) Cocaine abuse during pregnancy: Its effects on infant motor development— a clinical perspective. *Topics in Acute Care and Trauma Rehabilitation, 2,* 59–69.

School–wide behavior management systems: A promising practice for safer schools (1997) *Research Connections in Special Education,* 1, whole issue.

Schopler, E., Reichler, R.J., De Vellis, R.F., and Daly, K., (1980) Toward objective classification of childhood autism: Childhood Autism Rating Scale (CARS) *Journal of Autism and Developmental Disorders, 19,* 91–103.

Schorr Ribera, H.K. (1987) Ethnicity and culture as relevant rehabilitation factors in families with children with disabilities. In M. Seligman (Ed.) *The family with a handicapped child* (2nd. ed.) Boston, MA: Allyn and Bacon.

Schorr, L.B. (1988) *Within our reach.* New York: Doubleday.

Schrader, B. and Valus A. (1990) Disabled learners as able teachers: A cross–age tutoring project. *Academic Therapy, 25,* 589–597.

Schreibman, L. and Charlop, M.H. (1989) Infantile autism. In T.H. Ollendick and M. Hersen (Eds.) *Handbook of child psychopathology* (2nd. ed.) New York: Plenum.

Schroedel, J. (1992) Helping adolescents and young adults who are deaf make career decisions. *Volta Review, 93,* 37–46.

Schroeder, E. (1989) Literacy: The key to opportunity. *Journal of Visual Impairment and Blindness, 83,* 290–293.

Schroeder, F.K. (1996) Perceptions of braille usage by legally blind adults. *Journal of Visual Impairment and Blindness, 90,* 210–218.

Schumaker, J.B. and Deshler, D.D. (1988). Implementing the Regular Education Initiative in secondary schools: A different ball game. *Journal of Learning Disabilities, 21,* 36–42.

Schumm, J.S. and Vaughn, S. (1995) Meaningful professional development in students with disabilities. *Remedial and Special Education, 16,* 344–353.

Schunk, D.H. (1987) Peer models and children's behavioral change. *Review of Educational Research, 57,* 149–174.

Schvaneveldt, J.D., Lindauer, S.L.K., and Young, M.H. (1990) Childrens' understanding of AIDS: A developmental viewpoint. *Family Relations, 39,* 33–335.

Schwartz M.F. (1988) *Stuttering solved.* New York: National Center for Stuttering.

Schwartz, L.L. (1980) Advocacy for the neglected gifted: Females. *Gifted Child Quarterly, 24,* 113–117.

Schwartz, M.H., Wolfe, J.N., and Cassar, R. (1997) Predicting teacher referrals of emotionally disturbed children. *Psychology in the Schools*, 34, 51–61.

Schwartz, R.H. and Yaffe, S.J. (1980) (Eds.) *Drugs and chemical risks to the fetus and newborn*. New York: Alan R. Liss.

Scott, E.P. (1982) *Your visually impaired child: A guide for teachers*. Baltimore, MD: University Park Press.

Scott, J.L. and Sarkee, M.D. (1982) *Vocational special needs* (2nd. ed.) Alsep, IL: Technical Publishers.

Scott, R. (1969) The socialization of blind children. In D. Joslin (Ed.), *Handbook of socialization theory and research*. New York: Rand McNally.

Scruggs, T.E. and Mastropieri, M.A. (1989) Reconstructive elaborations: A model for content area learning. *American Educational Research Journal*, 26, 311–327.

Scruggs, T.E. and Mastropieri, M.A. (1990) The case for mnemonic instruction: From laboratory investigations to classroom applications. *Journal of Special Education*, 24, 7–32.

Scruggs, T.E. and Mastropieri, M.A. (1996) Teacher perceptions of mainstreaming/inclusion: A research synthesis. *Exceptional Children*, 63, 59–74.

Seguin, E. (1864) Origin of treatment and training of idiots. In M. Rosen, G.R. Clark, and M.S. Kivitz (Eds.) (1976) *The history of mental retardation* (Vol. 1) Baltimore, MD: University Park Press.

Seidel, V.P., Chadwick, O.F.D., and Rutter, M. (1975) Psychological disorders in crippled children: A comparative study with and without bone damage. *Genetic Psychology Monograph*, 75, 255–335.

Seligman, M. (1991) Siblings of disabled brothers and sisters. In M. Seligman (Ed.) *The family with a handicapped child* (2nd. ed.) Boston, MA: Allyn and Bacon.

Semel, E. (1970). *Sound–Order–Sense*. Chigago, IL: Follett.

Semel, E. and Wiig, E. (1980) *Clinical Evaluation of Language Functions*. Columbus, OH: Merrill.

Semmel, M.I., Abernathy, T.V., Butera, G., and Lesar, S. (1991) Teacher perception of the regular education initiative. *Exceptional Children*, 58, 9–23.

Senior, E.M. (1986) Learning disabled or merely mislabeled? The plight of the developmentally young child. *Childhood Education*, 62, 161–165.

Seyfarth, J. Hill, J.W., Orelone, F., McMillan, J., and Wehman, P. (1985) Factors influencing parents' vocational aspirations for their retarded children. In P. Wehman and J.W. Hill (Eds.) *Competitive employment for persons with mental retardation: From research to practice* (pp. 315–331, vol. 1) Richmond, VA: Virginia Commonwealth University.

Shaffer, D.R. (1985) *Developmental psychology: Theory, research, and applications*. Monterey, CA: Brooks/Cole.

Shah, A. and Holmes. N. (1985) Brief report: The use of the Leiter International Performance Scale with autistic children. *Journal of Autism and Developmental Disorders*, 15, 195–203.

Shah, R. (1985) Lecture presented to Ed. 416, U.B.C.

Shames, G. and Florance, C. (1982) Disorders of fluency. In G. Shames and E. Wiig (Eds.) *Human communication disorders*. Columbus, OH: Merrill.

Shames, G.H. and Wiig, E. (1990) *Human communication disorders* (3rd. ed.) Columbus, OH: Merrill

Shank, M.S. (1990) Old enough but too young for school. *Academic Therapy*, 25, 579–581.

Shanker, A. (1994, January 9) School rules. *New York Times*. Sec. 4. p. 7.

Shantz, C.U. (1987) Conflicts between children. *Child Development*, 58, 283–305.

Shaughnessy, M.F. and Mahan, Y, (1991) Adaptive behavior in the secondary learning disabled child. *BC Journal of Special Education*, 15, 101–110.

Shaver, K., Boughman, J., and Nance, W. (1985) Congenital rubella syndrome and diabetes: A review of epidemiologic, genetic, and immunologic factors. *American Annals of the Deaf*, 85, 526–532.

Shaywitz, S.E. and Shaywitz, B.A. (1987) Attention deficit disorder: Current perspectives. Paper presented at the National Conference on Learning Disabilities. Bethesda, MD: National institute for Child Health and Human Development.

Shea, T.M. and Bauer, A.M. (1991) *Parents and teachers of children with exceptionalities: A handbook for collaboration.* (2nd. ed.) Boston, MA: Allyn and Bacon.

Shell, P.M. (1981) Straining the system: Serving low–incidence handicapped children in an urban setting. *Exceptional Education Quarterly*, 2, 1–10.

Shinn, M.R., Tindal, G.A., and Spera, D.A. (1987) Special education referrals as an index of teacher tolerance: Are teachers imperfect tests? *Exceptional Children*, 54, 32–40.

Shirmer, B.R. (1997) Boosting reading success. *Teaching Exceptional Children*, 30, 52–55.

Shivers, J.S. and Fait, H.F. (1985) *Special recreational services: Therapeutic and adapted*. Philadelphia, PA: Lea and Felsiger.

Shonkoff, J. and Meisels, S. (1990) Early childhood intervention. In S. Meisels and J. Shonkoff (Eds.) *Handbook of early intervention* (pp. 3–32) New York: Cambridge University Press.

Shonkoff, J.P. and Hauser–Cram, P. (1987) Early intervention for disabled infants and their families: A quantitative anaylsis. *Pediatrics*, 80, 650–658.

Shore, B. and Tsiamis, A. (1986) Identification by provision: Limited field test of a radical alternative for identifying gifted children. In K. Heller and J. Feldhusen (Eds.) *Identifying and nurturing the gifted* (pp. 93–102). Toronto: Hans Huber.

Siegel, S., Robert, M., and Gaylord–Ross, R. (1992) A follow–along study of participants in a longitudinal transition program for youths with mild disabilities. *Exceptional Children, 58*, 346–356.

Siegler, R.S. and Kotovsky, K. (1985) Two levels of giftedness: Shall ever the twain meet? In R.J. Sternberg and J.E. Davidson (Eds.) *Conceptions of giftedness* (pp. 417–435) New York: Cambridge University Press.

Sigafoos, J., Cole, D.A., and McQuarter, (1987) Current practices in the assessment of students with severe handicaps. *Journal of the Association for Persons with Severe Handicaps, 12*, 264–273.

Sigelman C.K. and Shaffer, D.R. (1991) *Life–span human development.* Pacific Grove, CA: Brooks/Cole.

Silberman, R. (1981) A comparison of visual functioning in hearing–impaired children and normally hearing children. *Volta Review, 83*, 95–104.

Silva, P.A. (1980) The prevalence, stability and significance of developmental language delays in preschool children. *Developmental Medicine and Child Neurology, 22*, 768–777.

Silverman, F.H. and Paulus, P.G. (1989) Peer reactions to teenagers who substitute /w/ for /r/. *Language, Speech and Hearing Services in Schools, 20*, 219–221.

Silverman, L.K. (1989) Invisible gifts, invisible handicap. *Roeper Review, 12*, 37–42.

Silverman, S.R. (1967) Education of the deaf. In L.E. Travis (Ed.) *Handbook of speech pathology.* New York: Appleton Century–Crofts.

Silverstein, R. (1985) The legal necessity for residential schools serving deaf, blind, and multiply impaired children. *Journal of Visual Impairment and Blindness, 79*, 145–149.

Simen, R.J. and Rogers, R.C. (1989) School psychology and medical diagnosis: The fragile x syndrome. *Psychology in the Schools, 26*, 380–388.

Simon, E.W., Toll, D.M., and Whitehair P.M. (1994) A naturistic appproach to the validation of facilitated communication. *Journal of Autism and Developmental Disorders, 24*, 647–657.

Simonds, R.J. and Rogers, M.F. (1992) Epidemiology of HIV in children and other populations. In A. Crocker, H. Cohen, and T. Kastner (Eds.) *HIV infection and developmental disabilities: A resource for service providers* (pp. 3–13). Baltimore, MD: Brookes.

Simpson, R.L. and Myles, B. S. (1993) Successful integration of children with autism in mainstreamed settings. *Focus on Autistic Behavior, 7*, 1–13.

Sinnot–Oswald, M., Gliner, J.A., Spencer, K.C. (1991) Supported and sheltered employment: Quality of life issues among workers with disabilities. *Education and Training in Mental Retardation, 9*, 388–397.

Siperstein, G.N. and Leffert, J.S. (1997) Comparisons of socially accepted and rejected children with mental retardation. *American Journal on Mental Retardation, 101*, 339–351.

Sirvis, B. (1988) Students with special heath care needs.

Teaching Exceptional Children, 29 40–44.

Sisson, L.A., Van Hasselt, V.B., and Hersen, M. (1987) Psychological approaches with deaf–blind persons: Strategies and issues in research and treatment. *Clinical Psychology Review, 7*, 303–328.

Sitlington, P.L and Okolo, C.M. (1987) Statewide survey of vocational educators: Attitudes, training, and involvement with handicapped learners. *Journal of Career Development, 13*, 21–29.

Sitlington, P.L., Frank, A.R., and Carson, R. (1992) Adult adjustment among high school graduates with mild disabilities. *Exceptional Children, 59*, 221–233.

Siwolop, S. and Mohs, M. (1985, February) The war on Down syndrome. *Discover*, pp. 67–73.

Skelly, M. (1979) *Amer–Ind gestural code based on universal American Indian hand talk.* New York: Elsivien.

Slavin, R.R., Madden, N.E., Kariviet, N.L., Liverman, B.J., and Dolan, L. (1990) Success for all: First year outcomes of a comprehensive plan for reforming urban education. *AER Journal, 27*, 255–278.

Slee, R. (1997) Inclusion or assimilation? Sociological explorations of the foundations of theories of special education. *Educational Foundations, 11*, 55–71.

Sleeter, C.E and Grant, C.A. (1994) *Making choices for multicultural education: Five approaches to race, class, and gender.* New York: Merrill.

Sleeter, C.E. (1986) Learning disabilities: The social construction of a special education category. *Exceptional Children, 53*, 46–54.

Sloane, D.C. and Sloane, B.C. (1990) AIDS in schools: A comprehensive initiative. *McGill Journal of Education, 25*, 205–228.

Smith S.C. and Scott, J.J. (1990) *The collaborative school.* Oregon: ERIC/NASSP.

Smith, A.J., Del'aunne, W., and Geruschat, D.R. (1992) Low vision mobility problems: Perceptions of O and M specialists and persons with low vision. *Journal of Visual Impairment and Blindness, 86*, 58–62.

Smith, B. (1995, June) Implications of the Eaton case. *Alberta CEC, 5*, p. 7.

Smith, B. (1996, summer). Implications of the Eaton case. *Keeping in Touch*, p. 9.

Smith, C.B. (1991) Literature for gifted and talented. *The Reading Teacher, 44*, 608–609.

Smith, C.R. (1991) *LD: The interaction of learner, task and setting* (2nd. ed.) Boston, MA: Allyn and Bacon.

Smith, D.D. and Luckasson, R. (1995). *Introduction to special education: Teaching in an age of challenge* (2nd. ed.) Needham Heights, MA: Allyn and Bacon.

Smith, D.D. and Robinson, S. (1986) Educating the learning disabled. In R.J. Morris and B. Blatt (Eds.) *Special education: Research and trends* (pp. 222–248). New York: Pergamon.

Smith, G.J., Edelen–Smith, P.J., and Stodden R.A. (1995)

How to avoid the seven pitfalls of systematic planning. *Teaching Exceptional Children*, 27, 42–47.

Smith, J.O. (1992) Falling through the cracks: Rehabilitation services for adults with learning disabilities. *Exceptional Children*, 58, 451–460.

Smith, S.D. and Pennington, B.F. (1987) Genetic influences. In K.A. Kavale and S.R. Forness (Eds.) *Handbook of learning disabilities (vol. 1) Dimensions and diagnosis* (pp. 49–75). San Diego, CA: College–Hill.

Smith, S.P. (1978) Some (not all) facts about asthma. *Journal of School Health*, 48, 311.

Smith, S.W. (1990) Comparison of Individualized Education Programs (IEPS) of students with behavioral disorders and learning disabilities. *The Journal of Special Education*, 24, 85–100.

Snell, M.E. (1987) *Systematic instruction of persons with severe handicaps* (3rd. ed.) Columbus, OH: Merrill.

Snow, C. (1987) Relevance of the notion of a critical period of language acquisition. In M.H. Bornstein (Ed.) *Sensitive periods in development: Interdisciplinary perspectives.*(pp. 183–210) Hillsdale, NJ: Erlbaum.

Soare, P.L. and Raimondi, A. (1977) Intellectual and perceptual–motor characteristics of treated myelomeningocele children. *American Journal of Diseases in Children, 131,* 199–204.

Soucy, M. and Andrews, J. (1997) The underlying structures of autism: An exploratory factor analytic study. *Canadian Journal of School Psychology,* 13, 85–98.

Southern, W.T., Jones, E.D., and Fiscus, E.D. (1989) Practitioner objections to the academic acceleration of gifted children. *Gifted Child Quarterly*, 33, 29–35.

Spain, B. (1972) Verbal and performance ability in pre–school spina bifida children. *Developmental Medicine and Child Neurology, 27,* 155.

Sparrow, S.S., Balla, D.A., and Cicchetti, D.V. (1984) *Vineland Adaptive Behavior Scale.* Circle Pines, MN: American Guidance Services.

Spitz, R.V., Tallal, P., Flax, J., and Benasich A.A. (1997) Look who's talking: A prospective study on familial transmission of language impairments. *Journal of Speech, Language and Hearing Research*, 40, 990–1001.

Spradlin, J.E. and Siegel, G.M. (1982) Language training in natural and clinical environments. *Journal of Speech and Hearing Disorders*, 47, 2–6.

Spring, C. and Sandoval, J. (1976). Food additives and hyperkenesis: A critical evaluation of the evidence. *Journal of Learning Disabilities*, 9, 560–569.

Sprinthall, N.A. and Sprinthall, R.C. (1990) *Educational psychology: A developmental approach* (5th. ed) New York: Random House.

Squires, D. (1992, June) Forum 11: An overview, *Keeping in Touch*, pp, 2–3.

Stainback, S. ad Stainback, W. (1985) The merger of special and regular education: Can it be done? *Exceptional Children,* 51, 517–521.

Stainback, S. and Stainback, W. (1988) Educating students with severe disabilities. *Teaching Exceptional Children, 21,* 16–19.

Stainback, S., Stainback, W., and Mauer, S. (1976) Training teachers for the severely and profoundly handicapped: A new frontier. *Exceptional Children. 42,* 203–210.

Stainback, W. and Stainback, S. (1984) A rationale for the merger of special and regular education. *Exceptional Children,* 51, 102–111.

Stainback, W., Stainback, S., and Stefanich, G. (1996) Learning together in inclusive classrooms: What about the curriculum? *Teaching Exceptional Children*, 28, 14–19.

Stanley, J.C. (1979) The study and facilitation of talent for mathematics. In A.H. Passow (Ed.) *The gifted and talented: Their education and development. Seventy eighth yearbook of the National Society for the Study of Education.* Chicago, Il: University of Chicago Press.

Stanley, J.C. and Benbow, C.P. (1982) Educating mathematically precocious youths: Twelve policy recommendations. *Educational Researcher, 11,* 4–9.

Stanley, J.C. and Benbow, C.P. (1986) Extremely young college gaduates: Evidence of their success. *College and University,* 58, 361–371.

Statement of policy approved for bilingual/bicultural program –Ontario (1993). *Deaf Education,* 2, 1–2.

Staub, D. and Hunt, P. (1993) The effects of social interaction training on high school peer tutors of schoolmates with severe disabilities. *Exceptional Children,* 60, 41–57.

Steele, B.F. (1986) Notes on the lasting effects of early child abuse throughout the life cycle. *Child Abuse and Neglect, 10,* 283–291.

Steere, D.E., Wood, R., Panscofar, E.L., and Rucker, R.E. (1993) Vocational training for secondary–level students with severe disabilities. *Teaching Exceptional Children,* 25, 7–11.

Steffenburg, S., Gillberg, C., Hellgren, L., Andersson, L., Gillberg, I.C., Jakonsson, G., and Bohman M. (1989) A twin study of autism in Denmark, Finland, Iceland, Norway, and Sweden. *Journal of Child Psychology and Psychiatry*, 30, 405–416.

Stein, R.E. and Riessman, C.K. (1978) Impact on family scale. In S.E. McLindess–Mott and T. Braeger (1988) The impact on family scale: An adaptation for families of children with handicaps. *Journal of the Division for Early Childhood,* 12, 217–223.

Stephens, O. (1989) Braille— Implications for living. *Journal of Visual Impairment and Blindness,* 83, 288–289.

Sternberg, R.J. (1987) A unified theory of intellectual exceptionality. In J.D. Day and J.G. Borkowski (Eds.) *Intelligence and exceptionality: New directions for theory, assessment and instructional practices* (pp. 135–172). Norwood, NJ: Ablex.

Sternberg, R.J. and Davidson, J.E. (1986) (Eds.) *Conceptions of giftedness.* New York: Cambridge University Press.

Sternberg, R.J., Conway, B.E., Ketron, J.L., and Bernstein, M. (1981) People's conceptions of intelligence. *Journal of Personality and Social Psychology*, 41, 37–55.

Stevens, D.D. and Englert, C.S. (1993) Making writing systems work. *Teaching Exceptional Children*, 26, 34–39.

Stewart, D.A. (1984) Mainstreaming deaf children: A different perspective. *The ACHEI Journal*, 10, 91–104.

Stewart, D.A. and Ahamatsu, C.T. (1988) The coming of age of American Sign Language. *Anthropology and Education Quarterly*, 19, 235–252.

Stewart, G.A. (1994) External validity of attention deficit disorder without hyperactivity: A review of the evidence. *Canadian Journal of School Psychology*, 10, 15–25,

Stillman, R. (Ed.) (1978) *The Callier–Azusa Scale*. Dallas, TX: Callier Center for Communication Disorders, University of Texas at Dallas.

Stodden, R. and Boone, R. (1987) Assessing transition services for handicapped youth: A cooperative interagency approach. *Exceptional Children*, 53, 537–545.

Stoel–Gammon, C. and Otomo, K. (1986) Babbling development of hearing–impaired and normally hearing subjects. *Journal of Speech and Hearing Disorders*, 51, 33–41.

Stoker, R.G. (1983) On computers and the hearing impaired. *Volta Review*, 85, 364–365.

Stokoe, W.C., Jr. and Battiston, R. (1975) *Sign language, mental health and satisfactory interaction*. Washington, DC: Linguistic Research Laboratory, Gallaudet College,

Stone, P. and Adam, A. (1986) Is your child wearing the right hearing aid? Principles for selecting and maintaining amplification. *Volta Review*, 88, 45–54.

Stoneman, Z. (1993) The effects of attitude on preschool integration. In C. Peck, S. Odom, and D. Bricker (Eds.) *Integrating young children with disabilities into community programs: Ecological perspectives on research and implementation* (pp. 223–248) Baltimore, MD: Brookes.

Stoneman, Z., Brody, G.H., Davis, C.H., and Crapps, J.M. (1988). Childcare responsibilities, peer relations, and sibling conflict: Older siblings of mentally retarded children. *American Journal on Mental Deficiency*, 93, 174–183.

Story, C.M. (1985) Facilitation of learning: A micro–ethnographic study of the teacher of the gifted. *Gifted Child Quarterly*, 29, 155–159.

Strag, G. (1972). Comparative behavior ratings of parents with severe mentally retarded, special learning disability and normal children. *Journal of Learning Disabilities*, 5, 631–635.

Strain, P.S., Sainato, D.M., and Maheady, L. (1984) Toward a functional assessment of severely handicapped learners. *Educational Psychologist*, 19, 180–187.

Streissguth, A.P., Barr, H.M., and Martin, D.C. (1983) Maternal alcohol use and neonatal habituation assessed with the Brazelton Scale. *Child Development*, 54, 1109–1118.

Streissguth, A.P., Herman, D.S., and Smith, D.W. (1978) Intelligence, behavior and dysmorphonensis in the fetal alcohol syndrome: A report on 20 patients. *Journal of Pediatrics*, 92, 363–367.

Stromsness, M.M. (1993) Sexualy abused women with mental retardation: Hidden victims, absent resources. *Women and Therapy*, 14, 139–152.

Stuckless, E.R. (1991) Reflections on bilingual, bicultural education for deaf children: Some concerns about current advocacy and trends. *American Annals of the Deaf*, 136, 270–277.

Studer, J.R. (1993/94) Listen so that parents will speak. *Childhood Education*, 70, 74–76.

Sugai, G. and Maheady, L. (1988) Cultural diversity and individual assessment for behavior disorders. *Teaching Exceptional Children*, 21, 28–31.

Sullivan. M. (1988) *A comparative anaylsis of dropouts and non drop–outs in Ontario secondary schools*. Toronto: Ontario Ministry of Education.

Suran, G.B. and Rizzo, J.V. (1983) *Special children: An integrative approach* (2nd ed.). Glenview, IL: Scott Foresman.

Swanson, H.L. (Ed.) (1987) *Memory and learning disabilities: Advances in learning and behavioral disabilities*. Greenwich, CT: JAI Press.

Swanson, J.M. and Kinsbourne, M. (1980) *Artificial food colourings impair the learning of hyperactive children*. Report to the Nutrition Foundation, Hospital for Sick Children, Toronto.

Swanson, S. and Howell, C. (1996) Test anxiety in adolescents with learning disabilities and behavior disorders. *Exceptional Children*, 62, 389–397.

Swiatek, M.A. and Benbow, C.P. (1991) Ten–year longitudinal follow–up of ability–matched accelerated and unaccelerated gifted students. *Journal of Educational Psychology*, 83, 528–538.

Sydney, J. and Minner, S. (1984) The influence of sibling information on the placement recommendations of special class teachers. *Behavioral Disorders*, 10, 43–45.

Szymanski, E.M. (1994) Transition: Life–span and life–space considerations for empowerement. *Exceptional Children*, 60, 402–410.

Tager–Flusberg, H., Calkins, S., Nolin, T., Baumberger, T., Anderson, M., and Chadwick–Deas, A. (1990) A longitudinal study of language acquisition in autistic and Down syndrome children. *Journal of Autism and Developmental Disorders*, 20, 1–21.

Tannenbaum, A.J. (1962) *Adolescent attitudes toward academic brilliance*. New York: Bureau of Publications, Teachers College, Columbia University.

Tarr, J.E. and Macklin, M. (1987) Cocaine. *Pediatric Clinics of North America*, 34, 319–331.

Taylor, D.R. (1990, November/ December) Special education: A legal quagmire. *ATA Magazine*, pp. 40–43.

Taylor, I.K. (1976) *Introduction to psycholinguistics*. New York: Holt, Rinehart and Winston.

Taylor, R.L., Richards, S.B., Goldstein, P.A., and Schilit, J. (1997) Teacher perceptions of inclusive settings. *Teaching Exceptional Children, 29,* 50–54.

Telford, C. W. and Sawrey, J. M. (1981) *The exceptional individual* (4th. ed.) Englewood Cliffs, NJ: Prentice–Hall.

Teplin, S.W. (1995) Visual impairment in infants and young children. *Infants and Young Children,* 8, 18–51.

Terman, L. and Oden, M.H. (1959) *Genetic studies of genius: The gifted population at mid–life* (vol. 5). Stanford, CA: Stanford University Press.

Terman, L.M. (1926) *Genetic studies of genius: Mental and physical traits of a thousand gifted children* (2nd. ed.) Stanford, CA: Stanford University Press

Terman, L.M. and Oden, M.H. (1951) The Stanford studies of the gifted. In P. Witty (Ed.) *The gifted child.* Lexington, MA: D.C. Heath.

Tew, B. and Lawrence, K. (1975) The effects of hydro-cephalus on intelligence, visual perception, and school attainment. *Developmental Medicine and Neurology,* 17(supp. 35), 129–134.

Thompson, L.J. (1971). Language disabilities in men of eminence. *Journal of Learning Disabilities,* 4, 34–44.

Thompson, R. (1976) The severely handicapped: A new horizon. *Exceptional Children,* 43, 141–143.

Thorp, E. K. and McCollum, J. A. (1988) Defining the infancy specialization in early childhood special education. In J. B. Jordan, J. J. Gallagher, P. L. Huntinger, and M. B. Karnes (Eds.) *Early childhood special education: Birth to three* (pp. 147–162). Reston, VA: Council for Exceptional Children.

Thousand, J., Fox, T., Reid, R., Godek, J., Williams, W., and Fox, W. (1986) *The homecoming model: Educating students who present intensive educational challenges within educational environments.* Vermont: University of Vermont, Burlington.

Tiessen, J. (1996, winter) Orthotics and prosthetics: Fit and fashion join a tradition of function. *Disability Today,* pp. 23–25.

Tingey-Michaelis, C. (1985) Early intervention: Is certification necessary? *Teacher Education and Special Education,* 8, 91–97.

Tjossem, T. (1976) *Intervention strategies for high-risk infants and young children.* Baltimore, MD: University Park Press.

Tobin, M.J. and Hill, E.W. (1988) Visually impaired teenagers: Ambitions, attitudes, and interests. *Journal of Visual Impairment and Blindness,* 82, 414–416.

Topping, K. (1989, March) Peer tutoring and paired reading: Combining two powerful techniques. *The Reading Teacher,* pp. 488–494.

Torgenson, J.K. (1988) Studies of children with learning disabilities who perform poorly on memory span task. *Journal of Learning Disabilities,* 21, 605–612.

Torrance, E.P. (1966) *The Torrance Tests of Creative Thinking: Norms and technical manual.* Princeton, NJ: Personnel Press.

Torrance, E.P. (1969) Creative positives of disadvantaged children and youth. *Gifted Child Quarterly, 13,* 71–81.

Tower, C.C. (1984) *Child abuse and neglect: A teacher's handbook for detection, reporting and classroom management.* Washington, DC: National Education Association.

Transition programs help students with disabilities succeed (1997) *CEC Today,* 3, 1, 13.

Tredgold, A.F. (1908). *Mental deficiency.* London: Bailliere, Tindall and Cox.

Treffert, D.A. (1970) Epidemiology of infantile autism. *Archives of General Psychiatry,* 23, 431–438.

Treffinger, D. (1986) Research on creativity. *Gifted Child Quarterly,* 30, 15–19.

Treffinger, D.J. (1991) School reform and gifted education— Opportunities and issues. *Gifted Child Quarterly,* 35, 6–25.

Trief, E., Duckman, R., Morse, A.R., and Silberman, R.K. (1989) Retinopathy of prematurity. *Journal of Visual Impairment and Blindness,* 83, 500–504.

Tsai, L. and Stewart, M.A. (1983) Etiological implications of maternal age and birth order in infantile autism. *Journal of Autism and Developmental Disabilities,* 13, 57–65.

Tur-Kaspa, H. and Bryan T. (1995) Teachers' ratings of the social competence and school adjustment of students with LD in elementary and junior high school. *Journal of Learning Disabilities,* 28, 44–52.

Turnbull, A.P., Summers, J.A., and Brotherston, M.J. (1983) *The impact of young handicapped children on families: Future research directions.* University of Kansas, Lawrence: Kansas Research and Training Center on Independent Living.

Turner, K.D. and Szymaski, E.M. (1990) Work adjustment of people with congenital disabilities: A longitudinal perspective from birth to adulthood. *Journal of Rehabilitation,* 56, 19–24.

Tuttle, F.B., Becker, L.A., and Sousa, J.A. (1988) *Characteristics and identification of gifted and talented students* (3rd. ed.) Washington, DC: NEA Publications.

Tyler, J.S and Mira, M.P. (1993) Educational modifications for students with head injuries. *Teaching Exceptional Children,* 25, 24–27.

Udvani–Solner, A. (1996) Examining teachers' thinking: Constructing a process to design curriculum adaptations. *Remedial and Special Education,* 17, 245–254.

Udvani–Solner, A., Jorgessen, J., and Guchrane, G, (1992) Longitudinal vocational curriculum: The foundation for effective transition. In F. Rusch, L. De Stefano, J. Chadsey–Rusch, L.A. Phelps, and E. Szymanski (Eds.) *Transition from school to adult life: models, linkages, and policy* (pp. 285–320). Sycamore, IL: Sycamore Publishing.

United States Department of Health, Education and Welfare (1977). Education of Handicapped Children: Implementation of Part B of the Education of the Handicapped Act. *Federal Register, 42*(163).

Vallecorsa, A.L. and Garriss, E. (1990) Story composition skills of middle grade students with learning disabilities. *Exceptional Children, 57,* 48–54.

Van Dijk, J. (1982) *Rubella handicapped children: The effects of bilateral cataract and/or hearing impairment on behavior and learning.* The Netherlands: Swets and Zeitlinger.

Van Dyke, D.C. and Fox, A.A. (1990) Fetal drug exposure and its possible implications for learning in the preschool and school age population. *Journal of Learning Disabilities, 23,* 160–163.

Van Osdol, W.R. and Shane, D.B. (1982) *An introduction to exceptional children.* Dubuque, IO: William C. Brown.

Van Riper, C. and Emerick, L. (1990) *Speech correction: An introduction to speech pathology and audiology* (8th ed.) Englewood Cliffs, NJ: Prentice Hall.

Van Tassel Baska J., Landau, M., and Olszewski, P. (1985) Toward developing an appropriate math/science curriculum for gifted learners. *Journal for Education of the Gifted, 7,* 257–272.

Van Tassel Baska, J. (1987) The ineffectiveness of the pull–out model in gifted education: A minority perspective. *Journal for the Education of the Gifted, 10,* 255–264.

Van Tassel–Baska, J. (1989). Appropriate curriculum for gifted learners. *Educational Leadership, 4,* 13–15.

Vander Kolk, C.J. and Bright, B.C. (1983) Albinism: A survey of attitudes and behavior. *Journal of Visual Impairment and Blindness, 77,* 49–51.

Vanpoelvoorde, L. and Shaughnessy, M.F. (1991) Parental reactions to cleft palate children. *BC Journal of Special Education, 15,* 276–283.

Vargo, B. (1995) Are withdrawn children "at risk?" *Canadian Journal of School Psychology, 11,* 166–177.

Vasquez, C.A. (1994) Brief report: A multitask controlled evaluation of facilitated communication. *Journal of Autism and Developmental Disorders, 24,* 369–379.

Vaughn, S., Schumm, J.S., and Kouzekanani, K. (1993) What do students with learning disabilities think when general education teachers make adaptations? *Journal of Learning Disabilities, 26,* 545–555.

Vaughn, V.L., Feldhusen, J.F., and Asher, J.W. (1991). Meta–analyses and review of research on pull–out programs in gifted education. *Gifted Child Quarterly, 35,* 92–98.

Vergason, G.A. and Anderegg, M.L. (1993) Rich and Ross: A mixed message. *Exceptional Children, 59,* 475–476.

Vergason, G.A. and Anderegg, M.L. (1997) The ins and outs of special education terminology. *Teaching Exceptional Children, 29,* 34–39.

Verhaaran, P. and Connor, F.P. (1981) Physical disabilities. In J.M. Kauffman and D.P. Hallahan (Eds.) *Handbook of special education* (pp. 248–289). Englewood Cliffs, NJ: Prentice Hall.

Vernon, M. (1969) *Multiply handicapped deaf children: Medical, educational and psychological implications.* Washington, DC: Council for Exceptional Children.

Vihman, M.M. (1986) Individual differences in babbling and early speech: Predicting to age three. In B. Lindbloom and R. Zitterstrom (Eds.) *Precursors of early speech* (pp. 95–112) Basingstoke, Hampshire: MacMillan.

Villaruel, B.A., Martin, C.A., and Dickson, W.P. (1985) Using a microcomputer to create social interactions among handicapped and nonhandicapped children in a mainstream preschool. Paper presented at AAMD, Denver.

Vitello, S.J. and Soskin, R.M. (1985) *Mental retardation: Its social and legal context.* Englewood Cliffs, NJ: Prentice–Hall.

Voignier, R.R. and Bridgewater, S.C. (1980) Allergies in young children. *Young Children, 35,* 67–70.

Volkmar, F.R., Sparrow, S.S., Gourdeau, D., Cichetti, D.V., Paul, R., and Cohen, D.J. (1987) Social deficits in autism: An operational approach using the Vineland Adaptive Behavior Scale. *Journal of the American Academy of Child and Adult Psychiatry, 26,* 156–161.

Vorhees, C.V. and Mollnow, E. (1987) Behavioral teratogenesis: Long–term influences from early exposure to environmental agents. In J.D. Osfosky (Ed.) *Handbook of infant development* (pp. 913–972). New York: Wiley.

Waggoner, K. and Wilgosh, L. (1990) Concerns of families of children with learning disabilities. *Journal of Learning Disabilities, 23,* 97–98, 113.

Wagner, M., Newman, L., D'Amico, R., Jay, E.D., Butler–Nalin, P., Marder, C., and Cox, R. (1991, September) *Youth with disabilities: How are they doing? The first comprehensive report fromm the National Longitudinal Transition Study of Special Education Students.* Menlo Park, CA: SRI International.

Wahler, R. and Dumas, J.E. (1986) "A chip off the old block": Some interpersonal characteristics of coercive children across generations. In P.Strain, M. Guralanick, and H.M. Walker (Eds.) *Children's social behavior: Development, assessment and modification* (pp. 49–91) Orlando, FL: Academic Press.

Walberg, H.J. (1991) Improving school science in advanced and developed countries. *Review of Educational Research, 61,* 25–69.

Walker, H. (1983) *Walker Problem Behavior Identification*

Checklist – Revised. Los Angeles, CA: Western Psychological Services.

Walker, H. and Rankin, R. (1983) Assessing the behavior expectations and demands of less restrictive settings. *Journal of Special Education, 21, 56–82,*

Walker, H.M. and Bullis, M. (1991) Behavior disorders and the social context of regular class integration: A conceptual dilemma? In J.W. Lloyd, N.N. Singh, and A.C Repp (Eds) *The regular education initiative: Alternative perspectives on concepts, issues, and models* (pp. 75–93). Sycamore, IL: Sycamore.

Walker, H.M., Shinn, M.R.D., O'Neill, R.E., and Ramsey, E., (1987) A longitudinal assessment of the antisocial behavior in boys: Rationale, methodology, and first year results. *Remedial and Special Education*, 8, 7–16.

Walker, M.B. (1992, 1993, Dec./Jan) Helping crack–affected children succeed. *Educational Leadership*, pp. 57–60.

Wallace, I.F., Gravel, J.S., McCartan, C.M., and Ruben, R.J. (1988) Otitis media and language development at 1 year of age. *Journal of Speech and Hearing Disorders*, 53, 245–251.

Warren, D. (1984) *Blindness and early child development.* New York: American Foundation for the Blind.

Warren, P. (1988) *Teachers and the law*. St. John's: Memorial University.

Warren, S.F., Alpert, C.L., and Kaiser, A.P. (1988) An optimal learning environment for infants and toddlers with severe handicaps. In E.L. Meyen, G.A. Vergason, and R.D. Whelan (Eds.) *Effective instructional strategies for exceptional children* (pp. 139–156). Denver, CO: Love.

Warren, W. and Hasenstab, S. (1986) Self concept of severely to profoundly hearing–impaired children. *Volta Review*, 88, 289–295.

Wasik, B.H., Bryant, D.M., and Lyons, C.M. (1990) *Home visiting: Procedures for helping families.* Newbury Park, CA: Sage.

Watt, D.L.E. and Roessingh, H. (1993, October) Dropout—Fall out–Push out: Results from a longitudinal study of the educational progress of high school ESL students. Paper presented at the Alberta Teachers Association ESL Council, Calgary.

Watt, D.L.E. and Roessingh, H. (1994) ESL dropouts: The myth of educational equality. *Alberta Journal of Educationl Research*, 50, 283–296.

Watters, B. (1980) Special education in the Northwest Territories. In M. Csapo and L. Goguen (Eds.) *Special education across Canada: Issues and concerns for the '80s.* Vancouver: Centre for Human Development and Research.

Webb, J.T., Meckstroth, E.A., and Tolan, S.S. (1982) *Guiding the gifted child: A practical source for parents and teachers.* Columbus, OH: Ohio Psychology Publishing.

Webb, T.P., Bundey, S.E., Thake, A.I., and Todd, J. (1986) Population incidence and segregation ratios in Martin–Bell syndrome. *American Journal of Medical Genetics*, 23, 573–580.

Wechsler, D. (1991) *Wechsler Intelligence Scale for Children–3rd. ed* New York: Psychological Corporation.

Weiner, J. Harris, P.J. and Shirer, C. (1990) Achievement and social behavioral correlates of peer status in LD children. *Learning Disability Quarterly*, 13, 114–127.

Weiner, L. and Septimus, A. (1991) Psyhosocial consideration and support for the child and family. In P.A. Pizzo and C.M. Wilfert (Eds.) *Pediatric AIDS: The challenge of HIV infants, children and adolescents* (pp. 577–594). Baltimore, MD: Williams and Wilkins.

Weishaar, M.K. and Boyle, J.R. (1997, fall) Notetaking for students with disabilities. *CEC Today.*

Weiss, G. and Hechtman, L. (1979). The hyperactive child syndrome. *Science*, 205, 1348–1353.

Weiss, G. and Hechtman, L.T. (1986) *Hyperactive children grown up.* New York: Guilford.

Weiss, J.B. and Weiss, J. (1981) Use of the talking calculator to improve mathematical skills. *Journal of Visual Impairment and Blindness*, 75, 61–63.

Weiss, P. and Gallagher, J.J. (1982) *Report on education of the gifted* (vol. 2) Chapel Hill, NC: Frank Porter Graham Child Development Center.

Weissberg, R.P. and Allen, J.P. (1986) Promoting children's social skills and adaptive interpersonal behavior. In B.A. Edelstein and I. Michelson (Eds.) *Handbook of prevention.* New York: Plenum.

Weitzman, M., Gortmaker, S.L., Sobol, A.M., and Perrin, J.M. (1992) Recent trends in the prevalence and severity of childhood asthma. *Journal of the American Medical Association*, 268, 2673–2677.

Weller, C. and Sipherd, C. (1982). The learning disabled woman: Implications for the workforce. *Journal of Rehabilitation*, 48, 67–70.

Wenar, C. (1994) *Developmental psychopathology* (3rd. ed.) New York: McGraw Hill.

Wenz–Gross, M. and Siperstein, G.N. (1997) Importance of social support in the adjustment of children with learning problems. *Exceptional Children*, 63, 183–193.

Wesanko, E. (1990, June) Long term consequences of communication disorders. *Keeping in Touch*, p.2.

West, J.F. and Cannon, G. (1987) Essential collaborative consultation competencies for regular and special educators. *Journal of Learning Disabilities*, 21, 56–63.

Westby, C.E. (1992) Whole language and learners with mild handicaps. *Focus on Exceptional Children*, 24, 3–16.

Whalen, C.K. (1989) Attention deficit and hyperactivity disorders. In T.H. Ollendick and M. Hersen (Eds.) *Handbook of child psychopathology* (2nd. ed.) (pp. 131–169). New York: Wiley.

White, K.R. Bush, D., and Casto, G. (1986) Let the past be prologue: Learning from previous reviews of early intervention efficacy research. *Journal of Special*

Education, 19, 417–428.

White, L. (1974) Organic factors and psychophysiology in childhood schizophrenia. *Psychological Bulletin, 81,* 238–255.

Whitlock, M.S. and Du Cette, J.P. (1989) Outstanding and average teachers of the gifted: A comparative study. *Gifted Child Quarterly, 33,* 15–21.

Whitman, B.C., Simpson, G.B., and Compton, W.C. (1986) Relationship of otitis media and language impairment in adolescents with Down syndrome. *Mental Retardation, 24,* 353–356.

Whitman, T.L. and Scibak, J.W. (1979) Behavior modification research with the severely and profoundly retarded. In N.R. Ellis (Ed.) *Handbook of mental deficiency: Psychological theory and research* (2nd. ed.) Hillsdale, NJ: Lawrence Erlbaum.

Whitmore, J. (1985, November) Creating appropriate conditions for gifted students in the regular school program. Paper presented at the British Columbia Council for Exceptional Children conference.

Whitmore, J.R. (1979) The etiology of underachievement in highly gifted young children. *Journal for the Education of the Gifted, 3,* 38–51.

Whitmore, J.R. (1980) *Giftedness, conflict and underachievement.* Boston, MA: Allyn and Bacon.

Whitmore, J.R. (1988) Gifted children at risk for learning difficulties. *Teaching Exceptional Children, 20,* 10–14.

Whitmore, J.R. and Maker, J. (1985) *Intellectual giftedness in disabled person*s. Rockville, MD: Pen.

Whitworth, J. (1993) Special education: Addressing complex health needs. *Clearing House, 67,* 68–69.

Whorf, B. (1956) *Language, thought and reality.* Cambridge, MA: MIT Press.

Wicks–Nelson, R. and Israel, A.C. (1991) *Behavior disorders of childhood* (2nd. ed.) Englewood Cliffs, NJ: Prentice–Hall.

Widom, C.S. (1989) Does violence beget violence? A critical examination of the literature. *Psychological Bulletin, 106,* 3–28.

Wiggins, S.B. and Behrmann, M.M. (1988) Increasing independence through community learning. *Teaching Exceptional Children, 21,* 20–24.

Wiig, E. (1982) Language disabilities in the school–aged child. In G. Shames and E. Wiig (Eds.) *Human communication disorders.* Columbus, OH: Merrill.

Wiig, E.H. and Semel, E. (1976) *Language disabilities in children and adolescents.* Columbus, OH: Merrill.

Wikler, L., Wasow, M., and Hatfield, E. (1981) Chronic sorrow revisited: Parent vs professional depiction of the adjustment of parents of mentally retarded children. *American Journal of Orthopsychiatry, 51,* 63–70.

Wilcox, B. and Bellamy, G.T. (1982) *Design of high school programs for severely handicapped students.* Baltimore, MD: Brooks.

Wilczenski, F.L. (1992) Measuring attitudes toward inclusion. *Psychology in the Schools, 29,* 306–312.

Wilgosh, L. (1990, December) Issues in education and daily living for families of children with disabilities. *Alberta Journal of Educational Research, 36,* 299–309.

Will, M. (1986) Educating students with learning problems: A shared responsibility. *Exceptional Children, 52,* 405–411.

Williams, B.F., Howard, V.F., and McLaughlin TF (1994) Fetal alcohol syndrome: Developmental characteristics and directions for further research. *Education and Treatment of Children, 17,* 86–97.

Williams, F. (1980) *Creativity Assessment Package.* Buffalo, NY: D.O.K. Publishers.

Williams, J., Sharp, G., Bates, S., Griebel, M., Lange, B., Spence, G.T., and Thomas, P. (1996) Academic achievement and behavioral ratings in children with absence and complex partial epilepsy. *Education and Treatment of Children, 19,* 143–152.

Williams, W. and Rox, T.J. (1996) Planning for inclusion: A practical process. *Teaching Exceptional Children, 28,* 6–13.

Willings, D. (1983) Issues in career choice for gifted students. *Teaching Exceptional Children, 15,* 266–233.

Willis, S. (1995, December) Inclusion gains ground. *Education Update, 27,* pp.1, 6, 8,.

Wilson, R.J. and Humphries, T. (1986) The impact of recent legislation on the role of Canadian school psychologists. *Canadian Journal of School Psychology, 2,* 1–6.

Wingert, P. and Kantrowitz, B. (1997, October 27) Why Andy couldn't read. *Newsweek,* pp.56–64.

Winitz, H. (1975) *From syllable to conversation.* Baltimore, MD: University Park Press.

Winton, P.J. and Turnbull, A.P. (1981) Parent involvement as viewed by parents of preschool handicapped children. *Topics in Early Childhood Special Education, 1,* 11–19.

Winzer, M. A. (1997) *Special education in early childhood: An inclusive approach.* Toronto: Allyn and Bacon.

Winzer, M.A. (1989) *Closing the gap: Special learners in regular classrooms.* Toronto: Copp Clark Pitman.

Winzer, M.A. (1993) *The history of special education: From isolation to integration.* Washington, DC: Gallaudet University Press.

Winzer, M.A. (1995). *Educational psychology in Canadian classrooms* (2nd. ed.) Toronto: Allyn and Bacon.

Winzer, M.A. and Mazurek, K. (1998). *Special education in multicultural contexts.* Columbus, OH: Merrill.

Wolery, M. (1991) Instruction in early childhood special education: "Seeing through a glass darkly ... knowing in part." *Exceptional Children, 58,* 127–135.

Wolf, D., Bixby, J., and Gardiner, H. (1991) To use their minds well: Investigating newer forms of student assessment. In G. Grant (Ed.) *Review of educational research* (vol. 17) (pp. 31–74) Washington, DC: American Education Research Association.

Wolf, J.S. and Stephens, T.M. (1982) Gifted and talented. In N. Haring (Ed.) *Exceptional children and youth: An introduction to special education.* Columbus, OH: Merrill.

Wolman, B.B. (1978) *Children's fears.* New York: Grosset and Dunlap.

Wood, F.H. (1982) Living with the emotionally distrubed: Burden or opportunity? *B.C. Journal of Special Education,* 6, 1–10.

World Health Organization (1980) *International classification of impairments, disabilities and handicaps.* Geneva: World Health Organization.

Yarter, B.H. (1980) Speech and language programs for the Down's population. *Seminars in Speech, Language and Hearing, 1,* 49–61.

Yewchuk, C. (1984) Gifted education in Alberta: Current developments. *Special Education in Canada, 58,* 142–143.

Ylvisaker, M.(1986). Language and communication disorders following pediatric injury. *Journal of Head Trauma Rehabilitation,* 1, 48–56.

Yoder, P., Kaiser, A., and Alpert, C. (1991) An exploratory study of interaction between language teaching methods and child characteristics. *Journal of Speech and Hearing Research,* 34, 155–167.

York, J. and Vandercook, T. (1991) Designing an integrated program for learners with severe disabilities. *Teaching Exceptional Children,* 23, 22–25.

York, J., Vandercook, T., MacDonald, C., Herse–Neff, C., and Caughey, E. (1992) Feedback about integrating middle–school students with severe disabilities in general education classes. *Exceptional Children,* 58, 244–259.

Young, P. (1980) *Asthma and allergies: An optimistic future.* Washington, DC: NIH Publications, No. 80–388.

Youngblade, C.M. and Bibby. J. (1989) Child maltreatment, infant–parent attachment, security, and dysfunctional peer relationships in toddler–hood. *Topics in Early Childhood Special Education,* 9, 1–16.

Ysseldyke, J.E. (1987) Classification of handicapped students. In M.C. Wang, M.C Reynolds, and H.J. Walberg (Eds.) *Handbook of special education: Research and practice. vol. 1: Learner characteristics and adaptive edcuation* (pp. 253–272). New York: Pergamon.

Ysseldyke, J.E. and Algozzine, B. (1990) *Introduction to special education* (2nd. ed.) Boston, MA: Allyn and Bacon.

Ysseldyke, J.E. and Christenson, S.L. (1987) Evaluating students' instructional environments. *Remedial and Special Education,* 8, 17–24.

Ysseldyke, J.E., Algozzine, B., and Thurlow, M.L. (1992) *Critical issues in special eduction.* Boston, MA: Houghton and Mifflin.

Ysseldyke, J.E., Thurlow, J., Wesson, C., Algozzine, B., and Deno, S. (1983) Generalizations from five years of research on assessment and decision making: The University of Minnesota Institute. *Exceptional Education Quarterly,* 4, 75–93.

Yura, M. (1987) Family subsystem functions and disabled children: Some conceptual issues. *Marriage and Family Review,* 11, 135–151.

Zaragoza, N., Vaughn, S., and McIntosh, R. (1991) Social skills intervention and children with behavioral problems: A review. *Behavioural Disorders,* 16, 260–275.

Zeitlin, S. and Williamson, G.G. (1986) Early intervention of infants and toddlers. *Teaching Exceptional Children,* 19, 57–59.

Zemlin, W.R. (1990) Anatomy and physiology of speech. In G.H. Shames and E.H. Wiig (Eds.) *Human communication disorders* (3rd. ed.) Columbus, OH: Merrill.

Zentall, S.S. (1993) Research on the educational implications of attention deficit hyperactivity disorder. *Exceptional Children,* 60, 143–153.

Zetlin, A. and Hossenini, A. (1989) Six postschool case studies of mildly learning handicapped young adults. *Exceptional Children,* 55, 405–411.

Zetlin, A. and Murtaugh, M. (1988) Friendship patterns of mentally handicapped and nonhandicapped high school students. *American Journal on Mental Retardation,* 92, 447–454.

Zetlin, A. and Murtaugh, M. (1990) Whatever happened to those with borderline IQS? *American Journal on Mental Retardation,* 94, 463–469.

Ziegler, S. and Rosenstein–Manner M (1991) *Bullying at school: Toronto in an international context.* Toronto: Toronto Board of Education. ERIC Doc No Ed 328 848

Zigler, E., Balla, D., and Hodapp, R. (1984) On the definition and classification of mental retardation. *American Journal on Mental Deficiency,* 89, 215–230.

Zigmond, N., Jenkins, J., Fuchs, L.S., Deno, S., Fuchs, D., Baker, J.N., Jenkins, L., and Couthino, M. (1995) Special education in restructured schools: Findings from three multi–year studies. *Phi Delta Kappan,* 76, 531–540.

Zigmond, N., Kerr, M.M., Brown, G.M., and Harris, A.L. (1984, April) School survival skills in secondary school age special education students. Paper presented at AERA, New Orleans.

Zigmond, N., Levine, E., and Laurie, T.E. (1985) Managing the mainstream: An analysis of teachers' attitudes and student performance in mainstream high school programs. *Journal of Learning Disabilities,* 18, 535–541.

Zimmerman, I., Sheener, V., and Pond, R. (1979) *The Preschool Language Scale* (Revised ed.). Columbus, OH: Merrill.

Zirpoli, T., Snell, M., and Lloyd, B. (1987) Characteristics of persons with mental retardation who have been abused by caregivers. *The Journal of Special Education,* 21, 31–41.

Zirpoli, T.J. (1990) Physical abuse: Are children with disabilities at greater risk? *Intervention in School and Clinic*, 26, 6–11.

Zuk, G.H. (1962) The cultural dilemma and spiritual crisis of the family with a handicapped child. *Exceptional Children*, 28, 405–408.

Subject Index*

*Entries in **bold** are defined in glossary.

Author Index

Photo Credits